THE FUTURE OF
THE INTERNATIONAL LEGAL ORDER

VOLUME I

Trends and Patterns

THE FUTURE OF THE
INTERNATIONAL LEGAL ORDER

EDITED BY CYRIL E. BLACK
AND RICHARD A. FALK

Written under the auspices of the
Center of International Studies,
Princeton University

A list of other Center publications
appears at the back of the book.

THE FUTURE
OF THE INTERNATIONAL
LEGAL ORDER

VOLUME I

Trends and Patterns

EDITED BY RICHARD A. FALK

AND CYRIL E. BLACK

PRINCETON UNIVERSITY PRESS

PRINCETON, NEW JERSEY, 1969

Foreword

THIS volume on *Trends and Patterns* is the first in a five-volume collaborative series on *The Future of the International Legal Order*. Volume II, which will be published shortly, deals with *Wealth and Resources*. Volumes III and IV, which are now in preparation, are devoted to *Conflict Management* and *The Structure of the International Environment*. Volume V will be concerned with the problems of forming an international consensus in regard to the proper role of law in the international order during the next two or three decades.

This series has been organized and edited under the auspices of the Center of International Studies, Princeton University, with the assistance of a grant from the Ford Foundation. The views presented in these volumes are those of the authors of the individual chapters, and do not necessarily represent those of the contributors as a group, of the Center of International Studies, or of the Ford Foundation.

The editors wish to take this opportunity to express their gratitude to Marjorie Putney of the Princeton University Press, and to Jane G. McDowall and Priscilla Bryan of the staff of the Center of International Studies, for the careful attention that they have devoted to the production of this volume.

CYRIL E. BLACK
RICHARD A. FALK

The Future of
the International Legal Order:
A General Introduction

AT THIS point in world history it seems especially important to deepen our understanding of the evolving character of the international legal order. This series of volumes, arising out of a collaborative enterprise of scholars throughout the world, emphasizes the prospects for improving the quality of legal order in international society in the decades ahead, which is roughly the period of time that remains in the twentieth century.

In planning this project we have felt it useful to assume that there would be no major change in the structure of international society during the period that concerns us. For this reason we will not be emphasizing those orientations toward the future that rest their analysis upon the plausibility of shifting the focus of dominant power from the sovereign state to global international institutions. It may well be that no decentralized system of international order, even if reformed in several respects, is capable of meeting the emerging challenges posed by political change, weapons of mass destruction, overpopulation, pollution, and resource depletion. Nevertheless, we are skeptical about building public and elite attitudes and incentives that would be needed to induce national governments to merge their sovereignty and create a single world state in the near future.

We have set as our task, therefore, an inquiry into what sorts of developments within the present structure of international society might improve the prospects for peace, welfare, and dignity in the world. In studying the near future in a systematic and comprehensive fashion we hope that we might help with the process of adapting policy to the requirements of this period that lies ahead. In a world of such rapid change—the rate and pervasiveness of change being itself an attribute of this evolving world—it becomes more imperative than ever before to use human energies to anticipate problems as far in advance as possible.

A serious concern with the future of the international legal order needs to begin with a clear distinction between what is feasible and what is desirable. It is in the spirit of delimiting the domain of what is feasible that we find that the sovereign state is here to stay for the rest of the century. More specifically, states will retain predominant command over human loyalties and physical resources in the period that we propose to deal with. A world of sovereign states also implies a complex set of relationships involving conflict, competition, and cooperation. The competitive element in international life pervasively threatens to erupt into violence. On all levels of human organization we encounter evidences of pride and self-serving perception that shape national claims in a fashion that is typically insensitive to the claims and interests of the other side in an international relationship. This possibility of mutual insensitivity may result in unreasonable international behavior: each side is likely to be convinced that its cause is just, its actions reasonable and that the contentions and behavior of its adversary are unjust and unreasonable. Self-destructive international behavior may result from such an encounter of opposed wills and contradictory perceptions. The moderation of violent politics, then, is one crucial ingredient of the evolving future. We can no more anticipate the withering away of intergroup violence in world affairs than we can hope it will be managed more effectively through the creation of a world governmental structure. Neither of these possibilities is likely to occur in the near future.

At the same time, there is an important area of creative discretion whereby the more destructive forms of conflict can be avoided altogether or moderated to a significant extent. The faith that animates this scholarly enterprise is that an awareness of the challenges of the future is one way of mobilizing the will and resources needed to meet these challenges more effectively (see Chapter I of the first volume for relevant elaboration). Such a faith assumes a balance of reasonableness in human affairs that can be influenced by argument, evidence, and a creative sense of alternative. For instance, it would seem to be more feasible to bring the problems of world food supply under control by planning for future overpopulation than by reacting after the fact to its actuality. But this feasibility depends on persuasively stating the case that greater hardship and disorder are likely to result by such a date if present population growth continues, and that this outcome can be avoided by taking very drastic steps to reduce population growth. These steps may be more easily taken if states confronted by this neo-Malthusian vision can be induced to act calmly together, and if the richer, less concerned states can perceive that their own interests will be served by cooperative action. The recent development of new strains of wheat, corn, and rice that promise to increase food productivity by several orders of magnitude provides a further breathing spell during which new policies aimed at limiting population can be put into operation.

The prospects for improving world legal order in the near future depend partly on an understanding of the importance of timing. The Limited Test Ban Treaty of 1963 was finally agreed upon at a point in the nuclear arms competition when neither side felt that the other would gain an important advantage thereby. We need to know more about the factors that contribute to optimal timing of regulatory efforts in international affairs. Certainly part of the task is an awareness of the various interests at stake and a sense as to which of these interests can be preserved by various types of action. International lawyers have not always been imaginative about clarifying the techniques available by which to promote common interests in world affairs.

In trying to stimulate a focus on emerging international challenges, we have urged our participants to direct their attention in these volumes toward matters of both method and substance. As to method, ways need to be developed that facilitate the depiction and analysis of the near future within a suitably systematic and comprehensive framework. Much creative scholarship is currently being directed toward learning how to think better about relevant problem areas. Until very recently the discipline of law was largely preoccupied with inert data—such as judicial decisions, treaties, statutes, juridical commentary—or it was devoted to the explication of formal constitutional structure. The emphasis was static and mostly on the past: even future-oriented thinking was static—consisting of an alternative structure projected in the form of a utopia. We need the tools and concepts to study and explain the dynamic aspects of legal process, how law grows over time in response to a variety of extralegal pressures. It becomes essential to comprehend the relationship between law and the overall social order. Lawyers do not have all of the requisite skills to grasp the extralegal environment, and a serious collaboration with the social sciences becomes essential to the enterprise. In these volumes we have tried to bring together international lawyers who have seemed "open" to the dynamic side of legal order with social scientists who are sensitive to the relevance of milieu to the prospects for legal order in international society.

Part of the motivation for undertaking this project is to emphasize the importance of studying the future during a period of rapid, and often threatening change. A further part of the motivation is undoubtedly an expression of secular rationalism that implies a disillusionment with all deterministic accounts of the future, whether those that portray an inevitable future on the basis of a theory of history or those that spring from a belief in the certainty of human progress. The orientation that we adopt regards responsibility for the future as fully belonging to men who alone have the capacity to shape their future for good or ill by using the resources at their disposal with intelligence. We accept the limits imposed upon human discretion by the relatively rigid constraints of the power structure and its supporting base in human allegiance, and hope to activate human ingenuity in relation to that sector of the environment that appears most susceptible to beneficial manipulation. More specifically, we are seeking to enlist the imagination of international lawyers in this effort to interpret and then shape the rapidly changing environment that is a prime attribute of the history of our times. An animating purpose is to discover bridges that lead from the realms of thought to the realms of action. The discovery of these bridges and their careful specification with respect to the role of international law also may discourage the tendency to offer a false choice between legalism and cynical realism in the conduct of foreign policy. This dichotomy continues to induce many close students of international behavior to neglect the relevance of normative considerations.

In the course of this enterprise we need to make use of perspectives drawn from differing cultural, ideological, socioeconomic, and geographic circumstances. The capacity to modify the international environment through legal means depends on the degree to which voluntary cooperation among principal national and regional power groupings becomes possible. The quality of international cooperation, in turn, depends on the convergence of values and interests, as well as upon the degree to which rigid varieties of conflict persist. The Arab countries and Israel have the material basis for wide-ranging cooperative action in the Middle East, but the emotional nature of their opposition to one another appears to preclude coordinated action for the indefinite future, regardless of perceived mutual benefit. Students of the international legal order should begin work on a map of expectations and preferences that will sharpen the general awareness of what is feasible, under what conditions, and by what means.

Because international legal order will continue to depend so heavily upon volition it is important to assess the content of self-interest, as perceived by different dominant elites throughout the international system. Coercion as an instrument of legislative change may also play a certain marginal role to the extent that a communitywide consensus, including the principal world states, can be obtained. The questions of international legal order arising from the continuation of racism and colonialism in the countries of Southern Africa pose a test as to whether a global consensus can mobilize the capabilities to translate value preferences about race relations and national autonomy into behavioral results. At present, it would appear that the organized international community can only mobilize effective power to act, and only then selectively, in a peace-keeping capacity; the enforcement of legislative claims tends to be sporadic even in those areas where a value consensus of principal states does obtain.

Certain special sectors of international life may become increasingly susceptible to central systems of management. Such activities as the exploration of space, the exploitation of the mineral and food resources in the oceans, satellite communication systems, and climate control are illustrative of activities that may lend themselves to supranational regulation. Competitive national operation in these areas may engender costly rivalries that undermine common interests. For such a subject matter a future-oriented approach to legal order might usefully devise regimes for specialized control that can be brought into being before patterns of national rivalry grow entrenched.

The scope of cooperative action in the near future depends on the specific interaction patterns of functional, cultural, and ideological variables, as well as on the general climate of international relations. The characteristics of each subject matter will also help determine which forms of coordinated action are most feasible given a particular configuration of variables. Functional variables may be expected to predominate in matters of health and resource allocation, in space, in the oceans, and in communications; cultural variables will probably predominate in matters of human rights and dispute settlement; and ideological variables will be likely to predominate in matters of peace and security. Such patterns of predominance are tendencies that may themselves be subject to considerable specific variations as to time and place.

There are no sweeping generalizations that promise much guidance. Among the important tasks, however, are the identification of the changes in norms, procedures, and institutions reflecting the national, regional, and functional interests that may challenge the existing international order; and the elaboration of institutional means to adapt the international legal order to the management of foreseeable conflicts of interest and to strengthen its capacity for peaceful change.

It is a focus of this sort that we hope to encourage throughout this enterprise. The inquiry itself, together with a dialogue among those who write from different perspectives, is what is most needed now. It is still premature to propose action when the structure of thought remains so tentative. The vitality and usefulness of international law will depend on the continuous rediscovery of its own relevance to the world of action, a relevance that accepts the realities of power and values but identifies what can nevertheless be done.

CYRIL E. BLACK
RICHARD A. FALK

June 1969

Contents

PART III. THE REGIONAL PERSPECTIVE

Part I
The Framework

CHAPTER 1

Challenges to an Evolving
Legal Order

CYRIL E. BLACK

ORDER AND CHANGE

THE PURPOSE of international law is to devise and maintain a system of order for the family of nations, and the principal challenge to an orderly international system is the process of change that is transforming the societies of the world in a fundamental and bewildering fashion. An international legal order must have roots in an established system that institutionalizes continuities and formalizes precedents, but it must also be adaptable to changes in the system directly affecting that order.

The task of this chapter is to project and predict the character of these changes in a near future of perhaps twenty years or more, or a period comparable to that which has elapsed since the Second World War. The changes that have taken place in the last twenty or thirty years are sufficiently momentous to make one cautious in any attempt to see into the future. Indeed, an eminent philosopher of history has asserted that "The historian's business is to know the past, not to know the future; and whenever historians claim to be able to determine the future in advance of its happening, we may know with certainty that something has gone wrong with their fundamental conception of history."[1]

At the same time, as behavioral scientists if not as historians, it is possible to discuss certain main trends in the development of the societies of the world that are not likely within the near future either to come to a sudden and complete halt or to change to such an extent as to distort in unrecognizable ways the patterns of development that can be discerned in the recent past. Even in societies where great revolutions have occurred, trends of development tend to flatten out when seen in the perspective of a decade or two. The annual rates of economic and social change that are possible to societies at a similar level of development do not in fact vary more than a few percentage points over long periods of time. It is these long-term changes that concern us as we seek to discern the evolving challenges to the international legal order.

[1] R. G. Collingwood, *The Idea of History* (Oxford 1946), 54.

In conveying an understanding of the underlying forces of change and their implications for the international legal order, a general description will first be given of the character of the modern age at the societal level. This will be followed by a discussion of the prevailing images of the near future in contemporary writing, and of the challenges to the international legal order that are not primarily those that involve ideologies and great men but rather those that involve the political, economic, and social development of societies, and their relationships with each other.

THE CHARACTER OF THE MODERN ERA

Let us for the sake of simplicity discuss the features common to all modern societies in terms of five characteristics: intellectual, political, economic, social, and psychological—some such compartmentalization is necessary if the vast complexity of human activity is to be discussed in brief scope.[2]

Priority should be given to the intellectual realm, since man's understanding and control over his environment lies at the heart of the process that we are discussing. Not very much has in fact changed in historical times except man's knowledge, for the physical environment has not evolved significantly since man began to make and record history. One can trace the origins of modern knowledge in Western Europe to the renaissance of the twelfth century, when interest in classical learning was revived and the possibility of a rational explanation of all phenomena came to be recognized. In no other sphere is the contrast between the traditional and the modern more striking than in the intellectual. Traditional knowledge is subjective, sacred, and relatively unchanging—modern knowledge is objective, empirical, and dynamic.

Historians describe the evolution of Western man's conception of his development in terms of a Renaissance, a Reformation and Counter-Reformation, and a modern era, and this traditional periodization is still serviceable if it is not taken too literally. The extent to which this intellectual revolution has been a product of Europe is particularly striking, even after one has taken into account the significant contributions made by other peoples. The most familiar manifestations of this growth of knowledge have been in science and technology. Goods and services can be produced in quantities exceeding by many times the production possible in traditional societies. At the same time, all other branches of knowledge have been imbued with the values of empiricism. The prospects for both human betterment and for catastrophic destruction are greatly enhanced. One speaks of

[2] The view of the modern era in this section is based on C. E. Black, *The Dynamics of Modernization: A Study of Comparative History* (New York 1966), 1-94.

these developments in the past tense, because so much has already changed, but in the advanced countries the growth of knowledge has never been so rapid as it is today.

As it has affected political organization, the essential characteristic of modernization has been the creation of national states, based on a common heritage of language, religion, or shared experiences. At the same time, governments have tended to extend their authority to all sectors of society on a national and local basis. Pre-modern governments are concerned primarily with a few central functions. As they modernize, governments increasingly tend to accumulate functions formerly performed by the province, district, tribe, or family.

In the economic sphere, modernization has led to the centralization of economic activity, and especially of fiscal and monetary policy. Few policies are more characteristic of modernization than the establishment of currencies valid for an entire society and the management of such currencies in the interest of economic growth. The emphasis on the formation and investment of capital has also been a feature of modernizing societies. The area in which goods and services are exchanged has expanded, and local barriers to travel and trade have gradually been broken down. At the same time, technical improvements have led to mass production, to rapid growth in per capita productivity, and to an increasing division of labor.

There are also significant social changes that are common to all modernizing societies, despite the great diversity of human experience. Typical has been the social mobility that has permitted individuals to break away from traditional restraints, accompanied by an increasing acceptance of universalism in membership criteria. There has also been a proliferation of specialized membership units. Individuals who were formerly members of only a family, a village, and a religion, have increasingly found themselves related organizationally to innumerable groupings with political, social, economic, and other functions. The transition from an agrarian to an industrial way of life has generally led to the phenomenal growth of population, an increasing proportion of which has moved from the countryside to urban centers.

One tends to think of modernization in terms that embrace large sectors of humanity, yet it is with the individual that history must in the last analysis come to terms—and indeed the individual psyche has been profoundly affected by this process. The individual has been called upon to transfer his loyalties from the traditional influences of the family and the immediate community to larger groups and more cosmopolitan symbols. Where individuals once looked to the elders in their own environment for guidance as to behavior and belief, they increasingly find it necessary to turn for such guidance to intangible organizations frequently national or international in scope.

This change has brought with it a greater responsibility of the individual for personal decisions and attitudes, and at the same time has resulted in the creation of "masses" of people subject to common impulses and responsive to simple slogans.

Such in brief has been the impact of modernization, and in a general sense it has come to be accepted as synonymous with "progress" —as marking a notable enrichment of human potentialities. At the same time it must be recognized that the construction of a new way of life inevitably involves the destruction of the old. If modernization has been one of the most widely welcomed revolutions in human experience, it has also been systematically disruptive of traditional norms of thought and action.

The authority of traditional political institutions has been weakened, and political power has frequently been reallocated to new groups before they have gained adequate experience. This has resulted in endless political mismanagement and strife. Economic institutions adapted to small production units in an agrarian society have been undermined, and many have had to seek new employment. Urbanization has resulted in the extensive uprooting of rural populations, resulting in a loss of traditionally intimate social relations. The adoption by a literate minority of goals of modernization far in advance of local conditions, has tended to lead to the abandonment of traditional institutions and values before new ones have been created to take their place. The breakdown of traditional systems of individual guidance and decision-making has led to the weakening of personal and institutional relations on which individual security has been based. Nationalism, which is generally a modernizing force in societies striving for unity and independence, frequently exerts a regressive influence once national goals have been achieved.

The process of modernization is too complex to permit the discussion of its many ramifications in brief scope, but its essential features may be seen in terms of programs of modernization as expressed through political leadership. Formal systems of government can readily be identified, but these do not necessarily reflect very accurately the changing problems of political leaders. Stages of economic growth, in turn, evolve within the framework of politically organized societies and are dependent on political initiative and regulation. At the same time, economic growth is not as readily subject to periodization, although valuable attempts have been made in this direction. It is even less easy to periodize the evolution of the intellectual, social, and psychological aspects of modernization. Political affairs, by contrast, are relatively explicit. Although the periodization of political modernization still raises many controversial issues, and remains essentially arbitrary, the range of controversy is limited as compared with other aspects of society.

Let us therefore describe political modernization in terms of four successive phases or problems: the challenge of modernity in a traditional society; the transition from traditional to modernizing leadership; economic and social transformation; and the formation of an integrated society.

The first problem confronting modernizing societies is that in which modern ideas first begin to have an impact on a traditional society, without as yet causing a profound upheaval. In the case of the early modernizers, it is the phase in which the new knowledge is developed. In the case of the later modernizers, it is the phase in which modern ideas first begin to penetrate significantly from more modern societies. In both cases, there results a disaffection from the traditional way of life on the part of a minority of the ruling oligarchy, and the beginnings of a modernizing movement. Among the later modernizers, threatened militarily or ideologically by more modern neighbors, and prodded by the modernizing minority within the country, this not infrequently leads to the phenomenon of limited or defensive modernization. This is a form of superficial modernization, in which the bureaucracy, army, and other institutions are reorganized along modern lines for the purpose of preserving the traditional system. Throughout this phase, political power remains relatively unchallenged in the hands of traditionally minded leaders.

The most dramatic problem confronting modernizing societies is the transition from traditional to modernizing leadership. This is the phase of active political revolution, in which leaders in both central and local government who subscribe to traditional views and policies are gradually replaced by leaders dedicated to the introduction of what they regard as modernizing reforms. This process has several characteristics that distinguish it from earlier and later phases.

One is the explicit formulation of programs that propose to introduce institutional changes which correspond to the existing understanding of the functions made possible by the growth of modern knowledge. In the earlier-modernizing societies these programs tend to be based largely on abstract principles, drawn ultimately from the application of reason and pragmatism to human affairs. These earlier-modernizing societies in turn provide models for the programs of modernizing leaders in those societies that develop somewhat later. Before the transition from traditional to modernizing leadership such problems can often not even be discussed freely in public and are not formally advocated, whereas at a later stage political controversies center on the details of the program and not on the value of a modern as opposed to a traditional outlook.

The transition from traditional to modernizing leadership is also accompanied by concrete changes in the institutional structure of a society. A modernizing program cannot be said to be effective until the legal obstacles to the transformation from a predominantly agrarian to a predominantly industrial way of life have been removed. The commercialization of agriculture, through land reform or by other means, is generally the most important single feature of this institutional change since the great majority of the inhabitants of societies at this stage are engaged in agriculture.

This phase is also for most societies a critical period of nation-building. Only in a relatively few cases has there been a continuity of statehood and territory between traditional and modern societies. More frequently the transition to modernizing leadership has involved the unification of disparate territories, the disintegration of dynastic empires, and the liberation of colonies. Traditional leaders have generally been committed to the political forms inherited from the past, and have sought to defend them. Modernizing leaders have generally regarded the creation of new political forms as essential to their image of a modern society.

The transition from traditional to modernizing leadership generally takes at least a quarter of a century, and often much longer. It is not merely a question of deposing a king or a cabinet, but of replacing or at least changing the outlook of a substantial proportion of the national and local leaders of a society. It is also a period of violence—of civil wars, revolutions, and often foreign wars. At the same time it is an essential process, for not until modernizing leaders hold political power can fundamental economic and social changes be introduced.

When modernizing leaders first gain effective political power, their countries are in an early stage of economic and social development. Whether in the societies of Western Europe in the seventeenth, eighteenth, and early nineteenth centuries, or in Asia, Latin America, and Africa in the late nineteenth and twentieth, three-quarters or more of the population are still engaged in agriculture or in other forms of primary production. Indeed, a considerably larger proportion of the populations in England and France was engaged in manufacturing and urban pursuits at the time of their revolutions in the seventeenth and eighteenth centuries than is the case with many of the societies that have embarked on programs of modernization in recent years.

The policy problems involved in the transformation of societies from a predominantly agrarian to a predominantly industrial way of life—from an occupational structure in which three-quarters or more of the economically active population are engaged in agriculture, forestry, hunting, and fishing, to one in which a similar proportion is engaged in urban and industrial pursuits—are the essence of the process of change that concerns us here. A transformation of this scope has never been accomplished in less than a century, and it has generally taken a good deal longer. It involves not the relatively simple task of seizing power, but the infinitely more complex and subtle one of adapting the long-established ideas and institutions of a society to the values and functions derived from a new and, in recent years, very rapidly changing body of knowledge.

The transfer of political power from traditional to modernizing leaders may take many years and lead to much bloodshed, but it is a relatively simple task compared to the policy problems involved in the economic and social transformation of a society. The principal reason for this is that changes in political leadership involve relatively few people, while economic and social changes must sooner or later affect the entire population of a society. All values, traditions, customs, and assumptions are affected in some degree, and not infrequently they are affected very drastically. The policy problems raised by this process of transformation are far too numerous and complex, and too little understood even today, to permit the achievement of any consensus among political leaders. Too many interest groups are affected in too many contradictory and unpredictable ways to permit an orderly discussion and implementation of a policy of modernization. Even societies controlled by highly centralized political organizations have not avoided the prolonged and often bloody confrontation of a wide range of conflicting theories and programs that have continued to be storm-centers of controversy for many years.

There is no fully satisfactory criterion for determining when a society has become "modern," and indeed it must be assumed that the adaptation of institutions to changing functions will continue as long as knowledge continues to grow. One can nevertheless describe societies as more or less advanced in the process of modernization on the basis of a variety of criteria such as per capita production, urbanization, literacy, the development of mass communications, and so on, for the measurement of which reasonably accurate statistics are available. These various indices appear to be most satisfactorily reflected in the fundamental social feature of modernization that is represented by the gradual transfer of the bulk of the population from agrarian to urban employment. It is only under industrial and urban conditions that the integration of various discrete groups that make up a society can take place effectively, and that the problems of political modernization are fully faced. Let us assume that by the time three-quarters of the economically active population of a society are engaged in occupations other than agriculture, forestry, hunting, and fishing it may be regarded as sufficiently advanced so that its political problems are predominantly concerned with social integration in an urban and industrial setting. To the extent that comparative statistics permit an accurate definition of this degree of integration, fourteen societies —the advanced West European and English-speaking societies—may be considered to be in this phase.[3]

What is here described as the integration of society is the result achieved thus far in the most advanced countries in their efforts to adapt traditional institutions to the functions made possible by the growth of knowledge in modern times. The process has gone this far in only a relatively few societies, and the consequences at the societal level have already given rise to considerable controversy. The benefits in terms of widespread diffusion of consumer goods, education, and social welfare are generally recognized, and the possibility of a widespread satisfaction of material needs is within sight. At the same time, fears have been expressed that the degree of integration that makes these benefits possible will also lead to a significant blunting of individual creativity. Some equate societal integration with a "mass society" in which the spontaneous and fruitful interaction of diverse professional, economic, social, ethnic, political, and religious groups and organizations will be inhibited and eventually suppressed by a monolithic and technocratic central bureaucracy. These fears have not thus far been justified, and among the advanced societies only Germany has succumbed to a brief but violent pathological period of totalitarian rule. The other advanced societies have retained the essential values of diversity. Since only a small proportion of humanity has thus far experienced life in an integrated society, it remains to be seen what forms it may take in the future.

This synoptic sketch at the societal level of the character of the modern era is designed to convey a generalized conception of the contrasts between tradition and modernity and of the process of change involved in the transformation of societies, and it leads to certain conclusions regarding the present state of the international system. It has been noted that, in the interpretation just summarized, only some fourteen societies with a population of about half a billion may be regarded as sharing the characteristics attributed to integrated societies. Even these are in a relatively early stage of integration, and are in fact changing more rapidly in many respects than the less developed societies. Modernization is a process that has no end so long as knowledge continues to grow, and modernity is simply a relative term employed in contrast to tradition as a means of dramatizing change by comparing two slices of time.

Another fifty or more societies with a population of some 2.5 billion

[3] This category embraces the 14 countries designated as "high mass-consumption" societies in Bruce M. Russett, and others, eds., *World Handbook of Political and Social Indicators* (New Haven 1964), 293-303, in a ranking of 107 societies based on a composite index of critical economic and social variables.

are primarily concerned with economic and social transformation and have not yet made the full transition from a predominantly agrarian to a predominantly industrial way of life. An even larger number of societies, with almost a billion inhabitants, are still in the throes of the consolidation of modernizing leadership and are not yet prepared to devote their full attention to problems of economic development and social change. Another forty societies, finally, with a population of some 25 to 30 million, are still under traditional leadership and foreign rule.

The effects of this process of modernizing change on the international system during the past half century have been profound. No less than seventy societies, with more than a billion inhabitants, have been emancipated from direct foreign rule. At the same time, many others have been freed from lesser and partial degrees of subservience. The existence of rapid change is generally recognized, but its nature, scope, and direction are still a matter of controversy. In seeking to understand its significance, let us review some of the prevalent images of the near future before presenting some conjectures regarding the challenges that may be presented to the international legal order.

IMAGES OF THE NEAR FUTURE

The history of thought is rich in images of the future, but more often than not these futures are imagined in a spirit of criticism of the present and in the hope of solving or escaping the problems of contemporary existence. Most ideologies include an image of the future that is designed to influence and often to determine the present. Leaders see their policies and programs of today as plans and preparations for a future, and indeed all policy decisions imply an expected result in the near future that justifies the investments and sacrifices of today. Whether philosophers envisage a stable solution of human problems in a foreseeable future—as did Hegel and Marx— or a continuation into the indefinite future of fluctuations that they have observed in the past and the present (as is the case with many contemporary social scientists), the image of the future is profoundly concerned with the present.

In discussing the prevailing images of the near future that are useful in envisaging the challenges to an evolving legal order, one must seek to distinguish between those that arise primarily from a concern with the amelioration of the present and those that seek in a consciously objective spirit to consider the elements of the present that are likely to change significantly in the near future, and the probable rate of this change. This is a difficult distinction to make, because images of the future tend to arise from considerations of current problems, and to this extent affect the future that they seek to describe. Man makes his future as he makes his present, and his images of the future are a vital part of this process.[4]

In seeking to make a distinction between eschatology and utopia, and predictions and conjectures based on such objective analysis as is today possible, particular attention should be given to those images of the future that are based on an explanation of the past and present. It is not possible to know even the near future in any detailed or comprehensive sense, but it is possible to identify the institutional continuities, developmental trends, systemic structures and values, central problems, and relationships of constants and variables that have proven to be reasonably reliable. Even if a forecast does no more than suggest and evaluate a range of possibilities, it limits to this extent the uncertainties that lie ahead.[5]

Existing images of the near future suffer not only from an entanglement of analysis with hopes and a concern for ideal models, but most of them are also limited by their concern for restricted parts of the world. Mankind as a whole, to the extent that it is a subject of concern to those interested in the future, is frequently taken into account in name only. The great majority of the views expressed about the future are concerned with "the West," or the particular society of the writer, or some other limited segment of the human family. The number of modern images of the near future that is concerned with mankind, and hence with the international order in the broadest sense, is relatively limited. Those concerned with the future are no less ethnocentric than other theorists, and it is still exceptional to find one who is concerned with the world beyond his own society or group of societies.

Within the relatively limited range of seriously held and reasonably useful images of the near future, discussion will be focussed here on three categories: those predominantly imbued with the liberal tradition of the West European and English-speaking countries; those inspired by the ideology of Marxism-Leninism; and those that base their conjectures on the scholarly and comparative analysis of contemporary societies by scholars in the social sciences.

The conception in the Western liberal tradition of a Great Society toward which all societies are evolving, and the process by which this goal will be achieved, have been the subject of many treatises. The characteristic features of the contemporary work on this subject can

---

[4] These problems are extensively discussed in F. L. Polak, *The Images of the Future* (2 vols.; Leiden 1961).

[5] A. Kaplan, A. L. Skogstad, and M. A. Girshick, "The Prediction of Social and Technological Events," *Public Opinion Quarterly*, xxv (Spring 1950), 93-110; Daniel Bell, "Twelve Modes of Prediction—A Preliminary Sorting of Approaches in the Social Sciences," *Daedalus*, xcii (Summer 1964), 845-80; and Bertrand de Jouvenel, *L'Art de la conjecture* (Paris 1964).

best be appreciated in the light of the state of the art half a century ago. A convenient place to start is the work of the scholar who coined the term the Great Society. It is significant that Wallas chose as his subtitle "a psychological analysis," for he recognized that the types of social change with which he was concerned depended ultimately on a transformation of the attitudes and way of life of every individual.

Wallas defined the Great Society as "the whole result" of the transformation of civilized life "by a series of inventions which have abolished the old limits to the creation of mechanical force, the carriage of men and goods, and communication by written and spoken words. One effect of this transformation is a general change of social scale. Men find themselves working and thinking and feeling in relation to an environment, which, both in its worldwide extension and its intimate connection with all sides of human existence, is without precedent in the history of the world."[6]

Wallas wrote in a spirit of disillusionment with the results of the Great Society, and of concern that the fragmentation and atomization that he saw as characterizing it would lead to drift. This drift he attributed to the "unrelated specialism"[7] of its intellectual leadership, and the purpose of his book was to explore the contributions that psychology could make to the general problems of social organization that confronted the Great Society. His was thus a study of social psychology, and his purpose was to find out how the human disposition of instinct and intelligence could be oriented toward a good life in the new environment created by the Great Society.

What is significant about Wallas' work is that he was concerned with the central problem of advanced societies—how to provide at the society-wide level the degree of social integration that exists in traditional societies at the community level. Indeed, in his concluding remarks he writes that "if I try to make for myself a visual picture of the social system which I would desire for England and America, there come before me a recollection of those Norwegian towns and villages where everyone . . . seemed to respect themselves, to be capable of Happiness as well as of pleasure and excitement, because they were near the Mean in the employment of all their faculties."[8]

This characteristic ethnocentrism of the Western liberal tradition, which equates "Happiness" with a known Western experience (in this case Norwegian), is also reflected in the writings of a more important representative of this tradition—Woodrow Wilson. Wilson saw all government as passing through four stages: "a first stage in which the government was master, the people veritable subjects; a

[6] Graham Wallas, *The Great Society: A Psychological Analysis* (New York 1914) , 3.
[7] Same, 15.
[8] Same, 368.

second in which the government, ceasing to be master by sheer force and unquestioned authority, remained master by virtue of its insights and sagacity, its readiness and fitness to lead; a third in which both sorts of mastery failed it and it found itself face to face with leaders of the people who were bent upon controlling it, a period of deep agitation and full of the signs of change; and a fourth in which the leaders of the people themselves became the government, and the development was complete."[9]

Wilson's subsequent development of these four stages makes it clear that he intended them to embrace all of mankind, for he cites Russia, China, Turkey, and Africa in the course of his discussion. He also asserts that in the fourth "and final" stage, it was "inevitable" that the leaders of the people would themselves take charge of the government.[10] Two forms of this government were possible: the English parliamentary form, and the American form which Wilson designated initially by Walter Bagehot's term "presidential" but for which he preferred to use the term "constitutional." The image of the near future clearly implicit in Wilson's periodization is one in which the less developed societies would be moving toward the fourth stage, after which political change would cease.

This analysis was published in 1908, at the end of Wilson's academic career, and his subsequent preoccupation with politics prevented him from elaborating on it. At the time of writing he regarded England, the United States, and other societies enjoying civil liberties under constitutional guarantees as already in the final stage. He apparently saw the First World War, especially after the entry of the United States, as an opportunity to free the peoples of other societies from the constraints of unrepresentative rulers, and the League of Nations was to introduce constitutional principles on a worldwide basis. What he envisaged was not necessarily a near future, however, for in 1908 he regarded China and Russia as still in the first stage, in which he classed both feudalism and enlightened despotism. It would nevertheless be unfair to probe this system of periodization too deeply, for Wilson presented it only as a brief sketch prefatory to his discussion of constitutional government in the United States. It is significant, at the same time, as revealing the views held by one of the most prominent representatives of the Western liberal tradition in the first quarter of the twentieth century.

A leading representative of the contemporary form of this Western liberal tradition, which stresses the freedom of man to determine his own destiny, is Karl R. Popper. Although his major work is in the

---

[9] Woodrow Wilson, *Constitutional Government in the United States* (New York 1908) , 28.
[10] Same, 40.

field of political theory and is not concerned with specific societies or schemes of periodization, he establishes strong negative and positive positions that imply an image of the future. He argues against the view that history, and hence the future, is predetermined by immutable laws. He favors the view that man is free to create his own history and future. History has no meaning in itself, but it has the meaning that man gives it. Popper argues for piecemeal social engineering, for the redressing of specific inequities, in an open society in which institutions are attuned to the rational and critical processes of man.[11] While Popper's work does not suggest a specific near future, it carries the implication that one can and should work for open societies in which pragmatic solutions to functional problems are sought by rational means.

Other contemporary writing in the Western liberal tradition resembles the work of Popper in that it is profoundly engaged in arguments with differing points of view and is implicit rather than explicit in its view of the future. The large literature that defends the claims of open as against closed societies, to appropriate Popper's terminology, is concerned principally with the English-speaking and West European societies. That aspect of the literature in this tradition which deals with the later-modernizing societies is inclined to assume that the values of the Western liberal tradition will prevail if they are skillfully supported against the threats that beset them. Those who consider themselves adherents of the Western liberal tradition nevertheless tend to take the future for granted and are not inclined to regard the forecasting of futures as an important enterprise. This school of thought is therefore not very helpful in considering the challenges that may face the international legal order in the near future.

This attitude in regard to the future stands in sharp contrast to that of the Marxist-Leninists, for whom the future is a matter of major concern that plays a vital role in the conduct of policy and in the justification of the sacrifices that are demanded of citizens. In its contemporary form, Marxism-Leninism sees a world of societies that are at different stages in the evolution from primitive-communalism through slavery, feudalism, and capitalism, to a final stage of socialism that "opens up for humanity unlimited opportunities of progress, both in the development of the productive forces and in all other spheres of the life of society."[12] "Socialism" in this context refers not to the various forms of welfare state but only to the systems prevalent in countries governed by Communist parties. Marxism-Leninism

[11] Karl R. Popper, *The Open Society and Its Enemies* (rev. edn., Princeton 1950), 154-64, 453-63.
[12] *Fundamentals of Marxism-Leninism* (2nd edn., Moscow 1963), 133.

maintains that the general direction of the movement of societies through these stages is governed by historical laws that do not depend on human consciousness. At the same time it recognizes that the detailed implementation of these laws depends on the interaction of many forces, including the human qualities of individual leaders. The general laws of social development are known as "historical materialism," familiar to students of Marxism, and provide a basis for predicting the future that is regarded as scientific by adherents of this doctrine.

The point of departure of the Marxist-Leninist view of the near future is a present in which fourteen states embracing one-third of the world's population are in the final stage of socialism, led by the Soviet Union. At the other end of the scale a few backward societies still live in primitive-communal, slave, and feudal systems. The majority of the world's population, however, lives in societies that are either capitalist or under the influence of capitalist societies. The near future is thus seen as a struggle between two world systems, capitalist and socialist. In this struggle the socialist leaders are confronted with the twofold task of "building socialism" within the societies they control to the fully developed form known as "communism"; and of taking advantage in the rest of the world of situations conducive to the success of the inevitable—as they see it—proletarian revolutions in capitalist societies.[13] It is on this issue, among others —the costs and prospects of a policy of supporting revolutions—that the Soviet and Chinese leaders have become engaged in an acute ideological struggle. While both seek to avoid a general nuclear war, the Chinese leaders are much more optimistic than the Soviet regarding the prospects of early and relatively inexpensive revolutions.

The Soviet leaders, believing that "The development of human society from capitalism to socialism *is a universal historical process*,"[14] are prepared to rely on the gradual processes of domestic change in other countries. These processes can be encouraged both by the example of Soviet achievements and by direct assistance to revolutionary movements when this can be given without risk of general war. This is the essence of "peaceful coexistence"—the avoidance of major wars between socialist and capitalist countries during the period when the latter are considered by Marxist-Leninist theory to be evolving inevitably toward socialism.[15]

This dynamic view of "peaceful coexistence" is sustained by the belief that the final victory of socialism, in its fully developed form of communism, is inevitable. Views about the future are inextricably

---

13 Same, 476-508.
14 Same, 507 (italics in original).
15 Same, 469-73.

interwoven with views about the past and the present, and in this respect, as in so many others, official Soviet views differ markedly from those prevalent in the West European and English-speaking countries. Scholars in the latter countries who have concerned themselves with these matters are in general agreement that, regardless of current political institutions and economic policies, there are certain key problems that all countries encounter and must resolve as they become more advanced and integrated politically, economically, and socially. In this view, the Soviet Union is now resolving in its own way problems that the more advanced countries encountered ten, twenty, or more years ago. The near future of Soviet society can thus be envisaged in terms of its confrontation with problems that the more integrated societies are facing today, and it is assumed that institutional diversity will persist among societies despite the convergence of the functional problems that they face. In the Marxist-Leninist interpretation, the problems common to industrialized, integrated societies play a secondary role, and the dominant fact is the institutional framework. In this view a socialized society of the Soviet type is the only institutional system capable of coping with the problems of advanced development, and other institutional forms will in due course have to recognize the superiority of Soviet institutions and conform to their norms.[16]

The image of the near future projected by Marxism-Leninism is thus the dynamic development toward communism in the one-third of the world that is already at the socialist stage, and in the remaining two-thirds of the world the gradual transfer of power to leaders of the proletariat through socialist revolutions. This transfer of power will take place by peaceful means where possible, but the likelihood of nonpeaceful transfers—internal wars and possibly localized international conflicts—must also be envisaged. No timetable is set for this development, but it is formally asserted that by 1980 the Soviet national income per capita will exceed that of the United States by at least 50 percent.[17]

[16] M. B. Mitin and V. S. Semenov, "Dvizhenie chelovechestva k kommunizmu i burzhuaznaia kontseptsiia 'edinogo industrial'nogo obshchestva'" [The movement of mankind toward Communism and the bourgeois conception of a "common industrial society"], *Voprosy filosofii,* XIX (May 1965), 35-46, provides an authoritative juxtaposition of the Marxist-Leninist and social science views of the future.

[17] *Fundamentals,* 694. See also Thomas P. Thornton, ed., *The Third World in Soviet Perspective* (Princeton 1965). The preference of a minority of Soviet intellectuals for cooperation among the industrialized states in solving the problems of mankind, reflected in the unpublished essay of Academician Andrei D. Sakharov (translated in the *New York Times,* July 22, 1968), met with a firm reaffirmation of the official interpretation by Dr. Viktor A. Cheprakov in an article on "Problems of the Last Third of the Century" in *Izvestia* (translated in the *New York Times,* August 19, 1968).

It is significant that neither the Western liberal nor the Marxist-Leninist images of the near future is based on a scholarly analysis of the contemporary scene. Both assume in a markedly ethnocentric fashion the universal validity of the experience of a limited portion of humanity, and base their faith rather dogmatically on social theories developed a century or more ago. Neither view contributes very substantially to an understanding of the challenges to an evolving world order in the near future, except insofar as they reveal the underlying assumptions of some of the world's leading policy makers. More positive results can be expected only on the basis of scholarly comparative studies of contemporary societies.

It is not inappropriate to look for such results now that concern for the future has come to occupy the attention of important groups of scholars in the social sciences. In the United States, extensive work in projections and forecasting is being done by the RAND Corporation, the Institute for Defense Analyses, and the Office of Science and Technology. Private organizations concerned with this type of work include the Hudson Institute, the Institute for the Future, and Resources for the Future. The United Nations, the Organization for European Economic Cooperation, and the Organization for Economic Cooperation and Development also publish studies in technical fields related especially to problems of population, manpower, economic growth, and technological forecasting. Those concerned with more general problems of political, economic, and social development in the near future include a growing number of independent scholars, as well as such organizations as the *Société d'études et de documentation économiques, industrielles, et sociales,* which publishes the *Bulletin SEDEIS* in French and *Prognosis* in English; the *Centre d'études prospectives* (Association Gaston Berger), which publishes *Prospectives*; and the American Academy of Arts and Sciences, which publishes *Daedalus.* The journals *Futuribles* (Geneva), *Futurist* (Washington), *Futures* (London), and *Futurum* (Meisenheim) are also devoted to problems of projection and forecasting. The Soviet Sociological Association has established a Social Prediction Research Committee, and in Japan the Economic Research Center has sponsored an international conference on "The World in 2000."

It is superficially paradoxical, but logically understandable, that prediction is more difficult in the exact sciences than in the inexact. This is because change in the exact sciences depends on knowledge developed by relatively few individuals who can grasp and to a certain extent manipulate the myriad of variables involved. One thinking individual, or a team of well-equipped specialists, may be able to make dramatic changes in a specialized field of research in a relatively short time. Prediction in the exact sciences is thus concerned less with what is objectively possible, than with a knowledge of the areas in which scholars and governments are likely to invest massive effort.

In the inexact sciences—anthropology, law, political science, sociology, history, and many aspects of economics and psychology—change depends on altering the institutions and values of a great majority of the population of a society or even of the world. Matters involving whole populations do not normally change at a rate of more than a very few percentage points a year, and hence prediction is less difficult than in matters where rapid rates of change are common. This contrast in the logic of predictability between the exact and inexact sciences is conditional, of course, on a similar level of knowledge. Much less is known about societies than about nature, and probably less systematic effort is being made to study societies, but a significant amount of thought has been devoted in recent years to the development of methods of foreseeing future developments. The use of analogies, and the study of cause and effect both in individual fields and in the analysis of whole systems, are now the subject of a large literature.[18]

More sophisticated techniques have also been developed that seek to analyze international problems in terms of the perspective, environment, and values systems of the participants, and the strategies, outcomes, and effects of their actions. Some of the most thorough and imaginative work in international law has employed this framework of analysis.[19] In more technical fields, considerable success has been achieved by the careful interrogation of relatively few specialists working on the frontiers of research.[20]

Change in the international order is not a field in which much work has been done, and there are relatively few studies that seek to foresee the principal structural changes that are likely to occur in the international system. The main conclusions of these studies may be summarized briefly, before turning to a more general consideration of the evolving challenges to the international legal order.

[18] The most comprehensive general introduction to this literature is Lewis H. Mayo and Ernest M. Jones, "Legal-Policy Decision Process: Alternative Thinking and the Prediction Function," *George Washington Law Review*, xxxiii (October 1964), 318-456.

[19] Elaborated in Myres S. McDougal and Florentino P. Feliciano, *Law and Minimum Public Order: The Legal Regulation of International Coercion* (New Haven 1961); and other works by McDougal, Harold D. Lasswell, and their associates.

[20] Olaf Helmer, *Social Technology* (New York 1966), esp. 44-96; Theodore J. Gordon, *The Future* (New York 1965); John McHale, *The Future of the Future* (New York 1969); and the working document on *Technological Forecasting in Perspective*, prepared by Erich Jantsch for OECD (Paris 1966), with a valuable bibliography.

A study concerned primarily with stages of economic growth, for example, stresses the differing levels of development of the societies of the world and the tendency of the more mature to take military advantage of those that are at a less developed stage. In the long run, when the dominant larger societies all reach the stage of high mass consumption, the gaps between their military capabilities will be narrowed and the prospects for a consensus regarding the maintenance of international order will be good. In the meantime, however, the movement of many societies from preconditions, through take-off, and toward maturity will continue to be a source of international disorder. The image of the near future projected by this stage-of-growth approach is one of increasing danger of international disorder unless the major powers can impose a system of order during the transitional phase.[21]

Another study similarly based on economic considerations, although set in a political framework, sees all societies as developing through stages of primitive unification, industrialization, national welfare, and abundance. It reaches the conclusion, with important implications for the international order, that the conditions of national development in the near future are more likely to favor totalitarian than democratic political systems.[22]

An alternative economic interpretation describes development in terms of the emphasis placed on agriculture, industry, and services. The transition from industry to services represents in this view a "tertiary revolution," which only a dozen countries with 14 percent of the world's population have thus far experienced. Another 13 percent of mankind is in the industrial stage, and the balance of 73 percent still live in agrarian societies. The service society is seen as one in which the average working life of the individual will be 40,000 hours, in a biological life of 700,000 hours, and in which problems of education and leisure will play an increasingly prominent role.[23] The implication for the near future of this view is that the great majority of the nations comprising the international system are still on the threshold of great economic and social transformation and that their capacity for participation in the society of nations will for many years be in a state of flux.

A comparative sociological study of the role of landlords and peas-

[21] W. W. Rostow, *The Stages of Economic Growth* (Cambridge, England 1960), esp. 106-44.

[22] A.F.K. Organski, *The Stages of Political Development* (New York 1965), esp. 220-21.

[23] Maurice Lengellé, *La révolution tertiaire* (Paris 1966); and Jean Fourastié, *La civilisation de 1975* (Paris 1959), and *Les 40,000 heures: Inventaire de l'avenir* (Paris 1965). Some of these themes are also developed in Alain Touraine, *Sociologie de l'action* (Paris 1965).

ants in the transformation of societies from an agrarian to an industrial way of life, contrasts the democratic pattern of England, France, and the United States, with the fascist pattern of Germany and Japan, and the communist pattern of Russia and China. It suggests that to the extent that the landlord-peasant relations in the newly independent nations resemble the third pattern more than the first two, many nations may be faced with peasant revolutions in the near future.[24]

Those more concerned with politics than with economics are impressed by the profound problems faced by the less developed nations as they seek to create modern states. The division between developed and undeveloped countries is seen as posing continuing problems in the future, but the strains are more likely to be economic, social, and psychological, than political or military. The division between one-party and multi-party political systems is seen less in terms of ideology than of historical and political ecology. It is recognized that under modern conditions a viable government must be capable of responding flexibly to rapidly evolving domestic conditions. In this sense, political scientists are inclined to join with economists in envisaging a society of nations in the near future in which the great majority of the participants will be undergoing the destabilizing experience of rapid and prolonged domestic transformation.[25]

Political scientists are also concerned with the complexities resulting from the likelihood that many of the new nations will not be able to exercise their statehood in a manner conducive to international stability. This presents for the near future the problem of an adjustment between the needs expressed by the less developed nations comprising a majority of mankind, and the standards already established by the states that developed earlier. Accompanying these disparities in levels of development is the interpenetration of nations, especially the participation of the more advanced in the affairs of the less advanced, which provides fertile ground for instability. The central problem for the near future will thus be to seek to counteract this instability by direct action upon the revolution of modernization.[26]

The more comprehensive efforts at prediction generally stress the technical problems of advanced societies more than the political

24 Barrington Moore, Jr., *Social Origins of Dictatorship and Democracy: Lord and Peasant in the Making of the Modern World* (Boston 1966), 413-83.

25 Lucian W. Pye, *Aspects of Political Development* (Boston 1966), 190-200; and the works of Raymond Aron, esp. *Démocratie et totalitarisme* (Paris 1965), 341-74.

26 Dankwart A. Rustow, *A World of Nations: Problems of Political Modernization* (Washington, D. C. 1967), and Manfred Halpern, "The Revolution of Modernization in National and International Society," in Carl J. Friedrich, ed., *Revolution* (New York 1966), 178-214.

problems of a future international order. The results thus far available of the work of the Hudson Institute and the Commission on the Year 2000 offer no analysis of the nature of political change in the years ahead. Their conjectures therefore tend to be strong on creative imagination and weak on persuasive power. They seek, in short, to predict what will happen without suggesting why.[27]

A more analytical political approach stresses the requisites of stability in terms of the direction, control, resources, and capacities of participants in the international system. The development of the resources and capacities of the participants is likely to be increasingly destabilizing to the international system in the near future. Ideological direction and political control of these resources and capacities will require a major effort on the part of elites that are capable of appreciating and affecting this problem.[28] Other images of the near future focus on the transition from a bipolar to a multipolar or multibloc international system, which would initially integrate on a regional basis and ultimately integrate with each other. This transition will be a slow one, however, and will result in the full range of sources of controversy that nations have faced in the past.[29]

Scholars who approach the problem from a social and behavioral point of view are particularly impressed by the destabilizing effects of modernization in the less developed societies, and the likelihood that there will also be an exacerbation of continuing instabilities in the advanced societies. The international order in the near future is thus likely to be profoundly unsettled by the interacting instabilities of states at differing levels of development. The work thus far published along these lines is primarily theoretical, and the view of the future that it reflects is presented in only the most general terms, but it is persuasive in its analysis of the perils of rapid change.[30] This expectation of instability—continuing and perhaps growing—is accompanied by a recognition of the importance of traditional institutions, and the belief that the values and norms of societies in

[27] Herman Kahn and Anthony J. Wiener, *The Year 2000: A Framework for Speculation on the Next Thirty-Three Years* (New York 1967) , and Daniel Bell and others, "Toward the Year 2000: Work in Progress," *Daedalus*, xcvi (Summer 1967) , 639-988.

[28] Richard N. Rosecrance, *Action and Reaction in World Politics: International Systems in Perspective* (Boston 1963) , 296-306.

[29] Morton A. Kaplan and Nicholas deB. Katzenbach, *The Political Foundations of International Law* (New York 1961) ; Roger D. Masters, "A Multi-Bloc Model of the International System," *American Political Science Review*, lv (December 1961) , 780-98; and Wolfgang Friedmann, *An Introduction to World Politics* (5th edn., New York 1965) , 348-55.

[30] Marion J. Levy, Jr., *Modernization and the Structure of Societies: A Setting for International Affairs* (2 vols.; Princeton 1966) , esp. ii, 790-94; David E. Apter, *The Politics of Modernization* (Chicago 1965) , 422-63; and Samuel P. Huntington, *Political Order in Changing Societies* (New Haven 1968) .

the near future are likely to be congruent with those that they have inherited and internalized. This view has led to a reexamination of historical institutions as a means of foreseeing dominant continuing trends.[31]

At the other end of the generality-specificity spectrum, detailed statistical work is also being done that demonstrates the possibility of determining rates of development in individual indices of social change and of providing the basis for statistical prediction. This procedure is useful in conveying an impression of orders of magnitude, but it cannot foresee variations in rates of development that may result from changes in leadership and in the environment of national policy.[32]

The new Soviet school of sociology, which has developed in the 1960's, has begun to produce valuable studies based on detailed research in Soviet industrial areas. There is also an important development of social and behavioral studies in Eastern Europe which, like the Soviet, is not rigidly limited by ideological considerations.[33]

This brief summary of images of the future held by contemporary social scientists draws on an acquaintance with European writing. Many of the works referred to draw also on the scholarship of other national traditions, however, and to this extent the range of views considered is representative of those prevailing in the world at large among scholars concerned with problems of the near future.[34]

EVOLVING CHALLENGES TO INTERNATIONAL LAW

The conceptions of the near future in contemporary writing representing the Western liberal, Marxist-Leninist, and social science points of view reflect such a wide variety of alternatives that it would not be very useful to seek a consensus embracing the entire range of views. There are nevertheless certain central themes, especially in

[31] Ralph Braibanti and Joseph J. Spengler, eds., *Tradition, Values, and Socio-Economic Development* (Durham, N. C. 1961) ; Clifford Geertz, ed., *Old Societies and New States: The Quest for Modernity in Asia and Africa* (New York 1963) ; and Lucian W. Pye and Sidney Verba, eds., *Political Culture and Political Development* (Princeton 1965) .

[32] Karl W. Deutsch, "Social Mobilization and Political Development," *American Political Science Review*, LV (September 1961) , 493-514; and Russett, *World Handbook*.

[33] George Fischer, ed., *Science and Ideology in Soviet Society* (New York 1967) , 13-29; and G. B. Osipov, ed., *Sotsiologiia v SSSR* [Sociology in the USSR] (2 vols., Moscow 1965) , provide a good introduction to this subject. Radovan Richta, and others, *Civilization at the Crossroads: Social and Human Implications of the Technological Revolution* (New York 1969) , represents a significant Czechoslovak interpretation of the contemporary crisis and the most important contribution from Eastern Europe to the discussion of this subject.

[34] The very considerable social science literature in this field may be followed in the annual bibliographies on anthropology, economics, history, political science, and sociology published by UNESCO.

the work of social scientists, that permit one to identify those challenges to the international legal order that are likely to loom large, and to distinguish between those that are more likely to arise in the near and the more distant future. These may for convenience be grouped under four headings: national development, regionalism, international functionalism, and international government.[35]

National Development

There is probably no characteristic of the near future that has been the subject of more general agreement than the fact that the countries of the world are at widely differing levels of development and are modernizing at varying rates and in diverse patterns. There are diversities first of all in the traditional heritage of institutions, which form the starting point in each society for adaptation to modern functions. There are also diversities among societies as to their size, base of resources and skills, and the point in time relative to other societies at which they have confronted the challenge of modernity, made the transition to modernizing leadership, and undertaken intensive economic and social development.

The fundamental effect of this diversity in the international order of the near future is the instability that it engenders. In large numbers of societies, encompassing the majority of the world's peoples, in which political leaders have not yet achieved a consensus as to policies of modernization, continuing revolutions, coups d'état, purges, and other forms of instability and unrest may be anticipated. It is most likely that there will be as many as ten or twenty abrupt and violent changes of leadership every year for the foreseeable future in the over one hundred independent countries that are still relatively less advanced. There are also forty or more dependent societies that are still seeking national liberation. These societies tend to see instability and violence as a natural setting for independence, and to regard international order as the guardian of the status quo.

Although much of this instability is essentially domestic, it casts a long shadow over the international order because it makes these societies readily accessible to international intervention. In an international system in which the power relations between major countries with widely differing policies of modernization are still delicately balanced, these countries are subject to an irresistible temptation to seek influence within the unstable societies as a means of guiding their policies. The world is not in a state of civil war, but the leaders of the several major programs of modernization seek allies and associates in a situation that they perceive in terms of a system of coali-

[35] This section draws on Black, 95-174, which makes use of the large literature in this field, as well as on the monographic literature cited in the footnotes that follow.

tion politics in which a country lost to one ideology or program of modernization is a country gained by a rival or adversary. This view of world politics is encouraged not only by the reality of military strategy, where territory and populations and resources count heavily in the balance of power, but also by the politics of the United Nations, where each member has a vote and where many issues of at least marginal importance are resolved on the basis of majority votes. To this extent world politics is like national politics, in which no leader can be indifferent to the views of the other participants. There is no reason to believe that this form of international politics which has predominated in the 1950's and 1960's will not continue unabated into the near future.[36]

For international organization and administration this situation bordering on anarchy presents many problems. More specifically, for international law it involves a reconsideration of the practice regarding recognition of new governments and states, and also of insurgent, belligerent, and provisional governments. It also raises questions regarding the right of national existence and self-defense, and the laws of war as they affect internal war, methods of warfare, treatment of prisoners, and relations among belligerents. When these aspects of international law were formulated, principally in the era before the First World War, they were concerned primarily with formal, declared wars between well-established governments. Under the circumstances that exist today and seem likely to continue into the near future, this formalized conflict has been replaced by a much more fluid type of war in which the principals, and their friends, vary their roles in a bewildering fashion. The rigid established rules of recognition and nonintervention are normally violated, and under a strict interpretation of international law the major states have no alternatives but to act illegally.[37]

Regionalism

The various kinds of regional groupings may be considered in terms of two main types: those that represent an evolution beyond national sovereignty on the part of states already integrated, with the explicit aim of fusing their societies into new political units; and those groupings that are designed to further common political or economic interests without any substantial surrender of sovereignty. Both types of regional groupings, in turn, should be distinguished from the con-

---

36 See esp. Harry Eckstein, ed., *Internal War: Problems and Approaches* (New York 1964) ; and James N. Rosenau, ed., *International Aspects of Civil Strife* (Princeton 1964) , and *Linkage Politics: Essays on the Convergence of National and International Systems* (New York 1969) .

37 See esp. Richard A. Falk, "Janus Tormented: The International Law of Internal War," Rosenau, ed., *International Aspects of Civil Strife*, 185-248.

federations and federations formed by societies within a common ethnic background that mark an intermediate stage in the process of national unification. It is the development of the first type of regionalism, already well under way in Western Europe, that will be of primary concern to international law in the near future.

The mechanism by which states integrate into regions is essentially the same as that by which relatively autonomous villages, communities, towns, provinces, and principalities become integrated into national states as the bulk of the inhabitants move over several generations from agricultural to urban and service occupations. The whole of mankind is now organized on the basis of sovereign states, which are the principal actors in the formation and implementation of international law. Yet the functional needs that led the constituent communities in individual societies to integrate—political and economic advantage, reflected ultimately in the effort to find a form of organization that will yield a maximum per capita return for social effort—operate equally among societies as within them.

The principal difference is that national states are normally formed on the basis of language or other common experience whereas international integration usually has greater barriers of antagonism to overcome. Yet it should be recalled that even the most cohesive of national states have gone through periods of bitter internal strife in the course of nation-building, and the differences between a France and a Germany today may be no greater than those between a Normandy and a Burgundy or a Bavaria and a Prussia in earlier periods. Parts of Western Europe have already achieved a degree of success as a region, and the logic of regional integration, given the proper conditions, is powerfully persuasive.[38]

This first type of integration can only occur among societies that are already integrated themselves, and outside of Western Europe only the United States, Canada, Australia, and New Zealand may be said to have advanced to this point. These latter countries cooperate closely, but for a variety of reasons are not yet seeking to integrate. Quite distinct in terms of the problems they represent are the countries forming the second type of regional groupings, blocs, and alliances systems, which function within the framework of established international law.

Regional integration, by contrast, calls for as full a revision of international law as was required originally in municipal law when national legislation was codified in the advanced societies in the eight-

---

[38] Elmer Plischke, ed., *Systems of Integrating the International Community* (Princeton 1964); Amitai Etzioni, *Political Unification: A Comparative Study of Leaders and Forces* (New York 1965); and Bruce M. Russett, *International Regions and the International System: A Study in Political Ecology* (Chicago 1967).

eenth and nineteenth centuries. The norms of the participating countries must be adjusted to each other, and something resembling a common regional law must emerge. This revision must encompass the entire range of law, including not only that involving the relations of the higher organs of government, and of functional economic and social relations, but also that affecting individual human rights. Indeed, as a system of regional law develops, it in a sense ceases to be "international" and comes to resemble the municipal law of a confederation or federation.[39]

The development of politically integrated regions also calls for corresponding changes in the means by which law is determined. The roles of heads of states, cabinet ministers, and diplomatic and consular agents, in the negotiation of international agreements, would eventually be transformed to resemble the roles of the members of legislative institutions in sovereign states. As international regional law would come to be legislated rather than negotiated, the role of regional courts would resemble that of domestic courts. Integrated regions would thus resemble an integrated state in macrocosm and an integrated world in microcosm, and would establish the institutional as well as the procedural precedents for a worldwide integration in the distant future.

This conception of regional integration as an intermediate phase of worldwide integration, although except for Western Europe integrated regionalism is a matter for the distant rather than the near future, also embraces the development of the second type of nonintegrated regional blocs of varying types. As an international system that would be an alternative to one composed primarily of national states, one or more integrated regions might interact with regional groupings of more loosely associated countries to form an international system that might resemble the concert of Europe in the nineteenth century in its ability to control and direct international relations.[40]

International Functionalism

One of the areas of most rapid change in the international order is the development of international functional institutions. Although these are created by sovereign states to perform functions in their common interest, they eventually develop a life of their own and in

---

[39] A. H. Robertson, *The Council of Europe: Its Structure, Functions, and Achievements* (2nd edn., New York 1961) ; Robinson O. Everett, ed., *European Regional Communities: A New Era on the Old Continent* (New York 1962) ; Guy Van Oudenhove, *The Political Parties in the European Parliament* (Leiden 1965) ; and the documents and articles in the *European Yearbook* (The Hague 1955—) .

[40] Masters, 797-98; and Lord Gladwyn, "World Order and the Nation-State—A Regional Approach," *Daedalus*, xcv (Spring 1966) , 694-703.

substance if not in form they acquire supranational authority. The impact of modern knowledge on traditional institutions results in the development of many functions that are beyond the capacities of a single state to control. International functionalism thus represents an area of concern to international law that is distinct both from municipal and from regional law.[41]

Some aspects of international functionalism are already well developed and are not likely to change radically in the near future. These include the International Labor Organization, a classic example of an international functional body, and the many international organizations concerned with health, communication, transportation, finance, and commerce.

There are other areas, however, where it seems clear that a largely new body of international law and practice will have to be established in the near future. One of these areas is arms control. Only the very first steps have been taken toward an international system of arms control, yet to the very considerable existing problems in this area new ones will soon be added. It is anticipated that by 1980 the tactical use of nuclear weapons will be significantly enlarged, many new weapons and devices of varying lethal potential will be developed, and the rapid mobility of armed forces to any point on the earth will be possible. Even more than today, the security of mankind in the near future will depend on its ability to control the use of these weapons.[42]

Closely related to arms control as an area calling for international functional action in the near future is outer space. The intensive research and engineering that is in process permits no doubt that this will be one of the most important areas calling for the establishment of legal norms in the near as well as in the distant future. The demarcation of space, the relationship of national to international interests, and the use of space for communication, transportation, espionage, and warfare, are some of the problems that will have to be resolved in the near future. Just beyond the near future, questions regarding sovereignty over celestial bodies, the exploitation of mineral resources in space, and related matters, are also likely to arise.[43] Some of these questions can be resolved by analogy with established norms, but others will require imaginative efforts at innovation.

[41] The fullest treatment of this subject is Ernst B. Haas, *Beyond the Nation-State: Functionalism and International Organization* (Stanford 1964); see also James Patrick Sewell, *Functionalism and World Politics* (Princeton 1966).

[42] Gordon and Helmer, esp. 32-39.

[43] Myres S. McDougal, Harold D. Lasswell, and Ivan A. Vlasic, *Law and Public Order in Space* (New Haven 1963); and C. Wilfred Jenks, *Space Law* (New York 1965). See also Karl W. Deutsch, "Outer Space and International Politics: A Look to 1988," Joseph M. Goldsen, ed., *Outer Space in World Politics* (New York 1963), 139-74.

International Government

The absorption of international law into a worldwide municipal law when nations pool their sovereignties will not take place in the foreseeable future. Experience with nation-building, and with the initial phase of regional integration in Western Europe, has demonstrated that effective government is not possible until the component units are sufficiently close in regard to norms, institutions, and levels of development that they can be brought under a common legal system without gross forms of compulsion. The countries of Western Europe which have shared a common religion and culture for many centuries, and share a reasonably narrow range of levels of development, are only now after two catastrophic wars in the twentieth century able to reconcile themselves to integration. It is not likely that the world will be ready for integration in the near future.

It is not difficult to imagine in the abstract a United Nations with teeth,[44] capable of governing the world the way national states govern countries. But states are not people, and the logic of integration tends to militate against the conception of a world government composed of national states. Experience with integrated regionalism suggests that international integration is more likely to be achieved through integration at a lower level, by means of the growth or fusion first of integrated states into integrated regions and later between integrated regions, than by a worldwide federation of distinct sovereignties. Neither the international nor the inter-regional approach, or possible alternative roads to international integration, are practicable in the near future.

There are other roles for international government in the near future, however, that are likely to call for the imaginative development of international law. Not the least of these is the maintenance and development of the United Nations within its present framework as a forum for the discussion of issues of common concern to mankind and for the evolution of a consensus regarding norms and objectives.[45]

The United Nations is already directly or indirectly responsible for coordinating the activities of the various international functional or-

[44] Grenville Clark and Louis B. Sohn, *World Peace Through World Law* (Cambridge, Mass. 1958) ; and Lincoln P. Bloomfield, *A World Effectively Controlled by the United Nations*, Study Memorandum No. 7, Institute for Defense Analyses (March 10, 1963) . The World Order Models Project, organized by Saul H. Mendlovitz under the auspices of the World Law Fund, is concerned with the prospects for bringing about a world order system change by the decade of the 1990's.

[45] See esp. Norman J. Padelford and Leland M. Goodrich, eds., *The United Nations: Accomplishments and Prospects*, published as a special issue of *International Organization*, xix (Summer 1965) ; and Rosalyn Higgins, *The Development of International Law Through the Political Organs of the United Nations* (London 1963) .

ganizations now in existence, and it has an opportunity in the near future to further the development of international law as it relates to these activities. The organization and procedures of the International Court of Justice, the principal judicial organ of the United Nations, would also benefit from imaginative review.

At the territorial level, the Antarctic Treaty of 1959 points to the need for further elaboration of international law as it applies to strategic areas. There is a growing number of situations in which the established principles of international law could be adapted to new problems of neutralization and demilitarization of states, parts of states, waterways, and other areas in dispute.[46] It is possible that in the near future oceanography will develop to a point where there will be international competition for the use of the mineral and biological resources of the oceans and the underlying land. Methods of climate control may also develop to the point where the interests of many states will be affected. These are both areas where international law and procedures could be imaginatively developed.

Substantial achievements in international law at both the functional and the territorial levels depend not only on experience and imagination, but also on the development of a conception of international law common to all of mankind. This exists today to the extent that treaties ratified by the sovereign states form a kind of international legislation binding on the signatories. Beyond this nucleus of agreed law, however, there is a wide area where diverse ideologies, points of view, national interests, and ethnic traditions make agreement difficult.[47]

An issue that is likely to continue into the near future is the effort of the Soviet leaders to obtain general recognition of their view that international law should be brought into accord with the principles of "peaceful coexistence." These principles assume that all states will inevitably become socialist—in the Soviet meaning of the term—and that international law should be interpreted in the light of this assumption. The difference in this case is less in the specific legal concepts, although such differences exist, but rather in the spirit in which they are interpreted. Until there is agreement regarding the fact and logic of the diversity in the outlook and interests of states that will prevail in the near future, and the acceptance of principles of international law that recognize and overarch this diversity, the foundations cannot be laid for a common law of mankind.[48]

[46] Cyril E. Black, Richard A. Falk, Klaus Knorr, and Oran R. Young, *Neutralization and World Politics* (Princeton 1968).

[47] C. Wilfred Jenks, *The Common Law of Mankind* (New York 1958); and George Schwarzenberger, *The Frontiers of International Law* (London 1962), esp. 274-313.

[48] The Soviet case is stated in F. I. Kozhevnikov, ed., *Mezhdunarodnoe pravo* [International Law] (Moscow 1964), 66-93; and G. I. Tunkin, *Droit international*

The Challenge of the Next Generation

Fundamental to the scholarly study of the international legal order in the next generation is the need to strike a balance between a concern with ultimate solutions for future problems that can now be seen with some clarity and a preoccupation with international issues that are immediately upon us. The key to such a balance lies in an understanding of the forces of change that are at work today and the limits on change represented by the human, institutional, and physical environment.

It is understandable that a generation which has experienced two world wars and the possibility of widespread destruction of life by nuclear weapons is inclined to seek solutions that will establish once and for all a universal system of international order. It is a challenging task to design institutions of world government that will give a universe of societies the degree of legality that well-ordered national governments are able to achieve today. A universal legal order of this degree of stability would only be possible under conditions of an international consensus in regard to values and goals such as exists within individual societies. There is no such consensus at present, and the turmoil of the present age stands witness to the diversity of cultures and ideologies that motivate different groups of national leaders and to the many dimensions of distances that separate the one hundred and fifty or more politically organized societies that inhabit the globe.

A more immediate challenge than that of constructing an ideal world in theory is that of foreseeing and anticipating the practical problems confronting the international legal order a generation at a time, in an effort to achieve at least the degree of international consensus necessary to avoid violence and destruction if an acceptable degree of international order is to be achieved. It is to this task that these volumes are devoted.

---

public (Paris 1965), 19-62. This case is criticized in Leon Lipson, "Peaceful Coexistence," *Law and Contemporary Problems*, xxix (1964), 871-81; and Bernard Dutoit, *Coexistence et droit international à la lumière de la doctrine soviétique* (Paris 1966).

CHAPTER 2

The Interplay of Westphalia and Charter Conceptions of International Legal Order

RICHARD A. FALK

THERE ARE many useful ways to speculate about the future.[1] This chapter is concerned with identifying certain evolutionary trends that seem to be influencing the shape and substance of the international legal order.[2] Inquiry is organized around a comparison between the Westphalia and the Charter conceptions of international legal order. The Westphalia conception, taking its name from the peace treaties of 1648, constitutes the classical framework of legal constraint postulated to regulate a highly decentralized world of sovereign states; this conception yields a permissive, voluntaristic system of law stressing matters of the allocation of competence among sovereign states.

The Charter conception taking its name from the United Nations Charter, constitutes a major modification of the Westphalia system in a number of critical respects bearing on the status of war, the role of national sovereignty, and the degree to which authority structures are centralized.[3]

In the contemporary international system the Charter conception is far from fully realized, the Westphalia conception is far from fully

---

[1] A growing literature is concerned with speculation about the future. Several books are particularly useful as introductions. E.g. Erich Jantsch, *Technological Forecasting in Perspective* (Paris, Organization for Economic Cooperation and Development, 1967); Fred A. Polak, *The Image of the Future* (2 vols., Dobbs Ferry, N. Y. 1961); Bertrand de Jouvenel, *The Art of Conjecture* (New York, 1967); Herman Kahn and Anthony J. Wiener, *The Year 2000—A Framework for Speculation on the Next Thirty-Three Years* (New York 1967).

[2] As such, its emphasis is upon evolution within the existing system rather than with speculation about alternative international systems and the conditions of their emergence. For a discussion of this distinction see Falk, *Legal Order in a Violent World* (Princeton 1968), 8-38. A useful comparative analysis of alternative international systems is to be found in Oran R. Young, *The World System: Present Characteristics and Future Prospects* (Hudson Institute [HI-277-D], August 29, 1963).

[3] The Charter conception is a continuation, in most essential respects, of the modifications of international society embodied in the ideas leading to the formation of the League of Nations. In some sense, it might be more accurate to compare the Westphalia conception with the Covenant conception. However, since the League is defunct, it seems more suitable merely to take note of the formation of the League as a critical date and to suggest sources for those interested in a comparison between the Charter and the Covenant. On this see Inis L. Claude, Jr., *Swords into Plowshares* (New York, 3rd rev. edn., 1964), Chapters I-II; Falk and Saul H. Mendlovitz, eds., *The Strategy of World Order: The United Nations* (New York 1966), Vol. III, 5-36.

displaced.[4] The purpose of calling attention to these two conceptions is to specify the prospects for a fuller realization of the Charter conception of international legal order in the years ahead by pointing to some relevant trends in belief and attitude. To promote this purpose, however, it is essential to emphasize the extent to which Westphalia considerations continue to prevail as a consequence of the national control of military power and human loyalty. The focus upon the interplay between these two conceptions of normative orientation is intended to contribute a basis for speculation about the future of international legal order. Such a procedure does not imply that the Westphalia and Charter conceptions are the only important ordering logics at work in contemporary international society. And, in fact, later in the chapter there will be some discussion of such other ordering conceptions as spheres of influence, rules of the game, deterrence, and decentralized modes of law enforcement.

Before discussing the salient attributes of the Westphalia and Charter conceptions some attention will be given to conceptual tools of analysis. Discussion of world order issues has been typically blurred by vague definitions and by a confused relationship between description and prescription.[5] The first section of this chapter tries to be explicit about some of these issues.

THE COORDINATES OF ANALYSIS

What Is the International Legal Order?

The international legal order is here conceived of as an aggregate conception embodying those structures and processes by which authority is created, applied, and transformed in international society. The distinctive focus, then, is upon the authority system as an attribute of the wider extralegal conception of an international system. Authority

---

[4] These two conceptions of international legal order are ideal type characterizations that purport only to approximate the actual contours of behavior and order. Such intellectual constructs are useful in developing highly abstract images, but they must be adapted to the specific character of various sectors of international life.

[5] The study of legal order is complicated by a simultaneous concern with static and dynamic aspects. This double concern engenders a mixture of descriptive and prescriptive modes of analysis, as the data are being appreciated in light of certain perceived inadequacies, and one strategy of reform is to present "the ought" as the "is." In international societal affairs uncertainty as to the character of legal standards applicable to certain kinds of behavior makes it necessary for the decision-maker to exercise discretion, to choose. Myres S. McDougal and his associates at Yale University have worked out an entire jurisprudence of international law around this central issue of guiding decision toward the realization of certain values postulated as preferences. For McDougal's orientation see Chapter 3. It seems clear that given such a value-realizing emphasis it is impossible and undesirable to act as if there can be an entirely satisfactory separation of description and prescription. At the very least, however, clarity of explanation allows a reader to know the way in which a particular author proposes to treat the distinction.

is understood to encompass established expectations and traditions about who is entitled to make and implement decisions; the authority perspective also is concerned with patterns of compliance that suggest a positive, if imprecise, correlation between the authoritative decision and the behavior undertaken in relation thereto.[6] In effect, the international legal order is a socio-historical product of convergent perspectives of formal authority and actual behavior.[7] The decentralized character of the present system of international legal order complicates the task of specifying the prevailing profile of authority. It is difficult, for instance, to deal realistically with "spheres of influence" that are tacitly and reciprocally acknowledged by principal sovereign states as creating special prerogatives about the exercise of national power.[8] For instance, the role of the United States in Latin America or the role of the Soviet Union in Eastern Europe are critical aspects of the constituted authority system that exists in international life even though these roles cannot be explained in terms of formal norms or even by reference to formal processes of decision.[9] To exclude these patterns of control from a conception of the international legal order tends to produce an artificially formalistic and legalistic conception, one that over-clarifies the distinction between the realm of law and the realm of politics in international affairs. To assimilate completely *de facto* regimes of control into a conception of the international legal order, however, would endanger a confusion of law and power such that it would no longer be meaningful to distinguish the standards of international law from the patterns of international politics.[10] We seek here an

[6] There is a very suggestive discussion of authority, and its relationship to behavior, in Kenneth S. Carlston, *Law and Organization in World Society* (Urbana 1962) , 64-123.

[7] This viewpoint is well formulated in Oscar Schachter, "Towards a Theory of International Obligation," 8 *Virginia Journal of International Law*, 300-22 (1968) .

[8] For some discussion of the role of "spheres" or "zones" of *de facto* authority see pp. 41-69.

[9] In certain instances, these extraterritorial prerogatives are given formal or quasi-formal legitimacy. The validation of colonial title is, of course, one kind of example. Another more subtle kind of legitimacy is that given the Monroe Doctrine by Article 21 of the Covenant of the League of Nations. Article 21 reads: "Nothing in this Covenant shall be deemed to affect the validity of international engagements, such as treaties of arbitration or regional understandings like the Monroe Doctrine, for securing the maintenance of peace." See comment on Article 21 in Ronald J. Yalem, *Regionalism and World Order* (Washington, D. C. 1965) , 39-40. Professor Yalem reflects, perhaps, too narrow a view of international order when he concludes "the Monroe Doctrine was in no sense a regional understanding. It was a unilateral declaration of policy by the United States without any standing under international law." (39-40) Surely, this is true in formal terms of consensual authority, but claims to exercise authority that are acquiesced in by the community create expectations that are given *de facto* respect even if not accorded full *de jure* validity.

[10] The intellectual risks of such a confusion are well identified in Stanley Hoffmann, *The State of War* (New York 1965) , 123-33.

intermediate position, one that maintains the distinctiveness of legal order while managing to be responsive to the extralegal setting of politics, history, and morality.[11] In this spirit, the study of international law—as the specialized and disciplined inquiry into the structure and process of authority—gives the legal dimension in international relations the status of a quasi-dependent variable. By quasi-dependence is meant that law both tends to reflect and to be shaped by the international system as a whole and serves or may serve as a strategy by which to participate in or transform the international system.[12] As a consequence of such a conception of the international legal order it is essential to identify the wider systemic setting and to consider the strategic potentialities available in the various arenas of authority for system-reform and system-transformation.[13]

In this chapter attention will be given to the general characteristics of the present system of international legal order: its most characteristic and general level of existence.[14] The relatively permanent elements of structure are used as delimiting features: the number and kind of units, bases of international obligation, external aims and domestic public order systems, stakes and modalities of conflict, frameworks of constraint, and forms of conflict settlement.[15] Attention will also be given to dynamic elements of process: emerging units, converging and diverging external aims, alterations in the pattern of conflict, and shifts in loyalty and belief. Stanley Hoffmann has identified as "The law of the political framework—the network of agreements that define the conditions and some of the rules of the political game among states."[16] It is this structural framework, as distinct from the substance of specific rules and doctrine, that is the concern of this chapter.

[11] An attempt to specify this intermediate position is to be found in Falk, *The Status of Law in International Society* (Princeton 1969), Chapter III.

[12] This is the major theme of a series of lectures: Falk, "The New States and International Legal Order," 118 Hague Academy Recueil des Cours 1-103 (1966).

[13] Such an undertaking is the explicit orientation of Morton A. Kaplan and Nicholas deB. Katzenbach, *The Political Foundations of International Law* (New York 1961); see also Oran R. Young, "A Systemic Approach to International Politics," Research Monograph No. 33, June 30, 1968.

[14] There are many recent efforts at characterization. See e.g. Stanley Hoffmann, *Gulliver's Troubles, or the Setting of American Foreign Policy* (New York 1968), 10-51; George Liska, *Imperial America—The International Politics of Primacy* (Baltimore 1967).

[15] Cf. the formulations of Ernst B. Haas in Chapter 6.

[16] Hoffmann, *Gulliver's Troubles*, 97 n8; such a conception is somewhat static as it considers only "conditions" and "rules." International legal order is dynamic in the most fundamental sense—the principal participants evolve the conditions and rules through their patterns of action. An act, especially if effectively asserted and justified in legal rhetoric, tends to acquire status as a precedent. Expectations about what is lawful are influenced by the precedents of the past, even in situations in which the initial precedent itself rested on a shaky legal foundation.

The macro-level of depiction facilitates socio-historical and analytic comparison of distinct systems of international legal order. Socio-historical systems are those that have existed at some stage in the actual development of international society. A system of international legal order need not be global in scope; in fact, it might be argued that only since the end of World War II has there existed an international legal order of global dimension.[17] A comprehensive mapping of earlier systems of international legal order would involve the description of several distinct, but overlapping, partial systems.[18]

Analytic systems of international legal order are models of authority patterns that can be posited for consideration whether or not they have actually existed.[19] For instance, a world state or a world empire can be modeled for recommendation and study; it makes no difference to the intellectual integrity of the effort whether such a model has existed or even whether it is ever likely to exist. Nevertheless, models of the international legal order that are alternatives to the existing system are usually set forth in the spirit of either advocacy or prophecy. Utopian literature is concerned normally with depicting a better world order that overcomes the deficiencies of the existing system, whereas science fiction is concerned with various kinds of prophecy, often arising out of more or less plausible trend projections.[20] Both types of speculation tend to specify some alternative conception to highlight the deficiency of what exists or to provide the means of its cure.

It would seem most desirable to adopt a comparative method for the study of alternative systems of international legal order. Such

17 Cf. B.V.A. Röling, *International Law in an Expanded World* (Amsterdam 1960). Even in the late 1960's there are important formal exclusions from participation, most notably the two successor states to Germany and the Peoples Republic of China.

18 For preliminary depiction see Richard N. Rosecrance, *Action and Reaction in World Politics* (Boston 1963). See also Raymond Aron, *Peace and War—A Theory of International Relations* (New York 1966), 94-149.

19 The most ambitious effort in this direction remains Morton A. Kaplan, *System and Process in International Politics* (New York 1957); for other helpful studies that facilitate relevant forms of model-building see Kenneth E. Boulding, *Conflict and Defense: A General Theory* (New York 1962); Karl W. Deutsch, *The Nerves of Government* (Glencoe, Ill. 1963), esp. 3-50.

20 Cf. Polak, *Image of the Future*; Glenn Negley and J. Max Patrick, eds., *The Quest for Utopia: An Anthology of Imaginary Writings* (New York 1952); Karl Mannheim, *Ideology and Utopia* (New York n.d., original published in English 1936, in German 1929); "Utopia," *Daedalus* (Spring 1965), 271-519; Martin Buber, *Paths in Utopia* (London 1949).

The spirit of utopian literature can be reconstructionist in the sense of offering a plan for a better world that its author believes desirable and attainable. Such literature can also be satiric in character, projecting into the future a deteriorated image of the present, not because its author hopes for that world, but precisely because he fears it. This latter genre, sometimes styled anti-utopian, seeks to promote reform of the present by issuing a warning about the future.

a comparative method facilitates sharper delineation of the present system and a better appreciation of the relative desirability and at-tainability of alternatives to it.

The consideration of several models of the international legal order calls attention to the transition problem, i.e. to the problem of sys-tem-change on the macro-level of international society that is entailed in moving from an existing system to a preferred system.[21] To study transition processes underscores a managerial impulse—"Where will we be in the year 2000 or 2100 is far more a problem in control and anticipation than in prediction."[22] The objective of such an under-taking is to conceive of the future as an arena in which choice in the present can be influenced by evidence, analysis, argument, education, and learning of the range of future possibilities.[23]

Within the existing system of the international legal order there are various trends and countertrends. The evaluation of trends and countertrends presupposes value orientations: as Daniel Bell writes "the problem of the future consists in defining one's priorities and making the necessary commitments."[24] To carry forward this method of inquiry we will postulate five highly abstract preferences that may on occasion interact nonharmoniously so as to make an explanation of priorities necessary in each setting of decision:

1. The minimization of violence;

2. The promotion of human rights of individuals and groups, espe-cially national autonomy and racial equality;

3. The transfer of wealth and income from rich states to poor states;

4. The equitable participation of diverse cultures, regions, and ideologies in a composite system of global order;

5. The growth of supranational and international institutions.[25]

---

21 See Hoffmann, Gulliver's Troubles, 343-64; Young, The World System, 4:7-4:18, 5:7-5:13, 6:2-6:10.

22 Martin Shubik, "Information, Rationality, and Free Choice in a Future Demo-cratic Society," Daedalus (Summer 1967) , 771-78, at 775.

23 A pioneer enterprise in this direction was Gunnar Myrdal, An American Dilemma (New York 1944) ; a more relevant substantive study based on such a methodology is Johan Galtung, "On the Future of the International System," Journal of Peace Research, 4 (1967) , 305-33.

24 Daniel Bell, "The Year 2000—The Trajectory of an Idea," Daedalus (Summer 1967) , 639-51, at 646.

25 A very tentative, initial acknowledgment of the following criticism directed at my past work: "One difficulty in the way of Professor Falk's efforts to formulate an international law that embraces both the noncommunist and communist worlds resides, thus, in his unwillingness to postulate a comprehensive set of inclusive poli-cies, for which he as a scholar is willing to take responsibility in recommendation, relevant to appraising the detailed practices of both sets of participants." Myres S. McDougal, Harold D. Lasswell, and W. Michael Reisman, "Theories About Inter-national Law: Prologue to a Configurative Jurisprudence," 8 Virginia Journal of International Law, 188-299, at 288 (1968) .

Priorities could be postulated in noncontextual or categorical form such that, for instance, recourse to violence is never justifiable. It seems preferable, however, to establish priorities within specific contexts of choice or to endorse authoritative procedures as competent to establish priorities. For instance, an international institution may be endowed with the competence to authorize violence to promote collective security, anti-colonialism, or racial equality. The Southern African issues of racism and colonialism illustrate a setting wherein it appears increasingly appropriate for community institutions to suspend prohibitions upon violence so as to secure other valued ends.[26] The failure of the Security Council of the United Nations in 1961 to oppose India's forcible seizure of Goa was a vivid instance in which a constituted international organ established a priority schedule on an *ad hoc* basis.[27]

In studying the future of the international legal order several prominent issues emerge: (1) alternative conceptions; (2) transition prospects and strategies; and (3) trends and countertrends within the existing system; (3) may prove to be the most rewarding focus as the prospects for (1) and (2) are not very favorable. No major structural modifications of international society appear likely to occur in the twentieth century unless a general nuclear war takes place. Over a longer term, an evolutionary erosion of the existing national locus of power and loyalty seem likely to take place, but such trends are indefinite and their eventual impact difficult to anticipate. The existing system of international legal order appears resistant to drastic change through conscious redirection, whether in the form of agreement by sovereign states or by a transnational political movement.

[26] There is, of course, the correlative question about the extent to which priorities can be established by regional and national actors in circumstances where the organs of the global actor cannot or do not come to a decision. What are the residual capacities of subordinate actors to set priorities, especially in situations where the use of political violence is being authorized? Under what circumstances can the Arab League or the Organization of African Unity legitimize a contemplated use of violence to deal with an intra-regional adversary? Can even the United Arab Republic or Tanzania confer legitimacy on use of violence against a foreign state, at least to the extent of providing money, arms, and sanctuaries for insurgent and guerrilla groups? These questions probe the surface of a complex subject. There are different degrees of nonaction, authorization, and participation, as well as different normative expectations as to what it is permissible for various actors to do. There is a need for a systematic statement of these interrelations between different kinds of *actors* in different kinds of *conflict*.

[27] That is, norms precluding recourse to international violence were subordinated to norms invalidating colonial title; other factors of preference and capability entered in. The fact that Goa was "an enclave," not "a state," meant that there was some ambiguity as to whether India was making an internal use of force protected from international scrutiny by the domestic jurisdiction principle or was making an external use of force subject to the prohibition that force is illegal except in self-defense.

The strategic variable in assessing prospects for change is the extent to which capabilities to wage war will remain under the control of national governments, and the further extent to which the leadership of a few of these governments have predominant capabilities as compared to the remainder. Of course, many sub-variables are associated with the future of the nation-state as the organizing power center of international life.[28] It is especially important to gauge regional integration, cosmopolitan belief systems, and the proliferation of nuclear weapons technology in relation to the role and function of the state.

In general preliminary terms it seems most likely to project a hierarchically administered horizontal legal order into the near future. It is hierarchically administered as a consequence of the special role exerted by principal actors; it is horizontal as a consequence of decentralized decision-making persisting for the most vital subject-matter.[29] There is, in other words, sufficient inertia in the present system that it is unreasonable to expect significant cumulative trends toward either the refeudalization of international society by the breakup of states into nonautonomous units or toward its unification by voluntary or coercive means.[30] Arthur C. Clarke has aptly written that "It is impossible to predict the future, and all attempts to do so in any detail appear ludicrous within a few years." But a "futurology" of international law is not in vain. "[T]o describe the future" means, as Clarke puts it, to "define the boundaries within which possible futures must lie."[31] Although Clarke is concerned primarily with the impacts of science and technology on the future, his orientation is suggestive, as well, for political and legal studies. Amitai Etzioni has expressed a comparable orientation toward the future, one set in a subject-matter closely related to the international legal order—community-building and social action.[32] Etzioni invents a neologism "contextuating orientation" to express the idea of a limited range of plausible future contexts worthy of serious scrutiny.[33] He is also concerned with identifying a preferred future and describing the processes by which the relevant goals are most likely to be

[28] In assessing this future, Stanley Hoffmann's differentiation of national consciousness, national situation, and nationalism is suggestive. See Stanley Hoffmann, "Obstinate or Obsolete? The Fate of the Nation-State and the Case of Western Europe," *Daedalus* (Summer 1966), 862-915, at 867-69.

[29] Illustrative of such decentralization is the continuing unwillingness of even advanced non-Communist states to entrust the power of decision to international institutions in the event of a dispute touching upon serious issues.

[30] Such a distinction is relied upon in Falk, *The Status of Law*, Chapter XXI; see also Carl J. Friederich, *Man and His Government* (New York 1963), 567-609.

[31] Arthur C. Clarke, *Profiles of the Future* (New York 1964), XI.

[32] Amitai Etzioni, *The Active Society* (New York 1968), 550-613.

[33] Same, 155-63, 668.

attained. Such a strategy of inquiry is equally appropriate for examining the future of the international legal order.

World order literature is often flawed by its sentimental naiveté, by its implicit faith that what appears desirable is automatically attainable.[34] Little attention is given in this aspirational literature to problems of transforming power relations and redirecting loyalty patterns in international society.[35] And yet these structures of power relations and loyalty patterns are typical ingredients of a social system capable of maintaining itself against pressures for change. Reasoned persuasion does not by itself provide any realistic prospect for altering the structure of international society.[36] World order analyses have in the past emphasized some sort of plan that is supposed to appeal to the rational intellect as preferable to the present system of world order.[37] The projection of a preferred future system of world order is not likely to be relevant to the historical future unless the awesome problem of attainability is confronted with great seriousness. Such a problem is, above all, one of studying the transfer of power and authority under various kinds of functional stress and depicting the nature of a new cosmopolitan ideology that would dissipate the hold of the state upon the loyalty of the individual and substitute new myths and symbols capable of arousing widespread support.[38]

The consequence of a more practical orientation, then, is to refocus a study of the future of world order on the specific problems of political engineering: What is desired? Under what conditions can it be attained? What can be done to bring these conditions about? In a world of hostile ideologies, of states at different levels of economic and political development, and of different patterns of belief and fear there is bound to be a very limited consensus on means, ends, and prospects. Without consensus the only strategy of directed change for a system as decentralized as international society would appear to entail coercion leading to wider systems of domination—imperial world order systems—lacking any genuine sense of community at-

[34] For criticism of this defect in analysis see Falk, "The Revolution in Peace Education," *Saturday Review* (May 21, 1966), 59-61, 77.

[35] For a very significant exception see W. Warren Wagar, *The City of Man* (Baltimore 1967).

[36] The reasons why this is so have been ably stated by Walter C. Schiffer, *The Legal Community of Mankind* (New York 1954), esp. 273-301. See also F. H. Hinsley, *Power and the Pursuit of Peace* (Cambridge 1963).

[37] The most widely known contemporary plan of this variety is Grenville Clark and Louis B. Sohn, *World Peace Through World Law* (Cambridge, 3rd rev. edn., 1966); for a very persuasive analysis of the reasons why such a reasonable objective is unattainable see the numerous writings of Reinhold Niebuhr. See especially *The Structure of Nations and Empires* (New York 1959); *The Children of Light and the Children of Darkness* (New York 1944).

[38] A recent book is quite suggestive along these lines, despite its narrower focus. Robert Gilpin, *France in the Age of the Scientific State* (Princeton 1968).

tachment by many caught within the imperial net. A dilemma is posed by the difficulties of consensus-formation and the dangers and deficiencies of domination that expresses the basic quality of the current international situation. Bipolarity on the fundamental level of stalemating any effort by a principal sovereign state to achieve overarching domination is a further aspect of the dilemma of world order. The diagnostic consequence is to predicate the persistence of the present international system, including its quasi-dependent authority pattern.

FIVE DIMENSIONS OF INTERNATIONAL LEGAL ORDER

Surprisingly little effort has been given to a specification of the attributes of the present system of international legal order. Until we have a clear image of the present system it is impossible either to interpret trends or assess proposals and prospects for change. In this section of the chapter a preliminary profile of the present system will be attempted. Heavy emphasis will be given to the role of authority perspectives—expectations about permissible standards and procedures of behavior.

There are problems of *characterization* created by my unwillingness to accept a conservative interpretation of the province of legal authority[39] as delimited by formal expression of consent by sovereign states. The authority system operative in international society is specified here to encompass *de facto* regimes that can come into effective being without any dependence upon the rhetoric or technique of lawyers —for instance, through the manipulation of the so-called rules of the game.[40] In opposite fashion, the authority system is also specified to include *de jure* regimes extant without much prospect of behavioral impact—for instance, the human rights provisions of the United Nations Charter or the General Assembly Resolution adopting the Principles of the Nuremberg Judgment.[41] The main objective of this

[39] An excellent presentation of these issues is to be found in Schachter, "A Theory of International Obligation," 306-22; also useful is Clive Parry, *Sources and Evidence of International Law* (Manchester 1965).

[40] Suggestive writings include C.A.W. Manning, *The Nature of International Society* (London 1962), 64-181; Anatol Rapoport, *Fights, Games, and Debates* (Ann Arbor 1960); T. C. Schelling, *Arms and Influence* (New Haven 1966).

[41] The General Assembly unanimously affirmed "the principles of international law recognized by the Charter of the Nuremberg Tribunal and the judgment of the Tribunal" on December 11, 1946, G. A. Res. 95 (I). The same Resolution also directed the International Law Commission to formulate these principles as part of an overall effort to evolve a codification of "offenses against the peace and security of mankind, or of an International Criminal Code." For a summary of United Nations activity in relation to the Nuremberg Principles see Louis B. Sohn, ed., *Cases on United Nations Law* (Brooklyn 1956), 969-70; for formulation of the Nuremberg Principles, and a summary of their discussion in the Sixth (Legal) Committee of the General Assembly see same, 970-83.

analysis is to obtain a clear image of the limiting conditions that affect the world order potentialities of the existing system. Such an image may emerge more clearly if the roles of different forms of authority and quasi-authority in ordering the conduct of international life can be clearly identified.

The problem of world order is initially one of description. How does the existing system function? It is always problematic to explain the existence of order in a political system that lacks governmental institutions.

International lawyers have grappled for several centuries with the challenge to find an adequate account of the nature and function of law in international society. The principal mode of successful explanation is to relate international law to the specific features of the international environment. It is important to understand that legal order is a quasi-dependent variable in *any* social and political setting. For this reason it is a mistake to suppose that the domestic legal order of a modern state is a paradigm for any legal system, and that the quality of a *particular* legal system depends on how closely it resembles the structure and appearance of domestic law. The first step toward grasping international legal order is to become liberated from such an imprisoning notion of paradigms. The second step is to appreciate that international society is bound to possess a decentralized form of legal order that corresponds to its decentralized social and political structure. The third step is to build up an integrated notion of the distinctive characteristics of the sort of decentralized legal order that has emerged in international society. And the fourth step is to gain insight into the growth potentialities of such a decentralized legal order, both potentialities for sector centralization in certain subject-matter or for certain sub-systems of relations and potentialities for enhancing decentralized modes of legal order.

On the basis of such an effort to grasp the international legal order as a distinctive legal system, it is possible to consider the principal components of authority and its implementation within the present framework of world affairs. Predominant emphasis will be placed upon the roles of the Westphalia and Charter conceptions, but other components will be briefly noted so as to present a reasonably comprehensive description of the current character of international order. The following components of the international legal order will be considered in sequence:

1. The Westphalia Conception;
2. The Charter Conception;
3. Geo-Political Conceptions (sphere of influence, deterrence) ;

4. Rules of the Game;
5. Decentralized Modes of Implementation.

1. THE WESTPHALIA CONCEPTION.[42] The basic formal ordering conception in international society since the seventeenth century has been the coordination of sovereign state units. It is convenient to identify this conception with the Peace of Westphalia of 1648, a dramatic event in the process of transition from medieval society to the modern world. Medieval society was dominated by the image of a Christian commonwealth, a world order system hierarchically organized beneath the sway of the Pope and the Holy Roman Empire.[43] Westphalia evolved a new image of coordinated states, each sovereign within its territorial sphere. A jurisprudential debate has proceeded through the centuries between advocates of natural law who proclaim the objective nature of obligation in international affairs and the advocates of positivist thought who stress the essential role of national consent in the formation of international obligation.[44] By and large, the naturalist position is a legacy of the medieval period, seeking to sustain the unity of international society by substituting a universal normative order for the institutional disintegration entailed by the collapse of imperial and papal authority. In general, positivistic thinking prevailed until after World War I, culminating in the treatise of Emmerich de Vattel who managed, without abandoning the rhetoric of natural law, to provide a doctrinal base for sovereignty in international society through his idea that the state could only be legally bound to the extent that it had given its consent.[45]

The Westphalia conception—giving legal status to a growing exercise of authority on a national level—has provided the main outline of structure and process in international society up to and including the present period. Sovereign states remain the dominant actors in international society and the contents of international law in its most formal sense is the result of voluntary action by states, exhibited either in the form of express agreement (treaties), tacit agreement (custom), or through the effective assertion of claims to control behavior in specified ways.

The state, as a spatial unit, results in the fundamental ordering of international relations through a central reliance on territorial con-

[42] An analysis of the Westphalia conception as it applies to ocean fishery disputes is to be found in Falk, *The Status of Law*, Chapter xx.

[43] Well-explicated in Leo Gross, "The Peace of Westphalia, 1648-1948," 42 *American Journal of International Law*, 20-41 (1948).

[44] A useful discussion of these issues is to be found in James L. Brierly, *The Basis of Obligation in International Law and Other Papers* (Oxford 1958), 1-67, Percy Corbett, *Law and Society in the Relation of States* (New York 1951), 17-89.

[45] Emmerich de Vattel, *The Law of Nations* (Washington 1916).

ceptions. Respect for the boundary of states is crucial and results in derivative legal ideas of territorial jurisdiction, sovereign equality, and nonintervention. The confirmation of the exclusive internal governing authority of the national government followed from the triumph of nationalism over feudalism, another feature of the Westphalia system. Jurisdictional ideas about the reciprocal allocation of authority to govern territorially distinct units of space achieved great prominence through the logic of Westphalia. Mutual respect for territorial supremacy within well-defined boundaries provided a formal basis for international peace and a mutually beneficial endorsement of authority to govern the internal life of national societies. The oceans were an unregulated arena, originally a place of danger and chaos, but gradually, after a period of sporadic sovereign appropriation, subjected to the thinking of Westphalia. The horizontal structure of international society precluded the emergence of a super-sovereign of the oceans or even some community regime of organized cooperation. Ships were given identity through national registration and regulated as a "floating territory" when on the high seas. Cooperative norms emerged through practice and agreement to promote common interests in safety, conservation, and convenience.[46] All states were made competent to pursue and capture "pirate" (non-flag) vessels, and otherwise to make unencumbered use of the oceans.[47]

The spirit of Westphalia did not prohibit recourse to war. In fact, the decision to wage war was vested in the sovereign, the highest source of legal authority in international society.[48] The role of international law as measured by the coordination of sovereign wills evolved the status of neutrality to enable the differentiation of participant from belligerent states according to legal standards and procedures that protected the two categories of interests.[49] In addition, rules governing the conduct of war evolved by custom and treaty, in

[46] For a very ample documentation of these processes see Myres S. McDougal and William T. Burke, *The Public Order of the Oceans* (New Haven 1962), esp. 1-88, 730-1140.

[47] Related claims to regulate extranational activity have resulted from the increasing interdependence of complex patterns of human behavior. One prominent and controversial area of such regulatory activity has involved the extension of the American antitrust laws to cover certain foreign operations alleged to have an anti-competitive impact on the United States economy. For a survey and analysis of the pattern of claim in the extraterritorial antitrust area see Falk, *The Status of Law*, Chapter IX.

[48] The growth of rules of international law restricting the right to wage war is described in Quincy Wright, *The Role of Law in the Elimination of War* (Dobbs Ferry, N. Y. 1961); see further Ian Brownlie, *International Law and the Use of Force by States* (London 1963).

[49] See Myres S. McDougal and Florentino P. Feliciano, *Law and Minimum World Public Order* (New Haven 1961), 384-519.

a manner comparable to the law of the oceans, to serve common interests in safeguarding prisoners of war, caring for the sick and wounded, and exempting certain targets from attack and prohibiting some weapons from use. The idea of neutrality and the laws of war have suffered serious encroachment as a consequence of the progressive change in the character of war from a conflict between professional armies to a conflict between adversary societies. In modern warfare anything that weakens the enemy society tends to help the war effort, and there is little willingness on the part of belligerents to indulge neutral trade or to respect targets as "nonmilitary."[50] Neutrality rested on the presupposition that neutral states could engage in nonmilitary commerce with either side or even with both sides in a war without encroaching upon serious belligerent concerns. Neutrality also presupposes a balance-of-power mentality in which the stakes of conflict are limited and in which wars are not fought to transform the system.[51] In a bipolar world, or even in a highly heterogeneous international society,[52] principal states will tend to be drawn to one or the other side in a struggle and the stakes may involve the polar affiliation of a unit, and hence alter "the balance" prevailing in the system. Also the resurgence of a normative attitude toward warfare in the twentieth century, especially in the years since the Kellogg-Briand Pact of 1928, have produced some shift to a collective security consciousness. That is, the logic of neutrality is challenged by normative pressures to protect the victims of aggression.

Many attributes of the contemporary world render the state system less credible as a basis for organizing international society than in the past.[53] States are not nearly so autonomous in the present world with respect either to matters of security or welfare.[54] The territoriality of action does not provide as satisfactory a basis for allocating legal authority as it did at an earlier stage in international society. Communications, transportation, a world culture, and a world economy unify demands about internal social and political

[50] For a strong argument that the changing patterns of warfare require revision of the laws of war see Josef Kunz, *The Changing Law of Nations* (Columbus 1968), 831-68; in the context of the Vietnam War see John Gerassi, *North Vietnam: A Documentary* (New York 1968); Kuno Knoebel, *Victor Charlie—The Face of War in Vietnam* (New York 1967).

[51] On the conception of a moderate (as distinct from a revolutionary) international system see Hoffmann, *Gulliver's Troubles*, 17-21, 356-64.

[52] On heterogeneity, see Aron, *Peace and War*, 99-104, 373-403.

[53] For useful specification of state system see William D. Coplin, "International Law and Assumptions about the State System," *World Politics*, 17 (1964), 615-35.

[54] Such an argument is mainly related to security issues in John H. Herz, *International Politics in the Atomic Age* (New York 1959); to welfare issues in Gunnar Myrdal, *Beyond the Welfare State* (New Haven 1960); to circumvention via the growth of functional international organization in Ernst B. Haas, *Beyond the Nation-State—Functionalism and International Organization* (Stanford 1964).

life. Interdependence makes all states vulnerable to the effects of decisions made outside their boundaries on matters as distinct as nuclear weapons testing and currency devaluation. Nuclear weaponry and electronic guidance systems makes every state vulnerable to destruction at the will of a rival national power center. These factors appear to explain some loosening of the bonds between the individual and the state, especially in the principal societies possessing relatively democratic national traditions.[55] Transnational, regional, and even cosmopolitan trends are evident in behavioral and loyalty patterns.[56]

On a more formal level the Westphalia conception has been augmented by the emergence of international institutions, especially the League of Nations and the United Nations. Discretionary recourse to war has been formally repudiated. Community claims to create obligations are being increasingly asserted. The collapse of colonialism has created an international system in which the active participants in international society represent the major cultures, races, stages of development, ideology, and domestic public order systems.

At the same time the Westphalia conception remains very significantly central to the organization of international society. National governments retain predominant, if occasionally challenged, authority and control over events within territorial boundaries. Sovereign consent remains critical to the formation of serious new international obligations.[57] The retention of military capabilities at the national level ensures the continuing supremacy of state decisions in the area of war and peace. International institutions, with some notable exceptions, operate as instrumentalities for the realization of national purposes rather than as autonomous actors. The basic postulates of the Westphalia conception continue to hold true for the early decades of the nuclear age. Despite the political vitality of the Westphalia conception, its increasing inability to satisfy the needs of individuals and states is a social fact of prime importance for our time. At each stage of international history there has existed a peculiar tension between the logic of sovereign equality central to Westphalia thinking and the actualities of inequality in national wealth, power, and disposition.

[55] Quite different trends are evident in nation-building settings and in the relatively more authoritarian and totalitarian societies.

[56] See Galtung, "Future of the International System."

[57] As has been explained by McDougal and Burke, *Public Order of the Oceans*, and Schachter, "A Theory of International Obligations," there has always been some compromise between "consent" and functional imperatives in the processes of formation of customary international law. See also Karol Wolfke, *Custom in Present International Law* (Warsaw 1964).

The actuality of hierarchy has always influenced the shape of international society, especially the relations between the dominant states and the rest of the world. The Westphalia conception through its acceptance of force as a potential source of legitimation was able to accommodate in its authority system some of the consequences of inequality. This accommodation is most dramatically expressed by the legitimacy attached to peace treaties imposed by the victor in war.[58] The validity of imposed peace treaties contrasts sharply with the treatment of imposed contracts in domestic law wherein proof of duress or coercion relieves a party from the burden of performance. Efforts to qualify the legitimacy attached to effective uses of force in international society, such as the sponsorship by the United States in the 1930's of a doctrine of nonrecognition of territorial gains achieved by illegal force (the so-called Stimson Doctrine), have not been successful in altering the basic derivation of sovereign status from the facts (not the legal basis) of effective occupation.[59] At the same time, the involuntary "acceptance" of obligations under the temporary circumstances of defeat is not likely to produce a stable settlement of a dispute. Instead, a "revisionist" attitude toward such a treaty regime is likely to emerge after a period of recovery. The Versailles solution of World War I is the most dramatic example of the unstable, counter-intentional effects of an imposed peace treaty; the consequent burst of German revisionism has seemed to serve as a learning experience for statesmen about the limits to which it is self-serving to impose burdens on a defeated country in the guise of a consensual, formally binding treaty of peace. There is a growing understanding that a stable settlement of conflict needs to be correlated with what will be acceptable to the parties after the circumstances of defeat diminish or disappear. Such an attitude toward longer-term stability guided Western thinking about a peace settlement after World War II. Therefore, despite the formal validity of imposed peace treaties, their sociopolitical disadvantages tend to limit their role in the present international legal order, especially in the relations among principal sovereign units.

The colonial system—as with all *de jure* imperial relationships—rests upon the legitimation of a structure of domination; in addition, as has been already noted, quasi-legitimate spheres of influence accorded primary sovereign states also leads to structures of partial

[58] For an assessment of the juridical validation of coercion in the form of imposed treaties of peace see Julius Stone, "De Victoribus Victis: The International Law Commission and Imposed Treaties of Peace," 8 *Virginia Journal of International Law*, 356-73 (1968).

[59] For a short, but useful discussion of the Stimson Doctrine, its rationale and effects, see Herbert W. Briggs, ed., *The Law of Nations* (New York, 2nd edn., 1952), 847-48.

domination that are at odds with the ideology of sovereign equality. The contemporary reassertion of national autonomy throughout the world has been accompanied naturally enough by profound bitterness and skepticism on the part of Afro-Asian leaders about the validity of traditional international law.[60] The notion of oligarchy in international society has been perpetuated in our time on a political level by the distinction between nuclear and nonnuclear powers and on the authority level by vesting a veto in the five permanent members of the Security Council.[61]

To acknowledge hierarchy and oligarchy in the international system is not to imply that the Westphalia major premise of sovereign equality is something altogether nominal or epiphenomenal. In many areas of international life, including virtually all matters of international routine, the legal notions of sovereign equality enjoy political vitality. Despite power differentials, South Africa respects the great inconvenience that results from the refusal of black African states to allow overflight of their territory by South African commercial aircraft. The United States reimburses its fishermen seized many miles from the Western coast of Latin America even though it regards the claims of exclusive fishing rights and the implementing seizure as contrary to international law.[62] An ambassador from a weak state is likely to enjoy virtually the same formal prerogatives as the ambassador from a strong state. The legal implementation of the ideas of sovereign equality are overwhelmingly descriptive of the ordering processes at work in international society. In sum, then, the Westphalia conception remains fundamental to the ordering of international society despite a variety of functional and ideological strains upon it.[63] The national government remains the most exclusive source of territorial authority and the decisions and agreement of national governments continue to provide the most important sources of international authority.

2. THE CHARTER CONCEPTION. A second main dimension of the international legal order centers upon the normative conceptions embodied

[60] For some consideration of these matters see Falk, "The New States and International Legal Order," 118 *Hague Recueil des Cours,* 1-102 (1966); a more fundamental depiction of the alienation that follows from the colonial experience is to be found in the play "The Blacks" by Jean Genet. See also Frantz Fanon, *The Wretched of the Earth* (New York 1963).

[61] The phenomenon of neocolonialism also needs to be examined. It would be desirable to assess the functional dimensions of colonial rulership and then use these dimensions to assess allegations of neocolonial equivalencies.

[62] Cf. "Foreign Seizure of U. S. Fishing Vessels," Congressional Hearing before the Subcommittee on Fisheries and Wildlife Conservation, 90th Cong., 1st Sess., June 22, 1967.

[63] For a statement of the attitudes of socialist countries toward the present system of international order see Wojciech Morawiecki, "Institutional and Political Conditions of Participation of Socialist States in International Organizations: A Polish View," *International Organization,* 22 (Spring 1968), 494-507.

in the United Nations Charter. The Charter conception overlaps in many respect the Westphalia conception, but it also complements this conception by centralizing some cooperative activities and contradicts this conception to the extent that community-oriented procedures comes to displace sovereignty-oriented procedures.[64] On a formal level of norms these two dominant conceptions of international order are reconciled in Article 2, the provision of the Charter that sets out the Principles that are supposed to control the operation of the Organization; from the perspective of reconciliation Article 2 (1) and 2 (7) are particularly relevant, the former stating that "the Organization shall be based on the principle of sovereign equality of all its Members" and the latter asserting that "nothing contained in the present Charter shall authorize the United Nations to intervene in matters which are essentially within the domestic jurisdiction of any state or shall require the Members to submit such matters to settlement under the present Charter." Thus the critical ideas of Westphalia involving sovereign equality and domestic jurisdiction are formally perpetuated in the Charter. The tension between the two conceptions of international legal order arises from certain other formal imperatives embodied in the Charter, modes of procedure by which "decisions" are reached and implemented, and patterns of practice that have evolved over the history of the Organization. A few of the more significant points of tension will now be taken up to illustrate the relationship between Westphalia and Charter approaches to world legal order.[65]

Status of War and Violence. The Charter purports to prohibit all recourse to force in the relations among states except individual or collective self-defense against an armed attack.[66] There is a sharp un-

[64] To derive the juridical basis of the Charter see R. B. Russell and J. E. Muther, *A History of the United Nations Charter* (Washington, D. C. 1958) ; for comparison of Covenant of the League of Nations and Charter of the United Nations see sources cited in note 3.

[65] A parallel analysis of centralizing and atomizing tendencies of thought and action is examined in a very thoughtful, imaginative essay. See Hedley Bull, "The Grotian Conception of International Society," in Herbert Butterfield and Martin Wight, eds., *Diplomatic Investigations* (London, 1966) , 51-73.

[66] The relevant Charter provisions are Article 2 (4) and 51; there has been a great deal of legal analysis devoted to the textual and contextual implications of the interrelations between the prohibition on the use of force and the authorization of self-defense; there are related issues concerned with the obligations to report a claim of self-defense to the Security Council, the procedural duty in Article 33 to exhaust pacific remedies, and the ambiguous status of various uses of forces made under mandate of a regional institution (Chapter VIII of the Charter) or in pursuance of a collective defense arrangement (Chapter VII of the Charter). Some of the basic interpretive issues are considered in McDougal and Feliciano, *World Public Order*, 121-260; see also D. W. Bowett, *Self-Defense in International Law* (Manchester 1958); Julius Stone, *Aggression and World Order* (Berkeley, 1958) ; Louis Henkin, "Force, Intervention and Neutrality in Contemporary International Law," *Proceedings American Society of International Law 1963*, 147-62.

resolved debate as to the scope of self-defense centering especially on whether allegations of covert infiltration or sporadic border infringement constitute "an armed attack" for Charter purposes. In General Assembly Resolution 2131 (XX), Declaration on Inadmissibility of Intervention, the ambiguity is maintained by condemning armed intervention and forms of interference with the sovereign character of a foreign state as "synonymous with aggression."[67] Article 51 makes self-defense available only "if an armed attack occurs" and makes no reference to aggression;[68] presumably "armed attack" is a narrower notion than aggression, and hence there is no real implication that action in self-defense is compatible with the Charter undertaken in response to aggressive acts that do not amount to an armed attack. In the absence of an authoritative definition of "armed attack" the formal scope of permissible force under the Charter will remain beclouded by controversy and subject to the vagaries of auto-interpretation.[69]

But the problem of clarification is vastly more complicated even than this. Article 51 asserts that "Nothing in the present Charter shall impair the inherent right of individual or collective self-defense . . . until the Security Council has taken the measures necessary to maintain international peace and security." Furthermore, "Measures taken by Members in the exercise of this right of self-defense shall be immediately reported to the Security Council and shall not in any way affect the authority and responsibility of the Security Council under the present Charter to take at any time such action as it deems necessary in order to maintain or restore international peace and security." But suppose the Security Council fails to reach any deter-

[67] For convenient text of G. A. Res. 2131 (XX), December 21, 1965 see Louis B. Sohn, ed., *Basic Documents of the United Nations* (Brooklyn, 2nd rev. edn., 1968).

[68] As some commentators have noted, the French text of Article 51 uses the broader, more inclusive phrase "aggression armée" in place of "armed attack." As both texts are authoritative there is some ground for rejecting a strict construction of the English version. For a perceptive comment along these lines see Hardy C. Dillard, "Law and Conflict: Some Current Dilemmas," 24 *Washington and Lee Law Review*, 177-204, at 199-200 n. 28.

[69] There are great difficulties of application in real-world situations arising from the occasional arbitrariness of identifying as "aggressor" the state that makes the initial recourse to force. Given alignments and the patterns of group voting in the political organs of the United Nations it is not possible to entrust the power of authoritative decision fully to the organized international community. Pariah states such as South Africa, Portugal, and Israel cannot expect to receive a norm-guided determination of a dispute involving a controversial use of force. The primacy of policy-implementation over norm-implementation is another way of expressing this attribute of the international system. Of course, if the community of states can engage in norm-creation, then some of the apparent contradiction between normative and policy imperatives can be eliminated. Efforts at norm-creation have taken place in relation to "apartheid" and "colonialism." For a favorable juridical assessment of these claims see Falk, *The Status of Law*, Chapter vi.

mination? Or suppose the member state fails to report immediately its exercise of self-defense?[70] These formal gaps are of particular importance because states have been reluctant to fulfill their procedural duty to submit claims to act in self-defense to the Security Council and the Security Council has often been unable to mobilize a relevant voting consensus whenever the issue touched closely upon the central Soviet-American international rivalry. In earlier years of the Organization, the United States sought to transfer competence to the General Assembly in the event that the Security Council was paralyzed by a veto or a division of sentiment.[71] The growth of more militant and anti-Western sentiment in the General Assembly, largely as a consequence of the expansion of Afro-Asian representation, and the outcome of the financing controversy disclosing the limits of Assembly effectiveness in peace and security matters involving superpower rivalry has fostered a gradual realization that it is either futile or self-defeating to circumvent the Security Council. But such a realization also means that the United Nations is characteristically unable to interpret authoritatively whether a state is properly acting in self-defense or in violation of the Charter. The Organization is thus also often unable to identify which participant to a conflict is the aggressor and which is victim. Without such identification taking place it is impossible to establish a juridical basis for action in collective security, although it remains possible to suspend juridical judgment, and exert influence to end violence and sustain a cease-fire.

The central consequence of these limits on the capacity of principal organs of the United Nations to interpret and apply its own Charter provisions is to revive the logic of Westphalia for many problems in the area of war and peace, especially those problems involving the direct participation of principal sovereign states. National governments self-interpret and self-apply the provisions of the Charter; the foreseeable consequence is to produce adversary rationalizations couched in the prevailing legal rhetoric.[72] In practical effect, however, principal states tend to reserve for national decision the determination of discretion as the use of force. Shifts in beliefs about the utility of military power,

[70] For some data see "Submission of the Vietnam Conflict to the United Nations," Hearings before U. S. Senate Foreign Relations Committee, 90th Cong., 1st Sess., October 26, 27, and November 2, 1967.

[71] G. A. Res. 377 A (V), November 3, 1957; for convenient text see Sohn, *Basic Documents of the U.N.*, 99-102.

[72] E.g. compare Legal Adviser of the Department of State, "The Legality of U. S. Participation in the Defense of Viet-Nam," in Falk, ed., *The Vietnam War and International Law* (Princeton 1968), 583-603; Consultative Council of the Lawyers Committee on American Policy Towards Vietnam, *Vietnam and International Law* (Flanders, N. J., 2nd edn., 1968); John Norton Moore, James L. Underwood, in collaboration with Myres S. McDougal, "The Lawfulness of United States Assistance to the Republic of Viet-Nam," 5 *Duquesne University Law Review*, 235-352 (1967).

concern about escalation, and some socialization of national elites in terms of Charter conceptions are among the factors that differentiate current patterns of decentralized decision-making on war/peace problems from earlier patterns.[73] The gradual reorientation of national elites toward the impartial acceptance of world community legal standards may be the most significant, if occasionally invisible, contemporary trend in support of world order. The Charter conception, by its authoritative formulation of governing norms, is a crucial factor encouraging this trend. The principal organs of the United Nations often provide communication facilities wherein international adversaries meet in periods of crisis and violence. Invoking norms to rationalize a national position may lead to a gradual assimilation of the normative directive as part of what is perceived to be reasonable behavior. In effect, the Charter conception through its application and invocation in the organization settings of the United Nations contributes to a vast global learning experience, the effects of which are difficult to calculate.[74]

A further element of the Charter conception of authority, as it applies to governing the use of military power, entails a commitment to the logic of collective security.[75] The United Nations is entitled to use military power if its organs have acted in accordance with their own procedures. In any event, there is no higher decision-maker that can pass judgment upon a contested use of force by the political organs of the United Nations. There is no reason to suppose that the International Court of Justice would do more than render an Advisory Opinion on such a question.[76]

Members of the United Nations are obligated in Article 2 (5) to give the United Nations "every assistance in any action it takes in accordance with the present Charter, and shall refrain from giving assistance to any state against which the United Nations is taking preventive or enforcement action." In a complementary fashion the

[73] Many of these factors are discussed in Klaus Knorr, *On the Uses of Military Power in the Nuclear Age* (Princeton 1966) .

[74] Such a suggestive viewpoint is developed in Kenneth E. Boulding, "The Learning and Reality-Testing Process in the International System," *Journal of International Affairs* 21 (1967) , 1-15.

[75] For skeptical assessments of the record and prospects for collective security see Roland N. Stromberg, *Collective Security and American Foreign Policy* (New York 1963) ; Bull, "Grotian Conception."

[76] The experience of noncompliance by objecting members of the Organization with the Advisory Opinion of the Court in the financing context does not encourage present reliance on this mode of dispute settlement. For the various opinions of the International Court of Justice see Certain Expenses of the United Nations (Article 17, Paragraph 2, of the Charter) , Advisory Opinion, ICJ Reports 1962, pp. 151-308. For the wider setting of the financing crisis see John C. Stoessinger and Associates, *Financing and the United Nations System* (Washington 1964) ; Falk and Mendlovitz, *Strategy of World Order*, Vol. 4, 693-789.

Draft Declaration on Rights and Duties of States in Article 10 requires that "every State has the duty to refrain from giving assistance
to any state which is acting in violation of Article 9 [prohibition on
illegal use or threat of force], or against which the United Nations is
taking preventive or enforcement action."[77] In both documents the
essence of the legal duty is to support the United Nations in its effort
to establish peace and security. A state is obliged to defer to community judgment in a situation of conflict and violence. Such an obligation appears to take precedence over inconsistent duties arising from
an alliance and over a policy preference for impartiality and
neutrality.[78]

In practice, however, states have not been willing to support action by the United Nations with which they disagreed. The problem
has been minimized to some extent because it has been difficult to
organize support for action in situations of real confrontation between principal members. The U.N. Emergency Force organized after
the Sinai Campaign of 1956 and the Congo Operation of 1960-1964
are two examples of action by the United Nations in the face of a
split Organization. In both instances, however, an initial consensus
was lost in the course of carrying out a mission deliberately couched in
ambiguous directives so as to obscure the underlying conflict of objectives. The financing crisis arose from a backlash created by disappointment with the United Nations and expressing, perhaps, the concern of some members, especially France and the Soviet Union, that
the Organization was infringing upon the prerogatives of state
sovereignty.

The Charter conception of international order rests heavily upon
the capacity of the international community to mount collective action based on a fair-minded interpretation of certain shared norms.[79]
Such an approach can only hope to succeed if most states, especially
principal states, are prepared to accord priority to Charter rules and
procedures.[80] The effect of such priority is to subordinate alliance

[77] For convenient text see Sohn, *Basic Documents of the U.N.*, 26-27.

[78] Article 103 of the United Nations Charter reads as follows: "In the event of a
conflict between the obligations of the Members of the United Nations under the
present Charter and their obligations under any other international agreement, their
obligations under the present Charter shall prevail." Cf. also the consideration in
other settings of the alleged existence of a *Jus Cogens*. See Egon Schwelb, "Some
Aspects of International *Jus Cogens* as Formulated by the International Law Commission," 61 *American Journal of International Law*, 946-75 (1967).

[79] Deep skepticism as to this possibility is the central theme of Stone, *Aggression
and World Order* (Berkeley 1958).

[80] For a discussion of the uncertain relationship between a treaty regime such as
the Charter and its "amendment" through the practice of the Organization see
Ervin P. Hexner, "Teleological Interpretation of Basic Instruments of Public International Organizations" in Salo Engel, ed., *Law, State, and International Legal
Order—Essays in Honor of Hans Kelsen* (Knoxville 1964), 119-38.

relations and balance-of-power considerations. In the nomenclature of this chapter, the Charter conception can only become embodied in international life to the extent that Westphalia approaches to national security lose their political vitality. Behavioral patterns in international society continue to exhibit the strength of alliance relationships; the main directions of foreign policy are chosen for reasons of ideological sympathy, cultural affinity, and calculations of national advantage. That is, despite formal adherence to the Charter, national governments retain a discretionary approach toward issues of war and peace, and refuse to be bound by the will of the international community or by the norms and procedures of international law. The political splits in international society have impeded implementation of the provisions in the United Nations Charter designed to provide the Organization with a semi-autonomous international peace force.[81] Partly as a consequence of the limited prospects for effective U.N. action, potential victims of attack continue to look outside the Organization for the principal bases of national security. Most states rely mainly on their own deterrent capabilities to discourage encroachment by neighbors or adversaries. The vast majority depend upon military assistance to build up these national capabilities. Alliances supplement national efforts, resting upon a collective security rationale that unites one sector of the international system in defensive opposition against another.[82] From the perspective of man-hours, resources, and military capabilities far more security emphasis is placed upon decentralized approaches than upon the more centralized approach of the Charter. In sum, then, the Westphalia approaches to war and peace remain dominant within international society and have not yet been seriously displaced by the competing Charter conception.[83]

At the same time the Charter conception is not without great significance. In the event a consensus on ends and means can be reached within the United Nations then prospects for peace-keeping or peaceful settlement are considerable. On rare occasion, principal states have upheld Charter norms at the expense of alliance partners, as was done by the United States after Great Britain, France, and Israel invaded the Sinai Peninsula in 1956. More normally, however,

[81] Articles 43-47 of the Charter have never been seriously implemented. For consideration of the Charter expectation and its foreshortened realization see Ruth B. Russell, *The United Nations and United States Security Policy* (Washington 1968), 47-60, 119-21.

[82] For searching analyses of alliances as an attribute of the present system of international relations see George Liska, *Nations in Alliance—The Limits of Interdependence* (Baltimore 1962); Liska, *Alliances and the Third World* (Baltimore 1968).

[83] See Inis L. Claude, *Power and International Relations* (New York 1962), 94-204; see also Bull, "The Grotian Conception."

the Organization can only hope to mobilize a consensus to oppose the use of violence when principal states agree on the identity of the wrongdoer and on the direction of policy response. Small conflicts at the margin of regional and sub-regional concern can be kept within tolerable limits by this means. For instance, in both Cyprus and the Yemen the United Nations has been able to play a peace-keeping role.

In general, then, governments continue to base national security planning upon Westphalia calculations. The Charter conception has greatly changed the rhetoric of diplomatic discourse, and this change in rhetoric may gradually produce shifts in attitude and behavior. As well, the institutional setting provided by the United Nations is an excellent forum for adversary communication and facilitates the identification and implementation of converging interests. The United Nations has changed the international environment more by facilitating international communications than by translating the norms of the Charter into operational rules of conduct. Finally, for states or groups of states with little military capability but with extensive political support from other governments, the United Nations provides a mobilization arena, within which to encourage the sharpening of sentiment. Such a process has been an essential part of African efforts to mobilize global support for their insistence on the elimination of racism and colonialism from the continent.

Basis for Obligation. The Westphalia conception of international order rests upon the essential role of consent in the process of forming international obligations.[84] The Charter conception superficially respects, or at least contains nothing to contradict, this traditional mode of law-creation.[85] Among the recent developments that have encouraged a growing role for consensus as a law-creating energy are the following: (1) The functional needs of unified regulation in an increasingly interdependent world; (2) the increase in the number of active national participants in international life; (3) the cosmopolitan sentiments generated by the existence of the United Nations; (4) the emergence of a global public opinion on many issues of international importance; (5) parallel developments on a domestic level in both socialistic and capitalistic societies that involve the displacement of individual choice and responsibility by community choice and responsibility.[86]

[84] For elaboration see references already cited in notes 44 and 56.

[85] Challenges directed at traditional modes of law-creation are considered in Falk, *The Status of Law*, Chapters v and vi; see also Falk and Mendlovitz, *Strategy of World Order*, Vol. III, 39-122.

[86] Daniel Bell has written that "domestically the United States is becoming a *communal* society rather than a *contractual* one. Rights and claims against the community are becoming central." See Bell, "A Summary by the Chairman," in symposium, "Toward the Year 2000: Work in Progress," *Daedalus* (Summer 1967),

In several distinct subject-matter areas the General Assembly has come increasingly to formulate its "recommendations" and "declarations" in legal rhetoric. From a technical point of view, it would be possible to contend that the General Assembly is only giving formal expression to what the majority of its membership regards to be obligatory in any event. Given an expanded international society that needs and demands more rapid formulations of governing standards, the Assembly resolution can be understood as a modern adjunct to the traditional mode of law-creation by "international custom." The processes of growth of customary international law always involved some rather artificial notions about implicit consent, practice done with a sense of obligation, and the passage of requisite time. In actuality, rules of customary international law were often both expressions of majoritarian sentiment and rapidly emergent, the authoritativeness of an alleged rule depending heavily upon the behavior of a few principal sovereign states who kept adequate records of their diplomatic practice. The General Assembly of the United Nations has carried this aspect of customary law-creation much further, and has found a measure of support for the legitimacy of its activities in the recent jurisprudence of the International Court of Justice.[87]

Among the sorts of issues that have been the subject of Assembly law-creation are the following:

1. The prohibition of nuclear weapons;
2. The withdrawal of legitimacy from colonial regimes;
3. The condemnation of racial discrimination as endangering international peace and as justifying coercive and interventionary undertakings;
4. The banning of nuclear weapons in outer space;
5. The acceptance of certain welfare responsibilities by developed countries in relation to poorer countries;
6. The enunciation of rules and procedures of operations internal to the United Nations and the interpretation of provisions of the Charter.

The importance of such law-creating acts varies greatly from context to context. The quality of the supporting majority is very important, especially whether the real targets of regulation join in the consensus. In certain contexts, a resolution may be almost a func-

---

975-77, at 977. Such a statement of trend contrasts interestingly with the celebrated earlier distinction of Sir Henry Maine between *status* and *contract*, suggesting that modern society was a product of the transition from status to contract.

[87] E.g. especially the Dissenting Opinion of Judge Tanaka, South West Africa Cases, Second Phase, I.C.J. Reports, July 18, 1966, 244-324, esp. at 278-301. See also Falk, *The Status of Law*, Chapter v.

tional equivalent to an international treaty; such was the case, for instance, with respect to the resolution banning the introduction of orbital weapons into outer space.[88] In other contexts, the resolution may only posit aspirational standards as a technique of promoting an eventual legal standard; such was the case, for instance, with respect to the resolution prohibiting the use of nuclear weapons.[89] Other resolutions are designed to mobilize community action, put pressure on principal states, in contexts in which there is an adversary relationship between the organized international community and a particular state or group of states; such has been the case, for instance, with respect to the escalating confrontation between the General Assembly and South Africa over the issues of racial discrimination and over the status of South West Africa.

It is impossible to examine this development in any detail here. What has been described in the setting of the General Assembly is taking place in other international bodies of a more specialized nature. There is a noticeable drift toward consensus as a basis of legitimation; the will of the international community acquires a certain degree of legislative status when it manifests itself through formal actions of international institutions. These trends are indefinite and uneven, but their cumulative effect challenges the fundamental ordering principle of the Westphalia conception—that is, the centrality of the will or volitional behavior of individual sovereign states. Law-creation by consensus has the effect of overriding the opposition of a minority of states, and withdraws from the ideology of national sovereignty the prerogatives of a veto. A sovereign state may be bound over its opposition in a growing number of international situations, although the consequences of being bound to varying degrees remain indefinite; it remains important for a government to have "a sense of obligation." Treaties are still the most assured way, at least over the short run, of engendering a sense of obligation which gives some assurance of a willingness or intention to comply. Most technical international institutions have voting rules that allow the majority to prevail, although there are great differences from institution to institution in defining what constitutes a requisite majority for various kinds of votes.

There is no doubt, however, that the Charter conception, with its increasing emphasis on the claims of the Afro-Asian majority, is challenging and eroding the consent-oriented basis of Westphalia thinking. At the same time, states have not shown any dramatic willingness to defer to community claims directed against their central

[88] See in this connection Adrian S. Fisher, "Arms Control and Disarmament in International Law," 50 *Virginia Law Review*, 1200-19 (1964).
[89] G.A. Res. 1653 (XVI), November 24, 1961.

interests or traditional prerogatives. Sovereign acquiescence continues to be an element in establishing "a sense of obligation" on the part of government elites. It is this sense of obligation, far more than any mechanism of enforcement, that makes for effective adherence to international standards of behavior. National governments have not shown much disposition to be responsive to community claims posited in the form of General Assembly resolutions. Westphalia conceptions about law-creation remain very much alive, although Charter developments are posing a formidable challenge. Most of the important considerations in evaluating these trends are sociological rather than juridical, depending for their basic interpretation upon the attitudes, beliefs, and actions of elites in national governments and in international institutions. If the officials formulating the claims *think* that the mode of formulation has a law-creating effect—imposes some sense of obligation in relation to some standard of behavior—then this expectation has a bearing on how officials on the national level perceive and react. At this point, the evidence of trend and countertrend is difficult to evaluate. The future shape of international society will reflect the progress of this ongoing struggle between a consensus-oriented and a consent-oriented international society. It represents one of the critical issue-areas of transition in the international political system.

Constitutional Authority. The Charter of the United Nations in Article 2 (6) claims competence to ensure that states which are not members of the United Nations act in accordance with these principles [that is, the other provisions of Article 2] so far as may be necessary for the maintenance of "international peace and security."[90] The significant point here is that the United Nations Organization claims for itself whatever authority is necessary to establish global peace and security. The Charter embodies the claim and the Organization gives its continuing effect. Article 2 (6) is a significant provision (one that carries forward the approach of Article 17 of the League Covenant) because it relies on a treaty instrument such as the Charter to establish the basis for communitywide authority that might be extended to nonparticipants in the treaty regime. This authority claim embraces nonmembers and nonparticipants in the original formulation of the Charter. If the United Nations achieved universal membership, or close to it, then the basis of Article 2 (6) would be consensual in the minimum sense that all major states had formally acquiesced in some form. But given the exclusion of mainland China from the Organization there is some question as to the con-

---

[90] For an extended discussion of the significance of Article 2 (6) see Falk, *The Status of Law,* Chapter VII.

stitutional authority of the United Nations to act for world peace outside the scope of its membership.

From the point of view of an evolving international legal order,
however, it seems clear to emphasize a trend toward claiming constitutional status for international institutions within the scope of their
purported competence. The claim embodied in Article 2 (6) is paralleled in the practice of regional organizations such as the Arab
League, Organization of African Unity, and the Organization of
American States. These institutions act on the assumption of regionwide competence that is not constricted by the nonparticipation
of some national units within the region.

The development of constitutional authority for international institutions is complementary to the evolution of legislative authority
discussed in the preceding section. In the latter case, the will of
the relevant community is endowed with law-creating effect despite
dissent, whether from members or not; in the latter case, the constitutional status of the organization allows its competence to extend
beyond the activities of its members, and regardless of whether nonmembers assent or are given an opportunity to join. Since international
institutions remain voluntary associations of states their stature depends upon a basic consensus as to ends and means and upon a level
of participation that includes most, if not all, of the relevant states
concerned. If states withdraw from, are excluded by, or do not seek
to join an institution that claims constitutional status, then its claim
is jeopardized. Given the decentralized quality of international society
the exercise of constitutional authority rests upon tacit acquiescence
by all states most of the time. If there is a loss of complete participation, then there exists always the possibility of establishing a second
international institution that repudiates the claims of the first and
contends that it is the "true" source of constitutional authority.
Therefore, the Charter claim to control nonmembers depends upon
the organizational unity of the United Nations, which in turn depends upon quasi-universal participation. Again it is worth noticing
Article 2 (6) as an important developmental trend that may be reshap-
ing the structure of international order in subtle ways that cannot yet
be fully discerned.

Erosion of Domestic Jurisdiction. We have mentioned the saving
clause in Article 2 (7) of the Charter that promises to uphold the
domestic jurisdiction of states. The idea of domestic jurisdiction being invested exclusively in national governments is a prime element
of the Westphalia conception. The abiding strength of this idea is
suggested by the reluctance of states, even on the part of those states
most committed to the growth of a stable system of world order, to
entrust international institutions with the capacity to determine what

falls within domestic jurisdiction. The famous debate occasioned by the Connally Reservation to the United States acceptance of the compulsory jurisdiction of the International Court of Justice[91] is a familiar illustration of this reluctance to allow any risk of intrusion on matters thought to be within domestic jurisdiction. Most states have not even gone as far as the United States and have refused to accept the compulsory jurisdiction of the Court in any form whatsoever. In essence, the competence of international tribunals remains dependent on voluntary submission. The Westphalia confirmation of sovereign discretion remains paramount with respect to third-party settlement of disputes.

At the same time the practice of the Organization has increasingly removed from domestic jurisdiction various subject-matter in the area of human rights. The struggle to oppose apartheid in South Africa has created a whole range of precedents involving the claimed competence of the organized international community to determine for itself whether a particular national policy is within the reserved domain of domestic jurisdiction. Certainly in 1945 when the United Nations came into being it was widely assumed that policies used by a government to regulate internal race relations would have been thought to fall squarely within domestic jurisdiction. But the critical issue governing the shifting contents of domestic jurisdiction is the locus of authority to characterize subject-matter as domestic or international. If, as has been increasingly the case, the international community is unified in its assertion of competence to make this judgment, then the appeals of a national government to some earlier understanding of the domestic jurisdiction principle are not likely to have much bearing on authority trends. The United Nations as an organization possesses an almost unquestioned competence to determine what constitutes a threat to international peace and security, and by so determining, possesses the capacity to internationalize the status of a particular question. Over South Africa's vigorous objection, the policies of apartheid have been increasingly internationalized in this manner. It makes little juridical difference that the threat to the peace comes from hostility toward apartheid by foreign countries rather than from the policies themselves. The essential juridical ingredients of this legal claim are a strong consensus within the United

[91] It will be recalled that the essential provision of the Connally Reservation precludes the World Court from adjudicating any controversy that the United States Government determines to be within its domestic jurisdiction. For convenient text of the United States Declaration of August 1946 accepting the compulsory jurisdiction of the Court subject to the Connally Reservation see Sohn, *Basic Documents of the U.N.* 272; for text of the optional clause permitting states to file declarations accepting compulsory jurisdiction, Article 26 of the Statute of the International Court of Justice see Sohn, 227-28.

Nations and the expression of this consensus in a series of formal acts
by the principal organs of the U.N. There has been parallel experience in other areas, especially arising from the Unilateral Declaration
of Independence in 1965 by the Smith regime in Rhodesia and in connection with the various efforts of the United Nations to oppose
Portuguese colonialism in Africa.

This experience of the 1960's has established a rather rich body of
precedents that can be shifted to other settings in subsequent years.
The establishment of a competence to act in the first instance is
more difficult normally than is its repetition and extrapolation in the
future.[92] There is a kind of common law energy that builds up expectations as to the character of permissible kinds of undertakings. A
precedent established by overwhelming consensus (South Africa) or
by overwhelming military superiority ("defensive quarantine" in the
Cuban missile crisis), can be invoked in less compelling future circumstances. Thus the trend toward further erosion of the reserved domain of national governments may be expected to accelerate in the
decades ahead. Such an expectation is reinforced by the fragmentation of national loyalty patterns in such a way that domestic pressures
to conform national behavior to international standards are likely to
grow stronger. As well, the functional necessities of unified regulation
make the state a less autonomous unit for the conduct of practical affairs. So long as fishing resources were abundant, conservation and
management efforts were not needed. But given the technology of
long-distance fishing operations and the pressures on the world food
supply, there is need to allocate fishing rights on the basis of managerial principles and to secure the reliable implementation of these
principles. For an anadromous species of fish, such as salmon, it is
obviously necessary to extend regulatory efforts to internal waters.
This illustration is but one of many that could be given to show the
erosion of traditional spheres of exclusive national authority as a consequence of technological developments and functional imperatives.
Form follows function in organizing human affairs (as well as in organizing architectural space), and function appears increasingly
to be eroding national forms and evolving supranational and multi-
national forms.

In this respect, the functional foundations of the Westphalia conception are weakening. Modern communications, transportation, highly specialized technologies of space and oceans, interdependencies in
currencies, employment patterns, commodity pricing, and international trade are among the factors making for a world ever-less constituted by autonomous national states reciprocally deferring to exclusive patterns of territorial jurisdiction. Territorial space is declin-

---

[92] This is one of the principal findings of Haas, *Beyond the Nation-State*, 429-97.

ing as an indicator of formal authority. This decline is symbolized by the decreasing capacity of most governments to be able to provide for national security and national welfare. The ideology and practice of foreign aid expresses one dimension of this pressure upon the Westphalia conception at the unit level. In the present world, to put the point provocatively, the great majority of weak and poor states ultimately depend, for whatever marginal viability they may possess, upon the interventionary policies of the few strong and rich states.[93] The Charter conception of world legal order, as expressed in such recent developments as UNCTAD-I and II and the Tehran Conference of 1968 on Human Rights, is evolving a primitive base for a welfare state on a world level.[94] Such an evolution, if it continues, will be of crucial importance in shaping the near future of the international legal order.[95]

Supranational Professionalism. There is a growing kind of cosmopolitanism arising from the proliferation of contact between various kinds of professional groups located in different national societies.[96] Science, for instance, is becoming an increasingly supranational enterprise. Cross-national loyalties evolve and there is a tendency to form opinions on a basis less expressive of place of national affiliation. The great growth of specialized international agencies, and the parallel development of nongovernmental and intergovernmental international organizations, is part of this continuing process. The ease and growth of travel, the emergence of "world companies" without any real national center of operations, and the beginnings of global television and telephone coverage are further expressions of this supranationalization of human experience.[97]

It is difficult to assess such developments, and even more difficult to

[93] An interventionary capability often reflects relational factors of size, propinquity, access, modes, and geopolitical status. For example, a militant African state might, although a feeble power if measured in European terms, have a considerable sub-regional capability for military intervention. Another state may be able to make use of hostile propaganda to incite revolution in a neighboring state that is much more powerful than it is in terms of conventional military struggle.

[94] For an assessment of recent developments pertaining to the economic dimension of the North-South split see Branislav Gosovic, "UNCTAD: North-South Encounter," *International Conciliation*, No. 568 (May 1968), 1-80. Raymond Aron is skeptical about the capacity of the poor states to maintain a sufficiently cohesive position to influence the future character of international society. See *Progress and Disillusion—The Dialectics of Modern Society* (New York 1968), 176-79.

[95] For creative speculation along these lines see Myrdal, *Beyond the Welfare State*; Myrdal, *The Asian Drama* (New York, 3 vols., 1968); Gustavo Lagos, *International Stratification and Underdeveloped Countries* (Chapel Hill, N. C. 1963).

[96] See, in general, Vincent Rock, *The Strategy of Interdependence* (New York 1964); on the specific role of supranationalizing trends see Galtung, "The Future of the International System."

[97] See e.g. address by George W. Ball, "Some Implications of the World Company," Pace College, May 2, 1968 (mimeo.).

anticipate their future impact. We can anticipate an expanding international civil service and an increase in supranational professional role-playing. These trends are reinforced by certain diffusion effects that seem to link sub-elites in various countries more closely to one another than to their own national circumstances. Such cross-national linkages were evident, for instance, in the wave of student insurgencies that sprung up around the world during the spring of 1968; comparable linkages are more tentatively developing between the cause of black militancy in the United States and anti-apartheid efforts of black African states. A further source of support for this kind of supranationalizing of outlook has been sponsored by church organizations, given a sense of political relevance by the ecumenicism that has swept through Christianity in the wake of the Johannine revival of the Catholic Church.

Within domestic societies, especially those organized according to the principles of liberal democracy, there is evidence of increasing alienation of individuals from the nation-state as the central focus of their political loyalty.[98] More individuals appear socialized by Charter norms about violence than ever before in human history. The peace movement in the United States during the Vietnam War is probably the most dramatic example of the limits of national loyalty. The effort to organize draft resistance has rested heavily on normative considerations, especially drawing on legal standards of limitation applicable to recourse and conduct of war.[99] In several prominent domestic trials, defendants have attempted to introduce international law arguments to justify their refusal to cooperate with the Vietnam War effort. Courts in the United States have refused so far to examine the substance of these contentions, concluding that such issues are nonjusticiable because the subject-matter of war and peace is entrusted to the discretion of the executive branch of government. The "Political Questions Doctrine" is also invoked to explain why domestic courts cannot examine the substance of arguments about the legality of war and warfare. It is an important event that such issues are being raised in a serious fashion. The reluctance of domestic courts to adjudicate seems to be a legacy of Westphalia thinking with respect to the discretionary nature of sovereign decisions to wage war. Charter norms provide guidelines, the head of state is otherwise obliged to conduct the affairs of government within a framework of legal restraint, and the precedents of war crimes trials after World War II suggest an aggregate trend toward more cosmo-

[98] Such evidence is analyzed in Falk, *The Status of Law*, Chapter XXIII.

[99] My own analysis of this question is contained in a preface to *In the Name of America*, Clergy and Laymen Concerned About Vietnam (Annandale, Va. 1968), 22-27.

politan orientations of legal assessment than executive self-determination; the Judgment at Nuremberg surely established that the king can do wrong when it comes to war. Individuals are increasingly appealing above the heads of their elected national officials to global norms and procedures. These patterns of protest and appeal are currently at a rudimentary stage of assertion, but they represent important indications about what is going to happen in international society in the near future in the event that further cosmopolitan support develops.

The Charter is important in these settings because it provides individuals with a set of authoritative reference points that can be invoked against a national government that acts as though it was subject only to the minimal constraints of the Westphalia conception. On the level of individual loyalty, as on the level of elite predisposition, we live at a time of normative tension between the relatively permissive Westphalia restraints and the relatively restrictive Charter restraints. The two bodies of normative guidance coexist in uneasy irresolution, the clarity and proportionality of their eventual relationship depending on future events.

Supplemental Conceptions. As already suggested, the normative choices embodied in the Westphalia and Charter conceptions are qualified and complemented by certain additional ordering mechanisms at work in international society. These additional mechanisms are not "supplemental" in this sense of enjoying a secondary importance. On the contrary. The subordinate treatment is a consequence of the questionable normative status of these conceptions rather than their lesser impact on the shape of international behavior.

3. GEO-POLITICAL CONCEPTIONS. The stability of national boundaries is a consequence, to some indefinite extent, of the role of the predominant power wielded by principal sovereign states. Neither the Westphalia conception of sovereign units nor the Charter conception of a nascent world community can comprehend within its juridical logic the role of "spheres of influence," the special ordering prerogatives implicitly asserted by principal states and ambivalently acquiesced in by the rest of international society. The mapping of these "spheres of influence," a task beyond the scope of this chapter is definitely a critical aspect of the quality of existing order, and the remapping prospect is an important element in the near future. It is also very relevant to assess whether Westphalia and Charter conceptions will erode the quasi-imperial claims and practices of principal sovereign states in the decades ahead.

The relationship between the Soviet Union and Eastern Europe or between the United States and Latin America are illustrative of clearly delimited spheres of influence wherein interventionary preroga-tives exist. These spheres of influence are not symmetrical with one another, nor is the pattern of interventionary prerogative within any particular sphere stable through time. Each sphere can be conceived of as a sub-system possessing its own properties and its distinctive links to the global system.[100] For instance, the attitude of the United Nations has been obviously more supportive of United States patterns of hemi-spheric dominance than it has been of Soviet patterns of East European dominance; in 1956 the United Nations censured the Soviet military suppression of the Hungarian uprising, whereas the United States has been successful to date in avoiding censure for such assertion of prerog-atives as taking a role in overthrowing the Arbenz regime of Guatemala in 1954, in organizing and financing the Bay of Pigs invasion in 1961, and in conducting the Dominican intervention in 1965.[101] These asser-tions of a kind of "quasi-authority" to act within a fairly clearly delim-ited sphere of influence is an ordering conception based on an imperial logic that appears to contradict both the consensual sovereignty of Westphalia thinking and the will of the community notion underlying Charter thinking. Therefore, observers seeking a normatively self-consistent conception of international order are bound either to ex-clude the reality of spheres of influence or to deny these spheres any normative status.

Secondary spheres of influence also exist based upon unequal power relations of sovereign units within regional sub-systems. Militant ac-tors such as Cuba under Castro, Ghana under Nkrumah, and the United Arab Republic under Nasser, intervene, to some extent suc-cessfully, within their respective sub-systemic settings. Some efforts to establish spheres of influence generate intense geopolitical opposition. The United States role in Southeast Asia since 1950 is partly a con-sequence of its determination to resist Chinese efforts to establish such a sphere of influence over the states contiguous to her borders. The Vietnam War is a culmination of an American exaggeration of the geopolitical dimension of post-colonial Asian conflict. It is an exag-geration because the forces of struggle in Vietnam are animated pri-marily by nationalistic considerations—the impulse toward national independence, modernization, and unity.

The relations between a dominant actor and its sphere undergo sharp shifts through time. Interventionary prerogatives may be mod-

---

[100] See useful analysis along these lines in Oran R. Young, "Political Discon-tinuities in the International System," *World Politics*, 20 (April 1968), 369-92.

[101] For useful accounts of the action of the United Nations in relation to Soviet intervention in Hungary and United States intervention in Latin America see Louis B. Sohn, ed., *Cases on United Nations Law* (Brooklyn 1967), 634-79, 862-990; see also Inis L. Claude, Jr., "The OAS, the UN, and the United States," *Inter-national Conciliation*, No. 547 (March 1964).

erated or intensified. The history of the role of the United States in Latin America illustrates clearly the various swings of the pendulum in response to factors taking place within the sphere and those directed at the sphere from outside.[102] The efforts of Latin American statesmen to secure a greater measure of autonomy in their relations with the United States was rewarded with the Good Neighbor Policy of the 1930's. This abandonment in doctrine and practice of the interventionary statecraft typical of the later stages of the Monroe Doctrine approach was, in part, an acceptance of the logic of Westphalia as the true basis of international relations. However, with the challenge to hemispheric solidarity posed by militant world ideologies, such as Nazism, Fascism, and Communism, a United States revival of interventionary diplomacy occurred based on the assertion of special prerogatives. A thin mantle of regionalism has been draped over the renewed assertion of unilateral prerogatives by the United States. This effort to reconcile present diplomatic patterns with the earlier relinquishment of the Monroe Doctrine has not been fully persuasive, yet it does illustrate the impact of intervening normative variables: the revival of an active sphere of influence being moderated by its earlier renunciation.

Similarly, the Soviet experience of intervention in 1956 may have moderated its imperial prerogatives in East Europe throughout the subsequent period so as to avoid the need for a recurrence. The military pressure directed against the Dubcek regime in Czechoslovakia since 1968 contrasts at least in severity with the brutal coercion directed twelve years earlier at the Nagy regime. The Soviet claims against Czechoslovakia have been very extreme in the sense that they have concerned the domestic social and economic policies being pursued by a popular and stable government in Prague; there was no significant domestic unrest in Czechoslovakia *until* Soviet troops entered the country in August of 1968.

The normative point is that the existence of discernable spheres of influence is an important ingredient of the present system of international order. Expectations about the tolerable range of intervention are shaped by whether the locus of controversy is within or without a sphere of influence. To illustrate, the United States' response would have been very different if the Soviet Union was dealing with a West European country in the manner that relations with Czechoslovakia were conducted in 1968. Similarly, the ostracism of Cuba from the inter-American system is partially a consequence of its being situated within what had been regarded as the United States sphere of influ-

[102] Some consideration of these issues in Falk, *Legal Order in a Violent World* (Princeton 1968), 156-223.

ence. Many dangerous political conflicts arise when a secondary unit seeks to repudiate the policies and prerogatives of the dominant actor within a sub-systemic sphere.

The role of deterrence is closely linked to norms of international order which incorporate some appreciation of spheres of influence. States are deterred by the added perception that a state is acting within certain prescribed limits. If such action is within a discerned sphere, then it may be tolerated in a manner that it would not be outside such a sphere. Threatened retaliation normally does not include "intra-sphere" aggression, but is limited to either "inter-sphere" aggression or to situations wherein contradictory or ambiguous geopolitical perceptions are experienced by rival governments. One major cause of war is the failure to delimit spheres of influence in a sufficiently clear way to establish shared expectations. The problem of delimitation is vastly complicated by the fact, already alluded to, that the very existence of spheres of influence contradicts the prevailing ordering ideals of Westphalia and the Charter. A geopolitical input, although very apparent in the structure of world affairs, is ideologically abhorrent to the subordinate units. Such abhorrence has been clearly manifest on many occasions in the ex-colonial sectors of the world, but never more vividly than during the Security Council debate which followed the Stanleyville Operation of 1964, justified as a humanitarian rescue of hostages in the West and attacked as a neocolonialist venture by militant statesmen of black Africa.[103]

4. RULES OF THE GAME. A further basis for order in international society arises from patterns of mutual adherence to "rules of the game." These are rules that do not qualify as legal rules, at least if the criteria of qualification are established by the traditional sources of international law. At the same time, these rules of the game moderate the scope and magnitude of conflict, and create an important secondary line of normative defense in the event that primary rules governing the conduct of states have failed to prevent violence.

Rules of the game are standards of behavior to which adherence corresponds with widely shared community expectations as to the character of reasonable behavior; a departure from a rule of the game, as with the departure from any rule of order, is likely to generate some escalatory response on the part of adversely affected actors, provided such actors possess the capability to make or threaten a credible response. Mutual adherence maintains some kind of framework of restraint even in situations of chaos, crisis, and warfare.

The nature and function of rules of the game can be illustrated

---

[103] For discussion see same, 324-35.

in connection with the subject-matter of civil strife. Several rules of major significance appear to exist:

1. Nuclear weapons will not be introduced into battle by a belligerent;
2. Counterinterventionary targets will be limited to the territory wherein the civil strife is taking place;
3. States furnishing assistance short of combat troops to either interventionary or counterinterventionary actors will not be treated as belligerents.

The primary rules of intervention have not been very successful in prohibiting overt and covert forms of third-party participation in civil strife. These rules of the game are designed to moderate the destabilizing effects of third-party participation, assuming it takes place. The Vietnam War has been a major testing ground for the lim-bility of rules of the game is especially dependent on the self-restraint ber 1968 the United States violated rule (2) by bombing targets in North Vietnam; the pattern of violation was very significant because the targets struck in North Vietnam were so numerous and so functionally diffuse in relation to the war in South Vietnam (i.e. targets were not limited to supply lines and sanctuaries).[104] The stability of rules of the game is especially dependent on the self-restraint of principal states. Although a pattern of departure does not nullify a rule of the game, it does set a negative precedent of considerable weight for prospective violators in the future. Dominant states cannot induce compliance to these rules of restraint if their own behavior exhibits nonconformity. Atmospheric nuclear testing by the United States and the Soviet Union is a negative precedent of such strength that it virtually nullifies any effort by these two states to object to subsequent testing claims of China and France.

As with the geopolitical map superimposed on the Westphalia map of sovereign states, there is need for a comprehensive classification of rules of the game applicable to various subject-matter, their mode of creation, interpretation, and termination, and their degree of significance for a general theory of international order. Clearly, however, the *de facto* patterns of order should be described in a way that allows for the inclusion of rules of the game or of some more apt designation for these rules.

5. DECENTRALIZED MODES OF INTERNATIONAL ORDER. The Westphalia conception includes the idea that national governments are the basic sources of order in international society. National governments provide territorial order and share in authority to attach national law

---

[104] For a description of the United States bombing patterns in North Vietnam see Gerassi, *North Vietnam: A Documentary* (New York 1968).

to activity on the oceans and in air space. Various allocational doctrines have evolved to identify which of several national governments can apply its regulatory authority in situations of overlapping concern. Doctrines of sovereign and diplomatic immunity, act of state, and various kinds of extraterritorial jurisdiction carry out the basic postulates of the Westphalia system; decentralized legal control by sovereign states.

In addition, however, to this jurisdictional kind of decentralization there exist a growing number of situations that allow national institutions to act as agents of the international system. Domestic courts can supply judicial institutions for the adjudication of international controversies, national legislative organs can posit and clarify standards of international behavior, and the executive branch can implement sanctioning procedures to promote international enforcement processes.[105] National institutions, without efforts at explicit coordination on an international basis, can reinforce the ordering potential of the international system. The contribution to an evolving legal order depends upon the extent to which decentralized processes operate as *agents* of the world community enjoying independence from directives of national policy. A tradition of independence and an explicit appreciation of the ordering contributions that could be made might increase the prospects for national institutions. As matters now stand, national institutions tend to apply international law in such a manner as to assure its conformity with national policy.

A special case of decentralized ordering concerns an activity such as piracy which is universally condemned. Each state has the capacity to apprehend "pirates" on behalf of the overall international community. A somewhat comparable competence was claimed by Israel when it prosecuted Adolf Eichmann as a war criminal. Those individuals who have recourse to litigation in the United States to question the legality of the Vietnam War by invoking norms embodied in the Charter or in the Nuremberg Judgment are also trying to convert a domestic court into an agent of an emerging international system of order, an agent that accords precedence to the norms of international law when these norms come into conflict with the dictates of national policy.

A Note in Conclusion

The main effort of this chapter has been to specify the five principal dimensions of the international legal order. These dimensions seem likely to remain the most prominent bases of order in the decades just ahead, and so the analytical relevance of such concep-

---

[105] For extended consideration see Falk, *The Role of Domestic Courts in the International Legal Order* (Syracuse 1964).

tions is unlikely to be superseded soon. On the basis of this conceptual framework it would be possible to assess the near future for any sector of international life. This chapter, then, tries to develop some tools for thinking about the future of the international legal order, and needs to be supplemented by detailed empirical studies. In studying the future we are concerned with trends, preferences, and strategies to shape trends in the general direction of preferences.

Part II
The Global Perspectives

CHAPTER 3

The World Constitutive Process
of Authoritative Decision

MYRES S. McDOUGAL

HAROLD D. LASSWELL

W. MICHAEL REISMAN

THE FRAME of reference essential for discussion of the world constitutive process is the world social process. The fundamental point emerging from a survey of that process is that today the scientific observer is justified in referring to a "world community": the level of interaction among the inhabitants of the earth has reached a degree of intensity that includes both interdetermination and widespread explicit recognition of the facts of such interdetermination. To interact is to influence and be influenced, whether the influence is recognized or unrecognized. During the centuries when there were practically no contacts between middle and South America and the other inhabitants of the globe, the peoples of the world did not maintain a level of reciprocal influencing (recognized or otherwise) sufficient to justify an observer of global affairs to speak of a world community. Similarly, it would be inappropriate to refer to an inclusive context of interaction when the empires of Rome and China were flourishing. There were few acknowledged or unacknowledged connections between them. To identify a global community today, it may be noted, does not require that one find a transnational exchange of people or goods or reciprocally amiable perspectives. The interflow of such values is not the only index of interaction. Interaction occurs at the level of full subjective awareness when participants take one another into consideration; consideration may involve weighing the other as a potential enemy and remaining aloof from all trade, travel, or combat.[1]

---

[1] The word "community" has a notoriously broad reference. The meaning which we attribute to the term will be apparent in this chapter. At the expense of belaboring the point, it may be worth emphasizing that we employ "community" as an interpersonal concept, based on both the subjectivities and operations of participants; hence community or communities can exist at differing levels of intensity among an aggregate of participants. Many of the elements of community cited in definitions contributed by, e.g. Parsons, *The Social System* (1951), 91; Mercer, *The American Community* (1956), 27 and others are possible indices for determining the existence or absence of the requisite subjectivities, but are not, in and of themselves, necessary components. In particular, specialization of function and institutionalization of power-decision processes are an indication of the complexity, rather than of the

In any community, as the level of interaction among peoples approaches a critical intensity, it becomes apparent to key decision-makers in all affected groups that certain stable modes of dealing with the other can be more beneficial than allowing relative instability to continue. Stable practices may provide for minimum contact, a relationship exemplified by the "silent trading" arrangements among tribes who leave commodities for exchange at a definite location and achieve ratios of give-and-take without face-to-face association or discussion. It is perceived by all concerned that common interests are served, since all parties are better off in terms of net value gain than they would otherwise be. We can refer to such trading societies as comprising a community since they are territorially defined in reference to one another and share a set of reciprocal demands, expectations, identities, and operational patterns.[2] Any deviation from emerging prescriptive norms arouses vigorous demands to reinstate the relationship, perhaps by employing negative sanctions (penalties) against any norm violator. Where interactions are more abundant and varied, specialized institutional practices begin to appear. The latter are expected to provide a decision process capable of sustaining stable contact, or restoring severed relations.

The development, with global reach, of a network of practices specialized to decision is the distinctive problem with which we are presently concerned. A world constitutive process of authoritative decision includes the establishment of an authoritative decision process in the world community, and its subsequent maintenance, modification, or even termination. An examination of the world social process would indicate its dynamic character in the attempt of participants to optimize their preferred events or values. Hence the emergence of a measure of uniformity of expectation about the practices that are appropriately used in the world decision process is to be accounted for by operation of the postulate of maximization; according to this postulate, those who conform to, rather than flout, these practices ex-

---

existence, of a community. While de Visscher's injunction about the necessity of assuming an international community (*Theory and Reality in Public International Law* [Corbett trans., 1957], 99) is happily supported by the flow of events on the global scale, we feel that the tasks facing decision-makers and scholars are best performed when grounded on examination of the plenum of social reality rather than on Cartesian postulates.

[2] Interactive patterns within the contemporary global arena manifest wide variety in their degree of organization and complexity and do not exclude examples of "silent trading" even in situations where more explicit forms of collaboration could be negotiated. An example of current "silent trading" between major powers is the US-USSR exchange of moon photos. On May 26, 1966, the United States received the pictures taken on Luna 9. They were not part of an exchange agreement and were unsolicited. On June 1, 1966, the State Department subsequently disclosed, the pictures taken by the American Surveyor 1 were sent to more than 100 nations, including the USSR (*New York Times*, June 10, 1966, 8, col. 3).

pect, on the whole, to be better off by conformity than by deviation. The changing features of "world constitutional law" are to be understood by perceiving the intimacy of interplay between law and the entire social process of the world community.

It is pertinent to review, in this regard, a series of key conceptions. The inhabitants of the contemporary globe are, unquestionably, the members of a "group," not merely an "aggregate," since they share a sufficiently high frequency of perspectives and interaction. Enough evidence is readily available, despite the absence of appropriate intelligence agencies to describe frequencies, to support the assertion that transnational perceptions of interaction are numerous. No agreement exists among scholars about the minimum magnitudes essential to support the characterization of a "group." But the study of the content of the mass media of communication[3] and the data gathered in survey research amply sustain any reasonable conception. A group, as commonly understood, refers to participants sharing a high frequency of perspectives, but not necessarily having a territorial base. When a group is territorially based, it is appropriate to speak of it as a community. The obvious importance of territory as a base and scope value is expressed in this distinction between group and community. The interdetermination of peoples on a global scale and the pervasiveness of its perception justify the characterization of a "world community."

The world community is the scene of many effective decisions that involve more than one of the organized bodies-politic conventionally called nation-states. Specialized institutional practices cross boundaries; there are, for example, arrangements for sending and receiving negotiating agents and expectations have arisen about their treatment. These expectations include the assumption that if the decision-elite of one body-politic violates the usual freedom given to the agents of another, the elite of the latter will adopt deprivational measures against the offending state. Clearly it is a question of arrangements that are genuinely effective across particular boundaries, and that are sustained by sanctions of potential severity, sanctions of noncooperation or even of organized violence.

The example demonstrates a decision process going beyond effective power and including the characteristic features of authority: the

---

[3] Ennis, "The Social Structure of Communication Systems: A Theoretical Proposal," *1961 Studies in Public Communications*, 130, has observed that audiences, though dispersed, assume many of the characteristics of a social group and may even manifest a fairly high degree of organization in their behavior. A hypothesis meriting investigation is the degree to which and the conditions under which transnational communications media—both diplomatic and ideological—"communitize" their audiences. It may be necessary to draft a radically new map of sociopolitical subcommunities of the world as the magnitude of transnational communications increases.

prescriptive norm refers to the management of agents *and* it is assumed that sanctions are properly used if, in a contingent factual situation, the norm is disregarded. By authority is meant expectations of appropriateness in regard to the phases of effective decision processes. These expectations specifically relate to personnel appropriately endowed with decision-making power; the objectives they should pursue; the physical, temporal, and institutional features of the situations in which lawful decisions are made; the values which may be used to sustain decision, and so forth. There can be no automatic assumption of identity between formal and actually controlling institutional structures and expectations of authority. Genuine expectations of authority are discerned by contextual examination of past decision as well as by the utilization of all the techniques of the social sciences for assessing the current subjectivities of individuals. In the optimum public order which we recommend, the expectations of *all* individuals equally comprise authority. In extant public order systems, full universality and democracy are rarely achieved. The expectations and demands of the effective elites of a polity may be the dominant element of authority in a particular community; a sizable segment of the population may be in a state of folk culture with little or no notion of many phases of authoritative decision. An instrumental goal of a public order of human dignity is of course the equipping of all individuals for full participation in authoritative decision.

No decision process, whatever the size of the community, is wholly effective. The aggregate degree of effectiveness of an authority system must be sufficient to sustain expectations of future decision largely in conformity with demanded authority. The precise degree of effectiveness or "control" required for "law"—whether in international or national arenas—cannot, thus, be stated absolutely; it is a function of context and will vary. An authoritative and controlling decision can be contrasted with decisions involving only effective power ("naked power") or "pretended power." We see "naked power" in action when a strong empire coerces a weak neighboring polity and no one seeks to protect the weaker power. We identify "pretended power" when a superseded monarch vainly claims acceptance as the legitimate head of the body-politic from which he has been expelled.[4]

The larger decision process referred to above, despite its rudimentary character, is of immediate concern to us in the present context since it provides a constitutive example. We are referring to the circumstances in which the principal bodies-politic of the globe, acting in their role as participants in the world community, established the sending and receiving of agents as part of their authorita-

---

[4] For detailed discussion of power in its different manifestations, see Lasswell and Kaplan, *Power and Society* (1950), 75ff.

tive decision process. The constitutive act was the stabilizing act. It consolidated perspectives and operations in an institutional practice that was employed as both authoritative and controlling in the power process of the world community.

An examination of the world community context corroborates the view that, within limits, a global system of public order has come into existence that comprises a constitutive process in which authoritative decision institutions have taken form and which utilizes these institutions to protect and extend itself and also to contribute to the shaping and sharing of values other than power. The constitutive process is authoritative power exercised to provide an institutional framework for decision and to allocate indispensable functions; the particular decisions which emerge from this process may be specialized to the shaping and sharing of wealth, enlightenment, and all other values.

These distinctions are matters of relative emphasis, not exclusion; every use of authoritative power has some influence, however slight, on the predispositions and capabilities that are part of the decision process. Simultaneously, they affect other values; in fact, *all* values, in varying degrees. Respect, for example, is always at stake in every act of decision.

Over the centuries, the skeleton of shared practice that was originally little more than an exchange of intermediaries has broadened and grown into an encompassing system of bilateral, multilateral, and administrative arrangements. A globally inclusive system of public order, though operative, is visibly incomplete, proving inadequate to the task of maintaining a minimum level of world public order. An inventory of the arena of world politics must, further, distinguish more than a single, universal structure and acknowledge multilateral or regional systems that may suddenly or gradually change their relationships to one another.

At a high level of abstraction, most of the elites of the world community are united in giving verbal deference to words that formulate a common set of goals for universal order. These objectives are compatible with the conception of human dignity, a goal that finds expression in the Charter of the United Nations, in multilateral agreements, such as the instruments that define the rights of man, and in the enormous volume of national enactments and proclamations.[5] Any hesitation that we have to use these statements of aspiration to justify the conception of an all-inclusive public order arises from the definitional requirement that a structure of legality must go beyond words to expectations that are substantially corroborated by deeds.

[5] See Lauterpacht, *International Law and Human Rights* (1950); for a recent brief survey, see Schwelb, *Human Rights and the International Community* (1964).

An accepted body of prescriptive sentences is not enough; the linguistic patterns must be applied with relative frequency when the contingent circumstances to which they refer occur. Scholars and decision-makers do not, and need not, concur in setting the ratio of opportunity to application that must prevail if a given practice of decision is to be called "legal." The one essential point is that they not insist upon an impracticable degree of harmony in these matters, but rather develop a shared willingness to tolerate neither the extreme of words minus deeds, nor that of deeds minus legitimizing expectations.

More than words are involved in another and perhaps deeper sense than that which requires a specified frequency of conformity. It is meaningful to refer to authoritative decision as process, since the term process can easily be used to imply a context of interaction that has achieved a relatively high degree of stability, not chaos.[6] The constitutive process of the world community as a whole, and of its component territories, is the most rewarding frame of reference for international legal study and management, not only because different specific statements, perspectives, and operations can be kept in contextual relationship to one another, but because the problem-solving tasks with which the legal scholar, adviser, and decision-maker are faced can be most successfully managed in the "process" frame.

These most fundamental problem-solving tasks, no less indispensable to the decision-maker than to the scholar, can be summarized as follows:

1. Clarification of the goals of decision;
2. Description of the trends toward or away from the realization of these goals;
3. Analysis of the constellation of conditioning factors that appear to have affected past decision;
4. Projection of probable future developments, assuming no influence by the observer;
5. Formulation of particular objectives and strategies that contribute, at minimum net cost and risk, to the realization of preferred goals.

The process frame of reference can be utilized to provide a plan of inquiry that moves from the most comprehensive and abstract configuration to the most specific detail relevant to the problem-solving tasks. We have made use of the fundamental schema for characterizing the social process on the scale of the world community as a whole

[6] For pertinent reflections on the concept of process in the physical and social sciences, see Berlo, *The Process of Communication* (1960), 23-28.

or of each component context of interaction: *Man* (actors, participants) acts to optimize *values* (preferred events) through *institutions* affecting *resources*. The value-institution categories employed in the present framework of analysis are eight: power, or the giving and receiving of support in votes and fights; enlightenment, or the gathering processing, and dissemination of information; wealth, or control of resources; well-being, or safety, health, and comfort; skill, or opportunity to acquire and exercise capability in vocations, professions, and the arts; affection or intimacy, friendship and loyalty; respect, or recognition, whether personal or ascriptive; rectitude, or participation in forming and applying norms of responsible conduct. Note that any actor in the social process may be indulged or deprived in value terms, and that the whole process of interaction is "double phased" according to the shaping and sharing of values, and the institutional practices relatively specialized to the pre-outcome, outcome, and post-outcome phases of each value.

The previous pages have indicated how the institutions specialized to power have evolved in the world community; more specifically, how the confrontations among the participants in the social process of the world community and its subdivisions have led to the rise of systems of public order whose domain approximates every degree of universality or parochialism, and of value-scope and range. The power interactions that established authoritative arenas and formulated and allocated roles in decision are the constitutive processes with which we are most immediately concerned.

We have indicated that the observer-participant faced by the various problem-solving tasks, must position himself by clarifying the goals that he will postulate. Let it be explicit, in this connection, that we identify ourselves with the overriding goal of human dignity, which is the inclusive objective to which so much verbal, and even considerable behavioral, support is given in the modern world.

If the various tasks are to be performed in detail in reference to the past, present, and future of the constitutive process in the world community, an analytic framework is needed to bring into view the principal features of decision. "Conventional" analysis in terms of government organs and doctrines, an effective technique for certain problems, is on the whole, inappropriate for the study of international decision. Conventional usage must yield to "functional" analysis if comprehensive and realistic orientation is to be achieved. No dependable relationship exists between a structure that is called "governmental" in a particular body politic and the facts of authority and control. Analysts of comparative government are well aware of the truth of this observation for the understanding of the legal and political process at the national or sub-national level, since it is not unusual to discover, for example, that the authority formally provided in a written constitutional charter may be ignored, or totally redefined by unwritten practice. Similarly, when the international arena is examined, the presumed congruence of formal and actual authority of intergovernmental organizations may or may not be sustained by the concurrence of expectations necessary to justify a claim of actual constitutive authority. On a wide range of matters, the principal nation-states may—and do—continue to perceive one another as making the critical decisions, for which they accept, and reciprocally enforce, a substantial measure of responsibility.

Part of the functional approach recommended here is a conceptual technique for delineating the relevant aspects of any interpersonal interaction. Hence it is applied by first locating the decision—that is, choosing the phase at which a sequence of interactions appears to culminate. The culminating phase may be organized or unorganized; for example, it may be a formal agreement or a fight, a vote or a combination of unilateral assertion and passive acquiescence. The questions that are raised in phase analysis cover the outcome, pre-outcome, and post-outcome dimensions of the whole sequence:

1. Who acted or participated in roles of varying significance in the process which culminated in the decision? (*Participants*)

2. What were the significant perspectives of the participants? With whom were they identified? What value demands were they pursuing, with what expectations? (*Perspectives*)

3. Where and under what conditions were the participants interacting? (*Situations*)

4. What effective means for the achievement of their objectives were at the disposal of the different participants? (*Base Values*)

5. In what manner were these means or base values manipulated? (*Strategies*)

6. What was the immediate result—value allocation—of the process of interaction? (*Outcomes*)

7. What are the effects, of differing duration, of the process and outcome? (*Effects*)

Details pertinent to the performance of the requisite intellectual tasks will be adduced, for illustrative purposes only, for each phase. Furthermore, these seven aspects or "phases" of a decision process will be set in a wider context of conditions.

Since we are particularly concerned with the several outcomes that occur in the world arena, these decision outcomes are systematically examined to disclose the principal functions involved: *intelligence, promotion or recommendation, prescription, invocation,* application, *termination, appraisal.* In brief:

1. Intelligence is the obtaining, processing, and dissemination of information (including planning).
2. Promotion (or recommendation) is the advocacy of general policy.
3. Prescription is the crystallization of general policy in continuing community expectations.
4. Invocation is the provisional characterization of concrete circumstances in reference to prescriptions.
5. Application is the final characterization of concrete circumstances according to prescriptions.
6. Termination is the ending of a prescription and the disposition of legitimate expectations created when the prescription was in effect.
7. Appraisal is the evaluation of the manner and measure in which public policies have been put into effect and of the responsibility therefor.

In the following pages we set out, in most cursory outline, a framework of inquiry about the world constitutive process of authoritative decision.

PARTICIPANTS

All participants in world social process act in the constitutive process of authoritative decision.[7] Moreover, interdependence, one product of sustained high interaction, tends to restrict the unfettered employment of disparate bases of power, thus equalizing and democratizing participation. By a participant in constitutive process, as distinguished from the more general effective power process, we mean an individual or an entity which has at least minimum access to the process of authority in the sense that it can make claims or be subjected to claims. The traditional doctrinal position has been that only states are "subjects" of international law.[8] Yet there has always been a wide

---

[7] The discipline of international law, with its emphasis on inter-state relations, has been especially resistant to empirical examination of the actual participants in the world constitutive process of authoritative decision. As Lyman White described it more than a decade ago, the study of world affairs is:

in a state of development similar to the study of political science in the United States some decades ago when students gave attention only to the formally constituted branches of the government, not recognizing as they do now the important role of political parties and pressure groups," e.g. trade unions, chambers of commerce, churches. (White, *International Non-Governmental Organizations* [1951], 3.)

[8] For a general survey of the traditional views, see Briggs, *The Law of Nations* (2nd edn., 1952), 93-98. For contemporary treatment of the "subjectivity" of individuals and rather comprehensive references, see Friedmann, *The Changing Struc-*

discrepancy between this verbal doctrine and practice. While organized arenas have tended to set up rigid requirements for participation, unorganized arenas have not.[9] Where effective elites failed the "entrance requirements," they achieved a representation by transferring privity to an entity with access or by themselves taking a different participatory form. This practice has received authoritative approval.[10]

Since 1945, the trend has clearly moved toward broader participation. Rapidly proliferating new territorial units have been granted recognition, with no systematic reference to their ability to assume a responsible role in the constitutive process. In a different dimension, the *Reparations* case has confirmed the capacity of international organizations to participate in a number of organized arenas.[11] The status of individuals remains equivocal, though with trends toward wider recognition.[12] On the one hand, a document of the authority of the United Nations Charter states that the organization is founded by the "peoples of the world" rather than by the states of the world.[13] Yet practice is reluctant to grant an unqualified access to individuals to participate in a number of key arenas. While individuals have a relatively free access to unorganized arenas, states have proved jealous of their formerly exclusive position and have sought, in a variety of ways, to restrict or to regulate individual initiative in the constitutive process.[14]

Among the major classes of participants, we enumerate:

---

ture of International Law (1964), 232ff. It has proven easier for lawyers to preach an extended "subjectivity" than to practice it. Thus, Whiteman, in *Digest of International Law*, 1 (1963) includes "states and other entities" as subjects of international law. But the International Law Commission in attempting to apply a broader definition in the area of international agreements foundered. In 1962, it stated that treaties were agreements between: "states or other subjects of international law," *Report of the International Law Commission—1962*, GAOR, 17th Session, Supplement 9 (A/5209), 4. The difficulties inherent in restating traditional views in a manner comporting with current reality resulted in an atavism in later drafts. Thus, the 1965 version defines treaties as international agreements "between states," same, 20th Session, Supplement 9 (A/6009), 6.

[9] See, e.g. Article 4 of the Charter, Article 34 (1) of the Statute of the International Court of Justice. For discussion of the relation between institutionalization and participatory limitations, see section on Access.

[10] This practice is clearly demonstrated in one phase of the Hungarian-Rumanian Land Dispute (Optants Case): 8 LNOJ (1927), 354; in the Anglo-Iranian Oil Co. dispute, see Ford, *The Anglo-Iranian Oil Dispute of 1951-52* (1954), 91, and ICJ *Pleadings*, 66. Its most pervasive form is the practice of the diplomatic protection of nationals.

[11] Reparation for Injuries Suffered in the Service of the UN (Advisory Opinion) *ICJ Reports* (1949), 174.

[12] For a comprehensive survey of trends in context, see Jefferies, "The Individual and International Law" (unpublished dissertation, Yale Law School, 1954).

[13] Preamble, UN Charter, but note the conclusion of the preamble and the general reluctance of the Charter to specify procedures for individual participation.

[14] For an evaluation of American statutes and judicial decisions restricting partic-

Territorial Units

Control over territory, which continues to be a key resource for values, renders elites with territorial bases prime participants. This category includes the nation-state as well as different types of dependent territorial units. In certain cases, it may be convenient to include emerging state entities, i.e. elites in the process of consolidating a nation-state unit.[15]

Nation-states are relatively heterogeneous in structure when compared with one another or when examined internally. The flow of decision within each body politic is most intelligible in terms of the effective elite whose weight is expressed in the changing result. On analysis, the composition of the power elites of every nation-state can be shown to vary from the comparative stability of some small, though highly modernized states to the revolutionary turbulence or misleading totalitarian calm of societies in transition.

The internal process of decision is affected by the complexities of a division of institutional practice that strikes a variable balance between territorial centralization and decentralization, and degrees of pluralization. The bureaucratic and coalitional nature of contemporary society and government permits the development of sub-loyalties and idiosyncratic value goals in different sectors of society and departments of government. The same process renders authoritative and effective decision-making a complex sequence of component decisions, at each phase of which different individuals or groups may enjoy a dominant position in the shaping of decision. Any elite group manifests some degree of responsiveness to the pressures of sub-elites who are seeking to maximize their values in the internal arena of the nation-state. In view of the impact of such factors as these, effective delineation of the compound entity known as the nation-state must "pierce the veil of statehood" in attempting to discern probable trends of decision on constitutive matters at home or abroad.

Coordinations between elites of different nation-states can have important constitutive consequences. We analyze such coordinations according to the level of interdependence and the duration of the link, noting the existence of blocs, alliances, and alignments.

---

ipation by individuals in transnational interactions, see Vagts, "The Logan Act: Paper Tiger or Sleeping Giant?", 60 *American Journal of International Law*, 268, (1966).

15 The point at which entity "X" becomes a "nation-state" is elusive: see Emerson, *From Empire to Nation-State: The Rise to Self-Assertion of Asian and African Peoples* (1960), 89-188. Trends in authoritative decision exhibit their usual complementarity in this regard. The Paris Peace Conference appeared to give a quasi-state *locus standi* only to those elites representing "territorial groups" the powers had already decided to recognize. Postwar trends have, generally, been more liberal.

International Governmental Organizations

Participants in this category may be arranged in organizations the scope of whose value programs is general or specific. In the former category are found the United Nations complex as well as a number of regional organizations. The specific-value category is comprised of the so-called functional organizations. International organizations may be either participants or arenas in the constitutive process. Moreover, a variety of constitutive decisions may relate to some phase of the organizational process. Some organizations are specifically concerned with the constitutive process, while others, concerned with specific public-order features, have only a peripheral or indirect interest in constitutive decision.

Within organizations, attention must be paid to specific decisional entities. Thus, for example, the Secretariat, the Security Council, the General Assembly, and the Economic and Social Council would require special attention. Furthermore, predictable voting alignments, insofar as they exist, must be noted.[16]

Regional organizations may dominate the power process within their geographical area as well as act as composite participants in the comprehensive global process. Accordingly, regional organizations with scope value programs of varying generality or specificity require examination.

Political Parties

Political parties are ordinarily recognized as a nation-state rather than a transnational phenomenon. As global interaction intensifies and concentricity of identifications increases, entities seeking formal power in arenas larger than the nation-state may be expected to increase concomitantly. A transnational party may project a transnational program, i.e. one whose realization requires a coordinated acquisition of power in a number of states or in all states. It may have a solely national program but draw its inspiration, authority, or orders from participants based in other states. It may refer to a conglomeration of like-minded parties in different states, each of whose programs are national, but who coordinate policies because of the belief that

---

[16] For a survey of General Assembly voting alignments, see Alker and Russett, *World Politics in the General Assembly* (1966) ; Hovet, *Bloc Politics in the United Nations* (1960); Keohane, "Political Influence in the General Assembly," 557 *International Conciliation*, 11-13 (1966).

Quantitative analysis of UN voting patterns has proved and disproved the existence of blocs and alignments. It is pertinent to note that quantitative methods will be of heuristic and predictive value only if applied in a broad contextual framework. Until investigations have established that a few significant variables account for behavior—and we believe that this will not be proved—the isolation of a limited number of factors will only result in distortions. A vote out of context has no more significance than a case out of context.

realization of the desired national public order demands certain regional or global conditions which can be achieved only by other parties operating in other states. It may, finally, refer to fraternal parties in different states, which do not formally coordinate national activities, but keep one another apprised of general policies and activities.

A political party is distinguished from a political order by the degree of power-sharing in internal decision processes. Thus, a "party" manifests power-sharing in significant degree, while an "order" manifests elite power monopoly as its fundamental characteristic. In the following discussion, the term party will be used to include both phenomena, since the question of the degree of internal power-sharing of parties and orders will not be addressed; the distinction should, however, be kept in mind.

The leading example of a transnational party is the Communist party.[17] Schismatic divisions within world Communism have introduced marked changes in the formerly monolithic character of Communism.[18] The extent to which world Communism still constitutes an international system or order or the possible future conditions under which it will function as a system remains a matter for speculation.[19] A variety of other political parties operate transnationally, although they lack the ideological cohesion and organizational rigidity which once characterized international Communism. Religious, ethnic, and cultural bonds have proved to be an effective basis for transnational party collaboration. Common political goals have also served as an axis for transnational party collaboration. Acting on this basis, certain western political parties have undertaken to set up transnational organizational structures.[20]

In transnational parliamentary arenas, participants tend to group themselves in coordinations of varying stability, whose performance is not dissimilar from parties in national parliaments. Where, as in the Consultative Assembly of the Council of Europe, the actors are parliamentarians who have been conditioned to think in party terms, transnational party groupings and loyalties compete with national identifications.[21]

National parties frequently move into the international arena. Many opposition parties maintain shadow cabinets and "foreign of-

---

[17] Labedz, *International Communism after Khrushchev* (1965) ; see also the papers in Dallin, ed., *Diversity in International Communism: A Documentary Record* (1963).

[18] See Starobin, "Communism in Western Europe," *Foreign Affairs*, 44 (1965), 62.

[19] Modelski, *The Communist International System* (1961) ; Crankshaw, *The New Cold War: Moscow v. Peking* (1963).

[20] On the abundant literature of Christian Democracy, see Fogarty, *Christian Democracy in Western Europe 1820-1953* (1957) and generally the work of Allemeyer.

[21] Robertson, *The Law of International Institutions in Europe* (1961) , 38ff.

fices." In nation-states with democratic public-order systems, the allocation of representatives constituting national delegations to international organizations as well as to ad-hoc conferences is often determined on party lines. Although the incumbent party may be expected to control the delegation, opposing parties are represented, as a strategy of both good government (continuity) and good politics (shared responsibility for foreign policy decisions). Frequently, the individuals in these delegations are highly conscious of their dual role as both national and party representatives.[22]

Pressure Groups

We refer here to entities which attempt to influence authoritative decision in regard to specific matters, but do not project a total public-order program. Whereas political parties seek to gain formal power within the body politic in which they function, pressure groups are interested in influencing decision without assuming formal political power.

The United Nations complex offers an abundance of examples of pressure groups operating directly in organized international decision processes. The constitutive documents of the Economic and Social Council confer a consultative status upon a large number of private, nongovernmental organizations.[23] The incidents of the status vary, the lowest allowing no more than presence at the Council's deliberations and the highest permitting the organizations to enter items on the provisional agenda. Consultative status approximates a semi-official if limited participatory role. Pressure groups operate nonofficially in the UN as well. A variety of commercial entities maintain agents and, in certain cases, lobbies, at the United Nations. These lobbies function much as do their national counterparts. In addition to fulfilling the usual intelligence, promoting and appraising roles associated with pressure groups, they also may fulfill a quasi-invocatory function. Although only member-states may introduce items on the

[22] Thus, both Democratic and Republican members of Congress are accorded representation on the United States' delegation to the General Assembly. Similar policies of balanced delegation composition are pursued by a number of other democratic parliamentary states. Both Churchill and Attlee were present at the first phase of Potsdam. This is a well-known and oft-commented-upon phenomenon of the International Labor Organization and its unique Assembly structure. It has extended to other transnational parliamentary contexts, most noticeably those in which national delegations allocate special seats for labor representatives. See, for example, *New York Times*, May 11, 1966, 9, col. 1, reporting the repudiation and disassociation from a speech delivered by J. B. Bierne, of the U. S. labor movement by Secretary of Labor Wirtz and the U. S. efforts to remove the unamended speech from the record.

[23] As of December 1962, 10 organizations were accorded status "A," 124 status "B," and 198 status "C." For a brief survey see *Everyman's United Nations* (7th edn. 1964), 16-17.

agenda (with the exception of organizations of Consultative Status A in ECOSOC), an unofficial participant can have a matter placed on the agenda if he is able to obtain the sponsorship of a delegation member. In the future, it is not improbable that a significant number of agenda items will stem from the initiative of international pressure groups.

Private Associations

By private association, we mean a nongovernmental organization formed for the purpose of pursuing scope-values other than power.[24] A great many of these entities are "international" in membership, goals, and arena of activity. A significant number of private associations, however, are predominantly national, yet consciously aspire to affect the world value processes as part of their national program. Other private associations, with primarily national horizons, may have important indirect effects upon the global value and constitutive processes. The vast number of private associations operational in the constitutive process precludes a detailed description.[25] In the following pages, we illustrate by brief reference the leading participants and dominant trends within various values.

WEALTH: The number of international cartels is set by White at over 1,200 and he believes that during certain inter-war periods, they accounted for more than 42 percent of world trade.[26] However, the current extent of cartels or their functional equivalents is difficult to gauge.[27] Municipal legislation in several great trading states takes a stand against restrictive trade practices,[28] but certain activities, notably maritime and air transport, have been largely exempted. Application of antitrust legislation by national courts and administrative agencies has been irregular. Furthermore, anti-trust policies in differ-

[24] Our reference, it may be noted, is broader than that of Article 71 of the Charter and ECOSOC's implementing definition of "any international organization which is not established by intergovernmental agreement." Interestingly, ECOSOC's practice has construed its own definition broadly.

[25] The *Yearbook of International Organizations* (10th edn. 1964-65) describes 1,718 nongovernmental organizations. White, *Non-Governmental Organizations*, amply describes the richness of participation of NGO's. The organizations treated in these collections view themselves as NGO's. If we choose as the criterion of definition, operative groups whose activities have transnational impacts, though they do not view themselves as "international," the number of NGO's would be considerably greater.

[26] White, *Non-Governmental Organizations*, 41.

[27] See Lador-Lederer, *International Nongovernmental Organizations and Economic Entities* (1963), 247ff.

[28] See e.g. Fugate, "Antitrust Law and International Trade," Proehl, ed., *Legal Problems of International Trade* (1959), 387; Edwards, "Foreign Anti-Trust Laws in the 1960's," *Legal Problems in International Trade and Investment*, 57.

ent cultures show marked divergencies.[29] It has been suggested that the "New Deal of International Trade" means economic policy framed by international organizations rather than by private cartels.[30] In fact, the stillbirth of the International Trade Organization and the erratic record of GATT suggests that much of transnational trade policy is formulated, through direct or indirect communication, by participants engaged in international wealth processes.

The evolution of international business enterprises in the world social process has been subjected to detailed description and analysis in the literature.[31] As was noted earlier, many of these corporations act indirectly, through political parties, or directly upon international decision through international pressure groups. The larger international corporations negotiate directly with nation-state representatives in a modern form of diplomacy: agreements with these corporate giants may surpass treaties in terms of values affected[32] and may be constitutive prescription.

A number of private associations are concerned with the sharing rather than with the shaping of wealth. Foremost among these types of association are the labor unions. Although certain national unions pursue foreign policy objectives directly, as well as through participation in national decision processes, several composite participants are concerned predominantly with coordinating international efforts.

ENLIGHTENMENT: Private associations which seek enlightenment range over the entire spectrum of scientific and humanistic pursuits. International professional associations, concerned with exchanging information, collaborating in research and development, and generally maintaining contact with members in other countries are too numerous to discuss. Organizations concerned with philosophic or scientific education have been playing an increasingly important role.[33] Some have acquired or applied for consultative status with ECOSOC. Many pursue policies which are forwarded by conventional lobbying techniques. There are currently two major international student associations, one communist, the other generally anti-communist, both of which pursue indoctrination programs at the national and inter-

[29] For a survey, see Friedmann, *Anti-Trust Laws; A Comparative Symposium* (1956) ; Sakane, *Anti-Trust Legislations of the World* (1960).

[30] Lador-Lederer, *International Nongovernmental Organizations*, 273.

[31] See Borchard, "Relation of Bretton Woods Agreement to other Types of International Organization," *Supplement, New York University Law Review*, 99, 109-111 (1945); Timberg, "International Combines and National Sovereigns," 95 *University of Pennsylvania Law Review*, 575 (1947); Timberg, "Corporate Fictions: Logical Social and International Implications," 46 *Columbia Law Review*, 533 (1946).

[32] Jessup, *Modern Law of Nations* (1946) , 15-35.

[33] White, *Non-Governmental Organizations*, 95-132.

national level. The enlightenment role of the press will be discussed below.[34]

Since the great "Peace Movement" of the nineteenth century,[35] popular concern with the problems of international relations, international organization, and appropriate constitutive processes in the world arena has risen markedly. A mushrooming number of private associations have occupied themselves with these problems and many of them have filled important decision functions. The venerable *Institut de Droit International*, the International Law Association, the American Institute of International Law, the Academy of International Law, as well as numerous national and regional bar associations all appraise and recommend policies for constitutive decision.

Private international peace congresses were a frequent phenomenon of the nineteenth century. In a number of instances, they succeeded in initiating significant constitutive prescription. Thus, the International Association for Labor Legislation, created in 1900, was successful in its agitation for conventions on labor standards and was, in many ways, the predecessor and partial inspiration for the International Labor Organization. The International Red Cross has performed a similar promotive function. In the contemporary world, rapid communication and a growing intensity of interaction have led to a proliferation of such participants. The Pugwash conferences and the London Conference of Sanctions against South Africa, to name but two examples, may signal an increasing trend of private groups participating in the constitutive process in the future.[36]

SKILL: Many private associations concerned with the skill-value have been mentioned in passing in our discussion of wealth and enlightenment. A wide variety of associations have transnational activities and provide intelligence, recommendations, and appraisals to constitutive decision-makers relative to prescription and application in matters in which they have expertise. The enlarged possibilities for communication offered by highly specialized but universal technical languages present opportunities for contact and collaboration. Association with

---

[34] See sections on Intelligence and Promotion.

[35] For a survey of the activities of the peace movement at the end of the past century, see Davis, *The United States and the First Hague Peace Conference* (1962).

[36] It is interesting to note that while Pugwash has viewed governmental affiliation as contamination and has sought to avoid it militantly, the London Conference on Sanctions, which was initiated privately, sought from the beginning to transform itself into a quasi-governmental conference. The point appears to be that participants perceive application as dependent upon state power bases, but feel that appraisal can function effectively only if it is independent of states that are often the subject of examination.

a particular skill group may provide the basis for enduring transnational identifications.

The complexity of modern life has vaulted us into an age of specialists. Since many areas of public order concern prove too arcane for the general decision-maker, a practice of employing the specialist has developed. Legislatures frequently draw upon panels of experts in particular fields;[37] courts call expert witnesses; arbitration panels are not infrequently composed of members of that skill group which is the subject of litigation.[38] In these decision roles, skill group members play a larger and larger role in the clarification and projection of constitutive policy.

AFFECTION: Instruments of group identification—cultural, racial, linguistic, religious, professional—have long served as bases for private associations of diverse objectives. Irredentist group activities have been a subject of both protection and regulation in international law.[39] Groups without territorial bases have struggled to form nation-states by invoking the broad policy of self-determination. The "quasi-state" quality of these "groundless" groups and the fact that they have concluded international constitutive agreements has been a steady challenge to the traditional doctrine of "sovereignty."

Affection associations frequently operate on the national level, indirectly affecting the world constitutive process by shaping national policy. These groups may identify with particular ethnic, religious, or linguistic groups outside of their own state, attempting either to form their policy or to be an agent of it.

Affection associations—the extended family and kinship groups—are rarely given the attention which they merit and which approximate their influence on the world constitutive process. We cannot overlook the persisting role of influential families, especially the dynastic families whose members have a heavy stake in the defense or restoration of arrangements favorable to monarchical or feudal systems.

RECTITUDE: Some of the earliest nongovernmental international organizations have been religious associations. The Roman Catholic Church continues to be the organization with the most cohesive ideology and the most effective hierarchical structure.[40] The legal

---

[37] Newman and Surrey, *Legislation* (1955), 250ff.

[38] See White, *The Use of Experts by International Tribunals* (1965).

[39] See Feinberg, "The Legal Validity of the Undertakings Concerning Minorities and the Clausula Rebus Sic Stantibus," 5 *Scripta Hierosolymitana*, 95 (1958); Lador-Lederer, *Economic Entities*, 117-143; Robinson et al., *Were the Minority Treaties a Failure?* (1943).

[40] See Grubb and Booth, *The Church and International Relations*, 17 *Yearbook of World Affairs* (1963), 219.

status of the Church has been controversial in the literature, with agreement only on the proposition that the Church is *sui generis*.[41] The Vatican maintains a diplomatic corps and has a recognized treaty-making authority. The leader of the Church is a recognized international figure with important decision-making functions in the world constitutive process.[42]

A variety of other church and church-affiliated organizations operate on the transnational level, but none approaches the organization or sustained efficiency of the Roman Catholic Church. Of particular importance in the shaping of national public-order systems have been missionary societies and activities, Christian, Islamic, and Buddhist. The expanding national self-consciousness of the developing nations, formerly the challenge and, indeed, raison d'etre of much western missionary activity, will probably act to reduce the impact of missionary programs. The dominant flow of rectitude influence may follow an east-west rather than west-east course as in recent centuries.

Within democratic nation-states, numerous national private associations, primarily with national programs of rectitude scope-values, have found themselves increasingly concerned with global constitutive decisions. It is a commonplace that the American civil rights movement was affected and to a degree spurred by trends in African and Asian countries and that the movement has had a reciprocal effect on developments in those continents. Much of this reciprocal interaction has been indirect and unintended. However, many local reform movements, whose primary base of power is rectitude, have found it difficult to ignore the same "foreign" evils which they combat on the home front. Hence many of these groups are in the process of developing national and foreign programs.

WELL-BEING: One radical innovation of the post-war period has been the growth of *official* concern for the well-being of all people throughout the globe. The broadening of official activity in this area is a logical extension of a variety of cultural currents antedating the war; the political doctrine of self-determination, the political-economic doctrines of social justice, and so on, were ultimately grounded in concern for an equitable sharing of values for all people. The concern for well-being, formerly a prerogative of private transnational associations, has thus been largely subrogated to official processes. The United Nations, UNESCO, WHO, FAO, and the ILO,

---

[41] Lauterpacht-Oppenheim, *International Law* (8th edn., 1955), 254.

[42] Pope Paul addressed the General Assembly in 1965; although there was little objection, it is interesting to speculate on the basis of the Pontiff's appearance: head of state, leader of a world religion, pressure group, "corporation" or *sui generis*? The case of the Church seems to indicate that a participant with the appropriate bases can gain access to arenas of authority whether or not it is classified as a state.

to cite only the most prominent, have become major participants concerned with the shaping and sharing of well-being.

Though massive in goal and operation, official activities have not preempted the field. The private associations which have been traditionally concerned with well-being have continued to supplement official efforts. Many new associations, of varying durability, have been formed in response to new challenges to the safety and health of all individuals or of a particular subgroup in given circumstances. In periods of intense crisis private associations devoted to well-being have proven particularly indispensable. The excessive demands on official processes in crisis tend to diminish their efforts on behalf of well-being; private associations specialized to this value then become the principal supervisors. The International Red Cross, in addition to its work in alleviating the suffering attendant upon natural disaster, continues to concern itself with refugee problems and the administration of prescriptions governing belligerency.[43] It examines perforce the degree of compliance with the laws of war and its findings—official or otherwise—may have a sanction potential. HIAS and the JDC continue to play roles in the resettlement of refugees and in prescribing and maintaining standards of well-being and minimal respect for displaced persons. A number of private associations, religious and secular, particularly concern themselves with the well-being of children as well as with the general level of education in poverty-stricken countries.[44]

RESPECT: Parallel to the trend in well-being, there has been a great increase in official supervisory and enterprisory activities in processes specialized to respect. Detailed discussion of these activities is reserved for the *outcomes* phase, below. A useful index for gauging the upswing is the quantity of official and semi-official communications concerned with the respect of individuals: a cursory comparison of treaties, covenants, judicial decisions, diplomatic communications, and scholarly works regarding rectitude in two twenty-year periods— pre-1919 and post-1945—indicates an enormous growth. Traditional international law was, of course, not oblivious to this value. A trend from Roman stoicism through the classical Spanish school has emphasized that fundamental to an appropriate international order is the recognition of the innate value of every human being.[45] It is significant in this regard that both the London Agreement and the Nuremberg Tribunal tended to characterize their guiding norms as

---

[43] Werner, *La Croix Rouge et les Conventions de Genève* (1943); Coursier, *La Croix-Rouge Internationale* (1959).

[44] White, *Non-Governmental Organizations*, 166ff.

[45] For a survey of the trend, see Nussbaum, *A Concise History of the Law of Nations* (1947).

declaratory of customary international law rather than as innovative prescription.[46] Despite prescriptive precedents, however, processes of application have, until recently, been unorganized and sporadic. With the exception of "humanitarian intervention," the application of this value process has been left primarily in the hands of private rectitude-oriented associations. While the number of religiously based associations has not increased markedly, secular rectitude associations have multiplied many-fold as has the magnitude of their communications. The fact that many of these associations are primarily national in membership and goal has not impeded a flow of transnational activities and impacts.

Individuals

Individuals participate as the ultimate actors for all the composite participants as well as in their own right. In describing past trends and in undertaking to predict future behavior, the observer must be cognizant of a variety of characteristics of individual participants: culture, class, interest, personality, and past exposure to crisis.[47]

The adamant stance of some observers in refusing to recognize the individual as a subject of international law is currently based on a pseudo-empirical survey of the practice of organized arenas. Since individuals do not have a *locus standi* before the organized arenas which are examined, individuals are not, it is concluded, subjects of international law. The concealed assumption is that the organized arenas surveyed exhaust authoritative patterns of constitutive interaction. A more comprehensive survey of the range of constitutive arenas indicates that individuals with effective bases of power have always had access to a wide variety of arenas. A renewed emphasis upon the individual since the end of the Second World War has facilitated the access of more individuals to many organized constitutive arenas. Certain international tribunals, it may be noted, are open, as of right, to individuals.[48] Moreover, a variety of pressure groups and

46 Indeed, the tribunal construed the London Charter as perfecting its jurisdiction, but went beyond this in contending that many of the war crimes were previously proscribed by international law. See Briggs, *The Law of Nations* (2nd edn. 1952), 1020-21, for a catalogue of pertinent studies.

47 For discussion of many of these factors and for numerous references to UNESCO-sponsored studies in this area, see Klineberg, *The Human Dimension in International Relations* (1965). For a comprehensive treatment of the many roles of the individual in international law, see Jefferies, "The Individual and International Law" (unpublished dissertation, Yale Law School, 1954).

48 In regard to ad-hoc tribunals, reference may be had to international claims commissions. In regard to cogentive tribunals, note the Central American Court of Justice (1907-1917) which permitted a *locus standi* to nationals of the signatory states. Nonadjudicative arenas, such as the Permanent Mandates Commission of the League of Nations, the Trusteeship Council, the Fourth Committee of the General Assembly, the Committee of 24, and the Committee on Apartheid of the United

private associations concerned with the welfare of individuals place their base values at the disposal of private participants and further facilitate their participation in the global constitutive process.

The rapidity of communication in the contemporary world augments the potentialities for cross-boundary impact in the aggregate constitutive arena. This trend, if it continues, will further consolidate the arena. The transnational impact of an Onassis on the shaping and sharing of wealth hardly requires emphasis, since it occurs in a value process which has traditionally been susceptible to cross-cultural initiatives taken by individuals. Less conspicuous, perhaps, is the cross-cultural record as it relates to other value sectors. A comparison through time of the multi-value influence of Paul of Tarsus, Mohammed, Marx and Engels, Gandhi and Nehru on cultures other than their own, indicates that the interval required for an intense cross-cultural impact has progressively diminished to the point where a charismatic personality may expect to develop a global constituency within his own lifetime. The full dimensions of this trend are difficult to gauge.[49] It is currently common to characterize the nineteenth century as the era of the nation-state and the twentieth as the era of the international organization. Posterity may characterize our period as the renascent era of the individual.

PERSPECTIVES (EXPLICIT AND IMPLICIT OBJECTIVES OF PARTICIPANTS)

The reference here is to the objectives for which participants in the effective power process establish and maintain the constitutive process. Objectives are subjective events of "purpose" or "aim," and they are best inferred from the utterances of significant decision-makers, supplemented and assessed according to their deeds. Strictly speaking, the objectives are "demands" that are interconnected with "identities" and "expectations." We define a demand as "preference" or "volition"; hence it is an evaluation of a potential or actual event. The maker of a demand is an individual acting in the name of his own ego-identity, or in the name of a larger self, such as a nation-

Nations also accord access to individuals. A possible trend of preference for this form of invocation may be indicated by the European Convention on Human Rights of 1950 and the Committee against Racial Discrimination to be established by the Convention on the Elimination of All Forms of Racial Discrimination of 1965. For more treatment, see Jefferies, "The Individual and International Law."

[49] In this regard, the origins of the European community movement are extremely indicative of the potential role of the private individual. One man—Jean Monnet—had an enormous impact on the initiation of the community. See Yondorf, "Monnet and the Action Committee: The Formative Period of the European Communities," 19 *International Organization* (1965), 885. Mention may also be made of the significant role played by Raphael Lemkin in promoting the Genocide Convention.

state, with which his ego is identified. All matter of fact assumptions about past, present, or future events are expectations. Obviously, they may refer to the self as value-indulged or deprived in reference to others. Since the optimizing of value outcomes is the goal of participation in the constitutive, as in all other processes, the perspectives seem to provide both direction and intensity to the conduct of participants of all categories.

Fundamentally, international law is a process by which the peoples of the world clarify and implement their common interests in the shaping and sharing of values. By an interest, we refer to a value demand formulated in the name of an identity and supported by expectations that the demand is advantageous: ". . . more than wishes are involved in interests. Besides preference and volition there are patterns of expectation about the degree of congruence between events and demands."[50] It is possible to distinguish the expectation from the demand component of an interest and to consider the expectation in terms of validity, or high probability of descriptive truth (as determined by third-party observers). Interests are also open to relevant analysis according to whose value position is at stake. The constitutive interests of effective global elites may be distinguished as *common interests*—interests whose fulfillment will benefit the entire community and which are held in common by most effective elites —and *special interests*—demands made only by certain effective elites, whose fulfillment will benefit only one segment of the community with a corresponding deprivation to the rest. Insofar as they relate to the allocation of constitutive competence, common interests are further classifiable as *exclusive* if they primarily affect a single participant and *inclusive* if they primarily affect more than one participant. Common inclusive interests relate to the requirements of both minimum and optimum world order, whereas common exclusive interests relate to the minimum order and the sphere of value allocation left to the determination of each participant.

Common inclusive and common exclusive interests can be employed as concepts for either description or evaluation. When used descriptively, they depict who is or claims to be authorized to share in certain constitutive or public order decisions and who, in fact, does. Evaluatively, the distinction permits the observer to clarify and recommend, by reference to his own postulated and recommended goals, under what conditions decisions should be unilateral or plurilateral. We employ this distinction in place of the traditional dichotomy between "national" and "international" interests. The recommended terminology emphasizes that "national" interests may frequently be

50 McDougal, Lasswell, and Vlasic, *Law and Public Order in Space* (1963), 146.

common interests—inclusive or exclusive—a fact often obscured by the traditional dichotomy.[51]

Constitutive Policies

To identify the constitutive process of the world community is to demonstrate the presence of at least minimum stability of expectation about the decision flow by which authoritative and controlling decision processes are established and maintained. Relative stability does not necessarily imply that all phases and subphases of the constitutive process, or all facets of global public order, have been fully crystallized. In common with all human affairs, constitutive expectations are perpetually in flux, even to the point of partial disintegration during periods of conspicuous failure to sustain minimum public order. As a means of specifying the contemporary policies supported by the operations of a constitutive process, it is convenient to deal successively with elite objectives that are exhibited in reference to the different phases of the decision process.

Participants

Constitutive policies regarding participation may be summarized in terms of democracy and responsibility. Hence, within each participant class, universal participation is sought and any exclusions, postponements, or restrictions are made on the basis of either demonstrated or estimated inability or unwillingness to play a responsible role in the constitutive process. Trends in constitutive decision reflect the complementarities of this policy. While these complementarities are discernible in any competent review of the trend of decision in the constitutive process, it would be a mistake to suppose that they are applied at the same moment with equal emphasis. Since the end of World War II, and most emphatically since the early nineteen-fifties, many new states have been identified as authoritative participants even though questions relating to responsibility have been given minimum consideration. That many ex-colonial peoples are today represented abroad by leaders from their own cultural background is obviously true. However, this is often a very meager step toward democratic forms of public order since in not a few new states the inner process of decision is concentrated in the hands of a self-perpetuating few. It also augurs poorly for the capacity and determination of certain states to act responsibly in fulfilling their obligations to the common interest of all states in nurturing and sustaining at least minimum public order.[52]

[51] McDougal and Reisman, "The Changing Structure of International Law: Unchanging Theory for Inquiry," 65 *Columbia Law Review*, 813-14 (1965).

[52] See Judge Jessup's proposal on inclusive recognition procedures in Jessup, *A Modern Law of Nations* (1946), 48-50.

Perspectives (Objectives)

The articulated goals of the world constitutive process cover a range from minimum public order to many of the necessary components of an optimum public-order system. That minimum public order is a responsibility of the world community as a whole is formulated in the United Nations Charter and in the complex of Human Rights treaties and declarations in reference to every value institution process. It is possible to distinguish among objectives according to the intensity with which they are demanded and expected to be realized. A clue to intensity is that such demands are given operational priority and apparently are deemed subject to change only in formally prescribed procedures.[53]

Arenas (Structures of Authority)

In regard to arenas, constitutive policies may be summarized in terms of adequacy, with particular reference to economy and structural adaptation. The concern for adequacy has expressed itself in the formation of numerous arenas of widely varying composition and role, enabling participants, no matter what their formal relations, to collaborate in at least some decisions.[54] These diverse situations are not easy to describe in the tripartite categories so often used to analyze national systems.[55] Hence, the advantage of utilizing a richer system of phase and outcome analysis such as we employ in this article becomes clear. As a result, it is possible to choose the arena best adapted to a particular matter as recommended by the principle of economy. Since not all interaction is best served by the same degree or kind of organization, the policy of structural adaptation has wisely provided a wide variety of constitutive arenas, to fit the diverse requirements of the many participants in world politics.

Base Values

If the structures specialized to the tasks of the constitutive process are to obtain the desired impact they must have the necessary base values at their disposal. Major constitutive documents have created procedures for obtaining and centralizing the base values requisite

53 For a discussion of *jus cogens*, see section on Outcomes.

54 In an arena in which formal relations themselves constitute a multi-impact policy decision, a multiplicity of interactive patterns can permit communication without undesired ancillary effects, which might follow formal relations. Thus, for example, intergovernmental relations between China and the US, the two Germanys, Israel, and Jordan, etc. are possible. Moreover, since expected interactive patterns are "metacommunications," a variety of arenas can facilitate communication under different conditions.

55 1 Montesquieu, *The Spirit of the Laws*, 179ff. (Nugent trans., rev. 1900); for further discussion, see section on Outcomes.

to international organizations.[56] The degree to which practice conforms to goal varies according to context and arena. Even when the procedures originally prescribed have proved unworkable, novel improvisations have evolved[57] and have won acceptance by the Internanational Court as authoritative.[58]

Perspectives of authority are the most economical base values available in any process of decision. Accordingly, the constitutive process has sought to inculcate community-wide identification as a base of authoritative decision.

Strategies

Policies relating to the modalities by which the constitutive process and global public order are maintained are expressed in a preference for persuasive rather than coercive strategies; when the employment of coercive strategies is unavoidable, the preference is for inclusivity in their exercise. The United Nations Charter provides for the use of force only by the organized community and solely to maintain minimum order.[59] When the organized community is incapable of functioning in this sphere, the lawfulness of unilaterally applied coercive strategies is determined by reference to community goals of minimum order.[60] Public policy protects the private employment of diplomatic and ideological strategies, subject to regulation by reference to inclusive prescriptions.[61]

Outcomes

The outcomes that flow from the constitutive process are the decisions that delimit authoritative and controlling participation in the world arena. Fundamental policies guide the world community in restricting the role appropriate to action through inclusive community institutions. Since a basic preference is for initiatives to be taken as freely as possible throughout the world social process, disagreements unlikely to involve the use of coercion by the parties are left to "private" settlement until a community-wide decision-maker is invoked by at least one of the parties. The decision-maker then applies

[56] See Charter Articles 17, 43, 44, 45, 48; Articles 43, 46 and 54 of the Charter of Bogota.

[57] For survey and analysis, see Bowett et al., *United Nations Forces: A Legal Study of United Nations Practice* (1964).

[58] See *Certain Expenses of the United Nations*, 1962 *ICJ Reports*, 151 for application by the Court of the principle of effectiveness to such developments.

[59] See Article 2 (4); that this is a contingent allocation of authority is demonstrated by a variety of other provisions in the Charter. See especially Articles 51 and 52 and the delegatory power of Article 44.

[60] See McDougal and Feliciano, *Law and Minimum World Public Order* (1961), 143ff.

[61] See section on Strategies.

the prescriptions which, functionally characterized, belong to the "supervisory" code.

The "regulative" code prescribes limits beyond which private activities cannot go without provoking the decision-makers of the inclusive community to act to reinstate the previous limitations. The consequences of private deviations are expected to be sufficiently deprivational of common interests in the world community to require such measures.

The "enterprisory" code extends the role of inclusive community institutions to the continuous administration of activities that, if left in other hands, are expected to be relatively deprivational.

All prescriptions include sanctioning arrangements which are the indulgences or deprivations managed for the purpose of obtaining conformity to the prescribed norm. It is usually assumed that potential targets of sanction are capable of adapting their policies to the costs and risks involved. However, it is well understood that some individuals do not reach the minimum level of capability and therefore require "correction." They come within the purview of the corrective code.

Certain constitutive prescriptions are held with greater intensity than others. The prescriptions that are expected and demanded with greatest intensity are generally deemed to be terminable only by formal inclusive procedures. Norms of this category enjoy such doctrinal appellations as *jus cogens*, peremptory norms, or principles of natural law. That such norms are, and ought to be recognized is affirmed with exceptional unanimity and vigor; yet there has been almost universal dispute as to their content.[62] There is however little doubt that certain fundamental constitutive norms are held with expectations of greatest intensity and are less susceptible than others to unilateral modification and termination, since they are supported by a wide allocation of control. There are, of course, fundamental norms whose continued vitality depends upon the behavior of a few superpowers or even, in certain circumstances, upon the behavior of one participant. In terms of aggregate expectations, however, these norms

[62] Article 37 of the Draft Law of Treaties of the International Law Commission states that a treaty is void if it conflicts with a peremptory norm of international law; Article 45 provides for termination of an extant treaty by emergence of a new peremptory norm. The Commission was, however, unable to agree on any specific peremptory norm: Report of the International Law Commission—1963, GAOR 18th Session Supplement 9 (A/5509) 11, 23. Schwarzenberger, "International jus cogens?," 43 *Texas Law Review* (1965) argues that there are no peremptory norms and that the acceptance of such a doctrine is pernicious, in that it provides a new ground for defeating treaties. But this is to assume that treaties are denounced because of defective authority rather than defective control allocation. For a different view, see Verdross, "Jus Dispositivum and Jus Cogens in International Law," 60 *American Journal of International Law*, 55 (1966).

are fundamental because of their impact on the constitutive process and the general expectation that they will continue to be applied.[63]

ARENAS

We refer here to the patterns, of whatever degree of stability, in which participants interact in the constitutive process. Arenas vary enormously in degree of organization, which depends on the pattern of authority and control, and the degree of hierarchy or co-archy in the structure. The authoritative arenas of the world would be exceedingly visible if a unified globe had a single bureaucratic organization to give effect to the prescriptions of a world legislature, council, or ruler. Controlling arenas, as usual, could be expected to display somewhat variable patterns of congruence with these official structures, preparing the way for subsequent changes in the formal chart. Today's world is more co-archic than hierarchic since the nation-states, which play such a conspicuous role, are formally equal, and interact directly with one another (a bilateral arena), or in combinations of varying size, duration, and differentiation.

We first sketch the most important forms of arena found in the world as a whole, and then examine the practices that are employed to govern access by particular participants.

Establishment and Maintenance

An entirely systematic description of an arena would describe its role in reference to the performance of each of the seven outcome functions involved in constitutive decisions, including the several phases of pre-outcome, outcome, and post-outcome processes. Considerations of brevity call for heroic simplifications, after the manner, though not the detail, of the traditional tripartite scheme for identifying the organs of government.[64] We refer to five institutional structures,

[63] A comprehensive survey of the global constitutive process would include a description of the *public order* goals of the process. Public order goals are related to the aggregate of protected features of the different value processes. Protected participatory features would, for example, include who is permitted to participate, what prescriptions are designed to maintain or restrict these participants, and so forth. Protected features with respect to perspectives would include prescriptions relating to demands for the production and distribution of values within each value process. These are generally treated under such rubrics as "International Business Law" (wealth process), International Protection of Human Rights (affection, skill, enlightenment, and respect) etc. Protected base value features would include the prescriptive complex relating to sharable resources (the seas, international rivers, air space, outer space) and nonsharable resources (national territory, internal waters, natural resources, etc.). An example of a specific public order study may be found in McDougal and Burke, *Public Order of the Oceans: A Contemporary International Law of the Sea* (1962).

[64] See note 55. One can force transnational decision phenomena into Montesquieu's mold. The point, however, is the extent to which that framework aids in the performance of the intellectual tasks we seek to perform. The examination of decision

which recur in both official and unofficial interaction and which, in their varying degrees of organization, exhaust international interaction patterns.

1. INSTITUTIONAL STRUCTURES: (i) Diplomatic: An "official" diplomatic arena is the pattern of interaction between nation-state elites or their representatives. An "unofficial" diplomatic arena is the interaction between nonofficial elites or elite representatives. A variety of customary constitutive prescriptions are directed at facilitating official inter-elite communications. Thus, the concept of state recognition may initiate formal diplomatic contact, make operative the inviolability of the diplomat, his family and his habitat, and accord a confidential status to diplomatic communications. In the absence of formal relations, diplomatic contacts are maintained in unorganized situations.

(ii) Parliamentary-Diplomatic: Plurilateral elite contact, as in formal conferences, has until recently been a secondary trend. Its establishment requires a level of collaboration beyond that in the initiation of diplomatic contacts. Hence such arenas have lacked the spontaneity of formation which is characteristic of the diplomatic. Polycentric control contexts appear to favor parliamentary-diplomatic arenas.

(iii) Parliamentary: Parliamentary arenas[65] display a higher aggregate level of organization than do the two preceding arenas. Their decision dynamics are characterized by a doctrine of majority rule, continuity, and a measure of publicity, the development of which requires a minimum of prior constitutive agreement, and is fostered by a control context of comparatively equal bases of power or a doctrine calling for equality.

(iv) Adjudicative: These arenas are characterized by third-party decision as well as by a matrix of expectations calling for distinctive procedures and criteria of decision. Such an arena includes tribunals of all degrees of organization; in addition, there are relatively unorganized interaction situations. In either case a nonengaged party is the formally seised decision-maker. Stabilized expectations about the various phases of the process approach the point of mystique, a

---

functions (see section on Outcomes) will demonstrate that the relevant events are too complex for the traditional model.

[65] Rusk, "Parliamentary Diplomacy—Debate v. Negotiation," 26 *World Affairs Interpreter*, 121 (1955) and Jessup, "Parliamentary Diplomacy," 89 *Hague Recueil*, 185 (1957) use the term "parliamentary-diplomacy" for contexts in which a representative must be both a negotiator and a parliamentarian. This dual requirement exists in any plurilateral context. We distinguish further between contexts in which the ritual of voting as well as a number of other significant factors has a decision impact (parliamentary context) and those in which it has none (the traditional "conference" or parliamentary-diplomatic setting).

factor which, depending upon how it is exploited, works for or against a public order of human dignity. As a rule adjudicative arenas are secondary forms in the constitutive process, since they are usually created in connection with the administration of public order decisions.

(v) Executive Arenas: A relatively recent phenomenon in the constitutive process is the growth of transnational executive arenas to deal with the most important decision functions. Inclusive examples include international secretariats of both official and nonofficial participants. Earlier exclusive examples are the executives of nation-state and political party participants.

2. GEOGRAPHICAL RANGE: The geographic range of constitutive arenas varies from those which encompass the entire earth-space arena to arenas which are limited to extremely small groups of actors. We distinguish universal, general, plural, regional, bilateral, and single participant arenas of constitutive decision. The distinction is based on the scope of participation rather than on the scope of objective; depending upon the disposition of authority and control, single participant arenas may make constitutive decisions for the most comprehensive process.

(i) Universal: Universal participation typically takes place in an arena of minimal organization. The traditional example of universal participation, the plebiscite, is misleading in this respect. The maximum degree of organization required for plebiscites gives each individual a voice, but usually no real share in the power process. The closer an arena moves to universality, the more restricted its objectives become. As objectives broaden in scope and specificity, participation usually attenuates.[66]

(ii) General: General arenas comprise a majority of global elites and frequently project global programs. Less than global participation in these arenas may be attributed to a number of factors: the projected program may be unpopular with some participants or incompatible with their internal public order; active participants may bar other participants for a variety of reasons. For example, the presence of the excluded participants might impede effective operation of the arena, the arena may have been constituted specifically to counter their influence, or they have been barred from the arena as an incident of authoritative sanctioning procedures.

[66] The relation is illustrated by UPU and ITU, both of which supervise areas of interaction close enough to make a merger feasible and economical. UPU, with limited objectives, has the broadest institutionalized participation. ITU, whose objectives are more extensive, has a more restricted membership. At the other end of the continuum, the highest degree of specificity will be found in interactions between only two participants.

(iii) Plurilateral: These arenas comprise a group of participants, without necessary reference to geographical propinquity or common regional origin. Such arenas are usually formed to deal with specific problems.

(iv) Regional: Regional arenas are those which are largely restricted to participants inhabiting inter-identified geographical regions. These arenas are formed to deal with common regional problems or regional defence requirements.

(v) Bilateral: Much of the world constitutive process transpires in bilateral arenas; two participants, equipped with adequate bases of power and acting within a context favorable to maximizing these bases, jointly reach decisions of constitutive importance. Bilateral arenas range over the entire spectrum of possible degrees of organization. When highly organized, bilateral arenas stabilize expectations in regard to every phase of interaction. In other, less continuous, bilateral arenas, a measure of organization is supplied by reference to general practices (e.g. diplomatic, parliamentary-diplomatic, and so on). Bilateral arenas of low organization may include random meetings or indirect communications inferable only from behavior.

(vi) Unilateral: The reference here is to patterns of interaction occurring within a single participant, the outcome of which is a world constitutive decision. The relevant arena is often a relatively powerful participant in the total arena of world affairs; nevertheless, circumstances may favor the parallel development of such arenas among smaller participants.

3. DURATION (TEMPORAL FEATURES): Some patterns of interaction are relatively continuous; others are occasional or sporadic; still others are single occurrences, unlikely to recur. Although it is generally assumed that there is a direct correlation between repetition and ease of learning, it is not improbable that the stabilized prescriptions which constitute an organized arena are a combined function of numerous variables, of which repetition is but one. Some of the data compiled by Iklé suggest that the expectation of continuity is itself a conditioning, and often a self-fulfilling factor.[67] Strong expectations of continuity may increase demands to participate in an arena; expectations that an arena will soon become defunct or that it will be formally terminated usually intensifies the desire to avoid association with it.[68] The long-range advantages of participation in a constitutive arena may make short-range value renunciations quite palatable. Similarly, expectations of continuity in an arena may account for important nuances in intra-arenal behavior; it may, for example, seem

[67] Iklé, *How Nations Negotiate* (1964), 34-42.
[68] Same, 36-37.

impolitic to show open contempt for an arena whose durability potential is high.

4. CRISIS: When interacting participants share high expectations of violence, we characterize their interaction as establishing a "military" arena. If the expectation of violence is low, the arena is "civil." Since the aggregate international constitutive process is composed of many sub-arenas, both military and civil arenas may coexist. Elites in WHO, for example, may launch a campaign to wipe out trachoma at a time when the Security Council is paralyzed by an expectation of impending doom.

Crises are situations in which values are perceived as at stake in highly significant degree. It is not to be assumed that all participants are joined in expected deprivation of key values. True, such a crisis as a possible nuclear war may be perceived by all participants as inclusive, global, and deprivatory. In other crises, however, what may be viewed by one participant as imminent destruction may appear to another as providing an opportunity for a favorable reallocation of values. The emphatically subjective nature of crisis is nowhere better demonstrated than in current perspectives in regard to nuclear war. Allegedly such a war is not viewed as critical by the People's Republic of China;[69] what appears as a grave crisis to all other participants in the world constitutive process evidently seems to the Chinese elite as a contingency in which it would emerge with a maximized value position. A crisis may be initiated, sustained, or extended by a participant who perceives it as an appropriate instrument of his special interest. Hitler's hideous application of *Macht* diplomacy, the Leninist doctrine of inevitable war, and the strategy of "confrontation" provide examples of this phenomenon.

Demagogues have appreciated the utility of crisis as a means of consolidating an internal power position. Yet the effects of crisis need not and have not always been inimical to public order interests. Genuine crises may act to integrate disparate participants in collaborative patterns of interaction which extend far beyond a crisis period. Thus, the prospect of continued deprivation in war of well-being, respect, and rectitude—severe crises for participants in the world community whose personalities include demands for the enjoyment of these values by themselves and others—led to the formation of the International Red Cross, with discernible impacts on the constitutive process. A natural disaster generally excites unified international action for the alleviation of suffering, eliciting cooperation from individuals and groups who, though not themselves immediately threatened, nonetheless perceive the suffering of others as a personal value

[69] See CDSP 15:38 at 9. See CDSP 15:35 at 12.

deprivation. Another type of disaster—namely, possible Soviet domination of the continent—precipitated elite and popular support for European integration.

Future crises may introduce major structural changes in the world constitutive process. Consider the following construct: a space ship, from a planet inhabited by beings whose technological development and hence military potential far exceeds ours, lands on the earth. Elites of the world perceive in the intrusion a danger to their overall value position. The crisis might lead to attempts by nation-state elites to make separate alliances with the foreign planet, thus integrating the foreigner in the earth's constitutive process without structural changes. On the other hand, it might lead to the formation of a world government to which effective control is transferred in order to balance the power of the intruder. Analysis indicates that the determining factor in reactions to a perceived crisis is the perspective of elites: appreciation of the nature of the crisis and the net gains and net losses from alternate courses of action. We note that the projection of overpopulation and hence undernourishment of the globe— a crisis of the dimensions of the space ship—has as yet failed to introduce major structural changes in the constitutive process.[70] Either power elites fail to appreciate the crisis or they continue to assume that strategies short of structural change promise to yield the greatest net gain to their value position. We further note that the present constitutive structure of the globe in which coarchical elites are armed with nuclear weapons, and are free of effective hierarchical supervision or regulation, is widely denounced as a perpetual crisis endangering the future of man on earth; nevertheless, ameliorating structural changes have not been brought about. The effective elites of the globe presumably reject alternate courses of action on the assumption that net losses will be imposed upon their power position.

Recent studies of the effect of rising crisis upon national decision-making suggest that crisis mobilizes the internal and external adjustment mechanisms of nation-states, while simultaneously lowering the efficiency level of all decision functions. More particularly the significant impairment is in the capacity of elites to make rational decision.[71] No parallel study has been made of the effect of crisis on organized transnational arenas. However, the significant factors whose interrelations are decisive for the outcome of a crisis are not difficult to identify. Do the expectations of exposure to mounting common threat (or to a great affirmative opportunity) increase or de-

[70] See Bourgeois-Pichat, "Population Growth and Development," 556 *International Conciliation* (1966), 5-12, 75.

[71] North, Holsti et al., *Content Analysis: A Handbook with Applications for the Study of International Crisis* (1963), 159ff.

crease? Do changing common expectations strengthen or weaken the intensity with which a common identity is experienced and asserted? Do varying expectations and identifications affect positively or negatively the strength of demands to constitute a public order of power and other values?[72]

Some effects of crisis on important patterns of interaction are as follows: (i) Participants: Heightened crisis expectation maximizes the political power of specialists in violence. In view of their characteristic perspectives the inclusion of these elements can further increase crisis intensity; (ii) Objectives: Preservation of the value position of groups and individuals with whom identification is most intense becomes a paramount goal. Optimum order goals are supplanted by the most urgent minimum order considerations; (iii) Situations: Organized arenas with authoritative mandates for the realization of objectives, tend to include the principal loci of crisis, and to mobilize and centralize the base values required to resolve it. Value patterns depending upon stability of expectation (e.g. wealth) are disrupted within the crisis area; (iv) Bases of Power: As a crisis spreads territorially and pluralistically, participants strive to augment base values of all kinds available for centralized power purposes; (v) Strategies: The intensity of demand to employ coercive strategies rises proportionately with crisis expectations.

It will be noted that the foregoing discussion of the establishment and maintenance of arenas has seemingly been largely restricted to interactive situations that involve participants who are conventionally identified as nation-states or intergovernmental organizations of a transnational character. Let it be explicit that the constitutive process can only be fully revealed if the necessary research is done to estimate the genuine power significance of the arenas or arena-like situations in which all categories of participants in the world political process are involved. These include, for instance, the arenas established by interactions among powerful individuals who operate transnationally. They also include, in addition to the structures of political parties and pressure associations, the situations in which transnational groups chiefly concerned with values other than power interact. Hence all the "markets" established transnationally among

[72] Thus, crisis may have positive public order effects. In the recent phase of the Indo-Pakistani "Kashmir Dispute," the Security Council, under impending crisis, acted with a unity and impact which ordinarily proved unachievable. One cannot, of course, plot a future trend on one complex of events. However, the intensity with which assertions of the jurisdiction of the Security Council are made in periods of crisis provides an index of community perspectives—expectations and demands about jurisdictional authority. This index should, perhaps, be used to balance the over-cited British commentary on the U.N. Charter (A Commentary on the Charter . . . 1945, *Command* 6666, Miscellaneous No. 9, 1945), according to which a clash between big powers is supra-United Nations.

economic units, whether "governmental" or not, must be scrutinized to discover whether power expectations do in fact exist (as evidenced, for example, by effective informal policing of the market by its members). All situations specialized to enlightenment, skill, and other values are relevant.

Access

The patterns of interaction of any group can be distinguished along two continua: a compulsory-voluntary continuum and a restricted-open continuum. Some arenas can effectively require participation (including compliance with decision-outcomes), while others must depend upon voluntary participation and compliance. Some arenas are open to all actors who wish to participate, while others impose restrictions in varying degree. The arenas of the constitutive process range along both continua and are not, as some students contend, solely voluntary or consensual.[73] Compulsoriness arises from a perception of control and awareness of a disposition to employ it. Some organized arenas exercise direct control; others, indirect control. Certain arenas, without control bases of their own, may achieve a degree of compulsoriness by a conjuncture of circumstances in which nonmembers may force one participant into the arena.[74] When participants assume that they must submit to the pattern, an arena of maximum compulsoriness is stabilized.

Restrictions as to access are generally a function of organized arenas. As a rule unorganized arenas are open to any participant with effective power.

The general trend has been from decentralized to centralized, from coarchical toward hierarchical constitutive situations. Although nation-states frequently assert their "sovereignty" as a counterpoise to the trend toward inclusivity, the growing interdependence of the

[73] The root problem in discussions of compulsory jurisdiction has been the exclusive emphasis on documents rather than on perspectives and practice. Consent, it may be added, is a highly ambiguous communication; hence the interpretation and application of consent communications requires a policy structure more specific than the principle of *pacta sunt servanda*. See, generally, Lauterpacht, *The Development of International Law by the International Court* (1958), 91, 243, and Schechter, *Interpretation of Ambiguous Documents by International Administrative Tribunals* (1964), 130.

[74] In this respect, interdependence may become a factor for "compulsory jurisdiction"; peripheral participants, who will suffer consequential deprivations because of the conflict, will press the disputants into a highly organized arena specialized to decision by noncoercive means. Some examples of this phenomenon are the first phase of the Corfu Channel Case (Preliminary Objection, 1948 *ICJ Reports* 15) in which the Security Council sought to press the parties to the Court and the Honduras-Nicaragua Border War, in which the O.A.S. brought the parties to the Court. (Case Concerning the Arbitral Award Made by the King of Spain 23 XII 1906, 1960 *ICJ Reports* 192.) The concerted action of OAU members was a major factor in bringing Algeria and Morocco to arbitration in their border war of 1963-1964.

global arena has reversed matters; whereas formerly the maximization of all values was to be found in freedom from encumbrance, it is increasingly appreciated that maximization of values can now develop only through organized and centralized and regularly staffed decision-making structures.[75]

It has been argued, in certain quarters, that while collaborative activity may reach the point of organization in many value processes, it cannot be achieved in the global power process; in the latter, an uneasy state of co-existence is the most that can be expected. The fallacy of this view is demonstrated by the continual efforts of effective elites to establish and maintain organized power arenas. The current *Sturm und Drang* in these arenas may, therefore, be most appropriately interpreted not as an attempt to challenge the overall authority of the arena but rather as an effort to consolidate an internal power position. As indicated before, a comprehensive functional analysis of the constitutive arena as an inclusive aggregate would examine by proper empirical methods the interactive situation specialized to the shaping and sharing of every value.

In general, it can be said that the arenas of constitutive decision have become more differentiated. Since the growth of stable and refined practices at each phase of decision is a probable consequence of increasing and diversified interaction, differentiation will presumably increase in the future.

Numerous international constitutive documents express a policy of compulsory or cogentive jurisdiction over a variety of minimum order concerns. Trends register a movement toward increasing compulsoriness.

BASE VALUES

Base values are any potential means of influencing decisions.[76] Hence the values available as bases include the same categories of value that may be pursued as scope values (power, wealth, and so on). On analysis, it is evident that each value is composed of two components, one a pattern of symbols, the other a resource pattern. The symbol component includes the predispositions to adopt particular perspectives toward a participant and to engage in various operations that involve him. The resources are the physical magnitudes that fig-

---

[75] For elaboration and documentation in processes other than power, see Friedmann, *The Changing Structure of International Law* (1965); Jenks, *Law, Freedom and Welfare* (1963), 1-31.

[76] For illumination of the concept of base value, see Lasswell and Arens, *In Defense of Public Order* 14 (1961); same, "Toward a General Theory of Sanctions," 49 *Iowa Law Review*, 233-34 (1964); McDougal, "The Impact of International Law upon National Law: A Policy Oriented Perspective," 4 *South Dakota Law Review*, 25, 50-51 (1959).

ure in the operations. While the bases of power can, and often are measured in absolute terms (size of a standing army, destructive power of its weapons, ship tonnage, facilities which can be called upon for logistical support, and the like), it is ultimately the interpersonal or "operational" definition of bases which concerns us. Does a given participant perceive that values at his disposal are potential bases? Do other interacting participants perceive the relevant events in the same way or do they have a different or distorted view? The perspectives of any specified participant, as is obvious, may be singularly different from the more comprehensive view of the scientific observer.

The ultimately relational character of bases of power can be demonstrated by an examination of the value position of any single participant vis-à-vis others. Consider, for example, the *external* power at the disposal of a given nation-state in the arena of world politics. If the elite members of another state are favorably disposed toward the policy of giving support to the first state in pressing demands on a third state, the first state has power as a base value at its disposal which, besides including a favorable predisposition, also includes the added voting or fighting potential of the "allies." If the other states oppose the policy of the first state, that state may have a deficient external power position, in which the predispositions of the others can be expected to be employed against rather than in favor of the first state. This state may, however, be capable of realizing its policy by depending solely upon the resources and symbols at its own disposal, especially if the context tends to multiply their effectiveness. Even here, however, the observer must be wary of a purportedly complete enumeration of values, since an element in the viability of these bases will, once again, be the extent to which other participants perceive and appreciate them. The point is equally demonstrable by reference to values other than power. For example, a nation's external wealth includes all the claims to the services of resources that other states are disposed to honor. External prestige includes dispositions to give status to the nation and its members, together with favorable acts and physical tokens of esteem.

The task of establishing a constitutive relationship among the participants in the world arena proceeds by consolidating the symbols and resources required to allocate power. The scientific observer can demonstrate the occurrence of a constitutive relationship when at least a minimum level of stability is attained in authority and control. As indicated before, the perspectives of authority include expectations regarding the appropriate and demanded manipulation of values in the allocation of power. The requisite perspectives of control are the predispositions to establish and maintain an effective power allocation in harmony with authority, coupled with a sufficiency of resources to do so. Constitutive power is lawful; it is neither naked nor pretended (control without authority; authority asserted without control).

The policies relevant to the acquisition and management of base values in the constitutive process are principally policies of proportionality to the domain, range, and scope of decision. Since inclusive decisions seek to produce consequences of some considerable importance throughout the world community, it is obvious that the more inclusive the control of base values the more likely such decisions are to be implemented or enforced. The magnitudes involved must be measured according to the range and scope of the values to be affected. It is apparent from even the most cursory inspection that the risk remains high that the world constitutive process will not be able to mobilize base values adequate to all its inclusive objectives.

The situation is somewhat different in regard to the base values required to render exclusive competences effective. We call attention to the point that the only rational criterion available for an assignment of exclusive competence at the domestic (or less inclusive competence at the regional or general levels) is that the values at stake are highly localized in these domains, hence the common interest of the world community is in leaving determinations to be made by and for those directly concerned.[77] Presumably, the elite of a nation-state is able and willing to draw upon all its assets as bases for rendering its exclusive jurisdiction fully effective. We favor common recognition of a "police power" within every component body politic as a means of maintaining minimum order, but predicate the lawfulness of its exercise upon conformity with comprehensive common interests. Matters of police power which are initially delegated to exclusive authority are arrogated to inclusive review and termination if they are abused.

The shifting apportionment of base values between inclusive and exclusive spheres of jurisdiction is a fundamental feature of the world constitutive process. The chief trend is toward the attenuation of exclusive competence (domestic jurisdiction) and a broadening of inclusive authority. The scope of the present chapter allows no more than a brief survey of the important milestones in this development. Article 15 (8) of the Covenant of the League of Nations provided that should the relevant international agency find that the subject of a dispute, nominally within its jurisdiction, was "a matter which by in-

[77] See, e.g. Article 2 (7). Articles 51 and 52 of the Charter accord a contingent security jurisdiction to less than universal groupings, but require a reporting to the Council and modalities of application consistent with the Purposes and Principles of the Charter. Should the activities diverge from prescribed norm, they would cease to be lawful and the United Nations could assert a primary jurisdiction.

ternational law is solely within the domestic jurisdiction of that party," the organized community was not to intervene in the settlement.[78] Though domestic jurisdiction was to be determined "by international law," matters found to be within domestic jurisdiction, no matter what their impact upon general community security, were beyond the ambit of League jurisdiction. Indeed, the Permanent Court of International Justice subsequently held that though domestic jurisdiction might change through time, it was insulated from inclusive action at any given moment, unless it had been "internationalized" voluntarily by treaty.[79]

This construction is hardly an expression of optimum policy. Although the argument that domestic jurisdiction is determined by reference to community expectations and hence can change through time represented a dynamic conception, this view was largely nullified by the requirement of explicit formal agreement to any modification. This defect was ameliorated at UNCIO. Early drafts of the Charter had called for a provision parallel to Article 15 (8) of the Covenant.[80] At San Francisco, the entire concept of domestic jurisdiction was challenged as an erosion of the authority of the proposed organization.[81] The compromise proposal conceded the valid policies in a concept of domestic jurisdiction, yet asserted the primacy of the organized community to "pierce the veil" of domestic jurisdiction in the interests of minimum order. Article 2 (7) maintained a *domaine reservé*, but expressly rendered it inoperative if minimum order were threatened.[82]

In substantive matters of exclusive competence, the trend toward the attenuation of domestic jurisdiction is indeed dramatic. A perusal of the records of the United Nations as well as the practices of the complex of international organizations reveals that almost any matter has been treated as one of "international concern." In most cases, the inclusive examination of these matters has been countered by a claim of domestic jurisdiction.[83] The very fact that inclusive arenas

[78] "If the dispute between the parties is claimed by one of them [disputant states], and is found by the Council, to arise out of a matter which by international law is solely within the domestic jurisdiction of that party, the Council shall so report, and shall make no recommendation as to its settlement."

[79] Tunis-Morocco Nationality Decrees, *P.C.I.J.*, Series B, No. 4.

[80] Goodrich and Hambro, *Charter of the United Nations: Commentary and Documents* (1949), 110-11.

[81] Same, 111.

[82] "Nothing contained in the present Charter shall authorize the United Nations to intervene in matters which are essentially within the domestic jurisdiction of any state or shall require the members to submit such matters to settlement under the present Charter; *but this principle shall not prejudice the application of enforcement measures under Chapter VII.*"

[83] For an evaluation of these claims, see Higgins, *The Development of International Law through the Political Organs of the United Nations* (1963).

considered and possibly recommended action in regard to "domestic matters" is indicative of the trend toward limiting that domain. It is true that action beyond a hortatory or mandatory communication was often not taken because of the inadequate resources at the disposal of the inclusive decisional arena. Thus, the problem has not been one of articulate policy; such policies, as will be seen, generally hold that adequate bases of power should be at the disposal of inclusive arenas. The problem has been a discrepancy between preferred and formulated policy and actual deeds. In the following pages, we briefly survey policies, trends and projections in allocations between inclusive and exclusive competence in regard to each base value.

Power

Effective power continues to rest primarily in nation-state participants. Yet constitutive policy is rather unambiguous in its demand for inclusive control and application proportional to the basic task. Articles 43 and 45 of the Charter remain unimplemented,[84] but a variety of other devices for investing inclusive authority with effective power have been developed. Similar trends toward implementation of this policy may be noted in regional defense organizations.[85] Recent developments in the Organization of American States indicate a like development in that area,[86] and it is not improbable that contemporary demands in Africa will result in the formation of an implementing arm of the OAU.[87] A lawful regional activity must, of course, comply with the principles and purposes of the Charter.

Unquestionably there has been a great reluctance to cede power to inclusive processes, since global elites have thus far found it difficult to clarify their long-range common interests. The impeding conditions of mutual distrust and suspicion are subordinated only when

[84] These articles had envisaged a stable network of national military units which were to be on call for the Security Council. Their operation would, of course, have required a consensus among the permanent members. However, given such a consensus, the existence of a stand-by force would have added immeasurably to the confidence and impact of Council deliberations and decisions.

[85] Some material on the extent of inclusive control may be found in Bowett, *The Law of International Institutions* (1963) 150, 155, 197-201, regarding NATO, SEATO, CENTO, and the Warsaw Pact.

[86] There has been agreement in principle on the formation of an Inter-American Peace-Keeping Force as the implementing agent of the Charter and the Pact. Whether or not this particular agreement materializes, it seems clear that some implementing form will be created.

[87] While the OAU only supports anticolonialist rebel groups on the continent, it has discussed the possibility of joint forces against Southern Africa; such an instrument will probably be required to realize their express aims. See 554 *International Conciliation* (1965), 58-70.

a common threat is perceived; and when the crisis has passed nation-state elites tend to reassert their hegemony.[88]

There are indications that a changing constellation of conditioning
factors is mobilizing permanent support for more inclusively effective
power. Requirements of future security will presumably demand investments few nation-states can support unilaterally. Weapons are increasingly expensive and the proliferating sophistication of delivery
systems is draining significance from the concept of defense. Hence
security will of necessity become a more inclusive concern, requiring
the durable collaboration of groups of nation-states. (Paradoxically,
limited success in disarmament could well counteract this trend.)

Wealth

Constitutive policy favors a disposition of wealth adequate to support
authoritative processes of decision. Unfortunately, inclusive processes
rarely have direct control over wealth resources and hence are dependent on the goodwill of nation-state elites for the financing of
their activities.[89] Indeed, a recurring problem of international organizations has been to secure adequate finances permitting the operations necessary for minimum and maximum goals. The United Nations, for example, has no resource base of its own, and must turn to
annual contributions of members to support its activities. Wealthy
members thereby acquire a *de facto* veto power over activities of
which they do not approve; a possible result is the total paralysis of
the organization. In the recent "Expenses[90] Affair," the USSR and
France demonstrated that they could undermine peacekeeping operations of which they did not approve. Although the crisis has not
reached these dimensions in a number of functional organizations, the
lack of an adequate flow of funds does restrict their operations and
prevents the implementation of a variety of pressing programs.

There are a number of means by which authoritative organizations
might secure the necessary wealth base. Sharable resources could be
declared public international property, under the direction and at the

---

[88] Thus, it has been noted that French interest in the proposed EDU waned as
soon as *détente* with the European socialist states was on the horizon. Similarly,
France's current position vis-à-vis NATO may be explained by the fact that French
elites perceive no threat from those against whom NATO was formed. In a more
general sense, weaker participants may view international organizations as a means
of augmenting their power position, while stronger states view them as restrictions
on their power. This may be an imperfect assessment of long-range interests; for a
critique, see McDougal and Reisman, "The Changing Structure of International Law:
Unchanging Theory for Inquiry," 65 *Columbia Law Review*, 810-818 (1965).

[89] Exceptions to this condition are the economic agencies, which hold member
assets and the IAEA which has control over some nuclear material.

[90] Certain Expenses of the United Nations, 1962 *ICJ Reports*, 151.

disposal of international organizations. A low-keyed trend in this direction is suggested by the International Atomic Energy Agency. Another means would be the requirement that all national corporations operating transnationally secure an annual international license from the United Nations or from one of the economic agencies. This plan may prove to be palatable to corporate elites in capital-exporting countries, since when they venture abroad they frequently wish to shed their identifications with a rich country. This method would, furthermore, introduce a measure of international supervision to transnational processes which have become quite uncontrolled.[91] Changes in national tax legislation, permitting contributions to the United Nations to be deductible, or to constitute a national tax credit could serve as a short-term means of securing wealth. Paper increases only in "inclusive taxing power" achieve little. The problem is for authority to acquire a measure of control; the above solutions seek to accomplish the objective immediately by a larger application of authority.

Wealth malapportionment in inclusive processes is matched in exclusive ones. Owing to insufficient wealth bases many participants are incapable of adequately applying their exclusive competence. It is noteworthy that global policy is unequivocally committed to increasing the economic assets of all participants; a number of developmental programs are in the process of implementing this objective. However, relative growth rates indicate a continuing disparity. Nevertheless the relative rate may be an inappropriate index, since the tempo of infrastructural development in the poorer countries is expected to be somewhat retarded at first. Once the internal level of value-institutional growth has reached the "take-off point," the disparity in relative rates can be expected to diminish.

Enlightenment

A corollary of a public order of human dignity is wide sharing of enlightenment, both as a means of developing each individual to his maximum capacity and as a prerequisite of effective participation in global power processes. Constitutive policies expressly demand a free flow of enlightenment since informed opinion is expected to maximize rational behavior and to emphasize the advantages of common over special interests. The personnel engaged in inclusive processes is best informed about the world situation when it is widely recruited from capable people. Hence some of the most talented personnel of nation-states should be sent on to staff international organizations;

[91] See Barber, "Big, Bigger, Biggest: American Business Goes Global," 154 *New Republic*, 14 (April 30, 1966).

current trends, unfortunately, do not take this goal into account.[92]

It might be supposed that the trends toward universalizing the civilization of science and technology, and especially toward instantaneous communication, would concentrate tremendous assets in the hands of inclusive decision-makers. That such results may in fact follow is no mystery to the elites of nation-states and especially of the larger powers. Hence they have adopted a set of countermeasures designed to subordinate these innovations to the service of exclusive or even special interests.

The elites of closed societies in particular continue to regard controlled enlightenment as a positive base of power[93] and, conversely, unencumbered inquiry as a negative base. But infrequently, the intensely conditioned responses and highly distorted perspectives of the rank and file, which have resulted from selective and controlled enlightenment, have limited the decision options of these same elites. There is evidence for example that a number of expropriations and national realignments were decisions taken against the wishes and perceived long-range interests of totalitarian leaders as a politically expedient response to the strong and continuing demands inculcated in the rank and file of the body-politic.[94] Although the development of a xenophobic manicheanism may serve the short-range interests of a political leader or a political class, there is always a more extreme,

[92] Rubinstein, *The Soviets in International Organizations* (1964), 140. While secondment carried beyond a certain point can be deleterious to the international character of the civil service and can undermine its vital esprit de corps, it can, at the same time, give an international perspective to national officials, which may be carried back and applied when they resume their national posts. In view of the fact that so much international law is made by national officials, the most minimal transnational perspective will be a positive public order factor. A further consideration is the training which nationals of new states acquire in association with an international secretariat; this positive long-range result should be balanced against the relative inexperience which such seconded personnel bring to their international post. We do not ignore the fact that certain states have insisted upon secondment in order to restrict the internationalization of their citizens' perspectives. Exposure of even a year or two will, we believe, shape perspectives in a manner which is in the long-range interests of world public order. It should, of course, be obvious that secondment is an effective strategy only if there is, at the same time, a core of permanent international civil servants.

[93] See Barghoorn, *Soviet Foreign Propaganda* (1964), 3-29, for a survey of doctrine and practice.

[94] This construction is elaborated in Edwardes, *Asia in the Balance* (1962) in regard to Indonesian expropriations, but would appear applicable to many nationalizations in a number of countries. Certainly, expropriations have frequently proven counter-productive in short and long-term wealth terms. An anthropologist who has observed developing nations, compares expropriatory reactions as parallels to the Melanesian cargo cults. ". . . an increase in felt needs without any compensatory increase in expectations may cause frustrations leading to messianic or utopian movements . . . when such a gap between wants and expectations occurs among sophisticated people at the national level, the result may be 'utopian' expropriations of foreign and domestic capital." Erasmus, *Man Takes Control* (1961), 8-9.

more doctrinally pure position on which the opposition can insist. Under these circumstances, the politician who begins as a manipulator of restricted enlightenment will, in the end, be manipulated *by* it.

It is not difficult to propose base values and instruments of enlightenment that, if focused in the inclusive decision process, would strengthen and maintain the power prerequisites of minimum or even optimum public order. If current news originating in such world-inclusive sources should reach the rank and file of the global community, penetrating whatever barriers are raised against it, many parochial perspectives could be eroded. Similarly, a world board of education and basic culture could be put in charge of primary instruction, intent on disseminating a common frame of reference to clarify and strengthen the common interests of the whole community of man. High frequencies of transnational exchange of personnel are also indicated means of shared enlightenment.

Respect

Respect, as a base value of authoritative decision, is primarily negative in application, since decision-makers deprive nonconforming participants of approval and admiration. In order to be effective, the inclusive process must command a relative monopoly of respect and participants must share common views as to the specific components of the value.[95] The fact that the target of a respect sanction in international affairs generally resists such an application might suggest that it perceives itself threatened. However, it is not easy to demonstrate that such sanctions are effective. For instance, it is not clear that the sanctioned elites undergo severe psychic tension precipitated by the deprivation, or that other participants view the sanctioned party as, somehow, deprived. It is not improbable that respect deprivations are selected as sanctions by transnational bodies because they are the simplest and, possibly, the only ones available. One observer has noted that the parliamentary syndrome is to believe that a vote is equivalent to action,[96] and this point must be weighed before concluding that the impact is severely deprivational.

It is evident that before respect can be a significant instrument of public order there must be community-wide perspectives regarding the particular practices that convey or deny it. Such homogeneity

[95] Thus, Lasswell and Arens write: "one sign of tension in any society is an increase in the number of people who feel no shame when they flout lawfully prescribed rules and remain indifferent to the breach as committed by others. . . . If deprivations of respect are to operate formally and informally as sanctions of the public order system, it is evident that sanctioning measures must harmonize with the sentiments of the community . . . ," Lasswell and Arens, *Defense of Public Order,* 59 at 24-25.

[96] Bailey, *The Secretariat of the United Nations* (1962).

appears to depend on sufficiently intense levels of interaction to enable the participants to achieve a minimum level of familiarity and identification with one another. Before the rise of the territorial state, respect was accorded only to members of the family and tribe. As the world social process intensified and the state took form, common criteria of esteem began to emerge. In recent times, accelerating transnational interaction has been paced by a proliferation of universal normative standards of respect. If this trend continues, as is likely, respect will become a more effective base of constitutive decision.

Well-Being

The revolution of rising expectations has generated universal demands for the creation and maintenance of conditions conducive to the physical and psychic well-being of every individual. In the deepest sense, these demands are expressed as insistence that minimum order be maintained which in the contemporary world is a *sine qua non* of existence. More sweepingly, these demands relate to the inclusive supervision of conditions which can assure a production and allocation of values which are in accord with human dignity. These demands provide a strong base for action by the organized community against elite acts contrary to minimum or optimum order. Much of the work in the human rights sector and the supervisory role of a number of United Nations and functional organizations rest ultimately on shared demands to guarantee fundamental safety, health, and comfort to all human beings. Certainly such a demand underlies much of the "Trusteeship" concept as well as much of the work of the International Labor Organization.[97]

Denials of well-being are inseparable from the use of military weapons in the application of sanctions. In fact the connection between severe coercion as a form of power is so intimate in so many circumstances that a special task of analysis is often required to underline the point that severe deprivations may rely only to a very limited extent on actual or threatened destruction of life. Thus, although economic sanctions may provide widespread bankruptcy and unemployment, this is usually a far cry from mass killing or starvation.

Loyalty (Affection)

In a world traditionally divided against itself the constitutive process is not able to mobilize mass loyalty throughout the length and breadth of the world community as a means of obtaining consent to allocations of power. However, it is obvious to every qualified student of the problem of minimum or maximum public order that one of

[97] Jenks, *Law, Freedom, and Welfare*, 25-26.

the major long-range assets to be cultivated in the constitutive process is intense identification of individual egos with the inclusive self that comprises an authoritative and controlling world polity.

As a long-run factor in the social integration of the earth, we must not underestimate the intimate ties that cross national lines in inter-marriage and international friendship. The shattering prospect of separation is not one of the least of the considerations that often exercises a deterring effect on conflicts at every level.

Skill

The significance of skill as a base value in the constitutive process has been greatly enhanced in recent times by the spread of intense demands for modernization, hence for the achievement of a self-sustaining level of value shaping and sharing according to sophisticated standards of practice in every value-institution sector. The hope of obtaining assistance in programs of development is a factor tending to bring about responsible behavior on the part of most underdeveloped states; and the desire to obtain influence by inaugurating and continuing such programs is an inducement to giant powers to introduce some degree of stability into many international situations. The consequences of development are by no means uniformly positive, however, since conflicts are sometimes accentuated that limit the scope, range, and domain of constitutive trends.

Transnational operations are slowly improving their supply of administrative, diplomatic, informational, and other forms of skill,[98] and if these tendencies continue, the prospect of disrupting ongoing services may come to be a sanction of increasing importance to the consolidation of constitutive power on an inclusive scale.

Rectitude

In a homogeneous community, rectitude demands provide one of the most effective and economical bases of power. There have been historical periods in which rectitude provided such a base in large areas of the globe.[99] Undoubtedly, the rise of the nation-state had as one

[98] Secretary-General Thant has remarked on several occasions that the UN could alleviate tensions by presenting an intelligence flow to a broad audience which would be more accurate than that emanating from national media. See, in this regard, his address to the World Council of the YMCA, reported in the *New York Times*, August 9, 1965.

[99] Nussbaum argues that religious sanctions in international law were ineffective by the time Vitoria and Suarez had formulated them: "Just War—A Legal Concept?" 42 *Michigan Law Review*, 453, 463 (1943) and Friedmann contends that Vattel's "law of conscience" was a denial of international law: *Legal Theory* 34 (2nd edn. 1949); but Pound suggests that the law of conscience of a personal sovereign is clothed with a flesh absent from the desiccated concept of a state conscience: "Philosophic Theory and International Law," 1 *Bibliotheca Visseriana*, 71, 76 (1923). See

of its principal effects the shattering of Europe's inclusive rectitude system. Although the Catholic Church continued as a transnational repository of rectitude norms, its impact was often neutralized and overridden by national churches and secular systems of ethics. In periods of crisis, rectitude predispositions were frequently "nationalized" and drafted into the service of the state, and the glorification of state power became a conspicuous ideological current in a state, such as Germany, whose bid for unity and industrialization had been delayed. Despite these schisms, it is clear that the rectitude system interrelated with international law was primarily "Christian" and "European" until as recently as 1945. In the postwar "nation-state explosion," many non-European cultures became active participants in the international arena. The presence of effective non-European and frequently anti-European systems of rectitude has undermined even the semblance of a universal system. The German *Macht* school and its contemporary successor—the identification of international morality with national interest—represent the nadir of global rectitude.

Even a glance at the history of human culture shows that the early systems of rectitude were part of the syndrome of parochialism. Rectitude norms were restricted to the service of the tribe, the extended family, and the nuclear family. As identifications broadened, great systems of religious faith and morals came into existence and sometimes were turned to the service of huge imperial states. We have commented on the nation-centered systems of modern history; we should likewise take account of the fact that universal conceptions of human dignity have won their way to at least verbal acceptance on a vast scale. Although moralistic overtones are always present in every sanction attempted as part of the constitutive process, it is not possible to show convincing evidence of the impact of such affirmations.

The separation of church and state in many polities allows religious leaders to pursue collaborative activities across state boundaries without governmental interference. A possible outcome is a global system of *civic* rectitude that depends on clarity and relatively mild sanctions until world unity and stability bring about a firmer and more intensely supported body of norms.

STRATEGIES

Strategies are the modalities by which base values are manipulated in the decision-making process. For some purposes it is convenient to consider the strategies available for employment in constitutive proc-

also Corbett, *Morals, Law and Power in International Relations* (1956), 11, 14, 15, who suggests that rectitude demands operate, in varying degree, in all personalities and are a significant determinant in elite decision.

ess value by value. A certain simplification can be achieved, however, by classifying all strategies according to their characteristic reliance on the symbol or the resource component of values. We speak of *diplomacy* when communications are addressed by one elite to another, and of *ideological* strategy when communications are addressed to general audiences. When resources specialized as weapons are employed, we refer to *military* strategy; when the resources are specialized to production, the appropriate reference is to *economic* strategy.

The modalities of a particular strategy are affected by their relationship to the various pre-outcome phases. They vary according to the category of participant who initiates their use and the objectives toward which they are directed.

The more general perspectives of participants are an important factor. Thus preference for coercive strategies may be the result of a cultural pattern or a personal psychological deviation.[100] There is some evidence that positive identifications with targets tend to elicit strategies of a low degree of coercion, while negative identifications elicit higher degrees of coercion. Arenas of interaction affect the choice of strategy; for example, choice is narrowed as the differentiation of an arena increases. In highly elaborated arenas, stabilized expectations impede the range of eligible strategies, including perhaps the most coercive instrumentalities. Similarly, the base values at the disposal of a participant limit strategic policy.

All four categories of strategy are involved, though in varying degree and with different levels of planning, in all attempts to affect a constitutive outcome. The traditional conception of grand strategy emphasizes the importance of planning the total campaign in a way that allows for the optimum interplay among the subordinate instrumentalities of the strategic program. A serviceable distinction separates *primary* and *auxiliary* strategies, the former referring to the dominant value on which reliance is put, the latter to the supporting values employed.

Although military strategy implies a high degree of at least potential coercion, all strategies can vary in degree of intensity and in the extent to which they coerce or persuade their targets. Techniques of economic warfare, such as the boycott, asset-freezing, termination of aid or price-fixing, may in certain contexts, acquire a high degree of coerciveness. Diplomatic strategy (inter-elite communication) and ideological strategy may employ terror and threats. In all these strategies the point on the coercion continuum is plotted not by refer-

---

[100] Meisel, *The Myth of the Ruling Class: Gaetano Mosca and the "Elite"* (1958); Strachey, *The Unconscious Motives of War* (1957). But cf. Klineberg, *Human Dimensions.*

ence to a particular strategy but rather by reference to its effect upon those subjected to it. Concern with the modality rather than with the effect engendered has been a pitfall of traditional inquiry. More strictly, emphasis has often been put on the first part of an act—the employment of the instrument—rather than upon the character of the perspectives elicited by the relevant interaction. In discussions of aggression, for example, attention has usually been restricted to military strategy.[101] As transnational interaction became more intense and technology spread, the potentialities of other strategies broadened, and the rather incongruous term "indirect aggression" was coined. It referred to acts of aggression not employing the military instrumentality and not, therefore, authorizing the unilateral or community response that would be permissibly triggered by direct aggression. But both direct and indirect aggression can have the same outcomes and effects; concern with these is the perspective that underlies authoritative prohibition. The meretricious distinction introduced by overly rigid doctrine merely invited aggression by nonmilitary modalities, an invitation which was gratefully accepted and exploited by certain regimes.

The fragmented approach to strategies has precluded, to date, any empirical examination of the inter-relation between various modalities and, particularly, of the effect of crisis on strategic programs. Speaking speculatively, it would appear that strategies are agglutinative. The level of intensity of the primary strategy frequently determines the intensity of the auxiliary strategies. All phases of a process of interaction are affected by the level of crisis. Crisis probably dissolves numerous subjective restraints on intensely coercive strategies and thus acts to raise the level of coercion of all strategic forms.

Strategies are employed in order to create subjectivities in particular targets. Specifically, they communicate an image of how "A" intends to act and how "B," if he wishes to maximize his gains and/or minimize his losses, should react. The appropriate subjectivities are sought through two modalities: (i) communication without an accompanying application of resources, and (ii) a manipulation of resources, with or without explicit communication. Both of these modalities, of course, may affect perspectives, which are the effects most economically achieved by successful communication. Resource alterations may go far beyond simple communicative impacts, devastating the human and physical resources of the target. Both modalities are co-present, one being primary, the other (or others) auxiliary.

The diplomatic strategy as we have said refers to inter-elite communication. Elites are a function of context; hence different partici-

---

[101] See, for example, Convention for the Definition of Aggression, 147 *L.N.T.S.* 67, especially Article 3. (This continues to be the Soviet definition of aggression.)

pants may constitute elites in different situations. The ideological strategy refers to communication to the rank and file as the target audience. Diplomatic and ideological strategies are purely communicational when their modality is language or a language-equivalent, even though their content—e.g. threats—may draw upon military and economic strategies as auxiliary instruments. If a selective economic embargo is aimed at imposing deprivations upon the wealth-elite of a particular polity but imposes no serious deprivations upon the rest of the population, it is diplomatic in terms of target and economic in terms of applicative modality. It is trivial whether one characterizes this as primarily diplomatic or economic. What is significant is that a direct communication as well as an indirect communication by means of a resource application is aimed at an elite audience. A strategic program may incorporate the ideological modality. Broadcasts and leaflets dropped from planes may exhort the people to rise up against their established elites or to pursue a course of passive resistance. Even without a direct communication to the rank and file, the auxiliary ideological effects of the primary strategy may depend, among other things, upon the extent to which the rank and file identifies with or disassociates itself from the elite target.[102]

The military and economic strategies refer to modalities of resource application, without explicit reference to target. The terms will mean relatively little unless they are perceived in relation to the diplomatic and ideological modalities. Military and economic strategies are, essentially, reinforced communications, whose vehicle is the manipulation of resources. In general, they can be said to belong to an expanded category of "propaganda of the deed" rather than language or language-equivalencies.

In the most democratic constitutive process, strategies are employed inclusively rather than exclusively. Since inclusivity is a matter of expectations of authority, the actual agent of strategy application may be a nation-state acting in a *dédoublement fonctionnel*.[103] The dual-function role of effective participants, like the concept of self-help, is an expedient rather than a long-term goal,[104] which must be tolerated until the world achieves a more effective institutionalization of authority and control. The urgent challenge to scholars and students is to clarify the policies and the contingent events that will ren-

[102] Some examination of this factor may be found in Taubenfeld and Taubenfeld, "The Economic Weapon: The League of Nations and the United Nations," 58 *Proceedings of the American Society of International Law* (1964), 183, and Segal ed., *Sanctions Against South Africa* (1965).

[103] Scelle, "Le Phénomène juridique du dédoublement fonctionnel," Schätzel and Schlochauer, *Rechtsfragen der Internationalen Organisation* (1956), 324.

[104] See Reisman, "The Role of the Economic Agencies in the Enforcement of International Judgments and Awards," 19 *International Organization* (1965), 929, 933.

der strategy applications lawful.[105] The longer range goal of the international community is the application of constitutive strategies by joint authoritative action, preferably through international organizations. The realization of this goal is contingent upon the acquisition by these organizations of an adequate control base.

Joint application of strategies is a corollary of the principle recommended for all phases of the constitutive process: a sharing in decision and especially in responsibility. The opportunity for sharing in strategic decision is greatest in organized arenas, where the authoritative myth prescribes equality among all participants. The practice of engaging jointly in decision-making fosters responsibility among all who participate in the process. The authority of decision is increased and the symbolic enhancement of the result favors effective application against any possible challenger.[106] Whether constitutive strategies can be symbolic manipulations accompanied by parsimonious use of resources depends primarily, though not exclusively, upon the subjectivities of the targets. In a cohesive community, in which the doctrines and formulas of the established myth are internalized in the character structure of the personalities distributed throughout most strata of the population, nonconforming behavior or impulses toward such behavior set off auto-punitive mechanisms that may be triggered or intensified by sanction equivalents[107] rather than by measures requiring large resource involvement. In a noncohesive community, particularly one in which authority systems are in competition and conflict, community-wide symbolizations have failed to reach the requisite level of effectiveness or have fallen therefrom. Hence the conditioned subjectivities upon which strategy symbols depend for their operation do not obtain. On many matters of enormous pertinence to world security, no constitutive process has been consolidated, hence decision must rely on more than symbolic means of making itself effective. In sub-arenas, in which conditioned subjectivities do obtain, symbolic strategies are sufficient for many purposes.

Depending on their component elements, strategies relate to *assembling* or *processing*. At the processing stage, operations impinge directly on the targets, as when diplomatic messages, mass broadcasts, economic assistance, or military support are employed. A prerequisite of such final operations is the assembly of personnel and facilities in a form capable of generating the product. The constitutive process calls for stand-by units organized in routes and zones that can be

105 McDougal and Feliciano, *Law and Minimum World Public Order* (1961).
106 Lasswell and Arens, *Defense of Public Order*, 216.
107 Dession, "The Technique of Public Order: Evolving Concepts of Criminal Law," 5 *Buffalo Law Review*, 22, 32 (1955).

speedily mobilized to achieve and maintain the power allocations sought.

Considerations of economy and efficiency typically suggest that strategic programs give first priority to the processing of relatively symbol-rich strategies, and the sparing utilization of use-resources, including their manipulation to enhance communicative impact. We note in this context that the physical instruments specialized as communicative media are "signs" (they mediate between the subjective events of senders and receivers of messages). Nonsign resources, as has been said, invariably have some communicative effect, though they are relatively unspecialized to this function.

As noted earlier, when a constitutive process is thoroughly established, its strategies tend to combine rational persuasion with ritualized acceptance. A transition toward ritual acceptance occurs when troop movements are used to permit an elite to "save face" by giving in to a show of force.

Diplomatic Strategy

Styles of diplomacy have changed in the course of some three thousand years,[108] but the term, in its official sense, continues to denote communication between power elites. Nonofficial diplomacy refers to communication between elites of value processes other than power. There have been numerous changes in phases of the diplomatic process in the last thirty years. In participation, there has been a trend toward democratization of recruitment of diplomatic personnel.[109] Moreover, the cosmopolitan diplomat who would serve any master has been superseded by the national diplomat who serves only his own nation-state.[110] Recent surveys of diplomatic personnel indicate a trend toward uniformity in educational background and a trend toward specialization.[111] Diplomatic objectives have been broadened; formerly, contact was restricted to the host elites and the diplomatic corps. Currently, contact extends to all politically relevant strata of the host state, insofar as this is permitted.

The current breadth of diplomatic objectives accounts in some measure for the great increase in diplomatic activity. Many of the operations centered in a contemporary mission would not traditionally have been characterized as diplomatic. Changes in participants

---

[108] A brief historical survey of diplomatic techniques may be found in Wellesley, *Diplomacy in Fetters* (1945), 13-34.

[109] Ruge and Galtung, *Patterns of Diplomacy: A Study of Recruitment and Career Patterns in Norwegian Diplomacy*, 1965 *Journal of Peace Research*, 101, 116 and see n. 111.

[110] Wellesley, *Diplomacy*, 16ff.

[111] Ruge and Galtung, *Patterns of Diplomacy*, 123-24; Harr, *The Anatomy of the Foreign Service—A Statistical Profile* (1965), 14, 55, 60.

and objectives are reflected in the changed arenas in which diplomacy operates. The contemporary minister has moved from the chancellery and elite social contacts to the variegated value-institution situations where a broader spectrum of the population is found. The bases of the traditional European diplomat—skills and respect-status attributes—were transnational assets, since elites identified in a horizontal transnational plane rather than in a vertical domestic plane. Contact with many non-European cultures has neutralized much of this; and some European states have undertaken to immunize their representatives against respect and affection ties.[112]

Communication between the elites of different polities takes place only when the level of interaction between the polities is such that each elite group gains from some contact and loses if there is none. At the least frequent level of value-laden interaction, diplomacy is conducted exclusively by *ad hoc* envoy. With more interaction, diplomacy becomes "residential." With further increase, it permutates into "conference diplomacy" and "organizational diplomacy." At the most intense level of sustained interaction, diplomacy metamorphizes into a form of parliamentary representation. Contemporary diplomatic relations

> . . . correspond to an intermediate stage in the general growth of mankind into a world state. The major implication of this is that diplomacy must have come into existence at a point where interdependence between nations or city-states got beyond a certain threshold so that some institution was needed to stabilize the relationship and make it more predictable. A second implication is that this very institution of diplomacy will disappear or will gradually merge into a world government in due time.[113]

Although the current intermediate stage could be moving toward a stable system of organizational diplomacy, the earlier channels of constitutive interaction may continue, once again exemplifying the durability of established links.

The development toward organizational diplomacy will undoubtedly modify diplomatic personnel. Extended association with another state does tend to engender some enlarged, if conflicting, identifications.[114] However, these effects are relatively trivial when compared with the probable impact of authoritative international organizations which will probably increase *transnational* identifications, perhaps at the expense of nation-state loyalties, and culminate eventually

112 Thus Murphy, *Diplomat among Warriors* (1965) notes that he found it impossible to strike a personal relationship of the most minimal intimacy with any Soviet diplomat.

113 Ruge and Galtung, *Patterns of Diplomacy*, 102.

114 Same, 111-12.

in a neo-cosmopolitan diplomat. A possible countertrend may be the attenuation of the domestic policy-making role of diplomats. Continuing high levels of interaction within diplomatic corps will presumably influence their perspectives; as their intensity of contact increases, the norms of group authority will be clarified and applied, even though with relatively mild sanctions on individuals. Such a civic system of order will parallel and strengthen the impact of the expanding code of diplomacy.

The relative ease of communication in the modern world has promoted opportunities for quasi- and nonofficial diplomatic contact. In addition to national foreign offices—the traditional agencies of diplomacy—a number of other governmental components engage in diplomacy. Members of legislatures commonly junket abroad and establish direct intercourse with foreign elites at many levels. Branches of the armed services, establishing similar contacts, not infrequently work at cross-purposes with foreign offices.[115] Such uncoordinated diplomatic activities, though they increase the difficulty of disciplined policy-formation, prepare the way for the cross-national strategies that consolidate a world constitutive process.

Ideological Strategy

Ideological strategy—communication to an audience broader than specific elite groups—has a history almost as long, if not as illustrious, as diplomacy. Ancient polities frequently resorted to the manipulation of symbols, often sacred rather than secular in content, as a means of shaping mass perspectives and behavior. Emperor worship, for example, is an ideological strategy employed as a means of focusing disparate identifications on one personage. The concept of the crown in a number of current secular states is a vestigial remainder of this phenomenon. In a more comprehensive sense, many recurring cultural institutions were and continue to be ideological strategies.

The use of ideological strategy in transnational interactions, it is generally agreed, was profoundly affected by the French revolution.[116] This point in history marks the beginning of an accelerating proliferation of demands in the emerging constitutive process of the globe for the regulation of ideological strategies in a transnational context. In previous times, it was not uncommon for a belligerent to infiltrate agents, who were commissioned among other things to foment rumors in the hope of demoralizing the adversary's population. Similarly, the use of oracular predictions of victory served both

---

[115] For one account of this, see Schlesinger, *A Thousand Days* (1965), 199-200.

[116] Martin, *International Propaganda* (1958), 3-4, but see Fraser, *Propaganda* (1957), 30.

to bolster domestic morale and to erode the enemy's will to fight. The impact of these venerable examples was relatively limited, since they were chiefly restricted to military arenas in which the role of the general population was generally negligible, or at best peripheral.[117] Robespierre's program and doctrines designed to export the French revolution signaled an era of new importance for the deliberate encouragement of diffusion, especially by means of the ideological instrument. Monarchical Europe appreciated the danger posed to it and acted with unwonted unity and effectiveness.[118] The full impact of the ideological instrument was felt, however, only after the consolidation of nation-states and the improvement of technological channels for the transmission of messages.

Almost the first efforts at the scientific employment of official propaganda took place during World War I.[119] The USSR continued, thereafter, to use it as a major strategy in Europe, the Middle East, and the Far East.[120] In the inter-war period, attempts to regulate this instrumentality were the subject of bilateral treaties as well as numerous discussions in the League of Nations.[121] Although the Charter makes no express mention of such a strategy, the United Nations has discussed it on numerous occasions and draft conventions have been framed.[122] Nevertheless, it cannot be said that this strategy has as yet been subjected to organized, inclusive control. Claims continue to be brought in particular circumstances and decisions have been supported by unilateral measures, such as breach of diplomatic relations, radio jamming, and the like.

Ideological strategy has become a standard instrument of nation-states and of a large number of nonofficial participants in world politics. The specific modalities range from direct exhortation to apparently neutral "news." Propaganda awareness has reached such a pitch that it is not unusual for such assertions to be made as that by a Yugoslavian member who said, in the UN Sub-Commission on Freedom of Information and the Press: "I join the words 'information' and 'propaganda'. . . . Today there is no neutral news and no neutral

---

117 Morgenthau, *Politics among Nations* (3rd edn. 1960), 365-66.

118 Martin, *International Propaganda*, 6; Whitton and Larson, *Propaganda* (1963), 17ff.

For observations on the effect of these events on European transnational patterns, see Rosecrance, *Action and Reaction in World Politics* (1963), 79ff.

119 Barghoorn, *Soviet Foreign Propaganda*, n. 77, 3-6.

120 Martin, *International Propaganda*, 8.

121 Whitton and Larson, *Propaganda*, 34-38; Martin, *International Propaganda*, 89-95. Under the auspices of the League of Nations, the Convention on the Use of Broadcasting in the Cause of Peace was adopted. It has not been formally terminated and the General Assembly has considered its reactivation.

122 Same, 89-95. See, in this regard, the UN Draft Convention on the Freedom of Information and, in particular, Article 26 of the Draft Convention on Civil and Political Rights, Doc. A/6342 Annex 1.

information."[123] Available statistics indicate an enormous investment in this strategy in both current application as well as in preparatory and development research.[124] Available procedures for measuring the effects of this form of communication cannot always be
applied to transnational campaigns. There are, for example, often
insurmountable difficulties in applying the refined advertising evaluation techniques of American industry to foreign arenas.[125]

Every indication suggests that in the future the ideological strategy
will be even more intensively relied on. Satellite relay stations promise the expanded use of television to this end. The same stations will
further open the American continent to this instrument; both North
and South America have been relatively immune to such interventions in the past, owing to a concatenation of geographical factors
which impeded short-wave radio communication.[126] Rising costs are
likely to weed all but the most powerful participants from among
those who rely heavily on the ideological instrument.

Policy clarification in regard to the constitutive use of ideology
poses rather difficult problems. Assuming that maximum participation is a preferred criterion in the global constitutive process, ideological strategy, addressed to the broadest audience in the widest arena,
would appear to be highly suitable. But such a recommendation
typically assumes that the content of ideological communication is
matter of fact intelligence. However, it is commonplace to assert that
mass communication is designed to shape perspectives by a selective
presentation of facts which are therefore inaccurate or highly
biased.[127] The Charter of Bogota of the Organization of American
States indicates an awareness that the "intervention potential" of this
strategy is a means of hostile intervention.[128] Thus, the problem is
the specific content of communication or the objectives of the communicator and the degree of harmony with minimum and maximum
community goals.

Military Strategy

Control over the implements employed in military strategy remains
in the nation-state. Inclusive efforts to arrogate the sole privilege of
lawful use of force have, generally, been unsuccessful. Plans for main-

---

[123] Quoted in same, 12. See also Davison, *International Political Communication*
(1965).
[124] Whitton and Larson, *Propaganda*, 47-52; Davison, *International Political Communication* (1965).
[125] Meyerhoff, *The Strategy of Persuasion* (1965).
[126] Martin, *International Propaganda*, 22.
[127] Edwards, *Group Leaders Guide to Propaganda Analysis* (1938), 40; Lumley,
The Propaganda Menace (1933), cited in Martin, 44.
[128] See Articles 15 and 16 of the Charter of the Organization of American States;
cf. Article 3, 147 L.N.T.S. 69.

taining a permanent international military force, envisaged at UNCIO and expressed somewhat equivocally in the Charter, as the applicative arm of the inclusive community are stillborn.[129] Minimum world public order requires that military strategy be available for the maintenance of public order and be controlled in its exclusive application to all other areas. While a discernible trend toward inclusive application of the military strategy is emerging, global constitutive policies have concentrated primarily upon the regulation of exclusive military strategies and the development of criteria for the appraisal of nonofficial uses of the military instrument.

Thus far, Articles 43, 45 and 46 of the Charter have not been implemented. However, the inclusive community has demonstrated some capacity to react in concert to challenges to minimum order. The Korean action was an early success, but it is of interest to note that its initiation ultimately turned on the fortuitous absence of a vetoing power. Subsequent changes in the decision dynamics of the UN projected a security role for the General Assembly[130] as a result of which the United Nations successfully employed the military instrument, at differing levels of activity, in Suez and the Congo.[131] In certain contexts, an application of the military instrument by regional or individual entities may be recognized as constituting an inclusive operation.[132]

A promising development in the inclusive use of military strategy stems from the late Secretary-General Hammarskjold's doctrine of "preventive diplomacy." The Charter, though not unambiguous, tends to limit inclusive application of force to a breach of the peace or a situation that threatens global security.[133] Early interpretations generally construed the provisions to accord with a responsive rather than anticipatory role for the organization. Hammarskjold applied the articles of the Charter in a broader frame of reference, envisaging inclusive use of force in nominally internal disruptions, whenever a

129 See Articles 43 and 45 of the Charter. See Bowett et al., *United Nations Forces* (1964).

130 See "Uniting for Peace," General Assembly Resolution 377 V.

131 For an evaluation of the legal problems involved see The Hammarskjold Forum, *The U.N. in the Congo* (1964) and Schechter, "The Relation of Law, Politics and Action in the United Nations," *1963 Hague Recueil*, Vol. 1, 200ff.

132 For evaluation of the legal aspects of regional security claims, see Halderman, "Regional Enforcement Measures and the United Nations," 52 *Georgetown Law Review*, 89 (1963). See generally McDougal and Feliciano, *Law and Minimum World Public Order* (1961), 217ff.

133 Thus, at the core of the dispute between the United Nations and the Republic of South Africa is the seeming paradox that a "threat to the peace" can materialize by an African rather than South African breach. This is, of course, a most rigid construction. It is clear that an effective world public order must be capable of employing force, when necessary, to correct or ameliorate conditions inconsistent with public order principles.

plausible construct implied the emergence of a future threat to the peace.[134] The frightening alacrity with which events can transpire narrows the gap between prevention and rehabilitation; hence minimum world order may require an even more radical interpretation of "preventive diplomacy."[135]

In general, military strategy remains one of primarily exclusive rather than inclusive operation in the constitutive process. Military integration on the regional level suggests a possible trend toward inclusive control, though it has been argued, not without cogency, that inclusive integration is indefinitely postponed by the creation of "super-states." Where effective inclusive control over the military instrument has not been acquired, a body of inclusive prescriptions have been invoked to delimit the domain and circumstances in which military instruments of exclusive operation may be lawfully used.

Economic Strategy

Since transnational intergovernmental organizations have been given little direct control over economic resources, the strategies available to many components of the constitutive process have been relatively circumscribed. Modern states vary widely in the degree of inter-crisis responsibility that they take for the management of economic life, varying from socialist to relatively laissez-faire policies.

The contemporary world has become particularly sensitive to the long-range impact of economic factors owing to the importance attributed to modernization, which calls for the achievement of an economy capable of self-sustaining growth. It is generally acknowledged that political stability and the eventual sharing of power are heavily conditioned by the rate and magnitude of capital formation and consumption levels.

The most conspicuous strategies of economic manipulation are negative, taking the form of boycott of trade, loans, or skill. In a world that acts largely by parallel nation-state policies, the administrative arrangements required for successful boycotts are not easy to conclude, particularly when immediate advantages often accrue to those who fail to cooperate. Presumably as economies become more interdependent the growth of geographical specialization and a money-credit system will increase the vulnerability of nation-states. However, these tendencies are not allowed to work themselves out fully in large states. Hence economic strategies may prove in the long run to be instruments of the constitutive process when they rely more

[134] See GAOR: 12th Session, 690th Plenary Meeting, paras. 72-73; SCOR, 13th Year, 837th Meeting, paras. 10-16.

[135] On the necessity for and implications of "preventive politics," see Lasswell, *Psychopathology and Politics* (1934) .

on inducement than deprivation. Short term deprivations—such as loan deferment—may be efficacious as temporary expedients in a program designed to induce responsible transnational behavior.

Insofar as control over values relevant to effective operation in the wealth-process have remained largely in the hands of nation-state elites, the inclusive use of this modality in the constitutive process has been primarily supervisory. The absence of an effective taxing power has restricted the programs of international organizations and, more specifically, has limited the use of the economic strategy. A possible harbinger of an extended employment of this strategy in the future may be found in the economic agencies. Their credit powers and the capacity to withhold sorely needed loans could be an effective strategy.[136] Thus far, the agencies have employed this power only to support "international financial morality" and have eschewed any "political" role.[137] A broader perspective on the part of the personnel of these organizations could greatly enhance this potential instrument of international order.

Outcomes

The outcomes of the constitutive process may be most conveniently understood as culminations of the seven component functions which comprise the various types of decision: intelligence, promotion, prescription, invocation, application, termination, and appraisal. These are functional distinctions. Legal scholarship traditionally approached decision on the basis of the organic division of Montesquieu: the executive, the legislature, and the judiciary. Contemporary practice has added a fourth category: administration. These organic classifications were not honed to facilitate performance of the intellectual tasks required of students of authoritative decision. In response to this methodological problem, the Vienna school of jurisprudence developed a functional, as opposed to an organic, approach to constitutive problems, treating Montesquieu's amended classification as community functions rather than community organs.[138] Then without reference to formal constitutional label, the school undertook to determine by empirical examination which authorized individuals or groups within governmental structures fulfilled which functions.

The Vienna innovation introduced a new perspective, but suffered from several defects. Though it reacted against an organic approach, its functionalism operated within a traditional organic framework. The innovators began with a concept of formal government and ex-

136 Jenks, "Some Legal Aspects of the Financing of International Institutions," 28 *Transactions of the Grotius Society* (1943), 115.
137 Reisman, *Role of the Economic Agencies*, n. 104, 941-42.
138 The development has been noted and described in Klinghoffer, *Mishpat Minhali* (1957), 1-4.

amined only the functions which this formal government performed. Constitutive decisions which were made by nongovernmental organs escaped their attention. But no formal government monopolizes decision; many formal governments play no more than a minor or supporting role in constitutive decision-making in a national arena. Moreover, decision processes of a low degree of organization may not exhibit those stabilized patterns which we call governmental institutions. The restricted functionalism of the Vienna school is helpful only with a theoretical assumption that formal government monopolizes decision, an assumption which is difficult to sustain. In regard to transnational decision, the method is of extremely limited utility.

A second defect, stemming from the organic matrix of the Viennese approach was the derivation of only three functions, parallel to the three organs. Had the Viennese school been concerned with the aggregate of actual constitutive decisions in any segment of social process, it would have discovered that categories referring to only three dimensions of decision, and particularly those which they chose, could not provide a satisfactory instrument of analysis.

The authoritative process of constitutive decision may, obviously, be broken down into innumerable component functions. It is incumbent on the scholar to fashion an intellectual instrument to serve his objectives in the light of the data pertinent to his inquiry and a variety of such expediential considerations as economy and clarity. Our objective is the ascertainment and recommendation of policies and strategies for shaping the global constitutive process as a vehicle for a world public order of human dignity. Instrumental objectives are the assessment of past trends, the analysis of conditioning factors, and the projection of future trends. In the light of these objectives, we find it convenient to dissect constitutive decision into seven functions. For present purposes, it will suffice to set out, in brief form, a description of each function and an indication of the lines of relevant future research. This description follows the pattern of phase and value analysis which has been described and applied earlier.

For detailed description of the specialized process in which each particular function is performed, we find it convenient also to employ a sequence analysis of the components of the function which refers to events generally, though not always, following each other in a temporal order. It is clear, for example, that a reference to the process of prescription includes an initiation of the process, an exploration of facts, conditions, and projections, a formulation of policy, and finally a promulgation of prescription aimed at creating or sustaining expectations of policy choices—authority and control. Similarly, the function of application includes, sequentially, initiation, exploration of potentially relevant facts and prescriptions, an authoritative characterization of facts and prescriptions in which the decisional arts of interpretation, supplementation, and integration are operative, enforcement, and, finally, review.

It will be apparent that the seven decision functions themselves coincide with a frequently observed temporal order and are an inclusive form of sequence analysis. Strictly speaking, the categories employed to describe the often observed temporal order within each major decision function are "sub-sequence" analyses. It would be useful for many purposes to repeat the terminology of the seven major functions in the study of the flow of interactions within each one. This might, however, be somewhat confusing as to the level of analysis intended at any given moment. Hence a roughly equivalent set of terms is utilized to indicate that a sub-function of a major decision function is referred to, and, also, to obtain the advantage of some of the connotations conventionally associated with the operations to which reference is made.

Detailed analysis of decision functions is essential for the making of valid comparisons in various contexts. In small groups, there may be near identity in the temporal ordering of a function. Where a degree of specialization in decision-making is found, however, different participants, with different perspectives, possibly in different situations, manipulating different values in different strategies frequently operate at successive steps in performing an equivalent role. It is precisely because of a differentiation in sequential phases with potentially important value outcomes that it is necessary to clarify policy, on a lower level of generality, to delineate trends, analyze factors, and propose strategies for the component sequences of a function. We proceed now to a delineation of the seven functions we find convenient to distinguish.

Intelligence

The intelligence function comprises the gathering, evaluation, and dissemination of information relevant to decision-making, prediction based on the intelligence derived, and, in some cases, the planning for future contingencies. In general, there is some overlap of all functions; in the case of intelligence, relations are especially close with promotion or recommendation. This is particularly true in the world constitutive process where intelligence, disseminated by the use of ideological strategies becomes promotion.

The important sequential phases of intelligence are (1) gathering, (2) processing, and (3) dissemination. The processing phase itself is composed of a number of elements such as storage, retrieval, utilization, and so on. The community policies relevant to the constitutive intelligence function are dependability, comprehensiveness (contextuality), availability, and economy. A long-range goal is openness of participation to all interested actors in the constitutive process. It seems clear, however, that the realization of this policy will be deferred as long as elites feel themselves in a crisis situation and evaluate intelligence as an important base of power.

There are official and unofficial participants in the intelligence function. Contemporary government, though continuing to draw upon unofficial sources, has developed massive intelligence establishments of its own. In the West, this development has been particularly intense since the end of the Second World War. In the United States, interdepartmental rivalry and rapid changes in conditioning circumstances, coupled with lack of administrative foresight, has resulted in an often irrational web of intelligence agencies.[139] Studies based on defector reports suggest a parallel maze in the USSR.[140] Some of the output of these agencies is for public dissemination (without necessary acknowledgment of source) and is thus quasi-promotional. In the West, research and development projects are frequently contracted out to nonofficial entities, causing a delicate merger between institutions devoted to pure scholarship and the requirements of applied politics, the future social impacts of which are difficult to gauge.

Nonofficial participants who employ the ideological modality of dissemination include the press, radio, and television. The distinction between these mass media is introduced because studies of certain states have indicated that where the different media draw on different wealth elites for financial support—for example, through advertising—they highlight, suppress, and interpret events in significantly different ways.[141] In totalitarian systems, the media are government controlled and are employed as instruments of the power elite.[142] In pluralistic democracies, as the intensity of crisis rises, the freedom of nonofficial media is attenuated, both by direct government control and by indirect appeals for voluntary censorship allegedly in the interest of national security.[143]

Political parties and pressure and interest groups undertake explicit intelligence functions as part of their promotional activities, sending out private observers and maintaining private evaluating staffs. The intelligence which is gleaned may be beamed directly at decision-

[139] See, for description, De Gramont, *The Secret War* (1962), 124.

[140] Same, 129.

[141] Sakamoto, "The Japanese and Vietnam," 153 *New Republic* (September 4, 1965), 16.

[142] See Barghoorn, *Soviet Foreign Propaganda* (1964), 3-30; in Shabecoff, "East German Paper Holds the News Is Secondary," *New York Times*, April 16, 1966, p. 7, col. 4, Peter Lors, editor of *Neues Deutschland* is quoted as saying: "We do not regard ourselves as a source of information. . . . It may not be the classic role of the newspaper, but perhaps we are the truly modern newspaper.

[143] See Cohen, *The Press and Foreign Policy* (1963), 69ff.

makers or reserved for the formulation of private policy. Intense interactions affecting the shaping and sharing of wealth generate a demand for specific, current intelligence, which is supplied by specialized agencies of banks, investment houses, business counselling firms, and the like; the information so gathered often has fundamental constitutive importance. Individuals acting in their ordinary professional capacities—as social scientists, international lawyers, free-lance journalists—often fill official intelligence roles; they also play the same role in a private capacity.

The growth of organized transnational decision processes has, quite predictably, led to the initiation of specialized intelligence facilities. The United Nations press and information services employ the ideological instrument. Fact-finding missions, observers, and "presences" of the UN, the ILO, and regional organizations function primarily to service elite decision-makers.[144] International courts and tribunals frequently develop intelligence techniques to assist their decision-making.[145] Certain private associations act as intelligence participants in international decisions.

General community perspectives toward the gathering of intelligence have undergone far-reaching changes. Contemporary elite decision-makers have evidently decided that maximum knowledge of activities is fundamental to common security. Thus the "open skies" policy appears to be an unequivocal, international prescription.[146] Similarly, attitudes toward professional espionage have radically changed. Although national insecurities do not, as yet, tolerate ideologically or economically motivated traitors,[147] captured foreign agents have only rarely been given maximum sentences. The brisk barter trade in apprehended foreign operatives appears to be viewed with equanimity. Popular and professional protests regarding the CIA have been almost entirely directed against other than its intelligence functions. The public outcry which followed the discovery that NSA was monitoring and decoding diplomatic radio-telegraph correspondence seems to have been caused by the fact that the U.S. was reading the mail of its allies as well as its adversaries. Conversely, periodic discovery of listening devices in American embassies in socialist countries now gives rise to no more than perfunctory formal protest. These trends suggest both elite and rank and file appreciation of the contribution of effective and dependable intelligence for minimum

144 See Wainhouse et al., *International Peace Observation* (1966).

145 Judicial intelligence is traditionally adversarial. However, courts introduce their own findings via "notice" as well as *descentes sur les lieux*. But see Jenks, *The Prospects of International Adjudication* (1964), 604.

146 But see Wright, "Espionage and the Doctrine of Non-Intervention in Internal Affairs," Stanger, ed., *Essays on Espionage and International Law* (1962), 3.

147 West, *The New Meaning of Treason* (1964).

and maximum order goals. On the other hand, it is clear that important constitutive programs have been ineffective largely due to the absence of preliminary intelligence work. Foreign aid programs, for example, become notorious for their failure to gather the necessary intelligence before prescription and application.

In regard to the requisite perspectives of the personnel actually engaged in the intelligence function, the policy of responsibility is of primary importance. Responsibility, in addition to its reference to the necessary intelligence skills, includes independence and integrity. Intelligence investigators must manifest enough self-awareness to distinguish the trends they purport to describe from their own preferences about events. Considerable attention has been directed to the problem of the intelligence agent who gathers information to support his preferred prescriptions and applications. Recommendations for structural differentiations between intelligence and subsequent decision functions obscure the fact that the problem is essentially one of perspectives rather than organs. While a desirable function of intelligence may include the invention and tentative evaluation of a satisfactory policy proposal, accompanied by deliberate abstinence from factual distortion or agitation on behalf of a specific solution, the workability of the distinction ultimately depends on the personnel charged with responsibility for what is to be done.

The utility of power as a base value in this process needs no illumination. Wealth may be employed for maintaining a large open intelligence network as well as for the more sordid practice of buying information. Enlightenment and skill are used in devising techniques for finding and evaluating information as well as for predicting and planning. Personal enlightenment, in the sense of insight and understanding, improves the ultimate dependability of the tool devoted to the performance of this function.[148] Individuals may reveal or conceal information as a consequence of personal, family, or national loyalties (affection). Respect and rectitude motives may cause divulgement (e.g. apologias, memoirs explaining to posterity, and so on). These same values may be employed deprivationally for purposes of blackmail. Psychic and physical well-being will affect the efficiency of participants; inner conflict may, for instance, undermine loyalties and lead to the disclosure of information to a rival participant in world politics.

The process of intelligence employs both coercive and noncoercive strategies. Coercive strategies range from the "third degree," torture, brain-washing, and threats of deprivations to such technologically sophisticated violations of the person as "truth serums." Noncoercive

---

[148] Verba, "Assumptions of Rationality and Non-Rationality in Models of International Systems" in Knorr and Verba, *The International System* (1961), 93.

strategies include diplomatic methods, such as the personal interviewing techniques of the social scientist; ideological procedures, such
as mass interviewing, polling, content analysis, and economic tactics, such as acquiring information in exchange for coin of the realm.

The outcomes of the process of intelligence are a flow of data to
(or the withholding of information from) participants who are performing the other functions of constitutive decision. The questions
pertinent here relate to the extent of disclosure or nondisclosure of
gleaned intelligence. What intelligence is brought to the attention of
effective decision-makers? If realistic information was not made available, is this due to faulty channels of communication or to deliberate
blocking? To what extent do decision-makers take cognizance of the
intelligence from various sources or are likely to do so in the future?
How much influence has the flow of intelligence had on decisions
actually taken?

Promotion (Recommendation)

This function goes beyond passive recommending to active advocacy
of policy alternatives to authoritative decision-makers. A personality
system can be said to perform an inner promotional activity when
intensity of demand is added to expectations. The participants in a
decision process promote when they project their intensified demands
to authoritative prescribers. Hence promotion is a pressure operation
aimed at getting authoritative and controlling results. Its objective
is to transform promoters' demands into group prescriptions. As
noted before, this function often blends with intelligence. The extent
of the merger, when not deliberate, probably varies conversely with
the extent to which a given participant realistically perceives himself
and his personal psychic demands. At times the merger is imposed deliberately. Thus a recent study of the press notes that journalists are
often explicitly directed by their papers to mix reporting and evaluation; mere reporting of facts is rejected.[149] The fusion of functions is accelerated when purely promotional participants gather intelligence to aid in the propagation of their programs.

If the promotional function is to contribute fully to the world constitutive process, it is clear that it must be brought to conform to a
number of fundamental policies. Of primary importance is the encouragement of integrated policy: the promotion of common rather
than special interests. This implies that the channels of promotion
are open to all participants, and that strategies of persuasion rather
than coercion are used. In practice, a frequent barrier to adequate
performance of the function is domination of available channels by
promoters of special interests. Policies in favor of representativeness

149 Cohen, *The Press*, 22-25.

and of the cultivation of integrated policy can be brought into dynamic balance with policies in support of openness by means of structural regulation. Motivations of concern for the common interest and of responsibility can be encouraged, for example, by arranging for highly enlightened and disengaged individuals to operate at key phases of the promotional process.

Experience shows that within the departments of a single government, diverse policy alternatives may be promoted; obviously such a state of affairs gives expression to contrasting value sets and identifications. Hence it is incomplete and unrealistic to speak only of promotion as an official function. As with most functional analyses of the decision process the unity that is conventionally implied by the term "government" promptly shatters. Nongovernmental organs are intricately involved in the championing of public policy. The mass communications media typically engage in active promotion through editorial statements (direct promotion) and news culling, highlighting and interpreting (indirect promotion).[150] The media may direct their promotional messages to elite decision-makers or to a wider audience. Political parties and pressure groups often promote explicit programs whose constitutive impact is demonstrable. A phenomenon of rising frequency in pluralistic democracies is active participation in promotion by interest groups concerned with different aspects of the global constitutive process.

In transnational interaction, the nation-state plays a leading promotional role. Information agencies and consulates are among official outlets. Government radio, television, books, and periodicals move relatively freely across borders seeking both elite and rank-and-file audiences. The activities of a number of intergovernmental agencies are primarily promotional. Transnational interest groups of a private character also engage in constitutive promotional activities. Increasingly, they assume pressure group roles in organized transnational arenas.

As in the process of intelligence, all values may be employed in recommendations. However, certain arenas introduce limitations on the employment of some values. Frequently used symbols commonly draw on affection (national or group loyalties), respect (national honor, prestige, etc.), and rectitude (ideology, racial purity, etc.). Much of the communicational aspect of promotion is, in fact, a process of finding or fabricating a symbol of enough inclusivity to attract, concentrate, and manipulate the value bases of a disparate number of participants. As transnational interactions intensify and arenas enlarge, there will presumably be more attempts to formulate symbols of more inclusive common interest. On the verbal level, at least,

150 Same, 105.

this trend is clearly indicated in inclusive demands for minimum
order. However, as we have frequently commented, the scholar and
decision-maker must constantly distinguish verbalisms from more
overt indications of common willingness to move effectively toward
minimum world order. Special interests rarely present themselves
as such; the articulation of inclusive demands may be no more than a
hypocritical abuse of the opportunity to promote.

Promotional strategies are essentially communicational. They may
be either diplomatic—directed at elite groups—or ideological—directed at broader audiences. Since promotion is an agitational process,
directed at achieving authoritative prescriptions, strategies of a
high degree of coercion may be brought into play. Beyond a certain threshold, coercion becomes a component of the prescribing function. Before that threshold is reached, however, the effect of coercive
strategies is to limit the ambit of free choice of prescribers by sharply
increasing the costs of certain decisions which diverge from the outcomes sought by the promoters. Clearly there is no place for highly
coercive strategies in the promotional process of a public order of
human dignity.

Prescription

Prescription refers to the projection of policy for value shaping and
sharing accompanied by coordinate expectations of authority and control. As a process of communication, prescription proceeds on three
levels: (1) the designation of policy (fact contingencies, a norm,
and a sanction), (2) the communication of the authority of the policy, and (3) the communication of control intentions of the community to sustain it. Defined in this manner, prescription includes the
outcomes both of formally authoritative prescriptive processes and of
unorganized interaction.

Prescription is at once broader and more specific than the commonly used term "legislation." In conventional usage legislation is an
"organic" concept, deriving from the assumption that law is made by
a centralized legislature. Such an approach is inadequate for the study
of government anywhere, and especially of international law, since
there is little formal international legislation. Even within a relatively
organized community, the term legislation is often no more than a
procedural label, with little or no relevance to the question of creating expectations of authority and control. A significant amount of
what is conventionally identified as legislation is not prescription; in
fact, certain national legislatures are notorious for producing a voluminous statutory output, little of which can meet the functional requirements of a prescription. On the other hand, a considerable
amount of communication which cannot be traced to a legislature is

often treated as unqualified prescription. For example, the mongrel term "judicial legislation" is so common that it no longer astonishes lexical sensibilities.

In general, inherited terminology has become an obstacle to, rather than an instrumentality of, scholarship. Working within the frame of Article 38 of the Statute of the International Court[151] and seeking to extend it to cover the myriad patterns of world constitutive prescription, scholars have been forced to invent such fabulous terms as "binding recommendations,"[152] "instantaneous custom,"[153] and "pressure-cooked custom."[154] The emphasis on policy projection and the creation of expectations of authority and control immediately uncovers the vast and intricate web of international prescription. There is universal, general, regional, plurilateral, and bilateral prescription. Moreover, prescription is related to all the possible objectives of the value spectrum.

Processes of prescription occur in a wide variety of situations and the degree of institutionalization of the various component processes of prescription varies greatly. The sequence of a completed process of prescription is: (i) initiation; (ii) exploration of potentially relevant facts and policies; (iii) formulation, that is the characterization of the facts and policies accepted as relevant; and (iv) promulgative communication of the prescriptive content to the target audience.

The more important policies for constitutive prescription are promptness in initiation, comprehensiveness and contextuality in exploration, the conformity of prescriptive formulations to the basic goal values of the community, and effectiveness in promulgative communications to the target audience. The appropriate quantum of prescriptions will vary according to the context, particularly the absorptive capacity of the audience. Generally, however, the appropriate criterion is an adequate flow of prescriptions to support the public order without invasion of civic order.

The participants in the process of prescription may be broadly characterized as communicators and communicatees (audience). Any participant in constitutive activities may fill both roles. In the most comprehensive sense, all participants in social process are constantly communicating, explicitly as well as by implicit behavior, and

---

151 Article 38, generally treated as an authoritative statement of the "formal sources" of international law, gives agreements, custom, and general principles of law as the primary sources; judicial decisions and doctrinal writings as subsidiary sources.

152 Sloan, "The Binding Force of a 'Recommendation' of the General Assembly of the United Nations," 25 *British Yearbook of International Law* (1946), 1.

153 Bin Cheng, " 'Instant' International Customary Law?," 5 *Indian Journal of International Law*, 23 (1965).

154 Engel, "Procedures for the De Facto Revision of the Charter," 59 *Proceedings of the American Society of International Law*, 108 (1965).

the communications that are coordinated with authority and control intention become prescriptive. The problem of who is receiving these communications at any given time and place, and with what effects, is in continual need of comprehensive empirical examination.[155]

Prescriptive arenas, official and unofficial, are the five situations presented earlier.[156] These arenas are particularly relevant to the question of the degree of prescriptive authority of prescribers and the extent of prescriptive intention which accompanies their words and deeds. Authority, it will be recalled, is a set of common expectations; in regard to prescription, it is a set of expectations about who is authorized to prescribe community policy. A convenient set of indices for investigating these expectations of authority may be found in the concept of situational or contextual roles. Most participants, as all individuals, play different roles in different interactive patterns. These roles may provide indications of both expectations about the prescriptive authority of the communicator as well as of prescriptive intentions. Thus, nation-state officials in the parliamentary arena may be deemed authoritative prescribers by the world community, but their prescriptive authority may be deemed less if they communicate unilaterally in the executive arena. Similarly, communications made in a parliamentary-diplomatic arena may be assumed to contain a high prescriptive intention in contrast with statements made in a diplomatic arena.

All values are employed as bases in the process of prescription. Prescriptive strategies vary with the component of the prescription. The elements of the policy message are modulated by language rather than language-equivalents.[157] Authority is an attendant communication and is generally transmitted by implicit modalities such as situation, role, or auxiliary symbol.[158] Control intention—a communication of the capacity and willingness to apply effective power to support putative prescriptions—may be modulated by anticipatory action, reinforced statement, direct action, or reference to context.

Sequence analysis indicates that different sets of strategies are employed in the different phases of prescription. The difference is most marked in intra-arenal phases (initiation, exploration, and formulation) and promulgative strategies. The latter refer to the modalities by which a prescription, once formulated and decided, is communi-

---

[155] For a critical examination of the reception problem with particular attention to the inadequacy of available investigative techniques, see Klapper, *The Effects of Mass Communications* (1949).

[156] See section on Situations.

[157] Sapir, "Communication," 4 *Encyclopedia of Social Sciences* (1931), 81.

[158] Ruesch and Kees, *Non-Verbal Communication* (1958), 7, develop the concept of a metacommunication to describe implicit communications which explain how the primary communications are to be understood.

cated to an audience which does not participate directly in policy formulation. A constitutive prescription, it should be added, need not be publicized beyond the immediate prescribers. Thus a private "deal" between several nation-state elites can be effective constitutive prescription despite the fact that it is kept in confidence by the immediate prescribers. Promulgative strategies may comprise the ritual of a judicial decision, the signature and ratification of an international agreement, a parliamentary vote, and so on. Many of these acts, in addition to publicizing the communication, impart a degree of authority to it. Inter-arenal strategies, in contrast, include the modalities by which elite prescribers agree on a formulated prescription. Thus, in a diplomatic arena the strategies are comprised of the elements of bargaining theory, in a judicial arena the elements of small group dynamics, in a parliamentary arena the usual "political" strategies.

The outcome of a prescriptive process is the generation of the designated expectations in the target audience. The question of audience response—the degree and intensity of shared subjectivities resulting from prescriptive communications—is a fundamental problem in the study of this function. On a theoretical level, there is utility in assuming a "closed circuit." In fact, we know that many putative communications fail to engender the intended subjectivities in the target.[159] In certain cases, the circuit is not closed. In other cases, though closed, the effects are dysfunctional; expectations other than those intended by the communicator may be engendered or an overexposed audience may manifest "privatization" or "narcotization."[160] The improvement of prescriptive techniques, a root problem in international law, turns upon the effects of the process.

The initial challenge is the development of indices for determining when communications have prescriptive outcomes. The subjective elements—long appreciated by doctrines of customary law[161]—can be tapped by the employment of current social scientific techniques: manifest and latent content analysis, mass interview, intensive interviews, and participant observation. Work in this area can be accelerated and improved by development of a specialized field of prescriptive communication.

Invocation

Application is the authoritative characterization of facts in terms of their conformity or deviation from prescriptions and the possible application of control to reconstitute value outcomes discordant with

---

159 See Klapper, *Mass Communications.*

160 Wright, *Mass Communication: A Sociological Perspective* (1959) .

161 See Wolfke, *Custom in Present International Law* (1964) for survey of the literature.

prescribed policies and public order interests. In social process, however, it is generally impossible to move directly from prescription to application. The function of invocation refers to the *provisional* characterization of facts as deviating from prescribed policy and the *provisional* assertion of control to prevent or abate the deviation or to seize control of individuals or values necessary for subsequent application. Thus invocation refers to considerably more than the initiation of a process of application. In certain arenas, provisional characterizations of deviations may have enormous value consequences. The public statement by a Senator that an individual is engaged in subversive activities may result in enormous value deprivations, as may an article in a newspaper that a Senator is engaged in fraudulent activities. In neither of these cases is there a provisional application of control; mere provisional characterization sets civic sanctions in motion. If an individual is held without bail, summarily deported, refused entrance to a state, or killed by a police agent, the value deprivations attendant upon provisional characterizations may be even greater. It is precisely because of the potential value effects of invocation that it must be treated as a decision function; policy analysis must be directed to much more than the procedures for initiation of application.

The sequential phases of invocation are (1) initiation, (2) exploration of facts and policies, (3) provisional characterization and application of control, and (4) stimulation of applicative arenas.

Policy clarification in regard to invocation requires a balance between promptness and efficiency on the one hand, and adequate, safeguards against irremediable value deprivations on the other. Clearly, the public order demands promptness in initiating application in cases of divergences from prescribed policy. Invokers must be sufficiently authorized and motivated as well as accorded the necessary resource capability. The extent to which authority and control should be dispersed among all participants or concentrated in a specialized group of invokers must be determined by reference to context. The exploration and characterization phases of invocation should be executed by contextual analysis and with rationality in the provisional characterization. The use of coercion in provisional control applications should be carefully restricted. Official invokers having in high degree the qualities noted above may, nevertheless, impose severe value deprivations on innocent parties. If access to processes of invocation is broadened to include all participants, abuses as well as misinvocations may be expected. Rather than impose restrictive regulations on the invocative process, it is preferable to insist that all invocations be followed by authoritative applications: no invocation without application.

In institutionalized situations of interaction, invocation processes may be highly formalized and often restrictive in all their phases. In arenas of light organization, invocation is open to all effective participants and is frequently indistinguishable from the process of recommendation. Thus, a mild diplomatic note indicating dissatisfaction with the recipient's behavior and stating an intention to follow a counter-course may constitute the invocation of a process of constitutive decision, whose degree of organization is limited to the relay of communications through the diplomatic channel. In an even more unorganized sense, the behavior of one participant may evoke counter-behavior by another; the ultimate synthesized pattern of interaction will constitute a constitutive decision, which was invoked by the most indirect of communications.[162]

In arenas of a higher degree of organization, access qualifications may act to prevent wide participation in the function of invocation. The classic arena demonstrating this phenomenon is the International Court of Justice. Under the terms of its Statute, only "states" may appear before the Court.[163] In the Security Council and the General Assembly of the United Nations, invocation—placing a matter on the provisional agenda—is again restricted to states.[164] Although these practices limit the breadth of participation in this function, they rarely prevent effective participants from initiating application in an issue in which they perceive an interest. By a process of "mutable privity," excluded participants don the raiment appropriate to the arena to which access is sought. Thus, *Mavrommatis*[165] and *Nottebohm*[166] in effect "leased" state-cover in order to invoke decision and pursue claims in the Permanent Court and the International Court respectively. In the United Nations, while only a state can invoke through the agenda, a nonstate entity may effectively place a matter on the agenda by finding an acquiescent delegation member. This practice is not uncommon. In a more general sense, wherever a composite participant alone can invoke authoritative decision, all *infra-arenal* participants of the composite entity, with some measure of internal effective power, can move the appropriate organ of the composite participant to invoke transnational decision. Thus, the ultimate initiation of the process of invoking diplomatic protection of nationals is the intra-arenal claims of the deprived parties within the invoking nation-state.

162 See Schelling, *The Strategy of Conflict* (1963), 54ff.
163 Article 36, Statute of the International Court.
164 But see earlier section on Participants.
165 Series A/No. 2 at 6.
166 1953 *ICJ Reports* 3; 1955 *ICJ Reports* 4; in this case, the Court applied a doctrine of "genuine link" and found jurisdiction defective. The case has been criticized.

An effective global constitutive process of authoritative decision requires broad access to and participation in processes of invocation. Respect for and confidence in processes of authoritative decision are based, in no small part, on the ability of the individual to invoke decision when he feels that prescriptive misfeasance or nonfeasance has occasioned an unlawful value deprivation. Similarly, an effective minimum public order requires that centralized organs of the community be authorized and capable of invoking decisions when they perceive or anticipate a disruption of order. Although current access to invocation is not optimum, a trend toward the broadening of participation in this function is evident. The proliferation of new nation-states has accorded a large number of new elite groups access to organized arenas for invocation as well as for other decision functions. In certain regional groupings, individuals have been accorded a *locus standi* in invocation of transnational decision.[167] Reference has been made earlier to the access enjoyed by individuals to a number of constitutive arenas of a high degree of organization.[168] Of particular relevance here is the Trusteeship Council.[169] There has been a parallel broadening of the invocation function of centralized community organs. Thus, the Security Council and the Secretary-General play an invocatory role far greater than that accorded to their counterparts in the League of Nations.[170]

Application

Application represents the transformation of authoritatively prescribed policy into controlling event. Claimants, initiating decision, petition decision-makers whose manifest objectives are the application of prescriptions of constitutive and public order, to apply particular prescriptions to asserted events by management of the bases and strategies at their disposal. The temporal sequence of application is (i) initiation; (ii) exploration of potential facts and policies; (iii) characterization of facts and policies; (iv) enforcement; (v) review. The parallels with the prescriptive function should be noted. Whereas prescription is primarily prospective, application is immediate; hence a component function is enforcement or concrete implementa-

---

167 This was an innovation in the now defunct Central American Court of Justice. Under the European Convention on Human Rights, individuals may initiate an action before the Commission, though only that body and the contracting states have a right to bring the case before the Court. See Robertson, *Human Rights in Europe* (1963).

168 See earlier section Individuals.

169 For a survey of Trusteeship petitioning activity in the past year see *Issues Before the 20th General Assembly*, 554 *International Conciliation* (1965), 79-101.

170 See Schwebel, *The Secretary-General of the United Nations* (1952), 3-13, 84ff.

tion. Moreover, application includes as a component a review function; claimants may assert that an aspect of the prior phases of application was unlawful, thereby abrogating the characterization and terminating the enforcement. Prescription generally does not import review although its equivalent may be achieved, in certain cases, through the functions of appraisal and termination. There is a striking similarity between many of the procedures of invocation and application, particularly when the former involves an application of control. The functions are distinguished by reference to expectations of applicative authority. In appraising control applications, the decision-maker and the scholar should characterize them as provisional or definitive according to the public order impacts which will predictably follow.

Applicative policies, as they relate to the various sequential phases of the process, include promptness in initiation, comprehensive contextuality in exploration, choice in decision which is both realistic as to fact and in conformity to inclusive community policies, effectiveness and cost-consciousness in enforcement, and comprehensiveness in policy analysis and projected effect in review. Some of the most difficult policy problems of the law, though not confined to application, have traditionally been treated under this function. The problem of discovery, for example, requires a balance between the demands of realistic contextuality in exploration and the reserved domains of the civic order which should be protected from official interventions. The entire problem of circumstances in which appliers should refrain from positive decision, of which the "political question" doctrine is only an aspect, relates to the division of competence between coarchical appliers and the delicate problem of feasible enforcement. Parallel problems are encountered in the ambiguous policy of *forum non conveniens* by which appliers sometimes decline decision.

The arenas of application of the constitutive process include almost all situations of interaction. While much application takes place in official arenas, specialized in practice and in myth to that function, application, like prescription, is a component of all social interaction. All behavior is, in differing positive and negative degrees, application. The ubiquitous nature of application raises difficult quantitative problems for the observer.

Scholarly treatment of transnational application has broken from municipal conceptions, but has been seriously impeded by the assumption of requisite consensuality in inter-state application. The six basic processes recognized by doctrine are "good offices," "mediation," "commissions of enquiry," "conciliation," "arbitration," and "adjudication."[171] Theoretically, only the outcomes of the last two processes are "binding"; the outcomes of the other processes are essentially hortatory. In practice, different contexts have divested a "binding" arbitral or judicial decision of all effectiveness and invested it in the "nonbinding" pronouncements of a conciliation commission.[172] Theoretical difficulties with the control factor have led some scholars to extend the term "international adjudication," apparently, to cover all effective application. Wright, for example, states that "Broadly defined, adjudication includes dispute settlement by a political body such as the United Nations Security Council or a national legislature . . ."[173] On this line of analysis, it would not be surprising to find functionalists employing the term adjudication to cover unilateral decisions taken by an interested participant, if they accorded with general expectations; but to use the term "adjudication" in this manner obscures relevant differences in the various stable applicational arenas.

Application occurs in five contexts: adjudicative, parliamentary, parliamentary-diplomatic, diplomatic, and executive. In Western cultures, myth holds the courts to be the most appropriate arena of application. In non-Western cultures, this may not be the case;[174] moreover, many institutions which the Western anthropologist would characterize as adjudicative may partake more of the diplomatic or parliamentary. There is little need to illuminate the observation that national decision-makers have manifested no marked preference for this arena of application. The dominant applicative arena in transnational interaction has been the diplomatic. Formal constitutive documents, though paying obeisance to the appropriateness of courts for application, have implied a preference for parliamentary-diplomatic and parliamentary arenas. In a "unicentric" context, one which is currently found only on regional levels, one participant applies for others, on the basis of its inordinate power.

The base values employed in application vary according to arena and sequential phase. In pre-enforcement phases, there appears to be an inverse ratio between the degree of organization of the arena and participant freedom in base-value investment. In terms of authority, there is a clear demand for the employment of nonresource or symbolic values rather than tangible resources in more organized arenas. Of particular importance to the contemporary constitutive process is a clarification of rational base-value exploitation in the en-

171 For discussion see Sohn, "The Function of International Arbitration Today," *1962 Hague Recueil* 1-23.

172 Reisman. "The Review and Enforcement of International Judgements and Awards" (Unpublished thesis, Yale Law School, 1965), Chapters 3, 11.

173 Wright, "Adjudication," *Dictionary of the Social Sciences* (UNESCO, 1964), 9.

174 See Syatauw, *Some Newly Established Asian States and the Development of International Law* (1960).

forcement phase. While strategies directed at the rectitude and respect demands of individuals may be an effective enforcement base in a homogeneous community, the current context appears to require an effective power base for processes of enforcement. It is clear, of course, that an appliers' "preoccupation with enforceability"[175] will be a significant factor in formulation and characterization.

Strategies of application vary according to arena and to sequential phase. Thus, initiatory strategies vary markedly in an adjudicative and a diplomatic arena. Similarly, exploration in the adjudicative arena is, doctrinally, adversarial, while, in an executive arena, it may be collaborative. The effectiveness of constitutive application can be improved by a detailed analysis and evaluation of the different strategies employed in different arenas and their effects upon outcomes and goals.

The outcome of a successful application is a change in current value allocation and future behavior toward a greater conformity with constitutive and public order policies. It should be emphasized that we do not refer to a mechanistic application of sanctions— "evils" as John Austin revealingly called them[176]—to every deviation from prescribed norms. The minimum goal of application is the maintenance of public order; the maximum goal, the distribution of values and the conformity of behavior to the overriding policies of the world public order system. In different contexts, different applicative procedures and enforcement strategies will be required in order to realize these goals. Thus, depending upon the context, rehabilitative, deterrent, restorative, corrective, or preventive measures may be taken.[177] The imposition of deprivations and/or the according of indulgences are only lower-level implementations of the broader policy alternatives.

Termination

The termination function deals with the abrogation of extant prescriptions and provision for claims arising from disruption of an expected and demanded arrangement. Semantic or verbal termination —frequently implicit in codification—generally involves striking from the books statutes which are no longer expected and demanded: obsolescing the obsolete. Maintaining a congruence between expectations of authority and control and formally prescribed law is, of course, essential to an efficacious process of authoritative decision;

[175] Jenks, *The Prospects of International Adjudication* (1964), 667.

[176] Austin, *The Province of Jurisprudence Determined and the Uses of the Study of Jurisprudence* (Hart Introduction, 1954), 15.

[177] See generally Lasswell and Arens, *In Defense of Public Order* (1961) and Arens and Lasswell, "Toward a General Theory of Sanctions," 49 *Iowa Law Review*, 233 (1963).

hence provision should be made for semantic termination. However, such termination rarely stirs claims for compensation following major value reallocations; formal authority has been brought into line with expectations rather than vice versa. We are concerned here with community termination of extant authoritative expectations and demands. Termination may impose a deprivation upon those who have made good-faith value investments on the positive public order supposition that the prescriptions would continue; the deprivations may relate to both tangible assets as well as to the severe psychic dysphoria attendant on the collapse of an expected and demanded order. On the other hand, it may accord great indulgences to others, windfall indulgences to some, but not infrequently planned value gains to those who initiated the function. While both prescription and application may terminate expectations of authority, it is, in fact, the problem of claims arising on the abrogation of constitutive or public order features which distinguishes termination from the other functions.

The sequential phases of the process of termination are (1) initiation, (2) exploration, (3) cancellation, and (4) amelioration. The parallels of the first three phases with prescriptive sequences need no illumination. The fourth phase, amelioration, refers to the process of satisfying claims arising on termination and developing procedures which will both distribute losses equitably as well as consolidate support for the authoritative termination.

While community goals may survive a changing context, prescriptions embodying those goals will require reformulation or change as the facts upon which they were formulated are supplanted. Accordingly, an effective public order system requires a process of termination which is responsive to changes in the social process; without such a function, a legal system will be restricted to a minor or even negative role in social change. The primary policy of termination is, thus, reducing the cost of social change and encouraging changes in the appropriate directions. This policy will be served by the cultivation of a climate which is sympathetic to change. This, in turn, is contingent on the availability of procedures for minimizing the destructive impacts of explicit cancellation of prescriptions. Hence, constitutive termination should provide ease, promptness, and availability in initiation, comprehensiveness and dependability in exploration, cancellation in conformity with community goal values, and, finally, effectiveness in amelioration. Since orderly change will frequently turn on anticipatory satisfaction of termination claims, a balance must be struck between a reverence for the past yet a nonencumbrance of the future. Although value reallocations generally import fundamental changes, ill-effects can be mitigated by restricting windfall indulgences and irrational deprivations.

Participants in the termination function may be conveniently classified as terminators and affected parties. The latter class will include both deprivees as well as beneficiaries of a termination. These classifications are participatory roles; hence "terminators" may also be affected parties. Identification with an affected group turns on self-perceptions of participants: perceiving themselves as losers or gainers. Thus, although all participants of the global constitutive process may, at one time or another, participate in constitutive termination, participation in specific terminations may be highly restricted. A palace coup, for example, which involves a change of elite personnel but no change in perspectives or scope values is a termination of extremely restricted participation. Different constructs of future trends in the global constitutive process can eventually demonstrate, in differing degrees, democratic or oligarchic participation in termination.

Past trends in participation indicate a rising democratization of the function. Although the League's termination role was relatively stillborn, the General Assembly as well as a number of specialized committees are directly concerned with termination.[178] The economic agencies, in their developmental role, have insisted upon or aided termination of obsolete orders as a precondition for loans. Nation-states, of course, have played a major role in constitutive termination. General perspectives seem to indicate a willingness to disregard the old order and to accept terminations if there are appropriate ameliorative devices. The increasing perception of the utility of authority in maximizing values predisposes more participants to engage in authoritative termination.

Situations of termination have traditionally been unorganized. In the recent past, however, there has been a trend toward seeking termination in organized authoritative arenas, such as the United Nations, as well as ad-hoc international conferences.[179] Since elites perceiving themselves as deprived by an extant value allocation will seek the arena in which they can operate most effectively, use of organized international arenas for termination can be increased by a monopolization of authority by these arenas (tantamount to compulsory participation) and, at the same time, an adequate openness and flexibility in procedure assuring the prospect of some effective role for the dispossessed.

[178] Articles 13 and 14 of the Charter, among other things, aimed at a terminating function. In regard to specific constitutive terminations, reference may be had to the Assembly's role in creating special committees and itself dealing with the problems of colonialism.

[179] See n. 178. Consider the perhaps unsought terminating effects of the 1958 and 1960 Geneva Conventions on the Law of the Sea. Consider also the efforts of regional members to promulgate termination of general norms in restricted regional arenas.

All values contributing to power in a given context can serve as bases for cancellation. Great ingenuity must be employed in supplying bases for amelioration. Past trends in amelioration indicate a general preference for wealth or monetary compensations. Some attempt to find value equivalents for deprivations attendant on terminations may both compensate as well as reduce initial resistance and consolidate support for the termination. Thus, for example, land nationalization, which deprives a former elite of power, wealth, and respect, could be ameliorated by equality bonds which assure some power in national corporations (power and wealth). Noble titles, which have been stripped of benefits, might be retained (respect). Dispossessed workers could be retooled (skill). A frequent phenomenon in revolution-prone states is to make supplanted elites into ambassadors. This device permits them to retain some power, wealth, and respect, reducing, thereby, their antagonism to the change; it does not, however, allow them to control internal decision processes. A long-range goal is the development of a public order in which individuals identify intensely with the common interest. The mere call on their loyalty to undergo short-range value deprivations is, then, an effective base for termination.

Strategies of termination have been given narrow treatment in the literature. Emphasis has been placed on the diplomatic techniques of treaty denunciation.[180] A more comprehensive treatment would distinguish consensual and nonconsensual strategies of termination and the clarity of consciousness and the explicitness of the prescriptions to be terminated. Thus one might distinguish explicit terminations by mutual consent or unilateral denunciation and implicit termination (desuetude) by indirect communications.

The termination function has been, on the whole, neglected by doctrine. The effective global elites who sustain "international law" have, naturally, been concerned with retaining a context which maximizes their position. Hence, the oft-heard criticism that the law is status-quo-oriented. Although a number of devices for termination are recognized as lawful[181] and the General Assembly has been accorded an ambiguous terminating function,[182] the abrogation of constitutive and public order features has not been in step with the optimistic euphemism of peaceful change. On the basis of two decades of experience of great constitutive termination, it is clear that preferred

[180] See, e.g. Articles 28 to 34 of the Harvard Research, Draft Convention on the Law of Treaties, Part III, pp. 1096-1182.

[181] *Rebus sic stantibus, force majeure, "desuetude,"* mutual agreement etc. See Harvard Research, n. 180.

See also Articles 51ff. of the 1966 Draft Articles on the Law of Treaties prepared by the International Law Commission.

[182] See n. 178.

policy is the maximization of a community interest in terminating whatever arrangements are undermining commonly expected minimum and optimum order goals. Thus, termination is *ameliorative* rather than exclusively negative. The current challenge to the constitutive process is the development of terminating procedures facilitating adaptation to the demands of changing effective elites. These procedures should accomplish termination with minimum order, through peaceful procedures, and with a system of compensation which anticipates and deflects the resistance of participants perceiving a net deprivation in the impending termination.

Appraising

Appraisal refers to the function of assessing the degree of success of authoritative policies in realizing perceived constitutive goals and imposing responsibility and sanctions for discrepancies between them. Hence appraisal is concerned with the comprehensive performance of the constitutive process and the global public order. It is particularly important in a period in which conditioning factors are changing rapidly. Appraisal works within a framework of posited goals, but its outcome recommendations may clearly indicate the need for a reformulation of policy. The sequential phases of appraisal are (1) obtaining information about the process, (2) assessing the quality of performance, (3) reporting findings and recommendations to the appropriate audiences.

The efficiency of appraisal requires that scientific information about the decision process being examined be collected in the most rigorous manner. The skills necessary for appraisal can be maintained only if appraisal is continuous. Appraisal tends to be spasmodic, becoming active only when elite or rank-and-file members perceive a gap between goal and trend. The absence of the requisite fund of expertise frequently permits the process to degenerate into allegations of blame. If the function is to receive support, appraisers must manifest a high degree of impartiality. In its institutional aspects, this may require an assured and strong resource base. In its execution, appraisers must be contextual in method; each detail requires appraisal in the light of the whole set of community goals and the entire range of conditioning factors. Finally, the catharsis function of appraisal has positive public order consequences which should not be overlooked. The psychic tensions which can be generated in individuals by perception of a discrepancy between goal and practice can, if not dissipated, seriously undermine authoritative processes. While it may be impractical to incorporate all participants in authoritative appraisal, the outcome recommendations of the process should be communicated to all politically relevant strata of the population.

Participation in appraisal is probably the most democratic of functions. All participants—both official and nonofficial—are constantly evaluating authoritative decision in terms of the indulgences and deprivations which it occasions them or others with whom they identify or fail to identify. In its most primitive and private form, appraisal may be no more than the muttered "there ought to be a law" of the man in the street.[183] The spectrum extends through private citizen groups concerned with the evaluation of performance and goal and editorializing mass media. Scholars, meeting in a forum such as that convened here, introduce a high degree of specialization into private appraisal. Official decision-makers, both national and transnational, generally maintain specific organs, whose purpose is the appraisal of constitutive decision. Such decision-makers are also responsive, in varying degree, to the appraising communications of the rank and file.

Most of the base values which are employed in the process of intelligence are directly relevant to appraisal. In addition, certain bases are peculiarly important to the latter process. A minimum level of physical and psychic *well-being*, for example, is probably necessary for the initial inclination to undertake appraisal. Thus, value deprivations which are severe, and expectations that such deprivations will continue, may undermine the belief in the utility of appraisal and hence contribute to the further degeneration of the situation.[184] Many of the strategies which are employed in intelligence are put to comparable use in appraisal. In the third sequence of appraisal, however, the strategy of responsibility projection—ascribed or direct—is a unique element of appraisal.

While appraisal may concentrate upon patterns of value outcomes, a discrepancy between outcome and goal ultimately turns on the efficacy of all the prior decision functions. Hence appraisal, when performed correctly, is an ongoing evaluation of all aspects of constitutive decision. Creative and responsible appraisal, a necessity for a free society in a rapidly changing world, must emphasize this point. The mere observation that things are not as they should be is as limited in utility as it is in complexity. The constitutive process is not func-

[183] The spontaneous overt appraisal in which the rank and file indulges may be organized and to some extent checked by a regime so desiring. Thus, for example, in the People's Republic of China, all individuals participate in an institutionalized form of multi-value appraisal. The extent to which the individuals participating in such a process engage in genuine appraisal of all the gaps they perceive between goal and achievement, restricted appraisal of their own behavior's conformity to goals imposed from above, or "rubber stamp" approval of what is presented to them undoubtedly turns on what they deem to be the probable gains and losses of each alternative.

[184] For pertinent discussion, see Rivers, *Essays on the Depopulation of Melanesia* (1922).

tioning as demanded because of the ineffectiveness of one or perhaps all decision functions. The interacting defects will be discerned only if an appropriate map of decision is available, with the widest contextual scope. Without a systematic framework of inquiry, appraisal degenerates into jeremiad.

CHAPTER 4

Constitutional Structures and Processes
in the International Arena

MORTON A. KAPLAN

IT IS generally accepted that the social structure of international politics places constraints upon the possible variations in international norms. This assertion implies neither that law can be derived from social structure—for if that were true one could adopt or propose norms consistent with that structure regardless of whether these new norms fit into either the body of existing norms or a framework of legal reasoning—nor that there is a strict determinism between a systematic substructure and a normative superstructure, in which case one would expect the political and social structure to generate the norms of international law almost automatically. The first alternative would make law too much a matter of preference and dependent largely upon the perceived advantages accruing to the actors in adjusting or failing to adjust the law to actual or desired social structures. The second alternative would make law too little a matter of preference; it would derive the law from the political and social structure and divorce it from the values and choices by means of which we interact with the present to create the future.

International law, we can agree, is not a disembodied essence concocted from covenants, treaties, or customs, and unrelated to the social institutions that permit its observance. In the absence of central legislative organs, creative action by the member actors changes the international normative structure. If solemn treaty obligations enunciate intentions based upon reasonable expectation, that fact is a significant element for the process of juridical reasoning. Even when a norm is violated, referral to signs embodied in treaties of the existence of a norm may be important for later restorative actions that help to keep the norm alive and to maintain other important values as well. Sometimes, however, solemnly enunciated norms are based upon expectations that, although reasonable when first formed, are invalidated by later developments. The Charter of the United Nations, for instance, insists upon the outlawry of resort to arms except in self-defense. Yet some might—and I would—argue that the present structure of world politics is as far out of line with such a norm as current state practice would seem to indicate. In such a case —if I have correctly interpreted the situation—the attempt to avow the norm despite repeated and insistent violations may serve only to cast doubt upon the structure of international law generally. Too rigid an insistence upon an absolute ban on force may do a disservice to efforts to regulate the use of force and to maintain other norms that sustain important national and international values, including peace and security. Even within American domestic law judges make law; if wise, their creative efforts will be subsumed within a chain of legal reasoning that establishes a reasonable relationship with existing norms. There is perhaps even more reason in international law not to lose sight of legal logic; it is at least equally important not to become a prisoner of disembodied legal logic. Creative statesmanship that takes into account the (flexible) limits that the international system places on possible international norms retains the likelihood of developing norms constructively—and thus of enhancing important values, including that of a law-abiding international community —even while acquiescing in the demise of a solemnly agreed-to norm, at least in its pure and unrealistic wording.

The present international system seems to be evolving away from the loose bipolar system as we have known it. This will probably provide a number of opportunities for wise political leadership to help "legislate" the direction of change in the international political order and in the international legal order. Before turning to the future and the alternatives it may hold for us, it may be useful to return briefly to the past and to sketch some plausible relationships between the international social and political order and the international legal order. This may serve as a comparative foundation for our speculations concerning the future. To accomplish this purpose we will describe models of the "balance of power" international system and of the loose bipolar system to show the consequences they plausibly have for the international normative order. These models are not intended to be descriptive of reality. They are primarily analytic devices that permit one to test for internal consistency and for logical clarity. These models are abstracted from a much more complex world. This raises questions concerning the application of derivations from the models to the world that cannot be considered here. However, if appropriate caution is used, models such as these may provide illuminating insights.

"Balance of Power" Model

The "balance of power" model has the following characteristics.

1. The only actors in it are nation-states and thus there is no role differentiation in the model. This is a somewhat counterfactual assumption for there were other organizational forms such as the Dan-

ube Authority and the League of Nations during the historical "balance of power."

2. The goals of the major nations of the system are oriented toward the optimization of security. By this we mean that major nations will prefer a high probability for survival as major nations, even though this excludes the possibility of hegemony, to a moderate probability for hegemony combined with a moderate probability for elimination as a major actor. Most analysts would argue that Napoleon and Hitler did not operate according to this assumption. It is possible, although far from obvious, that the model would function differently were the assumption relaxed. There is sufficient factual validity to the assumption for large and interesting periods of history, however, to more than justify its use as a first-order approximation.

3. The weaponry in the system is not nuclear.

4. There are stochastic and unpredictable increases in productivity which, in time, unless compensated for, might destabilize the system. Therefore each actor seeks a margin of security above its proportionate share of the capabilities of the system.

5. There must be at least five major nations in the system. A two-nation system would be unstable. If either of the two nations gained a clear margin of superiority, it would be tempted to eliminate the other in order to guarantee that the other would not eliminate it, if, through some combination of circumstances, the ratio of capabilities were reversed. In a three-nation system, if there were a war of two nations against one, the probably victorious coalition would have some incentive to limit its demands upon the defeated nation. To eliminate the defeated nation would throw the victors into an unstable two-nation system. Under our assumptions, this would be undesirable, unless one nation could gain such an advantage from the elimination of the third that it could eliminate the second nation. But this would also give the second nation an incentive to combine with the third against the first unless it misunderstood its own interests. On the other hand, if the first nation refrains from sacrificing the third nation, that nation may later combine against it with the second nation in a subsequent war. And, if one of the victorious nations in this subsequent war sees some advantage in eliminating the first nation, it is dependent upon the ability of the only remaining nation to recognize that its own interests require it to oppose this. The reasoning here is inconclusive; therefore three is not a clear lower bound for stability. However, if there are at least five nations, it seems plausible that the argument for limitation in war would hold.

6. Each state, even though of great nation status, is likely to require allies to obtain its objectives. Thus it desires to maintain the existence of potential future alliance partners.

The assumptions specified give rise to the following essential rules of conduct:

(1) Act to increase capabilities but negotiate rather than fight.

(2) Fight rather than pass up an opportunity to increase capabilities.

(3) Stop fighting rather than eliminate an essential national actor.

(4) Act to oppose any coalition or single actor that tends to assume a position of predominance with respect to the rest of the system.

(5) Act to constrain actors who subscribe to supranational organizing principles.

(6) Permit defeated or constrained essential national actors to reenter the system as acceptable role partners or act to bring some previously inessential actor within the essential actor classification. Treat all essential actors as acceptable role partners.

The first two rules follow from the need for a margin of security in a world in which capabilities change stochastically. The third rule is essential for maintaining the availability of future coalition partners. The fourth and fifth rules recognize that deviant actors may destabilize the system by their actions or by the actions of their followers or cohorts within other nations. The sixth rule is also related to the need for potential alliance partners and warns against restricting one's own choices unnecessarily.

These rules are not descriptive rules. They are prescriptive rules. That is, under the governing assumptions, these are rules that states would follow in order to optimize their own security. Thus there is motivation to observe the rules, abstracting from other considerations, but no requirement to do so.

If the major nations follow the specified rules under the specified system conditions, there will be a number of consequences, some of which are obvious and others of which are not so obvious. Alliances will tend to be specific, of short duration, and to shift according to advantage, not according to ideologies (even without war). Wars will tend to be limited in objectives and the rules of war and the doctrine of nonintervention will tend to be observed.

Alliances will tend to be of short duration because permanent alliances would tend to undermine the "balancing" characteristics necessary for the security of the member states. Thus alliances will tend to be for specific objectives as determined by short-term interests. And to use a phrase current in the eighteenth and nineteenth centuries, nations will be disposed to act in terms of interest rather than in terms of sentiment. In short, there is, in this system, a general, although not necessarily consistent, identity between short-term and long-term interests.

The limitation of war in the "balance of power" system requires no further discussion.

We will not go into detail on the expected norms of international law except in a few specifics. One would expect belligerents to behave in ways consistent with maintaining the essential rules of the system since they are required for the security of all essential nations, including belligerents. For instance, behavior during the war or in occupation of territory that infuriated the population of an enemy state would probably preclude the possibility that such a state would be a potential future ally. Although this might not be the only constraint operating to enforce the rules of war, nonetheless it is an important factor tending in that direction.

The rule against intervention in the domestic affairs of another state—a rule violated on a number of occasions—also tends to be sustained under conditions of the model. If the intervention—for instance, in favor of rebels—were successful, there might be a permanent alliance between the states or a tutelage of one over the other. This would injure all other states in the system and thus would tend to draw their active opposition. For this reason the intervention would probably be unwise or unsuccessful. And if, for any reason, the intervention were unsuccessful, the state in which the intervention took place would probably have a serious revulsion for the interventionary state that would tend to make it a permanent enemy of that state. Even if the intervention is successful, the new government may oppose the aiding state to demonstrate its independence. Although these reasons are not absolutely compelling, they are strong enough to make likely rather general observance of the rule of nonintervention in the "balance of power" system.

It should be noted that other states by and large did not tend to intervene on the side of the government in the historic system; rather they merely maintained normal state relations and trade with the government. If the rebels grew strong enough, then the rules of belligerency would apply and other states would behave neutrally toward the belligerents, at least with respect to shipments of the articles of war or the goods of trade. These reasons are not dissimilar to those given above; intervention would have had potentially destabilizing consequences for the system and would have tended to be opposed by the other members of the system.

Recognition, whether of new governments or of new states, tended to follow universal norms in the "balance of power" system. Was there a definite territory? Did the government control the territory? Was there reasonable support on the part of the population or at least the absence of strong overt opposition? If these questions were answered affirmatively, then the government or state would tend to be recognized regardless of the form of internal government or regardless of its friendship or antipathy toward particular states. Although the act of recognition itself was a political act, so that the facts of the case did not absolutely require the act of recognition, nonetheless, with notable exceptions, there was fair concordance between rule and practice. Moreover, since nonrecognition was a political act, its consequences for international law were less than massive, the nonrecognized state merely being denied access to the privileges stemming from comity. Failure to recognize did not remove the duties and obligations under international law that nonrecognizing states had toward the nonrecognized state as a state. Even before the facts were clear that established the legitimacy of a government or a state, this did not imply a reign of anarchy with respect to the nonrecognized government or state. Intervention in its affairs would have been contrary to the rules of the system. Recognition may have been a political act and a negotiating tool in getting the new government or state to recognize its obligations under the rules of the international community, but it was not a weapon in a cold war designed to undercut its existence.

THE LOOSE BIPOLAR MODEL

A second model—one that has some relevance to present-day international politics—is that of the loose bipolar system. This model contains two blocs, each of which is led by a leading bloc actor. There is role differentiation in this model; in addition to blocs and bloc members, there are nations not joined to blocs and universal organizations as, for instance, the United Nations. The weaponry in this model is nuclear. In an age of efficient logistics and great organizational capacity, this latter feature is an essential element of the system; for, unless factors of scale precluded it, one would expect one of the blocs to overwhelm the other unless deterred by a weapons system such as a nuclear one.

This system operates according to the following simplified set of essential rules:

1. Blocs strive to increase their relative capabilities.

2. Blocs tend to be willing to run at least some risks to eliminate rival blocs.

3. Blocs tend to engage in major war rather than to permit rival blocs to attain predominance.

4. Blocs tend to subordinate objectives of the universal actor to objectives of the bloc but to subordinate objectives of the rival bloc to the universal actor.

5. Non-bloc actors tend to support the universal actor generally and specifically against the contrary objectives of the blocs.

6. Non-bloc actors tend to act to reduce the danger of war between blocs.

7. Non-bloc actors tend to be neutral between blocs except where important objectives of the universal actor are involved.

8. Blocs attempt to extend membership but tend to tolerate the status of non-bloc actors.

The first three rules reflect the uncertainties of the bipolar system and the need for at least a margin of security. Rule 4 is related to the need within the system for mediatory functions. Particularly in the nuclear age, mediatory activities help to coordinate conflicting blocs and to achieve an agreement short of nuclear war. This is similar to other types of bargaining situations in which optimal solutions for both conflicting parties are aided by the mediatory process. On the other hand, although these processes should be supported by the blocs, each bloc should nonetheless attempt to take advantage of any favorable opportunities to obtain better than a "fair" outcome. That is, maneuvering will take place and it will be related to situational advantages. Moreover, it is advantageous, even apart from the concept of mediatory functions, to subordinate the goals of one's opponents to those of the universal organization and to subordinate the goals of the organization to those of the bloc, provided this can be done with minimal inconsistency.

Universal organizations are major supports for the interests of actors not belonging to blocs—the greatest protection for them—insofar as they can be protected by universally applicable rules of conduct. Therefore non-bloc members have an interest in subordinating both blocs to the universal actors. This would become difficult, and probably impossible, in the event of major war; and minor wars might escalate into major wars. Hence, according to Rule 6, non-bloc actors are to reduce the danger of war between blocs. The non-bloc actors cannot properly fulfill these functions unless they remain neutral between the blocs; lack of neutrality would impede their mediatory functions and their support for the universal actor. On the other hand, a neutrality that threatened to undercut the universal actor would injure their interest. Thus Rule 7. Rule 8 emphasizes the fact that although extension of bloc membership is important to the bloc, the mediatory role is sufficiently important to the blocs to tolerate it and even possibly, under appropriate conditions, to support it.

The consequences of the rules are straightforward and for the most part have already been stated. Consequences: Alliances are long-term, are based on permanent and not shifting interests, and have ideological components; wars, except for the fear of nuclear weapons, tend

to be unlimited; however, the fear of nuclear war has a strong dampening effect on war; the universal organization tends to support mediatory and war-dampening activities; with respect to international
law, there are few restrictions on intervention and these arise mainly
out of the fear of escalation.

Some of the reasons for these consequences may now be stated. Alliances tend to be long-term and based on permanent interest; in
other words, there is a tendency in the system for bloc members to
support the leading member of the bloc even on issues where there
is a temporary divergence of short-term interests between them.
Moreover, there is a tendency for ideological congruity within the
blocs; for the kind of close association involved either requires organizational uniformity, as in the Communist bloc, or the kind of public
support and cultural similarity which helped at one time to support
NATO. If one bloc were organized according to long-term interests,
and other nations were not, the bloc might well gain its way on most
issues by splitting the opposition issue by issue.

There would be a tendency in this system for wars to be unlimited;
neither bloc would regard the other as a potential coalition partner.
The greatest inhibitor of a central confrontation lies in the nuclear
component and also perhaps in certain factors of scale that would
make administration of the world an extremely difficult, if not impossible, task.

As for the rule of intervention in international law, at least some
of the constraint present in the "balance of power" system would not
be operative in the loose bipolar system. The opposition to intervention would come from the other bloc and would not have the same
massive quality as in the "balance of power" system where most major
actors could be expected to oppose it; fear of confrontation and escalation nonetheless would inhibit intervention to some extent. In
areas where one bloc had easy access and the other did not, intervention would not be unlikely. Where both blocs had relatively similar
access, they might agree to insulate the area from bloc competition
or alternatively they might decide to compete for it. The decision
would depend upon the specifics of the situation; the model could not
be expected to give rise to a specific prediction on this point. One
factor inhibiting intervention would be the fear that the erosion of this
particular rule of law might tend to undermine the general system
of law. Although this fear might be a factor in decisions concerning intervention, the consequence feared is not so direct or so massive that
it would be likely to prove overriding; moreover, most interventions
would be indirect and covert.

One would expect the use of force to be permissible in this system;
the same factors that permit intervention also operate to permit the

use of force, the Charter of the United Nations to the contrary notwithstanding. Historically, Palestine, the Congo, Cyprus, Greece, Korea, Vietnam, Suez, Hungary, and various other episodes firmly illustrate the erosion of the so-called rule of law enunciated in the Charter. The bipolarity of the system tends to focus competition between the blocs and to produce a resort to force in those circumstances where one of the blocs has a clear preponderance of capabilities. The rule can to some extent be enforced against non-leading nations, as in the Suez case, or even in the Pakistan-Indian case. But it runs into greater difficulties in cases such as the Indian-Chinese case.

To some extent this stems from the fact that the bloc leaders have no desire for the continuance of a war that neither supports, especially since any armed conflict might lead to a central confrontation even if with low probability; the bloc leaders see no reason to risk even the lowest probabilities of a nuclear war if there is some convenient way of avoiding it and if there is no clear gain for the bloc leaders to be got from the use of force. Where the universal organization tends to dampen the armed confrontations and to mediate quarrels among non-leading nations, it therefore tends to reinforce the interests of the bloc leaders.

Recognition of states or of governments is based not on the criterion of control with reasonable support from the people within a region but is based upon the consequences of the act of recognition for bloc policy. Thus nonrecognition of East Germany, North Korea, or Communist China was, during the height of bipolarity, part of a program of political warfare designed to erode the position of these governments. This does not mean that nonrecognized states or governments are entirely without rights within the system or that unprovoked major acts of military warfare against them are permitted. However, whereas in the "balance of power" system the objective of nonrecognition is to secure the compliance of the nonrecognized state or government with the norms of the system, in the loose bipolar system the objective of nonrecognition is to weaken the international position of the nonrecognized state or government, and under favorable circumstances, to contribute to its demise.

FACTORS MAKING FOR A CHANGE

A number of features of the existing world make for greater divergence from the model of loose bipolarism than would perhaps permit retention of the model in its present form. First, however, mention will be made of those divergences of model from reality that have always been present but that do not clearly invalidate the model. In the model, uncommitted nations are not distinguished from bloc members by internal characteristics. In the real world, most of the uncommitted states are ex-colonies of the members of the NATO bloc. Their historical memories are conditioned by the fight against colonialism and by their fear of a reimposed colonialism, even if in the form of so-called neocolonialism. Their search for identity leads them to distinguish themselves from the former patron state and, even more specifically, from the leader of the NATO bloc, even though the United States has not historically been an imperialist power.

Most of the uncommitted states are also "colored." Although this characteristic should be irrelevant in countries that have values that are universalistic and achievement-oriented, historically this has not been the case. This creates resentment on the part of the uncommitted states against the members of NATO. In their fight against colonialism, most of the uncommitted nations have adopted some form of socialist or Marxist ideology. Although most of the uncommitted countries are not socialist in meaningful applications of that term, they nonetheless accept a number of intellectual corollaries of the socialist or Marxist position. Thus, it is widely believed among them—and even believed by many Western intellectuals—that capitalism is responsible for both colonialism and war.

The uncommitted countries are also by and large underdeveloped. Whereas in the nineteenth century, the newly developing countries, such as Japan, turned to Western Europe or to the United States for their models of development, there has been until recently a tendency among the contemporary developing nations to view either Russia or China as acceptable, or at least as partly acceptable, models.

One consequence of this set of conditions has been the emphasis of the uncommitted nations upon exterminating the remnants of colonialism, mostly through moral pressure or United Nations resolutions, and upon opposing so-called neocolonialist government among the uncommitted states. Thus a government in an uncommitted state that was relatively conservative, bound to NATO nations by treaty, or more concerned with its internal problems than with the export of revolution tended to find itself opposed by the more revolutionary uncommitted states, which at times even intervened in its internal affairs. Rather than lending support to the old rules of nonintervention, which necessarily suffer attrition as a consequence of the shift from the "balance of power" to bipolarity, the uncommitted states have tended to reinforce the shift away from this rule of law and even more narrowly to circumscribe its applicability. Although they have often attempted to distinguish between colonialist intervention and revolutionary intervention—a distinction the Soviet Union has also tried to maintain—and have not been entirely unsuccessful in this effort, nonetheless there has been a further weakening of the rule. These interventions sometimes threatened the stability of the bipolar system and the interests of NATO. A largely revolutionary world would probably be as inimical to American interests as a largely fascist world would have been. Such a world, even apart from conceptions of monolithicity, would confront the United States with strategic military problems and also, and perhaps even more importantly, with political problems that might affect both its systems of alliances and its internal institutional forms.

The above factors, however, would not by themselves necessarily produce instability or invalidate the model. Other factors may, however, invalidate the applicability of the model, although this is not completely clear.

Among the features eroding the loose bipolar system is the recovery, both political and economic, of Western Europe. Until 1948, the Communist parties of Italy and France seemed to pose a possible threat of violent revolution. The national economies of the occupied but liberated nations were slowly recovering from the havoc of war. Without the infusion of massive aid from the United States, social and political upheaval might easily have occurred. With more than six million men in its armies, the Soviet Union seemed to pose a threat of an immediate military nature. Although this threat never objectively existed in the form in which it was visualized, in the absence of the organized Western bloc that developed, Italy, France, or West Germany might have collapsed as Czechoslovakia did. Now that these nations are once again economically vigorous and politically stable and now that the threat of Soviet military action is visualized as only residual, national pride tends to counsel some degree of independent action. Moreover, the failure of Great Britain to join the Common Market upon its formation, the fear that a vigorous Germany might dominate a united Europe without Britain, and the specific policies followed by General de Gaulle that derive at least as much from his own ideology and view of the world as they do from external circumstances, seriously threaten the existence of NATO as an organized bloc and the Common Market as a supranational agency.

If the threat of Soviet military attack seems to have lessened, the likelihood of an American nuclear response to an actual attack by the Soviet Union also seems to have lessened. Before the Soviet Union acquired nuclear weapons, or even while its nuclear force was highly vulnerable to an American first strike, American nuclear retaliation for a Soviet attack was extremely credible. No doubt a massive Soviet attack out of the blue, that is, without provocation—and in the absence of a suitable conventional response—would still in all likelihood incur an American nuclear response. If, however, war were to develop in ambiguous circumstances, in which the Soviet Union suffered a plausible provocation, and after a prelude that gave much time for Americans to consider the potential damage to their own cities in the nuclear exchange, then although an American nuclear response is by no means precluded, neither does it appear quite so credible as it did in the early 1950's. Regardless of the motives that led General de Gaulle to emphasize the development of an independent French nuclear force, the fact that he has seen fit to call attention to the possibility that the United States would not use its nuclear force in defense of Europe is an indication that he felt the argument at least had some merit in securing support for his decisions. The failure of the Western allies to find some solution to this difficulty that satisfied jointly the needs of the United States and of the European nations no doubt has played a role in the weakening of NATO and hence in the growing instability of the loose bipolar system.

Problems of nuclear control may also have played a role, although it is difficult to say how large a role, in the rupture between China and the Soviet Union. Economic aid, personality conflicts, and conflicting national interests in border quarrels, may also have played important roles in this development. The quarrel between them has provided the other satellite parties with alternate founts of authority. The Communist bloc will not soon recover from the demonstration of the extent to which opposition between Socialist states can occur or from the shattering of the myth of the infallible leadership that resulted from Khrushchev's secret speech on Stalin in 1956.

The independence shown by China has had multifarious consequences within the Communist camp. Hungary and Rumania, for example, have been able to resist political pressures from Moscow and to develop at least partly independent policies that increase their support at home and that stabilize their regimes. These developments have increased the appeal of Communism by demonstrating that Communism can be at least in part an indigenous phenomenon and not merely a Moscovite plot. At the same time the world Communist movement has been weakened both by the fact that division exists and by the fact that the two leading Communist actors—Russia and China—must now expend much of their energies on the contest for the leadership of the bloc or, alternatively, in a contest to attract or to neutralize members of the other's bloc. Consequently they must turn much of their management capacity away from problems of international politics; this reinforces the reduction in their external opportunities that has resulted as a consequence of greater political and economic stability in the world. Thus the Communist bloc is no longer seen as a monolithic conspiratorial apparatus—an image that characterized much of the postwar debate.

If the Communist bloc is not seen as an imminent threat and if many believe that further liberalization will occur within the nations of that bloc, the world then will respond to a psychological détente, the logic of which may further reinforce the breakup of bipolarity. The assumption will be that an era of "good feelings" may promote international agreements and help to turn the world from a policy of blocs to one of independent states operating according to a flexible system of alignments.

The belief that détente helps to fragment bloc structure is not entirely wrong. Although the great breaks in the Soviet bloc—those of Yugoslavia, China, Albania, and temporarily of Hungary—did occur during periods of great international tension, the increases in autonomy and collegiality within the bloc are not entirely unrelated to the amelioration of world conflict. To some extent, similar processes are occurring within NATO, although both processes are much more complicated than generalizations concerning the détente imply. Moreover, even if the generalizations concerning the consequences of détente for internal bloc structure have some—but only some—validity, the relationship between détente and international agreement may radically overstate the importance of the psychological variable. The test ban agreement, after all, was reached subsequent to the Cuban missile crisis—a period of great tension in which restrained threat and counter-threat dominated the international scene. To the extent that détente implies moderate external policies and the likelihood of international agreement, the atmosphere of goodwill that is so highly valued in many circles may play only a minor role.

Some would argue—and I believe correctly—that the psychology of the détente mistakes the epiphenomena of international politics for the phenomena. Just as the popular images of the cold war were in part a response to the frustrated hopes of international cooperation that were held during the war period, the psychology of the détente is in part a reaction to the exaggerated fears of the cold war period. According to this view, Stalin's so-called aggressive policies were more likely responses to the opportunities and dangers that the immediate postwar period provided than they were to a generalized policy of expansion. It is also unlikely that Stalin's policies were the product of the uncontrolled nature of his power within the Soviet governmental system. On the other hand, Khrushchev's seemingly more passive policies—it must be remembered that Khrushchev initiated the Cuban missile crisis and sent troops into Hungary although Stalin only threatened Yugoslavia—responded more to lack of opportunity than to a generalized policy of agreement or to the benignity of a more moderate form of internal rule. If this is a correct interpretation, then expressions of goodwill and the amelioration of the internal Soviet regime, no matter how desirable the latter may be on humanitarian grounds, play little role in achieving international agreement. However, even if this view is correct, it is too subtle for the public. Subjective feelings, at least in the West, concerning the alleged fragility of the détente will probably continue to play a role in the formation of international policy and in the erosion of bipolarity.

Thus, the fact that confronts us is the possible, and even probable, erosion of bipolarity. If the loose bipolar system is becoming unstable, perhaps the model of loose bipolarity no longer functions very effectively as a representation of the world. We will, therefore, consider alternative models that, depending upon circumstances, might represent the alternative worlds that might evolve out of the present world. These systems may give us some insights into the kinds of international law that might accompany them.

Unit Veto System

We present here the model of an equilibrium system that conceivably could develop out of the existing international system. The unit veto system is a system in which each nation possesses a nuclear force capable of surviving a first strike by an enemy and of imposing unacceptable damage upon him. We consider this system before considering some more realistic alternatives because these more realistic alternatives do not constitute equilibrium models and because one or more of them are more closely related to the unit veto system than to the loose bipolar system.

Military alliances would be relatively meaningless in this world. Nuclear deterrence would be credible and effective. Conceivably minor military skirmishes would occur within a quite limited framework; presumably a strategy of limited strategic retaliation might be employed where the conventional forces of one side are too limited to halt successfully the armies of an opponent. Catalytic and anonymous wars would lack plausible motivation.

Nonmilitary, that is, political, interventions, would occur with relative frequency in this world. Such interventions could not easily be deterred by nuclear systems; the gap between penalty and transgression would be too huge to bear the burden of credibility; neither aggressor nor victim would likely be convinced by the argument for this kind of response. The universal organization, however, might well be employed by the other nations of the system to dampen such occurrences because of the danger, even if remote, of escalation. Yet, this will be an isolationist world in which the functions of the universal organization are largely underdeveloped. If the revolutionary ambitions of Russia and China, for instance, are likely to be dampened by lack of opportunity, the development of common interests is also likely to play a minimal role in this system. Neither law nor international organization will burgeon in this system. The citizens of the nation-states are likely to be suspicious of foreign nations, uninterested in the morals of quarrels or the morals of other regimes, and lacking in the assurance required for an articulated foreign policy. The dangers in this system may lie in the political deviancy that begins to develop within nations and in the withdrawal of affect from the external world. This will be a system with superficially low entropy that may suddenly flare up.

The systems presented below are not equilibrium models. They are neither highly analytical nor highly theoretical. However, by suitable adjustments at the parameters one might derive them either from the loose bipolar or unit veto models. Although some writers believe that future systems may be variants of a "balance of power" model, I do not agree; in my opinion the introduction of nuclear weapons and changes in scale make variations based on that model less probable than those adumbrated below. These nonequilibrium systems presumably would develop as the consequence of one or more parameter changes inconsistent with the equilibrium models discussed above. If these nonequilibrium systems are not exceptionally stable in their nature, they may nonetheless be maintained by favorable concatenations of circumstances. Most importantly, one can see how any of them could develop out of the present loose bipolar system as a consequence of changes in the parameters of this system. Thus they are useful intellectual tools for considering possible ranges of variation in international norms; we need to think not merely of the desirability of specific norms but also of the ways in which norms interact with international systems. Norms that are desirable when considered independently may either move us toward international systems the other aspects of which are undesirable or turn out to be unenforceable unless still other changes are made in the international system. Alternatively norms that are less desirable when considered independently may (or may not) help to promote international systems more in accord with our values. Perhaps even more important than the possible inconsistencies between specific norms and the development of alternative international systems will be the problem of relating national policy choices to either or both of these problems. We will not—and perhaps cannot—say much that is significant about these problems in one chapter. The systems described below, however, will be useful if they provide a framework within which the relevant policy choices can be discussed. Whether one thinks likely or unlikely the variations discussed, the style of thinking that underlies them may still prove useful.

Détente System

The détente system is one in which the United States and the Soviet Union are the two strongest nations in the system although they are confronted by other national challenges greater than those confronting them in the loose bipolar system. They are still highly competitive but are reasonably relaxed about their competition. The United States no longer finds it necessary to suspect Communist plots in revolutionary movements while the Soviet Union has learned that many of these distant revolutionary movements are so difficult to control and so alien in cultural background that they are not worth more than merely minor risks. China has alienated many of the uncommitted states, such as Indonesia, Algeria, and Cuba. Moreover, she is in her second generation of revolutionary leadership and is becoming more conservative. Nuclear diffusion has not extended beyond the United States, the Soviet Union, Great Britain, France, and China. The test ban has been extended to underground tests. France and China also have become signatories to this pact. Neither the United States nor the Soviet Union is capable of a credible first strike, and as a consequence either they refrain from increasing the size of their nuclear forces or they decrease them somewhat. France has withdrawn its armed forces from integrated NATO control; the pro-French faction in Germany has won a signal victory within German politics. As a consequence NATO becomes, as General de Gaulle demands, a loose alliance without integrative mechanisms. Rumania develops alternate ties to France to counterbalance its dependence upon the Soviet Union. Other signs of increased independence occur in the Communist bloc.

The anticolonial revolution has been carried to completion. The rule of nonintervention has been reestablished in international politics with support from both the United States and the Soviet Union. With both American and Soviet support, the United Nations Security Council condemns efforts by uncommitted nations to interfere in each other's activities. The rule on compensation in cases of expropriation is relaxed. The United Nations begins to play a strong role in the governance of space, celestial bodies, and polar regions. It also sets up a regime for the development of the mineral resources of the seas.

Breaches of the peace—or even wars—occasionally occur in this system but they do not directly involve any of the major nations. These wars are quickly regulated by the United Nations organization; observer teams are sent to prevent continuation of the fighting. A tradition develops of arbitration of major disputes. National courts increasingly apply international law. There are fewer restrictions on this process by either constitutional or legislative requirements within the national systems.

Recognition, as in the "balance of power" system, is based upon universalistic criteria. Recognition policy is no longer part of the arsenal of political warfare as in the loose bipolar system. However, the motivations that uphold recognition policy—as well as those that uphold noninterventionary norms—differ from those of the "balance of power" system. In the détente system these norms are desirable because they reduce those challenges to the existence of a regime or state that could involve the resort to force and increase the dangers of escalation. The mellowing of the Soviet Union—and to some extent of China—reduces the dangers of nonintervention and of universalistic treatment of new regimes and new states. The lack of cohesion of the blocs has similar consequences and also increases the difficulty of gaining support from one's own bloc for interventionary efforts. The rise of major nations either that are not in blocs or that pursue independent foreign policies reduces the pressure on the bloc leaders to assume that security depends upon their initiative in responding to revolutionary change in the world. Small changes no longer seem to threaten cumulative change as seemed to be the case in the loose bipolar system, viz., the case of Korea.

Four Bloc System

NATO has been dissolved. Western European nations including England have put together a nuclear force with a substantial second strike capability. This force has been integrated in a new organization based on the Common Market and including the Court of Human Rights. Constitutional democratic processes are guaranteed for all the European nations. The United States takes a special responsibility for Latin America and certain areas of Asia. It utilizes the OAS to intervene in Latin America to maintain constitutional processes within that region. It no longer intervenes globally; Europe now also has a capacity in, for instance, the Middle East or Africa comparable to that of the United States in Latin America. Therefore responsibility does not fall inescapably on the United States. The attractiveness of the Western European alternative has reduced the consensus supporting the governments of the Communist satellites in Europe. Consequently for the protection of their own regimes, they are forced to depend more on the Soviet Union. Thus Russian hegemony within the Eastern European bloc is reestablished. Southeast Asia has been neutralized. Communist China has entered the United Nations and has regularized its relationship with the United States. The rule of nonintervention applies in those areas that are not defined as bloc areas. Thus Japan, Africa, India, and certain portions of Southeast Asia fall within this rule. As none of the blocs aspires to control the world and as all now recognize the difficulty of controlling revolutions in developing nations, this rule is reasonably well-enforced.

There are many similarities to the détente system. Space, the Arctic regions, and the seas come under the control of the United Nations, except that the rules according to which this is done are established primarily by bargaining among the four blocs. The rule of expropriation also has been changed to give greater latitude to expropriating states. Some degree of compensation is demanded but not necessarily that amount that corresponds to the market values of the seized assets.

Recognition is usually based upon the criteria of control of territory and support, or at least lack of opposition, by a substantial part of the population. In areas of special sensitivity to the blocs, however, this rule is not followed. Thus, in Latin America, for instance, only republican forms of government are recognized. Those governments that do not provide for political competition have sanctions applied against them by the Organization of American States.

Resorts to force are regulated by a United Nations organ. Ad-hoc control, advisory, or observer groups are employed to separate the combatants. If these disputes are mediated or arbitrated, the blocs intervene to assure themselves that the principles of settlement are principles not discordant with their interests.

The influence of the uncommitted states is considerably smaller in this system than in either the loose bipolar or the détente system. Even in the détente system, the competition between the United States and the Soviet Union for the support of uncommitted states is likely to give such states considerable leverage. In the four bloc system, on the other hand, the existence of a number of alternatives reduces the pressure on any particular bloc to seek the support of any uncommitted state. As this holds for each of the blocs, the price to be paid for support is significantly lowered. Although in order to keep the Organization of American States viable the United States is quite likely to establish sets of economic arrangements that guard against violent fluctuations for the single-commodity countries, the global extension of rationalized procedures is less likely than in a bipolar system.

A variant of the four bloc system deserves consideration. The removal of the United States from Europe and the development of a united Europe exerts a major attraction upon the Soviet bloc. Instead, however, of clinging to the Soviet Union for support, the governments of at least some of the East European states begin to bring into the government only nominally Communist elements in order to foster consensus in the immediate period and association with the economically more vigorous European community in the future. As part of this process, they increase their treaty ties with one or more of the European nations and even enter into what might be regarded as alliances with them. In some of the Eastern European nations, these transitions take place smoothly. In others regime crises occur, as old guard Communist elements either rebel against these regimes, while calling on the Soviet Union for support, or take control of the government legally, while provoking revolutions against themselves in the process.

Developments past this point depend upon a context that has not been sketched here and that is obviously contingent in terms of prediction. Some of the potentialities are, however, obvious. The Soviet Union may also go through a regime crisis and may either intervene or not intervene with the consequences these decisions may have for the outbreak of war or the norms involving the use of force or intervention. Appeals may be made to a united Europe by either the governments or the revolutionaries, and the decisions made by Europe will also affect this set of norms. Attempts may be made to invoke United Nations procedures to pacify the situation. These may succeed, in which case there may be a major enhancement of international organization and world law. Alternatively the intervention by the United Nations may be so ineffective that the organization is discredited, its mediatory activities paralyzed, and the extension of its control over such areas as space and the seas inhibited. A situation parallel to that of the cold war may develop except that four blocs rather than two play major roles. Great instability may result.

Unstable Bloc System

The unstable bloc system is one in which the two major blocs have either begun to fragment or are well along in the process of fragmentation. Arms control agreements are minimal. Third area conflicts are extensive. Local outbreaks of violence are frequent. National liberation movements and internal revolt are rampant in the uncommitted areas. Qualitative aspects of the so-called arms race have made nuclear weapons cheaper and easier to acquire.

Although perhaps ten or fifteen nations have nuclear weapons systems in the unstable bloc system, the United States and the Soviet Union are the only nations with technologically advanced systems. The systems acquired by the United States and the Soviet Union have greatly increased accuracy in delivery, much greater efficiency in the use of warhead materials, and multiple warheads. Although increased mobility of missiles and extensive use of the seas have lowered the vulnerability to first strike of the US and USSR that otherwise would be present in the system in the absence of *these* qualitative improvements, other qualitative improvements, e.g., improved search techniques and increased delivery accuracy, make first strikes much less infeasible than they are at present. The increased instability in the relationships between the Soviet Union and the United States produces further fragmentation of the bloc structure, as the credibility of deterrence has been lessened.

The minor nuclear powers have systems that are good for minimum deterrence only. Their systems are highly vulnerable to first strike. They cannot do serious damage to the nuclear systems of the two major nuclear powers, and they are subject to rapid obsolescence. Alternatively, West Germany and Japan may develop large and sophisticated nuclear systems, while China may utilize its vast territory and large population to offset other deficiencies of its nuclear threat.

This is a system in which the leaders of the two blocs have a strong incentive to insulate themselves from quarrels that might escalate into nuclear war, even at the expense of deserting alliances of which they may be members. Growing recognition of this fact will tend to discredit the value of alliances and will also tend to free the more adventurous nations from the restraints that have previously characterized their behavior. Thus, for instance, a nation such as Rumania might seek support from France as well as from the Soviet Union. Inversely Hungary might turn to the protection of a nuclear-armed West Germany. West Germany, cut off from the support of both the United States and France, might reduce its pressure on East Germany, even to the extent, for instance, of giving tacit support to East German demands on Poland for ex-German territory. This nationalistic West Germany might make a deal with Communist China, in which it uses Chinese territory for nuclear experiments and, in exchange, provides technical aid. This might place great pressure on the Soviet Union, which then might turn either to the United States, or to a deal with either or both Germanies at Polish expense.

This system will be characterized by nuclear blackmail and unstable political coalitions. Although the need to avoid such a potentially unstable system would provide an incentive for the states of Europe to unite within the framework of a supranational organization and for the United States to provide them with the know-how to produce a stable nuclear system, by hypothesis, that alternative has been bypassed. As a consequence, resort to violence is widespread in this system. The United Nations is reduced to a debating body. Arms control agreements are minimal or nonexistent. Outer space, the seas, and the Arctic regions are not governed internationally but are sources of conflict. Recognition is used as a political weapon, and intervention in the affairs of other states is common. The uncommitted states will not be aided by other states to any considerable extent in their development efforts. There will be a general retrogression of international law.

One other variation of the unstable bloc system can be considered. This is a version in which the first strike potentiality of the United States and the Soviet Union is minimal, either because of improvements in antiballistic missile programs or because of failures in search procedures for sea-or-land-based mobile missiles. In this case, alliances would be possible between major and minor nuclear powers or among minor nuclear powers. But the former type of alliance would be inhibited by the small state's possession of nuclear arms. Possession would be a sign of independence and distrust. Moreover the large nuclear state would fear commitment (triggering) by the small nuclear power's use of the weapon. It would desire to insulate itself from a chain of actions that it could not control. And although a general alliance among most of the small states possessing nuclear forces might create a sizable nuclear force, unless there were exceptional political or cultural circumstances, the alliances would be susceptible to nuclear blackmail and splitting tactics.

Wars in this system would tend to be limited but the possibility of escalation would be greater than in the others. Limited direct confrontations between the United States and the Soviet Union might occur in non-European areas. A central confrontation might also occur. But as the danger of escalation beyond the limited war category would be very great, there would be strong pressure to avoid it.

The foreign policies of the United States and the Soviet Union would tend to be interventionist. American policy would tend toward conservatism, that is, toward the support of status quo, conservative regimes. Although one could argue that to retain the support of its own intellectuals, the United States would do better by supporting progressive regimes, American behavior will more likely support regimes opposed to change. There will be a consequent alienation of a considerable portion of the intellectual elite both within the United States and in other NATO states. Soviet policies will support to some extent national liberation movements but in a very cautious way. Additional "Hungaries" may occur that serve to disillusion Soviet intellectuals. Russia will also be torn between a desire to maintain solidarity with China and a fear of the strategic threat and organizational challenge that China presents to the Soviet Union. This will lead to inconsistencies in Soviet policy that conceivably could lead to the fragmentation of the satellite system. This again might produce East German pressure on Poland, depending upon a number of parameters that are too complicated to specify here.

The role of the United Nations will be primarily mediatory and adapted to dampening the consequences of outbreaks of violence.

Although each bloc will support political changes contrary to the interests of the opposing bloc, the efforts to secure a constitutional majority in the United Nations will generally prove ineffective. It is not likely that in this system the United Nations will acquire authority over outer space, celestial bodies, or arms control measures. The United Nations will prove ineffective in dampening local outbreaks of violence. Ad-hoc United Nations forces will become difficult to establish. Intervention and recognition policy will not be based on universalistic criteria but will not be used for purposes of political warfare quite as much as in the other variation of the unstable bloc system, as the blocs will introduce some small amount of constraint.

Development World

The model sketched here goes much further in its optimistic reading of world possibilities than any other of the models. It ignores the failures of development in so many nations, and the even more disheartening apparent failures in nation-building, as in the case of Nigeria, and instead adumbrates the outline of a world in which most of the more optimistic projections from the current world materialize.

In the development world, we would expect that a large number of successful regional groupings would enhance cooperation among the members of the region on both economic and political matters. Success in nation-building has stabilized the national political units. The internal social systems of the nations have developed sufficient infrastructure to provide satisfactory alternatives for those who lose out in political contests and thus to reduce the need for and the frequency of coercive politics. Increased internal political pluralism reduces the costs of political failure, provides alternative career lines and the potentiality for come-backs, and invests amalgamative activities with additional desirable alternative opportunities. Thus Africa and Latin America, for example, would form common markets and would establish the kinds of transportation and communication networks that they presently lack. There is now more intercommunication with Europe and the United States respectively than within the two geographical areas.

We assume that the Common Market flourishes, that with the demise of a general the Seven join the Market, and that the supranational features of the market are emphasized. The Commission on Human Rights becomes a full-fledged court of final constitutional review that sustains political liberalism as well as individual freedom. Although supranational features are less emphasized in Eastern Europe what had been known as the Soviet bloc develops self-regulating agencies in functional areas; these agencies operate either through COMECON or through more specialized and separate arrangements. Although the governments in Eastern Europe do not become democratic and remain, with a few exceptions, one-party systems, individual rights are much more regularized than had been the case in the past; and the freedom to move either within or outside the bloc becomes almost general.

The regime in China has meliorated. Although China has good relations with Korea and Vietnam, and is developing successfully, these nations do not enter into a regional grouping. Japan, which has emerged as the second most industrialized nation on earth, and which is pressing the United States strongly for world leadership, has a very strong aid program toward Southeast Asia. Most nations of this area have entered their own regional association through which Japanese aid and leadership is funnelled. Supranational characteristics of this association are weak, although there are a substantial number of regional cooperative arrangements.

The United States has retreated from global interventionism, although it has become the only "world" power with the incorporation of Australia, New Zealand, and the Philippines as American states. Israel has also joined this new grouping. With the death of the Israeli hope that the Arab states would make peace eventually and with the withdrawal of American protection to foreign states, except under United Nations auspices, incorporation of Israel into the American union remained the only solution for both nations. Cuba has also joined the American nation after a successful democratic revolution, as have the Dominican Republic, Haiti, and the former English West Indies.

The Arab states have formed their own regional association although development is retarded as a consequence of the replacement of oil by other energy sources. Some instability exists in the Arab Middle East as a consequence of internal instability and political extremism. United Nations controls, however, manage to dampen these instabilities.

The United Nations has assumed administration of outer space and the resources of the seas and, in particular, assures that all nations have equitable access to these resources. The United Nations also carries out arms control activities. A United Nations force also has nuclear weapons—to be used only under command of a Standing Committee and upon the authorization from the political organs of the United Nations. England has abandoned her independent nuclear force, as has France, although the European organization possesses a small nuclear force. Only the United States, the Soviet Union, and China possess individual national nuclear forces; and these are far smaller than presently existing forces. Moreover, there has been a widespread distribution of effective ABM systems to other nations and to regional organizations.

In case of civil war, the theories of neutrality and of intervention only in behalf of existing regimes have been discarded in favor of collective intervention organized by or under the terms of resolutions passed by the political organs of the United Nations and consonant with a universally agreed-upon set of standards. Thus interventions against existing governments would be permissible when these governments discriminated among their nationals according to race or religion (or some other unreasonable standard) with respect to their political rights; or when human or essential political rights were denied; or when access to information or freedom of movement was denied. The universal organization, however, would not authorize action prior to the outbreak of organized violence in the absence of a demonstration of widespread support for the demands of those in revolt, or except in circumstances that indicated that change could be brought about according to some reasonable schedule of human costs. When the revolutionaries sought to deny any of the specified values, the universal organization would authorize intervention in support of the existing government. Where the values were unclear or contested, the universal organization would authorize intervention on the side of those who would permit international supervision during a transitional period to help to enforce the stated values. Under these standards intervention under international authorization occurred in South Africa in favor of the blacks, in Kenya in favor of the whites, and in Cuba in favor of the democrats (prior to accession to the United States). In all these cases intervention was against the existing regime. In the cases of Uruguay and Venezuela, intervention occurred in favor of the existing governments.

Where possible, these interventions were organized by appropriate regional groupings whose findings of fact were subject to approval and whose decisions to act were subject to authorization by the universal organization, as in the Kenyan case. Occasionally, the actions were collective actions by the entire universal organization, as in the South African case, and occasionally by one or a few states, as when the United States, Mexico, and Brazil organized the action against Cuba. The case of Hungary was the only instance in which the United Nations authorized intervention against both the existing government and the findings of the appropriate regional body. In this case action was organized by the Western European organization when the Eastern European unit supported the Hungarian government in its repressive measures.

Discussion

These models obviously are not exhaustive of the alternatives that the future may provide. Also even within the models, depending upon variations in the parameters, there are multiple complications we have not even begun to sketch. As mentioned earlier, these are not equilibrium models. They are intended merely to permit discussion of the range of variation potentially inherent in the existing world situation. Despite these deficiencies in the models and in the discussion necessarily based upon them, it should nonetheless be apparent that national decisions seemingly unrelated to normative consequences may have extremely important side effects with respect to these normative consequences. For instance, present American policy designed to prevent nuclear diffusion may perhaps permit maintenance of a bipolar world with the prospects for world order inherent in that bipolarism. It may alternatively fail to prevent diffusion and also fail to encourage such alternatives as a European system, thus bypassing either a stabilized bipolarity or a four bloc system for a nonstable bloc system in which the restraints of international law are poorly developed. Even though bipolarity may provide a less stable legal structure than a "balance of power" system there are not improbable alternatives even less favorable for the development of international law than loose bipolarity. Even the détente, which is commonly regarded as one of the foundations of an expanded world legal order, may have the opposite consequences. It may help destabilize bipolarity at a time when the possible alternatives are worse from the standpoint of world order.

There are possible conflicts between the policies best designed to secure law-abiding behavior and those best designed to maintain the strategic interests of the United States. For instance, every time the United States engages in a Bay of Pigs, a Guatemalan coup, or even in bombing north of the seventeenth parallel in Vietnam, it weakens the already loosened fabric of international law. The failure to engage in such actions may injure American strategic interests. Yet American strategic interests, although not identical with the prospects for world order, are not unrelated to them. Sacrifice of these strategic interests may impede the development either of any kind of universalistic system of norms or of one consonant—or at least not inconsistent—with our values and interests. Questions of this kind are always difficult to assess; they involve choices at the margin, large uncertainties, and competing values. None is susceptible to dogmatic or facile answer such that one can assert "policy A builds law and policy B tears law apart," even with respect to the particular norm at issue.

The argument that the best way to build law is to act lawfully, although not entirely incorrect, obviously rests on a form of legal determinism that will not withstand serious analysis. Moreover, there are interests and values other than those that flow from the development of a system of international law.

Thus the truism that the United States has an interest in upholding, maintaining, and enlarging the area of international law obscures as much as it clarifies. There can be little doubt that if the United States could choose that world of all possible worlds in which it wished to participate as a nation, it would be a world organized according to strong principles of international law. It would be a world that maintained freedom of political choice for the peoples of the various nations; access to supranational and impartial tribunals for violations of human rights by national governments; noninterference in the affairs of individual nations except perhaps in pursuit of an international bill of rights; the outlawry of the use of force except in the pursuit of recognized common interests; objective standards for recognition; international governance of space, the seas, and Arctic regions; international control of violent fluctuations of the commodity markets; and developed supranational law in those geographic regions and functional areas where a common framework of customs, values, and economic development permit a highly developed set of common legal rules. Yet it defies at least this writer's imagination to project an institutional development that would support this kind of body of law. In a world in which we must choose from among a set of bad alternatives the least bad, we will continue to be confronted with hard and ambiguous choices. Some policies may seem best adapted to supporting the development of international institutions, others to implementing one or another international norm (perhaps at the expense of still some other international norm), others to promoting American strategic interests or political values. Some policies may seem to provide the greatest opportunity for the development of world order if they succeed. These may possibly create the greatest risks for maintaining even that minimal degree of world order we presently have should they fail.

No discussion at this level of generality could hope to provide any hard answers to such questions. The choices that will face our statesmen will be choices defined by the actual sets of circumstances that confront them—circumstances that are at best only vaguely predictable now. A discussion at this level of generality, however, may reveal some of the reasons why the choices are hard, what alternatives may compete for our attention, and what factors may play a role in our decision. It may also provide a framework within which our thoughts about the matter can be organized in advance, so that the choices may be perceived in terms of their intermediate as well as of their immediate contexts and consequences.

We have recently passed through an episode in which the United States sought to have the United Nations punish the Soviet Union for refusing to contribute toward the support of institutional measures that were incompatible with perceived Soviet interests. Suspension of Soviet membership obviously would have been incompatible with the functioning of the United Nations in a bipolar world. Yet in the absence of a genuine world consensus on institutions and values, was it not perhaps unreasonable to expect the Soviet Union to use its scarce resources to support measures designed to bring about a world community not in accord with Soviet values? Was not Soviet recalcitrance at least in part the consequence of an effort to shift the burden of intervention from the United States and its allies to an international organization whose useful functions in the international system were different from those which we attempted to impose on it? No doubt from the standpoint of the values the United States wanted to implement, United Nations ventures in the Congo, among others, were perceived as helpful. No doubt American and Western European intervention in the Congo was made easier by reason of United Nations cover. Perhaps failure to act would have produced chaos in the Congo and the disintegration of the Congolese state. Perhaps alternatively, though not surely, UN intervention prevented successful revolution by a radical Congolese grouping that would have squandered the resources of the Congo and that would have fettered the Congolese people with a bloodthirsty and inefficient tyranny. Surely, however, the actions taken were not designed to secure Soviet support for the peace-keeping activities of the United Nations, or for the role of the Secretary General; nor were they even designed to demonstrate to the Asian and African nations the development of "objective" and impartial enforcement procedures by the United Nations.

The UN has recently taken measures against the Rhodesians. It has yet to take measures against the Soviet bloc or other authoritarian nations for violations of human rights within national territory. Should action against Rhodesia be opposed on the ground either that it is a violation of domestic jurisdiction or that the Asian and African states will not support actions against violations of human rights when these involve the rights of white people? Alternatively should such actions be supported because they are politically expedient, because they constitute a first step toward widespread UN jurisdiction in the area of the violation of human rights, or because any good that can be supported constitutes an appropriate basis for action? How do such decisions affect the structural processes of international law and interact with other decisions to promote one or another of the alternative possible international systems?

We have not begun to discuss these questions; yet clearly they deserve systematic discussion. Generally laymen and also scholars have argued in terms of simplistic notions and of projections of existing lines of development. If scientific answers to these important questions cannot be obtained and if intuition will prove more important than quantification, symbolic logic, and sustained argument, yet systematic discussion is likely to reveal interconnections, turning points, and unconsidered alternatives that are essential to informed intuition and to selected empirical investigations that are related to these informed intuitions.

We have adumbrated the truism that law and international organization, if pursued too single-mindedly, may undercut the development of both law and organization. We can all agree that it would be unwise either to overstress the impact of the social and political structure of world politics on the normative structure of the international system or to fail to recognize the relationship between the two. We know that placing our ambitions too low forsakes the possibility of progress and that placing our ambitions too high may assure retrogression. What we lack is a sense of ordered relationship between national policy, international organization, international norm, and international system. In short, we are ignorant where we need knowledge and full of abstract generalization where we require articulated theory.

CHAPTER 5

World Parties and World Order

GEORGE MODELSKI

PARTIES are an essential feature of every modern political order. Indeed no state today could be judged complete unless backed by a party system of one kind or another. Statements to this effect raise few objections; but their obvious relevance to world politics at large is seldom, if ever, elaborated. For the thoughtful student such observations lead to some interesting questions: Is a party system a necessary element of a modern world order? Under what conditions and with what results could such a system emerge on the world scene?

In contemporary affairs parties are both an instrument of political struggle and a form of political cooperation. They operate most often at the national level and that is the context in which we have been accustomed to think of them. Certain parties—most notably Marxist parties—have long viewed their activities as global in nature; for them "workers of the world, unite" has never been an empty slogan. Nevertheless and to this day, world party politics remains an area in which (because of the scarcity of real world parties) imaginative construction of the future yields greater insights than painstaking empirical research.

"World party politics" is a phrase often used in this chapter and therefore demands clarification. We propose to use the phrase to refer to an arrangement of world politics wherein a political struggle at the world level is carried on by one, two, or more political organizations which correspond in essential features to national political parties as we know them. This means that world parties (systems of conflict and cooperation) can develop around the world political institutions (such as the United Nations) and on world issues (such as colonialism), and these parties contest and influence the process of debate and decision and seek to move events in directions desired by them. We would expect such world parties to be stable, permanent organizations primarily focusing on a broad range of world issues and acting to formulate *world* (not *national*) interests—even though such world interests may be seen through the distorting lenses of partisanship. The parties and party systems thus operating may or may not be related to parties active or operating at national or local levels, just as in federal systems national political organizations may or may not be geared to politics at the state or county levels. Such world parties form the subject of this chapter.

Conflict and cooperation are, of course, themes familiar to students of international relations. The form they have assumed most often in traditional contexts—the monarchical state system in Europe (1648-1914) and the contemporary universal nation-state system—have been alliances, blocs, coalitions, and bilateral and occasionally multilateral compacts but (most important for our purposes), always of an inter-governmental kind. Alliances exhibit analogies to world parties because they share the characteristic of being world-level cooperative entities; they must not, however, be viewed as identical. In addition to their governmental character the features which distinguish alliances from parties are their specific scope (often contained in explicit documents) and hence a tendency toward "selfishness" and "opportunism," their limited duration, and their frequent concern with war or war-like crises. Much effort is needed to keep the distinction in the forefront of our attention because most of what traditionally passes for international cooperation is precisely of this later kind.

Parties arise at the level of world politics only under certain favorable conditions, essentially those of considerable institutionalization. World parties, however, are almost nonexistent in the nation-state system composed of autonomous, self-sufficient nation-states that claim exclusive loyalties, exercise full territorial jurisdiction, and maintain links solely at the intergovernmental level. The pure nation-state system is, of course, no more than a model of world politics and we cannot be certain about the degree to which the real world now approximates the model. We can be more confident, however, in asserting that a trend exists in the direction of a more fully textured world society which is more favorable to the growth of world party politics.

WORLD SOCIETY AS A MODERN POLITICAL SYSTEM

Acceptance of the feasibility of a world party system depends on a general conception of politics and particularly of world politics. Those who see international relations as a realm characteristically different from domestic politics, one that deals with relations between autonomous political units acknowledging no common superior and each in complete control of its own means of violence,[1] expect cooperation and conflict at the international level to assume only the limited forms afforded by alliances, and they find nothing comparable occurring in national societies, especially well-integrated societies. However, if these same interactions are viewed as an arena of world politics in which universal processes of politics unfold in accordance with ap-

[1] Raymond Aron, *War and Peace: A Theory of International Relations* (New York 1966) (esp. the Introduction) is the most magisterial recent treatment of this conception; see also Stanley Hoffmann's *The State of War* (New York 1965), viii, 13-14.

plicable special circumstances, then an inquiry into world parties assumes some plausibility.

Yet we must note at the outset that the conventional diplomatic system, as well as conventional international law, are both organized on the basis of the first concept. They each take as their starting point what we have already described as the model of the pure nation-state system. This represents the world as divided between nation-states, each one of them controlled by one central government, responsible for all activities in its territory and each accorded monopoly control over the contacts of its nationals with all the outside world. The tendency of such a system is to discourage, if not to suppress as inimical to national loyalties and subversive of established governments, the cross-boundary contacts essential to a world party system. The conventional system is one of minimum contact and maximum self-sufficiency.

Doubt may be entertained whether the minimum contact–maximum self-sufficiency assumptions correctly represent conditions found in the contemporary world. Indeed they must be carefully scrutinized. A simple monopoly of control over extraterritorial interactions may be practicable and even acceptable in a situation of minimum contact and maximum self-sufficiency. But it becomes difficult to maintain and to justify when interactions occur at a high rate.

Concrete evidence that would allow us to evaluate these assumptions is hard to come by. Nor is the methodology for dealing with these questions well developed: how do we judge the self-sufficiency of small or large local communities within national societies? For in spite of obvious relevance as well as the wealth of impressionistic observations of the "world is getting smaller" variety the extent of global interdependence has not been authoritatively determined and changes in the degree of that interdependence have not been adequately studied.

The most popular index of global interdependence has traditionally been trade. United Nations Trade statistics allow us to estimate that in the last decade or so some 20 percent of world output passed each year through foreign trade. This is a substantial figure and it shows that the world's welfare substantially depends upon the state of international trade. There is however little concrete evidence to suggest whether this proportion has been rising or falling in recent years. Deutsch and Eckstein have cited evidence for a "law of declining importance of international trade" as industrialization makes national economies less dependent upon outside sources of commodities.[2]

2 Karl Deutsch and Alexander Eckstein, "National Industrialization and the Declining Share of the International Economic Sector 1890-1959," *World Politics*, 13, 2 (January 1961), 267-99.

(Deutsch's earlier work on international mail-flows has tended to show that since the turn of the century and for the world as a whole domestic mail has been rising at a higher rate than foreign mail, suggesting a law of the diminishing importance of foreign mail.) [3] Morgan has found however that the theorem is not supported in the income-trade patterns of some forty countries he has studied; he adduces evidence to show that in recent decades the developed, hence industrialized, countries have increased their dependence on foreign trade while underdeveloped economies typically have reduced such dependence. But both sets had by 1958-1959 a nearly identical degree of integration in the world economy, 20.1 percent for the underdeveloped and 21.5 for the developed countries.[4]

Global data tend to hide the great differences that exist in these respects among countries. The world's largest, most populous and politically most important countries are also among those proportionately least involved in international trade. Thus, for the United States, foreign trade in 1959 represented only 7 percent of its Gross National Product, for the Soviet Union, 5 percent; China, 9 percent; and India, 11 percent. By contrast, a large number of smaller countries, both developed and underdeveloped, depend upon foreign trade to a considerable extent: examples include (again in GNP percentages) Australia, 26; Britain, 30; New Zealand, 43; Ceylon, 63; Bolivia, 66; Netherlands, 74.[5] This means that the most powerful governments tend to be those least sensitive to the state of the world economy and hence possibly also world order.

At the political level global interdependence has risen dramatically as the result of the development of nuclear weapons and the consequent decline in the hard-shell which was thought to protect the territorial nation-state; John H. Herz's discussion of this problem has become a classic.[6] Empirical data to document greater political interaction is harder to come by. Partial data on centralization show that the rate of increase in the global function represented by the United Nations and the specialized agencies, however small that function is in absolute terms, is higher than the increase of resources devoted to national governmental purposes.[7] Data on interstate visits by po-

[3] Karl Deutsch, "Shifts in the Balance of Communication Flows: A Problem in the Measurement of International Relations," *Public Opinion Quarterly*, 20, No. 1 (Spring 1956), 143-60.

[4] Theodore Morgan, "Economic Relationships among Nations: The Pattern of Commodity Trade" in Bert F. Hoselitz ed., *Economics and the Idea of Mankind* (New York 1965), 161-63.

[5] Bruce Russett et al., *World Handbook of Political and Social Indicators* (New Haven 1964), 164-65.

[6] *International Politics in the Atomic Age* (New York 1959), esp. Part I.

[7] George Modelski, *Decentralization of Authority and Concentration of Power in International Systems* (mimeo., 1964), 5-10; Paul Smoker, "A Preliminary Study of

litical leaders of the highest rank (heads of state, heads of government, foreign ministers) reveal that face-to-face contacts at this level have risen dramatically in the past one hundred years, so as to constitute a qualitative change in the international system. Significant in particular is the amount of time now given to multilateral conferences. (Table I)

TABLE I

HIGH-LEVEL INTERSTATE VISITS, 1865, 1945, 1965

Number of States		Total visits	Visits to Multi-lateral Meetings
78	1865	18	—
77	1945	220	110
128	1965	1726	618

SOURCE: Inter-State Visits Project.

Incomplete evidence thus suggests that in the global system interdependence is substantial and may be rising especially in some aspects of political interaction; a model of world politics which derives its prescriptions from the postulates of maximum self-sufficiency would therefore seem to be inadequate on empirical grounds. But theoretical reflections too would dictate caution and argue its inherent instability. Because of its resistance to cross-national institutionalization the pure nation-state system does not contain within itself the means of its own self-maintenance. Because of the paucity of contacts within, it is conducive to polarization; it is too simple and too unspecialized a system to provide for its own regulation in case of serious conflict. A world in which the only regulatory mechanisms (those governing the production of autonomy and order on a global scale) are national governments, consisting most often of only a small number of great powers, is too brittle a structure to tolerate much stress.

These considerations suggest that the pure nation-state system model needs revision or replacement, even if the alternatives to it are not entirely clear. As we have seen in incomplete evidence, global interdependence is hardly of such uniform nature that the only logical alternative to the nation-state system is a world-government model of world politics, perhaps the one proposed by Clark and Sohn.[8] These two authors explore a model of limited world government consequent upon universal disarmament, the presumed destruction of all nuclear weapons, and transfer of the monopoly of force to the United Nations.

an International Integrative Subsystem" in *Proceedings of the International Peace Research Association Inaugural Conference* (Assen 1966), 40-43 documents the exponential rate at which nongovernmental international organizations have been forming in the period 1870-1961.

[8] *World Peace through World Law*, 3rd edn. (Cambridge 1967).

It would be hasty of any political scientist to assert that such a development could not occur during the span of one generation since profound changes of a revolutionary character take place almost daily. But for purposes of thinking effectively two or three decades ahead, this particular series of changes, based as it is to be on an unprecedented redistribution of the means of violence which have been the prime movers of the system of states for centuries, seems too bold to contemplate in earnest. It may be argued that the most positive achievement of the historic state system has been to consolidate a situation in which the means of force, instead of being monopolized, are distributed among a number of centers with some semblance of a balance of power. Proposals for the centralization of all power at one point therefore run counter to centuries of accumulated experience and advantage.

It should be pointed out, however, that the Clark-Sohn model requires, as do all models of world government, a world party system for effective operation. The authors themselves do not discuss parties or problems of party organization because these matters would not arise within the scope of amendments to the Charter of the United Nations; in any event, such matters rarely engage the interest of constitutional draftsmen. Even the United States Constitution ignores parties even though it is hard to image how it could work without them. We would surmise, however, that an effective world party system is a precondition of the Clark-Sohn model. Indeed, a world government could conceivably become, and could become so more easily than a less centralized system, the object of a seizure of power by a single party, hence an avenue through which single-party control could be established on a world scale.

Another model helpful in the discussion of alternative world orders is the model of the regional bloc system. Conceptually it raises problems which in the end are essentially those of a system composed of a few large states. The likelihood of world politics moving in that particular direction may not be very great, but may be greater than for a world government. A regional bloc system might, in some or all of the blocs, stimulate the growth of regional party politics. Notable developments have already occurred in this regard in Western Europe and will be discussed below. Caucus or clique politics of sorts have been evident in recent years in the Organization of African Unity—with its division between the radicals once led by Kwame Nkrumah, Sékou Touré, and Ben Bella, and the conservatives principally based upon party links established among French-speaking African leaders by men such as Houphouet Boigny of the Ivory Coast. The Arab world has witnessed a parallel division between socialist-leaning radicals, led by Nasser and driven on by groups such as the Baath Party centered in Syria (all-Arab in inspiration and international in organization), and the conservatives, organized by the rulers of Saudi Arabia. These rudimentary processes may also be observed in Latin America and in Asia, which presage the beginnings of regional party politics under favorable circumstances. They might gain strength if regional bloc organization increased. But as concerns global party politics they offer no particular promise except inasmuch as habits of cooperation learned at this level could be transferred to the world arena. Conceivably though, and certainly in the case of full-fledged blocs, such trends could take place only at the expense of global solidarity and as such they would tend to work to the detriment of world politics.

Thus to discuss world party politics in a more favorable context (we assign a higher probability to this than to the two preceding models), we require a world in which the political system is at once significantly decentralized and yet contains within it a variety of elements productive of autonomy and order. In this model we would not expect all such elements to reside solely or even predominantly in national governments—even though governments might be counted upon, in line with the doctrine of "dédoublement fonctionel," to contribute to the performance of global functions. Rather we expect it to be composed of a variety and multiplicity of organized units each contributing its own share of public goods. Let us call this the "multiple autonomy" model of world politics and, without excessively particularizing it at this stage, let us say that it would have to be a model in which parties are constitutive parts considered productive of order and autonomy.

For purposes of this model we are assuming, first, the existence of a world society within which such global activities as party systems can properly be anchored. By this we do *not* mean that all the world's inhabitants now constitute, or will resolve to form in the near or even distant future, one big happy family wherein everyone loves everyone. And by world society we do *not* mean the sum total of the world's social interactions but only those interactions that have global significance, that connote global interdependence, and stand opposite to tendencies of local or regional self-sufficiency. The location or geographical extension of these interactions is less important than their *potential* for worldwide impact and dispersion. In other words, we are interested not only in cross-boundary activities which in a crude sense are "international" (as foreign trade obviously is), but also in activities which locationally or organizationally or in some other respects could be national (e.g. a research laboratory) but whose operations (e.g. a new process) may have a world impact (thanks to a global communications network in that branch of science or technology).

There is a global network of political, economic, and cultural relationships in the broadest sense of these terms, and this network is moreover well-structured and articulated—we give the name of world society to this network. The principal components of this society would be the world's political institutions: the United Nations family, its members, and its associated and consultative organizations; the world economy which is composed of the world financial system, international corporations, global transport and communications networks; and world culture; including the great religions as well as, to borrow John Galbraith's phrase, the world's educational and scientific estate which is composed of world science and learning, the great universities, and the world's professions.

Second, we are further postulating a "multi-layer" concept of society, one which envisages social processes, including political activities, as occurring in a number of territorial layers.[9] For most purposes it will suffice to think of three such layers: the local, the national, and the global (in certain cases we might wish to add a "regional layer," as in the analysis of regional bloc processes). These three main layers are of course interconnected and in the ultimate and most basic sense constitute together one social universe, but such relatedness is never complete and for certain important purposes and especially those of analysis, these layers may be treated as relatively independent. Anterior judgment as to the "superiority" or "precedence" of any one of those layers over any of the others does not inhere in this analysis, but the shifting balance of interdependence between the layers and the varying evaluations to which they are subjected by their "constituents" are among the key constitutional problems of any social system. In this chapter we concentrate upon the global layer of society because within that layer world party politics must find its social context, its support, and its justification; attention needs to be drawn explicitly to this layer because its discernment often demands careful observation by nation-centered students of politics. That such a layer exists is beyond reasonable doubt, but its precise shape, strength, and location at any given time needs to be the object of careful and continuous research. As an initial hypothesis for purposes of study we expect that the growth of the world party system crucially depends upon the increased weight, scope, and autonomy of this global layer in a crucial way.

Third, in a loose and general sense, the global layer produces, discovers, discusses, and processes or fails to process, world problems. War may be cited as an example of a world problem, as may the

[9] This is an adaptation to world politics of Morton Grodzins' concept of the "marble cake of government" as set forth in *The American System: A New View of Government in the United States* (Chicago 1966) , ed., Daniel J. Elazar.

distribution of nuclear weapons, nuclear tests and air pollution, racial discrimination, the population explosion and inequalities in world income. We might assert that as a general rule world problems should optimally be handled at the world level, by the political and non-political, governmental and nongovernmental organizations that operate within it. But we know too that the institutions, organizations, and mechanisms at that level lack elaboration and resources or may be unevenly developed. They are no doubt better at identifying and discussing world problems than dealing with them; improved communications have clearly made an impact in this field; they have yet to evolve into effective problem solvers for world tasks. In the process of "dédoublement fonctionnel," such tasks will in some measure be attempted by national governments, especially those with identifiable or traditional interests and those alive to feelings of particular responsibility (as for instance, the United States government which in recent years has evinced special interest in the world food problem). However, we would not necessarily regard this as the only or necessarily the best way of dealing with such problems.

To sum up: world problems occur within that social layer which we call world society and they either do or do not concern world politics. Those bearing on autonomy and world order (all those we have named do) become issues of world politics and the concern of its institutions. It is around the processing of those issues and the contests to which they give rise that world parties may be expected to grow. In short, world party politics: (1) raises, debates, and resolves world problems; and (2) organizes the contest so that world political authority may pursue the processing of these problems.

The first function, the shaping of world debate, is probably the more important of the two functions—in its course alignments and alliances occur which persist and carry over to other debates and long-lasting values and preferences crystallize which, on occasion, may give shape and color to decades of world history. At other times, there might, of course, be no resolution. Take, for example, the issue of economic development as it has concerned world public opinion since early in the 1950's. A remarkable characteristic of that debate has been complete, worldwide unanimity on the desirability of industrialization and growth; a unanimity that supplies conclusive evidence that the global system is fully capable of producing consensus on basic values. This consensus is particularly surprising because that unanimous opinion was held in the highly developed areas which were most likely to benefit most from such growth as they developed still further, and was also held by the most backward areas which would find it more and more difficult to keep up the pace and would also be bearing the costs and the burdens of this process. There was also, of course, disagreement in this debate as to the methods and the speed of economic growth—the two main viewpoints coinciding with certain divisions in world public opinion—"free enterprise" *versus* "the planned economy." Participants in that debate would include government spokesmen and public officials of many states, businessmen, economists, professional men, and many others, on a variety of occasions and in many forums. We can say little that is concrete about the outcome of it because debates of this kind are, by their very nature, unstructured and, on the surface frequently inconclusive, but it would be hard to deny that the shape, as the quality, of the process of economic development in many countries over the past decade has not been substantially affected by it. It may well be through debates of this nature and others which may concern, for instance, the merits of democratic government, the value of space exploration, or the propriety of guerilla warfare, that the conceptions of what might be called the "world interest"[10] are from time to time formulated and reformulated. World parties can have a critical role in this process, as they serve not only to formulate the issues for debate and help influence their outcomes but also, and principally, help to relate one issue to another, reduce their mutual incompatibilities, and, finally, tie them up with the process of implementation.

Secondly, parties are concerned with positions of power and authority; they are devices to contest and fill such positions. Globally, the positions which are or can become objects of world party politics are of two kinds: (1) formal, in international organizations, and (2) informal, concerned with "world leadership." The formal posts are commonly associated with the central political organizations, such as the United Nations family, but may also extend to *ad hoc* international arrangements (such as the Indochina Truce Supervision Organizations) or to basically nonpolitical bodies, such as the International Olympic Committee. Most of these posts are subject to an election process. Among the important prizes in this election process in world bodies have been the office of Secretary-General of the United Nations, and the nonpermanent seats on the Security Council. Some elections to the latter have been sharply contested at considerable length and became the object of semi-party competition. Other coveted posts include judgeships on the International Court, seats on the Economic and Social Council, and the Presidency and the Vice-Presidencies of the General Assembly. Many of these positions are not fully elective since some are filled in part on considerations of rotation or geo-

---

[10] Kenneth Boulding, "The Concept of World Interest," ed., Hoselitz, *Idea of Mankind*, 41-62; the innovative role of parties is examined by Thomas Lowi in "Toward Functionalism in Political Science: The Case of Innovation in Party Systems," *American Political Science Review*, 57, No. 3 (1963), 570-83.

graphic distribution. There is, moreover, no one single post significant enough for its occupation to constitute a political victory. In respect to the Security Council at any rate, the United States has consistently succeeded in having its supporters and followers elected to the vacancies[11] but the limited powers of that body reduce the scope of this achievement.

More influential though less easily acquired are the informal positions of international leadership such as those of "world leader," "trusted mediator," "articulator of world interest." There can be little doubt that some such positions exist, yet it is far from easy to say much that is precise about them. Certain political figures, for instance John F. Kennedy, Dag Hammarskjold, Jan Smuts or, for that matter, Lord Russell, came to acquire positions of leadership or influence at certain periods which were global in significance. Such positions are attained through substantive achievement and the espousal of widely shared values. Those positions are easier to reach if candidates for it enjoy the support of a "world party" and they are easier to occupy if their holders continue to enjoy such backing, as though through continuous reelection. Here world party politics helps to conduct the "electoral campaign," and organizes support and rounds up votes for the candidates and the policies they espouse. In contemporary world society such processes are unstructured and party processes are only weakly built around them. Leadership is still commonly understood to appertain to countries, yet no country can lead or decide anything, only men can and if we look at the structure of world leadership we shall notice that it has always been exercised by men of special qualities. It is true that men from the larger and more powerful states have usually had a better chance of attaining such positions but they have never had a monopoly of them. The working of the party system tends to further equalize the chances of reaching such positions.

The stakes of world party politics can thus be twofold: (1) the molding of world values and world public opinion through debating world problems, (2) the occupancy of positions in the world authority system.

Some Elementary Concepts

Before we continue the discussion of world parties let us look at a few terms which are generally used in discussions of parties within

11 Marshall R. Singer and Barton Sensenis, III, "Elections Within the United Nations: An Experimental Study Utilizing Statistical Analysis," *International Organization*, 17 (Autumn 1963), 901-25. They conclude "at least since 1950 there has existed within the United Nations a pro-United States coalition on cold war issues, a coalition that has had enormous influence in United Nations elections . . . our data show that the nations elected to important offices are, in fact, the powerful nations closely aligned with the United States in the cold war and interdependent with it economically."

the framework of domestic politics. We shall note that the vocabulary of party politics is closely linked with that of electoral systems. This occurs even though some parties, e.g. totalitarian parties maintaining a single-party regime, hold on to power without the benefit of even show elections. The reason is that parties form part of the process of which elections are a manifestation; they function to maintain two-way communications flows between the electorate and those in authority. World party politics may or may not have an electoral basis but they, too, would serve to maintain that flow.

Constituency

The earth is now divided among a determinate number of independent national units of which there were 126 at the end of 1965. As all of them currently hold equal status, this means that each of these units plays the role of a separate constituency for purposes of representation in global political institutions; these national constituencies are the significant units of the world party system. Each one of these units is entitled to send the same number of representatives to international meetings at which it is represented, for instance five full delegates to United Nations General Assembly meetings. Frequently, of course, delegations are smaller than they could be, but this is unimportant because in most of these organizations each delegation is entitled to cast only one vote. "One state, one vote" is the general rule, with the exception of the financial and certain other technical bodies. For this reason the contemporary world political system may for all practical purposes be regarded as one of single-member constituencies.

We must bear in mind that the object of world party politics is not the "conquest" or the "winning" of national governments but ensuring that national constituencies select representatives committed to the achievement of certain objectives at the world level (the stakes of party politics have already been reviewed). While such achievement may be helped by developments at the national level, the connection is by no means a direct one. The complexion of the national government need have no simple or direct relationship to the representatives its constituency dispatches or instructs on the global level. Hence the task of world leadership should be thought to reside above all in the forming of policy and opinion at the world level rather than in altering the composition of national governments.

Two constituency characteristics may be remarked upon at this stage: national constituencies tend to be unequal (especially as regards population), and their boundaries tend to remain fixed. In essential features the world political system recalls British parliamentary politics of the eighteenth century as described in Sir Lewis Namier's celebrated work:[12] widely varying constituencies, some of them known as "rotten boroughs" (because they could be bought by and were often in the power of one man) , a network of personal and institutional relationships, and an emerging and already lively party system. The world too, is organized in a large number of greatly diverse units, unequal in all respects except that they are of equal status in international law. The importance attached moreover to the inviolability of national boundaries ensures that changes likely to equalize such inequalities are improbable except through voluntary schemes of federation or amalgamation, and those attempts have seldom been successful. In earlier eras, territorial boundaries were normally in flux; today they are virtually immutable.

Parliamentary arrangements of federal systems, of course, frequently comprise fixed constituencies: the United States Senate, for instance, has two seats for each of the states of the union irrespective of size or population, and is, also, more powerful than the House of Representatives whose membership is elected from constituencies basically equal in population and periodically redrawn in accord with census results. The fixed constituencies of the global system underscore the role of territoriality in world politics; they produce particularistic attachments and their spokesmen tend to view themselves (in Burke's classical distinction drawn in his speech to the electors of Bristol in 1774) as instructed agents and advocates and not as representatives. The unequal constituencies bring about unequal commitment to common goals; a lack of representativeness on the part of some and dearth of responsibility on the part of others. Neither feature prevents the rise of parties; it means that the resulting party system is likely to be a loose one.

The Electoral Process

Parliamentary assemblies may be recruited by election or by appointment. In world organizations, members are, as a rule, appointed, principally by authorities at the national level. This feature we refer to as the "vertical fusion" of the selection process, and we may recall too that for United States Senators selection by state legislatures (hence a degree of vertical fusion) obtained until early in the twentieth century. Direct election, hence a measure of vertical separation, came as the result of a Constitutional amendment in 1913. Some of the consequences of "vertical fusion" for the character of the global party system are: The most elementary and so familiar that its political implications are ignored, is the fact that the affiliation of the repre-

12 Lewis Namier, *The Structure of Politics at the Accession of George III*, 2nd edn. (London 1957) .

sentative at the global level is governed by changes in the political complexion of his national administration. Changes in the behavior of Cuban representatives at the United Nations after 1959 flowed from gradual alterations in the character of the authorities at home. This is certainly the way things move as a general rule, though if we checked a number of instances we might find that a great many changes of government at home had not led to alterations in the composition of delegations in New York. In principle, again, all delegations are subject to instructions from their home government, and yet here again delegates whose home office does not or because of weak communications cannot instruct them in detail on all issues, enjoy considerable latitude of choice, enabling them to develop some more advantageous "horizontal" links. This situation does nevertheless contrast strongly with political systems such as those in which the national level maintains a vertical separation from the state or local government level, and this is true not only of federal systems (in the United States a state may have a Republican governor but send two Democratic senators to Washington), but also in most countries that maintain some degree of local government and decentralization. Again, the world level has no electoral process for the whole system, no simultaneous election campaign during which issues common to that system could be generally debated. The present appointive, "fused" system therefore produces the effect of "staggered" elections.

Once more, these features of world politics do not destroy the possibility of a party system but severely influence its character. The fused character of the selection process militates against the growth of an autonomous world party system. In addition, the "staggering" of the selection process effects a lack of unity and makes it difficult to direct attention in an orderly fashion to a series of issues common to the system; rather issues are viewed only as they arise in crisis situations. The election mechanism of matching the debate of issues with changes in representation functions weakly at the global level.

Party Systems

A party system consists of (1) one or more political parties and (2) the rules and the procedures observed by the parties toward each other (or, in the case of the single party, toward its potential competitors). Parties are organizations for the conduct of the political struggle, and inasmuch as they are organizations and achieve the coordination of diverse activities, they require some degree of formal structure, of continuity, and of common values (among which values organizational loyalty would have a most important place). We would therefore distinguish them from cliques—unorganized, transient, and based on personal rather than organizational loyalties, and from temporary voting alignments on specific issues. Insofar as they engage in political competition, parties shape and organize the political contest, give it structure and regularity. We have already examined the principal stakes of party conflict; in world politics the stakes of party conflict (as distinct from the stakes of world politics in general) are not really high because they are now diffuse but they may increase; as they do rise, the importance of rules to govern this competition will also rise. The most important of these undoubtedly is the degree of tolerance parties are prepared to extend to each other's activities.

In summary, the study of party politics at the global level requires that we think of world politics in terms that we are not accustomed to use. Party politics can occur in conditions of world politics but its specific shape will be governed by the special character of that milieu. At all levels of politics, party systems reflect the polity and the society; we shall now examine how the decentralized character of world politics, and of world society, affects the world party system.

PARTIES IN A DECENTRALIZED SYSTEM

The modern party systems well-known to political scientists have been those of highly centralized states, e.g. those of Britain, France, or the Soviet Union. In such states the interplay of parties is almost absurdly simple and reduces itself, as in the case of British politics, to capturing a majority of seats in the House of Commons; in the Soviet system it is even simpler for it boils down to preventing the establishment of competitive organizations. The classical studies of political parties, such as that of Maurice Duverger[13] have been concerned primarily with those simple systems and have largely ignored the experience of federal systems in which the multi-layered nature of large-scale politics comes into view more clearly. Duverger himself describes the American party system as unique and hardly deals with it at all. As the nature and function of party politics substantially depend upon the type of political system, decentralization, which is the most characteristic feature of the global layer of politics, must clearly exert a profound influence.

General reflection alone would, indeed, suggest that a party system, and possibly a two-party system in particular, should be particularly important in a noncentralized polity. By definition such polities lack strong central political authority, such as a dominant central government, which customarily monopolizes the maintenance of order. If a noncentralized polity is to continue in an orderly fashion it has to devise and maintain other ways of integrating its diverse elements into a coherent whole. Several such forms of integration suggest them-

[13] M. Duverger, *Political Parties: Their Organization and Activity in the Modern State* (New York, 2nd edn., 1963).

selves; among those which occupy an important place are common values and a common culture, and possibly a common (centralized or noncentralized) economic and exchange system. Unfortunately the study of decentralized polities has been a field marked by underdevelopment and we cannot cite much evidence for or against these propositions from the existing literature. Further reflection also suggests however that parties and a party system might well have a crucial role to play in such polities because they are critically political institutions directly participating in the political competition. It could even be argued that under certain yet to be specified conditions, parties might be instrumental in maintaining a noncentralized political system. Limited, yet suggestive, evidence in support of this proposition comes from two directions: the experience of federal politics, and the study of certain patterns of tribal politics.

Centralization is always a matter of degree; among political systems at the national level, the federal state is the least centralized. Morton Grodzins recently depicted the United States federal system as one of "decentralization by mild chaos"; his research in a variety of fields has shown a relationship of interdependence between governmental decentralization and the structure of American parties which he calls the "decentralizers." "The parties," Grodzins wrote, "are responsible for both the existence and form of the considerable measure of decentralization that exists in the United States"; in fact they function as "decentralizers," that is as the mechanisms which make decentralization possible.[14] He is careful to point out that parties do not, of themselves, cause decentralization; that situation can be traced to a variety of political, social, and economic conditions. But they make it possible for a decentralized system to work at a high level of effectiveness. It may not be unreasonable to suppose that parties could play a similar role in other decentralized systems.

Evidence of a different kind comes from a report by Benet on the social and economic structure of Berber tribes in the highlands of Southern Morocco.[15] The most salient feature of their society is the complete absence of centralizing institutions. The Berbers are organized into segments or cantons each occupying territory of fairly equal size, usually a valley some 8 to 10 kilometers across. Observers have found that each canton possesses "an acute consciousness of its own singularity." In some ways this isolated highland society may

14 Grodzins, The American System, 385, 254-55.
15 F. Benet, "Explosive Markets: The Berber Highlands" 188-217; K. Polanyi et al., eds., Trade and Market in Early Empires (Glencoe 1957) , Benet's chief source is R. Montaigne, Les Berbères et le Makhazen dans le Sud du Maroc (Paris 1930).

be said to resemble an international system. As blood feuds and tribal clashes abound however, there is a need for integrative institutions. Markets fill this role in part and their influence indeed transcends the economic sphere. But what makes this society even more interesting for our purposes is the report that the cantons of the entire region "were affiliated to either one or the other of the two political parties which formed in this way intercantonal alliances." The result was a checkerboard pattern of party affiliation, the division of the cantons among the parties producing a form of equilibrium for the whole tribe. Observers regarded this division into parties as a guarantee of the survival of the cantons because in case of attack a canton could call upon the aid of other members of its party. Unfortunately the report says little else about the organization of these parties (as they consistently are called). We should have liked to know about the methods by which the parties coordinated their policies, carried out their decisions, and maintained solidarity. As it stands, the report carries interest because it deliberately links party politics to decentralization.

Superficial reasoning might lead to the view that noncentralized polities are inimical to political parties because such polities lack the strong focus which the contest for centralized authority, in a general election or in a coup d'état, lends to the functioning of the party system. The research cited suggests that decentralization, far from making parties superfluous, may indeed require them to play especially crucial roles. In other words and, if substantiated, this is a most important conclusion; we do not need a world state to have world parties, but we might have to have parties to operate a decentralized global system.

To explain such a conclusion we might have to argue that the role of parties in noncentralized systems is predicated upon the importance of personal contact in the functioning of "lateral" systems composed of segments of equal status. To a degree higher than hierarchical orders in which instructions travel down and information is expected to pass up the ladder irrespective of personal dispositions (even if the speed and the efficiency of that process may always be in doubt), systems of lateral organization depend on persuasion and bargaining and therefore also on personal, and frequently, face-to-face relationships.[16] Party organization may be envisaged as one of the essential ingredients assuring this condition.

[16] For an evaluation of the importance of "Personal Contact in Intergovernmental Organizations" see Chadwick Alger's paper in H. Kelman, ed., *International Behavior* (New York 1965), pp. 523-47; see also Chester Barnard's essay, "On Planning for World Government" in his *Organization and Management: Selected Papers* (New York 1948), 149-64.

PARLIAMENTARY AND EXTRA-PARLIAMENTARY WORLD PARTIES

"On the whole," writes Duverger, "the development of parties seems bound up with that of democracy, that is to say with the extension of popular suffrage and parliamentary prerogatives. The more political assemblies see their functions and independence grow, the more their members feel the need to group themselves according to what they have in common, so as to act in concert. The more the right to vote is extended and multiplied, the more necessary it becomes to organize the electors. . . . The rise of parties is thus bound up with the rise of parliamentary groups and electoral committees. Nevertheless some deviate from this general scheme. They originate outside the electoral and parliamentary cycle, and this fact is their most outstanding common characteristic."[17]

Duverger's distinction between parliamentary and extra-parliamentary parties is most apposite for our study because on the global level, too, we can readily distinguish these two basic types of party formation in embryo: the parliamentary party, essentially a form of persistent cooperation between delegates to the United Nations or other international organizations which takes the form of caucusing and bloc-voting, etc., and the extra-parliamentary party, of which the Communist Party is the principal example in its international manifestations and which owes its origins and principal strength to radical activities in national constituencies. At the global level, moreover, the process of extension of political participation is still in full swing and the extra-parliamentary fringe wields unusual strength. We could say that some of the difficulties of world politics reside in the necessity to combine in one global system parties of such diverse origin.

In recent decades "parliamentary diplomacy" has come to comprise an increasingly large share of world politics.[18] The practice of continuous multilateral conference devoted to nonspecific and frequently nontechnical subjects, the role of public and general debate in its proceedings, the importance of rules of procedure on such occasions, and the frequent resort to resolutions and other legislative acts has qualitatively changed the character of diplomacy and the skills required of national representatives. The processes have also brought about the necessity for such representatives to concert their action in a continuous fashion.

[17] Duverger, *Political Parties*, XXIII-XXIV.

[18] Philip P. Jessup, "Parliamentary Diplomacy: An Examination of the Legal Quality of the Rules of Procedure of Organs of the United Nations," *Recueil des Cours*, I (Leiden, 1957), 185-318; Jessup refers to an earlier definition of parliamentary diplomacy by Dean Rusk in *World Affairs Interpreter*, 26, No. 2 (Summer 1955), 121-22; for a discussion see also Herbert Spiro, *World Politics: The Global System* (Homewood, Ill., 1966), 134-53 and Hans Morgenthau, *Politics among Nations* (New York 1949), Chaps. 31, 32.

In his study of the United Nations General Assembly Sydney Bailey observes that "in an organization of States based on the principle of sovereign equality . . . a party system in the conventional sense has not evolved." But he does discuss the emergence of "an embryonic party system," and denies that the activities of organized groups in the Assembly are disreputable or tend to promote selfish sectional interests at the expense of moral principle. He distinguishes three types of association among states at the United Nations: the ad hoc coalition improvized to deal with a particular problem and which tends to disappear when the problem passes or changes in character; the caucusing group; and the bloc where states not only caucus together but also always act in unison. (The Communist group only falls into this last category) .[19]

Caucusing groups have been the most striking form of cooperation at the United Nations. The best known of these caucuses are the African and the Afro-Asian groups, the Latin Americans, the British Commonwealth, and the West European groups. The United Nations caucuses, largely and ostensibly based on regional affiliations, possess some attributes of parliamentary parties. They meet regularly, under a chairman and with an agenda; the meetings serve as occasions for coordinating voting positions (but without imposing binding decisions) , and they facilitate personal contact between members. The groups also arrange for nominations to positions reserved for regional representatives (e.g. for the Latin American seats on the Security Council) . While largely regional they also, in effect, represent groups characterized by a community of views and interests and exclude delegates alien to their own outlook (e.g. the Communist bloc; the African group excludes South Africa) . Their voting cohesion is far from perfect but shows consistency on some issues. One hesitates to call them parties mainly because they lack an explicit organization and explicit programs, because their membership overlaps a great deal, and because members themselves do not refer to them as parties.

Caucuses have been many in number, but parliamentary activity also has other occasions for expressing the views of delegates on contentious issues, among others through voting. Because of its simple yes-no structure of alternatives, voting by itself divides members of a parliamentary assembly into two basic groups each time a vote is taken. Ad hoc voting alignments may be subject to change, but in favorable conditions they tend to persist and form into groups of habitual co-voters. Hence overlaying the caucuses at the United Nations in recent years have been probably no more than three, and perhaps

[19] Sydney D. Bailey, *The General Assembly of the United Nations* (New York, rev. edn., 1964) , 21-24; see also Thomas Hovet, Jr., *Bloc Politics in the United Nations* (Cambridge, Mass. 1960) .

only two basic voting groups: the United States led coalition, the Communist bloc, and the Afro-Asian noncommitted groups, members of the last variously affiliating with one of the preceding two. Can we marshal data to show the existence of such groups? If they do exist, can they be regarded as world parties?

Alker and Russett[20] have carried out a factor analytical study of roll call votes at four United Nations General Assembly sessions in the period 1947 to 1961. The object of their study has been to determine who voted together, how frequently, and on what issues. Their analysis has revealed two main issues (or factors) underlying voting positions in the General Assembly: one of these they call the East-West factor—broadly those issues on which the Soviet Union is aligned on one side and the United States on the other and which include problem areas such as the cold war and colonialism; and the North-South factor—signifying issues such as nuclear tests and economic aid, on which the wealthier states and the great powers have lined up against the poorer and lesser states. A principal finding of the study is evidence that in the period under investigation the share of roll calls identifiable with the East-West factor has risen from 45 to 68 percent; the share of the next most important factor, the North-South factor, declined from 20 to 13 percent. Alker and Russett interpret this finding as proof of a tendency toward increasing polarization and express forebodings with regard to it; they seem to prefer a state of affairs in which delegates would not vote consistently to such a large degree.

I accept the Alker-Russett findings of the increasing saliency of the East-West factor but dispute their interpretation of the significance of this trend. I submit, as an alternative to their thesis, the proposition that the data disclose a trend toward the consolidation, in the General Assembly, of a two-party system; they, indeed, show that the scope of voting activity attributable to this system and reported by the East-West factor has risen to close to 70 percent. Inasmuch as such a trend discloses growing procedural consensus and increasing predictability in Assembly behavior, it makes for stability and might be regarded as a cause of satisfaction. It may be noted that over the same period specific cold-war issues have declined in weight while colonial issues, that is those on which the Soviet Union adopts Afro-Asian positions, have gained prominence.

Quite clearly we have here something that is coming close to a two-party system. But is this two-party system polarized, as Alker and Russett would have it, or is it normal? Surely lack of a multiplicity of issues leading to diverse voting positions is hardly by itself proof of polarization which is essentially a process whereby the conflicts divid-

[20] Hayward R. Alker and Bruce M. Russett, *World Politics in the General Assembly* (New Haven 1965).

ing a community not only coalesce but also become more intense. The United Kingdom is not a polarized political system merely because most of its political issues can be fitted into its two-party framework.[21] The data introduced by Alker and Russett to document the rising intensity of conflict is inconclusive and will be reviewed in the next section. In brief, since a two-party system is not, *ipso facto*, a polarized system (as Alker-Russett seem to assume and Parsons does not—see below), and the evidence is not convincing, we return to the earlier finding of the increasing weight of the East-West factor. This finding confirms our *prima facie* expectation that this particular parliamentary system shows the growing procedural accommodation and consensus that is characteristic of a "normal" two-party system.

A large proportion of United Nations delegates thus can be shown to act with considerable predictability. The two emerging voting groups in the General Assembly are the United States led coalition (West), and the loose alliance between the Soviet bloc and some Afro-Asian and Arab nations which is especially striking on colonial issues (East). Voting together does, in a fashion, constitute a significant act of cooperation. But is it evidence of the existence of parties or of a party system in the General Assembly? We would conclude in the negative from the available evidence, which, while it is suggestive, is not conclusive. We need more studies particularly and on activities other than roll calls and specifically on the point that cooperation between the Soviet Union and a significant number of Afro-Asians is close and continuous enough to amount to the creation of a new party.

Parliamentary parties in national systems have tended toward the conservative side of the political spectrum. Historically we have known them in Europe as the nineteenth-century parties of the middle class, parties of interest rather than parties of ideology. Their organization tended to be loose, with little stress laid upon parliamentary discipline and grassroots connections in the constituencies. All these represent characteristics that could with some justice be attributed to the emerging parliamentary parties in the United Nations system. This process would assume particular significance in the event that the Soviet Union should become an important participant in that system on account of its Afro-Asian alignments, for it might then win a stake within it and have something more to conserve.

Extra-parliamentary parties, as shown by Duverger, have on the whole, tended toward the radical pole of the political spectrum. In Europe they emerged late in the nineteenth century as protest movements against parliamentary underrepresentation of significant sections and interests; they grew, but less through personal links between

21 Spiro in *World Politics*, 84, doubts the applicability of the United Kingdom model to world politics and dubs this the Anglophile fallacy.

elected representatives than as constituency-based grassroots organizations founded on local political support. In time some of these organizations secured representation in parliaments, but parliamentary life never really became the central activity of these groups; the socialist and later the Communist parties were among the most active of these organizations.

The world Communist movement remains, as it has for decades, the most important example of an extra-parliamentary world party.[22] Conceived by Marx and Engels right from the start as an answer to the power of the "international bourgoisie" controlling the "capitalist world market," the workers' movement, spearheaded by socialist and Communist parties, was to be worldwide too. The Internationals, that is the organizations bringing together groups from many countries and ultimately from all over the world, became characteristic operating features of these parties. Contemporary Communism too may be viewed as a worldwide system of parties and even as a world party of loose organizational structure, with firm control of a number of national constituencies (its "safe seats") which contests power with other parties or organizations in a large number of the remaining constituencies.

On the eve of the Sino-Soviet split the Communist movement was a world organization that was impressive by any standard. It had grown in a few decades from a base which consisted of some seven parties, mostly in Europe, with a membership of 400,000 in 1917; to 56 parties and 4,200,000 members in 1939; 20,000,000 members in 1945; and to about 90 parties in all continents with a total membership of over 43 million in 1964.[23] Most of the membership was attributable to Communist parties in countries with a Communist government; nearly all the remaining parties were small and close to one-half of them contained less than 2,000 members each.

The organization of the world system of Communist parties has passed through a number of stages, the most important of which was represented by the Comintern (1919-1943). While it lasted, the Communist International was the largest and most tightly organized world party known to man. It was worldwide and so highly centralized that its directing organs were empowered, as a matter of statutory right and not merely as a fact of practical politics, to issue binding instructions to member parties. The organization was Moscow based right from the start and while in earlier years some effort was made to

[22] Cf. George Modelski, "Communism: The International System," *International Encyclopedia of the Social Sciences* (1968), Vol. III.

[23] United States Department of State, *World Strength of the Communist Party Organizations*, 17th Annual Report, January 1965 (Bureau of Intelligence and Research), 1-2; this is the single, most important, up-to-date source of global data on this subject.

bring a variety of the interests of member parties to bear upon the directing bodies, the Soviet party soon assumed a position of unchallenged power, legitimized by the article of faith, unquestioned during Stalin's lifetime, that the interests of the Soviet Union, the first Communist country, were to be supreme for Communists everywhere. Following Trotsky's defeat by Stalin the organization began to lose inner strength, even while it grew numerically. The Comintern suffered heavily during the Great Soviet Purges (1936-1939) because of its earlier association with Trotsky and the Soviet opposition. Its dissolution by Stalin in 1943 caused little surprise except to its headquarters staff who learnt of it from the newspapers.

The Comintern was the most elaborate world party known up to the present day and that is why it is of value to study the details of its organization. Some of the features of the Comintern were attributable to its character as a Communist party; we are particularly interested in those features which enabled it to "fulfill its role as a world party."[24] At the height of its power in the early 1930's the Comintern consisted of the following elements:

1. The Moscow headquarters, directed by the Executive Committee (composed of representatives of various parties) headed by the Presidium (both nominally governed by a World Congress); the General Secretariat headed a general and office staff of 2,000 to 2,500;

2. Representatives of national parties accredited to the Executive Committee, a form of party "diplomatic service"; but this was not the only channel of communication with the national parties; the Executive Committee was empowered to, and frequently exercised its right to, dispatch permanent and ad-hoc plenipotentiaries;

3. An international communications system controlled by the Executive Committee; this included bases, auxiliary offices, courier routes, and a radio network, and was used especially for clandestine activities and the transfer of financial resources;

4. International instructors, dispatched by the Executive Committee to provide guidance in special areas of activity (e.g. agitation, strikes, military problems);

5. The International Control Commission, a disciplinary body;

6. Branch offices with limited territorial jurisdiction (e.g. the West European Bureau, in Berlin until 1933, later in Copenhagen);

7. Associated mass organizations (such as the Red Trade Union International, the Communist Youth International, and the International Red Relief);

[24] Gunther Nollau, *International Communism and World Revolution: History and Method* (New York 1961), 125. The outline of Comintern organization is based on Chapter IV of this work, "The Organization and Methods of the Communist International."

8. Training schools and universities (including the Lenin School);
and

9. An international press service.

The Cominform (1947-1955) was but a pale shadow of the Comintern; Europe-oriented from the start, it never really got off the ground and was nothing more than one of the cloaks thinly veiling Soviet control over Eastern Europe. Since 1956 world Communist organization has been in a state of flux; there was at first a period of attempted coordination by means of international conferences and congresses (1957, 1960, 1963) without any continuing organization. Sino-Soviet confrontation of the mid-sixties made it difficult even to call general international meetings, let alone construct a new global organization. This would have to overcome not only the initial handicap of the unhappy memories of the Comintern and of Soviet domination over it but also cope with problems posed by the accession to power of a number of parties unwilling to take instructions liable to interfere with their own conceptions of the proper "road to socialism." In recent years the only remaining open coordinating element in the (Soviet wing of) world movement is the *World Marxist Review*, published in Prague (this is more important than appears on the surface because the Communist Party has traditionally regarded the press as a major arm of political activity); strenuous efforts to call a world Communist conference were resumed by the Soviet leadership in 1968. We can be sure that some residual elements of the Comintern organization remain to this day in Moscow, but the overall direction is no longer self-assured and its legitimacy is now in doubt.

For purposes of our own analysis the most interesting feature of the Communist system is its global range and its accepted goal of aspiring to global significance. In some ways the contemporary Communist system could be seen as the nucleus of a future possible world single-party system.[25] Yet it is astonishing that despite such long theoretical preparation and extended practical activity, the party has been singularly inept at operating at the world level, unable to reconcile the universal demand for national and other forms of autonomy with the requirements of maintaining and strengthening a world party system. The Comintern faltered because of "vertical fusion" blatant beyond belief: its entanglement in Soviet politics defeated the attempt to play a lasting role at the world level. Its conceptualization of world revolution as the conquest of power in one national state after another has been clearly inadequate. The present day Communist sterility with reference to world order and organization contrasts sharply

[25] George Modelski, *The Communist International System* (Research Monograph No. 9, Center of International Studies, Princeton University), 1960.

with earlier inventiveness in party organization and economic innovation. The Communist movement has been a failure as a world party.

We remarked earlier that Communist parties may be viewed as having emerged on the fringes of the parliamentary system, in part as a
protest against and in part as a complement to earlier parliamentary organizations. We have also observed that in the United Nations
process, by cooperating consistently with some Afro-Asians, Communist representatives could conceivably be joining more "normal" parliamentary activities. On the global scale too the Soviet brand of Communism could arguably be losing its revolutionary character. Sino-
Soviet disputes about correct methods of expanding Communism and
over the relative importance to be attached to peaceful coexistence
and to wars of national liberation may be seen in precisely this light.
If the Soviet branch of Communism is becoming less radical (and such
a process is by no means inevitable), then Peking's appeals to the "oppressed peoples of the world" may be an attempt to organize anew
the radical fringes of world politics, an attempt either to maintain
Communism's character as an extra-parliamentary and essentially revolutionary world party or else an attempt to found a new, truly revolutionary world party out of elements inadequately represented in the
contemporary international system.

Communist China's exertions at creating a new world party reached
a peak, as far as we know, in 1963-1966; they yet remain to be fully reported and understood. But we find that we are already prepared to
say that in this last case "vertical fusion" occurred at an even earlier
stage and in an even more acute form than in the Comintern. The
Cultural Revolution called a stop to such efforts and turned China
inward. But the lack of success so far and the internal difficulties of
China offer no conclusive proof that such an undertaking may not be
resumed later or indeed may not be repeated elsewhere with
greater vigor. For the fringes of any political system are a perpetual
breeding ground of new organizations and are particularly fertile
when such a system experiences a crisis. The process of political participation on a world scale is as yet incomplete and remains a source
of extra-parliamentary activity.

Concurrent with Peking's bid and coordinated with it in its later
stages has been President Sukarno's proclaimed desire to unite the
world's New Emerging Forces in one grand coalition bringing together,
potentially, three-quarters of the world peoples.[26] The grand ambitions and eloquent phraseology of this project proved no substitute
for the careful preparation, experience, and sound organization neces-

[26] A documentation of the earlier phase of this development may be found in
George Modelski, *The New Emerging Forces: Documents on the Ideology of Indonesian Foreign Policy* (Canberra 1963).

sary to maintain it. Indeed it is questionable whether any national government could launch such a scheme openly and hope for any success, even a government commanding a much sounder home base and greater financial and organizational resources than the Indonesian. With strong Chinese backing the idea reached a peak in 1964-1965 but the bubble soon burst and proved the most immediate cause of Sukarno's own downfall in 1966-1967. It deserves study as another attempt to organize an extra-parliamentary world coalition, even though Sukarno was never sure whether he wanted to build an alliance of governments or an organization of peoples, in other words, a world party.

The Communist and related parties are not, of course, the only instances of world parties with extra-parliamentary organizations. Socialist, liberal, Christian democratic, and peasant parties have each had or still possess international organizations[27] but none have been as striking or consistently significant as the groups aiming at the fringes of world society. In the nineteenth century the Anarchists organized an international movement of considerable scope and impact which for a time seriously competed for adherents with the socialists; the Anarchists' International still maintains a headquarters in Stockholm.[28] The Communist, Socialist, and Anarchist Internationals all drew upon the experience of secret societies which proliferated in eighteenth- and nineteenth-century Europe, were transnational, and were the direct antecedents of later world movements.[29]

We might remark, in conclusion, upon the affinity which extra-parliamentary world party activity has to political warfare, subversion, and other clandestine foreign policy operations. Thus when Hugh Dalton, a senior British Labour Party leader, urged, in the summer of 1940, the formation of a political warfare agency he saw it as an instrument for the creation of a "democratic international."[30] The Special Operation Executive established on his initiative and directed by him until 1945 did in fact succeed in organizing and coordinating extensive resistance and sabotage activities in occupied territories. These activities and the personal and organizational links then estab-

[27] For a survey see Jean Meynaud, *Les groupes de pression internationaux* (Lausanne: Etudes de science politique) 3 (1961) , Part I.

[28] Max Nomad, "The Anarchist Tradition," 57-92 in Milorad M. Drachkovitch, ed., *The Revolutionary Internationals 1864-1943* (Stanford 1966) .

[29] A general review may be found in Charles W. Heckenthorn, *The Secret Societies of all Ages and Countries* (University Books, 1965 reissue) ; Boris Nicolaevsky, "Secret Societies and the First International," in Drachkovitch, ed., *The Revolutionary Internationals*, 36-56, has traced the connection between "underground" (as contrasted to "official") Masonic lodges, in particular the Philadelphians, and the rise and fall of the First International.

[30] Quoted in M.R.D. Foot, *SOE in France: An Account of the Work of the British Special Operations Executive in France 1940-1944* (London 1966) , 8.

lished in turn had noticeable effect upon postwar party political arrangements throughout Western Europe and were instrumental in smoothing the way for far-reaching measures of political cooperation.

WORLD DISTRIBUTION OF POLITICAL PREFERENCES

In our discussion of United Nations parties we have already had the opportunity of referring to "normal" and to "polarized" or "revolutionary" political and party systems.[31] We may now look into these terms in greater detail and begin by positing that a "normal" party system is associated with normal (or "A" shaped) distribution of political preferences in the relevant political system, and that a polarized or revolutionary party system may be described by another type of distribution, best called "U" shaped. The major proposition underlying this discussion is the view that an "A" shaped distribution produces a stable party system and that a "U" shaped distribution does not.

At this point we assume therefore with Anthony Downs[32] that the distribution of political preferences is a major determinant of political life. As already indicated, it helps to shape the party system (and we might add to the just mentioned distributions the third type, namely the multimodal distribution which results in a multiparty system); it influences the stability and survival chances of that system; and, finally, it has much to do with the way in which new parties enter the political arena.

We assume, furthermore, that these considerations are equally pertinent in the global context. This means that, worldwide, individuals can be arranged along a scale measuring their political preferences. We surmise that for certain questions of wide concern such as development, war, or the character of national institutions such an arrangement would be meaningful. We surmise further that to arrive at a true picture of such a distribution the preferences of not all the inhabitants, or the adult inhabitants of the globe, need at this time be ascertained because world political issues may yet be the concern of only a minority of the people. We may also surmise further that the growth of world communications makes such an attempt feasible and that the same process is also leading toward the widening of the circle of people whose concerns enter the global layer. We surmise finally that developments of the next decades will make the knowledge about worldwide distributions of preferences increasingly significant.

Patterns of distribution of preferences may be illustrated with the help of the simple diagrams shown in Figure I a-c. Figure Ia shows

31 For an application of these concepts in a related field see George Modelski, "The International Settlement of Internal War" in J. Rosenau, ed., *International Aspects of Civil Strife* (Princeton 1964), 144ff.

32 *An Economic Theory of Democracy* (New York 1955), 139; see also R. A. Dahl, *A Preface to Democratic Theory* (Chicago 1956), 91-99.

an "A" shaped or normal distribution, Ib a "U" shaped or polarized distribution, and Figure Ic a multimodal distribution.

In each of these diagrams the horizontal axis measures the preference for a policy or value according to a scale of intensity. The scale may indicate preferences for a specific act or programs (such as type of government intervention in economic life or taxation measures) or it may indicate fundamental political value preferences according to some such general measure as a Left-to-Right scale indicating a person's preferences as being those of the extreme left, moderate left, center, moderate right, or extreme right variety. In general, the more specific the policy issues under review, the greater the need to think in terms of multidimensional preference planes. The more general the values, however, and in our discussion we are limiting ourselves to such general values, the more probable that a one-dimensional representation, such as that attempted in Figures I-IV, prove a satisfactory approximation.

The vertical axis of the diagrams measures the frequency with which any particular intensity of preference is held in a given political system. In its simplest form it indicates the number, or the proportion of individuals committed to a particular position. These could be individual voters or citizens, or the appointed or elected representatives in a parliamentary assembly. But it is hard to imagine how states or other organizations can be regarded as possessing political preferences or how data about the type of preferences exhibited by national delegates can be directly translated into data on world preference distributions.

We shall now try to complement these theoretical reflections by data on real distributions. We want to know: What is the world distribution of political preferences today? What shape might it assume two or three decades ahead? Unfortunately, the present state of our knowledge regarding worldwide preference distributions is largely inadequate.

FIGURE I

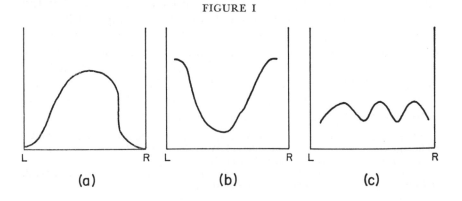

(a)　　　　　　(b)　　　　　　(c)

FIGURE II

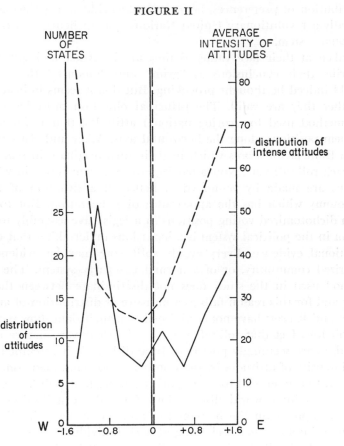

SOURCE: Alker and Russett, *World Politics in the General Assembly*, 203.

Alker and Russett's work is in part an attempt to answer such questions through the study of United Nations roll-call votes and, by implication, of the behavior of General Assembly delegates. As previously mentioned their major finding is an increasing polarization of voting positions, hence presumed instability in the UN system. "Bipolarity" they argue "accurately characterizes both the distribution of attitudes alone and the distribution of intense attitudes." More particularly "the polarization of attitudes in the General Assembly is on the upswing, not on the decline."[33] Their conclusion is based on trends deduced from data covering all the four years selected by them but may be illustrated by Figure II which reproduces a diagram showing the distribution of attitudes on East-West issues in 1961, as found by Alker and Russett. The two graphs clearly suggest a "U" shaped

[33] Alker and Russett, *World Politics in the General Assembly*, 196, 216.

distribution of preferences, hence a conflict-ridden, a polarized if not actually a revolutionary United Nations system; hence also the international system.

Taken at their face value, as they are by Alker and Russett who describe their conclusions as "grim" and "gloomy," these findings would indeed be thought provoking. But doubt seems indicated as to whether they are valid. The principal objection must be aimed at the method used for scoring national attitudes, that is for allotting to them positions along the horizontal axis. Alker and Russett derive them from factor scores which in their turn originate in scores given for each roll-call vote. Now a parliamentary system is one in which decisions are made by yes-no votes, hence in a situation of induced dichotomy which has the appearance of polarization. But to reason from dichotomized voting positions in a legislative assembly to polarization in the political system is a hazardous undertaking that calls for additional evidence. Every evenly split vote may be evidence of a polarized community, or of a normal two-party system. The scoring method used in the study does not discriminate between these two cases and for this reason fails as a measure of distribution of attitudes. Alker and Russett have not established that their data show more than the obvious fact that roll-call votes are by their very nature dichotomized, hence seemingly polarized. In addition, their attempt to measure intensity of attitudes by the number of speeches made on selected issues is too superficial to gauge such an important point. Finally, the attempt to infer world distributions from the distribution of attitudes computed on the basis of the number of *states* holding these attitudes implies equal weighting of each individual state—a position that may be justifiable if our questions are restricted to the situation in the General Assembly, but becomes most dubious if we attempt inferences to the state of the global system. Alker and Russett maintain their gloom despite such questionable deductions.

Let us try another, more direct approach, looking this time at the distribution of preferences not in the international assembly, but in the constituencies themselves. If we arranged the world's national political parties along a broadly left-to-right scale: Communist, left, center, conservative, and then added up the votes polled by such parties at the most recent general election we would get a global distribution of votes along that spectrum. Insofar as most of the political tendencies or movements such as Communism, etc. are worldwide, national elections might in part be interpreted as expressions of preference, not only on domestic but also on some global issues. The method has some obvious limitations. Some countries simply do not hold elections; there has been none in China, numerically a most important case, since the establishment of the Communist regime in

1949. In some other countries elections yield only limited information about political attitudes, notably so in the Soviet Union and in other one-party states. Finally, all such elections are national events conducted with the view to shaping national policy and only incidentally take account of world issues.

Figure IIIa-b summarizes election data for the 45 largest countries constituting 90 percent of the world's population in 1965. The voting figures refer to votes cast in the last national election prior to the end of 1965. In only three cases, China, China-Taiwan, and Spain, was there no election; two others have elections but no parties (Ethiopia, Afghanistan). In the great majority of cases votes were assigned to the chosen categories according to their designation in the State Department publication *World Strength of Communist Party Organizations*; in the remaining cases an effort was made to observe the same criteria. China aside, elections are now a process familiar to the overwhelming portion of the world's people.

Figure IIIa presents the spectrum of actual votes cast. Figure IIIb repeats this picture but has an additional entry, a notional figure of 350,000,000 for Communist China, placed to the left of the Communist position, on the assumption that in 1965 Chinese preference were already of a more radical type than the more orthodox Communist line. Figure IIIb is intended to illustrate the impact of newly enfranchised participants upon a political system and is in fact purely hypothetical.

In a vague and general sense Figure IIIa conveys the picture of a possibly multimodal distribution. Figure IIIb makes it clear that the entry of additional participants into the system might considerably radicalize it. But these conclusions are subject to large qualifications previously made at some length; they would moreover involve the assumption that the present day system of world politics faithfully translates such a constituency distribution into alignments at the global level. If the constituency distribution indeed were of this shape, and this is far from certain, might there not be some virtue in a political system which does not express it?

Let us try one other approach. If we agree that the distribution of political preferences may be determined by the distribution of incomes in the same political system (so that low incomes correlate with one set of preferences, e.g. radicalism, and high incomes with another, e.g. conservatism, by no means a self-evident proposition) we may wish to investigate this latter distribution on a world scale. We find, as illustrated in Figure IV on the basis of data for the years 1957-1959, a distribution that tends toward the "U" shape. The great majority of mankind earns extremely low incomes; the gap between this majority and the 15 to 20 percent affluent minority is tremendous. Prognosti-

FIGURE III

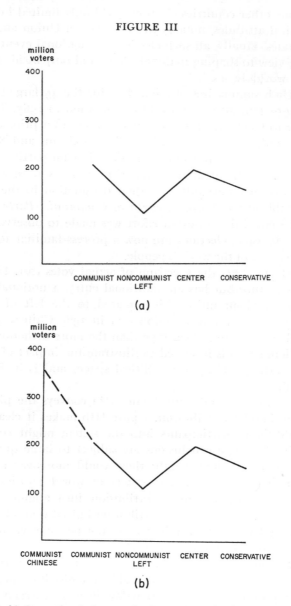

(a)

(b)

Sources: *World Strength of Communist Party Organizations* (1963-66); *Keesing's Archives; New York Times; International Comparative Political Parties Project,* Northwestern University.

Votes cast in national elections 1955-65 for Communist parties: 211,562,000; non-Communist left: 117,882,000; center parties: 190,187,000; conservative parties: 156,-842,000. Communist Chinese votes assumed in IIIb: 350,000,000.

cating from this one set of data only and assuming, furthermore, global awareness of this distribution as well as a value system that puts it into question, we would expect in the next two or three decades a tendency toward polarization, possibly through the formation of parties differentiated on the basis of support they are likely to receive from different world income groups.

Yet such a development is by no means inevitable. For one, world parties which could utilize such a trend may not emerge. Other things may change—the distribution of incomes may be altered. For instance, the rich may grow poorer because of expensive or devastating wars; incomes may be reallocated through aid measures worldwide in scope; or, finally, party alignments may crystallize in such fashion that on each side of the fence some rich would be linked with some poor, so that neither the rich nor the poor would present a united front. In this last case, a normal two-party system could yet evolve. The real question would be: in what circumstances is a rich-poor polarization likely and how would it be reflected in a party system? These are questions which go to the roots of the transformation process of political systems and they are still largely unanswered.

The future tendencies which can be discerned from our limited data do not therefore point conclusively toward polarization, that is toward

FIGURE IV

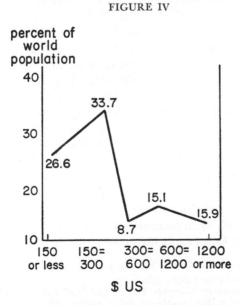

percent of
world
population

$ US

"Real" GNP per head of population

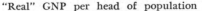

SOURCE: P. N. Rosenstein-Rodan, "International Aid for Underdeveloped Countries," 531 in Richard A. Falk and S. H. Mendlowitz, *The Strategy of World Order*, Vol. IV.

the widening of the gap between parties that might yet emerge. But they do suggest the likelihood of increasing radicalization of world politics and the continuation of a leftward drift of the center of the political system (familiar to students of the politics of certain phases in other societies), as freshly participating parts of the constituencies begin to present new unsettling demands. The way such a radicalization is handled is likely to be the key to the world politics of the next decades, and the operation of a party system may well become a crucial element in this process.

PARTIES AND ALLIANCES

"Nous ne coalisons pas les états, nous unissons des hommes,"[34] this was one of Jean Monnet's battle cries in his work to build "Europe." It enshrined the idea that European unity had to be built not primarily by means of governmental alliances, of coalitions designed to respond to sudden crises, but through the cultivation of politics at the grassroots level, by reaching not only governments but also men of influence, as well as the common man in all walks of life.

European unity thus was erected upon a large network of personal and organizational connections. Significant among these were the affinities established in World War II and in the early postwar years by the Christian Democratic Parties of Western Europe, so much so that the first institutional innovation of the new Europe, the Iron and Steel Community, was the work of Christian Democratic ministers in the three key countries of France, Italy, and West Germany. The formation of the European Parliament, a consultative body in the framework of the new European institutions, in turn led to the establishment of supranational, regional-level party groups. Three such groups now operate in accord with the standing orders of that body: The Christian Democrats, with some 45 percent of the seats in 1967, dominate the European Parliament and together with the Liberals form the governing coalition. The Socialists, with some 25 percent of the seats, perform the duties of the opposition.[35] This is the first example of explicit party formation in an otherwise international assembly and as such deserves careful study, even if it needs to be recognized that the activities of the political parties have been only one in the patchwork of influences instrumental in the mushrooming of new institutions; European-wide pressure groups, particularly of the

[34] Quoted in Richard Mayne, "The Role of Jean Monnet," *Government and Opposition*, 2, No. 3 (April-June 1967), 352.
[35] P. H. Merkl, "European Assembly Parties and National Delegations," *Journal of Conflict Resolution*, 8, No. 1 (March 1964), 50-64; Guy van Oudenhove, *The Political Parties in the European Parliament*, Leyden 1965; Gerda Zellentin, "Form and Function of the Opposition in the European Community," *Government and Opposition*, 2, No. 3, April-June 1967, 416-35.

professional type, and the steady growth of extensive personal links being other essential ingredients.

For this reason the contemporary politics of Western Europe is not coalition, alliance, nor bloc politics of the traditional sort which is familiar to us from treatises on diplomacy and international relations, but the politics of a kind of society in which party systems can and do work. We are reaffirming here the basic distinction, established in the introductory paragraphs of this chapter, and implied in Monnet's dictum quoted at the beginning of this section—between blocs, alliances, and coalitions on the one hand, and that type of association which goes by the name of world parties. Examples of each of these are not hard to find: the North Atlantic Treaty Organization, the Franco-Russian Alliance of 1890, or the coalition of nations which won World War II, are clear cases of the first and may be contrasted with the European parliamentary groups just mentioned or the instances of world parties previously reviewed.

The basic difference is this: blocs, alliances, and coalitions are all instances of collaboration between governments whereas world parties are and can be associations of individuals. Blocs, alliances, and coalitions are cooperative forms implicit in the nation-state system; they arise for certain specific purposes crucial to governments and have traditionally concerned defense and security, hence the expectation of war; they flourish in wars and in warlike situations. Blocs and similar structures are also preeminently activities in which great powers engage; without great powers there would also be no blocs. Dependent as they are on governments, blocs, alliances, and coalitions change as governments change. As each national government's most essential concerns focus on the nation, on affairs in its own territorial domain, and, not the least, on its own survival, alliances for external purposes reflect this egocentricity or even selfishness and opportunism and fade quickly when the explicit concerns which favored them pass away. Thus wartime coalitions habitually break up and blocs either disintegrate or lose their raison d'être. Blocs, alliances, and coalitions, as intergovernmental associations, tend to spill over into other types of association; thus the Franco-Russian alliance led to extensive French business ties in Russia and exports of capital; the NATO alliance fostered and clearly did not impede the growth of other Atlantic connections. Yet such induced links usually appear secondary: there was something distinctly artificial about NATO's attempts to create an Atlantic community, especially since such attempts increased at the same rate as the alliance grew weaker.

World parties, on the other hand, do not fundamentally depend upon governments. As pointed out earlier they cannot flourish in a system that is completely controlled by governments, hence governmental and interstate compacts can and do by-pass them. They are concerned with world issues and world issues may only in part be amenable to national governmental action; hence world parties must concern themselves with all those world institutions whose activities help to shape world issues.

As we have noticed present-day literature in the field of world party politics is scant. The most significant early discussion of this subject, Talcott Parsons' paper on "Polarization of the World and International Order," focused precisely on similarities between bloc and party systems. "An effective party system within a relatively stable national polity" wrote Parsons "constitutes a theoretical model which . . . is sufficiently similar to world bi-polarity to provide significant clues as to methods for achieving world order."[36] Parsons believed too that world polarization, as evidenced in the two-bloc system, far from indicating a breakdown of world order, was in fact indicative of the existence of a world community. He himself did not pursue this theoretical model at any great length and in any event felt it to be merely a matter of analogy, for he was not concerned with the emergence of "real" world parties, such as we have been discussing, but with the operating conditions of the bi-polar bloc system.

Yet we might speculate at this point that under certain conditions a two-bloc system could conceivably transform itself into a world two-party system. The general conditions of this process are those favoring a world party system and will be discussed in the next section. Nevertheless, we might add that a two-party system, while a sophisticated way of conducting politics and by no means a natural outcome of political processes, has several circumstances working in its favor: the tendency of legislative organs to produce yes-no decisions, hence the need to hold to consistent positions on one side or the other; the in-out situation in the occupancy of political positions; and the friend-enemy configuration of political combat. Such dichotomies are effective if oversimplified ways of handling life's problems and the two-party system institutionalizes them. The world's political issues, however, may not be open to such a degree of simplification and therefore the appearance of a multiparty system seems more likely. But it is possible that such an alignment might form and considering the bipolar structure of the postwar world, combined with the influence of Anglo-American types of political behavior on world politics, could yet induce a transition from two blocs to a two-party system.

[36] In Quincy Wright et al., eds., *Preventing World War III: Some Proposals* (New York 1962), 310-31; see also Talcott Parsons, "Order and Community in the International Social System," in J. Rosenau, ed., *International Politics and Foreign Policy: A Reader* (Glencoe 1961), 125-26.

Conditions for World Party Systems

We would, in the most general terms, predict the growth of world parties from the long-range trend which shows that the costs of communication continue to fall. If human associations and organizations are communications systems, then a fall in the costs of communications makes possible more inclusive forms for such associations and organizations. In the two to three decades ahead, improved electronic and satellite, air and rocket systems will make world organizations technically feasible at minimum cost. We could go further and assert that costs of communications may be falling at a rate faster than the costs of other facilities and may still continue to decline at a time when costs of other essential resources, such as food or space, will begin to show a rising trend. These tendencies might have even more compelling consequences for the developments we are investigating.

But technological and economic trends are inconclusive because they demonstrate the feasibility but not the necessity of certain changes. We have shown earlier that in some fundamental respects world politics are inimical to, even incompatible with the states system as it has developed in the past few centuries and even more so with the fully blown nation-state system of today. Therefore, when we speak of the emergence of a world party system, we are in fact discussing the probabilities of a substantial transformation in the existing arrangements of world politics: we are examining the possible emergence of a multiple autonomy system. Yet such arrangements, although undermined by technical and economic, and even political developments are notoriously hard to change.

In more specific terms only the prevalence of the following six conditions would significantly enlarge the probabilities of emergence for a world party system: (1) absence of general and conventional war; (2) strengthening of world society; (3) the number of states to be fairly large; (4) declining share of the great powers in world authority; (5) normalization of the world distribution of political preferences; and (6) broadening the scope of world issues.

All six of these conditions are significantly interdependent and the first of them is the most important and most pervasive in its effect. But they must be discussed separately and in relation to party systems in particular because they illuminate the breadth of changes in world politics which might be anticipated to occur.

1. ABSENCE OF GENERAL WAR: Most basically of all, world parties call for a no-war system. The great coalition wars of the past few centuries have played, in Europe and more recently in the world, the functions which periodic general elections exercise in more regularized systems.

They decided which states based on what territorial holdings would constitute the ruling directorate for at least a generation. The great settlements which marked the termination of such wars: Westphalia, 1648; Utrecht, 1715; Vienna, 1815; Versailles, 1919; Yalta-Potsdam, 1945 were more than conferences which drew up the terms of the peace. They were occasions on which the winning coalition settled the basic political issues of their century. World party competition for posts of influence on global issues may therefore be seen as the functional equivalent of the great wars of the past.

Party competition is not alone a substitute for, or an alternative to, general war. War and the expectation of war are incompatible with stable party competition on the global level. Political contest in a party system is a sophisticated, continuous, and finely regulated process of deciding issues and policies. War, by contrast, is a crude, spasmodic, and arbitrary procedure that can only be used once in a while. Resort to war creates conditions destructive of world party systems; it strengthens centralized governments and is the fundamental force maintaining the state and the nation-state system. The profound uncertainties it creates, particularly in respect to territorial sovereignty and the need for its protection from armed attack necessarily focuses loyalties on organs capable of giving such security and obstructs the growth of other wider and possibly worldwide links and loyalties. The expectation of war, moreover, transforms even the intervals of peace into preparatory stages for the next war. World war is the typical condition of "U" shaped, polarized, even revolutionary political systems; such systems do not promote the emergence of parties or their smooth functioning.

A war-less world in which fundamental security of the territorial variety would no longer be in constant jeopardy—this is the soil in which the rationalizing processes of party competition can take root. Can we achieve such a world? We might because mutual deterrence and a wide distribution of weapons might bring it about. But we also might not because even in the absence of general war, the expectation of it and the attendant emphasis on arms and defense questions perpetuates the conditions which maintain the nation-state system.

2. STRENGTHENING OF WORLD SOCIETY: We would expect a world party system to emerge beyond a certain threshold of minimum integration. The stronger the global "layer," and the more substantial the world society, the more probable the party system is to operate successfully. The strength of world society has a direct bearing upon the emergence of cross-cutting loyalties. The stronger the world society, the weaker and less exclusive can we expect loyalties at other levels to become. But since so far we have digested little information on this topic and have

little experience in estimating the strength of world society, nothing very precise can now be said about it.

By the strength (or weight) of world society we mean the quantity, intensity, and scope of communications and other interactions obtaining in this social system as compared with other relevant systems. We know for instance that in the two decades ending in 1965 the number of passenger-miles flown on international air routes had risen at least eleven-fold, that is by at least one order of magnitude. Indeed we can project this trend quite confidently at least two or three decades ahead. We would, therefore, be entitled to expect that the strength of world society has also risen, and furthermore, should also continue to rise. We maintain therefore that the amount of personal and face-to-face political interaction relevant to the creation and maintenance of a world party system must for this reason have increased and will go on increasing. But the precise significance of these developments still remains somewhat obscure.

3. LARGE NUMBER OF STATES: The number of nation-states into which the international system is subdivided bears some relationship to the likelihood of the emergence of a world party system. Specifically it may be argued that a drastic decline in the number of states, to a small number of presumably more self-sufficient blocs or regions of near-continental size would be unlikely to foster the feeling of global interdependence and therefore the growth of political activities on a world party pattern. By contrast, the present number of states, between 130 and around 150, offers the basis for the growth of semiparliamentary politics in existing international organizations. Some huge and unmanageable entities, such as China or India, might even benefit from subdivision, or at any rate from some looser type of association. Just as these two might be said to be too large, some other states are too small or too weak financially and in other respects. But it is also worth remembering that with the population relentlessly advancing in numbers, on present-day estimates, 75 states will in the year 2,000 have a population of more than 10 million, and of these, 22 will have populations in excess of 50 million. Countries of such size need and deserve political autonomy and direct representation of their interests at the global level.

We may add that the existence, in a political system, of a variety of political units, some very small and some very large, some very weak and some extremely powerful, helps to preserve within it a sense of equipoise and a degree of equality for all. In the American federal system Rhode Island or Nevada go along reasonably well with New York or California. The same situation might be expected to obtain in a well-built international system, for in that system the degree of permissible inequality between states could be even larger than in federal states.

4. GREAT POWERS DECLINE IN WORLD AUTHORITY: Closely related is the question of the role and significance of the great powers. In the state system as traditionally evolved the great powers assumed, by virtue of demonstrated strength but also of implicit consensus, the major share of authority over world affairs. What is more, in the world as constituted at the end of the last century—still held up as the master-period of diplomatic craftsmanship—the bulk of population, territory, wealth, and resources was in fact under the control of a small number of such powers. Lesser states hardly counted at all. Where political initiative as well as the complete capacity to act were the prerogative of only a few, variegated political life could hardly occur at all. For the future too, to the degree that the great powers assume and execute worldwide responsibilities, the viability and, indeed, the necessity for a party system are in doubt. In turn, the influence and the political weight of great powers may be traced directly to great wars; hence, the greater the incidence and the likelihood of wars, the greater the actual and potential role of great powers as the sole repositories of those arsenals without which such wars cannot be fought at all. Conversely and conceivably, therefore, the greater the dilution of military power possible through such processes as the dispersion of nuclear weapons, the lesser the influence of the erstwhile great powers and the greater the likelihood of a rich political life.

5. WORLD DISTRIBUTION OF POLITICAL PREFERENCES: As pointed out our knowledge of the world's distribution of political preferences is still minimal. But we would argue that a normal pattern in the distribution of preferences is optimal for the smooth functioning of a global party system. The grounds for asserting this have already been reviewed but we might add that a normal distribution indicates the existence of a consensus which every party system needs as the basis of its operations. Such consensus may in part be substantive—the desirability of avoiding a nuclear war of mutual annihilation, or it could be solely procedural and be based on a few fundamental rules of political competition. In party systems of more than one party, the most elementary such rule refers to accepting the existence of other parties. A group bent on destroying its competitors, e.g. through recourse to "world revolution," subverts the basic notions of a party system and manifests alienation from other parts of the community. Such a group might conceivably establish single-party world control, but this we would judge unlikely because of the practical and theoretical difficulties of such an undertaking.

Two conclusions emerge as of special import: The major groups in a world political contest would have to abandon any wish to destroy their rivals and accept each other's rights to political activity; this would entail a mutually respected allocation of rights and duties somewhat analogous to the entitlements of government and opposition parties in certain well-known political systems. Secondly, a party system would not tolerate the alienation of any sizable group or area because an alienated group can easily become the nucleus of a force capable of significantly disturbing if not polarizing the existing system. The processes by which a polarized or revolutionary system are normalized by means short of war are still ill understood and the academic observer can offer little more than caution. China in the grip of the Cultural Revolution seems a textbook example of an alienated if isolated complex; its impact upon the rest of the world can hardly be beneficial.

6. BROADENING WORLD ISSUES: We come finally to the scope of the issues to be processed by the world party system. The traditional state system despite its lack of institutionalization, did from time to time produce important political decisions. We have noted that peace settlements served as the occasions for taking such decisions, and, as time went on during the nineteenth century, occasional conferences of the great powers continued to settle questions arising from the settlement. Thus among the notable diplomatic meetings of that period were those which contended with the Belgian, Greek, Near Eastern, Congo-African, Cretan, and Moroccan problems. As can readily be seen, the common denominator of these issues was territoriality. The essence of great power government in the traditional system was its narrow scope evidenced most clearly by its concern for territorial questions: the apportionment of territory in the peace settlement and adjustments (e.g. the creation of new states) required by subsequent and unavoidable processes of change. While some other questions such as the slave trade, changes in international law or in the rules governing diplomatic precedence also became subject of international decision-making, the general rule holds good that the scope of nineteenth-century and earlier international government was limited in the main to territorial questions.

There was some logic to this. A system whose main concerns were territorial arrangements could afford to function intermittently. And when it did function it had to be called into being by a major war and had to be reconstructed by those who emerged victorious, or, at any rate, in the winning coalition of such an ordeal. The logic held fast until 1945, the last occasion for large-scale territorial revision by a great power coalition. But two trends now intervene: the recurrence of a great war is an unacceptable prospect; hence a territorial rear-rangement by a new great power concert cannot meaningfully be anticipated—the present territorial settlement might have to be accepted as permanent. Rather than concerning itself with territorial settlements the international community must of necessity direct its attention elsewhere. Thus, secondly, political life at the global level is now richer, is increasingly complex, and demands continuous (and not intermittent) attention. Territorial questions, once the mainstay of international agendas now plague them (e.g., Kashmir) as the unavoidable ballast. The global system already processes a variety of issues of wide scope and requires institutional arrangements for this continuous review. The United Nations family and other worldwide though nongovernmental organizations must all deal with them; a party system has considerable merit in coordinating such processing and promises a finer and a lower-cost capacity for dealing with them than the earlier power arrangements or the early experience of world organizations. Indeed, such great problem areas as the relations between rich and poor nations hardly seem amenable to other procedures.

Such are the conditions for the emergence of the global system of parties; the reader can himself assess the probability of this taking place. On balance, and assuming a decreasing expectation of general war, such prospects would appear good, yet he would have to be a confirmed optimist who would base prediction on the premise that the expectation of war is decreasing. But the pessimist should also bear in mind that party politics is a relatively recent invention even at the national level and has had less than one century to be fully tested even in the most favorably placed countries. Hence the slow growth of world parties should cause no surprise to one who maintains a perspective on world trends. But the main point of this analysis has been to bring out the dependence of parties and party systems upon the general makeup of world politics and the importance of changes on a wide front if such seemingly technical and organizational departures as those bound up with a party system can take hold on the global level.

SOME CONCLUSIONS

A world party system need not be regarded as the cure for all the ills that afflict international politics. Indeed, we might ask this fundamental question: Why parties? Why add this complication to an over-complex picture? The short answer must rely on the stubborn, intractable fact that people simply and most often disagree. Because people disagree, they need institutional arrangements for carrying on political affairs in spite of and in the face of such disagreement. Autonomy is one way of seeking cover from people who disagree with us, and war is the other when autonomy proves unviable. A party system is a third way of dealing with disagreements which, in favorable conditions, has been found to be both reliable and relatively inexpensive.

The principal advantages of a party system lie in its ability to organize the resolution of issues; the processing of such issues in a continuous, visible, and predictable manner is coming to be an essential condition of world order. But not to be ignored either is another service and that is the evocation of concern for the entire political system: it could be that political parties which form the principal links between the people and various organs of politics represent the element most vitally interested in maintaining the political system and the vitality of the life within it. World parties would be the builders, the bearers, and the defenders of the world political community.

World parties, are, however, only one component of necessary world order. Their full flowering depends on important changes in various elements of contemporary world politics. They depend too on adjustments in the system of law which has originally evolved in response to the need to regulate intergovernmental affairs. They may depend, too, on the carrying out of the transition from international law to world law.

International law as traditionally conceived has been the law of the nation-state system. Its most elaborate provisions have been those laying down the limits of sovereignty, the scope of territorial jurisdiction, and the rights and duties of governments and their representatives in such international intercourse as they engaged in, including, and, in particular, war. If the nation-state system is going through important changes in some of the directions discussed in this chapter, its law would be likely to change and develop too.

We would envisage the most substantial of such developments to be an explicit concern with the constitutional law of world society and with the definition of the multiple elements that must be brought within its scope. More particularly in respect of world parties, we would expect careful attention to rules governing party competition. The maintenance of a stable system of parties could become one of the more important areas of world society's interests. In place of rules consolidating exclusive national jurisdictions, monopoly of loyalties, and penalization of extranational linkages, we would look forward toward rules facilitating global political interaction. A firm legal order would prevail within a setting of a continuous and predictable system of politics responsive to a world society.

CHAPTER 6

Collective Security and the Future
International System*

ERNST B. HAAS

SOBER analysis and playful meditation cannot always be readily distinguished. Consider this image and its credibility, now and in 1980:

> The United Nations, now thirty-five years old, celebrated its twenty-first birthday in 1966. In the economic and social sphere, however, it did not truly come of age until after the U.N. Trade and Development Conference of 1969 decided to extend development assistance on an adequate scale, and in appropriate forms, to the United States of America. The decision represented a calculated risk, taken only after extended debate and complex behind-the-scenes negotiations. The Secretary-General and his staff, who favored this initiative, were active participants in the negotiations and were severely criticized by those opposed to the venture. Today, a decade later, it is still too early to say that the aid program begun in 1970 has been a success.[1]

Development assistance to the United States required a corps of 50,000 technicians. It was predicated on the assumption that rich and poor alike should serve as "host countries" for international cooperation and that the poor had as much to teach the rich as the other way around. The rich, according to accepted UN doctrine in 1980, do not devote enough attention and planning to general global welfare, the welfare world. Their economic planning apparatus is deficient. Political development and modernization have not kept pace with the call of the times. The Great Society was an admirable doctrine, but the country lacked the human and institutional infrastructure to carry it out. Hence the need for 50,000 foreign technicians.

FORECASTING, DEVELOPMENTAL MODELS, AND
THE RECONCILIATION SYSTEM

If we are committed to dispassionate social analysis, we have no legitimate way to label such a scenario as clearly preposterous. Stu-

* I gratefully acknowledge the financial support of the Institute of International Studies, University of California (Berkeley), in the preparation of this chapter. In addition, the chapter owes much to the comments of Rupert Emerson, Inis L. Claude, Jr., and Wolfram F. Hanrieder, as well as to the editorial and research assistance of Kathleen M. Wilson. But the responsibility for mistakes is mine alone.

[1] Robert E. Asher, "UN Aid to the United States: A Calculated Risk, A Retrospective Look from 1980." This elaborate and imaginative spoof was published in *International Development Review*, VII, No. 2 (June 1965), 15-19.

dents of international relations and organization have not exactly been ardent in their pursuit of images designed to capture the future —except in the field of military strategy and weaponry. Weapons, like economic development, are things to be counted and measured and correlated with the state of the industrial arts. Here one can marry statistical projection to conceivable future institutional arrangements. When we deal with human rights, collective legitimation of decisions, controls in outer space, the evolution of international law, and the maintenance of peace among more or less sovereign nations, we lack even these crutches.

Three Ways of Forecasting

Yet we need not simply dichotomize the effort at imagining the future between "prophecy," based on personal hopes and fears fed into a crystal ball, and "prediction." Prediction involves an appreciation of causative links between events; it rests on analysis; it produces contingent statements of the "if . . . then" variety. But even prediction cannot weight the causative importance of several simultaneously discernible trends, each of which may carry the United Nations in a direction different from the others if left unchecked. Which trend checks which? "At best," says I. L. Claude in seeking to make predictions of this kind, "one can state possibilities and probabilities, taking some comfort from the fact that part of what is unknown about the future of the United Nations is unknowable, given the role of indeterminate factors in the shaping of that future.[2]

The purpose of this chapter is to think about the future as it concerns the maintenance of peace by the United Nations. What will be the shape of the international system fifteen or twenty years hence? Will that system contain forces more (or less) likely to allow for the operation of collective security by the United Nations? Which of these forces will be the result of domestic conditions in the member states? Which forces will flow from purely international pressures, as filtered

2 Inis L. Claude, "Implications and Questions for the Future," in Norman J. Padelford and Leland M. Goodrich, eds., *The United Nations: Accomplishments and Prospects*, 837. Published as *International Organization*, XIX, No. 3 (Summer 1965); hereafter cited as Padelford and Goodrich. Among such "possibilities and probabilities" Claude lists the following: universality of UN membership, including Communist China; a growing verbal commitment to international economic development aid, unmatched by actual budgetary commitments on the part of the West and the Soviet Union; the systemic given for the practice of preventive diplomacy will continue to exist, but budgetary uncertainty may well curtail that practice; consequently, there may be a renaissance of the standard techniques of pacific settlement of disputes, based on conciliation and continuous negotiation rather than organizational intercession. The UN will be used more and more as an instrument for the collective legitimation of vital national policies, thus creating new norms and holding deviant states up to collective condemnation; this practice may well discourage negotiated peaceful settlement of disputes. The UN will become more useful to the members, but not necessarily stronger and more authoritative.

through the institutions of the UN? We must seek answers to these questions through a process of conceptualization which avoids the horns of the prophecy-prediction dilemma. How shall we do this?

In approaching this issue, it is useful to think in terms of three ways of dealing with the future. One involves the construction of utopias. Another uses various types of projections. A third—and this is the mode attempted here—makes use of selective developmental models in a systemic setting. The result is neither prophecy nor prediction. It is merely contingent forecasting based on articulate assumptions, established trends, and probable logical connections between these.

The construction of utopias is a necessary but very fallible exercise in imagination. Utopias concentrate on describing an end-state of an actual or imagined evolutionary process. They neglect the specification of causative links between the various temporal stages. They pay no attention to the unintended consequences of earlier steps and to the deflections of trends triggered by the unanticipated. Hence they do not concern themselves with countertrends. They lack a theory of process.

One type of utopianism simply posits the requisites of the good life as they appear in the mind of the writer. Then the social and economic institutions made necessary for the implementation of that good life are specified, thus translating normative requisites into human arrangements. The work of H. G. Wells, Thomas More, and Samuel Butler illustrates this genre. Another type of utopianism describes a future which is conceivable on the basis of extrapolating one or two currently discernible trends or features, such as automation and cybernation, space travel, or genetic manipulation. This variant very often gets mixed up with the exploration of a specific "problem" and wishes to solve it so that it is difficult to tell whether a consistent utopia is being painted or whether the writer is preoccupied with solving "the problem of automation," for example.[3] Examples of exercises of the imagination which proceed along these lines are Herman Kahn's scenarios on a future military world and especially his effort to sketch a future "beat America" in which the cult of personal consciousness expansion and alienation from organization-dominated life will have prevailed.[4] The critical anti-utopias of Huxley and Or-

[3] See Dennis Gabor, *Inventing the Future* (New York 1964), for an example of the mixture of problem-solving and utopia-construction. He, in turn, cites the fascinating evidence of an earlier effort at projection, the *Today and Tomorrow* collection of essays written between 1924 and 1932 by nearly 100 British intellectuals. The evidence is fascinating because most of the projections soon turned out to be wrong even when based on then discernible scientific breakthroughs. The *Futuribles* project of Bertrand de Jouvenel is a similar attempt. Serious science fiction also uses this method.

[4] From a memorandum submitted to the Commission on the Year 2000 of the American Academy of Arts and Sciences.

well follow exactly the same formula, though they satirize the future rather than hold it up for study or emulation.

Among writers dedicated to the study of international organizations, utopian thinking is one of the more common avocations. The world federalist's is one type of utopia: a future end-state called "nuclear catastrophe" is postulated as certain unless something dramatic is done to forestall it. This creates an urgent "need," generated by the "nuclear problem." The need is met by a set of prescriptions for the future world; these in turn are preached as self-evident truth. However, utopian thinking is no monopoly of reformers. A former Assistant Secretary of State for International Organization Affairs asked himself what requisites would have to be met by the United Nations in order that the organization may prevent wars twenty years hence. He found that these requisites include a halt to the proliferation of nuclear weapons, a ban on intervention contrary to the will of the legitimate government, the promotion of human rights through international measures, and a compromise among those who would vest control over UN peace-keeping in the Security Council and those who prefer the more "democratic" General Assembly. It is a happy circumstance that these larger requisites coincide with the policy of the U.S. Government.[5]

Among social scientists at least, systematic projection of trends is a more respectable—if less imaginative—way of dealing with the future. The most common method is the simple extrapolation of statistical trends. This is usually done for single and unconnected items or phenomena, lacking a link in any kind of process theory. Demography is one of the most sophisticated fields using this method; economic development projections are far cruder in terms of an appreciation of causes and causative links. The "Delphi Method" of forecasting suffers from the same weakness, being merely the average of the judgments of many experts not united by a commitment to process theory. Systematic forecasting models based on future expectations can be excellent devices for ordering data and arranging it in a manner suggesting the shape of the future, but they also lack a theory of causation and of process. Yet we could learn much by applying such models to the future performance of, say, the UN General Assembly even if the intervening links and connections are not spelled out.

Cybernetic models of large systems, such as that described by Karl Deutsch, pose a different kind of problem when we try to deal with the future.[6] Such models, especially if they are equipped with a sto-

[5] Harlan Cleveland, "The Evolution of Rising Responsibility," in Padelford and Goodrich, 828-34.

[6] Karl W. Deutsch, The Nerves of Government (New York 1963). For similar efforts along these lines, consider the TEMPER Simulation of international systems

chastic quality, contain an elaborate theory of social process and allow for several ways of making decisions and processing information. They fail us in that they have not so far specified the variables, not even the most strategic ones, which would produce inputs and eventually outputs. When we deal with the future of collective security we are, however, involved with a series of very specific variables: attitudinal, behavioral, institutional, and normative. How do we accommodate them? Only by including in the construct for which we opt the systematized lessons of the past, a patterned statement of strategic variables.

This brings us to the use of selective developmental models for purposes of forecasting. Most generally, such models require us to spell out a baseline for our projection: a starting date and a list of acting units that produce the inputs of which the trends are composed. The model also requires a specification of the units whose transformation is to be studied. Thus in the case of the UN, the units producing the inputs would be nation-states; the units being transformed might be international organizations, regional organizations, or the same nation-states, as the hypothesis may require.

Further, such models require us to spell out the operating characteristics of the unit, the recurrent features of behavior and structure which give it its peculiarity. Put differently, if we proceed in this fashion we have to set up ideal types of units whose life makes up the bulk of our concern. Next, we have to specify the key variables which we expect to operate as causative agents in bringing about change. Continuing with our example of the influence of nation-states on the future of the United Nations, such key independent variables might be the pace and kind of technological-scientific innovation and diffusion; the institutionalization of social engineering; the relationship between equality and meritocracy; or the number-density ratio of cities, populations, and agriculture. Finally, we must conceptualize the process whereby the key variables postulated are thought to effect the inputs produced by the acting units on the unit whose transformation is being projected. This may lead to an incremental theory of change or to a revolutionary one. In either event, a process theory is required to explain the way in which innovation takes place, how its results are diffused, and to tell us when the diffusion results in new inputs producing structural change. If we opt for an incremental theory of change as more nearly describing the normal pattern, we then have to face the issue of when a series of small changes adds up to a major

---

and the CRISISCOM model at M.I.T. For a discussion of some ongoing studies using strategic variables, see Charles A. McClelland, *Theory and the International System* (New York 1966), Chap. 4; Elton B. McNeil, ed., *The Nature of Human Conflict* (Englewood Cliffs 1965).

or qualitative change which could have been produced as a result of the process of change subsumed under a revolutionary theory.[7]

Developmental Models and Pluralism

For reasons which will become clear later, I shall opt for an incremental theory of change closely akin to the one embedded in the pluralistic model of American society and politics. I do so because I am convinced that the international system performs in many ways analogously to this model even though its component units are not necessarily pluralistic.[8] This choice is not dictated by my personal values as to the preferability of pluralism over rival theories of the social process, such as Marxism, psychodynamic therapeutic notions, or existentialist doctrines of commitment. I simply hold that the processes described by the incrementalist-pluralist thesis fit more accurately and more often the international process of change I wish to analyze, and I see no reason why events will soon make this "fit" obsolete. The possibility remains, however, that a series of incremental changes mediated by the process of pluralism may add up to an entirely novel set of relationships which will amount to a brand new system. If so, the result will still have been produced by forces not subsumable under the more chiliastic and dramatic conceptualizations of social change.

Having suggested the theory of social process and change that appears most useful, we must still decide between two types of developmental model. One way of proceeding involves the projection into the future of presently identifiable trends. The strategic variables named above could be selected, treated as independent causative agents, and the consequences they produce on the United Nations sketched on the assumption that each variable will continue to develop unchecked. Thus one might hazard hypotheses such as the following: (1) The unchecked movement toward scientific and technological innovation in all UN member states will cause concern over the increasing pace of social change unmatched by a clear picture as to where the social change will lead; hence the UN will be given the task of assessing the social change implications of scientific innovations.[9] (2) The

---

[7] My conception of the incremental process follows roughly the scheme developed by David Braybrooke and Charles E. Lindblom, *A Strategy of Decision* (New York 1963). The way in which this concept of change is incorporated into a theory of political decision-making and change in social structure is illustrated by Robert A. Dahl and Charles E. Lindblom, *Politics, Economics and Welfare* (New York 1953); Ralf Dahrendorf, *Class and Class Conflict in Industrial Society* (Stanford 1959); Ralf Dahrendorf, "Recent Change in the Class Structure of European Societies," in S. Graubard, ed., *A New Europe?* (Boston 1964).

[8] For evidence on this point, see my "Dynamic Environment and Stable System: The Role of Revolutionary Regimes in the United Nations," in Morton Kaplan, ed., *The Revolution in World Politics* (New York 1962).

[9] For a more elaborate development of this hypothesis, see my "Toward Controlling International Change," *World Politics*, xvii, No. 1 (October 1964).

dispute between egalitarianism within and among nations and the need for a technological-scientific elite to run the increasingly specialized artifacts on which modern society depends will be resolved so that formal and legal equality among all nations will be confirmed; but the people who, on behalf of these nations, will make crucial decisions will be increasingly part of an international meritocracy.

These hypotheses are not unreasonable because they are based on visible trends and do not conflict frontally with values now dominant in the world. However, they are still in the tradition of serious science fiction because they do not allow for countertrends and for the deflection of one projected variable by another. It probably makes more sense to view the future, if we use selective developmental models at all, as a series of vectors. Variables, in impinging on one another, merge and force the thrust of development into directions not clearly implicit in each projected variable, considered alone. But we have no way of stating such vectors quantitatively without massive simulation based on a theory of social process or several alternative theories. We are not in a position to do this. Hence the vector-like projection of strategic variables into the future does not, at the moment, appear feasible.

We shall therefore adopt a different kind of developmental model. It involves a projection of presently discernible variables relating to innovation and its diffusion *without* attempting to spell out which item will deflect which and by how much. Instead, I shall posit a future international arrangement as a "requisite" and ask myself which of the currently visible variables of change must work out in a certain way in order to meet the requisites of the future so specified. In this fashion, we gain some clarity as to what would have to happen in the attitudes and behavior patterns of nations to make possible the kind of United Nations sketched for 1985. This is not a utopian enterprise because the variables chosen are not the ones I happen to like or admire; nor is it a projection of my personal preferences into the future because the model I chose happens not to be my ideal either. The procedure also differs from the utopian projection because a theory of social process is explicitly stated.

The Reconciliation Model and Other Models of the International System

The construct chosen carries the label "reconciliation model."[10] It was developed by David E. Apter to describe the evolution of national states grappling with innovation and its diffusion, with ways and means of modernization and its political implications. Apter's purpose

---

[10] The term and the concept is borrowed and adapted from David E. Apter's work. See his *The Politics of Modernization* (Chicago 1965).

is to view the future of national states as determined by the selective developmental projection of key variables. The enterprise rests on an explicit functional logic but makes no claim as to applicability to international relations.

Why then choose a reconciliation model as requisite rather than develop a future from other models? Other possibilities, all defensible, would be an international social system model, a primitive system model, and various learning models. The reconciliation model was selected because it rests on a number of intellectual operations associated with "functionalism" and "functional analysis" which I have found useful for mapping international system change. The others, however, all share with the reconciliation model the clear virtue of breaking with the ingrained intellectual tradition of analytically separating "international" from "national" systems. They call attention to the fact that international politics is still politics and that the patterns found here are at most quantitatively different from those found within a state. In other words, all these ways of viewing international relations are united in breaking with the school of thought which concentrates on power and power relations as the crucial variable that is said to distinguish international from other kinds of politics. They also share a commitment to seeing all politics as possessing common features—such as the management of force, problems of legitimacy, patterns of elite recruitment, and participation—and therefore constitute a different type of systemic reasoning than is featured by writers who address themselves exclusively to "international systems." Finally, all these approaches are dedicated to the study of international politics in terms of the concepts and lessons implicit in our understanding of the structure and function of "society" in general.

Still, the three such approaches are not as helpful to our task as the fourth, the Apterian reconciliation system. The analytical "social systems" framework of Parsons and Levy, with its structural-functional method, has been applied to international systems by Fred Riggs and George Modelski.[11] I find their efforts of little help in coming to grips with the future of the UN. Their efforts are concentrated on typologies of political systems in developmental context—*agraria* versus *industria* for Modelski, *fused* versus *refracted* for Riggs—but not on

11 George Modelski, "Agraria and Industria: Two Models of the International System"; Fred W. Riggs, "International Relations as a Prismatic System" (both in Klaus Knorr and Sidney Verba, *The International System* [Princeton 1961]) . Talcott Parsons applied his system to the description and cautious projection of the current international system in an effort to demonstrate how the "systemic" properties of mixed hostile-cooperative relations may conduce to accommodation among opponents. He thereby introduces a dynamic quality to structural-functional analysis which neither Modelski nor Riggs accomplished. See Parsons, "Order and Community in the International System," in J. Rosenau, ed., *International Politics and Foreign Policy* (Glencoe 1961) , 120-30.

the process of change. The local and international characteristics of each type are suggestive; the way of getting from one to the other is still unclear.

Efforts have been made to state the similarities between "primitive political systems" and the international system, particularly so-called stateless primitive systems. The argument holds that such systems and international society are both functionally diffuse and that the lineage basis of the primitive system has its international counterpart in the notion of sovereign territoriality. The similarity goes further. Both systems lack a center with a monopoly on the legitimate use of force; hence decentralized redress of grievances through self-help prevails, thus easily leading to escalation. The systems also share periods of peace and security which stem from mutual restraint born of fear, the services of improvised mediators, and examples of *ad hoc* special institutions set up to carry out practical tasks of equal interest to all potential belligerents. Both possess the capacity to generate customary rules of law which grow so incrementally as to be mistaken for not existing at all. And so the *Nuer* look much like the United Nations. Further, the potential for UN development can be studied by analogy if we examine the evolution of the *Nuer*.[12] To which I must respond: *Structural* similarities at high levels of abstraction tell us nothing about the perceptions of the actors with respect to needs and tasks, about their bargaining styles, about the expansion or diminution of *functions* they wish on their institutions. And once we talk about functions it appears to me that the similarity between the *Nuer* and the UN becomes a bit strained.

The learning model of the international system comes much closer to our problem. It postulates a way of conceptualizing how the actors change their beliefs as a result of interaction so as to adopt new behavior patterns contributing to a possible transformation of the system. Here the example of the "developing polity" or the "modernizing system" is compelling; such polities are engaged in perpetual change, ambitious programs, roll reassignments, ideological evolution, and restratification. The Almond-Coleman scheme of conceptualizing input functions thus acquires relevance to international relations because it can help us sketch how socialization in international organizations changes, how interest articulation and aggregation are influenced by new demands and new structures.[13] When the effort is made to equip

---

[12] Roger D. Masters, "World Politics as a Primitive Political System," *World Politics*, XVI, No. 4 (July 1964); Chadwick F. Alger, "Comparison of Intranational and International Politics," *American Political Science Review*, LVII, No. 2 (June 1963), 414-19.

[13] Same, 409-14. Also Alger, "Participation in the United Nations as a Learning Experience." *Public Opinion Quarterly* (Fall 1963). For an essentially static approach to redefining international organizations as a "system" closely analogous to

this view of the political process with an explicit psychological learning theory, it would appear that we are making progress.[14] But are we?

The test of whether a system is being transformed or confirmed is not the learning ability of its actors as measured by their attitudes. That test is provided by attitudes translated into conduct. The affirmation that, after twenty years of close interaction in UN committees, national delegates appreciate each other's views more than before tells us little, unless their foreign ministries also issue different instructions on the basis of what has been "learned." Some conceptualize learning capacity, on the model of the stimulus-response theory, as following from stimulus strength, the timing of the response, reinforcement, and discriminating generalization. This theory is unlikely to tell us whether a meeting of democratic regimes or a conference of delegates from every conceivable kind of polity is more likely to achieve agreement on disarmament. Learning theory helps only if it is conceived as indirect, as mediated by the rational expectation of actors who bargain for lower and lower stakes as they weigh the possibilities of danger as against security. This, in turn, is best done by studying the changing output pattern of the system. In that way we observe behavior rather than attitudes.

The Reconciliation Model: Definition

A reconciliation model of politics features bargaining as its main decision-making technique, rather than coercion, ideological fervor, or traditional sanctions. The decisions made by its concrete institutions are always based on the kind of bargaining which implies that all antagonists remain in the game and continue to adhere to its rules *even though* no single actor ever wins a complete victory. The learning ability of large human aggregates, jockeying for advantage to realize their interests, may be very modest in such a setting; yet the adaptive powers of the constituent units are greater than those of the *Alur* and *Nuer* because the stakes are rarely very comprehensive and the calculus of survival can afford to be quietly rational.

A reconciliation model of politics can be specified further in terms of the values most commonly professed by its citizens and subjects and by the structuring of authority in it. Social values can be dichotomized as being "consummatory" or "instrumental" in nature. Consummatory values imply a devotion to the integral realization of strongly held beliefs; instrumental values involve a constant calculation of the adjust-

---

the Almond-Coleman scheme of a national polity, see Michael Haas, "A Functional Approach to International Organization," *Journal of Politics,* xxvii (1965), 498-517.

[14] An elaborate and ambitious effort of this kind is made by Henry Teune, "The Learning of Integrative Habits," in Philip E. Jacob and James V. Toscano, eds., *The Integration of Political Communities* (Philadelphia 1964).

ment of the proper means to achieve limited ends, and a willingnesss to settle for an approximation to one's beliefs. The reconciliation model, then clearly presupposes the prevalence of instrumental values. Authority can be viewed as being structured hierarchically or pyramidally. A hierarchical social system is divided into horizontal layers of status and power such that it is very difficult for individuals to pass upward to higher layers. A feudal or a caste-dominated society is rigidly hierarchical. A pyramidal ordering of authority, however, allows for some upward passage toward the apex of power on the part of individuals and groups initially located on or near the base of the pyramid. Reconciliation models are pyramidal.

But the international system would be hierarchical if *all* decisions were authoritatively made by the super powers and if no smaller state were ever permitted into the inner decision-making circle. Even though Apter conceives the international system as segmental rather than pyramidal, I suggest that the General Assembly be regarded as the base of the pyramid of authority, the Security Council (including its nonpermanent members) as the apex, and variously weighted committees and commissions in the intermediate ranges. The essence of the reconciliation model is the fact that no one group clearly rules to the exclusion of the demands of others, even though there may be less than perfect political participation, in law or in fact.

Now, a reconciliation version of the political system, just like any other version, must meet certain "functional" and "structural" requisites so that the system may survive. This is a formal way of saying that severe strains are imposed by clashing demands, none of which are ever fully satisfied, and yet none is supposed to be so stringent as to lead to the secession or rebellion of a dissatisfied constituent unit. The "functional requisites" of a reconciliation model of politics dictate that coercion be minimal, that there be a clear source of shared norms and a strong central symbolic referent, a mechanism for integrating the system which highlights public participation, and a source of identification with the system based on satisfaction. The "structural requisites" of the model demand that the political process highlight accountability to the public, possess a wide basis of recruitment, be flexible in the enforcement of norms, possess a mechanism for allocating resources that satisfies the constituents, and have a relationship with consent groups which gives them a sense of belonging.[15]

15 These formulations are all from Apter, *Politics of Modernization*, Chaps. 7, 11. As Apter uses the term, a reconciliation system is a more comprehensive rubric than "democracy." Democracies are a species in the genus "reconciliation system," but the genus would include such less-than-completely democratic polities as Britain and France during the nineteenth century, as well as contemporary Mexico, India, Turkey, the Philippines, and Senegal.

Our task now is the adaptation of this model to international relations. Because it is a bargaining model it assumes no radical breakthrough toward a world community either in terms of world federation or conquest by a single nation. The values professed in the practice of diplomacy and war—short of total conflict—are highly instrumental. Authority is structured in an essentially pyramidal fashion. Let me stress that we are talking about *international* systemic qualities here; the constituent units—the member states—may well be devoted to consummatory values and feature a hierarchical structure of authority. But a reconciliation model of the international system holds that relations among the units will be characterized by instrumental behavior and pyramidal authority relations *despite* the possible prevalence of the other characteristics at the national level.

The United Nations, in the past as now, illustrates my point. Certainly the bulk of its members are not reconciliation polities. Yet the systemic characteristics of the ensemble meet the reconciliation requisites (see page 238).

Thus the UN has functioned as a reconciliation polity. We hold that there is no firm evidence in the trends visible in the international environment now that the UN of 1985 will not also meet the reconciliation requisites. We therefore posit that the projected UN will be a reconciliation system, albeit under great strain because the functional requisites will be subjected to new and powerful demands while the structural requisites may be unable to adjust.

In 1985 as in the past, the international system will continue to exist and be given regulative tasks even though it will probably not succeed in changing the internal characteristics of its constituent units. The United Nations will remain highly "accountable" and not very "authoritative" vis-à-vis its member states. It will make new norms only in areas where the members continue to experience common or converging needs, and it will enforce these norms selectively and flexibly. Resources made available to the United Nations will probably increase, but their distribution will be subject to the same bargaining process which has existed so far and will not rest on an automatic and calculated international technocratic development plan. International civil servants will be recruited, as heretofore, on the basis of their technical skills *and* in proportion to the influence of their home government on the politics of the organization through a geographical representation formula subject to renegotiation. Consent groups, whether governments or private associations, cannot be coerced and must be coopted to ensure their support for organizational objectives. In this sense, then, the future international system will have the same characteristics as the present one. Because no one state will dominate it

Functional Requisite	How Met in National Polity	How Met in United Nations
Ratio of information available to the government to coercion practiced by it	High/low	High/low
Source of norms	Constitution, custom	Charter, custom
Mechanism of integration	Bureaucracy, articulate private groups	Bureaucracy, national delegations
Symbolic referent	Historical achievements	None available
Source of identification and loyalty	Satisfaction with performance of system	Satisfaction with performance of system

Structural Requisite	How Met in National Polity	How Met in United Nations
Ratio of authoritative decisions to accountability	Weak/strong	Weak/strong
Basis of recruitment	Skill, merit; group access	Skill, merit; national access
Enforcement of norms	Selective, flexible	Selective, flexible
Resource allocation	Mostly private decisions, market; some bargaining	All bargaining
Relation to consent groups	Cooptation	Cooptation

and all wish to remain in the game, it is condemned to be a bargaining system achieving sporadic and *ad hoc* reconciliation of national objectives.[16]

[16] This projection of the future reconciliation system is developed at length in my *Beyond the Nation-State* (Stanford 1964), Chap. 14. There, however, my concern was to hazard a judgment about the degree of integration the UN will have conferred upon its members as a result of its current programs, *despite* the probable decline of internal pluralism in the member states. Hence the pattern of bargaining was highlighted in order to explore its integrative potentialities in a setting of increasing heterogeneity and in order to predict where UN autonomy at the expense of the member states could nevertheless be expected. My present concern, however, is with the fate of collective security on the assumption that the system there sketched will obtain. The system is made "requisite" in order to see how collective security will fare in it.

Our question then becomes: in view of this projection, can we expect the UN to practice collective security in 1985 as it has been practiced since 1945? What would have to happen to the various factors certain to make for social change nationally and internationally so as to make possible the practice of collective security? Or, given the likelihood of certain kinds of change and the survival of a reconciliation system, is the practice of collective security going to be possible at all?[17]

SYSTEMS AND ENVIRONMENTS IN HISTORY

So far we have been concerned with requisite systems and the kind of forecasting required for matching social change and human aspirations with the requisites. We now return to the history of international relations. In terms of functional and structural requisites, the past and present international constellations represented the essence of a reconciliation system. This, however, tells us nothing about aspects of the system which differed in one decade from those of the next. It tells us nothing about the kinds of states which "lived in" in the system, their aims and objectives, their relative power, the means they adopted to gain their objectives, and the tasks which devolved on international organizations as a result.

Five Distinguishing Variables

Historical systems are differentiated from one another in terms of these variables: the number of actors, the internal characteristics of the actors, the relative power of the actors, the goals they pursue, the methods they adopt, and the outcomes of their conflicting goals and methods which they impose on the common structures they have set up, i.e., the "tasks" assigned to international organizations.[18] We hold that the outcomes are determined by the sum of the other variables: a major change in one of the several "input" variables will result in a different pattern of outcomes, thus resulting in a different type of system. Historical systems may be related to one another through the "feedback" effects of earlier outcomes on the actors, thus yielding new inputs, new outputs, new task patterns, and different inter-

[17] Claude, for example, tends to answer this question negatively for the immediate future. After analyzing the UN financial crisis and the manner in which it was resolved, he concludes that the inputs into the presently visible UN reconciliation system will result in a reduction of the collective security function. In part, he reaches this conclusion because he conceives of collective security in more ideal terms than I. Claude, "Questions for the Future" and *Power in International Relations* (New York 1962), Chaps. 4, 5, 8.

[18] This conceptualization of historical systems owes much to Richard N. Rosecrance, *Action and Reaction in World Politics* (Boston 1963) and to Stanley Hoffmann, "International Systems and International Law," in Knorr and Verba, *International System*. An earlier version of this formulation is contained in Haas, *Beyond the Nation-State*, Chap. 13.

national structures. But systems may also change because of autonomous developments in the character of the actors. In the history of the United Nations, at any rate, autonomous systems change has been a more pronounced phenomenon than change due to feedback effects. Still, both processes are at work and we conceptualize systems change as a continuous phenomenon due to both impulses.

1. NUMBER AND CHARACTER OF ACTORS: We shall confine the notion of "actor" to states which appear as members of universal international organizations: the League of Nations and the United Nations. The number grew from about 50 in the early life of the League to the present 122 in the UN. But the character of the member states changed even more dramatically and frequently. We are concerned, as before, with the impact of social and economic modernization on the nature of political regimes. Hence we shall continue to use Apter's typology, as amended, for establishing the distribution of key characteristics among actors in the historical international systems. The key types of polity are: reconciliation systems, mobilization systems, modernizing autocracies, authoritarian systems, modernizing oligarchies, and traditional oligarchies.[19]

A national reconciliation system was described above. Its values are preponderantly instrumental, its authority structure pyramidal, its government possesses much information regarding the society and economy and uses little coercion against it. Norms are sanctioned by the constitution and custom, history serves as a symbolic referent, integration is achieved by a bureaucracy working in close conjunction with private groups, and national identity rests on the satisfaction of the populace, which is "participant" in character.[20] Government is highly accountable, elites are recruited on the basis of individual skill and merit as well as on the basis of access, enforcement of norms is flexible, resource allocation rests on market forces or wide consultation with private enterprise, and consent groups are coopted into the governing structure.

[19] See Apter, *Politics of Modernization*. I have not used the system Apter calls "Military Oligarchy" because I believe that the forces it represents are just as frequently carried by nonmilitary oligarchies of dedicated intellectuals. I have instead adopted the distinction established by Edward Shils between "Modernizing" and "Traditional" oligarchies. See Shils, *Political Development in the New States* (Gravenhage 1962), 67, 75, 85. In addition, I have taken the liberty to re-label the system Apter calls "Neo-Mercantilism" as "Authoritarianism." This whole effort at establishing types of regimes, within the nexus of the modernization of society, economy, and polity, is an effort to achieve finer distinctions while reducing the number of categories initially used in *Beyond the Nation-State*, Chaps. 6, 7. Apter's types sum up variations in economic development, social modernity, and economic policy commitments, as well as dealing with political patterns.

[20] For these distinctions and their implications, see Gabriel Almond and Sidney Verba, *The Civic Culture* (Princeton 1964).

A mobilization system is the exact opposite. Consummatory values predominate and the authority structure is hierarchical. The single "party" serves as the source of norms and the integrational mechanism. A "political religion" provides symbolic referent and national identity. There is little accountability, recruitment into the elite rests on loyalty to the party, norms are rigidly enforced, resources allocated according to a plan, and consent groups manipulated. All national energies are "mobilized" to achieve dramatic and rapid modernization.

A modernizing autocracy attempts to attain rapid modernization by more modest means. The traditional ruler seeks to use and adapt traditional symbols, norms, integrational mechanisms, and sources of identity to cajole his subjects into modernity. The established religion is pressed into service if this is feasible in terms of the norms of that creed. Kingship is stressed, personal loyalty to the king determines recruitment, there is little accountability, consent groups are manipulated, and the allocation of resources is planned by the ruler to the extent that his limited skills permit. Unlike mobilization systems, modernizing autocracies frequently fail in controlling the social forces released by modernizing policies and thus become victims of their efforts at planned adaptation.

Authoritarian systems are milder and more relaxed forms of mobilization systems; sometimes they emerge after a harassed populace has succeeded in overthrowing a mobilization system which had failed to plan and manipulate consent groups successfully. Authoritarian systems hinge around the person of a "presidential monarch," an "elected" ruler who claims legitimacy on the basis of popular acclaim but who surrounds himself with the trappings of a court. Instrumental values dominate, but the authority structure tends to be hierarchical. Moderate amounts of coercion are used. The president himself attempts to be the source of new, modernizing, and progressive norms; he seeks to shape the new tradition, using a single party and a bureaucracy as the integrational device. National identity rests on the people's identification with the "new tradition" and also on the degree of satisfaction they experience. Personal merit and skill are important in recruitment, some accountability is maintained, and norms are enforced with moderation. While consent groups are both coopted and manipulated, the allocation of resources preserves a large sphere to private enterprise and mixed corporations. The modernizing policies of such a regime are relatively relaxed; dissent is not tolerated officially, but dissenting views can be heard privately and incorporated into the hierarchy through various informal devices. Authoritarian systems are the reasonably efficient dictatorships which can grow up in societies in which the bulk of the people have not yet evolved from the status of subjects to that of participants and where reconciliation systems were imported and superimposed from abroad.

A modernizing oligarchy lacks the structure and purpose of the authoritarian system. It is led by a junta of dedicated civilians or military people ruling over subjects or largely pre-modern people only dimly aware of their formal citizenship in a state. The authority structure is hierarchical in principle but far less efficient and rigorous in practice than that of the authoritarian system. Values are consummatory at the verbal level but tend toward the instrumental in practice. Formal links between government and society and economy are tenuous; the civil or military bureaucracy is neither large nor efficient, though committed to modernization. Modernizing oligarchies have no clear source of norms; only when young officers make up its personnel can the ethos of "the army" sometimes meet this requisite. Only then can "army life" serve as an integrational inspiration and a source of national identity. There is no accountability, consent groups are ignored, the enforcement of norms is rigid in principle but haphazard in practice, and recruitment to the elite rests on bureaucratic or personal identification with the junta seizing power. Modernizing oligarchies have little staying power; they readily develop into authoritarian or mobilization systems.

A traditional oligarchy has been spared the pangs of modernization. It is a system in which a small group of people, related in terms of family and status, control government, society, and economy. The bulk of the people live in tribal or village units under traditional rules and are outside the political system altogether. The small urban population is in the position of subject rather than participants—except through occasional anomic outbreaks. Values are neither consummatory nor instrumental; there are no real public values at all. The authority structure is hierarchical, and the oligarchy simply seeks to keep things the way they are. There is little information about the society and little coercion because there is so little government. It is hard to find evidence of any integrational integer, any central symbolic referent, or any source of norms other than the Church and the status values of the oligarchs. Certainly there is no national identity. Nor can one speak of consent groups or accountability outside the oligarchic circle. Resources are allocated purely on the basis of private— mostly foreign—market forces; recruitment into the elite rests on family ties. When modernization arrives, it is borne by the winds of accident and private enterprise, not by public policy.

2. DISTRIBUTION OF POWER: In classifying historical periods in terms of the relative international distribution of power, we must bear in mind two aspects of that elusive notion, "power." We must specify the *kinds*

of power we mean, such as nuclear capability, conventional military capability, economic-industrial capacity, and the ability to launch effective ideological, propaganda, and subversive offensives. We must then ask ourselves whether these kinds of power were distributed symmetrically, heterosymmetrically, or asymmetrically among the actors. A period in which all kinds of power were so distributed that two actors or two blocs shared them about evenly is characterized by symmetry. A period in which some third force possesses the kinds of power which *reduce* the aggregate ability of the major blocs to maneuver freely on the international stage in *equal proportions* is one of heterosymmetry. Finally, a period in which the third force or forces reduce the capability of the major centers in *unequal proportions* would be characterized by an asymmetrical distribution of power.

Further, we must specify how the distribution of these kinds of power is clustered around poles or into blocs. When single states "lead" or "dominate" (through alliances or otherwise) large segments of the globe we speak of a polar distribution, bipolar from 1947 until 1955, tripolar in the immediate aftermath of the Bandung Conference, and multipolar since the mass admission of African nations. Note that this multipolarity implied the introduction of a heterogeneous distribution of power *even though* the third pole possessed neither the nuclear nor the conventional military capability to cut into the slices possessed by the United States and the Soviet Union. Symmetry was destroyed because of the ideological-subversive capability of the third bloc and because of its ability to make claims on the economic-industrial capacity of the large powers. With the possible decline in the ability of single states to "lead" alliances, we may have to start speaking of "multibloc" clusterings of power in preference to "poles." The change in terminology obviously implies much more than a mere shift in words: a multibloc system permits far more room for maneuver and adjustment than a multipolar one because international agreements would have to be pre-negotiated within each bloc before full acceptance by all the blocs.[21]

With the specification of these categories relating to the nature of the units and their relative power, we have described some environmental aspects of historical systems. We now turn to the aims of the actors and to the methods they employ, thus describing the inputs

[21] This terminology and the concepts summed up by it were developed by Wolfram F. Hanrieder in "The International System: Bipolar or Multibloc?" *The Journal of Conflict Resolution*, IX, No. 3 (September 1964), 299-308. Hanrieder's conceptualization is a deliberate and successful effort to give the "pure power" categories of Morton Kaplan a wider scope and more relevance to historical systems. See also Roger D. Masters, "A Multi-Bloc Model of the International System," *American Political Science Review*, LV (1961).

into the system. When we finally deal with the task thus imposed on international organizations, we shall be describing the system's outputs.

3. AIMS OF STATES: Broadly speaking, the objectives of national foreign policy have always been classified as "revisionist" or "status quo"-oriented. States either wish to keep things as they are or work for a change favoring their goals. In talking about actor objectives in these terms we have in mind the substance of politics, the subject matter issues which make up the content of foreign policy; we have said nothing about the frames of reference that inform the specification of substantive issues. What are the major substantive issues of modern international relations on which states can line up as status quo or revisionist powers?

The legitimacy of existing political boundaries is one such issue. States demanding territorial adjustments, cessions of provinces, the removal of colonial administrations, and tribal reunification are revisionists; governments taking their stand on the legitimacy of borders at any one point—a position usually cloaked in the phrase "respect for international obligations and treaties"—are not. The expansion of a specific ideology, whether by conquest or propaganda linked with externally supported subversion, is another aspect of the same larger issue. The immediate relevance of this issue to the practice of collective security hardly requires comment. Another issue is international economics. Should there be a "natural" division of labor between raw material producers and industrial countries? Should there be a concerted effort to make everybody industrialize? Is the most-favored-nation clause an instrument of economic oppression or a device to assure equality? A revisionist state aims at the reduction of the superiority of the industrialized West; the West itself has taken a status-quo position much of the time. The universal protection of human rights, through international legal obligations and possibly intervention, is another issue area. Revisionists stress such a role; status-quo powers emphasize the domestic character of such questions. One may quibble over whether the disarmament and arms control question is a sub-aspect of the territorial and ideological security issue or whether it should be considered as an issue in its own right. Revisionists stress the danger of arms—the arms of other powers—while status-quo powers emphasize the need for caution and the demands of security. Finally, the promises and dangers of science and its relationship to social change has emerged as an international issue area; status-quo countries here tend to defend the promise of science and the need for unfettered diffusion of techniques and ideas while the revisionists are more alive to the implicit dangers. Note, however, that on this issue it is the developed countries who act as the revisionists.

4. METHODS OF STATES: Little need be said about the methods which states use to attain these objectives. What matters to us is which methods are predominant in any one historical system. The types of methods available do not change very rapidly. In the period which concerns us, means have included the marshaling of national armaments (both nuclear and conventional), strategic planning and counterplanning, the eventual institutionalization of the nuclear balance of terror, and reliance on it by the super powers. It has also included the fostering of conventional capability for the fighting of local and/or limited wars on the part of the super powers no less than an almost everybody else's part. In the inevitable confrontations which ensued, the dominant methods have been alliance-building, threat, and appeasement. The ideological dimension has seen the flowering of systematic propaganda, large-scale "international information" programs designed to praise the home state and to defame the opponent, the encouragement of dissident movements in the opponent's territory, and the support of subversive activity. In the realm of economics, the methods have included bilateral and multilateral technical assistance, international lending, emergency relief, and the granting of long-range development funds. Human rights have been extolled, by and large, as a way to hurt the opponent's image and to cater to the ideological commitments of third blocs. Disarmament negotiations have been featured to eliminate threats perceived symmetrically by all parties as well as to score propaganda points. Large-scale scientific conferences and much technical work by international agencies, including international inspection, have been the way of dealing with the issue area of science.

5. TASKS OF INTERNATIONAL ORGANIZATIONS: The purpose of this whole involved exercise is to determine how various combinations of environmental forces, aims, and methods of states mingle to produce "typical" task combinations for international organizations of universal membership. Abstract-systems theorizing would proceed by way of simulating the combination of all conceivable independent variables to see which type of organizational task mixture results. Historical-systems theorizing takes the shortcut of examining actual periods of history and then seeks to project probable changes in independent variables as the causative agents of a future system. The mixture of tasks which will concern us comprises the following ingredients.

Collective security is an ingredient of each historical system. Do security decisions rest on a big power consensus, on bargaining with third forces, on overwhelming majority support? Are bargains struck which involve other issue areas? How important are collective economic decisions favoring the revisionists in shaping collective security policy? Must human rights be protected in the process? Do third forces extract disarmament or national self-determination concessions in voting for a United Nations police force? In other words, our objective is to determine whether collective-security decisions rest on a combination of variables which bring in the other issue areas, thus widening the scope of bargaining, discussion, and international activity, or whether the maintenance of collective security is an isolated task unrelated to the growth or decline of overall United Nations activity. Our hypothesis, not unexpectedly, holds that the autonomy of the collective security task declines in proportion to the increase in the multipolarity and heterosymmetry of the power constellation.[22]

These, in gross terms, are the variables to be examined when we sketch a given historical system. But how does one system "die," so to speak, and another "enter life"? How do we explain transitions from one to another?

How Do Systems Change?

A preliminary question arises: Are we talking about the growth of a "new" system or about "transitions" within the same system? There is no absolute answer. Systems are creatures decanted by the social analyst and dematerialized by him. In requisite terms, we are not talking about new systems at all. Historically, the League of Nations in 1919 was a reconciliation system, as is the United Nations in 1967. For purposes of forecasting, we postulate that the international system of 1985 will also be a reconciliation system. To assume otherwise is to predict one of the following alternatives: (1) there will be a world state based on conquest; (2) there will be a world state based on voluntary federation or merger; (3) there will be no universal international system of any intensity because everybody will have gone back to isolationism, national or regional.

However, if we posit a system whose functional and structural requisites will remain unimpaired, we still remain in the dark as to the kinds of concrete relations which will produce behavior in conformity with the requisites. Here is where we return to historical systems. If we use the variables listed above in our delimitation of the systems, we inevitably encounter new clusters of behavior; that is, we reach a "boundary." When the "boundary" of a given system is breached, however, the new system which arises may still be—in requisite terms—a reconciliation system. Here we are concerned with transitions in his-

[22] However, the same hypothesis has been used to complain of the confusion, diffuseness, and lack of coordination between voting power and political responsibility, and the "mechanical" voting procedure increasingly used to cope with heterosymmetrical multipolarity in the United Nations. For such an argument, see Lawrence S. Finkelstein, "The United Nations: Then and Now," in Padelford and Goodrich, 367-93.

torical systems that breach their boundaries. For the sake of verbal convenience we speak of them as "new" systems even though, at a different level of abstraction, they are merely more of the same old thing.

Transitions from one historical system to another are rarely clear to the actors themselves. The finding that we have arrived at a "new" system is the property of the observer. How then do political leaders find out about this? After all, the character of the system is determined by their behavior. Transition from one system to another, therefore, must imply some kind of changed behavior. It is crucial to discover whether or not this changed behavior is the result of something learned by the decision-maker as a consequence of his international experiences.

Two alternative models of explaining international-systems change exist and both are equally plausible; but only one relies on a species of learning theory that can be linked up with the perceptions and experiences of actors in international organization. It is a kind of "learning" strange to psychologists and psychologically oriented students of socialization processes because it has little to do with the essentially nonrational—or at least nonpurposive—behavior patterns of subjects whose adjustment is measured in terms of intensity of or the timing of stimuli. It is a kind of learning which presupposes that actors make decisions that are "rational" for them in the sense that they are designed to achieve a definable political objective; but they may ultimately be "irrational" in the sense that the personal frame of reference of the decision-maker may correspond to all the well-known Lasswellian psychopathologies. This, however, would not matter for us. Insofar as the frame of reference yields articulate statements about the actor's desires and the objects desired from the international scene we can undertake a systematic analysis of how these desires change with experience. Learning, therefore, is a rational process of redefining objectives and changing methods as leaders discover that persistence with the initial aims is self-defeating or overly costly. Hence international bargaining may serve as a "school" in which such lessons are learned. Yet it is important to remember that we are not assuming that "learning" involves conversion to a new belief system, dramatic shifts in values, or convergencies that will suddenly yield love whereas the previous picture had been one of mutual hostility. The school of international bargaining yields no documented case of positive reenforcement that translates into a warm community of objectives.

Considered from the vantage point of the international system itself, we can express the functional-rational learning process differently. The initial objectives of states are the explicit purposes which lead to demands made of other states in international organizations. In order to gain acceptance of these purposes, a price has to be paid to the purposes of other states, perhaps in a different issue area. The purpose, once accepted by the organization, becomes its immediate task and its program is built around it. The program, however, cannot be fully realized because of faulty planning, inadequate power, low budgets, nor national opposition. Disappointment and the hope for better performance in the future is a consequence unintended by those who first framed the task. The lessons of what could and could not be done is "fed back" into the national states. They put forward new purposes. These can either increase or decrease the task of the organization. In either event, learning has taken place through the feedback process triggered by unintended consequences. Reformulated purposes may become "functional" for system transformation; hence we speak of them as "functions."

Two brief examples will illustrate this process. Frustration with Soviet opposition to the meeting of Western collective security demands led the United States to sponsor, and the UN to adopt, the Uniting for Peace Resolution. In 1950, it was thought that a Western-controlled General Assembly would vote the appropriate powers to a coalition of states eager to take on enforcement duties. It was an unintended consequence of this sudden catering to the small powers—especially as more were admitted in 1955—that these states proved exceedingly uninterested in meeting the purpose the United States had in mind in 1950. Hence, contrary to intentions, no new constitutional powers were bestowed on the General Assembly. The Uniting for Peace Resolution languished from disuse. As a second unforeseen consequence, however, the Secretary-General assumed prominence in the collective security issue area. With the Security Council deadlocked and the General Assembly unwilling or unable to act rapidly, the Secretary-General, in dispute after dispute after 1956, assumed the initiative in organizing UN collective measures with a certain measure of autonomy.[23]

The role of the General Assembly in making new international law illustrates a deceptive trend toward functional adaptation. As part of cold war and anticolonialist propaganda, various states at various times assumed the responsibility for having the General Assembly adopt declarations on human rights. Whatever the original intent, these declarations were soon used by other countries to press for changes in na-

[23] For a penetrating treatment of this theme, see Ruth B. Russell, "Changing Patterns of Constitutional Development," in Padelford and Goodrich, 410-28. She argues convincingly that "real" constitutional adjustments occur as a result of political bargaining which results from changing environmental impulses, whereas institutionally derived constitutional changes tend to be ignored.

tional policy, often in political contexts which had not been in the minds of the original sponsors. Some even argued that these declarations possess the force of law, if and when invoked often enough and respected in state practice. In short, as an unintended consequence of an immediate and expediential motive, new comprehensive international law is said to come into existence.[24] In fact, the reluctance of states to ratify conventions which result from the process—indeed the insistence that the declarations be transformed into conventions—suggests that the claim is hardly realistic. But it illustrates the functional logic of international learning.

This model of international-system transformation credits the international organization with the capacity to produce feedbacks capable of changing the environment.[25] There is an alternative model which puts the emphasis on autonomous changes at the national level. Developments in the various social, economic, and political sectors making up the environment are conceived as proceeding more rapidly and decisively than the national learning of international feedbacks. New demands will then also be put on the system's structures. These will still encounter other new or opposing demands. The structures may not gain any net power at the expense of the member states but will be transformed just the same because the new mix of demands will result in a different task for the organization. The point which bears repetition here is the absence of any learning on the part of the national decision-makers. The new task is purely the result of needs experienced at the national level and does not follow a previous period of related experience connected with the earlier task of the organization. The phenomenon of reevaluated national purpose is lacking.

System transformation can be explained with either model. But only the first one gives rise to net integration, whereas the second one results in a decentralized system that remains largely static. When feedbacks result in adaptive learning, the result is likely to be a stronger system with more autonomous power. When new tasks evolve from rapidly changing environmental impulses, the system's powers have barely a chance to keep up with the changing mixture of demands.

24 Leo Gross, in "The United Nations and the Rule of Law," Padelford and Goodrich, 537-61, makes the case for the deceptive nature of any UN legislative process. The Commission to Study the Organization of Peace, *New Dimensions for the United Nations: The Problems of the Next Decade* (17th Report, 1966) argues that declarations based on a profound consensus do have law-making force, an argument also advanced by the UN Secretariat in 1962.

25 The description of the integrative model of system transformation is the burden of my *Beyond the Nation-State*, Part I. The historical "testing" of the model led me to advance the chain of events subsumed here under the second model because the environment always changed faster than could be accounted for by systemic feedbacks. See *Beyond the Nation-State*, Chap. 13.

In the actual history of the United Nations and the specialized agencies, the second model comes closer to describing the truth. It is largely responsible for having given us a succession of reconciliation systems. I suspect that it will also give us the one the future has in store for us.

What are the limits of peaceful transition from one kind of reconciliation system to another? In our two models we have postulated the reaching of boundaries and the rearrangement of the system so that no violent breakdown occurs—such as would be implied by a world war or a massive retreat to isolationism on the part of everybody. But world wars do occur and Sukarno's Indonesia suggests that the attempt at full withdrawal may still be attempted. What limiting assumptions about transitional processes do we therefore have to make?

Hanrieder suggests that specific policy aims, such as the ones we discussed above, must be explained in terms of a larger frame of reference on the part of decision-makers. In providing such frames of reference, he is catapulting us beyond the old debate as to whether national policy is made in response to domestic impulses or international constraints. The answer, of course, is: in response to both. But we can do a little better than that.[26]

Actors make their decisions according to three possible frames of value reference. Material policy objectives may be derived purely from internal referents, as is the case in seeking routine commercial and technical relations. But nonmaterial values encountered at home as well as abroad also fall into this frame of reference provided their realization does not depend on any forces outside the state. Hence the idealistic devotion to higher living standards, natural law, peaceful change, and the like leads to policy demands of purely internal relevance. The New Dealer who preached international Keynesianism (without making specific claims that foreigners change their systems of banking) as well as the isolationist of the 1930's responded to internal referents.

An external referent dominates the making of policy whenever a given value demands a change of behavior on the part of foreign nations. Foreign policy based on a crusading ideology is the obvious example. Territorial revisionism is another. A policy devoted to reconstructing the world economic system is a third. Any policy which places the foreigner in a position desired by the home state, either in fact or in advocacy, responds to an externally focused value referent.

[26] Wolfram F. Hanrieder, "Actor Objectives and International Systems," *Journal of Politics*, XXVII (1965), 109-32. Hanrieder advances this scheme in an effort to deal with some of the ambiguities of Arnold Wolfers' classic, "The Pole of Power and the Pole of Indifference," *World Politics*, IV (1951), 39-63.

Finally, policy can be based on a systemic referent. No normative implication attaches to the impulse: it is simply perceived as existing. Most commonly, the systemic reference implies the desire of the state to safeguard its existence, granting the prevalence of a probably hostile system. Armament policies, in the absence of specific territorial or ideological claims, derive from such a referent. But accommodation in the United Nations—once that institution is taken for granted—may also be regarded as a systemic response.

These three frames of reference have very different implications for system transformation. Internal and external value referents are imbued with consummatory qualities. They refer to cherished beliefs, styles of life, and hallowed traditions. Systemic referents are highly instrumental and policies based on them lend themselves to bargaining and accommodation. It follows that international systems made up of states whose leaders respond to systemic frames of reference are more adaptable than others. Systems made up of a large number of countries devoted to violent policies involving external referents find it difficult to carry on negotiations. The League of Nations suffered accordingly after 1935. In brief, the peaceful transition of international systems is facilitated by two conditions: (1) the actors, or at least the most powerful, should respond to a systemic frame of value reference; (2) the actors should overwhelmingly be devoted to internal frames of value reference making no dramatic claims on foreigners.[27]

Historical Systems, 1919-1965

With these conceptual and methodological apologetics out of the way, we can now summarize the characteristics of the various reconciliation systems which have prevailed since 1919. Table 1 will summarize the environmental variables; Table 2 will deal with the inputs of states and the outputs rendered as organizational tasks. Note that the elements of actor learning involved in the transitions among systems are implicit in the evolution of the aims of states as we move forward from 1945. They also correlate closely with the changing distribution of power and the growing proportional share of all types of polities other than traditional oligarchies and reconciliation systems. I must caution, therefore, against any interpretation that the organizational task is somehow autonomous and that the character of the system can be assessed independently of the identity and attributes of the mem-

---

[27] Some support for this hypothesis can be found in a factor and content analysis of resolutions and votes on major collective security issues in all special and emergency sessions of the General Assembly. See Hayward R. Alker, Jr., "Supranationalism in the United Nations," Peace Research Society, *Papers* III (Chicago 1965), 197-212. Alker found that support for resolutions creating new powers and tasks for the UN in collective security operations came overwhelmingly from Western democracies and small ex-colonial nations in Asia and Africa.

ber states. On the contrary, Table 2 means that the tasks of the organization provide the dependent variable, with the aims of the states (as sorted in terms of the categories summarized in Table 1) serving as the independent variable. The methods chosen by the member states provide an intervening variable of such importance that at times it may acquire the position of independent causal force.

Further, I must call attention to the fact that what appears as one product of the independent and intervening variables—e.g., collective security—is a product only temporarily. It remains only a technique for maintaining peace—i.e., another intervening step—that owes its de-

TABLE 1

INTERNATIONAL ENVIRONMENTS,
1919-1965

Period	Polities (Number of League of Nations or UN members in each type, as a percentage of total membership)						Power Distribution
	Rec.	Mob.	M.A.	T.O.	M.O.	Auth.	
1919-1931 1925 League membership: 55	51	2	5	35	2	5	Unipolar victor group; isolated dissenters
1932-1940 1935 League membership: 57	33	7	10	37	2	10	Bipolar asymmetrical
1945-1947 1946 UN membership: 53a	43	11	6	34	4	2	Unipolar victor group
1948-1951 1950 UN membership: 60a	50	13	5	25	5	2	Tight bipolar symmetrical
1952-1955 1953 UN membership: 61a	46	13	7	19	8	7	Loose bipolar heterosymmetrical
1956-1960 1958 UN membership: 82a	43	19	15	10	6	7	Tripolar heterosymmetrical
1961-1965 1965 UN membership: 116a	37	19	9	6	7	22	Multipolar heterosymmetrical

a Does not include Ukraine and Byelorussia.

TABLE 2

INPUTS AND OUTPUTS IN INTERNATIONAL SYSTEMS,
1919-1965

Period	Aims of States	Methods of States	Tasks of International Organizations
1919-1931	Victors: preserve political status quo, colonial system, and global free enterprise Dissenters: territorial revisionism	Alliances, arms reduction, improve collective security against occasional protest from dissenters	Collective security based on a Big Power consensus to preserve the victors' peace settlement of 1919; short-term financial aid and emergency relief for victims of World War I; promote arms reduction; preserve free trade and freedom for private financial transactions
1932-1940	Victors: preserve entire status quo Dissenters: territorial enlargement, economic autarky	Victors: appeasement, slight rearmament Dissenters: subversion, propaganda, aggression, economic imperialism	None
1945-1947	Victors: preserve new political status quo, colonial system, global free enterprise Dissenters: not heard	Develop collective security through Big Power consensus, indoctrinate and reform vanquished states, return to competitive world trade and investment	Collective security through Big Power concert; emergency relief for victims of World War II; promote world trade rules stressing non-discrimination and unfettered investment; promote arms reduction
1948-1951	West: preserve total status quo East: expand into Europe and Asia, support nationalist and Communist revolts	Alliances, bilateral economic aid, multilateral technical aid, propaganda, collective security against East, limited war Subversion, aggression, propaganda, limited war, alliances	Collective security through authority delegated to U.S. and its allies; technical assistance; some regional economic planning for industrialization; Western-controlled human rights advocacy
1952-1955	West: preserve territorial status quo, cater to third forces otherwise East: aid nationalist and Communist revolts	Alliances, bilateral military and economic aid, nuclear buildup, propaganda Propaganda, subversion, nuclear buildup, alliances	Collective security through third-world mediation between East and West; more technical assistance; more general human rights advocacy; more varied technical services for under-developed countries

Period	Aims of States	Methods of States	Tasks of International Organizations
	Others: profit from cold war to further national and economic development	Agitation, revolts, economic planning	
1956-1960	West: adapt to third force by winning or neutralizing it. Spur global economic growth	Stabilize balance of terror, multilateral economic aid, UN to stabilize third force, economic regionalism	Collective security through cautious supranational leadership of UN Secretary - General; much more extensive economic aid; ambitious technical aid programs; collective intervention for decolonization and human rights
	East: adapt to third force by winning or neutralizing it, support decolonization (excludes China)	Stabilize balance of terror, bilateral military and economic aid to new nations, some support for UN aid programs, limited war, propaganda in new states	
	Others: profit from cold war to further national and economic development, contain cold war and nuclear arms, dislodge colonial powers	Aggression, limited war, secure more external military and economic aid, obtain legitimacy of total national self-determination	
1961-1965	West: same as above with Europe more eager to adapt than U.S., mute cold war	Cut back balance of terror, arms control, decolonize, supranational economic aid, spur trade, less stress on alliances - military aid - propaganda, cross - alliance ties	Collective security through supranational leadership and Big Power concert; massive human rights promotion and decolonization; new world trade norms; arms control; implications of science explored; great expansion of investment aid to developing countries
	East: same as above with U.S.S.R. most eager to adapt, mute cold war, reduce involvement in new countries while stressing decolonization (excludes China)	Cut back balance of terror, arms control, spur trade, economic aid, less stress on alliances-military aid - propaganda (after nuclear bid in Cuba), cross - alliance ties	
	Others: same as above (with three different blocs of unaligned states), reorganize world trade and finance system	Subversion, limited war, aggression, regional economic bloc formation	

gree of success to the operation of many other variables. Collective security, then, is not to be taken as an end product identical with "peace." The same is true of economic aid, protective measures for human rights, etc.

The UN and Collective Security

We should now proceed to analyze the past and future of collective security in terms of this conceptualization. But what is "collective security"? Some commentators treat the notion as if it were the equivalent of "peace" or the "maintenance of peace." American statesmen have implied that collective security means the same thing as American or free world security. Three closely related notions are commonly confused here: peaceful change, pacific settlement of disputes, and measures for dealing with threats to the peace and acts of aggression.[28] Yet all three share certain attributes which do differentiate a collective security arrangement from other international systems, such as the balance of power, the unit-veto system, or world government. All three require the existence of an intergovernmental *organization*, fixed *roles* for certain members or agencies, a basic set of *norms*, and an agreed *procedure* whereby the organization applies the norms to cases.

Collective Security and Peaceful Change

This said, "collective security" is the technique used by intergovernmental organizations to restrain the use of force among the members. It provides the norms and procedures for dealing with acts of aggression; it also includes the norms and procedures for inducing the members to delay hostilities, norms and procedures summed up under the label "pacific settlement of disputes." Finally, collective security also comprises the organization's own ability to use force against a member if pacific settlement fails. In terms of the norms of the UN, collective security is defined by the provisions of Chapters VI and VII of the Charter. The practice of collective security requires the existence, in the language of Article 34 of the Charter, of a "dispute" or a "situation which might lead to international friction or give rise to a dispute." The notion of peaceful change, by contrast, is more difficult to define. It covers "situations" which might lead to a dispute if permitted to fester, potential sources of strife already visible on the international horizon but not yet sufficiently congealed to enable the organization to find that State "A" has a specific complaint against

---

28 See Wolfram F. Hanrieder, "International Organization and International Systems," *Journal of Conflict Resolution* (September 1966), for an effort to render each of these notions as a separate "system" arranged on a conceptual continuum. My discussion below of the distinction between peaceful change and collective security is a slight adaptation of a portion of his demonstration.

State "B" which threatens the peace.[29] However, peaceful change is, like collective security, also a technique to keep the peace and it too makes use of the procedures of pacific settlement.

This distinction can be made clear by contrasting the modal attributes of collective security and peaceful change, though the distinction will not always stand the test of a specific organizational attempt to maintain peace. We can contrast the two in these terms:

	Collective Security	Peaceful Change
(1) Is the Organization concerned with the *internal* political attributes of the disputants (progressive vs. reactionary, democratic vs. tyrannical) ?	No	Maybe
(2) Is the Organization concerned with the realization of some new *international* values, such as national self-determination, economic equality?	No	Yes
(3) What degree of urgency prompts the Organization to act?	Aggression	Unrest
(4) Should the Organization act so as to use the dispute to transform the international system?	No	Maybe

To summarize, collective security aims at the preservation of the international status quo, deals with acts of aggression or imminent threats thereof, and is unconcerned with the domestic characteristics of the

[29] The UN Charter (Article 14) defines peaceful change as "the peaceful adjustment of any situation, regardless of origin, which it [the General Assembly] deems likely to impair the general welfare or friendly relations among nations, including situations resulting from a violation of the provisions of the present Charter." This includes dissatisfaction with the benefits obtained from the international economic system, opposition to colonialism, the desire to improve social standards, and the demand for the universal observation of human rights—all issue areas which could lead to real disputes. In the UN, such issues were to be dealt with by the Economic and Social Council, the Trusteeship Council, and the General Assembly. In fact, the creation of such new agencies as the Special Fund and the standing Assembly committees on colonialism testifies to the growth of a peaceful change task, as a result of dramatic environmental changes, far greater than anticipated by the drafters of the Charter. For an excellent discussion of the notion of "peaceful change," see Lincoln P. Bloomfield, *Evolution or Revolution* (Cambridge 1957) and Bloomfield, *The United Nations and U. S. Foreign Policy* (Boston 1960), Part IV.

disputants. Further, these measures are *instrumentally* informed: the objective is the preservation of peace or the punishing of aggression; it is not the *substantive* desire to aid in the establishment of a new norm.

Peaceful change, on the other hand, is the twin technique of peace-keeping that aims at heading off aggression by dealing with unrest so as to aid in the realization of new international values and to support "progressive" national forces. It is in this context that such new procedures as the "collective legitimation" of national policies come into their own, thus illustrating how the traditional pacific-settlement methods and the innovative expressions of world opinion can be combined as UN procedures to update the technique of peaceful change.[30]

This clarification, unfortunately, does not dispose of our conceptual troubles completely. The UN has attempted to combine the two operations in such cases as Palestine and the effort to dislodge France from North Africa (1950-1958). Broken into its analytical components, these actions show that collective security can sometimes be successful when peaceful change efforts fail, while peaceful change attempts unaccompanied by energetic collective measures may lead to nothing at all.

Operational and Other Theories of Collective Security

But there is an additional problem. Commentators differ with respect to a "theory" of collective security even when they accept the distinctions elaborated thus far. Consider the "ideal theory" of collective security, as tersely stated by A.F.K. Organski:

[30] Unfortunately, there is no agreement within the scholarly community on the proper use of these terms and concepts. This discussion is offered in the probably foolish hope of contributing to the evolution of such agreement. I. L. Claude has suggested that we scrap the notion of "collective security" altogether and substitute therefor terminology such as "peace promotion" to denote the full range of collective security-cum-peaceful change approaches. The more specific procedures of "peace promotion" would comprise "peacemaking" (including what we now call pacific settlement of disputes and the collective legitimation of innovation through UN resolutions); "peace-enforcement," or the marshalling of the measures associated with Chapter VII of the Charter and the Uniting for Peace Resolution; "peacekeeping," or the panoply of partial enforcement measures developed ad hoc by the UN since 1955 but falling short of formal sanctions. Such terminology, however, would not respect the fundamental analytical and practical distinctions between the operational assumptions of status-quo oriented and revisionist approaches.

For a discussion of the new procedure of "collective legitimation," see Inis L. Claude, Jr., "Collective Legitimization as a Political Function of the United Nations," *International Organization*, xx, No. 3 (Summer 1966). The use of the pacific settlement procedures, under the aegis of both the collective security and the peaceful change techniques, is elaborately and convincingly demonstrated by Mark W. Zacher, "The Secretary-General and the United Nations' Function of Peaceful Settlement," same (Autumn 1966).

The idea of collective security rests upon five assumptions that must prove to be correct if the idea is to work out in practice. They are:

1. In any armed combat, all nations will agree on which combatant is the aggressor. What's more, they will reach this agreement immediately, since rapid and united action is necessary if aggression is to be brought to a halt before extensive damage is done.

2. All nations are equally interested in stopping aggression from whatever source it comes. Preventing aggression is a value which overrides all others in international relations. Neither friendship nor economic advantage will stand in the way of action against an aggressor.

3. All nations are equally free and able to join in action against an aggressor.

4. The combined power of the collectivity, i.e., of all the nations in the world except the aggressor, will be great enough to overwhelm the aggressor.

5. Knowing that overwhelming power stands ready to be used against it, an aggressor nation will either sheathe its sword or go down in defeat.[31]

Organski believes that because only the last two requisites can ever be met in practice, collective security is a will-o'-the-wisp. Claude suggests that because the ideal requisites have not been met faithfully either in international practice or in the norms and procedures enshrined in the UN Charter, there is no real collective security but simply a rechristened balance of power system.[32]

To pitch the examination of an organizational task to an overly demanding definition is to invite disappointment "by definition." But the same can be said of a rival theory of collective security which rests on the diplomatic understandings that prevailed at the origin of a new organization. Unlike the ideal theory, the "diplomatic theory" defines the norms, procedures, and aims of collective security in terms of the consensus among the drafting countries which existed in 1919 and 1945. Instead of stating these as requisites, it enshrines them as the values of a new world order. Later departures from these norms in

---

[31] A.F.K. Organski, *World Politics* (New York 1958), 373.

[32] Inis L. Claude, Jr., *Power and International Relations* (New York 1962) and Claude, "The Management of Power in the Changing United Nations," *International Organization*, xv, No. 2 (Spring 1961). For a comprehensive critique of Claude's approach to collective security and a suggestion that we conceptualize the notion in terms of what actually happens in international organizations, see Ruth B. Russell, "The Management of Power and Political Organization: Some Observations on Inis L. Claude's Conceptual Approach," *International Organization* (Autumn 1961), 630-36. I share the position taken by Miss Russell.

the practice of the organization will then be greeted with cries of alarm and shouts of dismay as being "illegal" or "immoral." Thus the Soviet Union has stressed the "illegality" of collective security operations launched by the General Assembly or the Secretary-General; more circumspectly, United States spokesmen have recently warned of the "irresponsibility" and "immaturity" of Assembly majorities that refuse to follow the lead of the major powers.

The consensus which underlay the League of Nations can best be summarized as a devotion to the power of the "universal will of mankind," as enshrined in the unanimity voting formula of the League on all substantive issues. There could be no pacific settlement or enforcement against the will of a major power, of course, but even a minor power could block such action! As was made unambiguously clear by spokesmen for all the sponsoring governments of the San Francisco Conference which drafted the UN Charter, the unanimity of the Big Five was the condition *sine qua non* for pacific settlement and collective enforcement measures.[33] Collective security was to be something dispensed by a united concert of the major powers for the benefit of quarreling smaller nations. The Big Five were expected— and expected themselves—to settle their differences privately outside the UN. The consensual principle in this diplomatic theory was the notion of the "concert."

Must we conclude that there is no collective security simply because later events have illustrated the short life of these consensual principles? To do so would be to deny the possibility of the evolution of new norms and procedures arising from the ashes of a superseded principle; it would be to deny system-transformation following the path of either of the two models we have sketched. More important, to rest the study of collective security on either the ideal or the diplomatic theory implies that we simply ignore the *facts* of successful peace-preservation in situations which meet few of the requisites and none of the consensual patterns.

Hence we opt for an operational theory of collective security. We ask: What kind of technique did the UN use under what circumstances? What was the environmental constellation of forces when the technique was adopted? What kind of consensus did the members display in adopting a certain technique? How often and under what circumstances was the technique successful? In doing so we admit that

[33] The only possible exception (institutionalized after difficult negotiations with Stalin) is in paragraph 3 of Article 27 of the Charter: "provided that in decisions under Chapter VI and under paragraph 3 of Article 52, a party to a dispute shall abstain from voting." Permanent members cannot veto recommendations for pacific settlement or referrals of disputes to regional organizations when they are themselves parties. Security Council procedure has not actually lived up to this provision with clarity and consistency.

the ideal requisites are rarely met and that the diplomatic understandings are transitory. But since cases continue to be submitted to the UN—and are sometimes successfully dealt with—we are forced to ask the larger questions if we are concerned with the future as a result of the past.

This approach, however, should be differentiated from pure operationalism in the sense that no assumptions are being made at all. The assumptions explicitly incorporated in our approach are those referring to historical systems and to the two transformation models. A "collective security task" is viewed as the result of a bargaining process involving other issue areas as well. It is analytically integrated into the historical periods suggested by the size of the membership and the international distribution of power. Our leading proposition, then, is that different environments will produce different combinations in the aims of states and in the methods adopted, and that these will result in different combinations of tasks for the international organization. The unverified hypothesis is that each of these clusters will produce a specific consensual pattern making possible the use of certain peace-keeping techniques. These techniques will fit neither the ideal nor the diplomatic theory of collective security.

But how significant is it to study world peace-preservation solely in terms of disputes referred to international organizations? Do we not confine ourselves to a very small segment of the overall war-peace phenomenon by singling out international organizations? The statistics of disputes referred to the United Nations argue that we are not. During the League of Nations era, however, the situation was otherwise.

Thus between 1920 and 1937, there occurred 37 international "disputes," confrontations of the kind that qualify under our definition of quarrels which could trigger the collective security machinery. Of these 37 only 14 were referred to the League for settlement, or 38 percent. Six of the 14 were in some measure settled through League procedure. This gives the League a "success score" of 43 percent, granting the low percentage of total international disturbances which actually found their way to the Geneva council tables.[34]

The period 1945-1965 witnessed 108 disputes posing a possible threat to peace. Only 27 of these were not referred to any international organization.[35] This gives us a referral score of 75 percent, distributed as follows:

[34] My figures are based on the list of disputes referred to the League of Nations contained in James T. Shotwell and Marina Salvin, *Lessons on Security and Disarmament from the History of the League of Nations* (New York 1949).

[35] The following disputes were not referred to any international organization: border quarrels between Congo (Leopoldville) and all her neighbors, Somalia's claim on French Somaliland, the Indochina war (1946-1954), the Pushtunistan dispute, Soviet-Western controversy over the Japanese peace treaty, Japan's claim

Referred to United Nations: 45 (42%)
Referred to regional organizations: 26 (24%) [36]

Referred to United Nations and
regional organizations: 10 (9%) [37]

---

against the United States over the Ryukyu Islands, the Japanese-Korean controversy, the Vietnam war (1961——), the Sino-Indian war and related border disputes, Nepalese-Indian differences, Philippine claim on Sabah, the Rann of Kutch fighting, Soviet territorial demands on Turkey, Western-Soviet controversy over the German and East European peace treaties/NATO/Berlin access, British Guiana-Surinam boundary, Belize dispute, Falkland Islands, Iran-Iraq border disputes, tribal fighting and boundary delimitation on the Trucial Coast, British-Iran dispute over Bahrein, Egyptian-Sudanese border disputes, Lebanese complaints over Jordanian intervention, the Sino-Soviet dispute, the Polish-Soviet dispute (1956), the U.S.-Chinese situation (including Quemoy-Matsu fighting, U-2 flights, etc.), Spanish-Moroccan fighting at Ifni, Moroccan-Mauritanian boundary question.

The following procedure was used in arriving at the total of 55. Certain obviously related complaints were counted as one dispute even though complaints were lodged at separate times. Thus the Tunisian, Moroccan, and Algerian effort to dislodge the French was counted as one "North African" dispute. Complaints of violations of established truce arrangements (as in Palestine and Kashmir) were not counted as separate disputes; but a general breakdown of a truce by way of a new major campaign was (as in Suez and the India-Pakistan war of 1965). Generalized propaganda complaints (e.g. the use of bacteriological warfare in Korea) were not counted at all; usually they occurred in the context of a more specific dispute which was counted, even though they may have appeared as separate UN agenda items. In terms of periodization, a dispute was counted only once, during the period when it originated, even though it may have carried over into the next period.

It should be noted that this approach guards against the danger of distorted decision-making analyses by *not* ignoring the "dynamics of non-decision-making" stressed by Peter Bachrach and Morton Baratz, "Two Faces of Power," *American Political Science Review*, LVI, No. 4 (December 1962). My scores include the cases in which UN organs were unable to make a decision in addition to instances where decisions brought no results. If anything, they err on the side of UN failure because of the care and conservatism employed in crediting the UN with having settled an issue or aided in settlement. More charitable observers, for example, might argue that the UN deserves some credit for the settlement of the Panama Canal dispute between Panama and the United States. The Security Council voted to refer the dispute to the OAS. That organization, however, then deferred to bilateral negotiations between the parties, who arrived at a settlement. I did not credit the UN at all in this and similar situations.

The most complete and most recent list of disputes is contained in Carnegie Endowment for International Peace, *Synopses of United Nations Cases* (New York 1966). My figures, however, differ from the totals in that study because of slightly different criteria as to what a "dispute" is. The Carnegie list contains 69 rather than 55 UN "cases" because a number of situations I consider as typifying peaceful change were included, as well as a few propaganda-type resolutions. In addition, the Carnegie study lists far more than 27 disputes not referred either to the UN or to regional organizations. It arrived at its totals by counting several cases which were of little significance to international relations and posed no conceivable threat to peace, such as the lobster controversy between France and Brazil and various very hazy territorial claims on the part of new African states.

[36] Of these 26, the OAS was given 18; the Organization for African Unity 5; NATO 1; the Council of Europe 1; and the Arab League 1.

[37] Of these 10, 6 were referred to the OAS; 1 to the OAU; 1 to NATO; and 2 to the Arab League.

We derive our conclusions on collective security in operation from the 55 disputes referred to the United Nations.

Before presenting the data for these 55 disputes, we must make plain what was counted in each instance and how certain judgments were made.

Coding the Disputes

1. OBJECTIVE INFORMATION ON UN ACTION: Disputes were coded as to which organ of the UN was involved: the Security Council, the General Assembly, or both. In addition, we differentiated between the different types of action which each of these organs could adopt; naturally, a single dispute could be scored as having featured one, some, or all of these types of action. They are: (a) an appeal to the parties that they negotiate their differences bilaterally or refer the matter to a regional organization; (b) the launching of an inquiry into the facts of the dispute by the organ concerned; (c) the offer of collective mediation and/or conciliation by the organ concerned in the form of substantive resolutions designed to settle the dispute; (d) the appointment of a single mediator to work with the parties toward a settlement; (e) referral to the International Court of Justice for binding judicial settlement; (f) the issuing of a cease-fire order; (g) the establishment of a truce supervision force to patrol a cease-fire; (h) the creation of an international police force to separate the parties, maintain order, or disarm local forces; (i) the creation of a "Secretary-General's presence" in the trouble spot to facilitate adherence to UN resolutions and report to the Secretary-General; (j) the declaration of sanctions against one (or both) of the parties in the form of selective embargoes, trade boycotts, or military enforcement; and (k) the creation of a committee of experts to recommend measures to the parties and to the UN organ concerned. Such a committee has been used only in the case of the apartheid dispute with South Africa, after the failure of all of the other types of action. Finally, a given dispute was coded as "no action" if none of the UN organs was able or willing to adopt a resolution concerning it. This happened in 19 of our 55 cases. Decisions on how to code a given dispute were straightforward and required no judgment on the analyst's part.

2. HOSTILITIES: We also coded each dispute as to whether hostilities were involved, another operation involving no judgment. International hostilities as well as civil war were included and in some instances both of these forms of violence were involved.

3. POWER STATUS OF PARTIES: Disputes were classified as to the power possessed by the parties and with respect to their position in the world alliance system. Thus we used the following categories: (a)

disputes involving a major power (defined as a permanent member of the Security Council) ; (b) disputes involving two minor powers who are aligned within the same bloc; (c) disputes involving two minor powers who are members of opposing blocs; (d) disputes involving two minor powers, one of whom is aligned and the other unaligned; and (e) disputes involving two minor unaligned powers. Once more, no judgment was required in coding these matters.

4. TYPE OF ISSUE: We also want to know how the dispute fits into the major fissures and tensions of world politics. This question did require judgment on the part of the analyst that need not accord with the way the parties themselves saw their dispute. We considered the periods of world politics in which the UN systems have operated as marked by two meta-issues, the cold war and the anticolonial movement. Hence disputes were coded as (a) cold war, (b) colonial, and (c) other. The claims of the parties as to whether their grievances were "antiimperialistic" or designed to "maintain freedom" were given little credence in the scoring. The Malaysian-Indonesian dispute was scored as "other" and the Dominican intervention dispute as "cold war" even though some of the parties would not see it in that light.

5. TYPE OF POLITY: Wherever feasible, the parties were classified in terms of the nature of their domestic political system. The categories employed were taken from the Apter typology, as amended by me and described above. Two major limitations in this effort must be acknowledged. In 10 of the 55 disputes there were so many parties involved that a simple classification by pairs proved unrealistic because many types of polities were actually represented. These cases had to be excluded from some of the tabulations. Further, the judgment as to which type of polity actually describes a given country in a given systemic period is necessarily difficult because some of the desirable data are often lacking. In instances in which an assignment to a category was debatable, I engaged in consultations with colleagues and associates.

6. TYPE OF CONSENSUS IN THE UN: Consensual categories involve heavy conceptual judgments which take us some distance away from the factual scene and the explicit perceptions of the parties. These judgments flow from conceptual commitments on my part derived from the observational stance represented by the notion of a reconciliation system. They include first and foremost the institutional question of which decisional format was used to determine UN action: unanimity of the great powers in the Security Council, a two-thirds majority vote in the General Assembly, an initiative of the Secretary-General which is more or less rigorously ratified by either the Security Council or the General Assembly, or a prolonged bargaining pattern in either organ in which

a "third bloc" of some kind figured prominently. Secondly, a consensual category includes the question of the identity of the participating actors and of the pattern in which they group themselves in arriving at a collective decision. Briefly, we are here talking about the institutional and the behavioral dimensions which go into voting a decision. We distinguish between these seven consensual patterns:[38]

(a) Majority Will. The most uncomplicated consensual picture obtains when the necessary constitutional majority in the General Assembly opts for a given course of action without special bargaining or extensive manipulation on the part of a big power. A spontaneous majority will is the operative consensus when two-thirds of the members act in such a fashion. We should note that this type of consensus corresponds to the demands of the "ideal theory" of collective security and was made the institutional cornerstone of the League of Nations. Its prevalence in the history of the UN is difficult to detect.

(b) Concert. A decision is based on a concert if the minimal legal requirement for an affirmative vote in the Security Council is met, thus complying with the "diplomatic theory" of collective security associated with the origin of the UN Charter. A concert can take the form of the unanimous vote of the permanent members or manifest itself in the abstention of one or more. Concerts based on abstentions are themselves a constitutional innovation which, though pioneered by the Soviet Union in the Azerbaijan dispute, ran counter to the evident intent of the founders. The founders, as we know, had assumed that a permanent concert would come about because the major powers would successfully coordinate their foreign policies outside the UN. The operations of collective security, however, have shown us that ad-hoc concerts are a far more common and predictable phenomenon: the major powers may agree on action to be taken toward a given issue (Kashmir, Suez, Congo, Cyprus) despite—or perhaps because—they disagree on basic foreign policy. Each is driven to support UN action because this appears to be the most reasonable way of attaining its national interest. Hence we would expect this consensual pattern to show durability irrespective of historical systems and despite the failure of the original diplomatic theory.

[38] This discussion represents an elaboration and a rethinking of the scheme of interpretation advanced in my "Types of Collective Security: An Examination of Operational Concepts," *American Political Science Review* (March 1955). Majority will, permissive enforcement, concert, and balancing were introduced at that time as concepts summing up types of collective security, not more narrow types of consensus facilitating the use of the collective security techniques. The present effort adds the types of consensus which evolved after 1956 and seeks to refine the earlier categories. See Yashpal Tandon, "Consensus and Authority Behind United Nations Peacekeeping Operations," *International Organization*, XXI, No. 2 (Spring 1967), for a kindred effort to classify and analyze this phenomenon. The argument is confused, however, by the mixture of normative, descriptive, and explanatory categories.

(c) Permissive Enforcement. Collective security takes the form of a decentralized and largely national effort whenever the General Assembly "delegates" to a state or to a group of states the power to restrain or punish aggression. In such a situation the state which carries out its national policy under the aegis of the UN is "permitted" to use force in the name of the organization or engage in demonstrations of international authority short of force. This consensual pattern requires that a state or alliance indicates its willingness to engage in these acts *and* succeeds in obtaining a two-thirds vote of approval from the General Assembly. Only two disputes featured this consensus: the Balkan dispute (after 1947) and the Korean war in its earlier phases. The attempt to institutionalize this form of consensus through the "Little Assembly" and "Uniting for Peace" formulas was quite unsuccessful —essentially because the characteristics of the international system after 1952 militated against the mobilization of the appropriate majorities.

(d) Balancing. A consensus based on balancing can be organized either in the General Assembly or the Security Council. Balancing describes a situation in which a bloc of uncommitted or unaligned states (with respect to the dispute in question) intercedes between the major disputants and makes them accept a compromise formula. The most dramatic case of balancing is the second phase of the Korean war. Here, after the United States-led "United Nations force" began to encounter stiff Chinese resistance, states which had previously acquiesced in the permissive enforcement action began to have second thoughts. Asian states led by India and a number of NATO countries participating in the hostilities sought to induce the United States and the Soviet Union to settle for the *status quo ante* 1951. Balancing was particularly manifest in the formula finally adopted for screening and repatriating prisoners, controlled as it was by Indian troops and mediators. Here the General Assembly provided the forum for organizing the consensus which brought permissive enforcement to an end.

More recently, however, a form of balancing has been discernible in the Security Council in the absence of a previous permissive enforcement situation. Balancing there can be said to occur whenever the major powers take opposing positions *initially* with respect to action appropriate to a dispute. The balancing countries then attempt to introduce a resolution which will encompass some minimum common denominator spanning the gulf between the major power positions in the hope of persuading one side to abstain rather than vote against the course of action suggested. The eventual consensus thus involves a minimalist resolution offered by the unaligned countries sufficiently acceptable to one side as to make abstention possible. In a sense, this is a form of consensus based on a concert in that the major powers, for diverse reasons, opt in favor of the same course of action. However, the procedure differs sufficiently from an agreement negotiated directly between the major powers or based on "consensus" (i.e., no vote at all) as to warrant a distinct analytical reference. We must note that while during the Korean troubles the Asian unaligned bloc did the balancing, in more recent disputes there is no one bloc or country which assumes this role. Each dispute determines who will do the balancing; the meta-issue of the cold war no longer suffices to bring forth a stable definition of the mediator's role.[39]

(e) Permissive Engagement with Majority Will. The consensual formula featuring "permissive engagement" refers in all cases to the role the Secretary-General assumed after 1956. He did the "engaging" for the UN; he took the initiative in bringing the dispute to the attention of the members, and he usually proposed a specific course of action. This took the form of truce supervision, police forces, personal mediation, or the creation of his institutionalized "presence" in the troubled area. In many cases, the military and civilian organizations created to deal with the dispute were under the personal command of the Secretary-General.

But he still needed a consensus among the members to do this if he wanted to avoid the difficulties associated with the financial crisis. One type of permission to engage the UN can be given by the General Assembly acting through the two-thirds voting formula, thus sidestepping the possibility of a major power's opposing this course of action. This is what occurred in the Suez and Hungarian disputes.

(f) Permissive Engagement with Concert. On the other hand, there have been situations in which the permanent members of the Security Council have been willing to permit the Secretary-General to engage the UN in peace-keeping. Clearly, a tighter control over the UN's chief administrator can be exercised if this consensual formula applies because he is held accountable to a smaller body and to states able to back their attitudes with action. We may guess that as a result of the

---

[39] Thus Ireland and Malaya assumed the mediating role in balancing when the Assembly debated the Chinese invasion of Tibet. Bolivia and Uruguay took the role in the Security Council's 1965 discussion of the Rhodesian dispute, mediating between a minimalist British and a maximalist African set of demands, while France made consensus possible by abstaining. Bolivia, Norway, Morocco, and the Ivory Coast acted as balancers at various times in the Security Council's discussion of the South African race dispute, where consensus proved possible only because *all* the permanent members (except China) abstained at different times. Morocco and the Ivory Coast also acted as balancers in the Aden-Yemen border warfare dispute, the Stanleyville air rescue operation, and the Cambodian complaint of border violations by South Vietnamese and American troops. In the Aden dispute, the United Kingdom and the United States abstained; the resolution referring the Stanleyville situation to the Organization for African Unity was verbally opposed by the Soviet Union (which then voted for it), while France abstained; in the Cambodian/South Vietnamese dispute the Soviet Union did the abstaining.

financial crisis this consensual formula will be increasingly used to mount UN operations. All the characteristics we have noted above with respect to pure cases of the concert formula apply here as well, with the Secretary-General assuming a central role that is lacking in the pure concert situation.[40]

(g) Permissive Engagement with Balancing. The characteristics of a consensus based on mediation and bargaining between and among major powers and blocs in order to arrive at agreement with respect to a UN action also apply here. Some state or group of unaligned states has to assume a balancing role in order to obtain the necessary legal support for a resolution. This can occur either in the Security Council or in the General Assembly. Again, however, the added ingredient is the role assumed by the Secretary-General in proposing action and in offering his services for implementing measures in the field.[41]

7. DEGREE OF SUCCESS OF UN ACTION: The success the UN may or may not have achieved is the dependent variable of the whole enterprise. We must know which combinations of independent variables, mediated by what form of consensus in the organization, has produced successful outcomes. We must also know whether the pattern of success varies with the historical system.

How do we define "success"? One criterion of success is the frequency with which the UN succeeded in stopping hostilities once they had broken out, in most instances through the medium of a truce supervision organization. In the 55 disputes studied, hostilities occurred in 32 instances. Hostilities were stopped, largely as a result of UN action, in 10 cases. The more refined measure of success is the frequency with which various types of actions brought hostilities to a halt in various types of disputes and in a context of various kinds of polities.

Another measure of "success" is the frequency with which the UN managed to dispose of the major issue which caused the dispute in the first place. Here we ask when and how often the parties to the dispute accepted the form of action adopted by the UN and settled their difference on that basis. Again, we would want to know a frequency score with respect to types of action, types of polities and parties, and

40 Examples of permissive engagement based on a *de facto* concert are: the Yemen dispute, UN mediation in Laos (1959) and in the Thai-Cambodian border dispute (1960-1961), as well as during the Cuban missile crisis.

41 Permissive engagement based on balancing in the Security Council occurred during the Cyprus and India/Pakistan disputes (all non-Communist nonpermanent members acting as balancers). The Congo operation (with the Brazzaville countries doing the balancing), and the Lebanese-Jordan situations of 1958 (Japan as balancer) illustrate the same process in the General Assembly after Soviet vetoes in the Security Council.

kinds of disputes. Again, the frequency with which a given consensual pattern proved to be the applicable intervening variable is of interest. Our 55 disputes break down as follows with respect to the settlement of the issue:

Settled on the basis of the UN resolutions:	7
Settled in part on the basis of the UN resolution:	11
Settled wholly outside the UN:	13
Unsettled:	24

No credit can be claimed for the UN by including in our formula of "success" the disputes which, even though referred to the UN, were eventually settled by bilateral negotiation or regional organizations. On the other hand, we included in the "settled in part" figure disputes eventually settled outside the UN *if* the formula for outside settlement had actually been decided upon by the UN. We also included disputes in which the eventual settlement followed a portion of an earlier UN resolution or in which the UN was partly responsible for bringing about an improvement. Thus in the Balkan situation, the dispute ended because the Greek government won its civil war with the Communist rebels, partly as a result of aid from the West. However, that victory was facilitated by the fact that a UN truce mission patrolled the northern borders of Greece and made infiltration more difficult.

Success scores were then computed by dividing the instances of complete and partial acceptance of UN action by the total number of disputes, giving us a raw "success score" of 33 percent. In the consideration of each variable, the ratio was between those "successful" and "unsuccessful" aspects relevant to the disputes in question.

The Extent of Referral and Success

To these figures we now turn. Table 3 presents the list of disputes that we have identified as "successfully" handled after being referred to the UN. Table 4 summarizes the disputes in which hostilities were prominent.

Let us examine the degree of success achieved by the UN in aiding in the settlement of disputes. The success scores of the variables used are summarized in Table 5. One immediate conclusion jumps to the eye: the great incidence of disputes referred to the UN occurred during the initial "honeymoon" phase and during the later tripolar and multipolar power phases, with the greatest number in the most recent period. The frequent funeral orations pronounced for the UN by scholars in recent years have apparently not been heard by governments. Is the incidence of referrals negatively correlated with the occurrence of disputes which did not find their way to the UN? Again, the answer is no. The 27 disputes of the postwar era that were kept out of the UN by the parties are distributed as follows:

1945-1947	10
1948-1951	2
1952-1955	1
1956-1960	6
1961-1965	8

Only during the initial "honeymoon" period is the number of un-referred disputes almost as great as the number of disputes submitted to the UN. The reason has nothing to do with the popularity of the organization but merely reflects the statistical fact that a number of unresolved pre-World War II disputes were still alive in 1945 and reasserted themselves.

Which Disputes Are Successfully Settled?

What of the efficacy of the UN organs used and the types of action taken? The combined use of the Security Council and the General Assembly brings results most frequently; the General Assembly used in isolation is ineffective. None of the methods of pacific settlement and/or enforcement is useless. But only collective mediation/conciliation worked in more than half of the instances in which it was used. Truce maintenance is reasonably effective and various recommended enforcement measures have been of utility half of the time, though the Secretary-General's "presence" has not. Adjudication has been effective, but then it was used in only three instances.

Settlement occurs most frequently in the context of colonial issues, but the prophets of doom were wrong in holding that cold war disputes—by definition—are incapable of solution by the UN. A success score of one in four is not total ineffectiveness. It has also been suggested that the UN is good only for settling disputes among small states. The record proves this assertion wrong. Over one-third of the disputes involving a major power have been successfully settled; in fact, the success score is *lowest* for small power antagonists which are allies and for pairs of small unaligned nations.

The corresponding figures for disputes which involved hostilities are given in Table 6. The combined use of Security Council and General Assembly for the stopping of hostilities and the establishment of a truce is the most effective approach. The use of single mediators has been found equally effective in maintaining a truce. Indeed, there are very few cases in which the order to honor a truce was not obeyed by the parties, though occasional violations did occur. The Yemen and Angola cases are the outstanding instances of failure. The truce supervision organization in Yemen proved impotent and no effort to set

TABLE 3

DISPUTES REFERRED TO UN,
1945-1965

Period	Number	Disputes Referred to but Not Settled by UN	UN Settles or Helps Settle
1945-1947	11	French withdrawal from Levant Franco government in Spain Status of Trieste Kashmir Palestine South African race policies Revision of 1936 Suez Canal/ Sudan agreement	Azerbaijan Balkans Corfu Channel Indonesia

1948-1951	6	Berlin blockade
		Communist coup in Czecho-
		   slovakia
		Hyderabad
		Iran oil nationalization
			Korea
			Withdrawal of Republic of
			   China troops from Burma

1952-1955	3	North African decolonization Future status of Cyprus Guatemala	None
1956-1960	10	Hungary Syria/Turkey border Laos civil war Tibet South Tyrol U-2 flights	Suez war Lebanon/Jordan unrest Nicaragua/Honduras border Thai/Cambodia border

1961-1965	25	Civil unrest in Oman
		Cuba (Bay of Pigs)
		Cuban intervention in Domini-
		   can Republic
		Goa
		Iraq/Kuwait (U.K.)
		Portuguese colonies in Africa
		Cuban missile crisis
		U.K./Venezuela border
		Dominican intervention in Haiti
		Malaysia/Indonesia
		Senegal/Portugal border
		Yemen civil war
		Cyprus civil war
		Greece/Turkey hostile acts
		Panama Canal
		U.S./North Vietnam
		   (Gulf of Tonkin)
		U.S. intervention in Dominican
		   Republic
			Congo
			West Irian
			Bizerta
			Southern Rhodesia
			Aden/Yemen border
			Cambodia/South Vietnam
			   (U.S.)
			Stanleyville air rescue
			India-Pakistan war

TABLE 4

DISPUTES INVOLVING HOSTILITIES REFERRED TO UN
1945-1965

Period	Number	UN Fails in Maintaining Truce or Stopping Hostilities	UN Succeeds in Maintaining Truce or Stopping Hostilities
1945-1947	4	Balkans	Indonesia Kashmir Palestine
1948-1951	1	None	Korea
1952-1955	3	North African decolonization Future status of Cyprus Guatemala	None
1956-1960	5	Hungary Tibet Laos civil war	Suez war Lebanon/Jordan unrest
1961-1965	19	Bizerta Cuba (Bay of Pigs) Goa Portuguese colonies in Africa Cuban missile crisis Civil unrest in Oman Dominican intervention in Haiti Malaysia/Indonesia Senegal/Portugal border Yemen civil war Aden/Yemen border Cambodia/South Vietnam (U.S.) Stanleyville air rescue U.S./North Vietnam (Gulf of Tonkin) U.S. intervention in Dominican Republic	Congo West Irian Cyprus civil war India-Pakistan war

one up was made in Angola. Police forces, however, have been effective whenever they were created.

The picture is different when we examine the kinds of issues which called forth UN efforts to halt hostilities. Hostilities related to the cold war cannot be readily stopped by the UN. Hostilities unconnected with any of the major schisms of world politics are most frequently brought to a halt. Once a major power is involved in hostilities, the UN is not very often successful in inducing it to stop. However, it is successful in bringing wars between two unaligned countries to a halt in three out of four cases. Still, the UN is more often successful in inducing the major powers to stop fighting than in controlling small nations who are members of opposing alliances. It is simply not true that the practice of collective security has been doomed by the dominance and lack of responsiveness of the great powers, the omnipres-

TABLE 5

UN Performance: Settling Issues

(in percent)

Period	Organ			Action Taken[a]										
	Security Council	General Assembly	Both	Direct neg. and/or ref. to reg. org.	Inquiry	Collective mediation or conciliation	Single mediator	Adjudication	Cease-fire ordered	Truce supervision established	Enforcement, boycott, embargo	Police force	Secretary-General's "Presence"	Committee of experts
1945-1947 Average=36	43	—	25	38	43	57	0	100	33	33	25	—	0	—
1948-1951 Average=33	20	—	100	50	100	100	—	0	100	100	100	—	—	—
1952-1955 Average=0	0	0	—	0	—	—	—	—	—	—	—	—	—	—
1956-1960 Average=40	50	0	50	33	33	40	100	100	100	100	—	100	60	—
1961-1965 Average=32	25	33	50	40	40	56	50	—	50	33	67	67	43	0
1945-1965 Average=33	29	13	47	36	43	57	40	67	58	56	50	75	46	0
Number of Cases Total=55	31	8	15	25	16	23	5	3	12	9	8	4	13	1

Legend: —, no cases occurred.
[a] No action taken in 19 cases

ence of cold war issues, the role of ideology in world affairs, the advent of nuclear weapons, or any of the other developments held to be incompatible with the requisites of the ideal or the diplomatic theories.

Next, we must ask whether the figures suggest any evolution over time in the pattern of successful action. Is there a suggestion of a cumulative pattern, of successes in one period giving rise to expectations of new successes and thus inducing a better performance in subsequent periods? The data suggest no such trend. Performance in regard to the settlement of issues has remained fairly stable, with the temporary improvement in the period 1956-1960 apparently dissipated by the crisis over permissive engagement triggered by the Congo dispute. UN success in halting hostilities has declined sharply over the years, slipping from 75 percent during the first period to 21 percent in the

TABLE 5 (continued)

Issue			Power of Parties					Type of Consensus						
Colonial	Cold war	Other	Big power	Small powers, same bloc	Small powers, different blocs	One unaligned, other allied	Both unaligned	Majority will	Concert	Permissive enforcement	Balancing	Permissive engagement with majority will	Perm. engage. with concert	Perm. engage. with balancing
25	75	0	40	—	100	100	0	0	60	100	0	—	—	—
0	33	50	40	—	—	—	0	—	100	100	100	—	—	—
0	0	—	0	—	0	—	—	0	—	—	—	—	—	—
100	0	75	25	100	—	25	100	0	—	—	0	50	50	100
55	17	13	42	0	0	29	50	50	33	—	80	50	0	50
42	26	29	36	25	33	33	25	17	50	100	63	50	25	67
19	19	17	28	4	3	12	8	6	12	2	8	4	4	3

most recent. The complete success score during the period 1948-1951, since it includes only the Korean case, is of little statistical significance. Collective security, as an institutionalized organizational task, has shown no sign of producing any kind of cumulative patterns of satisfaction, acceptance, nor growth.

Is this sweeping conclusion equally true when we examine the success score with respect to UN organs, types of action, issues, and the power of the parties? Once more, the settlement of issues will be treated first. Wide oscillations characterize the effectiveness of the Security Council, and the General Assembly showed some effectiveness only in the most recent period. The referral of a dispute to both organs has retained its considerable effectiveness for the last ten years. No dramatic change over time is suggested by the data for appeals for direct negotiations, inquiry, mediation, and adjudication. Single mediators seem to have performed better in the two recent systems, prob-

TABLE 5 (continued)

Period	Reconciliation/ Reconciliation	Reconciliation/ Mobilization	Reconciliation/ Modernizing Autocracy	Reconciliation/ Authoritarian	Reconciliation/ Traditional Oligarchy	Reconciliation/ Modernizing Oligarchy	Mod. Autocracy/ Mobilization	Mod. Autocracy/ Mod. Autocracy	Trad. Oligarchy/ Mobilization	Trad. Oligarchy/ Trad. Oligarchy	Mod. Oligarchy/ Mod. Autocracy	Too many to work
						Domestic Political System of Parties						
1945-1947 Average=36	33	75	—	—	0	—	—	—	—	—	—	0
1948-1951 Average=33	0	50	—	—	—	—	—	—	—	—	—	0
1952-1955 Average=0	0	0	—	—	—	—	—	—	—	—	—	0
1956-1960 Average=40	0	33	—	—	—	0	—	100	—	100	—	—
1961-1965 Average=32	0	20	0	100	0	100	0	—	0	0	100	50
1945-1965 Average=33	10	40	0	100	0	50	0	100	0	50	100	30
Number of Cases Total=55	10	20	3	2	2	2	1	1	1	2	1	10

Legend: —, no cases occurred.
a No action taken in 19 cases.

ably because of the more heterogeneous and polarized international environment. Various enforcement measures—probably because they were recommended in colonial situations—have shown more consistent success in the period 1960-1965. The stationing of the Secretary-General's representative in a trouble spot showed a 60 percent success score during the Hammarskjold era but declined to 43 percent under his successor. As for the issues, the data are unambiguous: improvement in settling colonial disputes, consistent decline in successfully dealing with cold war disputes, and a sharp dip in the success curve on other disputes in the most recent periods. Time has brought no great change in the appreciable degree of UN success in dealing with the major powers and only slight improvement in cases where the parties involve one unaligned and one allied state (the 100 percent score during the first period including only the Indonesian case). On the other hand, the growing complexity of the international system does seem to imply that UN success is increasing in efforts involving two unaligned states.

The picture is very different when we turn to UN successes in stopping hostilities. Obviously, the Security Council's effectiveness in stopping hostilities has suffered over the years. The General Assembly remains ineffective (the 50 percent score in 1960-1965 being accounted for by the West Irian case) and recourse to both organs shows no net growth. The efficacy of bilateral negotiations, inquiry, and collective mediation/conciliation has declined sharply. Single mediators were effective during the first and the last periods. Truce maintenance and enforcement had been very successful until the most recent period. Police forces have retained their very high success scores, but the efficacy of a "presence" has declined. Not unexpectedly, UN successes with respect to all types of issues have declined, though "other" disputes have declined the least and colonial issues remain more amenable to UN intervention than cold war ones. Finally, the major powers are less amenable to accepting UN intervention in their wars now as compared to the previous periods, and the same is true of pairs of unaligned states and especially of situations involving one unaligned and one allied nation.

Certain conclusions seem inescapable regarding the evolution of the technique of collective security. The UN has shown more ability to function effectively with respect to settling certain kinds of disputes than in stopping wars, though in its first years the picture was the reverse. Colonial disputes of all kinds are the most likely to be settled successfully even if a major power is a party. Wars among pairs of unaligned states are stopped most readily, but with respect to the settlement of disputes the power of the parties seems to make little difference. Methods for the pacific settlement of disputes have become less effective over the years as mild enforcement measures, police forces and the Secretary-General have increased in potency—with the proviso that all this is true more for Hammarskjold than for U Thant.

Types of Consensus and Settlement of Disputes

These statistics have neglected the intervening variable of the consensual pattern, the manner in which the member states reach agreement on a course of action. I suggest that a causal understanding of why the UN succeeds or fails must attempt to link the power distribution of the system, the consensual patterns which prevail, and the type of issues to which they apply. This information is summarized in Table 7. What does it suggest?

A consensus based on majority will has emerged predominantly on colonial questions, twice on "other" questions which were of very little importance to world politics, and never on cold war matters. The only case in which some degree of success was scored is in the accept-

TABLE 6
UN Performance: Stopping Hostilities
(in percent)

Period	Organ			Action Taken[a]										
	Security Council	General Assembly	Both	Direct neg. and/or ref. to reg. org.	Inquiry	Collective mediation or conciliation	Single mediator	Adjudication	Cease-fire ordered	Truce supervision established	Enforcement, boycott, embargo	Police force	Secretary-General's "Presence"	Committee of experts
1945-1947 Average=75	100	—	50	75	75	75	100	—	100	100	100	—	100	—
1948-1951 Average=100	—	—	100	—	—	100	—	—	100	100	100	—	—	—
1952-1955 Average=0	0	0	—	0	—	—	—	—	—	—	—	—	—	—
1956-1960 Average=40	—	0	50	50	33	40	—	—	100	100	—	100	50	—
1961-1965 Average=21	8	50	40	13	0	38	100	—	33	67	50	100	14	—
1945-1965 Average=31	20	20	50	31	33	50	100	—	67	89	80	100	33	—
Number of Cases Total=32	15	5	12	16	12	18	4	—	12	9	5	4	12	—

Legend: —, no cases occurred.
[a] No action taken in 7 cases

ance by Britain of the General Assembly's demands with regard to Rhodesia. No past, present, or future importance should be attached to this way of approaching world security, not even in an increasingly multibloc systemic setting.

The concert has proved the most viable and effective approach, irrespective of international systemic conditions. It has been successful in all types of issues, even on cold war matters where the major powers were looking for a *modus vivendi*. If we project a future in which both cold war and colonial issues will decline in incidence, it is important to note the relative degree of success which attends the concert on "other" issues during the multipolar system which has prevailed most recently. Since even during the height of the cold war (1947-1951) the United States and the Soviet Union managed to agree on some disputes outside either's sphere of major interest, the

TABLE 6 (continued)

Issue			Power of Parties					Type of Consensus						
Colonial	Cold war	Other	Big power	Small powers, same bloc	Small powers, different blocs	One unaligned, other allied	Both unaligned	Majority will	Concert	Permissive enforcement	Balancing	Permissive engagement with majority will	Perm. engage. with concert	Perm. engage. with balancing
100	0	100	—	—	0	100	100	—	100	0	—	—	—	—
—	100	—	100	—	—	—	—	—	—	100	100	—	—	—
0	0	—	0	—	0	—	—	0	—	—	—	—	—	—
100	0	100	33	—	—	0	100	—	—	—	0	50	0	100
22	0	40	11	50	—	17	50	0	25	—	0	50	0	100
31	9	63	20	50	0	25	75	0	57	50	17	50	0	100
13	11	8	15	2	2	8	5	3	7	2	6	4	3	3

same possibility might be kept in mind if China were to assume a seat on the Security Council.

In all likelihood, permissive enforcement will never recur. It was a consensual pattern possible only under the membership and power distribution conditions of the first two periods. Success was due less to the internalization of new norms by the UN membership than to the systemic circumstances then prevailing. Permissive enforcement was confined to cold war issues and to the ability of one bloc to sweep along the membership. It is most doubtful that in a multibloc world such a feat could be repeated.

Balancing has gone through two distinct phases. The first involved simply the negotiated settlement of the Korean conflict, with a portion of the UN membership "balancing" between the aggressor and the UN Command carrying out the earlier mandate of the organization. This type of consensus depends on a previous permissive enforcement

TABLE 6 (continued)

Period	Reconciliation/ Reconciliation	Reconciliation/ Mobilization	Reconciliation/ Modernizing Autocracy	Reconciliation/ Authoritarian	Reconciliation/ Modernizing Oligarchy	Mod. Autocracy/ Mobilization	Trad. Oligarchy/ Trad. Oligarchy	Mod. Oligarchy/ Mod. Autocracy	Too many to work
	Domestic Political System of Parties								
1945-1947 Average=75	100	0	—	—	—	—	—	—	100
1948-1951 Average=100	—	100	—	—	—	—	—	—	—
1952-1955 Average=0	0	0	—	—	—	—	—	—	0
1956-1960 Average=40	—	40	—	—	—	—	—	—	—
1961-1965 Average=21	100	20	0	50	0	0	0	0	20
1945-1965 Average=31	75	31	0	50	0	0	0	0	29
Number of Cases	4	13	2	2	1	1	1	1	7
Total=32									

Legend: —, no cases occurred.
a No action taken in 7 cases.

decision and therefore is obsolete. Thus attention must be focused on the five cases of balancing which occurred under the very different circumstances of the most recent period. In three out of five colonial disputes, the consensus produced effective UN action; it worked in one cold war dispute in which the Soviet Union and the United States wished to minimize the damage, but it failed in the effort to save Tibet from China. There would seem to be no reason to suppose that in a multibloc or multipolar setting this approach to persuading the major powers—while ignoring the Secretary-General—could not increasingly apply to disputes which bear no relationship to the cold war or the colonial revolution.

The various patterns of permissive engagement did not come into existence until 1956. This is not due entirely to Dag Hammarskjold's tenets regarding the role of the Secretary-General and the drive toward

TABLE 7

UN Settlement of Disputes: Power Distribution, Consensus, Issues[o]

Power Distribution	Majority Will		Concert	Permissive Enforcement			Balancing	Permissive Engagement with Majority Will		Permissive Engagement with Concert			Permissive Engagement with Balancing	
	clnl.[a]	other[b]	clnl.[c]	c.war[d]	other[e]	c.war[f]	clnl.[g]	c.war[h]	clnl.[i]	c.war[j]	c.war[k]	other[l]	clnl.[m]	other[n]
Unipolar victor group	—	0 of 1	1 of 1	2 of 2	0 of 2	1 of 1	—	—	—	—	—	—	—	—
Tight bipolar symmetrical	—	—	—	—	1 of 1	1 of 1	—	1 of 1	—	—	—	—	—	—
Loose bipolar heterosymmetrical	0 of 2	—	—	—	—	—	—	—	—	—	—	—	—	—
Tripolar heterosymmetrical	—	0 of 1	—	—	—	—	—	0 of 1	1 of 1	0 of 1	0 of 1	1 of 1	—	1 of 1
Multipolar heterosymmetrical	1 of 2	—	1 of 3	—	1 of 3	—	3 of 5	1 of 1	1 of 1	—	0 of 1	0 of 1	—	0 of 1

Legend: clnl., colonial
c.war, cold war
—, no cases occurred

[a]North African decolonization
Future status of Cyprus
Portuguese colonies in Africa
Southern Rhodesia

[b]Franco government in Spain
South Tyrol

[c]Indonesia
Bizerta
Senegal/Portugal border
Panama Canal

[d]Azerbaijan
Corfu Channel

[e]Kashmir
Palestine
Withdrawal of Republic of China troops from Burma
Dominican intervention in Haiti
Greece/Turkey hostile acts
India-Pakistan war

[f]Balkans
Korea

[g]South African race policies
Portuguese colonies in Africa
Southern Rhodesia
Aden/Yemen border
Stanleyville air rescue

[h]Korea
Tibet
Cambodia/South Vietnam (U.S.)

[i]Suez war
West Irian

[j]Hungary

[k]Laos civil war
Cuban missile crisis

[l]Thai/Cambodia border
Yemen civil war

[m]Congo

[n]Lebanon/Jordan unrest
Cyprus civil war

[o]Disputes on which UN could reach no consensus:
French withdrawal from Levant
Status of Trieste
Revision of 1936 Suez Canal/Sudan Agreement
Berlin blockade
Communist coup in Czechoslovakia
Hyderabad
Iran oil nationalization
Guatemala
Syria/Turkey border
U-2 flights
Cuba (Bay of Pigs)
Cuban intervention in Dominican Republic
Goa
Iraq/Kuweit (U.K.)
Civil unrest in Oman
U.K./Venezuela border
Malaysia/Indonesia
U.S./North Vietnam (Gulf of Tonkin)
U.S. intervention in Dominican Republic

a UN which is less of a conference of states and more akin to a supra-national entity. It also required a loosening of the bipolar system, a more heterogeneous membership, and the tendency toward tripolar and multipolar diplomatic alignments outside the UN. Because issues and blocs were thus diffused and multiplied, the Secretary-General acquired the ability to maneuver for support, constructing different coalitions of supporters on different issues, and thus succeeded in gaining permission to "engage" the organization in collective security.

The Secretary-General succeeded in marshaling overwhelming majority support behind him in Suez and West Irian, both colonial issues. He failed dismally in Hungary, a cold war issue. He was never given the opportunity to try this consensual pattern on other issues. Since the colonial issue is passing, it is doubtful that a parallel degree of overwhelming enthusiasm for a delegation of power will emerge once more. Collective security in the future should not count on this type of consensus.

The concert has not often been useful in furnishing a basis of support for permissive engagement. The single case of success was an unimportant border dispute between Thailand and Cambodia. However, there is no real reason to suppose that if and when the major powers are indifferent to a local squabble, they would not let the Secretary-General try his hand at a settlement. We may therefore project that this consensual pattern may increase in importance as the cold war and the colonial context decline in importance.

This is even more true with respect to the marshaling of support for the Secretary-General by means of balancing. Note that this pattern was never used in a cold war dispute. Post-colonial situations will continue to plague the world for some time; civil wars between antagonistic ethnic groups are likely to multiply in the near future. I assume that a multipolar or multibloc world will act as a constraint on the United States and the Soviet Union. I assume that both superpowers are equally anxious to keep the other from profiting from such a disturbance. Both have an interest in letting some other agency deal with it in order to prevent escalation. At the same time, both remain eager to cater to blocs in the third world on somewhat different terms and may find it desirable to adopt a public pose which does not show their real motives. Balancing on the part of one bloc is thus given an opportunity to provide overt and tacit backing for the Secretary-General. An important future for this consensual pattern can be predicted.

These conclusions are supported by a tabulation of the consensual and issue patterns underlying the ability of the UN to stop hostilities, as summarized in Table 8. First of all, it should be noted that of the

TABLE 8

UN STOPS HOSTILITIES: POWER DISTRIBUTION, CONSENSUS, ISSUES[m]
(in percent)

Power Distribution	Majority will	Concert		Permissive enforcement	Balancing		Permissive engagement with majority will		Permissive engagement with concert		Permissive engagement with balancing	
	clnl.[a]	clnl.[b]	other[c]	c.war[d]	clnl.[e]	c.war[f]	clnl.[g]	c.war[h]	c.war[i]	other[j]	clnl.[k]	other[l]
Unipolar victor group	—	100 (N=1)	100 (N=2)	100 (N=1)	—	—	—	—	—	—	—	—
Tight bipolar symmetrical	—	—	—	100 (N=1)	—	100 (N=1)	—	—	—	—	—	—
Loose bipolar heterosymmetrical	0 (N=2)	—	—	—	—	—	—	—	—	—	—	—
Tripolar heterosymmetrical	100 (N=1)	—	—	—	—	0 (N=1)	100 (N=1)	0 (N=1)	0 (N=1)	—	—	100 (N=1)
Multipolar heterosymmetrical	—	50 (N=2)	0 (N=1)	—	67 (N=3)	100 (N=1)	100 (N=1)	—	0 (N=1)	0 (N=1)	100 (N=1)	100 (N=2)

Legend: clnl., colonial
   c.war, cold war
   —, no cases occurred

[a]North African decolonization
Future status of Cyprus
Portuguese colonies in Africa

[b]Indonesia
Bizerta
Senegal/Portugal border

[c]Kashmir
Palestine
Dominican intervention in Haiti
India-Pakistan war

[d]Balkans
Korea

[e]Portuguese colonies in Africa
Aden/Yemen border
Stanleyville air rescue

[f]Korea
Tibet
Cambodia/South Vietnam (U.S.)

[g]Suez war
West Irian

[h]Hungary

[i]Laos civil war
Cuban missile crisis

[j]Yemen civil war

[k]Congo

[l]Lebanon/Jordan unrest
Cyprus civil war

[m]Disputes with hostilities on which UN proved unable to reach a consensus:
Guatemala
Civil unrest in Oman
Cuba (Bay of Pigs)
Goa
Malaysia/Indonesia
U.S./North Vietnam (Gulf of Tonkin)
U.S. intervention in Dominican Republic

seven wars which the UN was unable to deal with for lack of consensus, four were cold war conflicts with the United States as a party. Once the major powers are involved in some kind of cold war hostilities, neither the concert nor a majority will are likely consensual patterns, as indicated by the absence of cold war cases in both columns. In two important instances the success score in Table 8 is better than in the corresponding columns in Table 7: "other" disputes handled by the concert method and by permissive engagement with balancing. The disputes in question are of great diagnostic significance and suggest some possibilities and limitations for the future of collective security.

The concert managed to stop hostilities in Kashmir and Palestine while unable to settle the underlying issue; permissive engagement based on balancing brought hostilities in Cyprus to a halt without succeeding in imposing a settlement. The reasons are not difficult to state: While the members of the UN were willing to marshal the forces and energy to establish and patrol a truce line, they were unwilling to coerce Pakistan, India, Israel, Greece, and Cyprus into accepting the conciliation and mediation proposals advanced by various UN organs and negotiators because each of these states is an important ally, client, or neutral from the national viewpoint of the major powers. Further, the concert broke down after a certain point in time though it existed at the onset of the disputes and thus permitted the establishment of the truce. In Kashmir and in Palestine, strong UN action following violations of the truce has proved impossible because the Soviet Union came to support India and the Arabs, respectively, while the United States backed Pakistan and Israel. In Cyprus, successful balancing was constrained by the unwillingness of the Soviet Union to give the UN forces an extended mandate and by Moscow's hesitation between supporting Makarios and neutrality. The Kashmir ad-hoc concert was reestablished in 1965 with the outbreak of large-scale fighting along the whole Indo-Pakistan border, though Soviet assent to UN action was again moderated by an insistence that the Secretary-General be forbidden from enlarging the truce supervision organization.

Collective Security and Types of Polities

This brings us to the major question which suggests itself to students of reconciliation systems: What kinds of polities tend to accept UN decisions on settling disputes and stopping hostilities? Do reconciliation polities respond more frequently than other kinds of polities? Briefly, does the success of the international reconciliation system depond in some measure on the behavior of national reconciliation polities? Answers are suggested by Tables 9 and 10.[42]

The data in Table 9 suggest that the success of the international reconciliation system *owes nothing* to the internal political mores and institutions of the member states. The UN success score for settling disputes among pairs of reconciliation polities stands at 10 percent; the figure for disputes between reconciliation polities and mobilization systems is a strong 40 percent; and the score for disputes between reconciliation polities on one side and modernizing oligarchies, authoritarianisms, and modernizing autocracies on the other stands at 33 percent. Table 10 changes this conclusion somewhat. When actual hostilities are involved, the UN success score for pairs of reconciliation polities rises to 50 percent, and for disputes involving reconciliation polities on one side and various systems on the other the score reaches 75 percent. We must bear in mind, however, that each of these clusters includes only four cases. The score for disputes between reconciliation polities and mobilization systems remains about the same.

Both tables support unequivocally the conclusion that a unipolar or tight bipolar power distribution is conducive to successful collective security operations between reconciliation and mobilization systems. It appears that such a power distribution—despite sharp ideological conflict—tends to imbue the parties with fear and caution *in the nuclear age*; no such restraint was apparent during the corresponding period in the life of the League of Nations. Further, both tables also permit us to conclude that a multipolar power distribution is conducive to successful collective security in cases involving a reconciliation polity scrapping with a modernizing oligarchy, modernizing autocracy, or authoritarian system. The data are heavily loaded with colonial disputes here, and our conclusion seems to hold true because the multipolar power picture also includes a considerable defense-and-guilt complex on the part of the reconciliation polities involved.

[42] These tables, but especially Table 10, present certain difficulties. Sixteen of the 55 disputes had to be excluded because of the smallness of certain polity samples and because the large number of parties in ten of the disputes precluded any meaningful sorting. Unfortunately, these excluded disputes contain the most interesting clues for the future of collective security because they covered a few instances of conflict between oligarchies, modernizing autocracies, and authoritarianisms. However, I am unwilling to hazard elaborate conclusions on the basis of such cases. Two Southeast Asian border disputes between modernizing autocracies were successfully settled, as was one such dispute between two Central American traditional oligarchies; three instances of civil wars and interventions involving a mobilization system as one party and a traditional oligarchy as the other were not successfully handled. In seven colonial disputes a large groups of heterogeneous Afro-Asian states complained against a Western country, leading to three successful UN operations. The disputes over Palestine, Franco Spain, and U.S. intervention in the Dominican Republic defy classification in terms of polities.

TABLE 9

UN Settlement: Power Distribution, Polities, Issues[a]
(in percent)

Power Distribution	Type of Polity and Issues							
	Reconciliation/ Reconciliation		Reconciliation/ Mobilization			Reconciliation/ Modernizing Autocracy/ Authoritarian/ Modernizing Oligarchy		
	clnl.[b]	other[c]	clnl.[d]	c.war[e]	other[f]	clnl.[g]	c.war[h]	other[i]
Unipolar victor group	50 (N=2)	0 (N=1)	—	75 (N=4)	—	0 (N=1)	—	—
Tight bipolar symmetrical	0 (N=1)	0 (N=1)	—	33 (N=3)	100 (N=1)	—	—	—
Loose bipolar heterosymmetrical	0 (N=1)	—	—	0 (N=1)	—	—	—	—
Tripolar hetero- symmetrical	—	0 (N=1)	100 (N=1)	0 (N=4)	100 (N=1)	—	0 (N=1)	—
Multipolar hetero- symmetrical	—	0 (N=3)	100 (N=1)	0 (N=3)	0 (N=1)	40 (N=5)	—	50 (N=2)

Legend: clnl., colonial
c.war, cold war
—, no cases occurred

[a] Some disputes were not tabulated. The following cases involved too small a sample of pairs of possibilities and were therefore excluded: Nicaragua/Honduras border, Thai/Cambodia border, Cambodia/South Vietnam (U.S.) (all successfully settled by UN); Cuban intervention in Dominican Republic, Dominican intervention in Haiti, Yemen civil war (none successfully settled).

The following disputes each involved more than three parties and could therefore not be summarized in terms of polity patterns: Congo, Southern Rhodesia, Stanleyville air rescue (all successfully settled); Franco government in Spain, Palestine, South African race policies, North African decolonization, civil unrest in Oman, Portuguese colonies in Africa, U.S. intervention in Dominican Republic (none successfully settled).

[b]French withdrawal from Levant
Indonesia
Iran oil nationalization
Future status of Cyprus

[c]Kashmir
Hyderabad
South Tyrol
U.K./Venezuela border
Cyprus civil war
Greece/Turkey hostile acts

[d]Suez war
West Irian

[e]Azerbaijan
Balkans
Corfu Channel
Status of Trieste
Berlin blockade
Communist coup in Czechoslovakia
Korea
Guatemala
Hungary
Laos civil war
Tibet
U-2 flights
Cuba (Bay of Pigs)
Cuban missile crisis
U.S./North Vietnam (Gulf of Tonkin)

[f]Withdrawal of Republic of China troops from Burma
Lebanon/Jordan unrest
Malaysia/Indonesia

[g]Revision of 1936 Suez Canal/ Sudan Agreement
Bizerta
Goa
Senegal/Portugal border
Aden/Yemen border
Panama Canal

[h]Syria/Turkey border

[i]Iraq/Kuwait (U.K.)
India-Pakistan war

TABLE 10

UN Stops Hostilities: Power Distribution, Polities, Issues[a]
(in percent)

| Power Distribution | Type of Polity and Issues | | | | | | |
| | Reconciliation/ Reconciliation | | Reconciliation/ Mobilization | | | Reconciliation/ Modernizing Autocracy/ Authoritarian/ Modernizing Oligarchy | |
	clnl.[b]	other[c]	clnl.[d]	c.war[e]	other[f]	clnl.[g]	other[h]
Unipolar victor group	100 (N=1)	0 (N=1)	—	100 (N=1)	—	—	—
Tight bipolar symmetrical	—	—	—	100 (N=1)	—	—	—
Loose bipolar heterosymmetrical	0 (N=1)	—	—	0 (N=1)	—	—	—
Tripolar hetero-symmetrical	—	—	100 (N=1)	0 (N=3)	100 (N=1)	—	—
Multipolar hetero-symmetrical	—	100 (N=1)	100 (N=1)	0 (N=3)	0 (N=1)	67 (N=3)	100 (N=1)

Legend: clnl., colonial
c.war, cold war
—, no cases occurred

[a]Cases excluded from Table excluded here also.

[b]Indonesia
Future status of Cyprus

[c]Kashmir
Cyprus civil war

[d]Suez war
West Irian

[e]Balkans
Korea
Guatemala
Hungary
Laos civil war
Tibet
Cuba (Bay of Pigs)
Cuban missile crisis

U.S./North Vietnam (Gulf of Tonkin)

[f]Lebanon/Jordan unrest
Malaysia/Indonesia

[g]Bizerta
Senegal/Portugal border
Aden/Yemen border

[h]India-Pakistan war

Unfortunately, we do not have any disputes pitting mobilization systems against each other. We have very few cases opposing oligarchies and authoritarian polities or modernizing autocracies. Since authoritarian polities will account for a rising percentage of the UN membership, any projection of a future collective security task will have to consider them keenly indeed. Our conclusion that the internal political systems of states bear no relationship to the UN's success in settling disputes therefore permits some optimism that the international reconciliation system has no need for a fixed number of members who are also committed to bargaining and peaceful adjustment of internal disputes.

The responsiveness of parties to disputes to UN action is only one side of the coin. We have an additional test for dealing with the problem of whether reconciliation polities are required to assure the functioning of collective security in a reconciliation-type UN. We must also inquire as to who furnishes the money, the troops, and the facilities in disputes involving hostilities. Such an inquiry leads us immediately back to the matter of consensus, legitimacy, and the UN financial crisis following the Congo operation.

Truce supervision and police forces were mobilized by the UN on eleven occasions. Four occurred before 1956 and did not involve the Secretary-General prominently: in the Balkans (UNSCOB), Kashmir (UNCIP), Palestine (UNTSO), and the Korean UN Command.[43] In the first three cases, the UN established special conciliation commissions in addition to the military forces charged with truce supervision and observation. In the fourth, no political organ existed other than the Committee of Sixteen whose members furnished troops in Korea. Financing did not pose a problem in any of these cases because the costs were borne by the nations furnishing the personnel and supplies. Who were the nations? Predominantly, they were Western reconciliation polities. NATO and SEATO countries accounted for thirteen of the sixteen Korean participants. American, Canadian, French, Italian, Dutch, and Scandinavian officers were predominant in UNSCOB, UNCIP, and UNTSO. It is certainly true that truce supervision during the first and second periods of UN history would have been impossible without the special stake which reconciliation polities felt they had in the organization.

After 1956, the pattern became very different. The seven UN operations requiring military forces include Suez (UNEF), Lebanon (UNOGIL), the Congo (ONUC), West Irian (UNTEA), Yemen (UNTSO again), Cyprus (UNFICYP), and India/Pakistan (UNIPOM). A special commission to advise the Secretary-General, who initiated each of these operations, was created in most cases, as was a special military command for each situation. The political commissions were devices enabling the Secretary-General to build variable coalitions of supporters in the Security Council and/or the General Assembly. Each military command had its own mandate and legal position involving little or no progressive institutionalization of UN authority and legitimacy from UNEF on. Uniformly, the superpowers were given no direct role in such operations.

Who staffed and financed these operations? UNOGIL, UNTEA, and UNTSO (Yemen) were paid for by the parties to the respective disputes. UNEF and ONUC were to be paid for from the regular UN

---

[43] In Indonesia a less complex procedure was used since the truce supervision personnel was furnished by the three powers who constituted the Committee of Good Offices.

budget as augmented by special assessments on all members. This triggered the financial crisis attendant upon French and Soviet failure to agree to the procedure despite the advisory opinion of the International Court of Justice authorizing it. In fact, these operations were paid for by the special UN bond issue and voluntary contributions. UNFICYP was financed exclusively by voluntary subscription on the part of those UN members willing and able to pay. The military personnel for UNTEA was furnished by Pakistan alone while the regular staff of UNTSO provided the abortive Yemen force. UNOGIL was staffed with officers from twenty nations from all parts of the globe and every conceivable kind of polity (except the large powers), though the largest number of officers came from Western reconciliation polities. Reconciliation polities predominated in UNEF, which contained military forces from small Western countries, India, and Yugoslavia. ONUC was staffed with troops from India, Ireland, Italy, four Scandinavian countries, and Canada—again predominantly from reconciliation polities. Also present were troops from Egypt, Ethiopia, Mali, Guinea, Indonesia, Ghana, and Nigeria. The mobilizations systems here represented proved most unreliable; all except Ghana withdrew their troops from the Congo when the operation took on a political coloration that did not fit into the national policies of these nations. Furthermore, the special position of the United States in UNEF and ONUC must be stressed. Even though no American personnel was used, it is no exaggeration to claim that without the heavy voluntary financial contribution of the United States and the transport facilities made available, neither operation could have been mounted. UNFICYP probably depended on the availability of British troops and facilities in Cyprus. We must conclude that the peacekeeping operations of the UN did rely very disproportionately on the services and responsiveness of reconciliation polities. Most of the reluctance to participate in compulsory or voluntary financing of such operations was voiced by oligarchies and authoritarian systems (on grounds of poverty) and mobilization systems (on grounds of principle and legitimacy).[44]

The Future of Collective Security

Our purpose in engaging in this exercise remains a projection of the future of collective security. But what can the past be squeezed into suggesting here? Clearly, the experience of the UN has been very dis-

[44] I have relied on the following excellent studies in this discussion: Jack Citrin, *United Nations Peacekeeping Activities: A Case Study in Organizational Task Expansion* (Denver 1965); William R. Frye, *A United Nations Peace Force* (New York 1957); Lincoln P. Bloomfield, ed., *International Military Forces* (Boston 1964); Ernest W. Lefever, *Crisis in the Congo* (Washington 1965); King Gordon, *UN in the Congo* (New York 1962); A. L. Burns and Nina Heathcote, *Peace-Keeping by U.N. Forces* (New York 1963); Gabriella E. Rosner, *The United Nations Emergency Force* (New York 1963).

continuous, and little evidence was uncovered that indicated a progressive and cumulative movement in a particular direction. Collective security was successfully practiced during the first period and again during the fourth, with the score declining during the most recent era. The institutionalization and legitimation of permissive engagement was suggested by the record of the fourth period; the more recent experiences of the UN argue a retreat from that position. What then can we project?

We can use the record of the past and probable outlines of the future system of international relations to exclude certain possibilities. Cold war disputes will decline in frequency but prove unamenable to collective security if the major powers are directly involved. Colonial disputes will disappear after the Portuguese and South African situations have been resolved, though their resolution will tax collective security procedures to the utmost. The Congo may turn out to have been nothing but a suggestive overture when Portugal's and South Africa's time comes. Consensus based on majority will and permissive enforcement will not recur in view of the multibloc character of the system. This leaves us with the likelihood of many post-colonial territorial disputes in the Afro-Asian world, ideological "international" civil wars in Latin America and Africa, and routine minor disagreements anywhere. The consensual patterns will be confined to concerts and balancing. The central question for the UN is whether such consensual arrangements will also feature permissive engagement and the attendant institutionalization of an autonomous supranational force.

This question brings us to the UN financial crisis. This often farcical interlude shows what the current international system permits and constrains in terms of permissive engagement. It also suggests what the immediate future of collective security will be.

As Stoessinger puts it, "The financial crisis of the United Nations does not indicate that the Organization has fallen into political collapse, but rather that the membership has not yet been willing to ratify and sustain its rise to a higher plane of development."[45] The issue was: (1) whether the entire membership should be compulsorily assessed according to some budgetary scale in the financing of peacekeeping operations authorized by the General Assembly; (2) whether the Court's opinion stressing the legality of such assessments should be obeyed; and (3) whether states defaulting on this obligation should be punished by being deprived of their vote in the General Assembly,

[45] John G. Stoessinger, *The United Nations and the Superpowers* (New York 1965), 110. This is the best short summary and analysis of the issue I have discovered, though it does not cover the work of the Committee of Thirty-Three.

as authorized under Article 19 of the Charter. Broadly speaking, the answer to all three questions turned out to be no.

Most underdeveloped African, Asian, and Latin American states opposed the compulsory assessment formula even though their share of the UNEF and ONUC costs had been reduced time after time through the initiation of several "special scales." They argued that the major industrialized powers should assume the burden of financing peacekeeping. France objected to the formula because it involved infringements on her sovereignty and intervention in internal affairs. The Soviet Union took the legal position that only action authorized by the Security Council was legitimate and that in other cases the aggressors should be made to pay for the cost of peacekeeping. The French and Soviet positions thus suggested that *only* the concert formula was to be legitimate in collective security operations and that permissive engagement be avoided. The United States, by dropping its campaign to have the General Assembly apply Article 19 against the holdouts, tacitly recognized that most of the membership did not wish to force the issue and was willing to settle for the concert even though this seemed to imply a quiet scrapping of the "Uniting for Peace" procedure.

Nevertheless, the work of the Special Committee on Peace-Keeping Operations created by the General Assembly in the spring of 1965, indicates that no hard-and-fast return to the concert is to be expected. In the first place, the Soviet Union intimated during the long negotiations that it was willing to make a substantial voluntary contribution to wipe out the debt incurred in operations previously held to be "illegal" *if* the principle of the Security Council's preeminence were reestablished. Secondly, the Soviets dropped their troika formula for staffing the Secretariat, originally put forward to prevent permissive engagement. They did demand during the Committee's sessions that the Security Council be recognized as the primary organ to conduct peacekeeping operations and that the long-dormant Military Staff Committee be revitalized for that purpose. They also admitted that the General Assembly had legitimate powers to make *recommendations* on collective security matters which might lead to the organization of peace forces; if so, contingents from socialist countries should be included in the future. France and India tended to support the Soviet position; the United States argued for the continued exercise of concurrent Security Council and Assembly jurisdiction; many of the smaller nations—while reluctant to make financial contributions—preferred a flexible arrangement under which both the Assembly and the Secretary-General would retain a role in peacekeeping.

The Committee's recommendations did little more than recognize the actual situation. Its first report recommended that: (1) the General Assembly carry on its work normally in accordance with its rules of procedure (i.e., continue its participation in collective security and work with the Secretary-General); (2) Article 19 would not be applied in questions relating to the financing of ONUC and UNEF; and (3) the financial difficulties of the UN are to be solved through voluntary contributions alone, with highly developed countries making substantial contributions.[46]

The immediate crisis surrounding the application of Article 19 was settled by virtue of this ingenious formula—but nothing else was. Two additional years of negotiations in the Committee of Thirty-Three contributed much discussion but little clarity. The General Assembly, for its part, deferred taking action on the troublesome issue, postponing a formal debate on the work of the Committee until the Special Session held in the spring of 1967.

At the time of writing, the most authoritative statement on the financial crisis and collective security is the resolution adopted in 1967 by the Assembly's Special Political Committee on the work of the Committee of Thirty-Three.[47] That text is eloquent in its comprehensiveness, in its eagerness to please partisans of Security Council primacy and

[46] UN Document A/5916, August 31, 1965. Other revealing information on the Committee is in Documents A/AC.121/5, A/5915, A/AC.121/L.2.

[47] *Comprehensive Review of the Whole Question of Peace-Keeping Operations in All Their Aspects* (doc. A/6603, 15 December 1966). The resolution reported out to the Assembly is in three parts. Part A resulted from a draft resolution presented by twelve small nations (European neutrals, African, Asian, Latin American); Part B is the result of a seven-power draft contributed by Argentina, Chile, Canada, Italy, Norway, Iran, and Nigeria, as amended by Ethiopia and it reflects a pronounced pro-Western viewpoint; Part C resulted from a Jamaican resolution.

The resolution creates, in Part A, a comprehensive formula for financing future peace-keeping arrangements, such that the permanent members assume responsibility for 70 percent of the costs in any year, provided that states not supporting the operation are not bound to pay and that no one state need pay more than 50 percent of the annual costs; other developed states would be responsible for 25 percent of annual expenses and the underdeveloped for the remaining 5 percent. Part B, however, while reaffirming the primacy of the Security Council, also praises the Assembly for having clear responsibilities in case of the Council's inability to act. Instead of offering a formula for financing action authorized by the UN, however, the various and well-known methods are merely enumerated and the need for a special scale is conceded if "heavy expenditures" are involved, with the underdeveloped nations then being responsible for 5 percent of annual expenses. Part B, as does Part C, again urges the Security Council to intensify its efforts to resolve the peace-keeping crisis and suggests measures for giving effect to Article 43 of the Charter.

The voting showed that only Part B comes close to having a two-thirds majority. It was supported by most of the Latin American and NATO nations, by one-third of the African and by nine Arab and Asian countries; it was opposed only by the Soviet bloc and a scattering of others, including France. The vote was 52 to 14, with 42 abstentions. Part A was adopted by a vote of 33 to 27, with 48 abstentions. Britain and the United States abstained, France and the Soviet Union opposed. The only sizable bloc of countries supporting Part A was African. Part C was adopted by the fluke vote of 20 to 5 with 80 abstentions, with the Communist members providing half of the affirmatives.

defenders of the stand-by role of the General Assembly. It seeks to protect the less developed nations from new financial burdens while sidestepping the exact shares of the permanent members. It safeguards the veto and reaffirms the means for getting around it. It wishes to explore new modes of peace-keeping while urging the implementation of the military provisions of Chapter VII of the Charter. The resolution, in settling nothing, provides the only possible approach to an eventual *modus vivendi* that is bound merely to continue the actual pattern of the last six years.

Balancing and the concert, with and without permissive engagement, continue to furnish the consensual basis for collective security. The financial crisis notwithstanding, the Secretary-General took the initiative in Cyprus even though he had to rely on voluntary contributions and was compelled to justify himself to a cautious Soviet Union every three months. And Soviet opposition to the rapid utilization of his services was more verbal than real as a concert quickly emerged in the India-Pakistan war. It remains true, however, that in order to forestall new efforts to alter the composition of the Secretariat, a distinction will have to be drawn between the personal role of the Secretary-General in collective security operations and the general participation of the Secretariat. Permissive engagement can flourish only if such a distinction is observed.[48]

Even then, the limits on permissive engagement are more sharply drawn now than was true five years ago. A comparison of the most recent disputes involving the mobilization of UN forces makes this quite clear. In order to be successful, permissive engagement (whether based on a concert or on balancing) cannot be undertaken unless the major military nations positively approve or, more likely, simply agree tacitly to refrain from unilateral intervention. Such a consensus need not last in order to facilitate the success of the operation. Experience shows that a major power alone is unable to bring such an operation to a halt, as shown decisively in the Congo. Further, small states must be willing to furnish the troops and large states voluntarily pay their expenses. The host country must be willing to admit the troops and the representatives of the Secretary-General and permit them to operate relatively freely. Host countries will not readily grant this permission if the UN force is given a sweeping and diffuse military-political mandate; but they may acquiesce in a diffuse task if it is permitted to evolve as a result of unintended consequences and strong consensus at the UN. The major powers (except the United States) will resist the granting of a wide mandate to the Secretary-General *ab initio*; but the record of recent disputes suggests that they will find it difficult to

---

[48] This point is strongly and convincingly made by Charles Winchmore, "The Secretariat: Retrospect and Prospect," in Padelford and Goodrich, 622-42.

oppose the evolution of such a task in specific situations and will have less opportunity to block it with the legitimation of the voluntary financial contribution formula. Most important perhaps, the role of the Secretary-General and the UN must be specific and limited and subject to the influence of the host country in order to make recourse to UN action an approach more attractive than reliance on bilateral or regional arrangements. The use made of the UN by President Makarios illustrates both the limits imposed by initial expectations and the evolution of unforeseen consequences. There is no reason to think that the leaders of authoritarian and modernizing oligarchic regimes likely to call on the UN would react much differently.[49]

Citrin is quite correct in summing up the growth of the collective security task in these somber terms:

> The ability of the United Nations to undertake military operations in the pursuit of international peace depends, in the contemporary world order, on the convergence of widely conflicting private interests. Since such a convergence is unlikely to be more than partial and very temporary, organizational task expansion in this area is an uneven and tenuous process. The benefits which are dispensed by several moderately successful instances of task performance, such as the programs of UNEF and UNOGIL, can be wiped out by one partial failure, such as ONUC. Furthermore, changes in the international environment can make irrelevant the authority that an international organization has laboriously built up over a period of years. In short, it is a hard struggle simply to stay even. Finally, when, as in the Congo and Cyprus, the Organization's leadership is able or forced to choose between alternative policies it is unlikely that either choice will be wholly satisfactory. Organizational task expansion in the military sphere, to repeat, continues to be largely attendant on changes in the international system.[50]

The future of collective security can also be envisaged by correlating the two consensual formulas likely to prevail with the degree of urgency or fear experienced by the major powers. This juxtaposition is illustrated in the matrix below.[51] The disputes placed in squares 1,

---

[49] For an elaboration of these conclusions, see Citrin, *U.N. Peacekeeping*, 63ff.

[50] Same, 69-70.

[51] I am greatly indebted to Mr. Peter Madian's undergraduate honors thesis in the Department of Political Science at the University of California (Berkeley) for this way of conceptualizing the future of peace-keeping forces. Norman Padelford offers a similar projection in his "Financing Peacekeeping: Politics and Crisis," in Padelford and Goodrich, 444-62. Padelford, taking into account all we have said about the political limits on future peace-keeping operations, sees a "negotiating area" from which future ad-hoc forces will derive their authorization. These will involve truce supervision missions, small police forces, and even UNEF-type operations. The consensual basis will be the *passive* acquiescence or resistance of countries like France

2, 4, and 5 involved reasonably energetic and successful UN operations and suggest that the major powers must at least experience some sense of urgency if action is to be taken on the basis of an energetic concert or the more passive balancing. The matrix also suggests very strongly that three kinds of disputes will not trigger any future collective security operations. First, direct confrontations between the major blocs will remain outside the scope of successful UN action. Second, post-colonial disputes considered to present few dangers to world peace will also be neglected. Finally, local disputes of little import with respect to world peace will not result in successful UN action whenever the parties are members of opposing blocs.

CONSENSUS FOR UN ACTION

		Concert	*Balancing*	*None*
	High	1 Early Congo India-Pakistan war	2 Later Congo Later Korea	3 Cuban Missile Crisis
Perception of Danger by Super-powers	*Medium*	4 Early Kashmir Early Palestine Indonesia Bizerta	5 Cyprus Lebanon Cambodia/ South Vietnam	6 Malaysia/ Indonesia U.S. in Dominican Republic Later Kashmir Later Palestine
	Low	7 Haiti/Domini- can Republic Laos civil war Yemen civil war	8 Portuguese Africa	9 Goa Guatemala Tibet

Angola and Southwest Africa may well become the Congos of tomorrow. Latin American countries may come to prefer the UN to the

and the Soviet Union and the enthusiastic (or at least moral) support of the small Western countries and India.

OAS for the resolution of future situations that resemble the trouble in the Dominican Republic. The trend is likely to gather momentum when continental disputes acquire ideological significance, when mobilization regimes fight modernizing autocracies or authoritarian rulers. These types of disputes will provide the milieu in which the collective security task will evolve. Goodrich is right in noting: "Since the essence of the UN's task is likely to be that of persuading the major powers to stand aside rather than become more involved . . . the requirements of preventive diplomacy will be better met by . . . using the forces of relatively uncommitted states."[52] He is also right in suspecting a limitation of this task in the future:

> The authors of the Charter recognized that in an international organization of sovereign states for keeping the peace, while there must also be a recognition of the interests of each member, large or small, there must also be recognition of the special position that the major powers must occupy in any system based upon voluntary cooperation. Recognition of this truth may result in limiting the activities of the UN in the maintenance of peace but it will assure a more substantial success in what it undertakes.[53]

GLOBAL TASKS AND THE UN OF THE FUTURE

Will a collective security task be able to flourish in the UN of 1985? Our historical analysis supports the contention that collective security has been practiced with varying degrees of effectiveness in each era despite different systemic and power characteristics. The periods of least effectiveness included the tight and loose bipolar situations, 1948-1955. Each period, though not with equal fidelity, met the structural and functional requisites of an international reconciliation system. Information remained high in comparison to coercion. The Charter and evolving custom provided the source of norms but no unambiguously legitimate symbolic referent. The integrational device was provided by the "learned" interaction pattern among the national delegations and later by the Secretary-General and the specialized staff he assembled for establishing his "presence" and for peace-keeping operations. The source of identification of the members with the UN was their satisfaction with the operations. Structurally, UN decisions were much weaker than the extent of UN accountability to the members, recruitment of personnel depended on both skill and the politics of

---

[52] Leland M. Goodrich, "The Maintenance of International Peace and Security," in Padelford and Goodrich, 442.

[53] Same, 443. Contrast this balanced view with the sweeping judgment of J. W. Burton that the future international system, despite the increased importance of nonalignment, will not permit a "real" collective security at all in *International Relations: A General Theory* (Cambridge 1965), 256-59.

access (with increasing access for the nonaligned Afro-Asians). Enforcement of norms was certainly selective and flexible. Resources
were allocated on the basis of continual bargaining and adjustment.
Consent groups were increasingly coopted into coalitions which varied
from issue to issue. As we would expect in the context of a pluralistic
setting, these requisites were met most perfectly during the tripolar
and multipolar periods. A pluralistic-incremental mode of social analysis merely sensitizes the observer to these features and enables him to
be reasonably systematic in his projections.

Why was there general satisfaction even though the overall rate of
UN success was confined to one case in three?[54] I argue that this surprising finding can be accounted for on two grounds: First, there
was no real alternative to the UN, or to another—and essentially identical—intergovernmental organization. No governing elite anywhere
favored energetic measures in favor of world government or consistent
isolationism. Even though certain elites might have preferred the active hegemony of single countries—whether based on conquest, liberation, or subversion—the network of regional agreements and opposing alliances outside the UN prevented the effective realization of any
such hope. If one also wished to have available a forum for taking up
issues that cut across alliances and regional arrangements, one was,
in effect, condemned to use the services provided only by the UN.

Second, it must be understood that collective security since 1956
has been practiced in the context of a tacit bargaining pattern that
also included peaceful decolonization, international economic development aid, and the protection of human rights. In a sense, politics
has become less "political" as the member countries become preoccupied with issues almost as important to them as military and territorial objectives. National self-determination has ceased to be a purely
political slogan; it has come to be understood also as a program including economic and human rights (though the rights are collective
rather than individual). The practice of collective security which
happened to satisfy Western objectives could be indirectly legitimated
by paying a price to non-Western countries in the currency of the
other issue areas; Soviet collective security objectives responded to the
same logic, though to a much lesser extent. In other words, not every
security issue had to be settled so as to satisfy each major nation or
bloc because compensating advantages could be and were provided

[54] An amazing amount of dissatisfaction with collective security operations was revealed in the Carnegie Endowment's multi-volume series of national studies of the
UN, dissatisfaction symmetrically distributed among Western industrialized and
Afro-Asian and Latin American underdeveloped countries. Yet the authority of UN
decisions did not decline. For a review and an evaluation of this material, see Haas,
"The Comparative Study of the United Nations," *World Politics*, XII, No. 2 (January
1960).

by the UN in other issue areas sometimes of greater importance to many nations. Relative satisfaction with the collective security task could be sustained because of an inter-functional and inter-regional tacit bargaining process.

This process was the result of rapidly changing social and economic forces within the member states, especially in the Afro-Asian and Latin American regions. Modernization, investment, industrialization, urbanization, the need for new sources of energy, immense population growth, public health, basic literacy, crash programs of technical education, and agricultural productivity all figure in these trends. The multi-pronged drive for modernization obviously had its origin in frustrations and dissatisfaction, but the efforts to meet the demands for modernization produced new frustrations and dissatisfactions—"economic and social imbalances"—which also make themselves felt in the foreign policy demands espoused by states. During the past ten years, these overlapping and contradictory pressures provided a field of maneuver and accommodation at the UN. The very open-ended character of this process is illustrated forcefully in the formula for the future of peacekeeping operations adopted by the General Assembly.

Will this continue to be true for the next decade or so? Will the forces of domestic social change so intermingle with international systemic impulses as to meet the structural and functional requisites of a future reconciliation system? The system could remain alive whether we postulate the "learning" model of system transformation or the model that stresses autonomous changes due to the environment. But whether it actually will, depends on the answers to these questions: (1) What will be the domestic pressures for change? (2) What will be the character of the environment of the international system of 1985? (3) What will be the distribution of power in 1985? Once these questions are answered, we can project the inputs and outputs of the system itself.

Future Domestic Pressures

True to our model of forecasting, no effort can be made to calculate the vectors of social-change pressure. The best we can do is list items. All countries will face the social and economic consequences of probable dramatic technological and scientific changes.[55] Fertility control will have been perfected. Synthetic materials will revolutionize the construction industry. Life will be longer because of successful organ transplantation and prosthesis. Weather forecasting will have been perfected. Central data storage will facilitate planning of all kinds.

[55] This material is taken from the results of several Delphi-type exercises undertaken by The Rand Corporation. T. J. Gordon and Olaf Helmer, *Report on a Long-Range Forecasting Study* (Rand Document P-2982, September 1964).

Automated language translators may ease the problems of multi-ethnic societies. In the industrial countries, moreover, the culture of plenty and leisure may well result in a more legitimate "beat" pattern in which the use of nonaddictive drugs will be socially acceptable and may give rise to new types of religious movements. Automation will have made tremendous inroads on the pattern of life in the more industrialized countries, though the impact in developing countries will be less. The most marked impact will be on teaching, data retrieval, office work, transportation, and industrial process control. The working week will be shorter and underemployment without loss of personal income will create many problems of leisure time investment. Space exploration will have advanced considerably to include manned lunar bases, manned fly-by missions to Venus and Mars, permanent orbital stations, nuclear propulsion, and manned and unmanned inspection and destruction of satellites. Possible future weapons systems include nonkilling devices, effective sensors for reconnaissance and intelligence gathering, temporarily incapacitating chemical and biological agents as well as lethal ones, use of computers and other automated equipment on the battlefield, mobile public-works and logistic units for reconstruction and refugee support, effective antimissile and antisubmarine defenses, and weapons using electromagnetic radiation, particle beams, and lasers. The more expensive of these weapons would be the monopoly of the industrial nations. Space exploration would also be monopolized by them. But the cheaper weapons could be generally available and pose a universal menace.

The social and economic problems implied defy cataloguing. A quantitative assessment in terms of mutual reenforcement or mutual neutralization is hard to imagine. I suspect that unsettling consequences for industrial countries will be greater than the impact on developing nations. The task of the latter is more clearly defined and provides a rationale for dealing with the dysfunctions of the modernization process, including decisions to slow down modernization. Suffering from a surfeit of success, in a way, industrial societies will also suffer the potential of several countervailing trends because of the absence of agreement on social goals and the difficulties of reconciling democracy and pluralism with overriding social purpose. Underdeveloped countries will suffer the results of more efficient agriculture in the form of accelerated urbanization and urban rootlessness. Their sense of insecurity in the face of weapons and space superiority on the part of developed nations may increase. Mass movements of discontent will grow as a result of improved education and communication unmatched by very rapid improvement in living standards, thus challenging traditional forms of social control *as well as* those provided by mobilization systems.

The Future International Environment

These speculations lead us to an inspired guess as to the environmental characteristics of the next international system. For the reasons discussed above, I consider it highly unlikely that any oligarchies and modernizing autocracies will survive by 1985. My projection is therefore confined to reasonably confident assertions as to the number of reconciliation, authoritarian, and mobilization polities and to likely alternatives in the more doubtful cases.

Established reconciliation systems in industrialized countries will survive, and they are likely to become even looser and more flexible in social texture and political cohesion as the logic of technology and leisure time acquires momentum. None will survive in Africa and few in Asia. Some of the Latin American countries (Chile, Venezuela, Uruguay, for instance) will succeed in cementing the reconciliation pattern which already prevails. Mobilization regimes will decline in importance. The European communist nations will have become more relaxed and benign authoritarianisms or even begin to approach a reconciliation polity as they experience the same technological-social syndrome already visible in the West. Mobilization polities in Africa will become fewer as their inefficiency and lack of flexibility combine to make them objects of popular discontent and overthrow; they will give rise to authoritarian regimes. The Asian communist states, however, will survive as mobilization polities. Authoritarian regimes will increase in number and show a great diversity of styles and institutions, but they will resemble one another in seeking to control and channel the scope and pace of modernization in order to avert the implications of some of the factors listed above. Table 11 summarizes my speculations.

I am unable to assert a "probable future" for 42 percent of the 135-member UN projected for 1985. The reasonable choices are between reconciliation and authoritarian systems, reconciliation and mobilization polities, and authoritarian and mobilization polities. For example, I consider it equally likely that Tunisia and Cyprus will either be reconciliation polities or authoritarian ones; neither the analytical categories nor the data here available permit a clear-cut choice. I cannot tell with any degree of probability whether Algeria will have a mobilization regime or an authoritarian one; the same is true of twenty other African nations. However, I am confident that they will *not* be reconciliation polities then even if they are at the moment. The same choice, for example, exists for the Dominican Republic, Panama, Jordan, Syria, and Indonesia. Oligarchies, modernizing autocracies, and presently unsuccessful mobilization polities provide the bulk of the candidates for these alternatives. Finally, a small number

TABLE 11

DISTRIBUTION OF POLITIES BY TYPE IN UN OF 1985
(Number of countries)

	Probable			Likely Alternatives			
	Reconciliation	Authoritarian	Mobilization	Reconciliation/ Authoritarian	Reconciliation/ Mobilization	Authoritarian/ Mobilization	Total
Europe	21	5	0	4	0	0	30
W. Hemisphere	10	1	1	3	3	8	26
Australasia	4	2	0	0	0	0	6
Asia	4	6	6	7	1	7	31
Africa	0	16	3	2	0	21	42
Total	39	30	10	16	4	36	135
Percentage of UN membership	28%	22%	8%	12%	3%	27%	100%

of countries may develop into either reconciliation or mobilization regimes, such as Argentina, Brazil, and Singapore.

If international reconciliation systems do not require a fixed number of national reconciliation polities to permit successful adjustment and bargaining and a minimum of a dozen or twenty such regimes to permit peacekeeping operations, these forecasts permit the projection that many crucial requisites of a future reconciliation-type UN can be met. Reconciliation polities will account for a minimum of 28 percent and a maximum of 43 percent of the membership; mobilization systems for a minimum of 8 percent and a maximum of 38 percent. The Soviet Union will not be a mobilization regime, though its place in the lineup will be taken by China. Authoritarian regimes will be ample in number and power for any balancing operations. All past systems suggest that such regimes make acceptable role-players in collective security operations. We shall have to see whether the social change patterns suggested in and among these countries will also meet the additional requisite of satisfaction through tacit inter-functional bargaining.

The Future International Distribution of Power

This brings us to the kind of power distribution likely in 1985. Instead of being multipolar, the new system will be a multibloc arrangement. The leadership role of such nations as the United States, Soviet Union, India, Egypt, Ivory Coast, and Ghana will be much less pronounced. An increasing and more uniform amount of technological, industrial, and human skill development will tend to diminish capability differentials within regions. The examples of declining consensus within NATO, the Warsaw Pact, the OAS, and the OAU also implies a reduction in the role of leading states or "poles." However, the blocs will not be identical or equally cohesive in all kinds of issues. A reduction of influence in the realm of economic capability will not be symmetrically distributed among East and West in the sense that both blocs lose equal increments to a third bloc, simply because there will be no single "third" bloc any longer. Furthermore, both blocs may lose different and unequal amounts of influence in the ideological and military realms, again to various blocs. Inter-functional and inter-regional bargaining will become much more complex, defying an easy reckoning of gains and losses. In short, the system of the future will be characterized by a multibloc asymmetric power distribution.

Let us project the probable blocs which will exist for purposes of economic development issues and economic-financial bargaining. There will be a Latin American Community, a Caribbean grouping, and a viable Central American Common Market. There will also be a self-contained East and Southeast Asian communist bloc, one or more African blocs, and a heterogeneous socialist Asian grouping. Together these will comprise the "developing nations" bloc within the UNCTAD of the future, confronting an industrialized bloc made up of a West European Community, Japan, a United States-Canadian component, and the European communist nations. Neither of the two super-groups will be very cohesive.

Considered in ideological-military terms, the blocs may be slightly different. On the communist side, there will be a European alliance somewhat looser and more egalitarian than the Warsaw Pact Organization and some kind of Asian communist alliance. These will correspond ideologically to the "Marxism" appropriate to the successors of Lenin's and Mao's states. Relations between these two need not be hostile. Will NATO survive? Writing in 1967, one is tempted to see 1985 as the culmination of trends quite clearly visible in the domestic life of the Atlantic nations and in their collective disagreements. NATO may disappear to give rise to a West European alliance with its own nuclear deterrent and a separate United States military establishment. The trouble with this projection is that few leaders on either side of the Atlantic really welcome it as of 1967 and that many actively oppose it for a variety of mixed motives. Thus NATO may survive because (de Gaulle aside) none of the alternatives to it really commands much enthusiasm, but NATO may lose in diplomatic and military significance as the cold war diminishes in intensity. The likely alternatives are between a weaker NATO and separate West European and United States military postures.

It is easier to think about future ideological than military groupings in the third world. None of the conceivable groupings there will possess the power, cohesion, unity of purpose, or strong central institutions which the communist and Western military and economic blocs possess now. Personal rivalries aside, it makes sense to think of two mutually antagonistic African blocs: one of authoritarian and another of mobilization polities, one reasonably friendly to the West, the other to China. Perhaps the same trend would be true of Latin America, though it is doubtful that an alliance of mobilization regimes will be permitted by the United States. It makes more sense to forecast a military-ideological grouping of reconciliation and authoritarian polities, retaining much looser ties with the United States than those maintained by the OAS now, and a number of isolated and bellicose mobilization polities. In Asia much depends on the future vigor of China and her allies. If Maoism remains forceful, we may forecast a defensive military-ideological grouping of authoritarian and reconciliation polities, including India, Indonesia, Malaysia, Iran, and the Philippines, and a few genuine neutrals, such as Burma, Nepal, and Afghanistan. If China were to become preoccupied with other matters, no military-ideological formations of any significance will emerge in Asia.

In the UN we would then have a minimum of six military blocs, or a maximum of ten, with a considerable number of neutral states. The cohesion of each is more than doubtful, as their central institutions will vary from tacit understandings among equals to more elaborate bonds.[56] Even if we assume a certain amount of nuclear proliferation, their military capacities will differ greatly. It is quite conceivable that some of the cheaper new weapons systems will be in general use and be employed effectively in domestic and regional counterinsurgency operations. This obviously would contribute to the internal stability of rapidly modernizing nations and to bloc strength. What matters most in the present context is that the military, economic, and ideological inputs of nations will no longer form a tight and coherent bundle and that blocs differentiated on a functional basis will appear as role players in the UN of the future.

Future Issues and Inputs

It is time we turned to the various issues of the future that constitute the source of inputs into the UN, inputs based on the needs perceived by the member states and thus related to patterns of domestic

[56] See the imaginative projection of blocs and of a multibloc world in Roger D. Masters, "A Multi-Bloc Model of the International System."

change. The issues will be considered here in the form of five "issue areas": self-determination and decolonization; human rights; economic development and financial aid; disarmament; and science and technology.

The only typical decolonization questions left over from the previous periods in UN history are those referring to the Portuguese in Africa and the future of South Africa. While the period from 1960 to 1965 can be given the label "decolonization era" because so much of the UN's energy was taken up with the implementation of the General Assembly's declaration on the complete terminiation of colonialism, little of this task will be left for subsequent periods. The resolution of the remaining "hard core" questions will probably not follow the pattern of reasonably peaceful change. In fact, the immediate future may well involve the application of the full panoply of collective security procedures to Africa. This done, the decolonization task of the UN will be accomplished, and the ideological and legal justification for the application of Chapters VI and VII of the Charter to this kind of situation will no longer prove feasible. The oppression of ethnic groups by the young states of Africa and Asia will not be treated as threats to world peace, despite the fact that practice is the reverse during the current period when the oppressor is white.

This means that the apparent increase in the competence and authority of the organization triggered by the decolonization issue will not carry over into the next phase. Several resolutions were adopted which were considered by many to have the force of a new law of self-determination, even though based merely on a two-thirds majority vote of the Assembly. Several committees of the Assembly have acquired powers of review, investigation, and admonition in a field considered very much as "essentially within the domestic jurisdiction" of states before 1960. But this accretion of power will not last. As Rupert Emerson sums up the matter: "It is not far off the mark to see the UN as rather reflecting the trend of opinion in the world than itself very decisively influencing it. . . . The UN could no more enforce its anticolonial decision after 1960 than before, but both the atmosphere and the facts of the case had undergone radical change."[57] Decolonization completed, the successor states are likely to be exceedingly jealous of

[57] Rupert Emerson, "Colonialism, Political Development and the UN," in Padelford and Goodrich, 490, 496. Emerson suggests that Assembly Resolution 1514 (XV) was in fact an amendment to the Charter. Ruth Russell in Padelford and Goodrich, 419-24, makes the same argument by suggesting that the combined pressure of the Afro-Asian and Soviet blocs made temporarily effective a Charter provision favoring national self-determination which had been understood very differently in 1945. She also argues that "these developments were more the result than the cause of the historical decolonization movement. But the world spotlight on the UN stage has misled many to credit the organization with more authority than it can in fact exert." (422)

the very powers they had denied their colonial antagonists and thus block the carry-over of UN constitutional evolution into the next system.

But is not the argument over national self-determination also a human rights issue? It is impossible to suppose that the claims to human freedom and dignity voiced in the context of decolonization will be heard more and more in the UN and be applied to all member states? It is not only possible but likely. I suspect, however, that the issue of human rights in the next system will no longer profit from being carried along by the prevalence of other issues.

In the past, the increased emphasis on the international protection of human rights owed its salience to the cold war and the colonial revolution. The cold war was responsible for the ILO conventions dealing with freedom of association, the right of collective bargaining, and forced labor because these texts were initially sponsored by Western governments in order to embarrass the communist nations. The colonial revolt was the godfather of the ILO convention dealing with discrimination in employment, the UNESCO convention on discrimination in education, and the 1965 UN convention on the elimination of all racial discrimination.[58] It should be noted that all these texts provide "strong" new norms because an international supervisory machinery is provided to hear and examine complaints of violation even though there is no possibility of enforcement against the will of the defendant.[59] The conventions dealing with genocide and the political rights of women, for example, contain no such provisions. The Universal Declaration on Human Rights has a most questionable status in law and the comprehensive International Covenants of Human Rights have not yet entered into force. Texts that do not owe their origin to some other issue area are neither strong nor successful in penetrating the international environment.

The strong arguments in favor of certain rights closely associated with decolonization will certainly not disappear from the international

[58] The self-serving origin of these texts is discussed by Louis Henkin, "The United Nations and Human Rights," in Padelford and Goodrich, 504-17. Henkin also stresses the fact that the cold war and anticolonial origin of certain standards does not imply that the beneficiaries of these claims will adhere to the standards in their own internal conduct. The UN conventions on genocide and the political rights of women and the ILO convention on equal pay for men and women are instances of human rights texts of autonomous origin. The same is true of the draft covenants on human rights.

[59] For a discussion of the ILO supervisory machinery, which was partly taken over in the UNESCO convention, see C. Wilfred Jenks, *Human Rights and International Labour Standards* (London 1960); Haas, *Beyond the Nation-State*, Chaps. 11, 12; E. A. Landy, *The Effectiveness of International Supervision* (London 1966). Similar provisions were included in the new UN Convention on the Elimination of All Forms of Racial Discrimination, General Assembly Resolution 2106(XX), approved by a vote of 106 to 0 to 1.

forum simply because decolonization will have been completed. Today there is some consensus that the denial of self-determination and racial equality constitute threats to the peace as well as violations of human rights. Why should this not be true in the future? The issues will certainly recur, perhaps with increasing frequency. But we may be skeptical of their salience in triggering concern and international action. The experience of the ILO suggests that certain kinds of polities are most receptive and responsive to international criticism and discussion regarding their violations of human rights. Predominantly, these have been reconciliation polities of recent origin anxious to demonstrate their respectability. Also, modernizing oligarchies eager to impress their own and foreign critics with their progressivism occasionally showed considerable responsiveness. However, the future international system will be populated by a very large number of authoritarian polities whose responsiveness to international criticism is open to considerable doubt. Violations of human rights will be particularly pronounced in settings where the rate and scope of social change is subject to deliberate governmental manipulation, i.e. in authoritarian and mobilization polities. These will not readily heed international admonitions, while older reconciliation polities do not require them. The international protection of human rights will be an issue area confined in salience to a relatively small number of young reconciliation polities.

Moreover, the international protection of human rights will no longer be able to profit from other issue areas. It must stand on its own feet as both the cold war and anticolonial stimulants fade into the background. To succeed as a task, it must be an autonomous and self-generating issue. The character of the future international system makes me doubt that this requisite will be met.

What about economic development and financial aid as future issues? I think that we are on the threshold of a dramatically different approach to economic issues that will have broad implications for this issue area and its link with other tasks. Hitherto, UN economic aid, financed largely by the Western industrial powers, has not been an autonomous issue area. The UN economic development machinery has expanded strikingly from the initially conservative IBRD and the modest technical assistance operations of the TAB to the much more powerful Special Fund and more generous lending and granting agencies now clustering around the Bank. Additional autonomous UN planning and research agencies are developing rapidly. At the same time, the scattered and self-preoccupied aid policies of the specialized agencies have been centralized and coordinated through the UN Development Program. These developments were a component of a tacit bargaining process between the West, the Soviet bloc, and the underdeveloped nations. The primary concern of the dispensers of aid—the West and the Soviets—was rooted in the interplay between the cold war and the colonial revolt. It was therefore closely connected with collective security concerns and peacekeeping operations.[60] Economic aid —bilateral and multilateral—was a method found useful to advance national objectives and to buy support in the third world. In order to maintain such a pattern, even a greatly multilateralized one, the economic aid task should *not* become autonomous and self-generating but remain tied to the other concerns. Otherwise there can be no tacit bargaining.

The events of the last few years, however, suggest that this task is about to become autonomous and self-generating. When the United States sought to influence the future of collective security by withholding its pledge to the Special Fund in 1964, it soon found it wise to abandon this stance and make its large contribution unconditionally. Economic development aid has acquired a consensual basis independent of other motives and concerns. Long-term planning for developing nations is being urged. They are being encouraged to seek planned paths to industrialization less closely dependent on heavy investment and shortcutting the technological-capital-intensive pattern of the West. The most-favored-nation clause as an operative norm of world trade is about to be scrapped. Internationally institutionalized discrimination in favor of developing countries is about to set in. Commodity price stabilization is becoming conceivable as a world policy on a more permanent and less piecemeal basis than in the past. UNCTAD symbolizes these developments and represents a formal and institutionalized forum in which seventy-seven developing nations face some thirty wealthy countries in a permanent dialogue.

These trends tend to take a world economic development policy out of the context of inter-functional bargaining, though they no doubt enhance the economic welfare of the underdeveloped. When massive new social and economic trends strike the members—more synthetics and automation in the West, more disruption of rural life and unbalanced industrialization in the third world—the resulting international issues will be negotiated on their merits. This is good for the finding

[60] Evidence on which these generalizations are based can be found in these studies: James P. Sewell, *Functionalism and World Politics* (Princeton 1966); Eugene R. Black, *The Diplomacy of Economic Development* (New York 1963); Stoessinger, *U.N. and the Superpowers*, Chaps. 8, 9; C. H. Alexandrowicz, *World Economic Agencies* (New York 1962); John G. Hadwen and J. Kaufman, *How United Nations Decisions are Made* (Leiden 1960); Jean Salmon, *Le Rôle des Organisations Internationales en Matière de Prêts et d'Emprunts* (New York 1958); Harold K. Jacobson, *The USSR and the UN's Economic and Social Activities* (South Bend 1963); C. Hart Schaaf and Russell H. Fifield, *The Lower Mekong* (New York 1963); the present United States position is illustrated in Richard N. Gardner, *In Pursuit of World Order* (New York 1964).

of solutions minimizing hardships; it is bad for finding a consensual basis for other international tasks, including collective security.

Is the field of disarmament and arms control likely to offer opportunities for inter-functional bargaining in the future? The lessons of the past allow very little optimism here. There have been almost continuous disarmament negotiations since 1945, yet in no sense have they constituted a task area or provided an issue which has been successfully pulled into a tacit bargaining pattern involving other issues and tasks. The future course of events seems here clearly delineated by the past. Substantively, the only agreements actually concluded have been arms control measures of a self-enforcing character, confirming the technological *status quo*. Weapons and weapons systems capable of destabilizing the balance of terror if one antagonist were to score a scientific breakthrough (excluding antimissile systems and space weapons) have been subjected to controls. Because these agreements are self-enforcing, no role of any kind has accrued to the UN except the capacity to register, *ex post facto*, ventures into space. We can only guess that with the diffusion of scientific and technological capability, other countries will come to share the fears of the super powers and also submit to the same minimal restraints.[61]

Analysts of bloc politics may take comfort from the fact that arms control and disarmament negotiations, whether formally under the aegis of the General Assembly or not, had displayed a bargaining pattern which differs from the consensual basis of collective security operations and resembles that of UNCTAD. While the United States and the Soviet Union provided the opposing poles, the smaller countries tended to mediate *en bloc* between the poles, most strikingly through the group of nonaligned states in the Geneva Seventeen-Nation conferences.[62] But we should note that this concern extends primarily to

[61] One piece of evidence of such a trend is the policy of the United States and the Soviet Union designed to upgrade the inspection powers of the International Atomic Energy Agency. The United States has, since the early 1960's, deliberately insisted that its bilateral nuclear aid agreements be placed under IAEA inspection rules. It has also placed some of its national reactor sites under IAEA inspection in an apparent effort to persuade other countries to do likewise. See Glenn T. Seaborg, "Existing Arrangements for International Control of Warlike Materials—5. The United States Program of Bilateral Safeguards," *Disarmament and Arms Control*, II, No. 4 (Autumn 1964), 422-33. The Soviet Union has insisted on a stronger IAEA to police the Non-Proliferation Treaty. This approach also tends to confirm the military status quo by preventing diversion of peaceful nuclear materials to military use, though it is *not* self-enforcing. One can at least speculate that a sense of shared fear may make possible the extension of this system to weapons systems yet to be perfected. On the other hand, most of the proposals for the creation of nuclear-free zones in many parts of the world stress self-enforcement.

[62] M. Samir Ahmed, "The Role of the Neutrals in the Geneva Negotiations," *Disarmament and Arms Control*, I, No. 1 (Summer 1963), 20-32. Gian Paolo Tozzoli, "The Geneva Negotiations as a Constituent Assembly," *Disarmament and Arms Control*, II, No. 2 (Spring 1964), 126-35. Excessive attention to this trend, however, can

nuclear weapons. Small countries, especially the newer ones, have yet to demonstrate a similar concern with general schemes involving conventional weapons and the arms of the future from which they are likely to derive additional security. It is therefore unrealistic to expect the kinds of convergences of interests which are capable of producing inter-functional trade-off patterns.

Is the extension of the arms race into near and outer space likely to introduce a new element? In the period being projected here, the major new technological development will be the perfection of surveillance satellites, ground-to-space and space-to-ground communication, and the use of manned orbiting laboratories and stations. If all the major nations possess the capability to engage in these activities, no need for inter-functional bargaining arises. Each will inspect everybody else; self-enforcement will be confirmed and no growth of centralized authority will be entailed. If only a few nations engage in these activities, there may still be no enlarged bargaining pattern as long as the capability is symmetrically distributed among the superpowers and confirms the balance of terror.[63]

One other possibility might be kept in mind suggesting the analogy of the IAEA's role in preventing the diversion of nuclear materials to warlike use. The agreement not to place orbiting weapons in space is probably self-enforcing through the use of surveillance satellites. But a proliferation of manned space stations—allegedly for scientific purposes—might offer another possibility. Presumably, only manned inspection of such stations could detect the actual character of the work going on there. Manned inspection, unless carried out by a neutral agency, is likely to be resented by the major powers. Yet they may wish to ascertain the friendly character of such facilities and there-

---

also lead to premature conclusions about the possibility of a larger consensus on these questions. See Philip E. Jacob, "The Disarmament Consensus," *International Organization*, xiv, No. 2 (Spring 1960), 233-60; Richard J. Barnet, *Who Wants Disarmament?* (Boston 1960). Because the smaller and newer nations have shown very little concern about new chemical, biological, and counterinsurgent weapons of smaller scope, the elaborate schemes presented by various peace research centers for the kind of police a "disarmed world" would need are utterly beside the point here. Such forces would naturally conduce to the benefit of the UN. In fact, they would transform it from a decentralized reconciliation system into something much tighter and authoritative. See, for instance, Arthur I. Waskow (and others), *Quis Custodiet? Controlling the Police in a Disarmed World* (Washington 1963). Such schemes are truly "utopian."

[63] Joseph M. Goldsen, ed., *Outer Space in World Politics* (New York 1963) presents ample argument and evidence in support of this line of projection. See especially Karl W. Deutsch's explicit projection for 1988, minimizing the likelihood for elaborate international tasks and forecasting more national preoccupation and self-reliance for the major nations. Daniel S. Cheever, "The UN and Disarmament," in Padelford and Goodrich, 463-83, comes to similar conclusions. He feels that the financial crisis and the probable return to the concert formula for providing a collective security consensus also freezes the present disarmament negotiation pattern.

fore come to favor manned space patrols under UN auspices. Once more, it is a desire to maintain a stable balance of terror which provides the motive for such a task, not a commitment to a different kind of world order. And once established, such a patrol no longer offers the opportunity for subsequent and more sweeping agreements.

This review of issue areas leaves us with one very speculative and uncharted sea of possibilities: the impact of science and technology generally. Do the probabilities enumerated earlier constitute areas of shared concern which might lead to demands and inputs on the part of various blocs so as to trigger a new inter-functional tacit bargaining pattern? Could one suppose that the eagerness of the Atlantic nations to obtain a financial basis for peace-keeping might be tacitly bartered for Indian or Indonesian desire to obtain more UN support in population control? Or that an American concern over the consequences of uncontrolled automation may be countered with demands for certain new types of investment aid by African nations, thus creating a bargaining situation in which collective security could find a new niche? Obviously, some reliance on science fiction becomes crucial in this kind of speculation, and our experience with space technology, science, and exploration furnishes a few guidelines for projection.

The multipolar heterosymmetrical era of the UN demonstrates rather sharply what kinds of new tasks scientific innovation in space has contributed; it demonstrates even more sharply which tasks have failed to evolve. In essence, the promise and the terrible dangers of uncontrolled space activity have resulted in limited agreement setting the ground rules for national action. They have involved, in Wolfgang Friedmann's terms, the "law of coexistence" and not the "law of cooperation." The UN has been the forum in which the space powers have agreed not to appropriate celestial bodies for national use and not to introduce armaments into space. Further, they have agreed that the UN Charter applies in space and have stated minimal rules regarding responsibility and liability for space activities as well as ownership and the right of return of space vehicles.[64] In other words, they have made space safe for peaceful national exploration. While there has been much sharing of scientific information, often through the channels of nongovernmental scientific organizations, there have also been limits to the amount of information released. There is nothing automatic and self-propelling about an ever-increasing amount of interest leading to more joint endeavors.[65] Even though sober pro-

[64] General Assembly Resolution 1962 (XVIII) , December 13, 1963, "Declaration of Legal Principles Governing Activity of States in the Exploration and Use of Outer Space."

[65] Rita and Howard J. Taubenfeld, *Man and Space: Politics, Law, Organization* (Dallas Monographs XI, 1964) , 10-12.

jections as well as science fiction have demonstrated what *could*
happen if there is no joint control over space activities, no new international issue area with a task of its own has developed. The Tauben-
felds sum up the picture:

> . . . the indicated conclusions on international scientific cooperation
> in space activities requires us to acknowledge that, where knowledge
> is, or could be power, the pursuit of knowledge is clearly a politi-
> cal activity. As a result, national investment in space science has
> turned out to be more sensitive and scientific cooperation has been
> less secure than other more mundane, more pressing, less mysterious
> forms of technical cooperation in space.[66]

I see no reason to suppose that things will work out differently in a
multibloc asymmetric system. Blocs of developing nations are most unlikely to acquire a space exploration capability in the near future,
though Europeans undoubtedly will go further with the efforts already under way. These probabilities do not suggest that there will
be much room or need for bargaining once the basic ground rules are
fixed. Once the International Telecommunications Union assesses radio frequencies, as it has done successfully, national or bloc activity
does not call for any new UN initiative unless and until the fear of
one bloc's acquiring a sharp military superiority grips the nations or
until uncontrolled space exploration triggers a wholly unforeseen catastrophe of a chemical, genetic, or epidemiological nature.

There are a few new tasks which involve some bargaining while
they take shape. One is suggested by the improvement of meteorology
and the possibility of weather control. Reconnaissance satellites may
soon provide enough weather information to enable man to undertake
counter-weather measures. Such steps do not stop at national frontiers
or respect national air space. Thus far, meteorological cooperation
takes the form of the World Meteorological Organization's dissemination of weather information collected by nationally owned satellites.
No nation will trust another to control the weather. It follows that
once one nation attempts such control, a new international bargaining situation is created which will permit some inter-functional activ-

---

[66] Same, 13. For somewhat more positive estimates, see also Howard J. Taubenfeld,
ed., *Space and Society* (Dobbs Ferry 1964) . For a thoughtful argument that international space cooperation has gone as far as the national security considerations of the
major powers will permit it to go, see Lincoln P. Bloomfield, "Outer Space and
International Cooperation," in Padelford and Goodrich, 603-21. Bloomfield also suggests the areas of joint concern in which further international regulatory activity is
conceivable despite the continuation of a conflict pattern. See his *Outer Space*
(Englewood Cliffs 1962) , 150ff. The United States, while praising past UN activity
and lauding more scientific cooperation, proposed no new regulatory activity for the
UN. See the statement by Arthur J. Goldberg to the General Assembly, December
18, 1965 in *Department of State Bulletin* (January 1966) , 163-67.

ity until the WMO acquires the task of controlling the weather. At that point, the task will become autonomous and self-generating and possibly of no more general significance for diplomatic activity than the work of the ITU on radio frequencies.

Consider another possibility. The almost certain perfection of communication satellites will make global direct television broadcasts possible. This involves the obvious issue of commercial competition for channels and audiences and advertising. But it may also involve an unforeseen political situation in that the entire globe can become an audience for national propaganda. The United States, Russia, and China can compete simultaneously for ideological support in everyone's living room, tent, adobe hut, and igloo. "It may be no exaggeration to say that priority in establishing the satellite communication system may determine whether, fifty years from now, Russian or English is the main language of mankind. The TV satellite is mightier than the ICBM, and intercontinental TV may indeed be the ultimate weapon."[67] In such a situation, the major and minor powers may suddenly acquire converging interests in UN control over TV broadcasting, again to preserve the *status quo*. And such an interest might conceivably keep open issues for some inter-functional bargaining.

Does the future suggest tasks when we turn to the exploitation of the ocean bottom, genetic manipulation, motivation control through drugs, automated teaching, and asymmetric population growth because of the uneven international use of contraceptives? Each of these topics has enormous political implications. Each could give rise to broad new issue areas. And since interest and concern are asymmetrically distributed, they could appear as constituents in a bargaining process also involving collective security. Can we hazard a projection that they will develop along such lines?

The UN Conference on the Application of Science and Technology for aiding the developing countries touched on these issues. The way in which the social and political implications of scientific innovation were explored presages no vital and negotiable new issue areas, however. Much concern was expressed over the destabilizing and problem-causing, rather than problem-solving, impact of unplanned and uncontrolled scientific techniques in underdeveloped countries; but the emphasis was placed on a more efficient *sharing* and *dissemination* of information rather than on the controlled *use* of innovative techniques. The Conference repeatedly warned that technological changes would not be painless and that the risks of rapid economic and social adaptation have to be accepted if people are to take their place in the modern world. New nations are to reorganize their training and research institutions so as to incorporate the scientific method into their own national ways of life instead of having to rely on the lessons

[67] Arthur C. Clarke as quoted by Bloomfield in Padelford and Goodrich, 607-08.

learned first by the West and simply accepting these as transplanted cultural items. The gaps in this process were stressed and the creation of new national and international agencies for closing them advocated. Shared dangers were sometimes suggested but not turned into an international task.

Only the World Health Organization came close to such a recognition. Its spokesmen pointed out that biomedical problems may well determine the future of mankind. They discussed the relationship between air and water pollution, soil contamination, chemical and genetic forces and the future of the world's health. And they suggested the creation of a World Center for Medical Research to deal with this nexus.[68] The Conference called for the creation of a new specialized agency to coordinate science, scientific training, and planning for development, but U Thant thought that better coordination of the ongoing programs of the specialized agencies would suffice. Eventually, a subcommittee of the Administrative Committee on Coordination was set up to achieve this objective!

Bargaining in the Future Reconciliation System

Such a solution reenforces a trend toward the *separate* planning of international measures *within* each major technological-scientific field and *within* each specialized agency. Separate national technical clienteles will be drawn into the process, as well as distinct national ministries. This trend will militate against any generalized attention to these issue areas. Perhaps, depending on how great the shared fears and hopes turn out to be, this will facilitate the reaching of a broad consensus on *each issue* and yield effective programs. But that is not our problem here. The very autonomy of such successful tasks will prevent their presence in a politicized inter-functional bargaining pattern. Functional analysis forces us to the conclusion that the more successful and self-contained a technical task turns out to be, the less relevance it will have for a world order dependent on generalized bargaining.

Our survey leads to the conclusion that the opportunities for inter-functional and inter-regional bargaining will be more restricted in 1985 than now. As far as domestic change impulses and inputs into the international system are concerned, we have seen that the bulk of presently interconnected issue areas will probably have become autonomous two decades hence. We have suggested the shape of the future

[68] United Nations Conference on the Application of Science and Technology for the Benefit of Less Developed Areas, *Science and Technology for Development: Report, I, World of Opportunity* (New York 1963), 221-40. See also the thematic presentations of the heads of all the major specialized agencies, 56-59, and their emphasis on the promise of planning and science, but never the destabilizing consequences implicit in this. The new UN Organization for Industrial Development may be a step in the direction of more central "scientific" planning.

regional blocs above, but a word must be added to explain what will happen to the current regional organizations and bargaining patterns in the process.

Several of the strongest UN blocs correspond almost exactly to apparently viable regional organizations. Thus the OAU corresponds to the African and the OAS (minus the United States) to the Latin American bloc; the Arab League corresponds exactly to the Arab bloc and the Warsaw Treaty Organization/Comecon to the Soviet bloc. The Commonwealth exists, with identical membership, both in and outside the UN. Why should we suppose that the preoccupations of these regional organizations will not remain alive as inputs into the UN bargaining process?

It is most unlikely that the Commonwealth will survive as a viable entity. Indeed, the present era suggests that in the UN it functions merely as an occasional mediator and balancer in situations when its members also constitute wavering actors in other blocs.[69] The Latin American members of the OAS have consistently turned to the UN rather than their regional organization when they sought protection against the United States. They will continue to do so. Further, they have turned away from the OAS for world trade and economic development purposes, relying on a UN agency—ECLA—for assistance and leadership on economic questions. LAFTA, the Central American Common Market, and the trend toward a Latin American Community suggest a progressive decline of the OAS.[70] As for the OAU, some students suggest that the viability of that organization will be confined to representing Africa in UNCTAD and in spurring continental economic development, especially if the UN's Economic Commission for Africa were to become a *de facto* unit in the OAU. Others dispute even this much viability and stress instead the ephemeral nature of the organization and of the African bloc, portending the division of Africa into several stronger subregional groupings.[71] The viability of the Arab League is so restricted even in this era as not to encourage any projection of greater cohesion and power in the fu-

[69] Geoffrey L. Goodwin, "The Commonwealth and the United Nations," in Padelford and Goodrich, 678-94.

[70] Bryce Wood and Minerva Morales M., "Latin America and the United Nations," in Padelford and Goodrich, 714-27. Glimpses of the regional ideology which may well characterize the future Latin American Community are given in Gustavo Lagos, *International Stratification and Underdeveloped Countries* (Chapel Hill 1963) and in Lagos, ed., *La Integración Latinoamericana* (Buenos Aires 1965).

[71] John Karefa-Smart, "Africa and the United Nations," in Padelford and Goodrich, 764-73. Albert Tevoedjre, *Pan-Africanism in Action* (Cambridge, Mass. 1965). Joseph S. Nye, "International Politics of Africa," unpublished paper, 1966. I. William Zartman, *International Relations in the New Africa* (Englewood Cliffs 1966). For Southeast Asia much the same case is made by Bernard K. Gordon, *The Dimensions of Conflict in Southeast Asia* (Englewood Cliffs 1966).

ture.[72] None of the present regional organizations will possess much cohesion with respect to any of the major issue areas except that of economic development. More important still, with the exception of concern over UNCTAD, interests will diverge so as to prevent the evolution of any stable pattern of inter-regional bargaining. The present groupings, either as UN blocs or as regional organizations, are not likely to function as aggregators of national interests capable of producing predictable bargaining behavior. Successor groups will be more preoccupied with concerns peculiar to each region while, at the same time, the issues that may spill over into the UN forum are tending toward greater functional specificity and autonomy.

What does this mean with respect to the practice of collective security? The decline of the present regional organizations contains two mutually inconsistent implications, one impeding and one favoring the UN's task. In the past and current eras, the UN's successful practice of collective security has frequently depended on the process of inter-regional bargaining, on the membership's respect for the reality of regionalism, and on the delegation of authority to regional agencies. In fact, the success of certain practices of universal collective security has been dependent on regionalism. Thus the UN utilized the Arab League in settling aspects of the Lebanese and Kuwait issues. The OAU was given authority to iron out the implications of the Congo civil war and the Stanleyville air rescue, as well as settling other regional issues not referred to the UN. The OAS was used more than once to apply pacific settlement techniques when no concert appeared possible in the Security Council and when one of the parties preferred an appeal to the UN to reliance on the OAS. The decline of current regional organizations may weaken the UN's ability to indulge in such practices.

Still, on many occasions regional organizations have engaged in collective military, or at least hostile, action contrary to UN policy or in defiance of the rules of Chapter VIII of the Charter. The Arab League's attack on Israel and the subsequent economic boycott is an instance. The military and economic measures voted by the OAU against Portugal go far beyond the sanctions authorized by the UN. OAS sanctions against Cuba and the Dominican Republic had not been authorized by the Security Council and caused the Soviet delegate to question their legality.[73] The decay of the present regional organizations may thus remove one source of collective violence which may be contrary to UN policy. Whether this is a net gain for universal

72 Robert W. Macdonald, *The League of Arab States* (Princeton 1965). Sylvia G. Haim, ed., *Arab Nationalism* (Berkeley 1962).

73 Francis O. Wilcox, "Regionalism and the United Nations," in Padelford and Goodrich, 789-811.

collective security, considering the simultaneous loss of pacific settlement support, must remain a moot point.

Politically, we shall have a system of blocs which will be differentiated along functional rather than clear geographical lines. And as each bloc is likely to represent a self-contained negotiating universe, the old inter-functional and inter-regional bargaining pattern cannot survive. Is this likely to weaken the norms of action and the legally sanctioned procedures of the current era? Two prominent jurists tend to draw precisely this conclusion from their analysis of the current system. Rosenne projects an increase in the purely voluntaristic character of international adjudication in political disputes. He sees in the evolution of the "preliminary objection" procedure before the ICJ evidence that the Court can participate in the peaceful settlement of disputes by avoiding a clear pronouncement of who is "guilty" or "not guilty." States before the Court will sacrifice less prestige if they lose a case on "preliminary" grounds, while still able to settle on the merits at a later point.[74] Julius Stone posits "realistic compliance goals" for jurists anxious to perfect the present and future international order. He warns that compliance must first be sought where there is existing law that is considered just by most states; "pressure for compliance with debatable rules or in debatable situations implies pressure for extended submission" to some authoritative—but non-existent—decision-maker.[75] Extended education of new states in the law must take place before such submission can be expected. This can be encouraged by increasing reliance on regional and specialized tribunals for dealing with the myriad petty disputes which do not challenge the major principles of world order. At the same time, the UN itself must defer more often to the law when it is clear and considered just, and the member states must refrain from equating unilateral imposition with compliance. An increase of respect for legal norms and procedures in the realm of collective security is scarcely implicit in this sober view.

Because the force of this analysis has come down on the side of the environmental "autonomous input" model, it is tempting to speculate about the future of the international order using the analogy of

[74] Shabtai Rosenne, "The Court and the Judicial Process," in Padelford and Goodrich, 518-36. Rosenne also suggests that the ICJ's advisory competence has developed autonomously and significantly and may further the institutionalization of UN activity. However, the ICJ's decision in the South West Africa cases and the reception accorded to that decision by most nations would seem to suggest that this analysis is very optimistic. See Richard A. Falk, "The South West Africa Cases: An Appraisal," *International Organization*, xxi, No. 1 (Winter 1967).

[75] Julius Stone, "Realistic Compliance Goals," *Proceedings of the American Society of International Law* (1964), 25. Stone adds a further "canon," an appeal to the new states to observe the law instead of merely demanding that the former colonial powers do so!

a domestic party system. Bipolarity, tripolarity, and multipolarity suggest strong similarities to bimodal and other distribution of voter preferences; further, the adjustment of political parties and their ideologies to such trends in the national electoral setting may have its counterpart in a UN voting trend in which extremes decline and a heterogeneous "middle" dominates.[76] Alker and Russett deliberately use such a construct in their analysis of the dimensions of voting in the General Assembly.[77] They hoped to demonstrate a trend toward a reduction in the bimodal distribution of preferences through the services of balancing blocs and the discovery of cross-cutting solidarities among the voters. Had they succeeded in illustrating such a behavior pattern, the systemic "learning" model of system transformation would have benefited. The General Assembly would then be accurately described in such terms and predictions made accordingly.

However, Alker and Russett discovered that their construct did *not* accurately describe the Assembly. They conclude that past and present consensual patterns permit of no projection into the future and that the intensity of attitude distribution is not tending toward a uniform pattern. "Knowing a state's allies on one dimension does not help in predicting with whom it will ally on another."[78] As the distinction between cold war and colonial issues decreases while the "East-West dimension" increases in salience, more violence and fewer bargains will occur. Cross-pressures on voters have declined, they find, with only the African nations continuing to be exposed to them. Further, they foresee a multibloc world possessing very little formal shape approximating that of political parties and no clear pattern in future voting alignments. The victory of environmental forces over the system-transforming capacity of the UN itself is implicit in this conclusion.

And so we reach the end of the prophetic road: *The UN of 1985 will be a reconciliation system.* The heterogeneity of the en-

[76] The classical work along these lines is that of Anthony Downs, *An Economic Theory of Democracy* (New York 1957).

[77] Hayward R. Alker, Jr. and Bruce M. Russett, *World Politics in the General Assembly* (New Haven 1965). See Chap. 8 for the elaboration of the model. It assumes that, as two major parties realize that neither can win a complete victory while each wishes to remain in the system, a third party will arise to challenge the appeal to the voters of both, thereby forcing them to make their positions approximate one another. All participants would therefore "learn" to moderate their demands, reduce ideological cleavages, increase consensus, and add to the legitimacy of UN institutions, thereby transforming them.

[78] Same, 215. Conclusions detracting from the learning model and supporting the argument of my analysis are developed on pp. 189-90, 242-50, 270-74, 289-93, 296. For a thoughtful discussion of ways to study the political role of the General Assembly without stumbling on the methodological difficulties found in the Alker-Russett work see Robert O. Keohane, "The Study of Political Influence in the General Assembly," *International Organization*, XXI, No. 2 (Spring 1967).

vironment, the prevailing polities, the distribution of power, and the structural and functional characteristics of relations between the nations and the international organization *do* meet the requisites posited. But, because most of the tasks of the organization will be autonomous, *the mingling of inputs and the production of outputs will not satisfy the requisites as well as does the present system. The UN then will be a reconciliation system unable to carry out the collective security task as well as does the current UN.* Future consensual patterns based on ad-hoc concerts are possible and even likely, but these may well tend toward a dictatorship of the big powers. Balancing is ever more necessary for successful collective security but less likely precisely because of the changing pattern of inter-functional and inter-regional bargaining. If the Security Council harbors the danger of big power dominance, the General Assembly hides the peril of flabby majorities without the collective will to act. No sermonizing in favor of "flexible" policies that call for moving between the two will provide a stable output pattern. What is good for most UN tasks is bad for collective security. The local forces of change will bring about a clustering of issue areas under which the institutionalization of world order itself is likely to become a subordinate function. And the possible increases in human welfare cannot count on a companion benefit in world peace.

CHAPTER 7

Participation of the "New" States in the International Legal Order of the Future

A. A. FATOUROS

AN ATTEMPT to look into the future multiplies the uncertainties and ambiguities with which our perception of the present is filled. As questionable conclusions are derived from unreliable data, and the uncertainties and schematizations on one point are combined with problematical predictions with respect to another, total uncertainty grows in geometrical progression. The final result is full of ambiguities and approximations, contingent upon a multitude of indefinite events; it ceases to be useful as a picture, however vague, of actuality, and it can only have the limited reality of an outline of patterns of possibilities. Still, while a significant difference in the degree of uncertainty does exist, the actual method of proceeding and the essential quality of the findings do not differ radically from those used or drawn in studies of the past or of that mixture of recent past and immediate future that we call the present. Not only is our understanding of past events uncertain and contingent, perhaps less than but not radically unlike our image of the future; more than that: to be validly perceived, the past must be approached in terms of the future.[1]

The peculiar character of the topic makes necessary a more explicit treatment of the limits, assumptions, and methods of the inquiry than is usually the case. Accordingly, the first section of this chapter is devoted to these questions. The next section deals with the new elements imported into the international legal order of today, and probably of the future, by the new states, while the third section examines their likely impact in terms of changes in general structures and methods. In drawing some brief conclusions from the study, the last section returns more specifically to the probabilities of future developments.

---

[1] In Alphonse de Waelhens' happy formulation of Heidegger's thought "le véritable historien se tourne en ordre principal vers l'avenir." A. de Waelhens, *La philosophie de Martin Heidegger* (Louvain 1942), 236-37. See Martin Heidegger, *Sein und Zeit* (8th edn., Tübingen 1957), p. 395; Trans. John Macquarrie and Edward Robinson, *Being and Time* (New York 1962), 447. And cf. Jean-Paul Sartre, *L'Etre et le Néant* (Paris 1943), 150-74; trans. Hazel Barnes, *Being and Nothingness* (New York 1956), 107-29.

PRELIMINARY OBSERVATIONS

Delimiting the Topic

The concept of an "international legal order" is not free of ambiguity, but it would be vain to try to explore its meaning in a few introductory paragraphs. Other chapters deal with it in a more comprehensive manner; from these I wish to retain the emphasis on the dynamic character of the concept.

In dealing with the future, certain chronological limits have to be imposed.[2] Outside of science fiction, only a relatively immediate future can be meaningfully dealt with in a study focused on social structures and interactions, rather than physical or technological developments, say, fifteen to twenty years from now, the decade of the 1980's. Our concern with the future is thus in essence but a way of focusing attention on important trends and features in the contemporary situation; conclusions are derived not from a free play of the imagination but from an extrapolation from present conditions.

Concern with the future eliminates one pseudo-problem that has been receiving far too much attention in legal literature. This is the question whether the rules of traditional international law continue to be in effect and to bind the new states. Two diametrically opposed views, as well as several intermediate ones, have been advanced. Some jurists support the view that the new states are automatically bound by the existing customary rules of international law the moment they become members of international society (subjects of international law). Others maintain the opposite, and question the binding force of legal rules which had been generally accepted before the new states appeared on the scene and which are founded on conditions radically different from the ones now existing. The question is of course irrelevant when the future is being considered since one can assume that twenty years from now the problem will be somehow resolved or at any rate outdated. But even with respect to the present, the real importance of this problem is minimal. While many arguments, pragmatic or metaphysical, can be used to support the one or the other position, the controversy has at best a merely symbolic significance. Like all legal systems, international law is not a fixed collection of immutable rules, it is the dynamic expression of a legal order, the external formulation of constantly changing relationships among the active participants in international life, whether formal subjects of in-

---

[2] A more elaborate discussion of what predicting the future means and the kinds of operations that it involves would take us too far afield. For some indications on the growing literature on this subject, see J. Meynaud, "A propos des spéculations sur l'avenir," *Revue Française de Science Politique*, 13 (1963), 666-88, and same, Vol. 15 (1965), 705-31; D. Bell, "The Study of the Future," *The Public Interest*, 1 (1965), 119-30.

ternational law (states, international organizations) or not (individuals, private corporations, or colonial "territories"). What is important therefore is whether and how far the rules and procedures of classical international law do correspond to present-day conditions and needs (one aspect of which is the emergence of the new states). It is the answer to this question that will determine the attitude of the new states toward contemporary international law.[3] If classical international law does not correspond to the needs and conditions of today, then, even if its rules are formally binding, they should change, and the task of jurists and statesmen is to study the methods and directions of such change. If, on the other hand, the established rules and institutions, or some of them, do correspond to present-day needs, then, even if they do not bind automatically the new states, the latter will accept them because it is to their interest to do so. The case where the special interests of a state or of a small group of states differ radically from the general interests of the international society presents a different question which is far from new and is known to all legal orders. In that context, the argument of lack of binding force should be seen as part of the pattern of the specific controversy in which it is raised.

The last component of the title is the concept of "new nations," whose actual content is by no means clear. Pierre Hassner has pointed out that there are at least five ways of naming, and thereby grouping, the states which constitute the object of his essay (and, to a great extent, of mine) and that to each of these ways corresponds a particular discipline or approach. One may refer to: (1) Newly independent countries (historical and, it may be added, legal, approach) ; (2) Underdeveloped countries (economic approach—at least in its origins) ; (3) Nonaligned (or neutralist) countries (political approach); (4) Afro-Asian countries (geographical approach) ; and (5) Third World countries (politico-geographical approach, according to M. Hassner, but perhaps economic and even cultural approach, as well).[4]

These categories overlap, of course: a state may belong to all five of them or to one or two only. Since, moreover, the terms are not precisely defined (nor is it necessary to become involved here in a complicated process of definition *per genus et differentiam*), it may

[3] In general agreement with this approach, see, e.g. the formulations of the problem in Jorge Castañeda, "The Underdeveloped Countries and the Development of International Law," *International Organization*, xv (1961), 38ff.; G. Abi-Saab, "The Newly Independent States and the Rules of International Law: An Outline," 8 *Howard Law Journal*, 95-121 (1962) ; Oliver J. Lissitzyn, *International Law Today and Tomorrow* (New York 1965), 72ff.

[4] P. Hassner, "Le système international et les nouveaux Etats," in J. B. Duroselle and J. Meyriat, eds., *La communauté internationale face aux jeunes états* (Paris 1964), 11, at 12-13. And see the longer list of possible tests for classification offered in Richard A. Falk, "The New States and International Legal Order," Hague Academy of International Law, 118 *Recueil des Cours* 1, 10 (1966).

be that for many purposes the contents of some of these categories coincide. Thus, the Afro-Asian countries are, by and large, the newly independent countries, as well, although some Afro-Asian countries (Liberia and Thailand, for example) are not newly independent, and some newly independent countries (Malta and Cyprus, for instance) are not Afro-Asian. Such exercises in elucidation are useful to the extent that they show that the borderlines of the concepts and categories mentioned are not rigidly fixed; the concepts themselves remain useful only as long as their "open-texture" is recognized.[5]

While keeping in mind the possibility of these distinctions, I shall assume in this essay that they are largely irrelevant for my purposes; accordingly, I shall use interchangeably most of the five terms listed above. To be sure, this involves an arbitrary disregard of certain differences; the Latin American states, for instance, are not newly independent, but they share many of the problems of the new states; moreover, they, as well as several other underdeveloped countries, are not generally considered as nonaligned. The present confused state of the last category, indeed, that of nonaligned nations, shows clearly the fluidity and relative character of such classifications. Disregard for these distinctions indicates, of course, something more than mere arbitrariness: it flows from a perception of certain features in the situation of the states in question as being most important and relevant for the present inquiry, namely, their stage of economic, social, and political development. Whenever the differences between the various concepts are of particular importance with respect to a specific question, the differentiation will be expressly made.

Assumptions and Limitations of the Inquiry

Preoccupation with the future makes necessary certain assumptions with respect to the environment (physical and otherwise) in which the central objects of this study will continue to exist. Thus it is necessary to assume that no major catastrophe (nuclear or other) will occur in the time span involved. Since this is by no means a certainty, it is impossible to treat it as anything but an assumption, even perhaps as merely an alternative assumption, leaving to strategists (or is it biologists?) the task of considering the exact consequences of the other alternative.

Another area of possible inquiry that will have to be assumed away is that of technology. I am thinking, in particular, of the technological

---

[5] For the concept of "open texture," see generally, F. Waissman, "Verifiability," in A.G.N. Flew, ed., *Essays on Logic and Language* (1st series, 1951), 117ff. And for its application in the legal context, see H.L.A. Hart, *The Concept of Law* (Oxford 1961), 119ff., and citations at 249.

developments which relate to warfare, on the one hand, and to the exploitation of natural resources and economic development in general, on the other. The element of unreality introduced by this assumption might be dispelled in part by arguing, on the basis of past experience, that any radical and revolutionary technological changes or discoveries made within the immediate future will become operative, so as to affect the economic situation of the majority of states, after a considerable span of time. This argument is not fully convincing, however, both because the pace of technological change is becoming constantly faster and because there is a significant difference between a situation where technological conditions are more or less like those of today, and a situation where the immediate application of revolutionary processes is validly expected within the (then) near future.

A third area where clearly unrealistic assumptions are necessary to avoid complicating excessively the present discussion is that of the "cold war." It is obvious that in the next fifteen or twenty years the relationships between the states of the so-called Western bloc and the states of the Soviet bloc, as well as among the members of each of these blocs, are going to change in many and significant respects. Indeed, it is quite doubtful whether the reference to "blocs" is even now realistic or meaningful. It is equally obvious that whatever changes occur will affect profoundly the position and role of the "new states," in the broad sense in which the term is used here. The evolution in the pattern of relations between the United States, the Soviet Union, and mainland China, for instance, is bound to influence substantially and immediately the position and attitudes of the states of the "third world." In spite of all this, these developments will be examined here only to a very limited extent. For the rest, the assumption will have to be made that the conditions of coexistence between ideologically opposed states and groups will continue to be in the future roughly similar to those prevailing today. That this assumption is quite unrealistic will be another factor to be taken into consideration when assessing the value of the findings and conclusions of this study.

Notes on Method and Sources

One basic problem in any study of the international conduct of the new states is the scarcity of relevant materials and documentation. No doubt, this scarcity has lessened somewhat in the past few years. It is now possible to rely not only on the official records of the United Nations organs (which present a most important but still limited and thereby distorted view of international relations) but also on numerous studies of the international conduct and relations of the new states. However, materials of a more specifically legal character, statements of positions couched in legal terms and relating to legal problems, continue to be quite scarce. Nonlegal materials can and should be used, of course, in order to deduce or derive conclusions regarding positions as to legal problems. Such materials, as evidence of actual state practice, are used in the study of the international law practice and position of the older countries, as well. But in their case there also exists an abundance of specifically legal documentation (treaties, court decisions, arbitral awards, opinions of legal advisers, official statements, etc.) which presents the legal side of the related problems. Such documents are rarer in the case of the new nations and, where they exist, their specifically legal content, i.e., the references to legal principles and rules and the use of legal reasoning and argumentation, is usually less important than the political or ideological content. As a result, while in the case of the older states the study of actual practice is used chiefly, though not exclusively, as a corrective to the legal interpretation given in or inferred from the materials mentioned, in the case of the newer states, again not without some notable exceptions, the nonlegal materials constitute the main or exclusive source for inferences as to legal positions. An additional element of ambiguity is thus introduced.

A related point, some particular aspects of which will be discussed later, is that the traditional legal concepts and terms may not be capable of fully expressing the position and attitudes of the new states. The legal principles, rules and approaches in use in international affairs have evolved out of the practice and needs of the older countries at a different historical period; they may not always fit the present conditions, in general, and the needs and intentions of the new states, in particular. (The phenomenon is not unique to international law; we still have some difficulty in describing and regulating property relations in an industrialized setting in terms originally evolved to account for and govern feudal relationships.) Since the new states continue, for a number of reasons, to utilize the traditional terms and concepts, departing from them rarely and somewhat erratically, a new element of ambiguity is introduced: the very attempt to formulate their position in traditional legal terms may in some cases distort the actual import of the actions or arguments involved.

Another source of materials, or more generally of experience, is to be found in history. More precisely it is to be found in the history of states which, at a certain time, found themselves in a situation which corresponds to that of the new states today.[6] Utilization of this

---

[6] As the illustrations in this chapter indicate, the states referred to are chiefly those of Eastern and Southern Europe and of Latin America at the close of the nineteenth century. The high incidence of references to modern Greek history is in a sense accidental: it so happens that that history is better known to me. Similar situa-

source necessarily brings in more ambiguity and uncertainty: which present and past situations "correspond" to one another is neither crystal-clear nor universally agreed upon. The "newness'" of the states concerned may provide a criterion of relative "objectivity": if all new states in the past have acted in a certain manner, it may be relatively easy to accept that the new states of today may or will act in the same manner (in more specifically legal terms, will seek to apply or strengthen certain rules or to encourage developments in certain directions). But "newness" in itself is not necessarily a proper test: the historical environment into which states emerge has changed in many ways and the "proper" reaction of new states may accordingly differ. In many cases, therefore, it is not the element of "newness" but other features of the states under consideration (military weakness, economic and political underdevelopment, etc.) that provide the needed link to past experience. And it has to be admitted, from the very start, that the choice of the "appropriate" features to establish analogies with the past imports the observer's own conclusions on at least some of the questions to be answered, thus unavoidably coloring the "objectivity" of his findings.

A third source, or method, is more difficult to define, since it involves extensive use of rational speculation as well as imagination. Given certain objective conditions and attitudes (cultural, political, social, and economic), certain goals and desires, and the facts as well as the appearances of contemporary international society, the probable claims, attitudes, and methods of at least some of the new states can be deduced with some assurance. What is involved is not only a rational process of deduction and correlation, but also "understanding," a feeling for human actions, reactions, and emotions. Such a deplorably unscientific method cannot provide quantifiable or even precise data, of course; but it can indicate possible (or probable) directions of future developments and open, at the very least, some useful avenues of inquiry.[7]

The Impact of the New States: Novel Features and Problems

Before considering the probable and actual effects of the emergence of the new states on the structure and methods of the international

tions and attitudes, however, can be found in the history of all Balkan states around that same period.

[7] For a concrete application of the method in question, see my "International Law and the Third World," 50 *Virginia Law Review*, 783ff. esp. at 799-817 (1964). It would be vain to attempt here to place this method in the context of current methodological inquiries in the social sciences; relevant and closely related questions seem to me to be raised in J. David Singer's, "The Level-of-Analysis Problem in International Relations," *World Politics*, 14 (1961), 77ff., esp. at 86ff.

legal order, some of the novel elements which these states have brought into international life should be examined. Some of them are altogether new; others, perhaps the great majority, have been long present and known but are today more acute and far more urgent. Correspondingly, while the problems which arise are in some instances new, in the majority of cases they are exacerbated forms of older problems, already known difficulties which have now been raised to a new level of importance.

Internal Political Conditions and International Law

Following the model of municipal private laws, in their treatment of companies and other associations with "legal personality," international law has consistently personified the states which are its subjects. With some qualifications and exceptions of uneven importance, it has treated states as if, in the last analysis, they were individual, physical, human beings.[8] That this approach is very useful cannot honestly be denied. It has indeed been a quite realistic approach, in differing ways over the years. Whether in the case of the princes and kings of early international law or in that of the democratic or totalitarian states of modern Europe and North America, it is possible and necessary to treat the governing officials as expressing the "will" of the state, either because the opinion of the "subjects" is held not to matter, or because it can reasonably be said to be fairly expressed by the officials. The cases in the past where this was obviously not so have been in the main exceptional. The legal doctrines and principles on the meaning and role of legitimacy[9] expressed the consensus on this point as well as the difficulties and doubts involved. Traditionally, legitimacy was judged in practice by both formal and informal criteria: constitutional procedures, on the one hand, and obvious consent and obedience of the bulk of the population, on the other. The potential conflict between the two was usually resolved in the affirmative, in favor of the recognition of legitimacy. This approach has always had its difficulties and problems, but these have generally

---

[8] This is, of course, a momentous oversimplification, but the reservations and qualifications that are needed do not affect the main argument of this section. For some earlier but still valid discussions of this question, see, J. L. Brierly, "The Rule of Law in International Society," *Acta Scandinavica Iuris Gentium*, 7 (1936), 3ff.; E. D. Dickinson, "The Analogy Between Natural Persons and International Persons in the Law of Nations," 26 *Yale Law Journal*, 564ff. (1917).

[9] I follow political science, rather than legal, usage in my use of this term here. Most legal discussions on this problem have occurred in the context of the law of recognition of governments. See esp. H. Lauterpacht, *Recognition in International Law* (Cambridge 1947), 87-140; Ti-Chiang Chen, *The International Law of Recognition*, L. C. Green, ed. (New York 1951), 97-130. For a political scientist's perceptive glance at this issue, see S. Hoffmann, "International Systems and International Law," *World Politics*, XIV (1961), 205-37, at 226 [reprinted in *The State of War* (New York 1965), 88-122, at 111-12].

been treated as due to exceptional situations or conditions. It was perhaps prophetically indicative of the causes of the future intensification of these difficulties that, until roughly the Second World War, international legal problems concerning legitimacy of officials were repeatedly and often intensely raised chiefly with respect to the Latin American republics.[10] In the Balkan states, where the social and economic conditions were essentially not dissimilar, such problems did not, in the main, arise,[11] in part, no doubt, because of the presence of formal legitimacy in the person of their kings.

With the appearance and growing importance of a great number of new states, the situation has radically changed. These are often "veneer states,"[12] in which no meaningful and reasonably stable relationship exists between the governing elites and the great bulk of the population. Both criteria of legitimacy are often indeterminate or lacking. There is often no convincing formal legitimacy, partly because the constitutional or political forms are too new and partly because they have been changed too often in their short life; neither is there (in many cases) any detectable substantive legitimacy, any evident degree of support of the government by the population, or, more generally, any proof of a meaningful relationship between the two. The fundamental opposition of a modernized and modernizing elite with a traditional and uninvolved rural majority (by no means uncommon in the past, but still peculiar in its present intensity) and an uprooted and semi-modernized urban proletariat, which is at the root of many of these problems,[13] is bound to affect the foreign policy and, more generally, the external position of the states concerned. In Stanley Hoffmann's phrase, these are "governments still in search of their nation."[14] The governing groups not only govern and represent, they are also trying to create, their nation. Political struggle, under these conditions, has an intensity and an importance unknown to past generations. Each change of government may involve radical changes in

---

[10] See the excellent treatment of the subject in C. Neale Ronning, *Law and Politics in Inter-American Diplomacy* (New York 1963), 6-32.

[11] But see the case of the Greek change of government in 1922, as briefly described in Lauterpacht, *Recognition*, 108, n2.

[12] This term has no derogatory implications; I owe it to Professor Kenneth S. Carlston, "Universality of International Law Today: Challenge and Response," 8 *Howard Law Journal*, 78-85, at 78 (1962).

[13] These problems have been the subject of many recent political science studies and even a few general theories are now appearing. Of the less systematic discussions, the most effective in exploring some facets of these problems are: René Dumont, *L'Afrique noire est mal partie* (Paris 1962); F. Fanon, *Les damnés de la terre* (Paris 1961), esp. at 113-51; B. Davidson, *Which Way Africa?* (New York 1964), 130-41 and passim; and T. L. Hodgkin, "The Relevance of 'Western' Ideas for the New African States," in J. R. Pennock, ed., *Self-Government in Modernizing Nations* (Englewood Cliffs, N. J. 1964), 50ff.

[14] S. Hoffmann, "International Systems," 230 [*The State of War*, 115].

domestic or foreign policy conceptions (although it does not necessarily do so in all cases). As a result, the succession of administrations or regimes as seen from the outside is not the smooth, more or less continuous process found in the past in the developed Western countries. Succession of governments becomes a complex discontinuous process, which the rules developed earlier are made to fit only with great difficulty.

As already suggested, the situation is not new in kind, but it is certainly novel in its incidence and intensity. To some extent, this is due to the pressure of time. Time was never so scarce a commodity as it is today. The conditions in today's world make impossible (or at least improbable) a slow, long-run development toward legitimization of existing authority. Regardless of their ability or inability to express themselves effectively, people are not prepared to wait a long time. Their attitude is in itself a factual datum, although it may even be objectively justifiable, since under present conditions far more is sacrificed when waiting than was the case in the past. This situation challenges basic assumptions of the existing international legal rules and processes.

The extent of the problem becomes evident when the attitude of new states toward prior commitments undertaken toward other states or, especially, toward foreign private investors is considered. In traditional international law, a basic distinction was made between commitments made before and those made after independence. In the case of international, intergovernmental, commitments made before a state's independence, the law allowed certain possibilities of revision or reconsideration.[15] The situation with respect to a state's commitments or obligations to private parties, entered into before independence, was less clear, but there is some authority in past practice for restricting or revising at least some such commitments once the state has acquired its independence.[16] In the case of commitments made after independence, however, the duty to respect the obligations undertaken was strictly accepted in traditional international law; exceptions to it were narrowly circumscribed. With respect to international treaties, the doctrine of the *clausula rebus sic stantibus* provides virtu-

[15] See generally D. P. O'Connell, *The Law of State Succession* (Cambridge 1956), 15-74.

[16] For a detailed inquiry, see same, 77ff., who admits some variance in the practice, although upholding as a general rule the binding force of such commitments. In recent years, denial of such binding force has been increasingly common, especially in the case of colonial territories acquiring independence. Characteristically, the UN General Assembly Resolution 1803 (XVII), 1962, on permanent sovereignty over natural resources, carefully excluded (on the basis of an initial Algerian amendment, to which one by the United States was substituted) the application of its provisions on expropriation to "property acquired before the accession to complete sovereignty of countries formerly under colonial rule."

ally the only escape valve. While the situation with respect to state commitments to aliens is too complex for summary treatment here, the general trend in the established legal policies (although not precisely in positive law) had been against allowing even a *rebus sic stantibus* type of exception.[17]

It cannot be denied that this position of the problem is useful and to a considerable extent necessary. A legal order needs some degree of predictability and consistency. The international legal order would be even more anarchical than it is if every government were allowed to repudiate the obligations undertaken by its predecessor. Nonetheless, it is also evident that in some cases the distinction is based on purely or predominantly formal criteria, in virtually total disregard of the substance. In the present situation, therefore, the attribution to it of critical importance in all cases may well be questioned. The growing feeling in favor of equality, the overwhelming wish for economic development, and the very fact of political development compel many citizens in new states to downgrade the importance of the difference between a colonial regime and a postcolonial loyalist ("neocolonialist," in the new terminology) type of regime. At the same time, as already noted, the differences between successive governments often are (or are considered as being) much more marked than in the past. It is of course possible to disregard these problems and stick to the traditional legal distinctions. But once the formal legal level is abandoned, it is increasingly difficult to support the solutions to which they lead. Is a concession granted to foreign investors by a corrupt, totalitarian government inherently more respectable than one granted by the colonial authorities before a territory has acquired its independence? The question may be posed in even broader (and more oversimplified) terms. Is a commitment, undertaken even toward a foreign state, by a government mindful solely of its political prestige and position or compelled by overwhelming pressures of foreign governments or private groups, always to be treated as a binding, voluntary undertaking? Clear-cut answers in either direction are easy; nonetheless, although they can be defended on a generalized basis, they are difficult to uphold when their ultimate substantive consequences in particular cases are considered.

[17] See the discussion and citations to the related literature in A. A. Fatouros, *Government Guarantees to Foreign Investors* (New York 1962), 232-338. And cf., more recently R. Y. Jennings, "State Contracts in International Law," *British Yearbook of International Law*, 37 (1961), 156ff.; C. F. Amerasinghe, "State Breaches of Contracts with Aliens and International Law," *American Journal of International Law*, 58 (1964), 881ff. Past legal policies in that connection emerge clearly from the materials collected in J. G. Wetter, "Diplomatic Assistance to Private Investment," 29 *University of Chicago Law Review*, 275ff. (1962); J. G. Wetter and S. M. Schwebel, "Some Little-Known Cases on Concessions," *British Yearbook of International Law*, 40 (1964), 183ff.

To raise the issue is not to answer it. The argument should not be overstated. It remains true that, in the main, states do respect their undertakings, toward other states or toward foreign companies. Moreover, not every change in government does, or can reasonably be expected to, result in a radical change in attitude on important issues; important common elements exist in the positions of even radically differing successive governments in any state. Although, therefore, the problems raised above are not mere exercises in speculation, the rules and principles of traditional international law retain much of their usefulness and wisdom, since the necessity for a minimum degree of stability and predictability in international relations continue to exist. But the questions remain, too.

Existing prospects for the near future enhance the importance of these questions. Given the overwhelming difficulties of the governments in the new states, radical, even catastrophic, internal developments cannot be excluded. It is true that actual regression is quite improbable. Even where it appears to take place, where the most chaotic breakdowns in the attributes of the modern state occur, what emerges is not the "traditional" tribal or feudal society of two or ten centuries ago, but a new form of society, clearly bearing the marks of the colonial past and of modern influences. In terms of probabilities, social, economic, and political stagnation is far more probable than regression; indeed, the experience of older developing countries in Latin America and Southern Europe would seem to indicate that stagnation is almost certain. If today some chances of avoiding it exist, it is chiefly or even solely because of the extent to which people in all states are involved in and have been affected by the revolution of rising expectations. At any rate, whether with or without stagnation, a long period of political instability is virtually certain, and such instability, perhaps coupled with partial but radical change, is bound to be a constant disturbing element in international relations.

Its presence, combined with the lack of a national consensus and indeed of a national reality behind the formal facade of a state structure in many new states, may affect developments in international law in many other ways. It raises serious obstacles to attempts to resolve international problems by bargaining, since it creates doubts as to the extent to which undertakings are going to be respected. And it makes it more difficult to accept solutions based on the existence and identification of an international "consensus," which would lead, for instance, to acceptance of the exercise of a "quasi-legislative" function by the General Assembly of the United Nations.[18] Since those who

18 See, Richard A. Falk, "On the Quasi-Legislative Competence of the General Assembly," 60 *American Journal of International Law*, 782-91 (1966). Awareness of this additional difficulty does not mean that such a function should necessarily be rejected; see text to notes 92-94.

will agree to a particular proposition advanced at any particular time will be but the unstable governing groups of a number of states, the effective consensus is shaky. A few revolutions or governmental changes, over a number of years, may radically change official attitudes and positions.

The Fusion of National and International Affairs

The internal situation in developing countries is important not only because it brings into prominence the whole *problématique* of legitimacy and ability to bind future generations, but also because at no other time were domestic and foreign affairs so intimately related, indeed for many purposes identical, as they are today. This fact has been stressed by many recent writers on international law and relations; in the present context, it can be treated only partially, chiefly with respect to the position and problems of the new states.

The closeness of the interrelationship is particularly evident in the case of civil war or other forms of "internal" violence. It is true that nationalist rebellions, i.e., revolutions directed at the assertion of the independence of a particular national group, were of international "concern" (involving varying degrees of direct or indirect intervention by foreign states) in the past, as well. This was less true in the case of purely internal rebellions (coups d'état, revolutions, civil wars) involving a struggle for control of the government.[19] Conditions have changed and the legal classifications and terminology evolved in a past era are hard to apply to contemporary policies and events.[20] It is evident that the phenomenon obtains, as well, in the absence of violence. In the world of today, "the interdependence of nations . . . makes it inevitable that each society's acts will have consequences within other societies. . . ."[21] As a result, "in certain respects national political systems now permeate, as well as depend on, each other and . . . their functioning now embraces actors who are not formally members of the system."[22] Such interpenetration occurs with respect to a

[19] This may be no more than an assumption, however, and a questionable one, at that. As will be developed below, indirect state intervention (short of actual warfare) by the great powers was by no means uncommon during the nineteenth century and was treated, accordingly, somewhat casually by all parties concerned. The established "facts" of past eras sometimes change in meaning and appearance, when studied in the light of present-day awareness of and heightened sensibility toward certain problems and certain kinds of conduct.

[20] See esp. Richard A. Falk, "Janus Tormented: The International Law of Internal War," in J. N. Rosenau, ed., *International Aspects of Civil Strife* (Princeton 1964), 185ff.; J. N. Rosenau, "Internal War as an International Event," same, 45ff. And cf. Raymond Aron, *Paix et Guerre entre les nations* (Paris 1962), 712ff.

[21] Rosenau, "Internal War as an International Event," 57.

[22] J. N. Rosenau, "Pre-theories and Theories of Foreign Policy," in R. B. Farrell, ed., *Approaches to Comparative and International Politics* (Evanston 1966), 27ff., at 63-64. Professor Rosenau's perceptive and far-reaching inquiry, same at 53-71, albeit brief and exploratory, is the best statement yet of the phenomenon discussed in this

multitude of actions and events, some of which possess an obvious international (that is to say, in the traditional sense, intergovernmental) component or aspect (for instance, economic assistance, cultural exchange programs, state propaganda activities) while others do not (for example, activities of tourists, journalists, businessmen, etc. or unofficial conduct of governmental officials).[23] Moreover, events which on the surface have no transnational (official or unofficial) side, such as the economic or political developments within a country, often have an international significance, i.e. have repercussions on the interests of other states; they are therefore of concern to such other states, which then may decide to act (or not to act) to protect or promote their interests.

To assess the importance and consequences of this situation, it is first necessary to identify the precise element in it which is new. The fact that there is a close relationship between the domestic and foreign affairs of all nations and that all nations, but particularly the weaker ones,[24] are subject to external influences, is in no way novel.[25] The three major parties in the newly created Kingdom of Greece, in the second quarter of the nineteenth century, were known respectively as the "French," the "British," and the "Russian" party.[26] This did

---

section. Another valuable study is Andrew M. Scott's *The Revolution in Statecraft— Informal Penetration* (New York 1965), where it is also stressed at an early point that "informal access is . . . characteristic of a wide range of conflict techniques, many of which do not involve arms and violence." (9) How far this is exclusively a modern phenomenon is discussed later in this section.

[23] Same, 17, distinguishes five main types of "informal access": " (1) informal government access; (2) quasi-governmental access; (3) non-governmental access; (4) informal access by an international organization; (5) informal access by a nation through the medium of an international organization." For some qualifications to Professor Scott's approach, see text to n. 31.

[24] Professor Rosenau, "Pre-theories," 68-69, suggests that a common feature of most penetration situations is "a shortage of capabilities on the part of the penetrated society and . . . an effort to compensate for, or take advantage of, this shortage underlies the participation of nonmembers in [the penetrated society's] politics." If "capability" is defined broadly enough, however, this explanation would come down to the fact that every nation has something that another nation wants (whether capital, technology, or natural resources). In other words, interpenetration is a function of interdependence.

[25] It may even be argued, indeed, that one of the classical tests used to determine which country was a "Great Power" was the extent of its accessibility to foreign, formal, and informal pressures and influence. On the concept of "Great Power" at the close of the nineteenth century, see the discussion in L. Oppenheim, *International Law*, I, *Peace* (1st edn., London 1905), 161-164; and J. Westlake, *Chapters on the Principles of International Law* (Cambridge 1894), 92-101.

[26] The Greek political situation of that time is described at length in, among others, G. Finlay, *History of Greece*, VII (Oxford 1877), 107-261; E. Driault and M. Lheritier, *Histoire diplomatique de la Grèce*, II (Paris 1925), 103-417. For a discussion of broader scope, see, L. S. Stavrianos, *The Balkans Since 1453* (New York 1958), 225-29. And see now, J. A. Petropulos, *Politics and Statecraft in the Kingdom of Greece 1833-1843* (Princeton 1968), by far the best and most exhaustive related study,

not show peculiar sincerity or classical clarity of thought—such parties were commonplace in the Balkans of that time; it was merely a manifestation of awareness of the importance, for a small, dependent, and weak nation, of the international factors, of the struggle for domination between foreign powers. If, under similar conditions, such a struggle did not take place, with respect to a state or a group of states, it was usually because a single power exercised undisputed hegemony over that particular state or region, or because the state in question had effectively isolated itself from the outside.[27]

The fact is not new, then.[28] What is new is the manner, the degree of intensity, and the extent of interpenetration. Its present-day causes can be found in a number of developments, the most important of which are probably the spread of communication facilities, the presence of the ideological conflict known as the cold war, and the increasing elimination of the distinction between private and public acts and domains of activity. The nineteenth-century conflicts between European powers involved clearly, and to a large extent avowedly, nothing more than differences in national interests, clashes in the pursuit of national power. The fundamental political and social structures of the powers themselves and of the states which were the objects of their "attentions" were most of the time not in issue.[29] Moreover, the economic liberalism which was increasingly dominant in Europe and North America established a clear and, within its framework, factual distinction between the public and private domains. It was possible, therefore, unequivocally to distinguish between the legal effects of public and private actions. The present situation is radically different. The ideological character of the conflict between the Soviet and the Western blocs is directly relevant to the new states, indeed doubly so, since the governments of the latter are presently engaged in both a national and a social revolution. They are building up nations, while at the same time (and, in part, in order to do it) they are engaged in building (or, in some cases, in resisting) a new social order.

---

with valuable insights into the relationship between domestic conditions and foreign influences.

27 The policy of the "Open Door" in nineteenth-century Asia should be seen, of course, as an attempt to eliminate that last category of states.

28 This lack of novelty is not merely a matter of historical interest; it is a factor that has to be taken into account in reaching conclusions on some legal aspects of the phenomenon under study.

29 Although the great powers did represent a limited spectrum of differences in domestic political orientation, still the international society of the time was basically homogeneous (politically and otherwise) rather than heterogeneous (as the present one is). For an analysis of the international society in terms of homogeneity and heterogeneity of systems, see Raymond Aron, *Paix et Guerre*, 103ff. and passim (citing in this connection, P. Papaligouras, *Théorie de la société internationale* [Genève 1941]).

Thus, both aspects of the cold war are relevant to their concerns: the conflict of power between the two blocs affects their preoccupation with national independence, while the ideological conflict between Communism and the "modified-free-enterprise-democratic-societies" of the West is directly relevant to their social revolution.

Under such conditions, political and social change within any of the new states is of direct concern, not only to the great powers of today, but also to each state's own neighbors whose politics may be directly affected. There is a short step from being concerned to doing something about it. "Informal penetration" has thus become today one of the primary instruments of foreign policy, utilized not only by the principal cold war competitors, but even by smaller states in their relations among themselves and with the great powers.[30] Harboring political refugees, training subversive groups, financing or supporting "friendly" political parties, or using paid lobbyists to influence legislative action are all forms of the same process.

While such deliberate pursuit of governmental policies is today the most important aspect of the process of interpenetration, the latter's manifestations are not limited to governmental action, official or unofficial.[31] Contacts between private persons, acting as individuals or as agents of private agencies (newspapers, firms, universities), with no significant relationship to or dependence on governmental action, play an important role, which is difficult to describe or assess. In a homogeneous international society, such contacts, to the extent that they do not involve covert governmental action, would be of negligible political importance. It is in the context of today's heterogeneous international society that they acquire their special significance. Contacts of this sort make it possible for one society, culture, or political regime to influence another, outside and regardless of governmental policies, formalities, and restraints.

[30] Scott, *Revolution in Statecraft,* gives the most extensive discussion of this aspect of interpenetration. In the more specific context of internal violence, see the essays in J. N. Rosenau, ed., *Aspects of Civil Strife,* and K. W. Deutsch, "External Involvement in Internal War," in H. Eckstein, ed., *Internal War* (Glencoe, Ill. 1964), 100ff.

[31] Scott, *Revolution in Statecraft,* although not unaware of the broader context, (cf. same, 17-19, 140), accepts such a limitation in the bulk of his study; this is particularly clear in his description of the states involved in terms of "penetrating" and "target" states. This view is perhaps justified with respect to the study of interpenetration in the context of the cold war; it becomes unduly restrictive when the totality of international relations is considered. Professor Rosenau, in his "Pre-theories," asserts at one point that "the existence of a penetrated system is determined by the presence of nonmembers who participate directly in a society's politics and not by their affiliations and responsibilities" (same, 68), but also discusses, in the main, the problems of official, governmental, penetration. Again, it is not merely a matter of emphasis or personal interest; I suspect that the adoption of a broad definition of the phenomenon at hand leads to partly different conclusions.

The importance of this form of interpenetration may become clearer if one or two typical situations are considered. It is, I suppose, indisputable that the United States Government exercises a high degree of influence within the international financial agencies, e.g. the World Bank, through its voting power and otherwise. This influence tends to be exaggerated sometimes, partly, I submit, because it is confused with another kind of influence, that of the top-level officials and advisers who, whether American or not, often represent the kind of thinking which is usually associated with the American (or, more broadly, Western European) "financial community." There is an important difference, of course, between policies which serve the national interests of a single country, or a group of countries, and policies which merely express the manner of thinking and attitudes prevalent in the country (or countries) in question, even though the two may on occasion coincide. When American (or Western) influence in the international financial agencies is decried, or merely stressed, by the representatives of developing countries, it is often the latter kind of influence that is involved, although the first kind is being referred to.[32] This confusion may obscure the actual situation and render more difficult the identification of the exact nature of the grievances and their possible satisfaction.

Again, although expatriate technical advisers, serving governments of developing countries in an individual capacity or as staff members of international agencies, have shown on the whole remarkable ability to adapt, not only their life but also their advice, to local conditions, the fact remains that their approach and ways of thinking are determined, at least in part, by their membership in their society, nation, and culture and by their having received their professional training within that environment. The advice they offer will therefore differ on occasion from that which would have been given by somebody else with a different background. Whose advice (and under what conditions) is appropriate for the particular country is a distinct question, the answer to which will depend on a variety of additional factors. What is important to note here is that the experts' advice may sometimes serve to advance the general interests of their country or culture, even though they may be acting in total good faith and not as agents of a foreign government. Whether this happens or not in fact, it is probable that it will be alleged to happen, again perhaps fully in good faith by those resenting such "foreign" influence.

The process of informal—and sometimes even unconscious—interpenetration is of particular importance to the new nations because in

---

[32] Confusing the two kinds of influence, or even not recognizing the distinction, may be, of course, a matter of policy, or even ideology, as in the case of the states of the Soviet bloc, as well as of some developing countries.

their present condition they are peculiarly susceptible to it. Although they too are subject to this process, the developed countries are less affected by it.[33] They offer fewer opportunities for the exercise of informal influence and they are generally able to provide native alternatives to the methods proposed from the outside; they possess, moreover, institutions and agencies (mostly private rather than official) which channel foreign influence and deprive it in part of its "foreignness." The many private associations or organizations operative in Western societies form, in at least some cases, transnational pressure groups which operate, through local affiliates, in more than one state.[34] They are agencies for spreading foreign influences, in one sense, but by adapting they also "nationalize" these influences.

The new and developing countries, in contrast, are wide open to influence. The difference between developed and less developed countries in this respect is not only one of degree, that is, that the latter are more often penetrated or vulnerable to penetration; it is also one of quality: the very features of the phenomenon differ. In Professor Scott's terms, the less developed countries are both technically and substantively accessible to foreign influence.[35] Their dependence on foreign or international assistance, technical and financial, public or private, with respect to a wide spectrum of activities (industry, finance, public and private administration, even foreign relations), opens up channels for the exercise of influence—again, not necessarily solely on the part of foreign governments or governmental officials.[36] The radical character of the process of social, cultural, and political change that is occurring within their societies provides fertile ground for such influence; the paucity of native alternatives, due to lack of experience, of training, or of a tradition in the fields involved, often limits their action to the choice between foreign alternatives. These countries, moreover, have not yet developed the institutions for channeling, restraining, and "nationalizing" foreign influences. The private

[33] The extent to which the states involved are "open" or "closed" societies is, of course, a relevant variable. See, Rosenau, "Pre-theories," 47ff.; and cf. R. B. Farrell, "Foreign Politics of Open and Closed Political Societies," in R. B. Farrell, ed., *Approaches to Comparative and International Politics* (Evanston 1966), 167ff.

[34] See, on this as yet largely unexplored aspect of the sociology of international law, J. Meynaud, *Les groupes de pression internationaux* (Lausanne 1961). And cf. G. Schwarzenberger, *Power Politics* (3d edn., New York 1964), 121-39.

[35] "A target that is vulnerable to a given form of informal penetration will be said to be 'accessible' . . . ." Scott, *Revolution in Statecraft*, 19. "Technical accessibility relates to the actual mechanics of penetration. . . . Substantive accessibility, on the other hand, involves the emotional and ideological response of the target population to the efforts at penetration." Same, 21. As already pointed out, there is no need to adopt here the "instrumental" bias implied in the author's choice of terms ("target," "efforts at . . .").

[36] To use Professor Rosenau's terms, developing countries are accessible, in varying degrees, to multi-issue penetration; see his "Pre-theories," 70-71, and, for an elucidation of the useful concept of "issue-areas," same, 71-88.

groups and associations active in the Western developed countries are either nonexistent in the new states or remain wholly foreign to the local society, despite the occasional presence of local affiliates. They are thus resented as representing foreign influences; more important, perhaps, they lose in the eyes of local inhabitants their private character, and they are treated as quasi-governmental agencies or institutions.[37]

Increasing awareness of interpenetration and of its extent is bound to have radical repercussions on the principles and rules of public international law and on the very conception of its operation. Traditional international law theory is based on the assumption that the national and international dimensions of state activity are separate and distinct.[38] The international legal order is thus conceived as a Leibnitzian world of monads, of state-units whose relations with one another are wholly external. The only state officials that can have a role in this scheme are the diplomat and the soldier. The informal interpenetration between states is typically treated as an exception, a departure (justified or not) from the "accepted norms" of international law; at best, it is sometimes perceived in recent years as an indication of the inevitability of "world government." Even where the reality and the nonexceptional character of interpenetration is acknowledged as a factual datum, it is still treated as a departure from, if not precisely a breach of, the legal norms in effect.[39] Awareness of historical continuity in this respect, of the presence of such interpenetration in the past, may help to qualify these conclusions.

Not only the name of the Balkan political parties, but the whole diplomatic history of Southern Europe in the nineteenth century shows clearly that no serious question as to foreign intervention was raised at the time, at least on the international level, unless the interference involved actual military action or threat of action (even those, of course, were by no means uncommon). Instead of asserting therefore that cases of interpenetration represented tolerated departures from an accepted formal norm of state conduct, it may be nearer the truth to say that the formal norm itself did not represent (was not accepted as) an actual legal rule, a rule generally felt as binding. The high incidence of "exceptions to the rule," in other words, should raise questions as

---

[37] For a first exploration of the attitudes and problems of the new states in this connection, see P. Gerbet, "Les nouveaux Etats et les organisations internationales," in J. B. Duroselle and J. Meyriat, *Les nouveaux états dans les relations internationales* (Paris 1962), 447ff., at 478-80.

[38] The chief factual bases for this assumption were the homogeneity of the legal order and the separation of the public and private domains of activity, on the basis of the dominant liberal-capitalist conceptions.

[39] Cf., e.g. Rosenau, "Pre-theories," 64-65; Rosenau, "Internal War as an International Event," 57.

to the effectiveness or validity of the rule itself, at least in its usual broad formulation.

It is then more exact to say that the process of interpenetration, in the past as now, is not strictly speaking a departure from the accepted legal norms, rather it lies outside the conceptual framework of traditional international law theory. It is not possible any more, however, to thus consistently ignore part of the reality of international life: the increase in the incidence and intensity of interpenetration is such that it is becoming broadly accepted that the dichotomy between external and internal affairs is no longer valid.[40] Moreover, states and their citizens have become today both more aware and more sensitive to lack of "independence"; real or imagined pressures, slights, and interventions are resented far more (and, to a degree, far more effectively) than before.[41] That this resentment is usually expressed in the traditional terms of public international law ("sovereignty," "equality," "independence") serves to diminish its impact and to distort its meaning, for contemporary reality cannot be properly understood in these traditional terms, at least not without radically revising their contents. It is furthermore rather shortsighted to treat interpenetration as an exclusively negative or undesirable phenomenon.[42] At this stage, it is a factual datum, not a legal concept. Still, different kinds, degrees and methods of interpenetration should not be treated in the same manner. Some methods, for example those involving use of force, must be regarded as clearly undesirable and thereby "illegal." Others, for instance cultural contacts, may be deemed clearly desirable. As to still others, e.g. economic penetration, much more study, elaboration, and clarification are needed before it is determined whether and under what conditions they are desirable or undesirable. There are few if any clearly established rules in this area and it is dangerous to rely on the half-truths incorporated in the formal expressions of conditions prevailing in past centuries. Here more than anywhere else perhaps, international reality is searching for its law.

International Personality and Attitude

An important facet of the external posture of new states today is that they place great value on their international personality and on the

---

[40] Pierre Hassner, "Le système international," 26, rightly points out that the internal-external distinction has a cultural, rather than merely political or legal, basis, and that the elimination of the external dimension is in part a consequence of the heterogeneity of the present international system; cf. n. 38.

[41] The increased sensitivity to pressures or intervention is a manifestation of the changed general attitude of new and developing countries to international affairs, to which the next section is devoted.

[42] That the fact of interpenetration, like that of interdependence, is often used to cover and justify intervention cannot be denied but this does not suffice to alter reality.

manner and extent of their participation in international life. Such
participation sometimes started before independence: revolutionary
parties and "governments" in still dependent territories often developed "foreign relations" with other states and with international organizations, appointing "official" representatives, for instance, in major
capitals and at the headquarters of international organizations and
taking part at conferences. Upon independence, with precious few
exceptions so far,[43] all new states have sought immediate entry into
the United Nations and most other international agencies and organizations. They all have established in a very short time ministries of foreign affairs and diplomatic services, with delegations at the
United Nations and networks of embassies.[44] Moreover, they have
generally perceived these institutions and agencies not as passive features of international personality but as instrumentalities for active
participation in international life.

It would be misleading, however, to consider active participation in
international affairs as being in itself a novel feature. In the past, as
well, weaker states have been intensely aware of the primary importance for them of the international dimension. Most Latin American and Balkan states at the turn of the century were deeply involved in international life; the few states that stayed outside it were,
even at that time, exceptional, although perhaps not as rare as today.
It is not then in the fact, or even extent, of participation that significant differences may be found between contemporary and earlier
new states; these lie rather in their basic attitudes toward the international society and perhaps in their actual role in it.

Around the turn of the century, even those states which, aware of
possibilities of gain through participation in international life, were
most active internationally, generally chose not to challenge the positions and attitudes of the great powers. Their leaders tried instead
to further the national interests of their states through an attitude
of compliance and, to call things by their name, subservience. This
was, for instance, the attitude adopted by Greece during most of the

[43] Western Samoa (pop. 130,000) decided, upon independence, not to seek membership in the United Nations, reportedly for economic reasons; see F.T.P. Plimp-
ton, "The U.N. Needs Family Planning," *New York Times Magazine*, September
18, 1966, 54ff., at 97. Control of its foreign affairs was delegated by treaty to
New Zealand.

[44] For some indications on the formal diplomatic activities and institutions of
new states, see, J.-L. Quermonne, "Les engagements internationaux des nouveaux
états," in J.-B. Duroselle and J. Meyriat, eds., *Les nouveaux états dans les relations internationales* (Paris 1962), 323ff., at 329-34; I. W. Zartman, *International
Relations in the New Africa* (Englewood Cliffs, N. J. 1966), 69-73; A. A. Fatouros,
"International Law and the Third World," 50 *Virginia Law Review*, 783ff. at 792-
93 (1964). The weakness of the existing diplomatic apparatus is rightly stressed
by L. Binder, "The New States in International Affairs," in R. A. Goldwin, ed.,
Beyond the Cold War (Chicago 1965), 195ff. at 207-08.

second half of the nineteenth century and the beginning of the twentieth, which became known, toward the end of that period, under the term "*attitude correcte.*"[45] It expressed itself in the exercise of restraint both in military action and in diplomatic claims and utterances, with the avowed aim of avoiding embarrassing the friendly great powers and thus deserve, at some later time, the reward of additional territory or other support of national objectives. In view of current feelings toward such "Uncle-Tom" attitudes, it should be stressed that this attitude was not necessarily typical of incompetent or cowardly politicians; it was also the position of wise and responsible statesmen wishing to promote effectively the national objectives of their states. It was their judgment that the best way in which these objectives could be promoted was through meritorious service to the great powers, rather than through opposition, vituperation, or creation of difficulties.

In his discussion of the political inequality of states and the rule of the great powers in the late nineteenth century, Westlake cites a characteristic example of the way in which the system worked. His argument is worth quoting *in extenso* for it is also indicative of the fact that the attitude described was not necessarily always detrimental to the interests of the smaller states. He starts by pointing out that "while [the Congress of] Berlin in 1878 reproduced on a smaller scale Vienna in 1814 and 1815, it was able to do so with less friction because the controlling authority of the great powers in Congress was no longer novel, but had sunk so far into European habits as to carry moral as well as material weight." He then goes on to illustrate:

> . . . Servia and Roumania had been semi-sovereign, with the power of entering into limited foreign relations: their independence was recognized. Montenegro had already been recognized as independent by all the great powers except England and Turkey: those powers also recognized its independence. The boundaries of all three were modified, Servia and Montenegro being enlarged and Roumania compelled to submit to an exchange of territory, and in all three it was provided that religion should be free and should be no cause of incapacity. Greece was an independent state of half a century's standing: an enlargement of her territory at the expense of Turkey was recommended to the latter by the other six great powers. Yet neither Roumania Servia Montenegro nor Greece

[45] The term appears to have been first used in a Greek note of 1905 to describe the Greek position concerning the Macedonian question and the related activities of the powers; see, E. Driault and M. Lheritier, *Histoire diplomatique de la Grèce*, v (Paris 1926), 537 n.1. It was repeated in 1909 in another official communication to describe the attitude of Greece with respect to the Cretan claims for union with Greece, thus becoming symbolic of the timid attitude of the successive Greek cabinets of the period.

was a party to the treaty of Berlin, nor was Greece a party to the protocol of the congress recommending the enlargement of her territory, nor was she a party to the convention of 24th May 1881 by which the seven great powers, Turkey being this time a party, fixed the limits of the enlargement which she was to receive. No doubt all these arrangements were subsequently accepted by the states concerned, and what was treated as an acceptance of her new limits had been obtained from Greece before the convention of 24th May 1881 was signed, but was not recited in the convention. Still, when no such acceptances were thought to be even formally necessary to a declaration of the will of Europe on the several matters, we can appreciate what political inequality is compatible in the European system with legal equality.[46]

The mere description of the earlier situation makes evident the gap that divides it from present conditions. The new states, perhaps not all of them, but certainly the most representative ones and those that set the pace and style for the others, tend to be self-assertive to a fault, rather than subservient. Today's "correct attitude" seems to be that of insistence on equality and legal principle and of verbal aggression. And it is characteristic of the degree of acceptance of this attitude that the great powers themselves despite their resentment of such attacks, complain most often not so much that they are being attacked but that the states involved are not attacking their opponents with equal vigor. This phenomenon represents a deliberate choice of temper in the conduct of foreign relations and is therefore important enough to justify further inquiry into its features and causes.

One facet of the new states' attitude is their insistence on state sovereignty as a basic principle of the international legal order and on the principle of complete equality of states which logically follows. Now both these principles are hardly newcomers in international affairs; they are both well-established in traditional international law and no state (at least no major power) has ever seriously suggested abandoning them or substantially reducing their importance (apparent exceptions generally involve either rhetorical arguments *in abstracto* or attempts to take advantage of existing factual situations to promote the interests of particular states). One of their chief functions, moreover, has always been to provide a shield for those who lack the actual (military or economic) power to defend themselves. The precariousness of political independence in many new states, coupled with the low degree (or even lack) of economic independence, provides then a realistic justification for their af-

---

46 J. Westlake, *Principles of International Law*, 99, 100. For a detailed discussion of this case and the whole problem, see, K. Wolfke, *Great and Small Powers in International Law from 1814 to 1920* (Wroclaw 1964), 64-75 and passim.

firmation and defence of these principles. The new element in the present situation appears to be their actual posture, their insistence on taking these principles seriously—more precisely, a tendency to accept them as normative statements concerning the substance as well as the form of international relations, thus treating them neither as merely formal legal statements (as "law-in-the-books") nor as descriptions of already existing factual conditions, but rather as objectives for the immediate future. This attitude is largely shaped by the recent historical experience of the states involved. In adopting it the new states are continuing on the international arena the struggle which they have already waged against their erstwhile colonial masters. Their pursuit of "total independence" is a direct offshoot of their desire for and acquisition of political independence. The latter is for them meaningful only as a first step toward the elimination of economic, social, even perhaps cultural, dependence on other states or cultures.[47]

While such stress on state sovereignty is rightly to be considered a manifestation of nationalism, an important qualification is necessary in the case of the new states: their brand of nationalism differs in significant ways from the nineteenth-century European nationalism to which the term usually refers. Whereas in nineteenth-century Europe, nationalism as the expression of a feeling of national unity came first and the desire, struggle for, and attainment of political independence followed, in the new states of Africa and Asia, nationalism as an operative force was born during and through the struggle against the colonial power.[48] It thus has retained the substantial social and economic features that colored the anticolonialist resentment at the origin of the struggle.

[47] See, P. González Casanova, "Internal and External Politics of Developing Countries," in R. B. Farrell, ed., *Approaches to Comparative and International Politics* (Evanston 1966), 131ff; Zartman, *The New Africa*, 58-59. It is chiefly in this context that it is valid to affirm that the new states are "revolutionary" in their attitudes and objectives; their struggle for total independence possesses revolutionary characteristics while at the same time their internal situation has been described, in some cases correctly, as involving a continuing revolution. It is, however, conducive to confusion rather than clarity to use the same term, without qualification, to describe the members of the Soviet group of states (with the possible exception of mainland China).

[48] From the constantly growing literature on the subject, see, J. S. Coleman, "Nationalism in Tropical Africa," in J. H. Kautsky, ed., *Political Change in Underdeveloped Countries* (New York 1962), 167ff.; J. H. Kautsky, "An Essay in the Politics of Development," same, 1ff., at 30-56; R. Emerson, *From Empire to Nation* (Cambridge, Mass. 1960); J. Y. Calvez, "Racines sociales et économiques des nationalismes du tiers monde," *Revue Française de Science Politique*, 15 (1965), 446ff. For a forceful description of the process of forging national feeling through anticolonialist struggle, see, Frantz Fanon, *Les damnés de la terre* (Paris 1961), and *L'an V de la révolution algérienne* (Paris 1959), 21-112.

The historical background also affects in another way the attitude of the new states: the anticolonialist past of their leaders largely determines the manner in which they present their states' case to foreign powers or before international assemblies.[49] The colonial situation has bred deep-rooted attitudes of hostility and aggressiveness which were expressed but not exhausted in the anticolonialist struggle (violent or not) that preceded independence. Even in mere terms of style, anticolonialist oratory is emotional, impassioned, and aggressive. These characteristics continue to dominate, in varying degrees, the external attitudes and manners of the officials of new states.

Another important feature should be noted, not because it is new but precisely because it represents a somewhat incongruous old element within an otherwise substantially novel attitude and manner. As may already have become evident, the new states have in the main chosen to move and pursue their objectives inside the framework of traditional international law. Whatever suggestions for radical structural legal change have been offered recently have come from scholars in the Western developed countries and, to some extent, from Latin America. The result is at first blush paradoxical, since today's "revolutionary" states thus appear highly conservative as far as the structure and principles of the existing international legal order are concerned.[50] It may be argued that the reason for this is that the present international legal order is in fact adequate and that within its confines the interests of all members of the world community may be reasonably pursued. There is some truth to this; the existing order does possess certain elements of flexibility and adaptability which allow it to reconcile diverse interests and, to a degree, resolve conflicts between its members. The adequacy of the legal order is not, however, the only way in which the conduct of the new states may be explained. It is surely relevant that the officials of these countries, and especially their jurists, have received their legal education in Western countries and have acquired the common ambivalent attitude of most private-law oriented lawyers toward international law: cynicism, downgrading of its role, and lack of precise knowledge, on the one

---

[49] For a brief attempt at a systematic inquiry into this question, see, R. A. Lystad, "Cultural and Psychological Factors," in V. McKay, ed., *African Diplomacy* (New York 1966), 91ff., esp. at 107-18. For some of the by now "classical" descriptions of the colonial psychological situation, see, O. Mannoni, *Psychologie de la colonisation* (Paris 1950), trans. P. Powesland, *Prospero and Caliban—The Psychology of Colonization* (New York 1964); A. Memmi, *Portrait du colonisé précédé du Portrait du colonisateur* (Paris 1957); and the two books by Frantz Fanon cited in n. 48.

[50] A similar paradox obtains in the case of the Soviet conceptions of international law. The reasons for the Soviet attitude, however, are not necessarily the same as those for the attitude of the new states. The dissimilarities in the situations of the two groups are important enough so that what may be wise policy for the one may not be for the other.

hand, combined with excessively idealistic notions and expectations founded on improperly drawn analogies from advanced municipal law systems, on the other. The scarcity of educated officials, which does not allow adequate concern for long-range policies and plans, and the lack of practical experience in diplomatic debate and negotiation on their part serve to strengthen the restrictive effects of traditional legal education.

It is not my contention that the diplomats of the new states should declare wholesale rejection of classical international law and should refuse to operate within its framework. Such action, indeed, would be precisely the kind of excessive and misguided gesture that is often offered as the only alternative to rigid acceptance of the status quo. It is rather a matter of being able to recognize and take advantage of existing opportunities for social and political change through legal methods and instruments—in the present context, for change of particular international institutions or principles or of other facets of the international legal order. The rigid wholesale adoption of a legalistic traditional viewpoint on international law seriously restricts the potentialities of the new states. These states admittedly have a very limited choice between alternatives in international political, economic, or legal relations; but they limit themselves further by failing to perceive and identify some of the alternatives which are in fact available.[51] This accounts in part for the fact that the actual impact of the actions and policies of the new states on the international legal order is far less radical and far-reaching than their rhetoric at the United Nations may lead one to expect. (Their lack of power, in its more traditional formulation, is, of course, another important reason for this.)

As an illustration, the problem of fusion of national and international affairs and of interpenetration between nations may be considered. The new states, in their present posture, are attempting to deal with this question by invoking the traditional notions of sovereignty and equality of states, notions based on the denial of the fact (or necessity) of interpenetration. The differentiations that may still be made (chiefly on the basis of actions or attitudes of the local government, e.g., invitation of foreign experts, requests for assistance, etc.) are rather elementary and quite inadequate. If a properly realistic and process-oriented view of international law were adopted, it might be possible to move toward a more effective legal regulation of foreign penetration and influence, based perhaps on such tests as degree, manner, and substantive content. To put it briefly, a condition

---

[51] The point is well made by Richard A. Falk, "The New States," 82, in the context of responses to the *South West Africa* decision of the International Court of Justice. And cf. same, 24.

for properly regulating certain situations is in most instances the recognition of their reality—and, perhaps, of the impossibility (or even
undesirability) of wholly avoiding them. A formalistic refusal to recognize realities is rarely an effective instrument in the pursuit of national or international objectives.

Nevertheless, although within a traditional framework, the new
states do express certain novel attitudes, the historical and political
causation of which is worthy of further inquiry. Although this cannot
be properly done here, certain general indications may be given which
will help in placing the attitudes in question in the context of the
present-day international environment.

There may be, no doubt, an element of naivete, of sheer lack of sophistication, at their origin. The responsible officials in the new states
may not be experienced or well-informed enough to realize that the
legal principles "in-the-books" were never intended to apply in practice, at least not to all states at all times. They may believe that such
principles as national sovereignty and legal equality afford them substantive elements of power. A related but distinct explanation may be
that the leaders of the new states are merely exuberantly enjoying
their newly acquired power by imitating the postures and actions of
former colonial officials and that they actually identify international
prestige and power with the pomp and circumstances of diplomatic
intercourse. In short, they act the way they do because they are not
aware of (or are not interested in) the underlying realities of international life. These explanations have some plausibility; they may
even be valid in some cases, as the innumerable stories of incompe-
tence and vanity that Western (and Soviet) diplomats and international lawyers relish in narrating would indicate. All the same, these
explanations are too easy. The new states' attitude turns out far too
often to serve directly their national interests to allow such an airy
dismissal of its realistic and rational basis. Indeed, those critics of the
new states' actions who insist on the "irresponsibility" of their conduct are really admitting that a rational basis does exist, that the new
states are attempting (properly or improperly) to wrest power away
from the "responsible" major powers and older states.

An important cause of the attitudes in question is the development
of "parliamentary diplomacy" in the United Nations and elsewhere,
which has given to the weaker states an opportunity to express themselves in the international forum and thereby a limited but real
power to influence decisions.[52] More generally, participation in international life, especially in the activities of international organizations,

---

[52] On the concept of "parliamentary diplomacy," see P. Jessup, "Parliamentary
Diplomacy," Hague Academy of International Law, 89 *Recueil des Cours* 185ff.
(1956).

has acquired today an important positive function and offers definite rewards in a variety of ways. Nonparticipation, or exclusion, has become indeed an effective sanction which may be used, directly or indirectly, by international organizations (or the majorities in them) to enforce compliance with the standards and rules they adopt.[53] These are good reasons for placing great emphasis on participation in international life. Moreover, the similarity in the operation of some international organs (e.g., the UN General Assembly) to parliamentary bodies in Western countries invites the same sort of high-pitched oratory that is typical of parliamentary debate in many countries (and not only underdeveloped ones). And the publicity given to the proceedings of such organizations, coupled with the intensity of interpenetration of internal and external affairs in the new states (of which such publicity may in part be considered a manifestation), induces the production of aggressive oratory directed (sometimes exclusively) to the home audience.

Another set of factors is also operative which is more difficult to describe or evaluate. There is today a general, objective as well as subjective, downgrading of power in international relations. On the legal plane this phenomenon has taken the form of the various suggestions, proposals, or attempts to make the use of force in international affairs illegal. It is not necessary to discuss here to what extent war and the use of armed force are today clearly illegal, or "unthinkable." For my purposes it is enough to note that armed force is not easily accepted any more as an instrument of large-scale legal change. No doubt, force is still used occasionally, with or without success, but extensive and formal legal as well as pragmatic limitations are now imposed on its use. This situation contrasts sharply with that of the late nineteenth century, when the use or threat of armed force was almost commonplace especially as against small states. The existence of limitations on the use of force necessarily favors those states which would normally be subjected to threats or actual use of force by other, stronger, states. It favors, therefore, the interests of the new states; it makes it possible for them to act in a far freer and even a more aggressive manner than the weaker states of fifty or sixty years ago.[54] However, it is useful to distinguish at this point between freedom of action and what may be called, for want of a better term, freedom of speech. The new states

[53] For an exploration of the function and importance of the sanction of nonparticipation, see, W. Friedmann, *The Changing Structure of International Law* (New York 1964), 61ff. and passim.

[54] They may even be tempted to abuse this freedom, a possibility suggested by many, but most responsibly explored by Julius Stone, in his *Aggression and World Order* (Berkeley 1958), 4ff., 161-74 and passim; *Quest for Survival* (New York 1961), 41-44. The point raised immediately following in the text is relevant here; moreover, irresponsible behavior is not and has never been an exclusive feature of the conduct of small states.

are free, within fairly broad limits, to speak in opposition or in a disagreeable manner to any particular great power. They are far less free to act, not only in military and other "tangible" matters, but even in such matters as voting in international organizations, since the stronger states possess various other methods of pressure and persuasion, short of the use or threat of armed force. That is to say, inequality in power is still a most important factor in international affairs. And the new states, individually considered, are extremely weak, by any objective test. It is only on few occasions (and with respect to few issues) that they are sufficiently united to be able to compete with other groups of states in terms of actual or potential power.

There is an additional reason for the present downgrading of armed force as a factor in international politics, and its operation is directly attributable to the new states. It can be best described as the dominance of an ideology holding that the traditional objective forms of power are of less value, moral as well as practical, in international affairs than they were held to be in the past and are still largely assumed to be by the Western and the Soviet bloc countries.[55] This ideology corresponds to the experience of many new states, especially those that acquired their independence after the Second World War. In the majority of cases, the military, political, and other objectively determinable preponderance of power was in the hands of the colonial regime; despite this, and for reasons which do not have to be examined here, the colonial territories did achieve their independence. It is, therefore, natural for them to hold that the role of power has been exaggerated. This is so to an even greater degree because this ideology corresponds as well to their present needs and conditions and is therefore convenient as well as reasonable and appealing. It is important to realize, however, that, at least in most cases, it is not power in general that is held to have lost its importance, but the kind of power —based on technology and wealth—that the developed countries possess, while the kinds of power that the new states can dispose of— based on the exact reverse factors of poverty and lack of technology—are considered as ultimately superior and more effective.[56] This last point may not always be clear; indeed, confusion as to the exact meaning of "power" may often exist in the minds of those propound-

[55] For a brief discussion of this attitude in the context of African affairs, see, Zartman, *The New Africa*, 145ff., who associates it with the works of Frantz Fanon (see n. 48). Fanon's emphasis on the positive role of violence in international affairs in, for instance, *Les damnés de la terre* (Paris 1961), 71ff., might seem paradoxical in this context, but it can be reconciled with the trend in question if the latter is understood in the manner suggested here.

[56] The family resemblance of this attitude to the "paper tiger" approach of the mainland Chinese government is obvious. It is not clear, however, how far the former has its origin in the latter; it appears more probable that they are both due to similar historical experience and, at this stage, fairly similar conditions and interests.

ing the ideology under discussion. In view of this fundamental ambiguity, it is not surprising that there is great uncertainty and controversy as to the identity of the values that override power and power politics.

While pretending to describe reality, the ideology of denigration of power is, like all ideologies,[57] essentially normative, rather than descriptive. Its existence and advocacy, on the other hand, strengthens considerably the ability and willingness of the leaders of the new states to exercise their "independent" verbal aggressiveness against the established powers, and thus the role of power in international affairs changes in fact partly as a result of the presence of this ideology.

The Impact of Cultural Diversity

Any discussion of the new elements brought by the new states into international life cannot ignore the cultural problems. There is continuing controversy as to the extent to which the differences between the cultural backgrounds of most new states and that of the Western states are affecting or will affect the content and structure of the future international legal order. The only valid answer is, of course, that nobody really knows at this time: there has been far too little inquiry into cultural differences in the context of their actual or possible effects on law and the legal order.[58] Certain preliminary observations as to the relevance of these differences may still be useful.

To begin with, our puzzlement and unease when confronted with the problem of the possible impact of differing cultural (and legal) traditions on international law are not merely a consequence of our lack of specific data but reflect a more fundamental ambiguity. They are a variant of a basic unresolved conflict in our current approach to development and modernization. Claude Lévi-Strauss' observations with respect to anthropology are valid with respect to law, as well:

> Contemporary anthropology . . . finds itself in a paradoxical situation. For it is out of a deep feeling of respect toward cultures other than our own that the doctrine of cultural relativism was evolved; and it now appears that this doctrine is deemed unacceptable by the very people on whose behalf it was upheld. Meanwhile, those ethnologists who favor unilinear evolutionism find unexpected support from people who desire nothing more than to share in the benefits of industrialization, and prefer to look

[57] For an elucidation of this overworked term, see, J. LaPalombara, "Decline of Ideology: A Dissent and an Interpretation," *American Political Science Review*, 60 (1966), 5ff., esp. 7.

[58] I agree thus with Richard A. Falk's conclusion, "The New States," 40. And see same, 26-43, for a perceptive discussion of the whole problem. Cf. also Lystad, "Psychological Factors," n. 49.

at themselves as temporarily backward rather than permanently different.[59]

We are willing to accept, with some effort, that a specific legal system or family of systems is not inherently or absolutely superior to all others; we recognize now that different legal systems fit different societies. At the same time, we have great difficulty in seeing any meaningful radical alteration of the existing international law system and its concepts that could be made on the basis of these other systems. What few differences and innovations have been suggested in recent years do not really affect the basic structure or the style of the existing system. Our cultural relativism remains pure and abstract; as far as any *praxis* is concerned, we too seem to operate on the unilinear evolution model. And as has already been noted, the spokesmen for the new states, rightly or wrongly, are the first to adopt and express their positions in terms located well within the traditional international legal structure and conceptualization.

An examination of the opinions that have been expressed on this issue supports this view of the matter.[60] With some oversimplification, the several distinct positions that have developed in the past few years may be roughly classed in two categories, the criterion for the distinction being the degree of importance attributed to cultural differences. The practical conclusions that are drawn, however, differ significantly within each category.

On the one hand, there are those who insist on the radical differences between the Western European (including of course, American or, at least, North American) cultural background and that of the new states. They stress the extent to which the former rests on the Christian and Greco-Roman heritage and on the attribution of high value to rationality, especially in legal and political matters. In contrast, the Asian and African states' cultural traditions have different religious and historical foundations, their established world views are different and their legal and political ideas have developed on different lines. On the basis of such argumentation (though with notable var-

[59] Claude Lévi-Strauss, "The Disappearance of Man," *The New York Review of Books*, VII, No. 1 (July 28, 1966), 6-8, at 7. It is essentially to the same conflict that George Balandier refers when discussing the "ambiguity" of modern Africa; see his *Afrique ambiguë* (Paris 1957, 1962) esp. at 279ff.

[60] For a bibliography of the abundant, although uneven and repetitive, literature on this topic, see G. Abi-Saab, ed., *Carnegie Endowment Conference on the Newly Independent States and International Law—Some Reflections and a Selected Bibliography* (Geneva 1963, mimeo.) esp. 31-35. See also, since then, A. A. Fatouros, "International Law and the Third World," 50 *Virginia Law Review*, 783ff., at 787-90 (1964); W. Friedmann, *The Changing Structure of International Law* (New York 1964), 297-324; A. Larson, W. Jenks, and others, *Sovereignty Within the Law* (New York 1965); O. Lissitzyn, *International Law—Today and Tomorrow* (New York 1965), 94ff.; and see Falk, n. 58.

iations in the degree of sophistication), some authors conclude that since the present international legal order is peculiarly Western European in its essence, the new states will have to adjust themselves to it, possibly through great effort, and they cannot be heard to complain of its lack of relevance to their own cultures. Other authors, however, conclude from the same premises that a greater effort should be made by the international community as a whole to adjust the present international law to the diverse cultures of its new members, and they see in the present lack of adjustment a prime danger for the international legal order.

On the other side are those who minimize the importance or relevance of whatever cultural differences there may be. Some argue, on the basis of extensive surveys of several legal systems and cultures, that such differences do not really exist with respect to the subjects which are central to an international legal order. Finally, some others dismiss the relevance of cultural differences to modern problems, pointing instead at attitudes and policies which are dictated by diverse interests, rather than values.

As usual, there seems to be some truth on all sides of the controversy. In the absence of the in-depth studies needed, one's choice is bound to be somewhat arbitrary. It is, however, significant that, possibly with one exception, the final conclusions of the supporters of these diverse positions do not vary too much: they all see existing international law as being here to stay. My own inclination is toward the very last of the views listed; certain further observations seem, however, necessary.

The historical background, to begin with, is only partially relevant; it certainly is not controlling. It cannot be disputed that modern public international law has its origins in the practice and theory of the Western states; although other international legal systems have been shown to have developed in other cultures, as well,[61] there is no indication that they have seriously influenced the prevailing system. Like all historical facts, however, the origin of the present international legal system has more than one possible meaning. It does show, on the one hand, that there is an intimate connection between Western culture and international law. On the other hand, it also points at the past utilization of international law by the Western states as an instrument of conquest and oppression. Again, Lévi-Strauss' remarks on anthropology are relevant (although not perhaps fully applicable) to international law:

[61] See, e.g. S. V. Viswanatha, *International Law in Ancient India* (Bombay 1925); C. J. Chacko, "India's Contribution to the Field of International Law Concepts," Hague Academy of International Law, 93 *Recueil des Cours*, 122ff. (1958); W. Friedmann, *Changing Structure*, 309-13.

Anthropology is not a dispassionate science like astronomy. . . . It is the outcome of an historical process which has made the larger part of mankind subservient to the other, and during which millions of innocent human beings have had their resources plundered, their institutions and beliefs destroyed while they themselves were ruthlessly killed, thrown into bondage, and contaminated by diseases they were unable to resist. Anthropology is daughter to this era of violence: Its capacity to assess more objectively the facts pertaining to the human condition reflects, on the epistemological level, a state of affairs in which one part of mankind treated the other as an object.[62]

The "obvious" conclusions, therefore, that can be drawn by relying on the historical record are more than one: it can be equally well argued either that the Western nations are entitled to and should be trusted with the further development of international law, for the common good of the world community, or that the whole of international law must be discarded because it is tainted with its past acceptance, and indeed legitimization, of colonial conquest.

The historical or antiquarian approach is to be avoided on another plane, as well. In approaching non-Western cultures, excessive attention should not be focused on the historical context to the detriment of awareness of present realities. Whatever the intrinsic importance and historical role of the classical Islamic religious and legal thinking, of Buddhist sacred texts and commentaries, or of pre-colonial Indian state practice, their relationship to the thinking and practice of modern Egyptian, Japanese, or Indian decision-makers corresponds at best to that between late medieval or perhaps Renaissance European thought and modern international law doctrine and practice. To assert that the writings of Grotius and Vitoria are not an unfailing guide to contemporary international law is not to deny their influence and importance. Similarly, any attempt to derive definite conclusions on current international problems from the "classical" theological or philosophical treatises and commentaries of Moslem or Buddhist sages is fraught with danger; not only will it probably lack persuasiveness but it may lead to self-deception.[63] As Wolfgang Friedmann

---

[62] Lévi-Strauss, "Disappearance of Man," 7.

[63] A good illustration of this danger is the recent attempt by an eminent scholar to show that Moslem law upholds the sanctity of contract between a sovereign and his subjects and adopts therefore a rigid *pacta sunt servanda* position with respect to concessions for the exploitation of natural resources. See, S. Habachy, "Property Right and Contract in Muslim Law," 62 *Columbia Law Review*, 450-73 (1962). The same demonstration could easily have been conducted by a Catholic or Protestant legal scholar or theologian as to medieval European canon law and it would have had exactly the same degree of relevance to the problem at hand (viz., the proper processes for allocating revenues from the exploitation of a country's natural resources).

has pointed out,[64] excessive emphasis on cultural and other "funda-mental" diversities, without any focus on current problems and atti-tudes, offers serious potentialities of distortion.

On the other hand, if by culture one refers to the complex aggre-gate of religious, philosophical, and historical traditions, it becomes evident that it is a factor that cannot be left out of consideration. While it is true that national interests rather than cultural back-grounds determine a modern (or modernizing) nation's foreign pol-icies and its attitude within and toward the international legal order, the perception of these interests and the manner of responding to such perception are significantly affected by the country's cultural tradition and by the hierarchy of values which that tradition dictates. The sen-sitivity of many new states to often trivial questions involving colonial-ism and its aftermath constitute specific patterns of behavior which correspond to perceptions of national interest determined by cultural tradition (including recent historical experience). In a more concrete context, the current negative attitude of Latin American states toward the Convention for the Settlement of Investment Disputes between States and Nationals of Other States sponsored by the World Bank is clearly attributable not to any intransigence in their policies regarding private foreign investment (with respect to which their attitude and practice has been far milder and more favorable than that of some other states, perhaps even some signatories of the said Convention) but to a long-established attitude toward the legal problems of the treatment of alien-owned property that by now forms so intimate a part of their political tradition that they cannot easily repudiate it.

THE IMPACT OF THE NEW STATES: THE CHANGED INTERNATIONAL LEGAL ORDER

The special features of the new states, those described above as well as others which cannot be listed or studied exhaustively here, will un-doubtedly affect the complex of structures, rules, and processes that we call the "international legal order." Other factors, as well, related or unrelated to the emergence of the new states, are bound to influ-ence it: the order's horizontal expansion (i.e. increase in the number and diversity of its constituent members), the changes in the scope of its subject-matter (i.e. concern with topics traditionally outside the scope of international law), the existence of nuclear weaponry, the conflict between the "super-powers," and so forth.[65] The final outcome will certainly be a changed legal order.

---

[64] Friedmann, *Changing Structure*, 321-22.

[65] From the abundant but uneven literature on the identity and effects of these factors, see W. Friedmann, *Changing Structure*, passim; R. Aron, *Paix et Guerre entre les nations*; Richard Falk, "The Adequacy of Contemporary Theories of Inter-national Law—Gaps in Legal Thinking," 50 *Virginia Law Review*, 231-65 (1964).

*The Claims for Law Reform: Actual and
Potential Legal Change*

It is by now commonplace to assert that the new states desire to change traditional international law. Their precise attitude, however, and the substance of their claims are in need of considerable elucidation, for distortions and misunderstandings abound.

At this stage, the new states seek to ascertain their interests and possibilities and to formulate their claims for legal change. These claims will be an important factor in the shaping of the future international legal order and should therefore be carefully studied, even though not all of them will ever materialize.[66] The prescriptions that will ultimately evolve are unlikely to coincide fully with them.[67]

The function of a legal order is to protect the existing allocation of resources (or "values") and, at least in advanced legal systems, to provide methods and procedures for orderly (i.e. nonviolent) changes in this allocation. Legal change or legal reform signifies then either an actual or a potential alteration in the prevailing pattern of distribution of resources. An actual alteration occurs when the legal measure involved is itself directed at changing the existing distribution; for instance when, in the national context, the property of certain persons or classes is expropriated, certain debts are remitted, or certain categories of slaves liberated. A potential alteration occurs when the existing legal rules, substantive or procedural, are amended to permit future changes in the distribution of resources; again in the national context, such a change occurs where a certain class is allowed to hold property, a previously disenfranchised group is given some political

[66] The national interests of any state or group of states do not necessarily coincide with the general (i.e. common) interests of the international community as a whole; on the other hand, neither do national interests necessarily and irreconcilably conflict with the general interests; furthermore, the ways in which national interests are conceived affect their relationship to the general interest. Although a fully impartial statement of general interests and objectives is impossible, there are degrees in partiality: therefore, when attempting to identify the general interests of the international community, one should try to remain aware of the influence of one's own national, cultural, or ideological background and avoid identifying, consciously or unconsciously, the special interests of one country or group of countries with those of the international community as a whole.

These caveats do not preclude the possibility that, in certain areas, the interests of the new states may coincide today with the general interests of the international society to a greater extent than those of the developed countries of either ideological bloc. At present, this may be regarded as a hypothesis or as a statement of personal visceral preference; further inquiry into its validity is however both possible and necessary. For a powerful affirmation of validity, see B.V.A. Röling, *International Law in an Expanded World* (Amsterdam 1960), 68ff.; and for some indications of the context of such an inquiry, see, Falk, "The New States," 15ff., 28, 79ff.

[67] On the factors operating in favor of the new states, see Fatouros, "The Third World," 794-97.

power, or slavery as a legal institution is abolished.[68] There are close similarities as well as important differences between these two kinds of legal change. In the short run the former method is more certain, for it works faster. However, it is an essentially static approach and subject to the danger that, if other basic legal rules or factual (social, political, technological, or economic) conditions are not changed, the initial situation may eventually revive. All through history, attempts at law reform have often failed because of inadequate attention to this danger. Legal change through alteration of the rules governing the methods of allocation of resources may in the long run have more far-reaching and more permanent effects; its results are, however, of little immediate benefit to the present generation and are basically uncertain since they may be negated by reversals in policy.[69]

In the context of the present international society, then, the new nations have (or should have) a dual objective. On the one hand, they wish to change certain present factual situations which came about because of past conditions and which are now protected by the existing legal rules. On the other hand, they wish to establish as law certain principles and processes which are presumably in their interest. The two objectives are related but not identical.

To change factual situations protected by law, a number of methods may be used.[70] The most common is that of formal negotiation. A new state may be in a position to induce the state (or states) benefiting from the existing situation to negotiate and, depending on a variety of factors (skill, bargaining position, situation at a particular moment, etc.), may succeed in effecting by common agreement the desired changes to the factual situations involved.[71]

[68] These two "kinds" of legal change represent, of course, but the two extremes of a continuum and are, indeed, rarely found in "pure" form. Attempts at actual law reform usually involve some changes in the framework of rules (potential reform) and vice versa. The distinction is of some usefulness, however, in an analysis of present and future law reform objectives and methods.

[69] A good illustration of the limitations of, as well as the interplay between, these two kinds of legal change is provided by the attempts at land reform, with a view to the protection of small land holders and the checking of the "powerful" (viz. the feudal landlords), in the Byzantium of the tenth century, under the Macedonian dynasty. The tale has been told and documented, in summary and in detail, by Georg Ostrogorski, in his *History of the Byzantine State*, trans. J. Hussey (New Brunswick, N.J. 1957), 241-44, 248-50, 253-57, 271-72; in the chapter on "Agrarian Conditions in the Byzantine Empire in the Middle Ages," in *Cambridge Economic History of Europe*, 1 (Cambridge 1941), 194ff., at 204-10; and in his article, "The Peasant's Pre-Emption Right—An Abortive Reform of the Macedonian Emperors," *Journal of Roman Studies*, 37 (1947), 117-26.

[70] Distinguishing between methods for the purpose of description and clarification does not imply, of course, that clear and well-marked borderlines separate each method or technique from the others, or that concurrent utilization of two or more methods is not possible.

[71] For two recent discussions of the relevant factors, see F. C. Iklé, *When Nations*

Another method is unilateral action. If the factual situation at issue exists within the new state and the latter has the physical power to change it, it may proceed to do so. The use of such measures in any specific case depends, of course, on several factors: the general attitude of the new state, the relative importance of the issue to either state concerned, the extent to which the situation can be changed by unilateral action, the probabilities of significant retaliatory action, etc. Often, unilateral action is but one of several reciprocal moves in a complex interplay of action and counteraction, which may finally reach results quite similar to those of negotiation.

These two methods involve to a certain extent the use of legal instruments and argumentation together with other kinds of arguments and instruments (political, moral, etc.). Although they may succeed in changing the particular situation, however, they do not generally establish clear legal principles by which future action of other states may be guided. Their function as precedents, though not nonexistent, is limited. Other methods, however, utilize primarily means and instruments which are specifically or predominantly legal.

A first such method consists in raising, *ex post facto*, questions as to the legal validity of the original transactions, which have endowed with legal sanction the factual situation involved. The new state argues, in this case, that the situation in question was never legally sanctioned, because it was based from the start on an illegal transaction or act. Two recent cases illustrate the uses of this method. The first instance is limited in its scope: the Prime Minister of Tanganyika stated in 1961 that his country would not consider itself bound by agreements concluded before its independence between Great Britain and Belgium, whereby the former granted to the latter a lease in perpetuity over certain sites in the ports of Kigoma and Dar es Salaam.[72] He argued that Britain as an administering authority under the mandate system had no power to grant rights in perpetuity over the territory involved. Such rights were therefore deemed "invalid," even though the Prime Minister also stated at the time that he did not necessarily consider everything done hitherto under the agreement in question as "unlawful." The second example is more far-reaching, indeed revolutionary in its implications: in defending its occupation of Goa, Damao, and Diu, the Indian Government argued that the initial colonial conquest of the cities and regions by the Portuguese

---

Negotiate (New York 1964) ; A. Lall, *Modern International Negotiation—Principles and Practice* (New York 1966) .

[72] See, Statement by the Prime Minister of Tanganyika before the Tanganyika National Assembly, November 30, 1961, in *International and Comparative Law Quarterly*, 11 (1962) , 1210ff., and in International Law Association, Committee on State Succession, *The Effect of Independence on Treaties* (London 1965) , at 370-73.

was in itself illegal and of no validity and that therefore Portugal never had sovereignty over these territories.[73]

Another method is to attribute to a certain fact or situation or to a certain legal transaction the power to affect radically all or some preexisting situations. Traditional international law recognizes essentially a single such case: under the accepted principles of the law of state succession, the acquisition of international personality by a state does affect the continuing legal effect of certain factual situations or legal relationships, without reflecting on their initial validity. Thus, the invalidation on the coming of independence of a treaty of alliance that originally covered a colonial territory does not imply that the treaty was invalid at the time of its original conclusion. On the same line of reasoning, it may be claimed that not only independence but the occurrence of other events, as well, may make possible the reexamination and possible invalidation of preexisting legal situations. This is, of course, but a broader phrasing of the doctrine of *rebus sic stantibus*. At a time of rapid and multifaceted change, when neither the extent nor the nature of future developments can be foreseen with any clarity, such a broad legal principle is necessary. Once it has been stated, it becomes necessary to inquire in depth on the areas and methods of its application. If abused or overextended, such a principle would destroy the necessary fabric of legal certainty. This possibility, however, is not in itself sufficient to preclude any application or development of the principle.

The methods described up to now relate to what was called an actual alteration of the law, a change of the factual situations and relationships protected by law, rather than of the law itself. A potential alteration involves that latter kind of change, a change either of legal rules, or of the structures of law-making and law-applying, the channels and institutions whereby legal rules are created or are given effect. The problems of structural legal change and of law-making are discussed briefly in the next section. At this point, it remains to stress the difficulties of such potential alteration, even at its simplest.

The case where a specific well-defined legal rule is not in the interest of a group of states, which therefore seek to have it changed, is exceptional, if not purely imaginary. In the present context, it is most difficult to identify particular legal rules or processes which are contrary to the interests of the new states. Several considerations are

---

[73] See, briefly, the excerpts from the statements of the Indian representative at the UN Security Council debate, reproduced in M. M. Whiteman, *Digest of International Law*, 2 (Washington, D. C. 1963), 1141ff. For a more detailed defense of this point of view, see, J. S. Bains, *India's International Disputes* (Bombay 1962), 195-208. And cf. Quincy Wright, "The Goa Incident," 56 *American Journal of International Law*, 617ff., esp. at 629-31 (1962); M. Flory, "Les implications juridiques de l'affaire de Goa," 8 *Annuaire Français de Droit International*, 476ff. (1962).

relevant. To begin with, international legal rules, like all legal pre-scriptions, rarely have a clear and well-established content. Secondly, even where the content can be identified, the precise effects of a legal principle, process, or rule are normally neither clear and certain nor easily identifiable. Moreover, the interests of the new states, or, more broadly, of the members of the so-called third world,[74] do not always coincide. In a great number of instances, which would cover, in all probability, a major part of the rules and principles of traditional international law, the interests of these states diverge. Indeed, there are probably only two general categories of problems where the in-terests of the members of the third world largely coincide—and this only *grosso modo*, with plenty of variations and minor differences—and these are the class of problems relating to economic development, and the problems of colonialism. Outside these categories, it is im-possible to identify at first glance the degree of coincidence of interests that would permit effective joint action.[75] (Cases where the interests of all members of the world community may coincide belong, of course, to a different class.) Finally, it should not be forgotten that state interests may and do vary over time. What is in the interest of a particular state or group of states at a specific moment may not be in its or their interest at a future date. As states develop in certain ways and in certain directions, their interests also change.[76] Such poten-tial changes of position are certainly relevant to the present inquiry, although, in the main, only if they are expected to occur reasonably soon; the very long run is usually left to take care of itself.

Changing Structures and Techniques in Law-Making

The central issue in the development of any legal order is not so much the problem of law enforcement as that of the process of law-making and legal change. The chief weakness of international law has ac-cordingly been not the lack of well-defined sanctions but that of clear, securely established and efficiently functioning procedures for making and changing the law.[77] The effective norms in international law are rarely clear and definite and there are few established and smoothly operating methods for the amendment of those among them which no longer serve their purposes well and for the creation of

[74] For a discussion of this term, see Fatouros, "The Third World," 784-85.

[75] And see also text to notes 82-88. For a stimulating agenda of needed research in this field, see Richard A. Falk, "The New States," 79-102.

[76] For a discussion and illustrations, see, W. Friedmann, *Changing Structure*, 55ff.

[77] A consequence of this has been that there are no clear tests or procedures by which the departure from the existing law that constitutes law-making can be distinguished from that which is lawbreaking. In the context of a community where much of the law is created through indefinite and nonformalized sets of reciprocal claims and restraints, this lack is particularly important.

new ones. The accepted doctrines of public international law and most of the related discussions and disputes have mainly served to obscure rather than clarify the situation in this respect. There is a general feeling today that the preexisting structures and processes are changing but there is no clear indication of the directions of change or of the features of the new processes and structures. This essay's venture into uncertainty is therefore here in a particularly indefinite and problematic area. The questions involved are so important, however, that the attempt must be made to identify among the actual or probable directions of change those that have a greater chance of success.

The traditional international legal order may have been Europocentric, but it was accepted by its subjects as single and universal. Today, it is increasingly accepted that, in addition to a central universal body of law (and a universal legal order), there exist several nonuniversal bodies of law and more than one legal suborder, distinguished from one another on geographical (regional), ideological, and perhaps cultural grounds.[78] This acceptance probably reflects a change in the observers' assumptions and predispositions as much as changes in the "objective" facts and situations observed.[79] To some extent (or from one point of view), the whole question is one of classification; by using various tests, singly or jointly, one may identify various groups of states.[80] But there is more to the matter than the satisfaction of a scholarly preference for logical order. The actual borderlines of the various groupings of states cut through logical dis-

[78] While several legal scholars agree as to the reality of this development, there is considerable controversy as to its significance and repercussions. Cf. C. W. Jenks, *The Common Law of Mankind* (New York 1958) , 14-19, 73-79; M. McDougal and H. Lasswell, "The Identification and Appraisal of Diverse Systems of Public Order," 53 *American Journal of International Law*, 1ff., esp. at 10 (1959), (reprinted in McDougal and associates, *Studies in World Public Order* [New Haven 1960], 3ff.) ; L. Sohn, "The Many Faces of International Law," 57 *American Journal of International Law*, 868ff. (1963) ; E. McWhinney, "Operational Methodology and Philosophy for Accommodation of the Contending Systems of International Law," 50 *Virginia Law Review*, 36ff., at 53 (1964) ; Friedmann, *Changing Structure*, passim; Fatouros, "The Third World," 818ff.

[79] For a parallel development in a sister discipline, compare the suggestions of a contemporary anthropologist, in the context of his search for a "theory of law" founded on the comparative study of primitive and nonprimitive societies. Leopold Pospisil starts by pointing out that "an individual usually does not participate directly in the life of the society as a whole. He is rather a member of a subgroup (or of several of them) , through which he takes part in social activities." He goes on to suggest that "law . . . is present not only on the society level but also in subgroups. . . . Many ethnographers assume that a given society has a single legal system. They either neglect legal phenomena on the subgroup levels or project these phenomena into the top society level and make them consistent with it. Instead of accepting this smoothed-out picture of a single legal system in a society, the writer suggests recognition of the fact that there are as many such systems as there are functional groups." Leopold Pospisil, *Kapauku Papuans and Their Law* (Yale University Publications in Anthropology No. 54, New Haven 1958) , 273-74

[80] See text to notes 4 and 5.

tinctions; their identification must rely not on general abstract tests and features but on perception and evaluation of actual conduct and official pronouncements, of political as well as cultural characteristics, and of images as well as realities.

The validity of any distinction depends in part on the purposes which it is designed to serve. For some purposes, the tripartite division of the world (Western states, Soviet bloc, and the third world) is still useful. For others, the distinction between several subgroups inside each of these main divisions is essential: in considering the problems of the relations among the states of the third world, for instance, it is vain to treat the group as a whole. There are few, if any, direct connections between the developing nations of Africa and those of Latin America, or even between the African and the Asian nations; their occasional coalitions inside universal organizations such as the United Nations hardly qualify as "direct relationships." Distinctions in regional terms are far more important in this context. For other purposes, finally, ideological or cultural tests may be more relevant. It must be stressed again, however, that not all logically possible distinctions are important or relevant in a study of the realities of the international scene; some of them are simply not operative enough to warrant their being taken into consideration.

It is not my purpose to study here in detail the problems of the divisions and subdivisions of the present international legal order. These problems, however, are particularly relevant to the present inquiry in two specific (and interrelated) connections and these will be further investigated.

In spite of the effects of modern developments in communication, relations with its neighbors remain a most important aspect of the international position of any state, particularly of a relatively weak state.[81] The relations of the new states with one another, therefore, cannot be left out of any consideration of their place in the international legal order. The assumption is too often made that, in view of their common features, problems, and objectives, the states of the third world are or will be united in pursuit of their common interests, as against the rest of the world. The rationality and desirability of such a course of action are one thing (or perhaps two) but its probability or reality is another matter. Historical experience easily shows that most warfare has been between neighbors. And the present picture of the concerns of the new states hardly refutes any conclusions drawn from history.

Using the situation in one region, Africa, as a sample, one finds that, in the political arena, the rivalries among African states are numerous

[81] The breadth of a country's circle of preoccupation is indeed a good indicator of its power in the international arena.

and well-documented.[82] Subversive activities against the governments of other states are commonplace.[83] Border disputes, however, have been relatively few—at least when seen against the background of the irrationality and uncertainty of existing territorial divisions.[84] The adoption in the Charter of Addis Ababa of the principle of respect of existing territorial divisions perhaps constitutes evidence of a realization of the irrationality of territorial disputes under present conditions and corresponds clearly, in content and causation, to the adoption of the principle of *uti possidetis* by the Latin American states.[85] Again, however, one has totally to disregard the teachings of history to believe that rationality and properly understood self-interest are the only operative principles in relations among states. The Latin American and Balkan experiences are less than encouraging in this respect. As this is being written, the Macedonian question is once again debated by Bulgaria, Yugoslavia, and Greece and, in Latin America, a new arms race is beginning to build up.[86]

In the economic domain, matters appear more encouraging at first glance. Economic development has been the one issue (apart from colonialism) around which all or almost all of the new states have rallied. It is the issue on which there appears to be the greatest amount of effective agreement among them as to objectives and methods, as the 1964 session of the United Nations Conference on Trade and Development has shown. It may be pessimistic but surely not unreasonable to suggest that this degree of unanimity may be due in part to

[82] For a survey of the situation in Africa, with abundant bibliographical references, see Zartman, *The New Africa*, 87-142.

[83] The colonial experience, the tradition of anticolonialist struggle and the present internal condition in many African countries (as well as in other countries, outside that region) have bred a familiarity with violence and a concomitant casual attitude toward the dangers of its use. To the extent that such attitudes are carried over from the internal to the international political arena, they represent a serious constant threat to regional and international peace.

[84] Cf. Zartman, *The New Africa*, 105-19; R. L. Kapil, "On the Conflict Potential of Inherited Boundaries in Africa," *World Politics*, 18 (1966), 656ff.; R. D. Hodgson and E. A. Stoneman, *The Changing Map of Africa* (Princeton 1963), 63-75. And cf., G. Reintanz, "Voelkerrechtliche Bemerkungen zu afrikanischen Grenzproblemen," in R. Arzinger and G. Brehme, eds., *Voelkerrechtliche Probleme der Jungen Nationalstaaten* (Berlin 1965), 127-42.

[85] See, Kapil, "Inherited Boundaries," 671; D. Thiam, *La politique étrangère des états africains* (Paris 1963), 97-103 (English edn., *The Foreign Policy of African States* [London 1965], 73-77); B. Boutros-Ghali, "The Addis Ababa Charter," *International Conciliation* (1964), 5ff., at 29-30. For brief discussions of and documentation on the Latin American practice, see, J. C. Puig, *Les principes du droit international public américain* (Paris 1954), 79-81; M. M. Whiteman, *Digest of International Law* 2 (Washington, D. C. 1963), 1086-88; G. Hackworth, *Digest of International Law*, 1 (Washington, D. C. 1940), 737-45.

[86] For an official U.S. statement, denying the latter, see L. Gordon, "Inter-American Cooperation: The Road Ahead," *Department of State Bulletin*, LV (1966) 946ff., at 950-51.

the relative lack of effectiveness, as of now, of international development efforts and procedures at the universal level. In matters of international trade, for instance, the chief competitors of most primary-product-exporting developing countries are other developing countries; their interests are therefore in actual or potential conflict (as the issue of the relationships between developing countries and the European Economic Community tends to make manifest). When and if the proposed preferences in favor of semi-finished manufactured products from developing countries come into effect, intensive competition among developing countries is likely to develop.[87] In the field of private foreign investment, as well, certain undesirable effects of the competition among developing countries in attracting investors are beginning to be identified: the possibility and perhaps presence of cut-throat bidding for investments through excessive tax and other incentives have been noted.[88] While such competition may help to increase the aggregate amount of foreign investment in developing countries (and thus have an "investment-creating effect," to adapt Viner's well-known distinction with respect to customs unions), it may also divert capital from worthwhile investments to less worthy but financially more attractive—because of the tax exemptions—projects (thus having an "investment-diverting effect"). Even apart from such effects, competition of this sort may reallocate the revenues from foreign investment to the disadvantage of the host countries (who would lose revenues from investments which would have been made anyway, even in the absence of tax incentives) and to the excessive advantage of some foreign investors, or even, under certain conditions, of the treasuries of their countries of origin.

These observations on actual and potential problems are not offered as evidence of the new states' "unworthiness," or as part of a thoroughly pessimistic view of their future, although some pessimism is warranted, at least to the extent of recognizing that the chances of success are not overwhelming. Moreover, in a study geared to the future, awareness of the actual and probable differences between the interests of the several new states and of the consequent chances for disputes of all kinds and proportions is particularly necessary.

The second context in which the question of the diversity and division of the present international legal order relates to the topic of this chapter is its influence on techniques of law-making. The multifaceted divisions of the international legal order have affected and will

[87] On this aspect of the problem of application of such preferences, see G. de Lacharrière, *Commerce extérieur et sous-développement* (Paris 1964), 247-54; G. Patterson, *Discrimination in International Trade, The Policy Issues 1945-1950* (Princeton 1966), 360-70.

[88] See, N. Kaldor, "The Role of Taxation in Economic Development," in Kaldor, *Essays on Economic Policy*, 1 (London 1964), 225ff., at 247-49.

eventually determine the processes and methods for making or changing legal rules and principles; the substance of the rules and principles involved and of the factual situations which they sanction will also be ultimately affected.

Within each of the several legal orders of today's international society, active processes of formal and informal law-making are functioning. There is no definite and permanent correspondence between the substance of a topic and the level of the group in which the principles and rules relating to it are being fashioned. There is, however, some rough correlation between topics and groups, to the extent at least that the legal processes in effect within certain groups are more important with respect to a given topic than those within other groups. Thus, although the problems of war and peace are relevant to all international legal orders, universal and nonuniversal, the principles and policies fashioned through the contacts of the bloc "leaders" (the United States, the Soviet Union, and possibly the People's Republic of China) are at this time more important than those developed within any one regional legal suborder and seriously affect the content of the latter.[89] The problems of international development, on the other hand, have yet to be effectively dealt with on a universal basis. Bilateral arrangements of many sorts and principles and understandings developed within regional or other groupings have been more effective in determining the legal terms of the relevant relationships between states.

The law-making procedures concerning international development operate at all the levels and forums of contemporary international society.[90] The most important arena of activity remains the national state; despite the adjective used, development is generally understood today as a process occurring within the limits of distinct territorial communities, even though it is acknowledged that it is affected by what happens outside each community. The purely or predominantly international dimensions of the development process and, as a consequence, of development policies, are as yet only obscurely per-

[89] Regional arms control schemes, for instance, may have better chances of success if prepared under universal auspices, as parts of a worldwide bargain. On the other hand, the assumption of a greater role by regional institutions in this field is probably desirable; it may offer better chances of peaceful solutions for relatively localized problems by insulating them from the worldwide ideological conflict. To the extent, however, that some regional groupings are dominated by a single major power (Latin America and the United States, Eastern Europe and the Soviet Union), actual or possible recourse to universal or near-universal groupings of states (viz. the United Nations) may paradoxically serve the same purposes, i.e. settlement of local issues through insulation from the ideological conflict.

[90] The listing in this paragraph constitutes but the summary of a discussion on the instruments of international law-making which I hope to develop elsewhere. For a recent discussion of these questions, see, W. Friedmann, *Changing Structure*, 117-51.

ceived. The unilateral action of states, whether with predominantly
domestic intentions and effects or in response to international or foreign stimuli, remains therefore the most important of the instruments
in international law-making in this field. To this must be added the
several more clearly international instruments: bilateral agreements,
concluded independently or as parts of networks of agreements clustered within a geographical region or around a dominant state; nonuniversal multilateral agreements, with or without a regional orientation[91] and whether or not setting up international organizations with
an independent capacity for action; and finally universal arrangements, such as the United Nations and some of its specialized agencies. It must be stressed that international law develops in this area,
as in others, not only out of the clearly juridical clauses of the instruments and decisions involved, but also (perhaps primarily) out
of the concrete arrangements, relationships, and structures provided
for or based on such instruments. At the same time, the more openly
law-making effects and activities of these agreements and institutions
play an important role: this is particularly true of at least some kinds
of multilateral treaties, of the activities of the International Law
Commission (chiefly with respect to the better settled and less controversial fields of the law), of those of the General Assembly of the
United Nations through some of its resolutions and, at least potentially, of the operation of the International Court of Justice and other
permanent or ad-hoc judicial institutions.

The emergence and participation of the new states will affect in several ways the existing structure of international law-making, but it is
not likely that its essential form will be radically changed. The role of
international institutions on the universal level (chiefly the United
Nations), as forums of negotiations, sounding boards for national or
factional position statements, and to a limited extent as law-making
institutions, will continue and it will probably acquire greater practical importance. Still, their law-making function, though real, will
continue to be limited. It will be expressed, as it is now, although at
a more intensive pace, through general declaratory statements of well-
accepted legal prescriptions, on the one hand, and compromise formulations of controversial prescriptions, on the other.[92] The latter are

---

[91] As already noted, the geographical region appears today to acquire increasing importance as a legally relevant unit in the international society.
This development is in itself a positive factor in the overall evolution of the international legal order, since it contributes to the intensification of international law-
making activities (even though not at the universal level) and the closer integration
of national units into international systems, which constitute subsystems of the
universal international legal order.

[92] While attention should properly be focused on such formulations of legal
prescriptions, it should not be forgotten that international organizations, like states,
make law not only by what they say, but also by what they do. Their practice

more important as vehicles of legal change, but their very character as compromises limits their total effectiveness. Such formulations necessarily allow several differing interpretations, often within a broad range of possibilities; accordingly, even though they do limit the area of dispute as to legal principle and perhaps illuminate the disputed core of the rule, they do not provide even minimally certain guidelines for legally sanctioned action.[93] To argue that the only (or the principal) method by which the international legal order can become more effective is through the creation of a central legislative organ (or the attribution of real legislative competence to existing organs)[94] seems to me, not merely unrealistic, but to disregard the peculiar characteristics of the international legal order, most fundamentally, its decentralized structure of authority. It is becoming increasingly evident that centralization of authority is not always, even within national societies, the most appropriate or effective structure. In the international context, much more inquiry and effort are needed to determine and devise possibilities and patterns of effective action in a decentralized setting, before choosing an alternative model.

From the "classical" formal sources of international law enumerated in Article 38 (1) of the Statute of the International Court of Justice, it is therefore the first, agreements, (bilateral and multilateral, including those with parties other than states) that will continue to play a preponderant role as instruments of legal change. The resulting picture is no doubt very complicated, but perhaps not as much as it would seem at first glance, on the basis of mere mathematical computations (number of countries times possible treaty subjects times number of countries). Certain features of the international law- (and treaty-) making process are important at this point.

First, the possibility that all states will contract with one another with respect to all subjects is purely theoretical. In practice, states conclude treaties on a considerable range of topics only with their neighbors and with a few more distant states (chiefly the more pow-

---

constitutes today one area where customary law is growing at a pace sufficiently rapid for our times. For an analysis of such practice, see, R. Higgins, *The Development of International Law Through the Political Organs of the United Nations* (London 1963).

[93] As an illustration of the strengths and weaknesses of this kind of statement, see the UN General Assembly Resolution 1803 (XVII), December 14, 1962, on permanent sovereignty over natural resources. This resolution advances international law in this highly sensitive area by reaffirming sovereignty over natural resources, while stressing the need for international cooperation in development, thus indicating the wide area of agreement on legal policy. With respect to the precise legal rules and standards that should govern, however, it provides little if any guidance; such texts neither can nor should attempt to attain precision in still unsettled areas of the law.

[94] For an able and near-persuasive statement of this position, see G. Clark and L. B. Sohn, *World Peace Through World Law* (2d rev. edn., Cambridge, Mass. 1964).

erful ones). Thus networks of treaties are developed, either focused on a single great power, party to all of the treaties, or spread over a region. Secondly, standardization may not be as highly developed in the case of treaties as it is in the case of international commercial contracts, but it undoubtedly exists and it is growing, its growth being in major part, but not exclusively, related to the development of networks of treaties. Thirdly, the extension of commercial concessions through the most-favored-nation clause has shown the way for devices for the automatic "universalization" of arrangements initially concluded between a few countries (especially where these arrangements do not involve the creation of institutions or organs).

There is no reason, moreover, why universal international organizations should not be involved in the elaboration of semistandardized, if not uniform, bilateral legal relationships, either by formulating plans, proposals, and model texts, or by providing procedures and institutional encouragement to negotiations leading to such arrangements. The procedures used within GATT, which involve establishing an active multilateral framework, chiefly but not exclusively for bilateral negotiations, with possible reference back and forth between the bilateral and the other levels, are one example of possibilities in this area. The institutional arrangements for the so-called conciliation procedures within UNCTAD are another example. The more technical dispute-settling procedures and negotiation arrangements within some of the specialized agencies of the UN or other international organizations provide yet another example. While bilateral and multilateral negotiations are constantly going on within all international organizations, they have not always been sufficiently institutionalized and they seem to operate (at least in theory) in the margin, rather than as the main focus, of the organizations' activities. A shift in focus (through minor changes of institutional structures, in some cases, and through mere changes in attitude, in others) may help to intensify and perhaps legitimize such processes of law-making.

It may already be clear that I believe that the role of the judicial process will continue to be relatively small. With respect to the kinds of radical change in the law that the new states are demanding or may demand, and which, more generally, are needed today, the "interstitial" law-making activity of the courts (even if the existing institutions were suddenly to become wedded to a theory of judicial activism) is far from sufficient.

It is then my submission that, aside from several important but not radical changes, there is little likelihood that the international legal order of the near future will be more definite or better organized than the present one. The horizontal character of state relationships, the vagueness of content of the legal norms in effect, and the confused overlapping of jurisdictions will continue to be principal characteristics of its essential structure.

Two New International Legal Principles

Discussion has focused up to now on the manner in which international law changes. It is time to turn briefly to the substantive content of current and future change. Predictions are most hazardous in this area, but it may be possible to identify certain general trends and to explore their possible evolution.

The main impact of the emergence of new states on the substance of international law has been felt until now in two areas: colonialism and international development. It has become quite clear by now that the legal status of colonial conquest and occupation has changed: colonialism as such, the occupation and exploitation of "backward" territories by Western powers on the ground that the "natives" are unable to govern themselves and to establish an independent state, is not legal any more, under international law—at least as far as present or future action is concerned. The legal status of the fruits of past actions is by no means as clear. Although the illegality of past colonial conquest and the corresponding invalidity of present situations based on it was the main legal proposition advanced by India to justify its occupation of Goa and the other Portuguese enclaves,[95] this position has not been supported frequently or consistently by the new states, apart from rhetorical statements of dubious effect. These states have generally shown a marked reluctance to draw ultimate logical conclusions from their vocal and insistent support of the principle of self-determination. The intensity of their affirmation of this principle has indeed tended to obscure their real position on the matter which is more limited and more realistic than it sounds at first.

The states of the third world are concerned not with self-determination as a general abstract principle but with the self-determination of colonial territories. The limitation is in part geographical: their preoccupation is directed at the territories of Asia and Africa (and, to a much less extent, Latin America). This is, of course, due to the historical accident (if accident it is) of the colonial conquest of these lands by the European powers. That it also is, however, a reflexion of realism and of an appreciation of the present state of the international legal order is shown by the reluctance of most new states to extend the application of the self-determination principle to boundary problems, on the one hand, and domestic politics, on the other. In general, the new states have strongly upheld the principle of territorial integrity, which in some cases directly contradicts that of self-determination.[96] They have, moreover, refused to extend the con-

95 See n. 73.
96 See n. 84, n. 85.

cept of self-determination, as an international legal principle, to cover the *desideratum* of effective participation of the people in government. As long as there is no clear distinction on racial or ethnic grounds between the governing and the governed, the new states have fairly consistently refused to see a question of international concern, thus setting well defined limits to the legal principle of the condemnation of colonialism which they have espoused and effectively promoted.

There is little doubt that, despite temporary setbacks and current frustrations, this principle forms today part of the law of nations. To the extent that problems exist in its application (and I do not wish to underestimate their importance), they relate chiefly to the liquidation of earlier situations, not to the future. To realize the legal effectiveness of the principle it is sufficient to speculate on possible reactions today if a European power tried to undertake a campaign of colonial conquest similar to those that were common and tolerated (if not fully established as legal) in the late nineteenth century.

The second legal principle that must be mentioned is far less certain in its content and, indeed, far less advanced at present in its formulation and in its acceptance as part of international law. Nevertheless, this emerging principle has today sufficient strength and is gathering enough impetus so that (by the time the future with which this essay is concerned has come) it should have become at least as well settled as the condemnation of colonial conquest.

The substance of the principle in question may be better understood if a rough and oversimplified analogy is used: present trends in international society may be understood as involving a movement which parallels that of the national societies in Western countries in the past century;[97] Sir Henry Maine's terminology, for all its need for correction, is useful in describing this process. In the recent past, the Western societies passed from a "status" order, with its inherent formal as well as factual inequalities, to the "contract stage," where a formal principle of equality before the law obtains: the rigidity of formal inequality is thereby eliminated, while at the same time the existing factual inequalities of power, wealth, etc. are allowed freely to operate. Partly as a result, however, of formal political equality, Western societies have now moved toward the "welfare state"— that is, the utilization of legal and political instruments to counterbalance and compensate for (and ultimately decrease) the existing inequalities of fact by assuring all members of the society of a certain minimum standard of welfare. With the passing of colonialism, which may be seen as the apotheosis of status, international society seems to

[97] For inspiration for this analogy, I am indebted, as is obvious, to Professor B. V. A. Röling's remarkable *International Law in an Expanded World* (Amsterdam 1960).

have reached the contract stage.[98] The developing countries, however, are now trying (not always with full awareness of what is involved) to induce a movement toward the next stage, which may be called that of the "welfare international legal order."[99]

Such a development involves acceptance and application of certain legal and political principles and the creation of institutional machinery to elaborate and implement them. A central such principle —or, perhaps, the essential feature of this basic movement—is the recognition of the inappropriateness of formal equality and reciprocity as governing principles of the relations between developed and developing countries and the consequent regulation of relationships on the basis of an awareness of, and of an attempt to counterbalance, existing factual inequalities. This principle has been variously named the "welfare" principle,[100] the principle of "the double standard,"[101] or the principle of "capability."[102] Whatever its ultimate appellation, this principle involves the abandonment of formal and immediate mutuality as the chief test of the "fairness" of international transactions. The principle would come into play where the contribution of one party to a specific transaction is not the strict equivalent, by market criteria, of that of the other party, and, more precisely, where the contribution of the wealthier or more powerful party is greater, by market criteria, than that of the weaker or poorer party. The elimination of the market test of immediate reciprocal advantage does not imply a disregard of the interests of one of the parties, but rather increased concern with the common, long-range, interests of the international community as a whole.

[98] Note, in that connection, how reminiscent some of the present defenses of freedom and sanctity of contract on the international level are of the domestic defenses of the same principle at the turn of the century.

[99] The greater acceptance of "socialist" doctrines by the new nations may account to some extent for their stressing techniques of planning and regulation rather than reliance on the so-called natural trends and processes. But in all societies, regulation and state intervention have been favored by those who expect to benefit. And today's "natural" processes are the result of yesterday's "interference."

[100] Röling, *Law in an Expanded World*, 77ff. and 83ff. refers to "protective law" and to "welfare law," whereas I would bring both under a single heading. See also, Friedmann, *Changing Structure*, 66-68, 275ff.

[101] See, A. A. Fatouros, "International Law and the Third World," 50 *Virginia Law Review*, 783-823, at 811ff (1964). The term is an adaptation of Gunnar Myrdal's "double standard of morality in international trade"; cf. his *An International Economy* (New York 1956), 288; *Beyond the Welfare State* (New Haven 1960), 205 and passim. Although descriptive and arresting this term is not fully satisfactory, for reasons explained elsewhere (see n. 107); "principle of asymmetry" seems more appropriate.

[102] H. D. Lasswell, "The Relevance of International Law to the Development Process," *American Society of International Law Proceedings*, v, 60 (1966), 1-8, at 4-8. I hope I am not betraying Professor Lasswell's thought in thus identifying the principle he referred to; cf. my "Comments," same, 18-21, and Professor Lasswell's remarks, same, 27.

The implementation of this principle in the present international legal order is not evident on first approach because of the peculiar structure of that order. In the national legal orders, the principle in question is implemented through legislation establishing labor law standards and procedures, social welfare agencies and principles, or various other principles, rules, and procedures (e.g. in taxation, housing, financing, etc.). Such implementation is properly considered not as a private law question but as a public, that is to say, a political matter; it proceeds therefore through the imposition of obligations and the creation of legal norms by the legislative organs without any apparent attempt at previously securing universal consent. The international legal order being a "horizontal" system,[103] the implementation of the principle in question proceeds chiefly through bilateral and multilateral arrangements between states; although legislative in character, these arrangements appear more similar to contractual transactions, as we know them from municipal law, than to legislative acts.[104]

The clearest case of application of this principle is, of course, that of international economic assistance. Much remains to be learned as to the exact relationships established by means of the multitude of formal instruments whereby capital, commodities, and technical assistance are provided.[105] The lack of mutuality, however, (at least in purely economic terms) is usually clear enough—indeed its actual extent is often exaggerated—and it implies a recognition of the need for a change in the existing allocation of resources, apart from any immediate, partial or attempted, *quid pro quo*. In this sense, it is highly desirable that economic assistance be further disentangled from the allegations of charity, indirect exploitation, or generosity that have tended to obscure its character.[106]

---

[103] Cf. Richard A. Falk's "International Jurisdiction: Horizontal and Vertical Conceptions of Legal Order," 32 *Temple Law Quarterly*, 295ff. (1959), reprinted in Falk, *The Role of Domestic Courts in the International Legal Order* (Syracuse 1964), 21ff.

[104] "The essence of a political situation, as opposed to one of agreement and routine, is that someone is trying to do something about which there is not agreement. . . . Political situations arise out of disagreement." J.D.B. Miller, *The Nature of Politics* (New York 1962), 14. This view of the political, however "correct" or useful as a theoretical instrument, is widespread enough so that the situations where there is agreement, or the appearance of agreement, are normally automatically considered as outside (or as something different than) politics.

[105] For two recent descriptions of patterns and policies, see W. Friedmann, G. Kalmanoff, and R. Meagher, *International Financial Aid* (New York 1966); I.M.D. Little and J. M. Clifford, *International Aid* (London 1965).

[106] The attempts of the United States Congress in the past few years to link foreign aid to the treatment of private foreign investment may thus be understood, perhaps paradoxically, as recognition of the close connection of aid and investment to a broader process of reallocation of resources.

Attempts or claims to interfere with the "natural" (i.e. market) process of allocation of resources are involved in other situations, as well, where some aura of reciprocity may still remain and hide the real nature of the process. A few such cases will be listed briefly here, subject to more elaborate developments elsewhere.[107] The current proposals for changes in the accepted pattern of legal regulation of international trade, with their deliberate abandonment of the principle of reciprocity in tariff concessions, certainly follow this approach.[108] A manifestation of the same trend may even be found in the recent acknowledgment by the United States Departments of State and Treasury that a new type of double taxation treaty is appropriate as between countries at different stages of economic development, because formal reciprocity in such a case is often profitable only to the developed country.[109] It is with respect to foreign private investment that the principle in question seems to have been most discussed, though in most instances without a clear understanding of the process or principle involved. I have attempted to show elsewhere[110] that the legal position of private foreign investment in developing countries should be restated in terms of the desirability of and necessity for international development and that a "double standard" may be formulated which would allow greater freedom of decision-making to the host country's government and, at the same time, protect to a reasonable extent the interests of the foreign investors.

Concluding Observations: When the New States Are No Longer New

One principal conclusion, which in a way underlies the whole discussion in this chapter, but has not yet been expressly stated, is that the present dichotomy between developed and underdeveloped coun-

---

[107] I discuss the problems of formulation and implementation of this principle in more detail in a forthcoming study.

[108] For earlier general statements, see, G. Myrdal, *International Economy*; S. Dell, *Trade Blocs and Common Markets* (New York 1963), esp. 367-68. These demands were forcefully expressed at the 1964 meeting of the United Nations Conference on Trade and Development and discussed widely thereafter; see esp. United Nations, *Towards a New Trade Policy for Development* (Report by the Secretary-General of UNCTAD, New York 1964) esp. 65ff. And cf. P. O. Proehl, "The Geneva Proposals to Reform International Trade: 'A Clear Convergence of Responsibilities'?" 33 *George Washington Law Review*, 1031-66 (1963) ; A. Etra, "Time for a Change: The UN Conference on Trade and Development," *Revue Belge de Droit International*, v, 1 (1966) , 50-67; de Lacharrière, *Commerce extérieur*, 121-47; Patterson, *Discrimination*, 347-84; H. G. Johnson, *Economic Policies Toward Less Developed Countries* (New York 1967) , 163-206.

[109] See, esp. the statements and discussions in U.S. Congress, *Tax Convention with Thailand—Hearings Before the Subcommittee of the [Senate] Committee on Foreign Relations* (Washington D. C. 1965) . And cf. S. Surrey, "The United States Tax System and International Tax Relationships," *Taxes*, 43 (1965) , 6ff.

[110] "The Third World"; and cf. n. 107.

tries in international society is going to continue in existence for the foreseeable future. In the past twenty years, since we have become aware of the problem, the gap between the two groups has widened rather than narrowed. The numerous causes of this phenomenon (population growth, technological gap, developmental bottlenecks, and "resistances," etc.) have been studied extensively, but by no means exhaustively, by now.[111] Whether this dichotomy is permanent is a difficult and perhaps impossible question; that it is bound to continue during the foreseeable future (indeed far longer than the "immediate" future considered in this essay) seems certain, on any realistic view of the matter. At the same time, our conceptual, technical, and technological apparatus will doubtless improve and we shall have by then a better grasp of the problem and a sharper and more definite picture of the gradations between development and underdevelopment.

Given the continuation of the present division of the world and of the attendant conflicts, the problems of legal regulation of interstate relations and indeed of the establishment of an effective international legal order will also continue in essentially their present forms. Bilateral and multilateral agreements, unilateral measures, decisions, and arrangements within international organizations and agencies will dominate the law-making process. While the trend toward centralization of authoritative decision-making will probably increase in intensity and effectiveness, it is probable that international law-making will continue to be almost as confused and frustrating as it is now.

As far as substantive legal principles are concerned, the condemnation of colonialism will probably become even more effective and positive a legal principle than it is now. Given the continuing division of the world into developed and underdeveloped countries and regions, the principle of the "double standard" or of "asymmetry" not only will continue to obtain, but is bound to grow in acceptance and precision of formulation. The areas of application are going to expand: we started with economic aid, now we acknowledge (or almost do) that the principle is relevant to private capital movements, international trade, and international fiscal relations. It is reasonable to expect that the developing nations will claim, and the developed ones will eventually admit, an obligation on the part of the latter to so structure their foreign (and even perhaps domestic) economic policies as not to harm—or so as to benefit—the economies of the former. In their role as foci of networks of bilateral treaties, and in view of the necessary legal and other skills at their disposition, the developed countries will be increasingly burdened with the responsibility for de-

[111] See esp. G. Myrdal, *Economic Theory and Under-Developed Regions* (London 1957).

vising acceptable procedures and arrangements that will maximize the benefits to be derived by the developing countries. The relationship between institutional and substantive arrangements is of essential importance, for the proper implementation of the principle of asymmetry or double standard demands full awareness of and meticulous attention to concrete details, such as the resource-endowment of countries, the structures and effects of their relationships, etc. A general declaration that "developed countries should help the less developed" may be of some help—and its very formulation as a legal, rather than moral, principle raises serious practical problems—but it is the actual relationships, the ways of sharing and allocating resources, that matter principally. These exist only *in concreto*, with respect to specific problems, to particular countries and sets of countries.

Any discussion of trends and possibilities is incomplete if it is not properly qualified by a reference to attitudes. It is, of course, simplistic, in international as in domestic problems, to reduce everything to a matter of attitude and to place the whole burden for social and political change on a precedent-shattering "change of heart." Legal forms and substantive prescriptions, legal and political procedures and institutions, economic trends, attitude changes, and technological innovations—all occur at the same time through a contemporaneous interlocking and interacting process. Recognition of such complexity, however, does not imply rejection of the need for changes in attitudes toward or even in the perception of the international legal order. In the succinct formulation of McDougal and Lasswell, "the effective authority of any legal system depends in the long run upon the common underlying interests of the participants in the system and their recognition of such common interests. . . ."[112] The two steps are properly distinguished: the perception of common interests may or may not presuppose their existence but in all cases it reflects a certain attitude, a willingness to see and to attribute importance to the interests in question. In this sense, the perception of interests is indissolubly tied to the values held by the person or persons concerned. As long as the international legal order is seen in the traditional terms of a loose external relationship between fully distinct units, no adequate foundation for the far-reaching implementation of principles such as that of "asymmetry" or "double standard" will exist. The present fellowship of terror, the states' tolerance of and cooperation with one another, under the inducement of fear of nuclear catastrophe, on the one hand, and revolutionary chaos, on the other, although a

[112] M. S. McDougal and H. D. Lasswell, "The Identification and Appraisal of Diverse Systems of Public Order," 53 *American Journal of International Law*, 1ff., at 5, reprinted in McDougal and associates, *Studies in World Public Order* (New Haven 1960) , 3ff., at 8.

closer relationship than the traditional concepts allow, is still too weak to suffice. Only in the presence of a positive intense conviction of the necessity for an international legal order in view of the long-run benefits flowing from its existence, will it be possible for the developed countries to make the short-run sacrifices demanded of them, and for the developing states to wait for future benefits without violently rejecting or undermining the present legal order. And this is the point on which uncertainty is most profound.

CHAPTER 8

Approaches to the Notion of
International Justice

JULIUS STONE

THE PURPOSE of this chapter is to examine certain approaches to justice as a measure for criticizing and reconstructing international law in the conditions of the contemporary world. It is not offered as a conclusion of any kind. It is written, of course, in awareness of the general tenor of preceding chapters, but its concern extends to debated ideas which those chapters have had to presuppose. I have to add immediately that the problems here approached in the international sphere presuppose in their turn the vast range of thought to which the writer recently dedicated his work, *Human Law and Human Justice* (1965). It is neither necessary (nor would it in any case be possible) to attempt to cover here the general ground in that substantial volume. Yet it would be naive to think that there can be any adequate approach to *international* justice without constant awareness of the present state of knowledge concerning justice in the municipal and general spheres.

I was confronted with deep perplexities about how to cover such an undertaking, and also with indecision about how and where it would be sensible to begin its performance. These perplexities continued to the end, long after it became clear what I wanted to write; and they remain even now in doubts whether the choices finally made were the best.

These choices finally dictated the ordering of this chapter under title headings which (because they are not self-evident) may be here briefly explained by way of introduction.

I. *Of Notions of Justice in General*: Justice in the international sphere, whatever be its specific differences from justice in general, involves the application of ideas which have largely been explored in the contexts of municipal law and of general philosophy. The opening section deals with some of these explorations and contexts in the hope that this may encourage a mood receptive to the more specific sections that follow.

II. *Of Natural Law and "Conscience" in the Growth and Criticism of International Law*: To a more than usual degree modern international law, as a nominate legal order, came into being on a rationale which served simultaneously as an instrument for its own self-criticiom. The reference, of course, is to its natural law foundations pegged out by Victoria and laid (as firmly as they may be said to have been laid at all hitherto) by Grotius. Granted the contrast between former centuries of Monarch-Sovereigns, and our modern world of State-Sovereigns, the double role of natural law (and the related "conscience" notion) as both progenitor of international law and of its precepts, and the censor of its justice, merits attention as a model of approach to the notion of international justice. It deserves early consideration, in this section, because of its successes, and also because of its failures. These latter, in particular, help us to focus on the limits of that particular approach, and also on some limits which may affect any approach whatsoever. Moreover, through its doctrine of the equality of nations, the natural law approach continues to be a fertile source of criticism even into our own times. The next section is devoted wholly to the remarkable career of the equality doctrine as a vehicle of justice-theorizing and criticism.

III. *Of the Equality of Nations Doctrine and International Justice*: Even apart from historical sources of the equality of nations doctrine in natural law theory, no study of international justice could prudently neglect it. For from its tangled exegesis emerged on one way or another the main justice-issues, for instance, concerning self-determination and self-preservation in modern conditions, economic justice between nations, and the entire role of state entities in the doing of international justice, which still affect the relations of states. These issues, and sometimes their outcome also, were secreted as a kind of by-product of endless struggles to give meaning to the doctrine of equality of nations as an axiom of international law, in a world in which, to an untutored mind, it appeared to be simply false.

IV. *Of the Approach to International Justice by Analogy from Justice in Municipal Law*: The immediately preceding sections, as now sketched, will have suggested some main issues of justice as they emerged historically in the doctrines and practice of international law. Sometimes, as with natural law and conscience, the intellectual bearers of the demands of justice were common both to municipal and to international law (Section II). Sometimes, as with the emanations from the doctrine of equality of nations, the bearer of these demands was a more specific product of the international context. In Section IV an attempt is made to approach the issues of international justice by proceeding outward, with due caution as to the limits of analogy, from our *present* understanding of justice in municipal societies.

V. *Of the Question whether States or Human Beings Are the Claimants and Beneficiaries of the International Justice Constituency*: Great difficulties affected attempted solutions of questions of international justice which offer no assurance of the entitlements of human beings as such. Yet when we insist on these entitlements, we confront no less grave questions. How far can the claims of justice made by or on behalf of states *inter se* be said really to represent the claims of human beings constituting their people? These questions go beyond mere *application* of criteria derived from the municipal sphere; they may go to the very preliminary question of applicability. And if (as is possible, *faute de mieux*) we must, nevertheless, use such criteria, we should keep very explicit the points at which our applications remain questionable.

VI. *Of the Present Role of States in Tasks of Just Economic Distribution within a Postulated Justice-Constituency of Mankind Administered by States*: Untidy and difficult of practical application as may seem the position thus reached, the intellect must accept and try to work with it. In a tentative essay toward this, Section VI approaches some long-term problems of international economic justice as they now confront both the developed and the developing states.

VII. *An Emergent Enclave of Justice?* The concluding section reapproaches, in the light of what has gone before, the relations between the enclaves of justice won and held by men in their mutual relations within their own municipal society, and those which seem to offer for governing their relations with the rest of mankind.

IT WILL BE apparent that the above issues bear on already well-known demands about the rights and duties of individual human beings under international customary or treaty law. There is already a substantial (if rather inconclusive) literature on these matters, including the international legal personality of individuals, their *locus standi* before international tribunals, their liabilities to punishment under an "international criminal law" of debated ambit, from the customary law of piracy to the post-Nuremberg principles concerning crimes against mankind. And, closely related to this last, there is a body of treaty and doctrinal law, as massive and promising on paper as it is frustratingly slow and meagre in its influence on the practice of states, about human rights and freedom from discrimination. For the most part, such demands arise by way of extension from the body of ideas concerning justice developed in municipal societies. On these ideas there is a vast literature, including recently the present writer's *Human Law and Human Justice* (1965) and *Social Dimensions of Law and Justice* (1966).

All this existing body of knowledge is the implicit starting point, rather than the subject matter, of the present explorations. The more specific questions of *international* justice, here to be explored, are at once less technical and more practical. They are less technical in the sense, for instance, that questions of "duties" of wealthier states to promote minimal levels of human subsistence or of how far each state is the proper arbiter of rights of personality of its individual subjects, are obviously less technical than questions of interpretation of declarations of human rights, or conventions against political or religious discrimination, or of the jurisdiction of international Courts, or of *locus standi* before them. They are also more practical questions, since they concern functional as distinct from merely verbal translation of ideas from the municipal to the international spheres. They are directed (for instance in relation to the notions of conscience, natural law, and equality of nations) to expose the limits and potentialities for the international sphere of the existing body of knowledge already referred to, as well as of such ideas of justice as are already built into the practice and doctrine of international law. Their drive, notably, is to find workable frames of thought in which to set demands for restitution for "historic wrongs," for the vast transfers of physical wealth and knowledge and skills associated with the development of poorly endowed nations, and for fixing appropriate stewardships for dispensing justice among mankind as we seek hopefully to move from speculative to working models of international justice.

I. Of Notions of Justice in General

When we try to bring down to earth the prophetic vision of the brotherhood of man, our tasks are difficult enough even within the more or less homogeneous and integrated constituency of a single municipal society. The difficulties arise not merely from man's age-old and continuing struggle to move from reality to vision, from control of present facts to achievement of ideals espoused. This continuing struggle in the face of past failures may, indeed, be among the more glorious and eternal marks of the human condition, as it is certainly central in the perplexities of the wise and informed in each generation. The main intellectual source of these perplexities resides in our inability to fix any hard core of irreducible meaning to the concept of justice which is *intellectually* convincing (as distinct from more or less plausible to some or others of us). As a result, such meaning as is confidently offered by some seems always no less confidently unacceptable to others, even among the most "objective" of thinkers within a single municipal society. We can often, it is true, move *toward* a transcending consensus by increasing the abstractness of our theoretical models and statements. But this invariably increases the difficulty we, in any case, have of emerging from our theorizings near enough to the facts of the here and now to make any decisive contribution to the problems which first drove us to theorize.

We were indeed able, in 1946, to feel that we had identified a certain hard core of the notion of justice in Western societies. This is that society shall be so organized that men's felt wants can be freely expressed; that law, in order to be just, must at least protect that expression and provide it with the channels through which it can compete effectively for (though not necessarily attain) the support of politically organized society.[1] Even this kind of "absolute," open-ended as it is in a material sense, cannot really be offered as valid for *all* municipal societies. For it presupposes a mobility and articulateness of demand found chiefly in Western democratic societies which has been less prominent in many civilizations. Furthermore, its meaning for a postulated international community is problematic until we have found some basis for translating the demands made by states into demands which would be made by the individuals who constitute their populations as these would be in the absence of modifying or suppressive or distorting influence of state entities. The question whether such a relation can be found still stands starkly in the path.

We have, in a more modest sense, also pointed to certain other precepts as having quasi-absolute standing for Western society. One precept is that the law's distribution of benefits and burdens should have regard to the goods and evils of this world, and should not relegate recompense to a world to come. Others are that action should be based on the maximum knowledge available which is pertinent to the subject matter; that it should respect principles of reciprocity and equality, of compensating for invasions, of rewarding for contributions to socially approved values and arrangements, and of punishing in due proportion, and also with due respect to the human dignity of the offender, the graver invasions of these values and arrangements. It is obvious, even as we thus summarize such precepts, that we at present think of their fulfilment as entrusted to the government of each state.[2] Even when deficient resources and developments are seen now as ground for international aid from other states or from specialized agencies, the distribution of benefits among human beings required by these precepts is jealously preserved for each donee government. The problems of justice as between states are thus cumulative on those of justice within municipal societies.

When we return to notions of justice in municipal societies and seek a basis of theory for adaptation to the international sphere, we immediately have to acknowledge the continuing reality of the con-

---

[1] Julius Stone, *The Province and Function of Law* (1946), 782-85.
[2] Julius Stone, *Human Law and Human Justice* (1966), 341-55, esp. 341-44 (hereafter cited as Stone, *Human Justice*).

frontation between the protagonists of natural law and positivism, of the cognitivist view of ethics and its doubters. And within any of these sprawling camps, and under whatever banners, we have to acknowledge continuing and perhaps increasing difficulties of communication. Partly, these are functions of the very elaboration and accompanying clash of ideas. The epochal struggles of past theorizings tend, if anything, to escalate and become more confused, rather than fade into mere doctrinal and literary history. And with all the confusions and cross-purposes, they still compete for the allegiance of all who have to think or act toward desired changes in the human condition. Moreover, in our generation, as in the past, contemporary conditions inevitably modify the understanding even of theorists tending to absolute positions. Natural lawyers constantly find themselves *engagés* in the actualities of their own times; their asserted "absolutes" have served, in different times and places, in social and political as well as legal matters, the forces both of radicalism and conservatism. This is, obviously, even more true for positivistic approaches to law, justice, and society.[3] And, finally, the continuing reality of the natural law-positivist confrontation for general legal purposes must be even greater for international law and justice. For whatever the merits of the general philosophical debate, the actual role of natural law in the foundation of modern international law was preeminent, and we have as yet been unable to build ultimate foundations which are any sounder than this. The permeation of the theory and practice of international law by natural law assumptions and approaches is thus an inescapable historical fact. So is the importance of these assumptions and approaches in the historical critiques of international law in terms of justice.

The clamor for human betterment, and for the use of law as an instrument toward this, are ever-recurrent in human history. That some notion like "justice" has been steadily associated with this clamor, playing a charismatic role in the major movements of human thought and action throughout the ages, is also a historical fact of immense importance. Appeals to justice as a means of moving men to the action which marshals power, as well as overthrows it, are associated with some of the most sublime and traumatic experiences of the family of men. It is also doubtful whether any historically known society with a stable differentiated legal order can be named where there was no awareness among its exponents and appliers of the relation of law to ethically approvable social arrangements, that is to "justice" in a broad sense. All this has tempted us to the attractive view that whatever its final definition or criteria, the notion of justice somehow

[3] For a fuller study of these struggles see Stone, *Human Justice.*

gives meaning to the tasks of men who work with the law, as the idea of beauty is thought to give meaning to the work of the artist.

It is all the more impressive, in view of this, and of the age-old emotional and intellectual alignments already investing the notion of "justice" on all sides, that men's yearnings toward it have shown themselves so irrepressible. In every generation, too, are to be found men, and often a substantial proportion of all men, who envision "justice" as raising issues not to be avoided; issues of more than a merely subjective nature; issues involved in present actualities; issues, finally, fit for pondering and provisional judgment, rather than dogma.

Such provisional judgment need not preclude the search for unchanging principles of justice valid for all times and places, such as those whose self-evidence may be intuitively perceived by a natural lawyer's "right reason," or those proceeding from the necessary postulate of the truly "free" individual will. It is to be expected, however, at the present stage of history, that judgment will be deeply sensitive to the actual conditions of man's social, economic, and political life at the particular time and place of judgment, and of the need for acceptable solutions to the actual problems of that time and place. In terms of method these actualities have, in the past, been reflected in tests of utility by reference to a Benthamite calculus of pleasure and pains in concrete situations, or of the actual purposes of men as adjusted by reference to "social purposes" or "social utility" or "social solidarity," as these have been thought to make themselves manifest in the observed facts of social life. They may, as with Rudolf Stammler and Joseph Kohler, struggle to place the reference to contemporary empirical actualities within universal philosophical ideas (in their cases, of Kantian and Hegelian origins respectively). They may, as with Radbruch and Pound, attempt to confront the actualities more frankly, with less philosophical aspiration, offering such practical tests as the capacity of law to satisfy to the maximum possible extent the demands which men make upon it. Such thinkers would urge, rather humbly, that men cannot await the decisive outcome of the search for an ultimate criterion of justice. For pragmatist approaches of this sort, best represented for law by Roscoe Pound, every sociological inquiry may simultaneously become an inquiry into justice, and any clear separation of these spheres tends to become impossible in practice.

We need not deceive ourselves concerning the indecisiveness thus far of the search for the ultimate criteria of justice in order to insist that it ought to go on. For there is good reason why the normative tasks of ethical and political philosophy (and the philosophy of justice that is an integral part of them) can never be finished as long as human society itself persists. Every substantial change in man and his environment calls for reexamination of existing values in their application to new situations. This call is more than ever insistent in a world of state-societies growing increasingly industrialized and mobile, powered now by an unprecedented technological explosion. Few a priori thinkers of the past have (as we have seen) ever succeeded in approaching their problems with a mind quite innocent of their own world. Few positivist-empiricists have been so sterile of emotion and ideals that they have succeeded in drawing no more from the "facts" observed than what was warranted by the "facts" themselves. If the champions of absolute criteria have not been able to establish them (or even to secure more stable consensus about them), the case of relativist criteria has as yet fared little better. Some limits must be set to the exaltation of the full role of time and place in basing a criterion of justice. For, unlimited, this role threatens to defeat itself in an age when too much is too long in rapid transition. King Time then becomes, not a wise mentor but a capricious tyrant, the gist of whose decrees cannot be foreseen from moment to moment, but only waited upon.

Formulae of justice sufficiently generalized to try to accommodate such shifts and intractabilities, for instance in the now rather fashionable terms of "equality" or "fairness," rarely get beyond restating the main problem. Linguistic analysis of the usage of the term "justice," while valuable for exposing our assumptions as to the evaluative reference of the term, especially in legal contexts, scarcely penetrates to problems of application in a particular time and place. Theories which take either "the sense of justice" or "the sense of injustice" as a basic datum, do indeed point to the wondrous persistence (observed above) of certain human yearnings. They also point to psychological (including psychiatric) matters which we should be more aware are involved in the justice-concern. Yet in their very simplification of this side of man's experience into "the sense" of justice or injustice, the problems of time and place not only remain unsolved, but become quite lost from view.

What has been said of the continued importance of the critique of law by justice in the municipal sphere, seems still more compelling in relation to the future of international law. With many municipal legal orders, at any rate, substantive and procedural norms, accepted legal ideas and legal techniques, and related institutions are sufficiently launched, sufficiently elaborated, and sufficiently dynamic to maintain overall direction for a substantial time even if attention to theory ceased. In the international legal order, more than three centuries of technical elaboration have not produced any assurance that its launching was a "take-off," rather than a series of forced landings or crashes. It is an order in which crisis is (as it were) normal; and crisis is the greatest catalyst of reexamination of goals and methods, and of the adequacy of the status quo. At the present stage of the international legal order, in which the number of participant states has more than doubled, and the range of cultures and of levels of their political, social, and economic capacity have become frighteningly diverse, even settled areas of the law are increasingly challenged and subjected to the questionings of justice. And these questionings extend beyond particular segments of the law to its very foundations, including the identity of its main participants and beneficiaries—states or human beings? And they present themselves, not only for our contemporary situation, but as deeply embedded in the very origins and history of international law.

II. OF NATURAL LAW AND "CONSCIENCE" IN THE GROWTH AND CRITICISM OF INTERNATIONAL LAW

The historical fact that most modern states first emerged as the personal domains of more or less absolute monarchs bears both on the formation of technical international law and on the criticism of that law and its operation by the norms of justice. The basis on which Grotius reconstructed an ordering to replace medieval authority and unity was an appeal to the rational and social nature of man. This offered norms to the newly emerged states for the avoidance of anarchy, deriving from their own nature as human communities, and from the common human nature of monarchs. The charismatic power, always manifest in the history of natural law, was of supreme importance for the beginnings of international law. Rejection by the new states of papal and imperial authority, and the bitter religious schisms of the time, excluded either superior secular power or divine authority as the source of the binding force of law on the new sovereigns. It was in this situation that a body of rules based on the natural law, a law deemed to emanate from men's inborn nature, offered itself. Since its claim to bind did not spring from any external human authority it could be acknowledged by the new national communities, or rather by the monarchs in whom these were personified, without impairing their new-won independence. Natural law, moreover, assumed thus to bind all men in common by the inner compulsion of their shared reason and sociality, had sufficient overtones of divine sanction to command respect without provoking disputations affecting the divine law as a revealed system.

Around this natural law frame Grotius marshaled not merely the secular practice of princes, who as men (Grotius argued) would necessarily manifest reason in their conduct of affairs, thus transcending the particular sectarian divisions of the day. He marshaled also materials from both the Old and the New Testaments, and from the ancient and modern, and the pagan and Christian worlds. And generally he thus reinforced the intellectual and emotional appeal of natural laws with the persuasiveness of post-Renaissance humanism, of the residue of Christian ethical consensus, and of the comfort of conformity to what was familiar.[4]

Insofar as the systematic exposition of the rules of international law by Grotius and his successors in fact went (as it obviously did) beyond the mere discovery of rules already binding on states, it was using the notion of the conscience of the monarchical head of state in a broad sense as a source of substantive technical law-making. In that broad sense even bodies of rules which have long ceased to be the center of serious frictions, like the immunities of heads of states and their representatives, the principle of exclusive jurisdiction of the territorial sovereign, the law and procedure of treaty-making, were accredited for state acceptance by the dictates of conscience. While the emerging idea of the state was still personified in the monarchical sovereign, we were still quite far from the present reification of state entities, in which the politically organized community and its apparatus of government are seen as transcending any particular persons, even though access and communication must be through persons holding particular status in it. Even to understand the notion of conscience in early international law we have to remember thus to dismantle our present more abstract notions of the state entity into its developing phases. This notion is then seen as a functional adaptation to the monarchical structure of the early European state. The historically available learning of natural law, and practical considerations of achieving consensus, thus combined to commend to early publicists the central role of appeal to the conscience of the monarch as a strategy for founding and elaborating the rules of international law.[5]

Concurrent, however, with this use of the appeal to conscience for "discovery" of rules of law as already technically binding, there was the continuing use of the notion as a channel of criticism of these rules. Students of English legal history will here recall the analogy of the operations of the English chancellor as "keeper of the King's conscience." On this basis he not only developed the comprehensive body of binding legal principles known as "equity," but also maintained a continuing interstitial criticism of the operation of the rules of

---

[4] See Julius Stone, *Legal Controls of International Conflict* (1954, 2 impr. with supplement, 1959) 7-18 (hereafter cited as Stone, *Legal Controls*), and the literature there cited; see esp. H. Lauterpacht, "The Grotian Tradition in International Law," 23 *British Yearbook of International Law*, 1-53 (1946).

[5] For a general discussion see section III of this chapter.

both common law and equity.[6] The role of "conscience" and of related natural law ideas down to the end of the eighteenth century
certainly parallels this; but it also has aspects (here of close interest)
which go beyond this analogy. For the appeal to the monarch's conscience also served in early international law thinking the function of
protest and *cri de coeur* in face of injustices which the publicists, owing
to inescapable facts of international life, saw no possible means of
alleviating by law. There is, perhaps, no better illustration of this
than the long, tortuous, and agonizing body of thought, from Grotius
down to the contemporary work of the International Law Commission, on the effect of duress (and in particular of the duress of war),
upon treaty undertakings thereby imposed.[6a]

Even the common law, which gave no civil action for duress, recognized (like the Roman law and its civil law successors) that a transaction entered into under duress can be held void at the instance of the
oppressed party. A treaty entered into by a sovereign after military
defeat, or to escape military defeat, obviously manifests duress of a
very extreme kind. It was to be expected, therefore, that from its beginnings the pioneers of international law were deeply perplexed
by the question whether such treaties were binding under the principle *pacta sunt servanda*. The principal writers concluded that such
treaties were binding and could not be avoided. But they usually accompanied this with solemn denunciations of oppressions by one
sovereign against another, and (more significantly for our purpose)
sometimes by the affirmation that it was in conscience the duty of
the dominant monarch to renegotiate the treaty so as to remove its oppressive features. The balancing of the affirmation of binding legal
force with eloquent denunciation and exhortations of this kind, serves
obviously to keep alive the demands of justice against the law, in a
limit-situation for which (as we shall shortly see) the law itself could
not adequately provide.

Vattel's exposition on this point, as on so many others, sharpens all
the contrasts involved.[7] On the binding force of peace treaties he
opens with the assertion not only that they are binding but that
it is "always disgraceful and absurd" for the weaker party to plead
either fear or constraint. He thought that the fairness of such treaties

---

[6] On this see Stone, *Human Justice*, 77-78; and Julius Stone, *Social Dimensions of
Law and Justice* (1966), 54-56 (hereafter cited as Stone, *Social Dimensions*).

[6a] For a later and rather fuller account of this matter see Julius Stone, *"De Victoribus Victis*: The International Law Commission and Imposed Treaties of Peace"
8 *Virginia Journal of International Law* 356-73 (1968).

[7] The text follows Vattel's general analysis in bk. iv, c.iv of his celebrated treatise, *The Law of Nations or Principles of Natural Law* (1768) trans. in Vol. III,
Classics of International Law (1916). The Chapter is entitled "The Observance
and the Breach of the Treaty of Peace."

must be judged, not in terms of peace-time relations, but in terms of the alternative evils which confront a state faced with the prospects of defeat and destruction. From this aspect the burdens of treaties of peace on the weaker party must be supported by the law, and he thought finally that ". . . common safety and welfare of Nations" required this.

The main legal position thus clear, Vattel proceeded to exhort sovereigns on matters of conscience and justice. They must not, for example, confuse genuine treaties of peace with treaties of oppression, as when an "ambitious and unjust conqueror subdues a Nation, and forces it to accept hard, disgraceful and unendurable terms of peace." Necessity may constrain the nation to submit to them. But this show of peace is not real peace; it is oppression of the constrained nation, which "endures" such a treaty only "so long as it lacks the means to free itself."[8]

Morally inspiring as this at first seems, close examination quickly suggests cautions as to its effect on law. "If ever a plea of constraint may be admitted," Vattel cautiously proceeds, it is only "against an agreement that does not merit the name of a treaty of peace, *against a forced submission to terms which are equally contrary to justice and all duties of humanity.*"[9] Natural law fidelity to promises "does not favor oppressors," for natural law is directed to the good of mankind, and he who violates all those principles should not be allowed to invoke them. Having put the burden of pleading on the constrained party as high as this, Vattel turns to the danger that abuse of the plea of constraint may impair the security of treaties of peace. He generously insists that this danger is a lesser evil than "allowing a regime of oppression to flourish perpetually" in defiance of both "human and divine justice," which of course increases the burden somewhat more.

The first caution then is that Vattel remains to the end ambiguous as to whether he is saying that *in law* such a treaty of peace is void, or merely that in fact such a treaty will not endure since the oppressed sovereign will repudiate it at the first opportunity. The second caution is that, even if he did mean the former, the range of treaties of peace which would be voidable for oppression would be narrow and also very difficult for the victim to establish. Since he is emphatic that it is even "disgraceful and absurd" for a defeated sovereign to complain that he was forced to accept onerous terms, at what point, and how, exactly, can the victim prove that terms are "contrary to justice and all duties of humanity," and that they violate "all" the principles of natural law, and are "mere oppression"? So sophisticated a thinker must have

[8] Same, bk. iv, c.iv, §37 at 356.
[9] (Emphasis added.)

known that such requirements for overcoming the binding force of treaties entered into under duress could rarely if ever be met, even if there had been an impartial forum (which, of course, there was not) with power to determine the applicability of such critical precepts.[10]

Finally, as already foreshadowed, it must be recognized that this whole problem of imposed treaties of peace represents what we have elsewhere described as a limit-situation for international law.[11] We have now to add the possibility that it represents a limit-situation also for any quickly approachable notion of international justice. And it is because a Vattel, as well as a Grotius and their classical colleagues were already aware of this, that they resorted to this kind of approach, on the dual level of clear rule of law, and eloquent admonishment of conscience.

The question posed usually arises when there has been a war between states, and one state bears the guilt of war-making. If that guilty state was defeated and had unfavorable terms imposed on it (as is likely to be the outcome of the Egyptian and Syrian adventures which led up to the Middle East crisis of 1967) there is little problem (at any rate for present purposes). The state got no fruits from its wrong, only burdens and penalties possibly according to its deserts. But if the guilty state is the victor, it will usually stipulate for benefits from the defeated state, often involving deep suffering on that state's people. We are all agreed that it is morally outrageous for the law to give effect to such a treaty. But our question is, how is the law to avoid giving effect to it?

By hypothesis, since the beneficiary is the victor he has the power to compel observance of the terms. By the same token no other states have been willing to engage the victor in a trial of force while the war is on; and *a fortiori* no other state is likely to begin a separate war to prevent enforcement of the terms after the peace treaty is signed. If no third state was willing to help the defeated state as an ally, it will not usually be willing to face the victor as a lone crusader for a more equitable treaty of peace.

Apart from anything which the law might do, therefore, the equitable revision of the terms of the wicked treaty of peace must wait until the power relations of victor and vanquished have changed. This may take only a few years, as when Italy was expelled from Ethiopia or Germany from the Sudetenland and Czechoslovakia, on their defeat in World War II, or it may take generations, as did the libera-

---

[10] Vattel's discussion of unequal treaties generally follows in essence the structure above analyzed, and is open to similar comment. See same, bk. ii, c.xii, §§180-81 at 166-67.

[11] See Julius Stone, *Quest for Survival* (1961), 63-71, from which this treatment is substantially derived.

tion of Poland from the partitioning powers in World War I, or it may remain uncertain into our own times, as with the Soviet seizure of the Balkan States, and of paramountcy over Finland, early in World War II. What happens, and how long it takes, is a function of changing power relations.

This is the harsh and naked truth of Mr. Khrushchev's observation a month or two before the abortive Summit Conference of 1960, that the present arrangement in Europe (meaning satellite Europe) were produced by war (an observation reasserted just as clearly, though perhaps less offensively, by Prime Minister Kosygin on February 9, 1967), and it could only be changed by war. "War" here includes such a confrontation by changing power relations as makes it not worthwhile for the erstwhile victor to try and maintain his gains by war. In substance, this was also Vattel's point, that the victim of a "treaty of oppression" will "endure" it only so long as it lacks means to throw it off. And this too is the harsh and naked truth which Washington recognized when it stopped dead in the tracks of a campaign for the "liberation" of satellite Europe on the very occasions when in East Germany and in Hungary, the opportunity to give effect to the program was offered to it, for it was offered only at a cost which might involve a general war.

If, therefore, the very nature of military victory creates a power situation in which the terms of the treaty of peace are firmly anchored until the situation itself changes, what attitudes can the law adopt as to the legality of these terms? Suppose the law says, conformably to our sense of justice as men, that these terms are null and void, and no other state must recognize that they have any legal effect. Can this deprive the victor of the fruits of these terms? Conceivably it might have a certain nuisance value, and it might even constitute a degree of moral pressure against the victor. Yet the basic fruits will usually be placed by the terms of peace within his actual grasp, which no mere nuisance tactics will relax; and as an aggressor he is unlikely to be sensitive to moral pressure. In substance, even if the legal rule squarely denied his titles under the peace treaty, he would still continue to enjoy the fruits, as Japan continued to do in Manchuria, despite the refusal of members of the League to recognize her title. But the story would not end there. For while such a last-ditch legal rule would not do much to check the victor or relieve the victim, it might produce dramatic and perhaps disastrous effects for the whole international legal order.

For whatever view be taken of the Japanese conquest of Manchuria, many other states in the world still had need to maintain legal relations of some sort with both Manchuria and Japan. If they, on the one hand, were not prepared by force to undo the Japanese conquest, and international law, on the other hand, forbade them to have any dealings on the basis of the status quo, then Japan and Manchuria would cease *pro tanto* to be within the international legal order at all. And this result might be as harmful to the rest of the world as it was to Japan. And since over a recent generation many states and areas of the world have become involved in such forcible changes, international law might find itself in the position of not extending at a particular time to a substantial number of the states and peoples of the world. And all this still without achieving the objective of really depriving the aggressor of the fruits of his aggression.

These, then, are the reasons why international law as well as the practice of states on which it is based have continued, even to the present day, to recognize the validity of the terms of a treaty of peace imposed by victor on vanquished. The lawyers have continued to express emphatically that the imposition of such terms violates natural justice, good conscience, and fairness. They have sometimes declared that the only way in which the victor can purge himself of the sin was to enter upon negotiations for a new treaty, on the basis of freedom and equality, with the defeated party. They shared, therefore, the general sense of moral outrage. But they saw no way in their world, any more than we can see one in ours, whereby international law can take unto itself sufficient power to defeat every victor at the moment of his victory.

In a world in which militarily strong states remain the supreme depositories of worldly power and collective organs wield only feeble power, and that only by the grace of those states, military victory by a state is a limit-situation for international law, as it is for the vanquished. But the choice before international law is in one way more difficult than the choice before the vanquished. For the vanquished it may be counted noble and even wise if, in the name of justice or some other high principle, they reject all terms and choose the path of self-immolation. But for international law there is really no alternative to accommodation with the victor as to his terms for the vanquished. The victor will have whatever way his power (tempered by his conscience) gives him, whatever international law may do.

The effect, in these circumstances, of refusing the limited accommodation will be but to destroy in whole or in part the international legal order generally. And in the case of a war in which the greatest military states are involved, this would but make it all the easier for the victor to impose on the world a whole new legal order tailor-made to suit his own interests. Insofar as the international legal order exists to mitigate as far as possible the rigors of life among states, and not for its own sake, there can be neither virtue, wisdom, nor nobility, much less any duty, to destroy itself in a polite and futile protest against those rigors which it cannot mitigate. It has neither the right nor the duty to commit suicide, when suicide can only increase the rigors on states and peoples. For this would be to sacrifice such modicum of justice as the rules do as yet embody, to a demand for justice in circumstances intractable to present redress.

We are now perhaps in a position to grasp one of the deepest paradoxes which affect the relations of states and the international legal order as they bear upon the human future. In most national societies the legal order is flexible beneath the hand of the legislator, and not dependent for judgment or enforcement on the moment-to-moment consent of citizens. Yet it is normally stable and robust for three main reasons. First, because the legislator continually molds the law more or less to the majority demands; second, because there is a monopoly in the organs of the state of the major means of violence; and third, because at a pinch this public force will overwhelm the force marshaled by marginal demands which refuse to accept the legislator's law or his judge's judgment.

Only rarely, in most national societies, do the forces of these marginal demands reach dimensions which the public force cannot overwhelm. When this happens, the stable and robust national legal order breaks. A new legal order is substituted, whether by a dictator, a constituent assembly, or other revolutionary instrument. This breach in the continuity of the legal order is what we mean in the strictest sense by revolution, because the public monopoly of force is so critical in a national legal order that, when this monopoly is broken, the legal order is also broken. This is why revolution within a state is usually accompanied by violence or threat of violence; such a successful challenge to the state's monopoly of force breaks the legal order. Such events are cataclysmic for a national society; they can no more be felt as normal events than an earthquake in San Francisco or Tokyo or Chile. In stable societies, they are sufficiently rare that men learn to live as if they will never recur.

When we move over to the international legal order all is topsy-turvy. Here we have an order not flexible under the hand of a legislator, but held rigid in the grip of states whose joint consent is necessary for change. Here we have, instead of a stability and robustness founded on a public monopoly of force, an absence of any substantial public force and the persistence of great concentrations of military power in the private hands of states. Here at a pinch the public force cannot prevail over the private force wielded by any of a substantial number of the members of the community; it can attempt at the most to marshal some of these private forces against others for public ends. This being so, the international legal order, unlike the legal orders within our own states, is frequently confronted in hostile fashion by a superior, and indeed overwhelmingly superior, force of its own members.

We have seen that when this happens inside a state, the state legal order breaks down, and a new legal order is established by those who wield the superior force. Revolution breaks one national legal order and substitutes another. But since this happens comparatively rarely, national legal orders can be regarded as comparatively stable. And here comes our paradox. For in the *international* legal order this hostile encounter with overwhelming private force commanded by single member states is an everyday, or at least an every-year, occurrence. If, therefore, the pattern of the national legal order were here followed, the international legal order, and any norms of justice which support it, would have a moth-like existence, fluttering inevitably and precariously year by year into the destructive flame of power.

To avoid so shiftless an existence, the international legal order takes the extraordinary course of providing by its own rules for its collision with overwhelming power. It allows the military victor through the imposed treaty of peace to incorporate his dictated terms into the body of international law, thus preserving at any rate the rest of the rules and its own continued existence. By this built-in device, it incorporates into the legal order the net result of what otherwise would be an extra-legal, or even an illegal, revolution. International law, in short, legalizes even that scale of transformation and destruction of legal rights which in national legal systems can come about only from legal revolution. The municipal legal system breaks under these strains; the international legal system is not broken, it merely operates.

FOR SUCH limit-situations the related criteria of the justness or unjustness of war (whether offered as doctrines of the law of God or of the law of nature and nations) were not able to sustain themselves as either religious or social or specifically legal controls. The doctrine of "the just war" as formulated by St. Augustine and incorporated by Grotius into his design for a modern international law, has been the repository into our own times of many noble aspirations for a righteous and peaceful world order. The doctrine, whatever its limits, has always been more flexible than some modern theses of the absolute illegality of all exercise of violence by individual states, and even than those admitting exceptions for self-defense, for internationally authorized violence, or the like. Those limits, in the Grotian design, sought to build the standards of justice into the precepts of law concerning resort to violence between nations. The enterprise still awaits consummation.[12] Certainly, this part of the design did not establish

---

[12] On this see Stone, *Legal Controls*, esp. 13-14, 16-17; and generally Julius Stone, *Aggression and World Order* (1958) (hereafter cited as Stone, *Aggression*) and

itself in the practice of the chancelleries. And in the doctrinal stream it succumbed in the next century to the Vatellian restructuring of war as a relation which international law licensed states to establish between themselves, and in which the duty of third states was to maintain neutrality between the belligerents unless they, in turn, chose actually to enter into the relation.[13]

Even if the doctrine were to establish itself as a part of international law, as some still think it may and should, its effectiveness for the control of violence between individual states would remain problematic. It has been ably suggested, indeed, in recent notable reexaminations by Robert W. Tucker, that forms of the just-war doctrine are implicit in the policies and conduct of the nuclear giant states of our own times, and that as expounded and practiced by them, the actual tendency of use of the doctrine may be to increase rather than decrease both the number of occasions and the level of violence. And it has also been thought that the doctrine, as now addressed impartially to secular states by the second Vatican Council, with all its great religious and ethical prestige, cannot even yet be stated precisely enough to exclude each state's freedom to interpret the requirements of justice in a manner as likely as not to continue the escalation.[14]

To challenge the implications of such an analysis would prerequire that we can somehow reverse the menacing tendency of state power to mold to its purposes the nationally acceptable versions of truth and justice which underlie conflicting interpretations of the "justness" of particular causes of war. But even if, as all of us must devoutly hope, such a pre-requirement could be met, this would still leave most difficult problems to be faced in an effort to exclude gross injustices from becoming tolerated in international law. That law would still from time to time be confronted with limit-situations in which it would have to choose between three alternatives so dour that only the third remains as a kind of Hobson's choice. First, it might choose to immolate itself in resistance to the will of the victor with little prospect of gain for mankind. Or, second, it might choose to seek desperately for sufficient power to defeat every victor at the moment of victory. Or, third, it might choose (as it has done hitherto) to incorporate the victor's terms into the body of international law,

---

the masterly exposition in R. W. Tucker, *The Just War* (1960), Tucker and others, *The Just War and Vatican Council II: A Critique* (1966). See also L. K. Miller, "The Contemporary Significance of the Doctrine of Just War," *World Politics* 16 (1963) 254-86.

[13] Cf. Stone, *Legal Controls*, esp. 381-82.

[14] See Tucker, *The Just War*; and P. Ramsey's attempted rebuttal of Tucker's critique, same, 68-72. It does no doubt neglect the pastoral milieu to subject the Pastoral Constitution to a purely analytical scrutiny.

thus preserving at any rate the rest of its own rules and the possibility of its own future growth.

Despite redoubtable efforts, the International Law Commission, led by its eminent Special Rapporteurs on the Law of Treaties, Sir Hersch Lauterpacht (1953), Sir Gerald Fitzmaurice (1958), and Sir Humphrey Waldock (1963), has tracked no clear legal path through this limit-situation for international law and justice created by these obstinate facts of power.[15] Sir Gerald's draft respected these facts, and on this ground, while it provided for the case of duress exercised against a state's negotiators, it offered no provision as to duress exercised against the state itself. He observed rather cogently that "the same compulsion . . . that procured the conclusion of the treaty will ensure its execution; and by the time, if ever, that circumstances permit its repudiation, it will have been carried out, and many steps taken under it will be reversible, if at all, only by further acts of violence." Basically this is near to the writer's own position, though we have struggled to analyze it more fully. So that it is the position of the other two Rapporteurs which here require attention.

Sir Hersch proposed that treaties "imposed" by threat or use of force "in violation of the principles of the Charter of the United Nations are invalid if so declared by the International Court of Justice at the request of any State."[16]

The essence of his position, which surely cannot sustain itself, was his full disjunction between what he admitted to be the lessons of "experience," on the one hand, and what he regards as an adequate basis of legislative endeavour. The former (he admitted in his concluding Note) "shows that the nullification of treaties imposed by force takes place not in pursuance of a judicial verdict but of a political action taken in conformity with changed conditions of power." Yet almost in the next sentence he reasserted that it is nevertheless a sufficient basis for a proposal to nullify such treaties that the rule as to the admissibility of war as an instrument for enforcing and creating legal rights has been changed. But, of course, this change in the rule will not neutralize the above lesson of experience until somehow, either force has ceased to be used between states, or international law has acquired sufficient power to make theoretical nullification effective

15 See respectively, *Yearbook I.L.C.* ii (1953), 147-52; same, ii (1958), 26, 38-39; same, ii (1963), 50-52 and 197-98; and 61 *American Journal of International Law*, 406-09 and 438-41 (1967). (This last is reprinted from U.N.G.A.O.R. 21st Session, Suppl. No. 9, A/6309/Rev. 1.) These will be hereafter referred to, in the above order as the "1953 Report," "1958 Report," "Second 1963 Waldock Report" (i.e. page span 50-52), and "Third 1963 Waldock Report" (i.e. page span 197-98) and finally, the "1966 Report."

16 See 1953 Report at 147; and Sir Humphrey's summation of Sir Hersch's view in Second 1963 Waldock Report at 53.

against the victor whose power imposed the treaty. Further, of course, his proposal could never in fact operate unless the issue of nullity was decided by the International Court, and such decisions could not be made unless the jurisdiction was accorded to the Court by consent of the states affected. Sir Hersch Lauterpacht made no serious effort to indicate how any of these indispensable conditions for success of the Article could be met. And, of course, the limits of the Court's performance in disputes involving grave political issues surrounded by legal doubts, such as the *Goa* and *South-West Africa Cases*,[17] scarcely indicate easy outcomes, even if these difficulties could be overcome.

On the surface, Sir Humphrey Waldock's first draft of the pertinent article (contained in his Second 1963 Report) follows in Sir Hersch's rather than Sir Gerald's view, in affirming the avoidance of imposed treaties of the nature designated. There are also, however, rather radical differences underlying these general similarities between the 1963 Second Waldock Report and the 1953 Lauterpacht proposals. And when the full implications of these differences are drawn out, they also indicate that the Waldock proposals, even if implemented, would produce (despite what appears at first sight) only marginal departures from the position under traditional international law.

In the first place, it will be recalled, the 1953 proposals on this matter could not come into significant effect except on the assumption (obviously a most unlikely one) that most states (including the militarily strong ones were willing to accept the compulsory jurisdiction of the International Court of Justice on such rather critical matters. Under the 1953 proposal nullity, then, could not arise except on a declaration by the Court whose jurisdiction has been accepted. Under the instant 1963 proposal, declaration of nullity or qualified denunciation or affirmation is a wholly unilateral act by the victim state.

A second difference between the proposals yields some rather surprising results. Under the 1953 proposal not only the victim state, but any other state (and even against the wish of the victim state) would have been entitled to move the Court to declare nullity. Under the Waldock 1963 proposal here examined only the victim state can act (by its unilateral declaration) to affect the treaty's validity. This latter means that validity of a treaty imposed by an aggressive victor could under this draft never be impugned unless and *until the victim state is willing* to take this action. And if we attend to what "willing" here means, it obviously must import that the power relations between victor and victim have become such that the victim no longer remained exposed to further retaliatory oppression by the victor. It further imports, *as regards any transfers already made* under the imposed treaty,

[17] See Stone, "The South-West Africa Case and Apartheid," *The Australian* (September 1966), 27, 28, 29.

that the power relations are so changed, that the erstwhile victim *can effectively demand* restitution, or at least *make the victor state willing* to make restitution.

It will be observed that the effect of Sir Humphrey's ostensibly innovatory proposal would be to leave the legal rights of the victim and victor rather unchanged from those under traditional rule. Under what *appears* to be a rule nullifying imposed treaties there would be produced substantially the same position as in any case existing under the traditional rule that imposed treaties of peace are valid. In both cases, if and so long as important changes do not occur in the power situation, the treaty will remain in legal force. In both cases also, if and when such changes *do* occur, the legal validity of the treaty will be removed, and its effects undone, whether in whole or in part. It is true that under the above innovating proposal the change in validity and undoing of its effects would arise from a declaration by the victim state operative in law under it. It is also true that under the traditional rule the change in validity arises from renegotiation between victor and victim, or from a new factual trial of predominance between them. But the underlying and main determinant of whether there will be any change in the validity of the imposed terms, and of how much change, is in both cases obviously the same.

Waldock's proposals in his Second 1963 Report range themselves, then, with Sir Gerald Fitzmaurice's and the present writer's position on this whole matter, rather than with that of Sir Hersch whom he set out to follow. And this is confirmed in still another way when we take note of Sir Hersch's great pains in 1953 to break his proposal away from the traditional rule of validity of imposed treaties. He recognized that even under the traditional rule nullification of such treaties did take place, and did so "in conformity with changed conditions of power" (1953, p. 15 Note, para. 2). It was to break from this that he gave a decisive voice to the International Court of Justice. This, and his insistence that acquiescence by the victim state could not prevent any third state from moving the Court to nullify the treaty, were of the essence of his rejection of the traditional rule. By leaving the challenge to validity wholly and solely to the victim state, Waldock is flatly rejecting those very features of the Lauterpacht proposal which in that writer's eyes, and in actual fact, are of the essence of its departure from the traditional law.

While *in its major lines*, therefore, the instant Waldock formula was a kind of tour de force, whereby the traditional rule of validity of imposed treaties was reaffirmed and endorsed in a treaty form only superficially novel, certain *marginal* novel effects can perhaps be detected. The most important of these relates to the degree of change in the power situation which is likely to mature into full or partial nullification of the imposed treaty. As regards those terms of the treaty which are not yet executed, for instance as to transfers of land or resources due but not yet made, a victim state under Waldock's "innovating" rule would be in a position to declare nullity as soon *as it approached* parity of power with its former victor. It could be argued that, contrarily, under the traditional rule of validity, the power of the victim state necessary in fact to compel the former victor to renegotiate must be more substantial. The legal act which alters the legal situation here requires more than the unilateral decision of the victim state. It requires negotiation which, in turn, implies sufficient power in the victims to induce active concurrence by the former dominator. Even if this argument were sustainable, however, the difference it would yield would still be only slight and uncertain. And it would be a serious question whether, in order to bring about so slight and uncertain an effect, it would be worthwhile to introduce into international law a wide-ranging new power of states to bring into doubt unilaterally the provisions of so important a class of treaties, with no provision for third party resolution of the resulting doubts. In assessing the gravity of these effects, we have to remember that the proposed power of unilateral nullification under the Second 1963 Report was only to arise when the force which imposed the treaty is unlawful under the Charter. For no informed authority can *reasonably* say that the exact limits of the lawful threat or use of force under the Charter is free from serious controversy.

As to such advantages as have already been physically seized and are now held by the aggressor-victor, or have been transferred to him under the terms of an imposed treaty, there would not appear to be even the above amount of difference of effect between Waldock's proposal and the traditional rule that imposed treaties are valid. Under neither can it be expected that restitution will *in fact* be made except under the pressure of a pronounced swing of power predominance to the victim state. In law, of course, insofar as items of such property involved move out of the physical control of the victor state into that of a third state, the courts of that third state may, if the new Convention is in force and applicable, adjudge it to the victim state. So, too, if an international tribunal came to have compulsory jurisdiction over the parties in respect of the subject-matter. Yet such contingencies are so casual and slight at the present phase of international relations as again to raise the doubts discussed in the last paragraph.

So that, finally, the main point which Sir Hersch and Sir Humphrey shared in the discussed drafts of 1953 and 1963 is a rather Platonic point. This is that no practical difficulties should prevent the elevation of the principle of nullity of the treaties in question to "the dignity of "a general principle of law recognized by civilized states" (Lauterpacht, 1953, para. 6), which "derives from the most fundamental provisions of the Charter" (Second 1963 Waldock Report, at 51).

In its post-1963 development Sir Humphrey Waldock's draft of the coercion of state article (formerly Article 12, then Article 36, and finally, in the 1966 draft, Article 49) was simplified further. As Article 49 it reads: "A treaty is void if its conclusion has been procured by the threat or use of force in violation of the principles of the Charter of the United Nations." While in general the Special Rapporteur seemed to maintain the positions in his Second 1963 Report, the revised text and comment show some important changes, not all of which may have been intended.[18]

In the first place, instead of requiring "nullification" to be declared by the coerced state, the new draft and its comment insist that the treaty is void without any step being taken by that or any other state. One effect might seem to be to bring the draft nearer to Sir Hersch Lauterpacht's original proposal of 1953, that any state whatsoever might apply to the International Court for a declaration of nullity. For, under this change the treaty, under the new Article 49, may be null even if the coerced state does not ask and does not even wish for this. Yet this apparent resemblance is ironically deceptive. For while in theory the Waldock draft leaves the treaty null without the need of any step by *any* state, it is difficult to see how in practice any state could assert its nullity unless the allegedly coerced state chose to do so.

The Waldock 1966 comment asserts indeed that any treaty within the article would be void *ab initio* even if the coerced state wished the treaty to operate. The plausible ground offered is that "this would enable the State concerned to take its decision," on a basis of "full legal equality" whether, if it wished those terms to continue in force, to conclude a new treaty of similar terms. (Comment, para. 6.) Yet, since this Waldock draft, unlike the Lauterpacht 1953 draft, provides no forum for determining when a treaty is null,[19] the net effect

[18] See 1966 Report at 406.

[19] Article 62 of the 1966 Draft concerning procedures of notice and the like for cases involving *inter alia* "invalidity" and "termination" of a treaty, has little or no bearing on this point. Not only do procedures involving notice seem irrelevant to the case of treaties whose voidity was declared, with extreme emphasis, to be *ab initio*. The Rapporteur's emphasis (it is recalled) was carried so far as to say that even if the victim state did not wish to void the treaty and indeed desired its continuance, the treaty would still be void. The victim would (he said) have to negotiate a new one with similar terms. It would certainly be inconsistent with this to say that voidity for duress under Article 49 is in some way conditional on fulfilment of the procedures of Article 62.

Moreover, if voidity under Article 49 were subject to the procedures of Article 62, this would also not affect the critique in the text. For the procedures of Article 62, paras. 1 and 2, even if they applied, do but set into motion processes which

must surely still be to leave to the victim state the liberty to raise or not to raise the plea of nullity. The only escape from this would be if it were always likely to be self-evident and agreed among the states affected whether a treaty fell within the article. Yet the Special Rapporteur is insistent that it is not only the presence of threat or use of force (which might be *comparatively* self-evident), but also violation thereby of "the principles of the United Nations," which are necessary for the article to apply. It is no doubt correct that Article 2 (4) prohibits the threat or use of force. It may also be said that this is a *"clear-cut"* prohibition (as the Rapporteur seems to be saying in para. 1 of his Comment) *within whatever may be the scope of Article 2, para. 4.* Sir Humphrey himself drew attention however (1966, para. 3 of Comment to Article 49) to the doubts surrounding the question whether the prohibition therein extends to less obvious *forms of coercion* than the merely physical, for example to "economic strangulation." And he should perhaps also have referred to even graver, as well as sharper and more complex, legal controversies as to the *range of circumstances in which* that prohibition operates, and therefore the entire application of Article 2 (4) to concrete cases of use of force. In the light of these doubts it must be said that the scope of the new Article 49 so far from being "clear-cut," is really profoundly obscure.

This obscurity represents a veritable Achilles' heel of Waldock's 1966 draft. Insofar as it exists, a cloud of doubt would be cast on the one hand, over a wide range of treaties, with no forum usually available either to clear it or to precipitate it into legal nullity. On the other hand, insofar as this last is so, it would usually fall to the allegedly coerced state to determine whether to confront its alleged oppressor with the plea of nullity. Its decision on this matter would necessarily be determined, in existing international conditions by considerations of power relations. The effects, then, would not be significantly different from those operative under customary law where the imposed

---

can only go beyond mere bilateral or multilateral diplomatic negotiation *if all the parties so agree.* Such mere negotiation would be an available recourse, even without Article 62; and its outcome would, under Article 62, depend on the realities of power just as much as under the traditional rule by which imposed treaties were valid, and changeable only by negotiation of a new treaty. Nor does Article 62 para. 3, providing for recourse to Article 33 of the United Nations Charter, thereby afford any forum competent of deciding the issue independently of the *ad hoc* consent of all parties at variance.

Finally, Article 62, para. 4, seems to make clear in so many words that the procedures described in that Article shall *not* affect (not merely, be it noted, shall not *prejudice*) "rights and obligations" of the parties with regard to "settlement of disputes" under *"any* provisions in force." So that even if we could plausibly read some designation of a competent forum into the preceding paragraphs (which we cannot) para. 4 would destroy this plausibility, and leave us still confronted by the difficulties raised in the text.

treaty is valid, but will if the power relations change sufficiently be renegotiated or denounced.[20]

There is another irony here. This relates to so-called "unequal treaties" when juxtaposed with the treaties imposed by duress just discussed. In relation to the latter, all three Rapporteurs, with their deeply divergent philosophies, seemed to agree in one respect. This was that the risks to general stability of treaty relations imported by a rule nullifying duress-induced treaties, would be least in the case of the extreme physical duress of military defeat. Correspondingly, they seem to agree that risks become greater as lesser pressures and coercions become involved, such as the merely economic and political. Sir Gerald Fitzmaurice's statement went straight to the present point. The argument for nullification, he thought, "must evidently be confined to the use or threat of *physical* force, since there are all too numerous ways in which a state might allege that it had been induced to enter into a treaty by pressure of some kind (for example, economic) ." If it were extended to the latter less gross situations "a dangerously wide door to the invalidation of treaties, and hence a threat to the stability of the treaty-making process, would be opened." Hence, if introduction of a nullity rule should be considered at all, it should "obviously" be "confined to the gross situations."[21] So, Sir Humphrey, too,[22] denied that a rule of nullification would unduly disturb the security of international treaties "unless 'coercion' is extended to cover other acts than the use or threat of force." If the nullifying invalidity were "confined to treaties procured by the use or threat of force," the danger of abuse would not be excessive. Other forms of pressure (he thought) "are much less capable of definition and much more liable to subjective appreciations." Moreover, the use of political and economic pressures are part of "the normal working of relations between States," and no criteria are available for drawing the line between the legitimate and illegitimate use of such pressures. It would thus be unsafe to extend nullification to any coercion "beyond the illegal use of force."[22a] The point was also clearly present though not

[20] Beside these rather old-fashioned difficulties, the points of real novelty in the 1966 Report are insignificant, even if technically interesting. One is that the Article was not to affect the validity *ab initio* of a coerced treaty entered into before "the modern law regarding the threat or use of force was established." This "modern law" at the latest came into effect with Article 2 (4) of the Charter; but the Special Rapporteur left it open as to whether it might not have come into effect earlier, and if so, when. On this most controversial issue see Stone, *Legal Controls*, 298-300, 324-27, and literature there cited.

[21] See 1958 Report, para. 62 at 38.

[22] See Second 1963 Waldock Report at 52.

[22a] At the first session of the Diplomatic Conference on the Law of Treaties, Vienna 1968, the interested delegations nevertheless made a *démarche* against this view of all the Rapporteurs. The Committee of the Whole adopted a draft declaration, to be included in the Final Act, condemning "the threat or use of pressure in any form,

so explicit in Lauterpacht's position (1953 Report, p. 149). He is careful to limit his proposed nullification to cases of "physical force or threats of force as distinguished from coercion not amounting to physical force." Even then he admitted that the borderline between was "not rigid," and that the nullifying coercion was not limited to compulsion resulting from war or "other use of direct physical force." It was precisely this uncertain line which led him to insist, in his own draft, that nullification could only be by the International Court. Without this (he thought) a nullification rule would have "disintegrating force in the treaty relations between States."

The Soviet Union's leaders have, as seen above, insisted on the binding force of treaties of peace imposed with the extreme of coercion and inequality. The deepest point of the present irony is reached when Soviet representatives and writers concurrently argue that treaties entered into under coercion, or of an "enslaving" nature, or otherwise disregarding the equality principle, or not corresponding to a state's "real will," are thereby void under international law.[23] No doubt it could be argued in resolution of the apparent conflict that the settlements which Khrushchev and Kosygin admitted were imposed by force and insisted could only be changed by force, were not imposed by *unlawful* force. It could also be said that even such as were based on arguably "unlawful" use of force (like the "absorption" of the Baltic States by the Soviet Union), were at the relevant time (prior to the coming into force of the United Nations Charter) not technically unlawful. Neither of these arguments, however, would dispose of problems of violation of the Kellogg-Briand Pact or the League Covenant itself, by such clear suppressions by force of both the territorial integrity and political independence of the states concerned.

A recent writer[24] has well pointed out that a criterion based on "inequality" as such would catch far too wide a range of treaties to serve as a criterion of such voidity. Some selection among "unequal" treaties is tacitly assumed by the campaign against "unequal" treaties;

---

military, political or economic, by any State in order to coerce another State to perform any act relating to the conclusion of a treaty in violation of the principles of sovereign equality of States and freedom of consent." (U.N. Press Release L/1854, Apl. 3, 1969, p. 2.) The *démarche*, however, when we try to give it legal meaning, confirms rather than weakens the position it attacks.

[23] See the valuable discussion in Ingrid Detter, "The Problem of Unequal Treaties," 15 *International and Comparative Law Quarterly*, 1068 at 1081-85 (hereafter cited as Detter, "Unequal Treaties"). Many of the comments of the Soviet Union and other Socialist countries were directed to the extension (or even translation) of the coercion article into terms of "leonine" treaties, e.g., certain ones accompanying grant of independence or economic aid. See, e.g., U.S.S.R., Bulgaria, Byelorussia, Czechoslovakia in A/CN 4/183 Add.1, pp. 9, 6, 3. Cf. these same states in A/CN 4/175 at pp. 264, 256.

[24] Detter, "Unequal Treaties," 1086-88.

but no objective means has been offered of delimiting those inequalities which avoid a treaty, from those which do not. Assertions of the voidity of "unequal" treaties thus simply vacillate between some imprecisely indicated *kind of* inequality, or some imprecisely indicated *kind of* coercion or inducement, or combination of these.

The more important point, however, is still that the imposed treaty of peace, on the validity of which Soviet practice rather indiscriminately insists, generally manifests *both inequality and coercion* in extreme forms. So that no *objective* criterion based on *the mere degree* of either or both of these elements can really explain the Soviet position, either. It thus becomes hard to avoid the conclusion that such elements when offered to support the Soviet thesis that "unequal" treaties are void, must be understood merely as referring to whatever treaties the protagonist, from his standpoint,[25] regards as too "unjust" to be tolerated. While thus rather strangely inadvertent to its full impact on the Soviet-type position, Miss Detter does correctly identify the central puzzle. This is that insofar as the validity of imposed treaties of peace "has never been put in question," the International Law Commission's proposal to make force or threat of force a ground of nullity, which is wide enough to invalidate most treaties of peace, would constitute "a complete innovation in international law." It is true, of course, that these proposals have been predicated on the *unlawfulness* of the coercion, and not on the coercion as such. But this increases the present paradox. For none of the many Soviet *bloc*, African, and Asian proposals for voidity of "unequal" treaties, include any similar additional requirement of unlawfulness in their inducement.[26] We have seen that inequality *simpliciter* will not do as a ground of avoidance; so that coercion in inducement must also be an element in avoidance of "unequal" treaties. If so, why should *unlawfulness* of the coercion be a necessary element for avoidance of the most oppressive and severely coerced treaty of peace, and yet not required at all for the presumably less severe coercions inducing "unequal" treaties?

Our present concern, however, is not to form any final view on the issues concerning "unequal treaties" (however defined), but with the relation of these to the limit situation set for the judgment of justice by the imposed treaty of peace. In relation to this, the controversy whether the *clausula rebus sic stantibus* provides an indirect means of release of the weaker party to "unequal treaties" (including imposed treaties of peace) is seen in a deeper, less sanguine, light. It

---

25 As when the examples offered are "treaties of assistance" which "in reality" secure "colonial rights," or agreements for military bases involving "surrender" of sovereignty; or agreements made as the "price" of freedom. The nonobjective evaluation is merely concealed in such emotive words as "colonial," "surrender," "price."

26 See n. 18.

is the same light in which both the doctrine and practice as to imposed treaties, from the classical writers to the latest Soviet utterances, cast the post-World War II arrangements in Europe. The decisive *res* which are *sic stantes* are then seen as the very power relations which established the status quo. And it is above all in this de facto sense, rather than in any merely technical legal one, that the status quo may be said to change with the *res* on which they rest.

Miss Detter's recent article was, of course, ostensibly directed to "unequal treaties" *other than* imposed treaties of peace. She felt free, accordingly, to seek a governing rule without making the very inquiry which for us here is crucial. This is as to why a rule which is the very opposite to what she finally supports for the lesser injustice of "unequal" treaties, is so unquestionable for the more outrageous injustice involved in the traditional rule of the validity of imposed treaties of peace. She seeks a criterion of invalidity for these less outrageously unjust treaties neither in the element of coercion, nor of inequality in negotiation, but in "extreme" inequality *as manifest in the contents* of the treaty in question. A treaty of complete surrender of sovereignty and extinction of the weaker party (she thinks) should be void; treaties manifesting equality in contents short of this should be avoidable at the instance of that party. Avoidance (she thinks) should be made before an international body, preferably in the General Assembly or "a non-political (sic!) subcommittee" of it, and decision "possibly by a majority vote."[27]

However admirable their objectives, such proposals ignore the real problems. Treaties of complete surrender of sovereignty will usually have been induced by dire coercion and even conquest. As to these it is difficult, as she herself seems to recognize concerning the imposed treaty of peace, to see how (short of some radical change in power relations) it can be avoided by the presumably extinct state. (Presumably she would not want to make void a mere voluntary merger of one political entity into another, analogous to that of Newfoundland into the Dominion of Canada.) As to "unequal treaties" of minor degree, which she would place in the "voidable" category, she has herself admitted (at 1807) that not all literally unequal treaties can be within it, since even the most impeccable treaties cannot "give all contracting parties the same profits." As already seen, she was also compelled to reject coercion in inducement as a possible criterion. So that, in the end, no criterion for distinguishing acceptable from unacceptable inequalities of contents, nor any other criterion for delimiting voidable from valid treaties in this regard has been offered by her or any other writers.

[27] Detter, "Unequal Treaties," 1086-89.

In these circumstances, her proposals amount to giving to the General Assembly a roving commission over practically all treaties, for these are almost always, like contracts are in municipal society, *open to the charge* that one party got the better bargain. In addition to the main thesis herein as to the limit-situations with which imposed treaties of peace confront both international law and justice, three other comments need to be made. One is that in international (as in municipal) society, we cannot base the judgment of justice on equality alone.[28] Another is that the time is obviously distant when any important group of states (except perhaps, for obvious reasons, some of the newer African states) would ever grant to the General Assembly or any other United Nations organ such a roving commission to probe and declare void any treaty they have made. Nor is it pleasant to contemplate the mixture of pandemonium and Tower of Babel which would arise if such a miracle did in fact occur.[29]

Unless the present volume is treated as referring to a future international legal order toward which no signs as yet point in actual international life, this gross and lamentable conflict of international legal bindingness with justice must be recognized as insoluble by merely legal invention.[30] The heart of the matter lies not in technical niceties about the effect of duress in vitiating treaties, but in the overall problem of regulating the use of coercion in international relations.[31] And in this regard we must say that, while international law may from time to time diminish the attractiveness of particular procedures and modes of violence and warfare among nations, the crucial determinants in the decisions relating to coercion between states seem still to lie outside the ambit of effective legal regulation. No

---

[28] See generally Stone, *Human Justice*, 325-35.

[29] The above critique is directed to the general concepts thus far offered to delimit treaties to be declared void. It does not exclude the possibility of delimiting more concrete classes of treaties to be void or voidable, *per se*, as it were. Such might be (without offering these as necessarily warranted, or adequately drafted) post-colonial treaties limiting a new state's opportunities of developing its overseas trade or conducting its foreign relations freely; or treaties involving a substantially total alienation (for instance under pressure of immediate distress) of a nation's economic assets; or concessions to a foreign state or other entity, manifesting what Roman law would have called *laesio enormis*, or gross inadequacy of the *quid pro quo*. Such precepts, by concreteness in their framing, could avoid both futile attempts to control uncontrollable limit-situations of power, and criteria (such as "unequal") which cast an excessive cloud over treaty law generally.

[30] Even if the thesis of J. W. Burton, *International Relations* (1965) as to the inadequacy of "power" as the main focus of concern had some general, long-term validity, it could not affect the present point. Nor can the noblest pacifism subdue it; see recently from a reflecting pacifist standpoint, J. Folliet, "A Dissection of Pacificism," *World Justice* 2 (1960-61), 162-77.

[31] The point was clearly made by Sir Gerald Fitzmaurice in his 1958 Report; and see Sir Humphrey Waldock's summation of it in Second 1963 Waldock Report, n. 15.

doubt events since World War II have checked the resort to *full scale* conventional war and even to nuclear war. But it is dubious whether this is the effect of the Charter rather than of nuclear retaliatory threat; and in any case international coercion has been rather sublimated into internal war, fostered by subversion and aid from outside powers. And some of the now *crucial* distinctions, for example between mere *intervention* in a civil war, and armed attacks on a state, have become (as the controversy concerning the bombing of North Vietnam, shows) rather remotely related to ideas of justice. Furthermore, concurrently with this reduction in grade of violence actually used, the highest grade of violence based on proliferating nuclear weapon technology constantly operates as the ultimate coercive "argument." The key to the containment of coercion (including threats of major coercion), in short, still lies in international politics rather than international law.[32]

WE DO NOT intend by all this to overlook our vastly increased moral responsibilities to perform important, even if not life-and-death, tasks. We must learn to acknowledge the finite limits of international law's capacity to contribute to the banishment of injustice from the relations of states. The unavoidable frustrations of history should not be allowed to weaken the search for feasible next steps, nor self-righteousness our will to understand and accommodate, nor dreams and yearnings our patience and will to wait.

The publicist critique and hedging of unjust law with appeals to conscience is, of course, rather repugnant to the positivist climate of thought. At least as a trans-individual phenomenon "conscience" is no longer respectable either philosophically or psychologically, though no doubt the fact of resort to it should still be grist to the mill of behavioral social science. It should also continue to be of interest to the student of international law and politics as the form through which ideas about international justice have expressed themselves. After all this is admitted, its overall impact today, outside the ethico-religious, political, and social milieu of its initial expression, is that of an anachronistic and even ethical curiosity.

One central factor in this change has been the general disappearance of the personal monarch and his domain as the prototype of the

---

[32] See in general Stone, *Aggression*; and same, "What Price Effectiveness?" and "Realistic Compliance Goals" in *Proceedings of the American Society of International Law* (1956), 198, and (1964), 24 respectively.

The issues arising from Article 35 of the Draft, rendering of no effect consent given on behalf of states by individual representatives coerced by "acts or threats directed against them in their personal capacities," are of course different and have not in the past been subject to the same difficulties. Para. 2 of Article 35 allows the aggrieved state to sever the tainted provisions if, under Article 47, they are severable in principle. On the meaning of "acts or threats" under Article 35, see Sir Humphrey Waldock, n. 16.

state. The "conscience" of European monarchs during the formative era of international law was relatively homogeneous, with shared values springing from relatively common religious and cultural traditions. States of political democratic form have, since the French and American revolutions, become increasingly complex and opaque. Often enough the key actors are not identifiable, and when they are identifiable, constitute an elite group in which those who influence decisions are not necessarily those who make them. The conscience appealed to would have to be a group conscience. Assuming such a notion to be sensible at all, the dictates of personal conscience would normally be blunted, if not wholly canceled, by the anonymity within it. Certainly no group conscience has prevented the impersonal state entity gaining its modern quasi-supernatural accouterments, nor (still increasingly) the power to mold national versions of truth and justice to whatever it adopts as its ends of action. And the very tendency toward "nationalization" of values is, of course, a flat negation of any decisive modern influence of "conscience," as the natural lawyers conceived this.

So far as we may admit, especially with the newer states of Asia and Africa, that the "conscience" of the leadership is less manipulated, the value of the notion is still undermined in other ways. Their admission to the community of states has constituted a creative infusion of many important and varied cultures of mankind. In the result, the massive accompanying diversification of religious and speculative traditions, makes it even more difficult to postulate some converging multinational conscience. Even when we have allowed for a degree of isomorphic religious and cultural tendencies within particular traditions or regions, such as Hinduism, Judaism, Islamism, and Christianity, or Asia and Europe, or East and West, little obvious guidance to the precepts of international law and justice springs from the "conscience" of the leaders of modern states.[33]

The difficulties of placing the notion of conscience into the service of the modern tasks of international justice comparably to its specific role in the traditions of international law and diplomacy are thus apparent enough. We may be dispensed, therefore, from examination of the very serious philosophical problems which also affect it. Is conscience innate, acquired, or in some degrees both? And if so in what precise sense? Is conscience a cognitive, emotive, or connative faculty? Or again, how does the conscience reconcile two of its own dictates when these appear to conflict? Can we speak of a group conscience

[33] See Julius Stone (ed.), *Indian Traditions and the Rule of Law Among Nations* (1960, being the Report of the All India Seminar on the Possible Contributions of Indian Traditions Concerning the Relations of Major Organised Groups to Contemporary Problems of International Law, published by University of Delhi). There is a summary and critique by D. Derett in *International and Comparative Law Quarterly*, 266 (1962).

at all? If so in what sense? The comparative neglect of such questions, even by modern ethicists themselves, no doubt testifies to the search in other directions for more acceptable bases of ethical obligation.[34] It is unnecessary for our present purposes to take any position as to the residual significance of the concept of conscience for the daily life of today's individuals, and as to whether it must be regarded as wholly abandoned for future ethical theory.

III. Of the Equality of Nations Doctrine
and International Justice

No inquiry about international justice can ignore the tangled story of the doctrine of equality of states. It is tempting, indeed, to infer from the rather limited guidance of the equality principle in municipal law thinking about justice that the doctrine of equality of states is more likely to lead us to different statements of problems, than to solutions.[35] Yet the rather specific history of international law, and the rather specific role of the equality doctrine in it, suggest that the political and sociological role of the doctrine may be of major importance. The existing literature tends to be analytical or historical;[36] and in the absence of definitive work on its political and sociological role, we can here at least attempt to sketch what may be involved.

In major respects the doctrine of equality repeats here the maneuvers familiar in municipal law. The equivocations which affect it are, however, even more numerous and interesting, and perhaps still more fruitful. For present purposes we can distinguish a clustering of no less than four equivocations each comprising pairs of ideas, and between these pairs (and within each of them) the use of the doctrine may swing in meaning, with striking differences of effect. There is, first, the swing between equality before the law of all *legal* persons (that is, persons recognized by law, and thus not embracing slaves in municipal law or "dependent" nations in international law), and the equality of all *"natural"* persons (that is, human beings in municipal and nations in international law). There is, second, even for the class of legal persons supposedly equal before the law, the equivocation between equal entitlement *to such rights as the law confers on* them, and the meaning that all are entitled in a substantive sense *to*

---

[34] But see recently P. Fuss, "Conscience" 74 *Ethics* (1963-64), 111-20; A. J. Bahm, "Theories of Conscience" 75 *Ethics* (1964-65), 128-31.

[35] On the principle of equality in relation to justice in national societies, see Stone, *Human Justice*, passim, esp. 325-35.

[36] We have in mind, in particular: (1) E. D. Dickinson, *The Equality of States in International Law* (1920); (2) J. Goebel, Jr., "The Equality of States" (pts. 1-3) 23 *Columbia Law Review*, 1, 113, 247 (1923), (later published in book form); and (3) P. H. Kooijmans, *The Doctrine of the Legal Equality of States* (1964). These will be hereafter cited by surname of author only.

equal rights. (This equivocation is also expressible as a contrast between equality before the law and factual and political inequality.) Third (as a special international law variation of this last, and thus worthy of separate attention), is the equivocation of which one side, the formal one, sees the equality of states as an aspect of state sovereignty, the reasoning being that entities each of which is deemed to be "supreme" but all of which coexist in one world must by this very fact be equal.[37] The other side of this pair is similar to that in the second equivocation, namely, equality of rights in a substantive sense; and it is mainly the complex relations surrounding the notion of sovereignty which has required separate treatment of this third equivocation. Fourth, the doctrine of equality of nations, if sought to be used as a basic principle of justice, draws in the perplexities of determining whether the claimants and beneficiaries of international justice consist of states, or whether they consist of the human beings who in their respective politically organized societies constitute these states.

The cluster of equivocations is amply nourished by two notable features of the history of international legal doctrines. For the classical writers, and indeed in a manner of talking which persisted almost until the nineteenth century, "sovereignty" and often statehood itself tended to be attributed to the personal monarch to whom the realm was deemed to belong.[38] So that when, for instance, the old writers spoke of duties of conscience, they meant the conscience *of a human being*, albeit the monarch. Moreover, insofar as the classical writers founded international legal rights and duties upon natural law, they proceeded by an analysis, more or less empirically sound, of the supposed rational and social nature of man, or in some cases of his *imbecilitas*, his inability to manage except by mutual respect and helpfulness vis-à-vis others. And, however artificial some of these analyses might become, the concepts which were the starting points of analysis were concepts pertaining to individual human beings. So that when, after a century and a half in which positivist theories struggled to substitute "the state" as their conceptual starting point, the title of individual human beings as claimants and beneficiaries of international justice is now agitated in our own times, the questions raised are not wholly new. They rather attach themselves, though

---

[37] Detter, "Unequal Treaties," is still inadvertent to these equivocations. She identified equality with an "inference" from "the idea of sovereignty" (1070, and see under "Third Equivocation"); and for the rest distinguishes only forensic equality" and equality in "exercise" of rights, relying in this respect on A. D. McNair, "Equality in International Law," 26 *Michigan Law Review*, 134-42 at 136 (1927).

[38] The assertions in this paragraph concern the dominant moods of publicist discourse, rather than any *invariable* usage by the writers concerned, and (of course) rather than the historical state of affairs in post-medieval Western societies.

not without great confusions, to many ideas agitated by the natural law antecedents of modern international law.

We shall, where material, have to refer to some of these as we explore the bearing of the rich history of the equality of states doctrine upon the present inquiry concerning international justice.[39] We acknowledge, of course, that the doctrine is in some sense a cardinal principle of contemporary international *law*, despite such modern inroads such as the privileged decision-making position of the permanent members of the Security Council. These no doubt increase the difficulties (in any case very great) of delimiting the sense in which the doctrine is law. But since our prime concern here is not with international law as it is, but with international justice, we are happily dispensed from most of these difficulties.

First Equivocation

The reference in the first equivocation swings, as we have seen, between equality of states and equality of certain natural persons or aggregates of such (for instance nations). When the reference is to the former, that is, to equality between states, to aggregates endowed with international legal personality, this is immediately of great negative importance to justice. For it excludes from legal entitlement all entities not yet so endowed. Insofar as protection by law is necessary for justice, this negative aspect imports a dispersed denial of justice to these other men or aggregates of men. When those excluded clamor for justice, the clamor tends to be for admission under the equality principle to the class of international legal persons. And it is in this connection that the present equivocation shows its fertile, creative side. It was easier, for example, for Vitoria to plead for justice to the indigenous South American peoples, by asserting that all "nations" *were* equally within the protection of international law under some principle like the equality of nations, than to argue that *in justice they ought to be brought within this protection.* So, in modern times, the "right" of self-determination, and the "principle" of anticolonialism, play similar roles, hovering between an assertion of law and a demand for justice.

This second reference of the present equivocation, which operates as a demand for justice upon law, may also (and perhaps best) be understood as a reaction to the negative implications of the first reference. Insofar as its demand succeed, the successful claimants become entitled as beneficiaries of the principle of equality of states under the first reference. They become legal persons whose battles for justice may now be fought with the weapons of international law.

[39] Goebel's outstanding work deserves greater attention than it has so far received on this aspect. See citation n. 36.

But, of course, other less successful entities still clamoring for justice remain excluded. Ordinarily, as with admission to other privileges, the *nouveau venu* will take his place alongside the old members in resisting the clamor of later aspirants to admission. But sometimes, as with most of today's emancipated colonial peoples, the successful new entrants become a kind of bloc lobbying for peoples still excluded, motivated both by principle and by the self-regarding aim of enhancing the voting power of like-minded states.

Once we see the creative virtue of the second reference of the equivocation under discussion, we are struck by a further paradox emerging from the chaos of debate. If we are inclined to regard international law as now entering a new phase, extending to twice the number of former states, we can interpret the consequences in terms of the equality principle thus. The increase in number of claimants and beneficiaries (states), proceeds from clamor of formerly excluded peoples in title of the equality-before-the-law principle. Equality is, as it were, a progenitor of the increased number of states. But these later admitted states are mostly, in the nature of the situation, less strong, less well-endowed, and less organizationally skilled, than the older states. This means that, *by their admission*, the range of *de facto* variations (that is, of inequalities in the material or political sense) tends to be increased. (We disregard, for the present purpose, older states, like Luxembourg or Monaco, which are generally and correctly regarded somewhat as curiosities, thrown up as products of power relations between other particular states.) We then have the intriguing paradox that the equality principle is at once a chief progenitor and a most troublesome problem-child of the international order. It has helped to transform a "world" order arrested at some line such as "Christendom," or "the civilized world," into one more fully horizoned. Yet this very transformation, by swelling the number of state-entities with newly admitted states from among weaker and less-privileged peoples, also deeply aggravated the problems of reducing material inequalities between states to acceptable levels.

This accentuation of *material inequalities* between states *equal before the law* is only the most troublesome of the problem-children of the creative second limb of this first equivocation. Another arises when insistence on the entitlement of all nations to equality before international law (in the sense of full legal personality or participation) *is pushed to extremes*. This produces an extension of the principle of self-determination of nations to a point which cannot be objectively delimited.[40] The guidance to justice from the principle, at

[40] Well manifest, of course, in the Declaration on the Granting of Independence to Colonial Countries and Peoples, in G.A. Resolution 1514 (XV). See also, on re-

best always open to political abuse, then tends to disappear alto-gether. To make present *dependence*, whether in title of the equality principle or otherwise, a sufficient ground for insisting on immediate *independence*, regardless of the will or ability of the particular people to be thrown on its own resources, puts the principle of equality in critical tension with the idea of justice.[41] For while independence is no doubt every people's ultimate rightful destiny, the justice of termi-nating (in the above sense) the responsibilities of particular more ad-vanced states to afford guidance and support, depends upon the tem-poral situation. Premature demands (when made in good faith) are consistent with an extreme interpretation of the principle of equality; when not made in good faith such demands may also serve well the military or political objectives of other states. In either case, however (and this is the point), what is consistent with equality still involves, at such a stage, a gross injustice to peoples who are not yet ready to be cast loose to control their own fate. The self-determination principle, thus inspired by an extreme version of the equality of *nations* prin-ciple, turns the grant of statehood into an imposition rather than an emancipation.[42]

The second problem-child of the equality principle brings forth its own, a problem *grand*-child. For indeterminacy of application, having thus opened the way for extraneous and extraneously motivated pres-sures to force a spurious legal independence which cannot in fact

---

lated aspects, G.A. Resolution 626 (VII) on National Sovereignty over National Resources. See other related U.N. and other declarations during and after World War II, collected in Detter, "Unequal Treaties," 1067, 1071-72.

[41] This should not be concealed by assertions of "the nation's subjective right, as already a juridical person, to pass from the larval to the more perfect State" (A. Bonnichon, "The Principle of Nationalities and Implied Ethical Requirements," *World Justice*, 7 (1965-66), 22-23. For a sharp critique of the irremediable in-determinacy of the self-determination principle, and of its consequent abuse in political warfare, see F. Peters, "The Right of Nations to Auto-Determination," *World Justice*, 4 (1962-63), 161-79. And on the related needs for a transitional phase of international cooperation between decolonization and independence, see F. Vito, ". . . Economic, Social and Cultural Transformation of the New African States," *World Justice*, 2 (1960-61), 147-62.

[42] As would be the case if the premature "anti-colonialist" pressure for early independence of Papua and East New Guinea succeeded. This would be imposed more on the indigenous peoples than on Australia and would yield nonviable state entities impairing prospects of later viability, and adding meanwhile to the in-stabilities of international politics. See Dr. Bowett's point that self-determination has "wider ramifications" than "decolonization," and Dr. Emerson's seminal identi-fication of the various "incarnations" of the self-determination principle. See D. W. Bowett, "Self-Determination and Political Rights in the Developing Countries"; R. Emerson, "Self-Determination," both in *Proceedings American Society of Interna-tional Law* 1966, 129-31, 131-41 respectively. See also on the problem of "mini-States," Margaret Broderick, "Associated Statehood: A New Form of Decolonization," 17 *International & Comparative Law Quarterly*, 368-403 (1968), Philip M. Allen, "Self-Determination in the Western Indian Ocean," *International Conciliation* No. 560 (1966).

be sustained, also opens the way to arbitrary subjection of some peoples' right of self-determination to that of others. Such manipulations are foci of self-interested concerns of the older states, so that all examples we might offer of this, such as the tribal struggles in the Congo, or Nigeria, or the Rhodesia problem, will be interpreted differently from different standpoints. We are content to rest on the general point, which is obviously of particular importance in the ethnic conditions of Africa as related to the often artificial post-colonial boundaries. Obviously, however, as but a thought on Malaya or Indonesia would show, it is not irrelevant to Asia either.

We might summarize the tendencies of this first equivocation of the equality principle under actual world conditions as follows. It tends to fulfill a basic precondition of the doing of international justice, by opening up the traditional legal order to hitherto excluded claimants and beneficiaries of justice. Implied in this, it tends to promote acceptance internationally of what we have seen may be one absolute precept of justice, namely, the maintenance of conditions in which all men may form and formulate their own interests and press these for legal support.[43] Yet, on the other hand, the limits of this opening up are so indeterminate as still to leave quite unclear the ambit of the justice-constituency within which these demands are to be adjusted.[44] This is so however much we relax the municipal model of this notion for purposes of international justice. And, of course, we continue in any case to confront here the chronic perplexities of translating demands of state entities into terms of genuine demands of the human beings within their care.

Second Equivocation

The second equivocation, that between equal standing of all states to enjoy such rights as international law confers upon them, and equality in the quantum of rights thus conferred, also turns on formal and creative references within it, interacting fruitfully on international justice. No doubt those who take doctrines at their face value as data for logical testing of their literal ambit easily conclude, though often with despair or cynicism, that the obvious factual inequalities between entitlements of states under international law challenge both these

[43] In this respect justice among states presupposes a similar irreducible minimum for doing justice to that in municipal societies. See Stone, *Human Justice*, 341-44, and *Social Dimensions*, 796-98. And see Section IV in this Chapter.

[44] Of course, I recognize that demands are in fact made by spokesmen for state entities, and that these demands can be analogized, to some extent, with those made by individuals and groups on the state within the national legal orders. The question is what value can be attached to the analogy, on which see Section V of this Chapter. And as to the specificity of some of these demands see W. Friedmann, "The Relevance of International Law to the Processes of Economic and Social Development" in Volume 2 of this series.

referencoo. For ouch incqualitioo (they fccl) flatly cxpuoc Lulli thc falsity of that reference of equality which asserts entitlement to equal quantities of rights, and the vacuity of the reference which asserts merely formal equality of standing to enjoy such rights as the law confers.

Yet in history (as distinct from logical analysis) neither version of this second equivocation can be lightly dismissed.[45] The equal quantum of rights reference, for example, despite its obvious variance for existing law, still operates *as a demand of justice for change in the law*. It exerted pressure, surely quite strong during the last century, for abolition of regimes, of capitulations, and of extraterritoriality such as long characterized Western-Asian relations.[46] One effect, certainly, of the factually erroneous assertion of equality in quantum of rights, was that such inequalities of status were challenged continually to justify themselves, and finally failed to do so. Even as positivist exposure of the error was reaching its zenith and as Africa was undergoing colonialist partition, the challenge against such inequalities gained power. So that when, after the World Wars, scores of non-European peoples have been accorded statehood, it has not been seriously suggested that inequalities of the type of the old capitulations should be imposed as a condition of this.

We are inclined to applaud the effect of this justice-demand operating through the equal quantum of rights reference in the present equivocation. But the same reference has also come into conflict with some forward looking movements in the international legal order. Since serious efforts began toward international organization in the late nineteenth century, small state insistence on equality has proved a constant obstacle, and often an absolute roadblock, as when it helped to defeat establishment of a Court of Arbitral Justice and an International Prize Court in 1907.[47] In the flowering of international legal organization of the sixty years which followed, the clash with this justice-demand continues to have its dramatic episodes, whether in United Nations voting and representation rules, or in the allocation

[45] See Goebel, n. 36, 113, esp. 113-16 and 140-41, for the antecedents of the equality principle as a "fundament" of the feudal system. Goebel's analysis is notable both for its valuable historical data and for his attack on the publicist tendency to identify the emergence of the equality principle with the advent of Grotius and the other founders of international law (the ". . . delusion that both science and law itself were born *anno* 1625. . . ."). See Stone, *Legal Controls*, 11.

[46] For a discriminating brief historical account of capitulations and extraterritorial from this present aspect, with useful documentation, see Detter, "Unequal Treaties," 1067, 1073-81. And also see generally, C. H. Alexandrowicz, *Introduction to the Theory of the Law of Nations in the East Indies in the 16th, 17th and 18th Centuries* (1967).

[47] The aftermath of indignation is well symbolized still in the polemics of P. J. Baker, "The Doctrine of Legal Equality of States," 4 (1923-24), *British Yearbook of International Law*, 1.

of budgetary burdens and benefits of this or other organizations. In such a context, of course, criticism of this reference of the equality doctrine is functional as well as analytical. In the demand for an equal quantum of legal rights within the new institutions, the doctrine flies in the face of actual economic, military, and political inequalities which, if these institutions were to prove viable, their constitution and operation had necessarily to take into account. Insofar as both stronger and weaker states benefit in the above regards from achievement of an organization's objectives, the relative capacity of states to contribute to the objectives must also be relevant to a just structuring of the organization.[48]

Third Equivocation

The third of this cluster of equivocations, we recall, closely paralleled the preceding one, except that here the first, the formal, reference within it bases the equality of states before the law on the sovereignty of each state, in all its tangle of doctrinal perplexities. Historically, indeed, both of these conceptions are deeply and independently involved in the emergence of the present decentralized international legal order from the medieval unities of the Holy Roman Empire and the Holy See. The ideas of equality and sovereignty were invoked in increasingly articulate form to free the temporal from the spiritual authority in the struggle between emperor and pope, and (overlapping in time with this), to make the emergent "national" monarchical states independent of both emperor and pope, and also of each other, yielding finally (with the fall of the empire) the system of sovereign states familiar to us. The equality principle already showed itself early, in speculation concerning the place of Christians and non-Christians in the *Ecclesia*, which may, in important respects, be a conceptual forerunner of modern ideas of the state.[49] The consolidation of the equality principle, in any case, was certainly a central fea-

---

[48] See generally on vote differentiations in international organizations H. Weinschell, "The Doctrine of Equality . . ." 45 *American Journal of International Law*, 417 (1951); B. Broms, *Equality of States in International Organisations* (1962). It of course affords very little guidance to say (e.g., recently with Detter, "Unequal Treaties," 1069, 1070) that "voting rights" should be the same "unless there is explicit agreement to another effect."

For the economic aspect of the capacity variations see Section VI of this Chapter.

[49] See the rich, even if somewhat forbidding, account of scholastic speculation in M. Wilks, *The Problem of Sovereignty in the Later Middle Ages: The Papal Monarchy with Augustinus Triumphus and the Publicists* (1963). It surveys the strife of scholastic ideas of the hierocrats and anti-hierocrats, the floundering of these and other contending schools of thought in the *via media* of Thomism, and sees an "intellectual schizophrenia" (characterized as "the endemic disease of the scholastics") as arising from fascination with the Thomistic synthesis. For the relevance of Aquinas' thought to jurisprudential endeavours *provided* the directions there specified are observed, see Stone, *Human Justice*, esp. 214-18.

ture of the order of monarchical states which emerged in the fifteenth and sixteenth centuries. As against the fading claims of Holy Roman emperor and pope each monarch, identified with his State, asserted the freedom and independence which Bodin classically expounded as "sovereignty." As against each other, within an international community of sovereigns, equality presented itself as a corollary of sovereignty, and both of these together as the best available principles of maintaining order in a world in which each controlled a defined territorial domain.

In Vattel's eighteenth century formulations, which served (as we shall shortly see) as a kind of bridge between the natural law and positivist bases of international law, the relation of the equality and sovereignty ("freedom" and "independence") doctrines is worked out. The doctrine of sovereignty, with equality as a corollary, became at his hands the very basis of international law, to the point, indeed, of serious emasculation of the key ideas of an international community and of a *binding* legal order. His classic statement is still worthy of quotation:

> Since men are by nature equal, and their individual rights and obligations the same, as coming equally from nature, Nations, which are composed of men and may be regarded as so many free persons living together in a state of nature, are by nature equal and hold from nature the same obligations and the same rights. Strength or weakness, in this case, counts for nothing. A dwarf is as much a man as a giant is; a small Republic is no less a sovereign State than the most powerful Kingdom.
>
> From this equality it necessarily follows that what is lawful or unlawful for one Nation is equally lawful or unlawful for every other Nation.
>
> A nation is therefore free to act as it pleases, so far as the Nation is under merely *internal* obligations without any *perfect external* obligation. If it abuse its liberty it acts wrongfully; but other Nations can not complain, since they have no right to dictate to it.
>
> Since Nations are free, independent, and equal, and since each has the right to decide in its conscience what it must do to fulfill its duties, the effect of this is to produce, before the world at least, a perfect equality of rights among Nations in the conduct of their affairs and in the pursuit of their policies. The intrinsic justice of their conduct is another matter which it is not for others to pass upon finally; so that what one may do another may do, and they must be regarded in the society of mankind as having equal rights.
>
> When differences arise each Nation in fact claims to have justice on its side, and neither of the interested parties nor other Nations

may decide the question. The one who is actually in the wrong sins against its conscience; but as it may possibly be in the right, it can not be accused of violating the laws of the society of Nations.

It must happen, then, on many occasions that Nations put up with certain things although in themselves unjust and worthy of condemnation, because they can not oppose them by force without transgressing the liberty of individual Nations and thus destroying the foundations of their natural society. And since they are bound to advance that society, we rightly presume that they have agreed to the principle just established.[50]

If (as we must) we read "free and independent" as equivalent to "sovereign," the interrelation with the equality principle, as well as all the accompanying mysteries as to the consequential nature of the binding force of international law, will be found embedded in these lines. Natural law sanctifies the equal "fundamental rights" of all states; and the content given to these equal rights then makes the force of any "governing" law problematical.

It is obvious from Vattel's further elaborations that he was not insensitive to the sea-change which his position brought to the natural law foundations inherited from earlier writers, and which he purported still to accept as the foundation of international law. He sought to escape the central difficulty, which has been well described as the "internal dialectic of sovereignty,"[51] by his well-known distinction between *droit nécessaire* and *droit volontaire*. The *droits parfaits*, emanating from the *droit nécessaire*, are for Vattel those rights of which no state can be deprived because they are indispensable to the very existence of a state and for that reason give rise to "perfect external obligations" of other states. These contrast with his *droits imparfaits* arising out of benevolent or humane considerations (*offices d'humanité*) but which cannot be enforced against states with regard to whom they are asserted, since to allow this would violate the principle of equality, destroying in this sense the foundations of "the natural society" of states.[52]

Vattel also elaborated the notion of *offices d'humanité*, governed by what he regarded as the "bold" principle that "each State owes to every other State all that it owes to itself, as far as the other is in need of its help and such help can be given without the State neglecting its duties towards itself." This (he thought) sprang from an "eternal and immutable law of nature," supported by various humanitarian and utilitarian considerations. Even as he asserted such duties of hu-

[50] Vattel, *Law of Nations*, 7-8.

[51] Cf. E. Reibstein, "Die Dialektik der souveränen Gleichheit bei Vattel" (1958) 19 *Zeitschrift für ausländisches öffentliches Recht und Völkerrecht*, 607-36. And see Stone, *Legal Controls*, 15-17, and the discussion in Kooijmans, 85-86.

[52] Vattel, *Law of Nations*, 7.

manity, Vattel was clearly aware of the tensions they created in his general position. He hastened to assure those who might regard such duties as repugnant to "wise statesmanship" that "Sovereign States . . . are much more self-sufficient than individual men, and mutual assistance is not so necessary among them, nor its practice so frequent." In any case, he added, a state's duties to itself, especially as to its security, require it to be much more careful than an individual in helping others.[53]

We have referred to the changed meaning of "nature" and "natural law" as Vattel used these to base his position. And it is necessary to understand this change to see his exact standpoint on equality, which is our present focus. For most of his predecessors, from Aristotle onward, the "nature" of man was his *ideal* nature, what he is in the fullest development of the faculties special to him; and these were seen by the classical writers as his rationality and sociality and sometimes his dependence on others. For Vattel, however, "nature" rather meant what it means to Hobbes—the "actual" rather than the "ideal" nature of the creature. For him, as for Hobbes, what is primary is not the *restraint* of "*natural law*," but the license of "*the state of nature*"—of men in their pre-social isolation, each self-dependent for survival.

It is, indeed, precisely because "natural law" consists of the principles applicable to men in their pre-social isolation that it is (in this view) apt for governing the relations of independent states. The condition of such states, recognizing no binding human law over them and no human superior, is precisely that of isolated men before civil society and its law arise. Only this kind of "natural" law can claim to control such civil anarchy. The precepts of the Vattelian natural law, therefore, on which his international law is based, must be derived from contemplation of such independent beings, from their "naturally" sanctioned claims, from the "rights" inherent in independence. The precepts must assure those rights of all states in a manner which allows them to coexist. Vattel's whole system is (on its theoretical side) an analysis of the precepts which (he thought) followed from these "fundamental rights" of states, illustrated richly by state practice.

The deeper implications of this position, which (as already stressed) bridges the naturalist and positivist strains of this body of thought, may be most clearly seen in connection with the fundamental

---

[53] Same, 113-20. He opens by admitting that state officials may regard the above principles as impolitic, and that "those astute leaders of Nations will turn into ridicule the doctrines in this Chapter." And at the end of §1 he answers his own doubt that men in power will follow "the Laws of Nature" by rumination that "to lose all hope of making an impression upon any of them would be to despair of human nature." Contemporary thought about justice must still maneuver between these same rocks of self-deception and despair.

right of self-preservation. Not only did each state, according to Vattel, have such a right, in pursuance of which any other rules of international law can if necessary be overridden; each state was also its own final judge whether a situation for the exercise of this right had arisen, and what action was necessary to implement it. On such a basis, the binding force of all rules became subject in the final resort to each state's discretion. The manner in which this *détournement* of natural law pointed towards the "conventional" or "consent" or "positivist" theories of international law, which became dominant in the nineteenth century, is clear in the present perspective.

One sign of this, indeed, was immediately apparent in the destruction of the Grotian theory of "the just war." In war situations, each belligerent's self-preservation is usually invoked: insofar as each is the final judge of what its self-preservation requires, each can in the external world (however it be *in foro conscientiae*) maintain its cause as just, without possibility of legal challenge. To that extent, the "just"—"unjust" distinction as applied to the causes of war became rather indecisive; and with it any basis on which third states might or should discriminate between the belligerents. Vattel's unchallenged position as founder of the modern law of neutrality is thus also seen to be organically related to his version of natural law, and to his mediating role between that law and positivism.[54]

It is easy to see against this background, that Vattel's stress on the *offices d'humanité* is part of an effort to stop short of the full implications of his own new positions. It is an effort in particular to show that the related ideas of sovereignty and equality do not exclude duties arising from sociality and interdependence. No doubt this outcome of "the dialectic of sovereignty" is transparently wavering. Yet it is a part of Vattel's position (not to speak of those of later full-fledged positivism) which is intensely relevant to enquiries concerning international justice. It may be somewhat fanciful to see in Vattel's struggle to have each state sovereign and equal to every other state, but nevertheless subject to unenforceable duties of helpfulness to its fellows, as a forerunner of our own problems. Yet we *are* still struggling to delimit the duty of aid to developing nations. And Vattel's *offices d'humanité* concept, in turn, itself seemed to echo the notion of "conscience" which the classical writers saw as somehow inhibiting the sovereign person of the monarch without yet constituting a binding legal obligation on him.[55]

---

[54] This account is adapted from Stone, *Legal Controls*, 15-17.

[55] The notion of conscience is, indeed, explicit within the above crucial distinction between perfect and imperfect rights. "Obligations," wrote Vattel, "are internal insofar as they bind the conscience and are deduced from the rules of our duty; they are external when considered relatively to other men as producing some right on their part. Internal obligations are always the same in nature,

The jealousy with which the new nations prize sovereignty and equality for themselves (*and therefore perforce have to concede it to other states*) makes it difficult to predicate any general legal duty of affording aid to them in terms of a limitation on the sovereignty of donor states over their resources. For the new states have successfully insisted (admittedly in order to secure their own exclusive power within their own domain, but still in general terms) on recognition of each state's sovereign rights over its own resources.[56] It is in these circumstances that the ex-colonial states and their spokesmen have had to elaborate the thesis (to be examined) which would rest the demand for aid to developing states on a duty of compensation and restitution springing from exploitations of the colonial era.[57] No question exceeds in importance that of determining whether we can find a convincing basis, here or elsewhere, for the duty of richer states to give such aid in terms of acceptable and feasible precepts of justice. Only thus can we escape both the wavering indeterminacy of the *offices d'humanité* notion, and the impracticality (as well, in any case, as the inadequacy) of the restitution notion.

We certainly need not attempt here to trace the somewhat wearisome story of post-Vattelian attempts to find a theoretically acceptable outcome of the "dialectic of sovereignty." The enterprise has continued to engage able minds into our own times. Whatever the esoteric construct invoked, be it auto-limitation of sovereignty, *Gemeinwille* or *Vereinbarung* of state wills, basic norms of *pacta sunt servanda* or custom, these efforts assume at least this consensus: That sovereignty (including the related equality doctrine) can only be a useful concept within an assumedly binding international legal order, if it be redefined in some less absolute form than Vattel, and before him Bodin, and after him Hegel, gave to it.[58] But even to this day this rather obvious truth is constantly obscured by the no less obvious weakness of international law enforcement which allows sovereign states to act often with as much impunity as if their sovereignty were absolute and unlimited. So that scholars have to continue, as late as 1965, to

---

though they may vary in degree: external obligations, however, are divided into *perfect* and *imperfect*, and the rights they give rise to are likewise *perfect* and *imperfect*." So that "external" obligations are "*imperfect*" when "the corresponding obligation depends upon the judgment of him who owes it." For, otherwise, "he would cease to have the right of deciding what are his obligations according to the law of conscience," when he "ought to be free" to decide such matters. Vattel, *Law of Nations*, 7. Other examples are ubiquitous in Vattel.

56 See Unner Kirdar, *The Structure of United Nations Economic Aid to Underdeveloped Countries* (1966), 231-32; R. Higgins, *Conflict of Interests: International Law in a Divided World* (1965), 47-98, esp. 51-54. And see Section v of this Chapter.

57 See Section v of this Chapter.

58 See generally Stone, *Legal Controls*, 30-32, and the literature there cited; and, in the context of the equality doctrine, Kooijmans, 131-39.

write notable books in order to demonstrate that state sovereignty is not unlimited but is subject to the limitations imposed by the international legal order.[59]

It is because of this involvement of the equality principle with the central mystery of the theory of sovereignty and the international legal order that we have separated off the present third equivocation. And this equivocation itself we must now proceed to specify. Its first meaning lies (as already seen) in the formal legal concept of the equality of all states *qua* sovereigns. At the height of nineteenth-century positivist writing this led to a kind of discrediting of the equality principle altogether. Westlake in 1904 felt that equality was "merely independence under a different name"; Lawrence that it was merely a historically given doctrine for which "there is no moral or jural necessity"; Funck-Brentano and Sorel that it was merely an ineffective ideal, and that the reality lay rather in the political inequality.[60] Dickinson, in the first systematic treatise on equality of states, declared after a historical survey that the doctrine was "a creation of publicists," and that it was meaningful only in relation to status before international law, and even there often affected by internal and external legal limitations on the "capacity for equal rights" of states.[61] Baker, in 1923, saw the equality principle as a "positive political danger," rejecting even Oppenheim's modest precepts of equality, and following Westlake (and with him Pollock) rather unquestioningly.[62] Even natural lawyers of this period echoed these conclusions, Lorimer (for example) declaring in 1872 that "all States are equally entitled to be recognized as States," but this did not mean that they were *equal* States, "because they are not equal States." Stowell, in 1931, climaxed this emasculation of the creative power of this equivocation. Recalling the Russian proverb that "paper endures all," he asserted that despite its historic pretensions the oft-proclaimed doctrine of equality of states "exists only between States of same rank in respect to the exercise of power."[63]

Here again therefore one reference in the equivocation is finally resolved into the mere formal (many would say empty) truth. It is in this sense that, if we postulate that a state as such is absolutely sovereign, then each state must be as absolutely sovereign as any other,

---

[59] See A. Larson, C. W. Jenks, eds., *Sovereignty within the Law* (1965). And see for a notable political theorist's approach, F. H. Hinsley, *Sovereignty* (1966).

[60] For general expositions see Dickinson, 100-48, esp. 131-44, and Kooijmans, 106-25.

[61] Dickinson, 334-36; and see Goebel's criticisms, n. 45.

[62] Baker, n. 47.

[63] And in this last respect he distinguished: (1) great powers; (2) small independent states; (3) dependent states and (4) the semi-civilized states. He thought that equality was only meaningful for the first two classes.

and therefore in this respect equal to every other. And here too the other reference is not to a formal but to an ethical and empirical truth. Vattel himself, even as he gave us the *locus classicus* of the first meaning, also imported the second by the side of it. For he placed there, as we have seen, the *offices d'humanité*, or duties arising from the special needs of other states. These were in effect directives of justice arising from the actual inequalities between states, the evidence of which was concealed by the formal equality of their sovereign status. And these directives, though ignored for the most part when the number and relations of states are fairly stable, as in nineteenth-century Europe, tend to come alive in times of rapid change. They share the creative potentiality which we have seen also to arise in the first and second equivocations. In the first, the justice demand was for admission of nations as natural aggregates of men to legal entitlement in general. In the second, the demand was for removal of prejudicial legal discrimination against some nations after they became international legal persons. In the present, the third equivocation, the justice demand is again focused on the needs of peoples already admitted to statehood, but it is a demand for positive assistance from other states in meeting the burdens of *de facto* inequality.

Fourth Equivocation

The fourth equivocation we detected beneath formulations as to equality of states or nations, is even more intensely relevant to contemporary efforts to speak meaningfully of international justice. The name *ius gentium* already had a rich and fruitful history when the founding thinkers adopted it to describe the law which Bentham renamed international law. It had been applied to the body of law which the Roman *praetor peregrinus* had made applicable to commerce involving foreigners, on the theory that its rules were common to the legal orders of all peoples in the world. As such it could be applied to all free men, as men, regardless of their origin and citizenship. When the classical international lawyers used this term its meaning had of course quietly slipped from "law common to men of all nations," to "law governing the relations between nations." Yet this was neither a quick nor a sharp transition. For the *ius gentium* of the Roman *praetor* was itself related to and sometimes quite indistinguishable in function from the no less active natural law, and it was upon a derivative of this same natural law that the classical writers built the foundations of modern international law. So that, as we have seen, early international law doctrines reflected by their starting points the rational and social nature of each human being, and by their reference to the conscience of the monarchical personification of the state, many principles of the law and justice of municipal societies.

We should not therefore be surprised to find the meaning in the principle of equality of states or nations also wavering somewhat uneasily between two (perhaps even three) references. One is, of course, to equality between state entities; the other is to equality between all the men and women who constitute the populations of such entities, that is, to all mankind. (We recall that the third possible reference, to "nations" as aggregates of human beings, has already been canvassed as part of our first detected equivocation.) The swing of the reference exclusively to state entities has dominated international law at least since Vattel. But in the two centuries since Vattel, and even before his time, the reference has also been to equality among all mankind, and to some kind of social ordering or community constituted by mankind. Since we still find ourselves confronted by a choice between these competing references and by the essential task of delimiting the constituency in which international justice is to be done, some account of the historical swing between the related competing ideas of the past is here necessary.[64]

As the secular national states were still struggling to throw off the embracing unities of the medieval empire and church, the weapons on both sides included the rich and complex body of theological learning. In particular the learning as to the *Ecclesia*—the mystical body of the church—with its varied range of meanings provided what some have thought to be the first concept of a community in the West. Clearly the *Ecclesia*, conceived as a *societas christiana* must have referred to the condition of individual human beings to whom souls, salvation, and damnation could be attributed.[65] When in the later Middle Ages the notion of *Ecclesia* was transmuted into a *societas*

[64] Discussions by ethical philosophers have not generally focused on the problems raised by these competing references. See, e.g., H. Sidgwick, *Elements of Politics* (1919), 285-97, passim; and for an antirational utilitarian position, B. Bosanquet, "Patriotism in the Perfect State" in *The International Crisis in its Ethical and Psychological Aspects* (1915), 138; and same, "The Function of State in Promoting the Unity of Mankind" in *Proceedings of the Aristotelian Society* (1917), 43-44. And, recently, from the standpoint of a rationalist ethic, M. Ginsberg, *Justice in Society* (1965), 196-97, asserts as "the axiom of justice" for states as for individuals, the Kantian principle that justice for our own state is justice also for other states. In this he bases the duties of states to transcend their own interests and work toward displacement of war by "a rule of law" (196-97). He recognizes (208) that practical implementation of these generalities is "complicated." One purpose here is to explore these and other "complications."

[65] See the interpretation of *Ecclesia* as "a universal mode of right living rather than as the actually existing community of mortals which endeavours to follow it." (Wilks, n. 49). But this writer's own discussion of the concept bears out its multiplicity of meanings in medieval theological literature. See recent main themes of J. V. Schall, "Ethics and International Affairs," *World Justice*, 6 (1964), 462-75; A. Dondeyne, "Cultural Encounters: True and False Universalisms," 3 (1962-63), same, 35-49. For an attempt to rebase the self-determination of nations on "the right of individuals demanding their own city," see A. Bonnichon, "The Principle of Nationalities and Implied Ethical Requirements," 7 (1965-66), same, 22-23.

humana, this might be expected to have reinforced the reference to human beings. Yet in the concreteness of history this transmutation served, by its recognition of human concerns lying beyond the pale of Christianity, to aid the emergence of purely secular political power, and its withdrawal, though *in the form of our modern state entities rather than a world community of individual human beings,* from overlordship of both church and Holy Roman empire.[66]

In the outcome of this particular struggle, therefore, there is the paradox that the notion of a community of mankind which emerged did not do so literally as such. What emerged was rather the system of territorially organized aggregates of men in states representing the more formal and static reference within the equivocation at present being considered. But *during* a struggle which lasted as long as this one it was not to be expected that issues would seem so clear-cut. Students of the matter have observed upon the lack of concern of the protagonists with explanation of what they meant by "community." They often themselves seemed to hover between the idea of a community of states or a community of mankind or an admixture of both, as when each state is thought of as embodied in its personal monarch. And these views, whether they proceed from various shades of Christian theology, or from secular anthropomorphic speculation, assume that states are agencies for the general good, and therefore that all of them contribute somehow by their activities to the realization of a perfect community of mankind.

It is because of his unusually early and clear articulation of the reference to the constituency of mankind, in which there was equality of entitlement among all peoples, Christian and non-Christian alike, that Vitoria's work has been thought outstanding. With great courage and progressiveness, he used this humanity-wide ideal to champion the cause of the Indians of South America.[67] The ideal itself, more or less explicitly, and still on the basis of divine prescription, is also espoused by Suarez and Gentile. (Its relation to the "law of the sons of Noah" affirmed by the rabbinic interpreters of the Old Testament may well be worth inquiry.) The transition to affirmation of the same variant of the equality principle is clear enough in Grotius, who af-

[66] For a fuller study of these currents of thoughts, necessarily oversimplified here, see Wilks, n. 49.

[67] See the classic treatment of the Spanish claims in relation to the Indians in Vitoria, *De Indis et de Iure Belli Relectiones,* trans. J. P. Bate, in *Classics of International Law* (1917), 163-87; and, in general, Introduction by E. Nys, 9-53. For a brief, but systematic summation, see J. B. Scott, *Law, the State and International Community* (1939), Vol. I, 310-23; and for a sensitive analysis and discriminating bibliography, A. Nussbaum, *A Concise History of the Law of Nations* (rev. edn. 1964), 79-84. On the implications of Vitoria's thesis for the doctrine of equality of states, see generally Kooijmans, 57-62.

firms a *unitas generis humani* grounded on man's specific attributes of natural reason and his *appetitus societatis.*

It is intriguing to think that under the very different "state of nature" of the Hobbesian type, yielding the pre-social *bellum omnium contra omnes,* equality would still prevail, and yet the mutuality of duties based on reason and sociality would be replaced by the merely self-regarding struggle of each for self-preservation. It seems better in an inquiry such as this, focused on justice within an assumed future international legal order, to regard this last variant of the equality principle as really negativing the idea of a community. And the same is to be said of Vattel's main positions, except so far as we have seen these to be qualified by his notion of *offices d'humanité.* For continuity with the Grotian affirmation we have to turn to Pufendorf's adjustment of it with the Hobbesian kind of thought. The *socialitas* of the Grotian tradition is tempered by Pufendorf into a sense of men's inability to stand alone, their *imbecilitas,* which drives them in the "state of nature" to the kind of cooperation which had matured into the formation of states. *As between states,* however, this maturation had not taken place, nor did Pufendorf think it shortly would, or necessarily should. States remained (he thought) capable of achieving the "purposes of legal security," in a "state of nature" governed by the principle of natural equality, all of them insisting on the maxim *superiorem non recognoscere.* On this basis, Pufendorf added, states were still capable of meeting among themselves "when necessary" for cooperation and mutual aid, in accordance with the natural interdependence proceeding from their *imbecilitas.*

It is obvious that an interdependence manifesting itself only in the *ad hoc* meetings thus indicated by Pufendorf is a vanishing point of the idea of the community of mankind in a world of sovereign states. Another vanishing point, found later in the same tradition, is at the opposite extreme. Wolff, in his engagement with the dialectic of sovereignty a century after the Grotian consolidation of the young law of nations, saw no other way of apprehending the binding force of its rules on equal states than to assume that this law is the law of the *civitas maxima,* a notional world polity transcending all particular states. In terms of a community of mankind organized in a world of sovereign and equal states, this concept is obviously an evasion of the problems. For in it the idea of community of mankind has been swallowed up by the national world polity. Conversely, the problem of how law can bind equal sovereign states has disappeared, because in their subordination to the *civitas maxima* the states are simply not sovereign.[68]

[68] See generally W. Schiffer, *The Legal Community of Mankind* (1964), for a too-neglected study of the development of the idea of a community of mankind,

Vattel, much influenced by Wolff in other aspects, did not follow him in this desperate attempt to end the troublesome dialectic of sovereignty. He reverted rather, as we have seen, to the fruitful equivocations between sovereignty and equality of states on the one hand, and to the duties of humanity on the other. His unrivaled influence on the practice of international law in the two centuries since he wrote, no doubt reflects predominantly the equality-sovereignty reference in this equivocation. Yet he also affords, along with Grotius, the most influential model for those later writers who were determined somehow to hold on also to the notion of a community of mankind, whose welfare should be the concern of all sovereign states. This model, of course, became increasingly difficult to follow as full secularization of the body of law whittled away ancillary support (as Grotius still had it) from a divinely supported natural law.

Yet in certain respects the tensions between the competing references within this fourth equivocation have eased in the present century. No doubt there is much rhetoric in the United Nations Charter's preambulatory invocation of "the *Peoples* of the United Nations," of faith in "fundamental human rights," and "the dignity of man," the "equal rights of men and women" (paired, despite the latent contradiction, with those of "nations large and small"), and in social progress and better standards of life, and the resolve "to employ international machinery for the promotion of the economic and social advancement of all peoples." Yet even within the modest limits of the operative provisions of the Charter, for instance for the Social and Economic and Trusteeship Council, and of developments like the technical assistance program, and the work of specialized agencies like the International Labor Organization, World Health Organization, and UNESCO, and the rest, the institutionalization of functions concerned with the welfare of mankind on a world scale have made some progress. And the fact that they are vested in entities other than sovereign states eases the strain of their coexistence with the more inward-looking residues of the doctrines of state sovereignty and equality. In this respect, at any rate, the "functional internationalism" of David Mitrany and his followers has been productive of realities.[69]

We must still beware, however, of mistaking this rather pragmatic psychological adjustment in our attitudes for a solution either of the basic theoretical or practical perplexities involved. It does not, for example, much ease the practical perplexities of stating in acceptable

---

outstanding for its detached but stimulating critique of classical and modern literature, and for the richness of the assembled data.

[69] And see for an admirable study in the full contemporary context, E. B. Haas, *Beyond the Nation State: Functionalism and International Organisation* (1964).

and feasible form the really critical precepts for redistributing world resources so as to produce a minimal standard of social and economic justice for men and women throughout the world. Even success in fuller integration of sovereignties in structures like the European Coal and Steel and Economic Communities gives only limited promise for the wider reaches of mankind, which lack the proximities, homogeneities, and symbiotic relations which largely explain regional success. So that the present writer has been and still remains rather skeptical of theses suggesting that, somehow, a community of mankind with its common law is already in course of establishment (if not, indeed, already established) in replacement of the traditional state system.[70] This skepticism in its turn, however, should not lead us to disdain the role that even integrative structures limited to given regions can play in promoting material and social welfare by increased efficiency of the integrating states, as a result of pooling and sharing skills and resources and of greater incentives to better management of men, money and resources. Above all, we should not disdain their role in widening the concerns of each nation to embrace the security, welfare, and progress of other nations within the region, and even in the wider international community. And it is possible that such beneficent outcomes may foster inter-regional integrations, no less beneficent, and gradually press the world of states towards a full community of mankind. Yet the certainty of such an outcome scarcely goes beyond the mere maturation of integrated regions into rather more powerful units of international rivalry and conflict.

We can at best perhaps believe, as Section VI below will show for the economic sphere, that we are in a tentative and perhaps intermediate stage somewhere before the emergence of a community of mankind. In the final outcome, not a little may yet turn on what sense man can make, in both head and heart, of the problems of international justice. In the meanwhile we remain, into our own days, confronted by the actuality of each state as the predominant decision-maker on all the vital matters concerning the use of its power and resources, and concerning the distribution among its own people of burdens and benefits which arise from these decisions. In this respect the idea of sovereign equality of states, embedded in the traditional law, still awaits the wisdom and the will capable of adapting

[70] See Julius Stone, "A Common Law for Mankind?" (1960) 1 *International Studies* (*New Delhi*), 414, main points in which seem to have gone unnoticed in Dr. Jenks' later restatement in *Sovereignty within the Law* (1965), n. 59 at 18.

There is also a related danger of overgeneralizing the potential role of experts in producing a community of mankind, from the example of the "Eurocrats" of regionalism in Europe. See Haas, 453-57.

it to the high purposes of assuring even minimum freedom and subsistence to the men and women of the world.[71]

In organizing the preceding sections around certain historically given equivocations, we did not mean to imply that these exhaust the relevance of the equality principle to international justice. We meant only to provide some guidance through the confusion of what has emerged from within the literature of international law itself. For example, Robert Tucker has recently drawn attention to the plausible hypothesis that one of the consequences of the replacement of the *bellum justum* doctrine by the principle of equality between combatant nations during time of war was the emergence of commonly accepted restraints on the conduct of warfare, leading to a degree of humanization.[72] There have also been attempts to identify all the several aspects of the equality principle which bear upon the relations of states—namely equality of "sharing" (related to freedom of decision), and equality of honor, estimation, and privilege.[73] The fact remains, however, that neither absolute denial nor absolute affirmation of the equality principle, nor elaborate distinctions between the values in respect of which equality can be claimed, illuminate much the more difficult contemporary problems of international justice.[74]

[71] For an examination, unrivaled in its objectivity, of the limited potentialities of functionalism as a decisive factor toward world integration (i.e. toward transformation of the international system à la David Mitrany) see Haas, esp. 429-58.

[72] In his *Just War and Vatican Council II: A Critique* (1966), 19-20.

[73] See R. McKeon in C. J. Friedrich and J. Chapman, eds., *Justice and Equality* (1963), VI, *Nomos*, 44-61, at 58-59. On Professor McKeon's more general positions see Stone, *Human Justice*, 327, n. 26, and see also the same author's restatement of some of these points in "The Concept of Mankind and Mental Health," *Ethics*, 77 (1966), 29, esp. 31-33.

Such classifications display rather clearly that the only equality at all entrenched in existing international law is equality before the law (analogously to the former position even in Western democratic municipal societies). Equality of voting has made progress in the General Assembly, with rather mixed results for organizational effectiveness; and, of course, the requirement of each state's consent for new obligations to arise is itself more potent than a mere vote. (As to the obviously related self-determination principle, see this Section under "First Equivocation" and R. Emerson, n. 42.) These features, however, as well as the absence of equality in sharing, honor and privilege in the international order, are, of course, clear enough in any case.

Professor McKeon adds useful insights concerning the meaning of "social justice" in terms of equality, and the dangers associated with equality of vote. He observes that "social justice" may be best understood as "equality in the satisfaction of basic needs," combined with equality under an impartial rule. Yet even this point obscures (by assuming that equality in subsistence *can* at present be combined with equality under an impartial rule) the fact that legal discriminations are necessary to turn *de facto* inequalities as to basic needs into the equality of which he speaks. So that the hard core of the problem lies, not in equality, but in finding the precepts of justice to guide the necessary discriminations.

[74] So M. Ginsberg, *Justice in Society* (1965), still asserts the controlling preeminence of "the principles of equality" among states, but simultaneously denies both that states *are* equal and that "States ought to be treated in the same way." The

As with the list of "values" which is so central a feature of Professor McDougal's policy-oriented legal science, national and international, the real difficulties begin after the values have been listed and named, either in general or for the particular conflict. It is after that, usually, that the crucial choices have to be made about which of them is to be sacrificed, and how far. For, except in the simplest cases, not all of them can be equally secured.[75]

We have to add, however, that the bitterest core of the debate as to equality, symbolized for instance in Stanley Hoffmann's denunciation of the principle as a "myth" obviously at odds with actual state ascendencies and dependencies,[76] can only be fully understood by moving outside that debate itself. For in terms of that debate, as we have seen, the rich cluster of equivocations which the equality formula covers forbids any simple "aye" or "no" to the cry of "myth," or to other similar skeptical positions which we have considered. In terms, for example, of the doctrine's reference to mere equality before the law, that is, the title of all states to assert before international law such benefits as that law confers, the cry of "myth" cannot literally stand. The deeper meaning of the cry of myth lies in the fact (which the emotive overtones of the equality slogan tend to conceal) that not merely the legal status of particular states, but their very existence and whole subsequent life, are usually the product of inequalities of power rather than of impartial principles of justice.

This meaning is important not merely for historians and cynics. It is also important in the search for precepts of international justice. For it reminds us that we may be compelled, even today and in the future, to recognize the existence of limit-situations in which justice cannot, in the very nature of the situation, be implemented by law. It is, then, rather for the areas that lie within these limits that we must concentrate efforts to frame and implement feasible precepts of justice. And this reinforces the point we separately reached, for example in the economic sphere, that international justice-theorizing will be more sensibly set toward minimum tolerable goals rather than toward maximum desirable ones, and that the tasks even then are well worth the dedication of all the energy and intelligence with which we are endowed.

---

equality is only in "entitlement to consideration," and "differences in treatment require justification in terms of relevant differences, and . . . shall be proportionate to the differences." What is "relevant" for the purpose of justifying different treatment then depends on "the rights and duties under consideration."

[75] For current statements by Professor McDougal see Chapter 3 and his contribution (with H. D. Lasswell) to the Symposium in 19 *Florida Law Review*, 486-513 (1966-67).

[76] See S. Hoffmann, "International Systems and International Law," 134 in Falk-Mendlovitz, 2, *Strategy*.

IV. OF THE APPROACH TO INTERNATIONAL JUSTICE BY ANALOGY FROM JUSTICE IN MUNICIPAL LAW

For an international society, as for municipal societies, theories of justice in their rich historical diversity of method and content, certainly provide a wealth of clues and hypotheses. Yet here, above all, in view of the special features of the international scene, we must stay acutely aware of the ingredients of time and place which went into their formulation and operation. Even when we try to see justice criteria as fully normative, transcending particular ideas about them, they still remain (in our experience of them) emanations of, as well as strivings from, particular conditions in a community in a particular time and place. So that, as a prerequisite for meaningful inquiries about what "justice" demands in a given situation, we must always identify and delimit what we have called "the justice-constituency," among whose members a "just" distribution is to be made. And if (as we so often assume) what the human beings affected regard as just is also in some way relevant to our criteria of justice, this point is reinforced.

For such an assumed international society, therefore, as for other societies, justice enquiries are doubly anchored in the contemporary facts. They are anchored, first, to the inquirer's own situation, including his time-position and his degree of awareness of what preceded and what now surrounds him. They are anchored, second, to some concrete constituency for which the inquiry is being made. These anchorages refer us to the claimants and beneficiaries of justice in concrete times and places, with their biological endowments and social inheritances, their physical and social environments, and their limited and tentative envisionings of the future. To speak of "justice" among any aggregate of beings, such as "the international community," implies that we can identify such a constituency, and even delimit its membership. We cannot, putting the point another way, make practical judgments about the substantial content of justice for *all* generations and *all* constituencies. No doubt, as we have elsewhere suggested, there may be in a given constituency at a given time some precepts which achieve a practical standing of near-absoluteness; but even these have had to be felt, and thought out, and fought out, at crucial points in social life and change. They have not been always there, biding their time to take the stage as the hurly-burly of social life and change allowed.

If, as is widely believed in the Western societies, justice is to be sought through mediation of the *meum* and *tuum*, of the conflicting claims of the human beings found within the territorial domain and legislative competence of the relevant justice-constituency, no less than four critical corollaries are implied for any society, be it municipal or international. First, this constituency must be so organized that all its members can express their felt needs, or demands. Second, it is by this process, which directs attention to the socio-cultural situation of men and women that material precepts of justice relevant to present actuality are sought. Third, implied in this, the tasks which face us are most centrally tasks of adjustments of conflicting demands, involving sacrifice of some. Finally, it is almost explicit in this approach that the claimants of justice whose demands set the stage for its drama, as well as its beneficiaries, must be human beings. This should not be concealed by careless use of notions such as "public interests," or "interests of the state" as a juristic person, and related notions which we shall shortly mention.

When we observe the efforts to achieve a just distribution among members in a particular justice-constituency, its achievements as they become stabilized in time may be thought of as historically won "enclaves of justice." Within these achievements are precepts which for the men of that constituency are recognized as worthy of acceptance, and may even come to appear as self-evident, and even quasi-absolute.

An enclave of justice occupied by the group is, as it were, a complex of attitudes and roles and expectations, and attendant values, expressed progressively in accepted precepts and explained and expanded in attendant theorizings, manifest in concrete segments of the group's arrangement and activities. From the standpoint of the outside observer it consists of empirically observable facts, even though within the group members it may be felt as productive of norms, and thus of obligations. When we say that theories of justice are emanations of the enclaves of justice held, it is to be stressed that the enclaves are not themselves theories of justice, nor substitutes to displace such theories as criteria of judgment. The theories are rather attempts (often competing attempts) to explain, or justify, or extend, or retract, or modify the ambit of the enclaves held. The enclaves themselves remain empirically given complexes—of environment, attitudes, demands, roles, expectations, felt obligations, and other facts of biological or social endowment—all held in a certain stability within tolerable tensions in the particular justice-constituency. Thus conceived, the enclave metaphor (for it is only as such that it is offered, and not as a new piece of conceptual apparatus for some future justice-theorizing) encourages certain orientations of mood and concern in those who address themselves to problems of justice. It directs us, for example, to the historical struggle of men, individually and in their societies, to achieve the gains which men now hold, as well as to the forces which threaten what is held, or support its defence, and to the emotional and intellectual commitments entailed. Above all, this metaphor raises the question whether, even if we are able to identify and delimit "the international justice constituency," we can point to any enclaves of justice as yet held within it.[77]

All the problems to which these provisional notions of "the justice-constituency" and "the enclave of justice" address themselves exist in more intense degree as we approach the questions of justice *between nations*. We can no doubt envision, in Isaiah's literal words, a world in which swords will be beaten into ploughshares, and nation will not lift up sword against nation. We can even accept that in a world of justice for all humanity all nations will have acknowledged some ultimate principle of embracing goodness, and the brotherhood among all men which this implies. And we should also recognize how important it is that men everywhere, especially in their rather grace-less condition, should have such visions kept clear and meaningful, by the devotion in each generation of some who refuse to be blinded or silenced by contemporary savagery, cynicism, or somnolence.[78]

After we have accepted all this we still encounter grave difficulties for clarity of thought about justice between nations. Among the gravest are those caused by the intrusion into the data with which the criteria of justice must operate, of the territorially based political organizations of states, each interposing itself between men of different nations. If these consisted of mere conduit pipes or channels of communication or distribution of benefits and burdens between all mankind, the difficulties would be serious enough. But the elements of the justice-evaluating process would not be critically different from those with which we have long wrestled, not without success, in the municipal sphere. But, of course, the role of the state cannot as yet be so limited, nor is there any prospect of its becoming so in the foreseeable future.

It is no doubt true, as many have sanguinely declared, that our century has seen great economic, political, and technological changes,

[77] For a fuller version of the notions here adumbrated see Stone, *Human Justice*, 322-55; Stone, *Social Dimensions*, 775-76 and 797-98.

[78] We should here recall, of course, E. Brunner's exposition of Isaiah's prophecy from his theological standpoint. "But Isaiah's lovely picture of the future is not contained in history: *it is the end of history*." In the same spirit (he says) the prophecies of world peace and world justice in the New Testament are based on the expectation that "the conditions of life in the reality of earthly history will entirely pass away." Brunner proceeds to say: "The reign of peace belongs to meta-history, *to the realm of eternal life*. The last ages of earthly history, however, are not looked to as times of perfect peace but as times of unprecedented world tumult." (Emphasis added.) See E. Brunner, *Justice and the Social Order*, trans. M. Hottinger (1956), 199-201. But contrast (supporting the use in the text) the interpretation in terms of actual Jewish religious doctrine, S. Greenberg, "Judaism and World Justice," *World Justice*, 5 (1963-64), 314, 321. And see, generally on the import of religiously inspired visions of human brotherhood, international justice, and world peace, N. Bentwich, *The Religious Foundations of Internationalism* (2nd edn. 1959) *passim*.

both of range and direction, including a phenomenal growth in global communications. It has also often been assumed that the facilities for physical communication must mature into increased human communication and understanding across frontiers, and interdependence of nations into world legal and political order. So that (this kind of thought concludes) the state will lose, before long, its traditional supernatural accouterments.

As regards direct *human* links across the frontiers of states, however, free from the controlling, mediating, or distorting influence of state policies, the realities fall far short of such wishfulness. Partly, of course, the obstacles lie in the very rise of so many new states, each concerned to project a national image at home and abroad, and to draw bargaining advantages internationally from the state identity thus symbolized. But resurgence rather than retreat of the role of the state extends also to old and strong states, as well as to new and weak ones, and to democratic states as well as communist and the various shades of totalitarian states. It bears heavily on the problem of identifying the international justice-constituency, and the enclaves of justice which may be said to be controlled within it. Marvelously swift and powerful mass communication media have provoked defensive measures by each state to limit, in the hinterlands now exposed to radio penetration, the matters to which its people's minds will be receptive. Opinion among the people of each state is increasingly conditioned by the mass media, even democratic governments limiting directly or indirectly the versions of truth and justice which can gain wide currency. Such trends bring into hazard even existing human links across state frontiers; they are not really neutralized by economic interdependence and rapid travel and communications.

This tendency towards direct or indirect control by the state of all socially important means of communication brings with it, then, what we have called "the nationalization of truth and justice." Within the rather insulated chambers of each state, the free exercise of the intellectual and moral faculties of men tends to yield place to acceptance of official versions. In matters of international concern, we face, in Richard Falk's words even a certain "nationalization of scholarship." In realms of the intellect and spirit, this reinforces rather than weakens the supernatural accouterments of the state. The dominance of "nationalized" values insulates men of each state from those of others; it also deprives them of effective criteria for criticizing their own government, and hinders spread of opinions across unfriendly frontiers. Each state is increasingly not only the powerful guardian of its human members as regards their material welfare and security and the fulfilment of their major aspirations. It is also a barrier, and a rack of torture for their values and sense of justice, and the transmission of these to their fellow men in other states.[79] The negative effects of these tendencies are further aggravated by the depersonalizing and stereotyping effects of technological progress. Modern weapons not only multiply destructive capabilities, but also depersonalize the destructive process by interposing time and distance, and mechanical contrivances, between the actors and the responsibility for horrors perpetrated on the victims. And since more efficient modern weapons fall increasingly within reach only of governments of states, it is obvious that the role of the state may well be in the ascendancy rather than on the wane.[80]

The caution thus given in terms of justice generally seems also implied in Kenneth Boulding's notable recent effort to articulate what might at present be meant by "the world economic interest." We are at best in a kind of purgatory in which, despite the rapid growth of economic and physical interdependencies, the functions and organs, and even the knowledge and techniques, required for common counseling, decision-making, and action to implement decisions, cannot yet be said to be in sight. The truth is the same whether we state it in terms of "world community," or in our own terms of "a human justice-constituency."[81] We must agree, no doubt, that the common concern of nations to eliminate economic misery and destitution already exists independently of state frontiers and ideological alignments, and despite deep disagreements about other aspects of international justice. We observed in 1946, in the context of Western municipal legal orders, that the assurance of minimal material standards of individual life was there already a substantially agreed end.[82] No doubt other factors, including bidding for diplomatic support, have helped to promote the remarkable growth of aid by more developed to less developed nations. But one factor, certainly, is the extension of the principle of municipal justice, that human dignity implies entitlement to a basic life subsistence, and that to this extent at least all members of a society are their brothers' keepers. There is much that can be said about international justice even on so modest a foundation, and we shall return to this point in our concluding section. Yet, in the relevant oper-

[79] For a somewhat fuller discussion see J. Stone, "International Law and International Society" 30 *Canadian Bar Review*, 169-74 (1952); and on human communication across frontiers see same, *Problems Confronting Sociological Enquiries Concerning International Law*, 89 *Recueil des Cours*, 65-180 (1956); and Stone, *Legal Controls*, xii-xliv. See related insights in F. J. Kutten, "Inter-Human Relations . . . ," *World Justice*, 2 (1960-61), 43-68, esp. 57-61; W. H. Roberts, "The International Political Common Good," *World Justice*, 2 (1960-61), 178-198.

[80] On this see also Stone, *Legal Controls*, 318-23 and 335-48.

[81] See Boulding, *Interest*, 507-08; and for parallel conclusions from a functionalist standpoint par excellence E. B. Haas, *Beyond the Nation State* (1964).

[82] See Julius Stone, *The Province and Function of Law* (1946) 595-99, 773-74.

ations of international aid, it is still each state which speaks with a conclusive voice for the human beings within it.

V. Of the Question Whether States or Human Beings Are the Claimants and Beneficiaries of the International Justice-Constituency

The preeminent role which we have seen to be reserved for each state's determinations, affects the following critical matters involved in the concept of humanity-wide justice.

1. The dispositions vis-à-vis other states and peoples of "goods" (in the widest sense, embracing all valued things, facilities, and skills) which lie, by reason of physical location and otherwise, within its control according to the existing international legal order.

2. The distribution of such goods among the human beings who constitute its people.

3. The assessment and assertion of the demands of its people against goods similarly controlled by other state entities, the distribution of which among mankind generally is a main part of the business of justice in the international field.

4. Decisions whether to place such power and resources as it controls at the service of the directives of humanity-wide justice.

5. Decisions whether to place such power and resources as it controls in opposition to the directives of humanity-wide justice.

6. Decisions to withhold such power and resources from participation in efforts to achieve humanity-wide justice.

Consequential upon these prerogatives of each state entity are certain special difficulties, also already referred to, of fixing what we have called the "constituency" relevant to *international* justice. Allocations among all mankind on the basis of one-man-to-one-entitlement will not do. Those who have to make the international judgments of justice (be these national or international agencies) must make the allocation to each state authority, which (at best) will then distribute among its human members according to criteria apt for its own municipal justice-constituency, or (at worst) arbitrarily or even not at all. No doubt we already have glimpses, in the operations of agencies like the World Bank, or European regional agencies or UN technical assistance, of devices for guiding or controlling the international redistribution of goods through to their allocation among human beings within the municipal societies concerned. They are, however, glimpses only. Moreover, the regional European experience, because of the highly developed reciprocity there present, is of limited persuasiveness for world purposes. For one thing, the high level of reciprocity among European regional participants is not typical of the world problem. The demands of cooperation and renunciation have not there involved such gross disparities of human living standards as those between Western and African and Asian nations. These demands have not had to overcome vast gaps in human cultures, or the heavy burdens of past one-way exploitations—burdens of resentment of the exploited, burdens of guilt of the exploiters. Unless we can develop such devices and the supporting convictions of peoples and their leaders to an incomparably higher stage, we are unlikely to enlarge these glimpses into the full prophetic vision of the humanity-wide justice-constituency.

We have also to reckon (among these consequences) the difficulty arising from the fact that, apart from men's basic presupposed rights (involved in human dignity) of forming and expressing their own interests, the justice that appears to be within human reach is somehow conditioned (if not determined) by the environment and experience in time of the particular justice-constituency. The judgment of justice also depends on the facts knowable and known at the point in time and space at which the decision-maker stands; and it was to accommodate such elements of experience and knowledge that we introduced the notion of enclaves of justice gained, held, extended, or lost by men in particular societies. Obviously when we try to use such notions on a humanity-wide basis, matters become very complicated by dint of the great number of peoples involved and the vast gulfs which divide their respective environments, cultures, and experiences. Directives of justice which seem to be thoroughly warranted in the enclaves held by some peoples, have little warrant and much incongruity for other peoples.[83] The legislator who may glean helpful directives for the internal life of each people may still have little or no guidance for a supposed society embracing many or all peoples.

There is, of course, no sharp line between the difficulties of intrastate and humanity-wide tasks of doing justice. There have been municipal societies, like the present South African polity (not to speak of numerous former ones, including those of ancient Greece), presenting acutely many of the difficulties affecting the humanity-wide tasks. These include sharp diversity of cultural patterns and experience

---

[83] For a powerful thesis that if the tendency to greater inequality is to be arrested, we must, even apart from economic trade and aid problems—and as a prerequisite—somehow produce transformations in the cultural and social systems in the world as a whole, and especially in the poorer countries struggling for development, see B. F. Hoselitz, "Unity and Diversity in Economic Structure" in Hoselitz (ed.), *Economics and the Idea of Mankind* (1965), 63-96, esp. 93-96.

See generally the brilliantly comprehensive study in Haas, 450-53, discussing the differences between the European Community and the now defunct West Indian Federation. The key to the failure of the latter organization would seem well-pointed in Haas's observation: "National and regional pluralism in the European case have been congruent; but the opposite seems to have been true in the West Indies."

with justice within a single society, and dualism or pluralism of ethical norms (and of entitlements under these) all deliberately maintained by state authority. But the challenge to the legitimacy of this, both by leaders of the oppressed segments, and by other states and peoples, and the bitter controversy which surrounds it, indicate that such a state of affairs is now marginal in municipal societies. While all societies, and not least the developing ones, show wide and varying defaults of justice by any standard, the view that such gross defaults within a municipal society can be normatively ethically justified is now exceptional. So that we might even hope that here, at least, is an enclave of justice which virtually all modern nations have now reconnoitered and either captured or resolved to capture. Yet, this is to speak only of what is professed by each municipal legislator toward his own people. The international legislator who will secure even such marginal entitlements of human beings as against their own recalcitrant government is still in the future. In this very case, the power and policies by which the South African government insulates white South Africans from sharing in the general moral growth of mankind symbolizes a central difficulty of framing a conception of justice on a humanity-wide scale which is not merely speculative.

Can we then escape such problems by treating the international justice-constituency as consisting of state entities themselves, leaving outside the ambit of *international* justice the relation of each to the human beings who compose it? This, indeed, is the common assumption of diplomatic and political discourse, which regularly personifies state entities, attributes demands and rights and duties to these, and appears to make judgments of justice on this basis. This facile (and in our view unacceptable) solution is found also in less relaxed discourse. The municipal analogue of it has been a main point of the present writer's criticisms of Pound's sociological theory of interests and its related theory of justice, and it is deeply relevant at this juncture in the argument.

IN HIS VIEW of the tasks of law and justice as centered on the satisfaction of human demands (or claims or interests), Pound asserted that there were three aspects of such demands. They could be viewed (he thought) as (1) individual interests, (2) social interests, and (3) public interests. He did not intend this division to suggest that "public" and "social" interests "belong" to (or are asserted by) the state or society as collective entities, as distinct from "individual" interests "belonging" to (or asserted by) human beings. He insisted, indeed, that all the interests (in his sense) which just law must take into account are interests of individual human beings. The interests he classified as "public" were merely (he thought) those asserted *by individ-*

uals in title of their stake in *political organization*, just as "social" interests were those so asserted in title of their stake in social life. Consequentially, he thought, each of these three "kinds" of interests was always translatable into the others. In order, apparently, to avoid distortions of judgment arising from men's varied emotional reactions to such symbols as "individual," "social," and "public," he urged that all conflicting interests presented to the judgment of justice should first be translated into terms of only one of them.

The present writer offered the view in 1946 (which he still maintains) that the category of "public interests," whatever its value for *technical legal* purposes, is barren and even misleading in the context of judgments of justice. For the interests here involved are by definition *de facto* demands which human beings press for support by the precepts and apparatus of the law. But it is apparent from all Pound's examples of "public interests" that they do not represent *de facto* human demands, but rather devices or other advantages created by law to protect such demands, or they represent demands which are more correctly seen as a "political" subdivision of the "social" aspects of such demands.

For justice in municipal legal orders, for example, it seems inapt to speak of "interests" either of the states' "personality" or "substance," or of the state as "*parens patriae.*" To do so is to take technical legal devices at their face value as judgments of justice, begging the question what justice *requires of law* as to the human demands involved. As to the "juristic personality" of a state, is not this, like that of a corporation, but a legal device to secure various interests of human beings protected by political organization? As to the state's supposed "interests of substance," are not the immunities of the state and its preferential position as a creditor vis-à-vis the citizen—insofar as they are well based at all, only legal devices for securing the social interest —in the security and efficiency of political institutions? No doubt, as to the state as "*parens patriae,*" we find legal apparatus of widely varying form and structure by which special attention is given to certain human demands, for instance as to care of dependents, or defectives, or national resources, or supervision of charities or other corporations. Such apparatus ranges from formidable statutory corporations and commissions, to informal administrative advisory committees, or heads of judicial jurisdiction like that over lunatics or minors. And it is especially tempting when some powerful state organ is involved, to think of it analogous to a human being as having "interests" or making demands for itself or for the state, and to call these "public interests." Yet there is here no difference in principle from slighter or more ephemeral legal devices or apparatus. The mere fact that the legal apparatus used to secure particular kinds of human demands are relatively powerful and sophisticated, cannot turn this apparatus into human beings, or their rights and powers into human demands, relevant to justice-determinations. This being so as to the notions of "public interests" or "interests of the state" in relation to justice in municipal law, the same *may* have to be said of such notions in relation to justice in the international sphere, unless of course, this is to be seen as a relation merely between state entities without reference to the human beings for which each of these acts.

With a surprising inadvertence to the difference between a state entity as arbiter of justice among its own human members, and a state entity as one of the members of an international community among whom justice is to be done, Pound also offered the supposed "absolute," of "fundamental" or "natural" "rights" of states under international law, for instance of self-preservation, independence, equality, and dignity, and of exclusive territorial jurisdiction and *imperium*, as examples of "public interests." Are these to be regarded as relevant to international justice? The question is tangled by the well-known ambiguity of such terms as "absolute," or "natural" rights. If by his use of these examples Pound intended to refer to rights conferred by international law—to legal rights—the examples are open to all the objections explained in the preceding paragraph. On this basis Pound's analogy between the "rights" of states under international law and the *de facto* claims of human beings within a municipal society is neither fruitful nor even acceptable. Modern international law still conceives such legal rights as held by states vis-à-vis other states and (with only minor exception) not by human beings at all. No doubt often legal rights are legal advantages which support more or less and more or less directly *some* human claims. Yet to *assume* that those claims coincide, or even closely correspond to legal rights of states under international law, is to beg questions of the sociology of international law, on the answers to which orderly thought about international justice also depends.

If, on the other hand, the terms "absolute," "fundamental" or "natural" rights are understood in this context as referring not to rights under positive international law, but to demands which a "higher" ("natural") law requires positive law to support by the conferment of legal rights, the objections to Pound's position are different, but no less serious. For whatever human claims are assumed to lie behind such "fundamental," "basic," or "natural" rights of a state under international law, these cannot, even if we regard them as demands justified by higher law, necessarily be coordinated with existing legal rights.

If, as I believe, these criticisms remain unanswered and unanswerable in terms of basic theory, they reinforce the obstacles which we

have seen to be presented by the compartmentalized system of territorial states to the framing of a conception of justice on a humanity-
wide basis. For the aggregate of state entities cannot *as such* constitute
a meaningful justice-constituency; and their existence also blocks that
access to the demands of men and women of all nations which is pre-
required for bringing them into a single justice-constituency.[84] A
looser way of saying this is that the operation of that sense of common
humanity, which is presupposed by a humanity-wide conception of justice, seems to be gravely inhibited.[85] We may still, even at this point,
try to maintain the prophetic vision, and devote ourselves to elaborating what would be its implications if the world could be changed so
that the obstacles presented by the existing state basis of organization
no longer existed. But this, of course, would have little bearing on
the immediate human future, nor on the confidence with which we
can look beyond this.[86]

IT IS TRUE, as already mentioned, that contemporary discourse, even
among the learned, often overlooks the need for choice between the
conception of "international justice" as justice between states (that is,
within a justice-constituency whose members, and therefore claimants
and beneficiaries, are states), and that conception of it which is humanity-wide justice (that is, within a justice-constituency whose members, and therefore claimants and beneficiaries, are all the men and
women of the world, regardless of the state to which they belong).
Diplomats and publicists seem to calculate in terms of state entitlement—but not entirely or consistently so. They also speak of justice to
Asians, or Indians, or Africans, or Bantus, or oppressed or less-developed or under-privileged peoples—but they deal in and with govern-

[84] On the related blocking ideologies see W. Stark, "Ideologies Around the Problem
of World Organisation," *World Justice*, 2 (1960-61), 435-44. And see the recognition
(though grudging) of these obstacles to the movement from "Welfare States" to a
"Welfare World Community" in V. A. Wreck, "Present Trends . . . in International
Law," *World Justice*, 4 (1962-63), 291-305, esp. 305.

[85] See W. H. Roberts, "The International Political Common Good," *World Justice*,
2 (1960-61), 178-98. This cardinal fact is too often glossed, even in the serious literature. See for random examples G. Del Vecchio, "Natural Law as the Foundation of a
Society of the Human Race," *World Justice*, 4 (1962-63), 307-14, who gets no nearer
the point than to say that the state's duty to assure justice to the individual is "a first
and unchallengeable condition of its very existence . . . the limit and essential condition of its lawful authority over individuals" (313). It does not correct this to
complain (same, 313) of the admission to the U.N. of so many states clearly in
default by such criteria, nor, with R. Bose, "Natural Law and International Law in
an Unstable International System," *World Justice*, 4 (1962-63), 314-33, to press the
claims of natural law and focus on "the mystery of society"; nor with F. J. Th.
Rutten, "Inter-Human Relations . . ." *World Justice*, 2 (1960-61), 43-68, esp. 56-58,
to lose sight of the state entity problem altogether by talking only of "peoples" and
"nations." And see L. Jannsens, "World Justice," *World Justice*, 1 (1959-60), 15-34,
esp. 30-34.

[86] See on this, Stone, *Social Dimensions*, 171-75; and see also same, 114-18.

ments of states. When aid to a developing country is under consideration, the number and poverty of its people and the responsibility to
them of the state apparatus, its degree of honesty or efficiency as a
channel to their welfare, are often dominant factors. With "territorial"
and "political" claims on the other hand, like those concerning frontiers or unification of states, calculation rarely goes beyond state entity
entitlement. Even when it seems to do so, it still usually stops at some
hypothetical entity—for instance at the claims to unity of the German or Chinese or Korean or Vietnamese "nation"—far short of the
demands of the human beings finally involved. (Optimistic theses after
World War I that territorial adjustments ought to be based on
plebiscites of the population affected have as yet come to very little.) [86a]
The supposed suppression or liberation (according to standpoint) of
the tens of millions of Chinese men and women subject to the one or
the other (Peking or Taiwan) Chinese governments is at best a subsidiary point in the Chinese question of our time, when it is not indeed but a flourish of political warfare. "Neutralist" slogans against
"strings" attached to bilateral aid are, not infrequently, directed
against the benefactor states' requirements that the aid given will in
fact be channeled to benefit the human beings who are its ostensible
beneficiaries. In this aspect, clamor against alleged interference by
other states, even in purported protection of human claims, is significantly parallel (though obviously somewhat more morally justifiable
than they) to South Africa's protests against interference in its "domestic affairs" which claims to vindicate the human rights of Bantus
in South Africa.

This ambivalence between the "state entity" and "human" frameworks in conceptualizing *international justice* has its technical legal
parallel in now chronic arguments as to whether, and if so in what
respects and to what extent, individuals as well as states are bearers of
rights and duties under international law. Even if, conservatively, we
exclude any direct legal personality of individuals under this law, the
vigorous growth of the opposed standpoint cannot be ignored. For it
imports at the least the thesis, here intensely relevant, that justice in
the international sphere requires that international law should be
changed so as to assure that just benefits and burdens lie directly on
human beings—and perhaps, indeed, that the legal personality of the
state entity be seen as merely instrumental to this assurance.[87]

[86a] The quotation marks within which the words "act of free choice" (in relation
to the future of West Irian) are usually enclosed in current discussions, speak
eloquently on this point.

[87] See for succinct statements Stone, *Legal Controls*, 118-19 and W. Friedmann,
Changing Structure of International Law (1964), 40-44, and the voluminous literature there mentioned.

We have already explained at the beginning of this Chapter that, since the more

What is most troublesome concerning this ambivalence is not the duality of focus, but the absence of sustained effort to draw some objective line between the occasions when one or the other is to be appealed to.[88] For the main point, that neither can serve as an *exclusive* basis of present thinking about international justice, does not exclude the possibility that each of them may, within some ascertainable limits, provide at least some practical bases of judgment. It is probable, indeed, that some coordinate operation of both, each in a delimited sphere, is the best we can hope for for the foreseeable future.

VI. Of the Present Role of States in Tasks of Just Economic Distribution within a Postulated Justice-Constituency of Mankind

Such a delimitation of the respective influences of the justice-constituency of state-entities, and that of the men and women of the world would have to proceed on some at least of the following series of propositions.

1. Insofar as international justice requires transfer of goods, including (here and in the following paragraph) services and skills, from peoples better endowed to those less endowed, these must relate predominantly to the elementary means of *material* advancement, food, raw materials, machine tools, know-how, and the capital necessary for achievement and development of these. To these must be added, in the actual world, and despite the dangers of wasteful diversion to concerns other than justice, the means of military security whether in the form of arms, finance for securing arms, and military training.

The negative aspects of this proposition are less obvious but no less important. For this first point makes clear that international justice cannot at present be primarily concerned with the protection of the *ordinary interests of human personality*, but only with the above ma-

---

technical legal aspects of this and related questions of the status of individuals in international law already enjoy a very substantial literature, they will not here be further considered.

88 For a seminal study of the history of certain of the basic ideas involved, see E. McKinley, "Mankind in the History of Economic Thought" in B. F. Hoselitz, ed., *Economics and the Idea of Mankind* (1965), 1-40, esp. 18ff. with summary at 36-40. Some of these ideas touch: (1) the possibility of seeing mankind as a single humanity for purposes of economic knowledge; (2) the acceptability of the individual as the "atom" which is at the base of social and economic construction, if the laws of interaction are to be understood; (3) the nation as a competing base for such understanding; (4) generally the metaphysical postulates on which modern systematic economics has proceeded; (5) the forms taken by the postulates of the possibility of economic progress and of the competing notion of equilibrium; (6) the challenge to this whole body of thought raised by its inapplicability to economies other than Western developed economies (esp. 35-40).

terial preconditions for these. This protection of personality interests still rests and is likely to continue to do so, on adjustments *within the justice-constituency of each state-society*. And this for two reasons. One is the crude, deplorable, but understandable fact, of the general refusal of state entities to allow routine intrusion of other states or of international agencies, for the protection of the men and women from their own power.[89] Another is the fact that even should this refusal soften, the wide variation of cultures and attendant values would still leave the authorities of each state as *prima facie* better qualified than any others for adjusting conflicting claims of personality among its citizenry.

2. Where (as is largely the case) justice requires transfers of such goods, services, and skills from one people to another for the purpose of accelerating the social and economic development of the receiving state, it is the latter which must be the final judge (after adequate counseling) of the scale, pace, and direction of such development.[90] This by necessary (though less pleasant) implication also imports that it must be the judge of distribution among its own population of the burdens imposed and benefits conferred by such development.

3. The last proposition indicates rather convincingly that the ideal of equal endowment of men and women throughout the world with material goods cannot, in any foreseeable future, be a practical prescription of *international* justice. When this is added to the earlier point that cultural diversity among the world's peoples makes it rather impractical for international justice to prescribe directly the equal enjoyment of rights of personality of all men and women, this may seem a grave renunciation of many noble hopes for world order. Yet powers can scarcely be said to be "renounced" which are not within our reach, so that we face not a "renunciation" but only the as yet rather unalterable present facts. Moreover, even when the limits are thus recognized, *we are still left with critical questions (shortly to be discussed) of minimum material endowment and the assurance of min-*

---

[89] See the caveats on the main themes in H. A. Rommen, "Towards the Internationalisation of Human Rights," *World Justice*, 1 (1959-60), 147, 173; and M. Hickey, "The Philosophical Argument for World Government," *World Justice*, 6 (1964), 185-210, esp. 202-10; K. N. Waltz, *Man, the State and War* (1959); P. T. de Chardin, "Sauvons L'Humanité" in L. S. Senghor, ed., *De Chardin et la Politique Africaine* (1962). On special attitudes of the Soviet Union relevant to this matter, see L. Friendl, "The Soviet Conception of International Law," *World Justice*, 2 (1960-61), 198-227, esp. 212-14, 226-27.

[90] This notwithstanding the fact that U.N. agencies, now performing such tasks in significant measure, do often make stipulations in specific agreements. I need scarcely add that, in my view, jealous cleaving to "absolute sovereignty" should not block attention by underdeveloped states to counsel and even stipulations offered in good faith by aiding organizations or states. In any case, the derogations from sovereignty of receiving states arising from stipulations *hitherto* are not really significant. (Note some unguarded expressions in U. Kirdar, n. 38.)

imal rights of personality. Questions of *minimum rights* of all mankind are one thing; those of *equality of rights* are another.

If we feel rebellious against this tempering of high aspirations, we should call to mind the stark realities which bid us submit. The solid hostility with which most peoples confront South African *apartheid* policies, and the naked power which supports them, is not a function of failure to realize social, educational, political, economic, and legal equality of South African Bantus with other peoples throughout the world. They would appear in fact, in some of these respects, to compare more than favorably with some other African peoples whose governments denounce *apartheid*. The hostility is rather against legally enforced permanent inequality of Bantus *as compared with white men of the same state*; and, in some respects, against failure to secure to them what can be regarded as an acceptable minimum. If we were to treat *equality* in these various respects among all mankind as a present imperative of international justice, we would face vastly uncomfortable, if not impossible, duties with regard to a large and varied range of modern states. The arbiter of international justice (to offer some random instances) would have to meddle with tempo and method of fulfilment not only of the emancipation of the Bantus of South Africa and Rhodesia but of the Indian commitment to abolish factually as well as legally the inequalities arising from the caste structure of Indian society. He would have to take sides in the chronic controversy concerning the million former Indians now in Ceylon, in the Malaysia-Singapore controversies concerning the Chinese in those countries, in the divisions within Indonesia, in Negro-white struggles in the United States, and in colored-white conflicts in the United Kingdom and other countries. He would have to wonder what can be made in terms of equality of all men and women of the forcible drafting of Katanga into the Congo, and Biafra into Nigeria, and to keep an eye on the treatment of their own peoples including their white inhabitants, by scores of new African and Asian states. Of such supervision these states (however zealous their desire to remold South African and Rhodesian societies) would surely be very intolerant indeed.

4. As foreshadowed under the preceding head, it can be stated with some confidence that international justice has come in the present age to import a duty upon more affluent states to foster achievement of minimal subsistence for all the people of the world. It may have been true, as Attlee observed in reaction to the general euphoria after World War II, that there was then still no "Welfare World" Government. Yet it is probably true in 1968 that the shortfall from minimum subsistence among any great mass of human beings in any country has come to be of routine concern for other states and international

organizations.[91] We shall consider in the next section how far this concern expresses a precept of justice between states which may be regarded as also already part of an enclave of justice *internationally* held.

The precept importing such a duty may come to be unconditional, but it certainly still falls short of this. It is difficult to see, even when aid is not channeled through the receiving state's apparatus, how donor states can be asked not to show concern as to who in fact benefits from the transfer. So far as this is so, donor states must also be entitled, consistent with justice, to weigh before they act, the record and prospects of a recipient government for concern and efficiency in attending to the needs of its people. Even more troubling is the further indeterminate qualification on this duty, which must surely arise when a receiving government fails to take such measures as are feasible to discourage levels of procreation which cannot be sustained on any reasonable projection of economic growth or availability of food.[92] On a matter at once so intimately private, and so momentously public, self-righteousness cannot be a prerogative of either giver or receiver. It is certainly difficult to see on what criteria of justice even the most affluent states can be required to make sacrifices to benefit the human beings involved when the government concerned is not ready to match these by a degree of responsibility and efficiency in its domestic policies.

5. It may be argued indeed that, in certain relations arising from history, the duty imposed upon donor states is not subject even to such mild conditions. Between some peoples and others, it may be said, lie heavy duties of this kind, duties of restitution and reparation for great historic wrongs. An Indian colleague has recently argued in a

[91] See the general theme of Kirdar, centered around U.N. aid projects. The U.N. Experts Report of 1954, indeed, formulated noneconomic criteria of underdevelopment in terms of individual human beings rather than states, and notably: (1) expectation of life at birth; (2) infant mortality rate; (3) per capita nutrition rate; (4) 5-14 year-old school population; (5) percentage of illiteracy by age and sex groups; (6) percentage unemployment; (7) distribution among economic groupings; (8) individual consumption as percentage of national revenue. See generally A. Shonfeld, *The Attack on World Poverty* (1960).

[92] See generally P. V. Sukhatme, ". . . Hunger as F.A.O. Sees It," *World Justice*, 5 (1963-64), 147-68. There are, of course, major controversies as to such projections. Among the prominent economist dissenters is, of course, Colin Clark. See, e.g., "The Earth Can Feed its People," *World Justice*, 1 (1959-66), 35-55 and "Demographic Problems on a World Scale," *World Justice*, 6 (1964), 436-40. See also the approach in John XXIII's Encyclical Letter *Mater et Magistra* under the rubric "Population Increase and Economic Development," on which see A. McCormack, "International Social Justice in *Mater et Magistra*," *World Justice*, 4 (1962-63), 52, 70-73, that ends on the note: "Why do you offer us contraceptives instead of bread?"; and see the modified view in P. Anciaux, "Ethical Aspects of Demographic Policy," *World Justice*, 5 (1963-64), 520. Much, of course, turns on the chronological relation of population growth and economic take-off: see A. Shonfeld, "The Attack on World Poverty," *World Justice*, 2 (1960-61), 444-65, esp. 464-65; A. Nevett, "Population and Resources in India," *World Justice*, 2 (1959-60), 466-88, esp. 488.

related context that the Indian use of force for the liberation of Goa in 1961 was a legally and morally justified reaction to the Portuguese conquest of Goa in 1510, no Indian Government having in the intervening four and a half centuries voluntarily accepted the legitimacy of the *status quo* subsisting during these centuries.[93] The gist of such a position cannot, of course, be as to rights under positive international law. For there it would confront rather settled doctrines of title by conquest and prescription, and the stale and endless juxtapositions of the legal contradictories of *ex iniuria non oritur ius* and *ex factis oritur ius*, not to speak of Charter obligations prohibiting use of force against the territorial integrity of other states. The gist of the argument must concern not law, but justice. And on this level it provokes the important question whether the mission of delineating a future international legal order which is acceptably just to all peoples should be burdened at the outset with the impossible preliminary task of expunging all the black record of collective wrongs of the past. Even if, in the Goa case, the charges against Portugal could be framed as a legal indictment, as well as a demand of justice, the main point would remain. Many of the epochs of man's history have been marked by the gravest moral and legal wrongs. But, of course, the logic of restitution and reparation with no benefit of prescription or reprieve, cannot stop at legal wrongs; indeed, its heart is rather as a demand for justice. No generation of men could hold the gate of reason against clamor to mend all the wrongs of all the generations of men that went before.

Assuming that we were to accept it as a part of the tasks of present international justice to right all historic wrongs between peoples, we would then confront the questions: How, if at all, are we to assess and liquidate wrongs committed by former generations of some peoples against those of others? After how many generations, and on what terms, could collective moral indebtedness in justice be written off, and the past left to bury its dead? To these we shall shortly turn. But before doing so it would be well to explore further the precept concerning oblivion of ancient wrongs. In preceding points concerning duties of aid to meet demands of subsistence, no regard was paid to wrongs committed by earlier generations of men. Because of deference, there shown to be unavoidable, to the claims of each state government to continue to make basic decisions of justice between man and man within the justice-constituency of its own people, the duties involved were practically rather than morally delimited. At the present point, the trend of argument seems to suggest that undoubted moral principles, this time of restitution and reparation, have also to

93 J. S. Bains, *India's International Disputes* (1966), 195-208.

yield place, again for the sake of practical progress toward a viably just international order.

Yet it has to be added that the attitudes here invoked in the name of feasibility, still imply moral effort and responsibility of a very high level. For international justice, as thus envisaged, still demands that some nations (largely but not only the ex-colonial Western powers) shall adopt a policy of sacrifice and helpfulness, on a basis other than self-interest or reciprocal material benefits, and to an extent measured only by their own capacity and the vast needs of states whose people lack subsistence. Conversely, this conception asks the present generation of many African and Asian nations to assume an attitude of uncalculating forgiveness towards wrongs of the past, and to accept help for implementing their national tasks in a spirit of common aspiration toward a better human future. The qualities to which all states and their peoples are thus summoned by these practical reasons thus have (I do believe) also the nobility of sane and constructive compassion. Indeed, in face of an irreversible history, and the choices to which history has brought our own generation of all the nations, the rapprochements of mutual compassion may well be of a higher moral order, as well as more practical, than any principles of restitution or reparation for past wrong. There is, finally, moral merit in recognizing the limits of the possible, and in refusing to allow the hard-won community of human endeavor to be destroyed by uncontrolled passions—whether of vengeful hatred or guilt-born fear. The irreversibility of most wrongs of past generations of nations joins with men's present aspirations for the common human future, to bid us rather forward, with eyes ahead.

6. It must now be stressed, moreover, that it is not merely practical urgencies and mutual compassion, but also the promise of technological advance in ways of peace which press in the direction here indicated. For even suppose that we were resolved to see the great and pervading wrongs of past generations righted by the making of present restitution and reparation; suppose, also, that it were feasible for the states concerned to make now the redistributions thus found due. Would it not still be doubtful, to say the least, how far such amounts could be decisive or even very significant in the struggle of the new states for rapid development in pursuit of subsistence? No conceivable extension of the principle of unjust enrichment, now emerging in the sphere of international agreements, could reach these more general problems of the historical relations, of exploitation and the like, between developed states and developing states generally. That principle, moreover, is one in which equities on both sides have to be taken into account. In many cases the entitlement of the ex-colonial people would have to be adjusted to allow for benefits already received. The

same relations which saw gross exploitation also often saw the transmission of substantial elements of educational, administrative, social, economic, and technological skills, and managerial and institutional resources, which later became part of the ex-colonial people's national inheritance and at least a first beginning of development. So that, even where former exploitation is clear, the reckoning and apportioning of losses and gains over a long and often obsolete association may prove neither feasible in theory nor decisive in practice in relation to the contemporary needs of developing states.[94]

Finally, we should remember that the very lapse of time usually involved, with the spectacular accompanying change in range and tempo of economic activity, has multiplied the scale of all the factors involved in the process of economic development, including gross national product, capital investment, and labor. All the capital extracted by the exploiters in a century from 1750 to 1850, if restored according to the present real values in 1966, would still be far short of what is essential for economic development of a now independent former colony. Aid which may become available to developing states under a principle geared to the needs of their contemporary development seems likely to exceed greatly even generous estimates of reparations due for wrongs of past centuries, before this multiplication of range and scale, and of technological capacity to produce. This, if it proved indeed to be so, could seal the bonds arising from mutual compassion with the insignia also of material success.[95]

7. Finally, in these propositions relevant to delineating an international justice-constituency, it must be said that the duty to make a suf-

[94] See W. Friedmann, n. 87, at 206-10 for further discussion in the context of an emergent principle of "unjust enrichment."

[95] This, indeed, is an area which calls on both sides of past wrongs for dynamic reorientation of "thought" and "passion" (R. McKeon's terms, in "The Concept of Mankind and Mental Health," *Ethics*, 77 (1966), 29, esp. 33-37. What this present discussion adds, however, is that the main warrant of success here is a function of the absence of practical alternatives, rather than of abstract ideals alone. Nor should the intellect be other than content to be brought thus close to religious and spiritual preoccupations. See, e.g., C. Santamaria, "In Search of a Concept of Peace," *World Justice*, 2 (1960-61), 5, esp. 23; S. Greenberg, "Judaism and World Justice," *World Justice*, 5 (1963-64), 314-21. See esp. the reminder (at 314) of the Old Testament doctrine that a world judged by the standards of justice, untempered by mercy, could not continue to exist. See J. F. Cronin, ". . . Thoughts on the International Common Good" same, 1 (1959-60), 299-317, esp. on the difference between the mood here invoked and "charity." And see the statement of the dedicated economist Barbara Ward, "The U.N. and the Decade of Development" same, 7 (1965-66), 308, esp. 333-35, precisely in terms of the Hebrew prophets. *Cf.* the call to Asian intellectuals to transcend their reactions to historical injustices in P.K.T. Sih, "The Mind of Asia . . . ," same, 3 (1961-62), 18-34.

Contrast the problem of deprivations of developing countries by continuing "unjust" monetary policies; see J. F. L. Bray, "Riches and Poverty," same, 2 (1960-61), 331-47, at 346. Such wrongs, so far as established, obviously demand remedial action in terms of "unjust enrichment."

ficient transfer of goods and skills to permit general attainment of minimal subsistence does not spring from the mere conscience, goodwill, and humane ideals of developed nations. Nor is the importance of the duty limited to men's material well-being. The duty emerges, in the present submission, from the harsh and otherwise intractable nature of the relations between them and the poorer states by whom they are surrounded, and to whom most of them are tied by this irreversible history. Were this not so, the position here taken would be open to the charge of naivete. It has, indeed, been suggested that, in psychological terms, fuller recognition of such a duty by the developed states (which are also the states most laden with armament expenditure) may produce a salutary diversion from fear of aggression and the resulting arms race, to constructive peaceable tasks of bringing the newer nations to political maturity and economic viability.[96] Such a diversion, it is said, would be reflected in a diminution of tensions and the fostering of a climate of minimum security. In a world where defense budgets could thus be substantially reduced, the argument proceeds, economic development of poorer nations could be significantly accelerated. Of course, the political and economic decisions leading to such changed use of resources would not be brought about merely because such therapeutic effects were to be anticipated, any more than from mere conscience, goodwill, and humane ideals. But once we see the nature of the imperatives which lie behind the duty of aid, it is not at all naive to acknowledge and to bring fully into the prognosis of the human future such likely accompanying psychological changes.[97]

The deep interlocking of ethical drives with long-term political and economic forevision and prudence in this area of human affairs can be illustrated in still another way. One of the earliest statements to articulate in modern terms the demand that more affluent states as-

[96] See the valuable analysis of such psychological components in O. Klineberg, *The Human Dimension of International Relations* (1963), 145-50. See on a more speculative level, the attempt to restate traditional—especially ethical-philosophical—discussions of "individual and society," within the frame of a "concept of mankind," in Richard McKeon "The Concept of Mankind and Mental Health," *Ethics* 77 (1966), 29-37. He considers the bearing of this concept on action in relation to (1) aspiration (31-33); (2) thought (33-35); (3) passions (35-37) and (4) morality (37).

[97] See O. Klineberg, n. 96. Much of current strategic thinking also emphasizes the pernicious consequences for world ordering, of the psychological insecurity and uncertainty involved in the "balance" of nuclear terror. See, e.g., main themes of H. Kahn, *On Thermo-nuclear War* (1960); and same *On Escalation: Metaphors and Scenarios* (1965); T. Schelling, *Arms and Influence* (1966); and B. Brodie, *Escalation and the Nuclear Option* (1966). And see generally the illuminating survey of styles and dimensions of contemporary strategic thinking in J. Chapman, "American Strategic Thinking" (1967), *Air University Review—Canadian Confederation Centennial Number* (professional journal of the United States Air Force), 25-33.

sume responsibility for assisting in the attainment of humanity-wide subsistence, is that of a theologian rather than an economist, or a political leader, or the authors of the Atlantic Charter, or an international official. It was in 1943 that Emil Brunner declared[98] that many problems, such as the colonial problem, depend for their solution on somehow detaching economic life from its too-exclusive connection with national political life. With nations, as with individuals, the wealth of the rich is unjust when it entails the poverty of others. So that such nations, when they persist in regarding their special economic advantages as their unqualified "due," and in excluding others from preserves commanded by their power, are contributing to future wars. Economic imperialism, in this sense of the preservation or enhancement of economic advantages by superior political power, strains all peaceful ordering. And for this reason (Brunner argued) "the most far-reaching detachment of world economy from power politics is one of the most urgent postulates of international justice." We have to understand this powerful action-oriented statement as framed within a theological position which identifies justice with love, but recognizes that this "is a message of that which lies beyond all earthly institutions," which is the fulfilment (and by that the end) of law, and what we restlessly struggle for amidst earthly justice and injustice.[99]

It is clear, indeed, that both sides of the ideological struggle have already (and repeatedly) referred to the great opportunities of human development, including that arising from international aid, if only resources now used for warlike preparations were diverted to constructive ends. No doubt this has often been of propagandist import, especially in maneuverings during disarmament negotiations; but the point is nevertheless well understood. We should not expect developed countries to decide suddenly to appropriate for international aid the amount of their last year's defense budget. But we can already see (for instance in relation to the United States economy and the Vietnam War, and the coupling of peace overtures with offers of massive aid for South East Asian states) that international aid programs exert a

[98] E. Brunner, n. 78 at 216.

[99] E. Brunner, 230. And see the next Section in this Chapter for Brunner's statement on the justice thus attainable in an *earthly* sense. We are aware, of course, in making this claim for Brunner, of the vigor of the attack on "economic imperialism" from the side of Communism and Socialism, but Brunner's message is directed to richer states of both camps. There are also, of course, significant bodies of wartime opinion which demanded action to give reality to "freedom from want" as a plank of the "five freedoms" of the Atlantic Charter. See, e.g., Julius Stone, *The Atlantic Charter* (1942), esp. cc.iii, vii, and viii. But this was before even the Marshall Plan, when thinking was rather in terms of just social ordering within states, for example by policies of "full employment," than of the massive transfers between nations which have now come into consideration.

steady psychological pressure in favor of arms reduction and military disengagement.[100] Progressively, therefore, as the duty of transfer in aid of the developing nations becomes recognized, and even fully institutionalized, we may also expect increased psychological and electoral pressures for the reduction of armament expenditure and reduction of international tension generally.

AN APPROACH to international justice in terms of contemporary urgencies has led us, rather inevitably, to the area of international economic relations. It may be important to ask, therefore, at this stage, what critical or confirmatory suggestions current economic thought has to offer. Kenneth Boulding has here recently explored whether it is possible to formulate with precision the meaning of "the world economic interest" as a final criterion by reference to which adjustment should be made.[101] The term "interest," as he here uses it, obviously does not refer to a *de facto* demand conflicting with other *de facto* demands, but rather to a judgment as to where final community advantage lies in resolving such a conflict. In this sense the notion "world economic interest" may be understood as a criterion of economic justice for adjusting the conflicting economic claims of individual men and women constituting mankind as a whole. Can "world economic interest" in this sense of a "world economic justice criterion" be given a meaning sufficiently determinate for practical use.

Clearly, before we can use the notion of "world economy" in this context, we would have to define a base "condition" of the economy, by reference to which improvement or setback, and therefore "world economic interest," could be measured. For, in economic theory, before we can speak of such "world economic interest," we have to formulate a condition, or a working model, of world economy by reference to which improvement and impairment in the realization of that interest can be measured. The prospect of evolving such a model (and we may in fact require, as Boulding himself observes, more than one such model) is itself problematic. Closely related to the above preliminary difficulty is the general matter already stressed of identifying

---

[100] See generally O. Klineberg, n. 96. And see recently the British proposal (at the end of February 1967) that to obviate foreign exchange problems arising from the stationing of British troops in West Germany, the latter country should buy British goods for supply to India or some other developing country. This kind of contribution of military activities to developmental financing is obviously marginal to the main problems.

[101] See K. E. Boulding, "The Concept of World Interest" in B. Hoselitz, ed., *Economics and the Idea of Mankind* (1965), 41-62. This article is reprinted in R. A. Falk and S. Mendlovitz, eds., *Strategy of World Order: Disarmament and Economic Development* 4 (1966), 494-515. (The latter reprint will hereafter be cited as Boulding, "Interest"; the Falk-Mendlovitz work itself as Falk-Mendlovitz, *Strategy*, with volume number.)

the relevant justice-constituency of all mankind (here the *economic* sectors of it) in operationally useful terms. If we assume, however, that such a base-line can be fixed, other major groups of problems still loom.

The first is that quantitative criteria of economic well-being, such as the commonly used per capita income, while they reflect the resources available for distribution within each state, do not adequately reflect the level of satisfaction of human demands or needs in all states. This difficulty is, of course, a function of the economic and cultural heterogeneity of the various peoples of the world. Standards of satisfaction of demands or needs relevant to developed economies, for example, may not be applicable to the less developed. What a given level or increase or decrease of per capita income means in terms of actual satisfaction of demands or needs of the men and women of one society may be vastly different from their meaning for those of other societies. This is a problem even if we always assume (as of course we cannot) a perfectly efficient and just distribution among the members of each state.

It is obvious, furthermore, that an increased aggregate of world resources (in whatever terms measured) will rarely mean also that there is a similar increase for every state comprised in that aggregate. Indeed, it may, and usually will, mean a decrease for some of them, raising a second group of problems as to how we should value such particular decreases as against aggregate increase.

Another, still more serious, problem arises even if we assume no decrease for any particular state within the aggregate increase. For aggregate increase may and usually will be so distributed among the various parts of "the world" (for instance, states) as to increase the inequalities already existing between rich and poor states. This difficulty quite transcends any merely quantitative criteria for economic justice. We refer to the question of inequality. For one great directive of social justice in the West for at least the last century has called for progressive diminution of merely accidental material inequalities between men. The spectacular rise of sentiment and practice in favor of economic aid for the developing nations suggest that this directive is transposing itself, at least inchoately, to the international scene. This suggestion draws strength from the historical relation of colonialism to economic inequality, and the now general condemnation of colonialism; as well as from the relation of economic distress to international tension.

"Just" economic action should, in this light, have as one aim the reduction of economic inequalities between states as regards the production, exchange, distribution, and consumption of wealth. It would then be a material precept of international justice that economic relations should be so arranged that economic inequalities between nations should be reduced. At one extreme, as already seen, economic *equality* among them is not attainable at present or in the foreseeable future; no precept of justice demanding it seems plausible. At the other extreme, it has not been too difficult to show that assistance by more developed to less-developed states, so as to enable the peoples of the latter to reach an adequate level of subsistence, is a basic precept of international justice. In between these, we can perhaps venture, as has just been done, a precept of justice for the reduction of *inequalities*.[102] Even, however, if we do (and this is the main point here) such a precept can afford little guidance for action until it has been adjusted in the concrete world situation with the precept requiring the maximization of aggregate "world" economic welfare or resources. Thus Boulding himself, in terms of his own analysis, recognizes (as already observed) that his criterion for aggregate maximization by reference to per capita income, would have to have built into it some kind of nonquantitative index of tolerable inequalities.[103]

If it were possible to devise criteria taking into account both the level of aggregate world resources and the effect on inequalities of distribution among states of raising resources to any given level, this problem could be solved, though at the cost of foregoing merely quantitative criteria. Such an enterprise would be hazardous in theory, and certainly very difficult to bring within general consensus. Up to what point can we say that a particular range of inequality should not debar measures to increase world resources? And at what point should inequality become a bar? On one side of the line we treat equality as irrelevant; on the other side as decisive. On one side, increase of world economic resources is decisive; on the other it is irrelevant.

What this means is that, even if we look only at *economic* justice, nonmaterial values (or disvalues) intrude—here the disvalue attributed to inequality *which cannot be justified*. And it is this last emphasized qualification which, of course, throws the whole problem beyond the range of merely economic calculation. It is, furthermore, not merely the disvalue of economic inequality which here complicates economic calculation.[104] The problems of social and cultural

102 For a study of the theory and practice of advanced countries which have tended to produce increasing inequality, and an offered approach for counteracting these tendencies in contemporary development aid, see B. Semnel, "On the Economics of Imperialism" (in B. F. Hoselitz, ed., *Economics and the Idea of Mankind* [1965], 193-232, esp. 229-32) . And on the cultural and social changes required, especially in the poorer states, for correcting the tendency to greater inequality see in the same volume, B. F. Hoselitz, "Unity and Diversity in Economic Structure," 62-97, esp. 93-97.

103 See Boulding, "Interest," 497-99.

104 So Boulding acknowledges that "any concept of world economic interest implies an ethical system of some sort" (511) , and that "technical economics alone

heterogeneity (as we have seen) already operate here also. Similar quantities of material wealth, even in terms of "real" values, may have radically different meanings for different peoples, quite apart from variations between individuals. What will qualify as socioeconomic betterment, or reduction of inequality, is affected not only by economic quantities but also by the psychological facts of the need, receptiveness, and expectations found in the social inheritance of such particular people. Furthermore, noneconomic values also bear vitally on the range of tolerable inequality insofar as inhibitions may arise from the control on the modes and therefore the rate of economic expansion. A given quantity of investment capital is more significant when it may trigger an "economic take-off" of a developing nation. The available ways of accumulating such capital may also be severely limited, in a country like India, by accepted ethico-political commitments. We must not think of this point merely in terms of literal sacred cows. For such commitments may also in fact close off methods of accumulating capital, such as the exploitation of labor so critical to the British economic take-off of an earlier century, and to that of the Soviet Union in our own times.[105] And the point is even clearer when we consider that in past times abuses such as trade in slaves or narcotics or the exploitation of child labor have been important sources of capital accumulation. Moral constraints against such methods now operate severely in economic development, aggravating the tasks of developing countries and placing them under inequality as difficult to overcome as time is to recall. Some of these restraints associated with anticolonialism and human rights are, ironically enough, expressions of the birthright of the newer states.

This last complication reemphasizes the earlier main argument as to the impracticality of compensating arithmetically for historic wrongs. Granted the irreversibility of history, the multiplied scale and tempo of modern economic processes, compulsion to respect present moral constraints on modes of economic development makes the earlier conclusion on this point even more compelling.

IT WAS AN earlier conclusion that the duty of the more developed states to help to assure a minimum human subsistence was virtually

cannot provide an unequivocal definition of world interest, although it can help in relating whatever definition is arrived at to the ethical system that is implied by it" (513). See generally same, 513-15.

[105] So, in extreme form, see B. F. Hoselitz's thesis, "Unity and Diversity in Economic Structure," in his *Economics and the Idea of Mankind* (1965), 62-97, esp. 97. See on cultural pressure for large families in relation to population problems, J. Delcourt, "The Birth Rate . . . Social and Cultural Aspects," *World Justice*, 2 (1963-64), 169-196; and, in relation to rural development M. L. Meyer, "Community Development and Developing Nations," same, 5 (1963-64), 208-29; and generally W. Banning, "Meeting of Cultures," same, 3 (1962-63), 5-18.

unconditional, and certainly not subject to any reciprocal material interests of donor states. This justice-imperative, we showed, is imposed by history and by the situations in which history has thrust the peoples concerned, as well as by ethical commitments which most of them and their government have already assumed.

At the same time, questions were raised concerning a too facile translation of interdependence into criteria of just organization and distribution. We did not challenge *the facts* of growing *physical and economic* interdependence of nations; we rather pointed out that these did not in themselves give forth criteria for international justice, but left us with the really hard problems of choosing and articulating these. We have now to add that, whatever the criteria, they could not be implemented by ordinary processes of international trade. For trade relations do not exist between numerous of the pairs of states involved, and the potentialities of the relations between most of the rest are too limited and varied. Here again Boulding's conclusions in economic terms march with our own. If a "world economic interest" could be postulated, its pursuit would have to be largely not by trade but by the operation of a world "grants economy."[106] And we would here make explicit the vital rider that useful directives for such a "grants economy" cannot be drawn from the notions of either "world economic interest" or "interdependence," unless we recognize the kind of justice imperative imposed by history on the relations of the more developed to most of the newer states.

No doubt appeals in the West for expanding aid programs seek support from quarters which favor internationalism and the emergence of a world community generally. But unless such programs are seen finally as requirements of international justice, the relations of leading economic powers to the developing states must remain one of grace, bounty, and dependence. If we are to refashion these relations into genuine interdependence, there must first be a great international reallocation of resources as a matter of present duty, rather than of mere bounty, or even enlightened long-term self-interest.

When we face the magnitude of transfer problems involved, it is clear that this imperative of international justice bears major corollaries concerning other competing uses of the resources of the developed states. It is apparent that there may be the severest competition between the defense-security function and that of achieving minimal standards of life for all mankind. As a practical matter, of course, allocations at present take place under decisions made *within* the polity of each military power; though the same point might conceivably

---

[106] Boulding, "Interest," 505-08.

become applicable to any comparable expenditure of international security forces, if these ever came into existence. There could, in the light of this corollary, be more than mere wishfulness behind promises of American and Soviet leaders to devote hypothetical savings from the fruits of successful peace or disarmament or armaments control negotiations to the advancement of the developing nations. Yet there is also required a serious adjustment of perspective by some of these latter nations, which have in the past been willing to exploit great power tension in the interests of their own national policy.

It would be fatuous to conclude that progress toward minimal subsistence required by a humanity-wide economic justice presupposes a world in which international security is attained without substantial arms expenditure. It is not fatuous to say that it is an important corollary of the precepts of international justice that expenditure on arms (and perhaps on other goals, such as space exploration) ought to be reduced as much and as quickly as possible. Only by wisely husbanding the world's resources can there emerge a genuine approach even to that degree of economic solidarity among nations implied in the common goal of minimum subsistence to all men.

We have to add, finally, in relation to the precept requiring aid to maintain general minimum subsistence, that other practical problems will remain even if the duty of the developed states in this regard be granted and criteria be achieved which take account both of factors maximizing world resources and those reducing inequalities between peoples to tolerable levels. One problem affects the division of the resources available for distribution. It is a common experience in federal states, where a system of grants from the center to the constituent states is part of governmental arrangements, that the very division of the resources available among the beneficiary states becomes a matter of regular contention among the authorities. This experience also shows, however, that this contentiousness can generally be held within bounds, and indeed reduced for the most part to subcriteria of relative entitlement, more or less routinely applied by impartial commissions. Another problem, perhaps more difficult, concerns the sharing of the burden of making aid available between the more developed states. It is a tribute to the degree of growth of techniques and attitudes already attuned to the concept of a community of mankind, that this problem seems far less formidable than it would have seemed thirty years ago. Adequate approaches to it are well tried in the allocation of burdens of such budgets as those of the United Nations, the International Monetary Fund, the World Bank, the International Development Association, and a score of other organizations, not to speak of the experience of quasi-public consortiums of private resources to meet particular emergencies, as with the recent economic crisis in Indonesia.[107]

No doubt as the scale of such operations grows, to meet the precept of a general minimal subsistence, such problems will come to have new aspects and new difficulties. There is no reason, however, to suppose that the techniques and criteria already employed for sharing benefits and burdens cannot be adequately developed further to meet them.[108]

VII. An Emergent Enclave of International Justice?

What the preceding section has exposed are some rational grounds for accepting as a precept of international justice that there is a duty on all the richer states to afford means for ensuring a minimum level of subsistence for the men and women of all countries. It was shown that, as an approach to righting wrongs of the past, such a precept would be more feasible and effective than any principle of restitution. It was also shown that its acceptance would provide valuable psychological incentives toward the further consolidation of an intelligible international justice-constituency, toward the development of world resources to meet the population pressure upon them, and toward the reduction of wasteful expenditures like those of armaments and space exploration. Can such a precept be regarded as emergent (if not already accepted) among the peoples concerned and the national and international decision-makers involved? In other words, assuming that we could delineate clearly an international justice-constituency, could this precept that minimum subsistence is thus to be assured within it by appropriate efforts and sacrifices, be regarded as within its enclaves of justice, or at least within such enclaves as are in process of being won?

In this inquiry there is one sure starting point, namely that the more developed states, those from whom the main sacrifices to fulfil such a precept would have to be expected, consist mostly either of Western

---

[107] For statistics up to 1965 of the distribution of burden of aid as between Communist *bloc* (288-89) and Western (281-88, 289-96), and for a breakdown of Western aid in terms of each donor's gross national product (311-512), see Kirdar on the pages indicated.

[108] In the mass of growing literature on development, going far beyond the present subject, see, e.g., W. W. Rostow, "The Take-Off into . . . Growth," *Economic Journal*, 66 (1956), 25-48; G. M. Meier and R. E. Baldwin, *Economic Development* (1957); A. O. Herschman, *The Strategy of Economic Development* (1958); B. Higgins, *Economic Development* (1959); B. F. Hoselitz, ed., *Theories of Economic Growth* (1960); W. W. Rostow, *Stages of Economic Growth* (1960); A. Shonfeld, *The Attack on World Poverty* (1960); I. Adelman, *Theories of Economic Growth* (1961); H. W. Singer, "Trends in Economic Thought in Underdevelopment," *Social Research* (Winter 1961), 387-414; N. A. Khan, *Problems of Growth of an Undeveloped Economy: India* (1962); J. Tinbergen, *Shaping the World Economy* (1962); E. E. Hagen, *On the Theory of Social Change* (1964); B. Ward, "The U.N. and the Decade of Development," *World Justice*, 7 (1965-66), 308-35.

capitalist democratic or Communist democratic states. Moreover it is on the whole true that, whatever the other differences between them, these states have accepted each within its own municipal justice constituency a precept asserting the right of all members to a minimum subsistence. It is also clear that up to a certain point (still far short of what fulfilment of the precept on a world scale would require) most of these states have already recognized a duty to aid underdeveloped countries to move toward subsistence. By participating in nation-building and economic development programs, both bilaterally and through international agencies, the developed nations, Communist and non-Communist alike, have entered upon this duty. No doubt other motives have often accompanied the sense of duty, including those of redeeming past sins of exploitation. But, with equal certainty, the dominant factor has been a degree of diffusion onto the international scene from the now firmly held enclaves of municipal justice constituencies, of precepts enjoining minimum subsistence for all.

Realistic assessment of the numerous technical and economic assistance programs undertaken by the United Nations since its inception (for example, in Unner Kirdar, *The Structure of United Nations Economic Aid to the Underdeveloped Countries* [1966]) shows already a substantial movement of capital and "know how," and the movement of personnel belonging to both developed and developing countries across state frontiers. The movement stirs hope of greater understanding, more efficient communication, and of commitment of individuals to a precept of international justice favoring a minimum subsistence for all men and women. And this may also bear some promise of gradual molding of traditional state entity motivations to embrace this commitment. Included here is some dampening of youthful economic nationalism among developing countries, which might otherwise be as negative a factor as political nationalism in obstructing fuller commitment. It may be premature, and provocative of futile controversy, to say with Kirdar that this emergent precept already creates "legal obligations." But as a precept of justice guiding modern statecraft the emergence of its broad outlines is clear enough.

The authenticity which marks the direction of these developments is (it is true), still obscured by the very inadequate scale of the resources involved in such multilateral operations as those of the United Nations, and by the mixed motivations which accompany the concurrent activities of providing aid by bilateral arrangements. As to the latter, for example, the United States has tended, even when bearing more than half of the burden of Western bilateral aid, to resist the establishment of U.N. developmental agencies such as the International Finance Corporation, SUNFED, and the United Nations Capital Fund, pleading her inability to extend her contributions in the absence of progress in worldwide disarmament. And generally developed countries are distrustful or at least reluctant before demands from developing countries for greater flow through multilateral channels.

The thesis that the latter are the more efficient channels for aiding developing countries toward subsistence is here confronted by the traditional power-political implications of bilateral aid, these latter being of course extraneous to the justice commitment which here concerns us. The fact that such extraneous elements will not apparently yield to mere frontal arguments on principle, signalizes the rather limited acceptance of the justice precept involved. A more potent line of persuasion in the long run is likely to be that formulated by Gunnar Myrdal:

> . . . a very important moral element of every scheme redistributing income, national as well as international, should be that the burden be shared in a just and equitable manner. It is not fair and will never be felt to be fair, that a man who lives in Stockholm, Geneva or Brussels should not share the burden of aid to underdeveloped countries equally with the man in the same income bracket living in Columbus, Ohio, in Detroit. . . . Most of the things which are imperfect and wrong in the present aid schemes spring from this lack of justice in their financing. . . . When international aid becomes unilateral . . . politics enters into its distribution.[109]

What is operative here to neutralize the extraneous drives of power politics is not, of course, the main justice precept itself concerning minimal subsistence, but a more general (and as we have seen, more richly ambiguous) precept of justice concerning equality. And the efficacy even of this principle is here likely to arise from its appeal to the self-interest of the major developed states, as against other developed states which have not assumed a proportionate burden. For the demand that all contribute according to their means only becomes persuasive when the contribution is on a common plan through a common channel, and contributors who claim to be bearing a disproportionate share of the burden can plausibly demonstrate that they are not already in more or less devious receipt of an adequate *quid pro quo*. The much discussed delay by the United States in 1966 in agreeing to make food shipments to relieve the then threatening Indian famine illustrates both these aspects of the motivation toward multilateral channeling. The delay was explained by the United States as intended to draw attention to her inability to continue, even in the medium term, to contribute the heavy share of India's needs that had come to be expected of her; and to the duty of other states to share this burden. And the

[109] G. Myrdal, *Beyond the Welfare State* (1960), 188-89.

rather limited sympathy with which this explanation was received in many quarters also illustrated the difficulty which confronts even a munificent bilateral contributor state, which protests the duty of other states to match its munificence. Still, the underlying demand for "equal sharing" of the burden of aid manifests once again the fertility of the general principle of equality. In this context the equality principle presses, along with other factors, toward the multilateralization of aid already emergent as a contemporary trend.

Yet, the important point for present purposes is that the question which persists in debate is not as to whether aid shall or shall not be given to the developing countries, but as to how much aid, and how transferred, and how the burden of affording it is to be distributed. Invocation of the aspirations of Article 55 for stability and well-being based on the equal rights of peoples, the securing of higher standards of living, full employment, and the conditions of economic and social progress and development, and the pledge of members of the United Nations in Article 56 "to take joint and separate action in cooperation with the Organisation for the achievement of the purposes set forth in Article 55," is of course common form in General Assembly Resolutions on technical and economic aid. The Marshall Plan, the the United Nations Charter, the Resolution of the British Labour Party in 1957 to dedicate at least 1 percent of the gross national income for economic aid, and a similar resolution passed by an overwhelming majority of the Council of Europe, all add to the evidence of some kind of precept of international justice already emergent at the mid-twentieth century.

A major shift towards multilateralization of the aid would, in this sense, signalize movement toward fuller acceptance of the justice precept under discussion; and it would also tend to reduce the wastage of aid arising from competition between donor *blocs*.[110] Yet, of course, it would be naive to think that even the most complete multilateralization would itself assure the full acceptance, let alone the implementation, of the justice precept concerning subsistence. The problems of adequacy of the aggregate of resources made available, whether bilaterally or multilaterally, for the needs of developing countries, as of proportionality to the capacities of the developed countries, would still remain. The fact that bilateral aid with its elements of wastage and of unjust allocation of benefits and sharing of responsibilities by contributing states, cannot adequately meet the growing needs of the

---

110 More significant than statistical contests between Western and Communist states as to their respective contributions to aid for economic development in Asia and Africa (see n. 107), are the effects of the Cold War on the distribution and use of aid. Thus recipient nations have often not been selected according to needs; and aid received has been excessively diverted to military purposes ancillary to Cold-War tensions.

developing countries, does not necessarily mean that multilateral aid would be bound to meet it. General use of the multilateral model, however, would be an important step toward increasing the aid which can be marshalled, as well as the doing of justice among both contributors and recipients. And it would also make progressively clearer the requirements of justice which press imperatively for the available resources to be made more adequate.

How far can the union of full commitments of these states within their municipal domain, with the beginnings of modest commitment in the world arena just discussed, be taken as evidence of an enclave won (or in process of being won) *in some assumed world-justice constituency?*[111] Can we say that the duty to assure a universal minimum subsistence is about to be or has already been established as part of the movement of international life? It is tempting to assume that since the domestic and foreign policies of these states are broadly controlled by the same leaders, the precepts of justice accepted by them in the domestic sphere can be regarded as equally established for the external relations of their state with other states. So far as the ethical acceptability of the precepts are concerned, the problems which arise seem not too difficult. The main one concerns the assurance with which the ruling elite of each state can ask its people to forego a modicum of their own affluence in order to raise less fortunate people nearer to subsistence. The question is made sharper by the fact that not the donors, but the governments of the receiving states, will control the use (or the waste) of the resources thus transferred. We are entitled to assume in the present enquiry, however, that such assurance can usually be afforded by further growth of appropriate transnational structures and processes, or by appropriate bilateral stipulations. Far more difficult are those problems which pertain not to ethical justifiability but to feasibility. Can we see democratic leaders maintaining the support of electors, at any point when the magnitude of the transfers to foreign nations for such purpose bites

111 It will be sufficiently clear from the text that the "enclave" notion is used in the text only as a metaphor yielding historical insight, rather than as an instrument of rigorous thought. I therefore feel reservations as well as interest toward efforts to develop my merely suggestive use of it into an "excursus in the realm of abstractions" avoiding "concrete problems of acute concern." (See I. Tammelo, "World Order and the 'Enclaves of Justice,'" 1 *Ottawa Law Review*, 1-35) (1966). It must be obvious that this takes my thought out of its essentially concrete historical frame. This last is on the whole well understood in A. Blackshield, "The Enclaves of Justice: The Meaning of a Jurisprudential Metaphor," 19 *Maine Law Review*, 131-180, esp. 136-38 (1967). Mr. Blackshield pinpoints well the ways in which the metaphor falls short of an instrument of rigorous thought, underlining limits within which I offered it. And his discussion of the processes of "internalisation" of precepts of justice in relation to it is a particularly promising contribution, developing from our oral discussions in Sydney, after publication of Stone, *Human Justice*, and Stone, *Social Dimensions*.

into the level of welfare benefits and personal affluence which domestic electors have grown to expect? It is now a truism in the domestic politics of states, that it is virtually impossible for a party which hopes to come to power to reduce substantially prevailing social welfare benefits. It is also a truism that the long-term effect of the struggle for votes is to produce a steady rise in these benefits, and that only looming economic disaster (as in contemporary Britain) can arrest these processes, and then only with difficulty. And the regular travails of American presidents in securing support for their foreign aid budgets are well known.

So far as national leaders are concerned, therefore, the mere depth and sincerity of their personal commitments to the principle that men and women of all peoples are entitled to a minimal subsistence, is no guarantee that they will be able to make this commitment good in the international sphere. So far as concerns electoral support, moreover, the issues presented by dedication of national resources to other nations, do not present themselves in the same light as transfers for the maintenance of subsistence within the national community. Within the *national*-justice constituency enclaves are already controlled which afford a psychological basis for the sacrifices entailed by obeying the precept. The precept has been not only articulated to rationalize actual developments; it has also been internalized, as grounding a recognized duty in the above sense, by the members of the community. While the corresponding precept for transfers from nation to nation has already been articulated, also in response to actual developments, it is doubtful whether the citizenries of many states have as yet internalized it sufficiently to base recognition of the duties of citizens to make substantial sacrifices in order to give it effect. And insofar as even the wealthiest societies, like the United States, still contain substantial population elements living (by local standards) at below subsistence level, the precept enjoining subsistence for *all of the nation* may be felt positively to conflict with that enjoining subsistence for *all mankind.*

Emil Brunner, without the advantage of hindsight of the extraordinary change of the generation since he wrote, clearly foreshadowed some of the tensions which this diffusion has brought. It is, he observed in 1943, in precisely this context of international justice in the economic sphere that it is "the tragic lot of really good statesmen that they are often forced by their people to act otherwise than their own insight dictates." And it may commonly happen that a nation's sense of justice "demands from [its leaders] a policy of justice to which they are personally disinclined." Effort in the cause of justice, even by the humblest citizen, is thus not quite vain, and none, not even that of the most powerful statesman, can ever quite attain its goal. Yet the ethical merit of such effort should not be mistaken for success, any more than men's mere knowledge of the requirements of justice should be mistaken for their willingness to fight and sacrifice for these. "It is a part of every man's natural disposition that he wishes to be *justly dealt with*, but it is by no means a part of man's nature to deal *justly with others* and to intend justice even when it runs counter to his own advantage."[112]

If this interim conclusion is somewhat discouraging for the theorists who have already, for a generation, convincingly elaborated the ethical, economic, and political merits of international economic aid, it also returns us to basic presuppositions of any careful inquiry concerning *international* justice. How far can we get with such an enterprise before we have to try and delineate a justice-constituency? And what constituency can we delineate here which will simultaneously embrace the human claims involved, and the rather inescapable interposing authority of state decision-makers? The precept of justice as to subsistence is held by democratic peoples as part of the enclaves of their own municipal-justice constituencies, representing ideas articulated from shared group experience, internalized by members of the group to the point of felt obligation, of acceptance even at a sacrifice, and then further institutionalized in the life of the group. Theories (including *merely* articulated precepts) of justice, tend to be operationally effective in democratic polities only when they have grown beyond mere articulation and become internalized in the attitudes of electors. The crucial mark of internalization lies in recognition of the obligation, if need be, to make sacrifices for the vindication of them.

From this operational standpoint a precept like that as to subsistence, already internalized and institutionalized within municipal justice-constituencies, is really not the same precept as that articulated or even theorized for the as yet undelineated justice-constituency of mankind. There are rather obvious differences between the direct mutuality of sacrifice and benefit within a national community, and the much more diffuse and long-term mutuality associated with subsistence for all mankind. In the no man's land between the actual operativeness of the *municipal* precept, and the hope for its analogical operative extension to all mankind, the battle to seize the corresponding enclave of *international* justice has still to be won. In this battle, radiating tendencies from enclaves and precepts municipally pioneered and held have no doubt a role to play; but the victory itself has to be won on its own ground, by men's acceptance of the obligations transcending their national communities which it implies.

Conceivably all the developed states in the world might come to have dictatorial leaders strong enough to dispose of the national re-

[112] See E. Brunner, 219, 228.

sources by their own independent decisions, and these leaders might transpose to the international sphere any precept as to minimum subsistence for all already established in their respective municipal spheres. But, of course, the prospect of the appearance of such a combination of humanity loving irresponsibles in the critical seats of power is not great. There is certainly no present reason to expect that Western democratic states will all come to be headed by such leaders; and the relaxation of restraints on consumption and on freedom of expression in Communist bloc countries is tending increasingly to assimilate their position on the present matter to that of political democracies.

After all needed caution, however, we are entitled to note some clear signs that the establishment of precepts as to the right of minimal subsistence at home, in the lives of the peoples of the developed states, is already extending itself to embrace all mankind. The internalization of this concern for mankind generally is already manifest to a degree in the modest sacrifice of national affluence which responsible governments have hitherto been able to accept on behalf of their peoples. The future task is to extend these bridgeheads nearer to the point at which a real attack can be made on the destitution of so many tens of millions of the peoples of the less developed states. In part the task is for the thinkers and political leaders of our generation. But in part it is the task of time, and the change which time brings. Even now the demographic and other scientific realities threatening the global food supply are infiltrating the minds of the run of citizens of the advanced countries. So is the relation of gross economic inequalities between nations to tensions and the danger of war. So is the monstrous dissipation of resources in the search for military security. From all this, and the promise of plenty from automation as yet only dimly seen, great developments are possible, both as to sacrifices needed, and men's readiness to make these. Institutionalization of performance of the precept through more governmental action, even when this is of little beyond a token nature, is already a strong ferment in the consciousness of ordinary citizens, sensitizing them to the international responsibilities which affluence brings, and internalizing the related precept. Escalation in the scale of aid, which is at the heart of the future task, is itself a cumulative process, and each people's will to sustain the sacrifices involved may paradoxically increase with the magnitude of what is demanded for the dignified sustenance of the whole family of man. All this, in turn, may help to liberate men from the bonds of merely "nationalized justice." For the deeds of feeding the hungry and healing the sick are readily understood and esteemed as ennobling by men of all nations. The task of beating swords into ploughshares is long and painful; yet the more men engage themselves upon it, the less likely are they to resort to the sword.

We were concerned at the outset to warn against too facile transpositions of enclaves and precepts from national justice constituencies to a vague and inchoate international constituency. We now stress that this leaves us, still, entitled to look with hope on the critical and complex interrelations between enclaves of justice already won in national spheres and the emerging enclaves of justice toward which men continue to struggle and stumble in their global neighborliness. Whether in warning or in hope, we need to go beyond the formulation of a merely conceivable notion of international economic justice. We need also to address ourselves, as has here been attempted, to questions of feasibility in terms of living societies of men and their leaders as we know them, and as they can be expected to develop. For by whatever approach, men can move forward only from where they are.[113]

[113] For this reason we should not be sanguine toward hopes that the fulfilment of worldwide "welfare" programs can serve as a *sufficient* lever for transforming the international "system." We here agree with this conclusion from E. Haas' massive study of the International Labour Organisation, in his *Beyond the Nation State* (1964), 126-458, esp. 429-59.

See as to the role of other "functional" activities in such transformation, e.g., economic planning, securing of human rights, same, 461-64, 492-97.

And see for a most perceptive statement, especially on the importance of various active choices and initiatives by receiving states and peoples, and adjustment of technical aid donors to these, Francis X. Sutton, *sub voce* "Technical Assistance," *International Encyclopedia of the Social Sciences*, 15 (1968), 565-76.

Part III

The Regional Perspective

CHAPTER 9

The Prospects for Regionalism in World Affairs

ELLEN FREY-WOUTERS

INTRODUCTION

AN IMPORTANT issue for every student of world order is the destiny of the nation-state. In the second part of the twentieth century, the fragmentation of the world into numerous separate political entities may be considered dangerous for peace. The majority of states are no longer truly sovereign and are increasingly dependent for their security on factors that extend far beyond their boundaries. This fragmentation is equally illogical for human welfare and economic development. Modern systems of production require raw materials, skills, and markets that few societies can any longer provide unilaterally. The heavy costs of autarchy often paralyze modernization and economic growth.

The weakness of the majority of states, particularly the developing countries, creates an unstable economic and political environment. These states easily become the victims of the power struggle among the big powers. The already industrialized nations have, so far, denied the new states full participation in the revision of the international political, economic, and legal system developed by the West. This has created dangerous, anti-Western revolutionary undercurrents in various parts of the world.

This is where the danger lies. A multitude of states—politically powerless and economically crippled—remain the basic units in present-day international politics.

Many argue in favor of a more integrated world, either under more centralized authority or through various regional political communities or through a combination of both. But there is little agreement on the exact formula for this new "Strategy of World Order."

The regionalist formula has already shown some viability. The search by various regional groupings of states for new forms of cooperation to advance common interests has become one of the most interesting developments in present-day international relations. Not only in the Western world, but on all continents there is a growing awareness that areas now artificially divided, politically and economically, in reality form "natural" units. The establishment of existing regional political communities and the planning of future ones demonstrate that the distribution of functions and sharing of authority within regions have already become facts of international life.

The new impetus given to the issues of regional integration has resulted in a considerable amount of scholarly discussion concerning the future—the features, aims, effects, and general rationale of regional groupings. Integrative efforts have confronted participant and observer alike with a number of fundamental questions.

One of the first questions to arise is whether continued regional integration is really possible in the world today? Will the broad sweep of history bring about the progressive integration of the many regions in the world, and are we observing the early stages of this process? Will a diversity of regional political communities supersede the nation-state—just as the dynastic state had replaced the feudal structure—as the likely result of historical and technological development? Various studies suggest that regional political integration cannot be expected to emerge as an automatic by-product of historical evolution. Definite political and administrative action has to be undertaken if political integration is to be attained.[1]

Will the existing regional political communities continue to develop in the face of major policy differences among their members? Or have they already become the victims of existing national and international forces? Hoffmann has argued that "the survival of nation-states" is primarily the outcome of two unique features of the present international system. "One, it is the first truly global international system: the regional subsystems have only a reduced autonomy . . . the domestic polities are dominated not so much by the region's problems as by purely local and purely global ones, which conspire to divert the region's members from the internal affairs of their area." The second unique feature "is the new set of conditions that govern and restrict the rule of force . . . the ideological legitimacy of the nation-state is protected by the relative and forced tameness of the world jungle . . . the atrophy of war removes the most pressing incentive [for unification]. What a nation-state cannot provide alone—in economics, or defense—it can still provide through means far less drastic than hara-kiri."[2]

Some other observers have questioned this "relative tameness." They have pointed out that the national situations, especially in the developing world, are increasingly becoming similar because of an overwhelming common external threat (in the form of neocolonialism and

1 See, for instance, Karl W. Deutsch and others, *Political Community and the North Atlantic Area* (Princeton 1957) , 22-29.

2 Stanley Hoffmann, "Obstinate or Obsolete? The Fate of the Nation-State and the Case of Western Europe," in *International Regionalism*, Joseph S. Nye, ed. (Boston 1968) , 180-81.

foreign interventions in civil wars) and because of the failure to achieve modernization. As a result, integration for survival may well become a necessity.[3]

Another question which arises is whether regional integration is really desirable in the world today? There is general agreement among observers that truly integrated regional organizations are revolutionary in nature. But their exact character, their structure, their probable development are not as yet thoroughly understood. The prescriptionists among the theorists of regional integration present the following main arguments in favor of regional integration:

1. Nationalism has become a luxury fit to be enjoyed only by the big powers. The integration of small and medium sized states located within a certain geographic region is an imperative. These states must collectively pursue the political and security goals that are no longer attainable unilaterally.

2. Regional economic cooperation holds out the promise of greater prosperity and a more stable economic system. In the developing countries, economic integration is necessary as a means of accelerating modernization and economic growth.

3. Regional integration creates more political cohesion to help defend the independence of the developing countries against big power interference. Regional institutions provide these states with an effective channel through which their demands and interests can be articulated, and a redistribution of political and economic power can then be achieved.

4. Regional integration contributes to world peace by creating political communities where there is a great probability of internal peaceful change in spite of the continuation of contending groups with mutually antagonistic interests.

As yet we know too little about the effects of these groupings to prove the validity of the above arguments. A number of questions present themselves. For example: Does the existence of these communities change the operating conditions of the relations between its members, or does it only introduce milder ways of forcing and controlling the weaker members? Do these communities have a lasting and positive impact on the national, regional, and international political processes, or is such impact insignificant or easily reversible? What are the effects of these groupings on the prospect of world integration or disintegration? Will the regional systems now emerging in many parts of the world become disruptive factors in the world structure, separating

---

[3] This argument is developed in Sidney Dell, *Trade Blocs and Common Markets* (New York 1966). See also Jorge Castaneda, "Pan Americanism and Regionalism: 'A Mexican View,'" *International Organization*, x (1965), 375-81.

groups of countries from one another? Or will these groups seek closer ties with one another?

To many, it seems far from self-evident that regionalism will bring about decisive progress toward the evolution of an effective world economic and political system. In their view, regional groupings will contribute toward a larger, world-wide community only if they support the growing powers of the central structure, not if they resist such development. Much will depend, accordingly, upon the capacity of the United Nations to reconcile the practices of regional organizations with its own actions in the sphere of world order and development.

This study is an attempt to explore and to suggest some tentative answers to the above questions. It will seek to clarify some of the uncertainties and ambiguities surrounding the theory of regional integration and to forecast the prospects for regional integration in the near future. It will examine the impact of regional integration on the political, economic, and legal system within the region. It will attempt to ascertain some of the achievements and failures of existing regional organizations in the present international system as well as their potential contribution to the establishment of a more stable world system of international order.

Each of these areas covers an extremely broad topic, and it is impossible to treat even one of them exhaustively in a single brief study. None of them, however, is wholly independent of the others and it is this interdependence that forms the focus of the present essay.

I

In order to ascertain the nature of regionalism, it is necessary first to clarify what constitutes a region. No generally accepted definition exists. The extent and character of a region varies with the criteria selected for analysis. Most of the efforts to delineate regions have made use of a wide variety of criteria, and theorists of the regionalism concept do not fully agree as to what the appropriate criteria are. As a result, the term "regional organization" has been used to describe regional as well as interregional, inner-directed as well as outer-directed, single-purpose as well as multi-functional associations. For the purpose of this study, the concept of a region and a regional organization will be defined rather narrowly. Geographical contiguity, perception of belonging to a distinctive community, interaction, interdependence, and common institutions will be considered the necessary criteria for a region. A regional organization will be defined as a permanent, both inner- and outer-directed multi-functional association, located in a particular geographic area, serving a number of states which are mutually interdependent and share certain common interests, needs, characteristics, and loyalties.

Two types of associations commonly called regional organizations do not fit the above definition and will be excluded from this study— collective security arrangements and inter-regional political groupings. The *collective security arrangements*, such as the North Atlantic Treaty Organization and the South East Asia Treaty Organization are primarily single-purpose associations, oriented toward externally motivated power factors. While on paper committed to the development of their regions, they have in practice made little or no contribution to the political or economic integration of their regions. They are more or less transitory arrangements, and cannot be expected to play an important role in the near future.

Inter-regional political groupings, of which the British Commonwealth and the Organization of American States are examples, have also proved to be insignificant as promoters of regional integration. In the case of the OAS, the great difference between the economic and political power of the U.S. and that of Latin American countries enables the highly industrialized, dominant power to undermine the cohesion of the associated, largely underdeveloped region. The specific interests of the U.S. are basically in opposition to those of Latin America, and economic and political relations between them have so far not been able to give rise to a genuine regional political community.

In this study, the OAS will therefore be excluded, with the exception of its relationship to the UN concerning maintenance of peace and security, since only with regard to OAS activities has this relationship between the UN and regional organizations been extensively discussed.

Until 1956, the Council for Mutual Economic Assistance served a similar purpose of great power domination over an adjoining area. The events of the post-Stalin era have changed the character and purpose of CMEA. Present methods of cooperation between the Soviet Union and the other members of CMEA are based to a large extent upon mutual agreement and compromise.[4] CMEA serves a number of states which are mutually interdependent and share common interests, needs, characteristics, and loyalties. CMEA, therefore, can be considered a permanent, primarily inner-directed regional organization which contributes to regional integration.

This study, then, will focus attention primarily on (1) the general political organizations, the Organization of Central American States, the League of Arab States, and the Organization of African Unity, and (2) the various common market arrangements in the developed and developing world, more particularly in the European Community,

---

[4] See Kazimierz Grzybowski, *The Socialist Commonwealth of Nations* (New Haven 1964), 2.

the Council for Mutual Economic Assistance, and the Latin American Free Trade Association. These organizations can be expected to remain in existence and to make a contribution to regional integration.

In efforts to describe regional integration, several conceptual frameworks have been employed. Some scholars have used the concept of regional integration to refer to the relationship among countries that no longer anticipate engaging in war with one another. Karl W. Deutsch et al. define integration as the "attainment, within a territory, of a 'sense of community' and of institutions and practices strong enough and wide-spread enough to assure for a 'long' time, dependable expectations of 'peaceful change' among its populations." According to this view, the combined territory of the U.S. and Canada, for example, constitutes an integrated "pluralistic security-community."[5] This concept of regional integration is too broad for the purpose of this study. Others have described the process by which nation-states within a certain area become integrated as "the federalizing process."[6] According to these writers, the integrative process is one in which an inter-state pattern of relations between more or less autonomous entities slowly evolves into a federal state. This concept of regional integration is too narrow to cover all the varied integrative processes occurring in different parts of the world. Whether or not integration will lead to the establishment of a new political state cannot be the only standard in its evaluation. In some cases, the formal merger of previously independent units into a single larger unitary or federal unit may take place. In other cases, the legal independence of separate governments will be retained and nothing more will be achieved than the formation of a regional community that maintains certain functional and political cooperative arrangements among its member states.

The degree of integration is sometimes measured on the basis of the formal legal relationship between the participating states: The term "international organization" is used to describe the less integrated one and "supranational organization" to describe those that are more integrated. These distinctions based on the legal structure are of limited value. The degree of integration does not necessarily coincide with the formal legal structure. The constitutional treaty of an organization may transfer certain functions to the decision-making bodies of the organization, but the transfer may prove to be ineffective. Conversely, a regional organization which (by definition) is not a federal state may have reached a higher degree of integration than is the case

[5] *Political Community*, 5-6.

[6] See, for example, Carl J. Friedrich, "International Federalism in Theory and Practice," in *Systems of Integrating the International Community* (New York 1964), 119-56.

with some federal states. For the purpose of this study the degree of integration will be measured along a continuum which can be conceived of mainly as a function of three interdependent variables. The most important of these is the effective transfer of functions from the state governments to the regional decision-making bodies. The second is the degree of interaction between the elites of the participating states, and the third is the more general societal interactions. The importance of this third variable is considerably less in transitional societies than in highly industrialized ones.[7] The relevance of these variables is based on the fact that effective transfer of functions and the accompanying and to some extent conditioning changes in the two other variables means that a political community comprising the region is brought into being or strengthened. This enables us to distinguish between different degrees of regional integration, as located on this continuum. It must be kept in mind that on a continuum of this kind there are no clear-cut stages—there are only gradual increases in integration, and one degree of integration cannot be sharply distinguished from the one immediately above or below. Nevertheless, it is useful to distinguish between "full political community," "minimum political community," and "regional arrangement."

A *full regional political community* exists when the major part of functions in an important field of government has effectively been transferred to the regional decision-making bodies and there has been some transfer of functions in other fields as well. In regard to an important range of functions, the constituent states no longer act as independent governmental units.[8] In addition, partly as a cause and partly as a consequence, a high degree of interaction has been achieved between the elites affected by these functions and, to an extent varying with the degree of development of the society, a corresponding increase in the societal interaction.

A *minimal regional political community* exists when at least *some* functions in an important field of government have been effectively transferred, accompanied by a certain measure of elite and societal interactions. When as yet no functions are effectively exercised by the regional decision-makers in spite of the fact that a regional organization has been established, we will refer to this simply as a *"regional arrangement."* The term *"regional organization"* will be used to describe any organization in a region, irrespective of the degree of integration reached.

---

[7] These variables are related to what Ernst B. Haas has called "process conditions." See "The Challenge of Regionalism," *International Organization*, XII (1959), 440-59.

[8] Same.

Essential to an understanding of the integrative process are reliable methods of identifying and measuring integrative and disintegrative factors. Because of the complexity of the integrative process, few coherent models have been worked out. Most of the existing images of regional community formation are fragmentary, consisting of isolated concepts, hypotheses, or generalizations. They are almost exclusively based upon the Western European integrative process and do not provide us with a general theory applicable to other regions as well.[9]

As yet we have too few cases to be able to make very sound generalizations about comparative regional integration. In addition, the various groupings manifest great diversity in aims, powers, institutions, and procedures, making it difficult to develop a genuinely comparative framework for political analysis. Significant differences can be discovered in the analysis of the integrative process, depending on the orientation of the national and regional decision-makers and the political, social, and economic realities of the region concerned. The participants in an integration scheme, for instance, may all be at an advanced level of political and economic development, as in Eastern and Western Europe; they may all be less developed, as in Africa and Central America; or they may differ considerably in their level of development, as in Latin America.

A comparative study of regional integration nevertheless suggests that certain factors more or less consistently affect the integrative process in all regions concerned. It is impossible to relate all relevant integrative and disintegrative factors to a general model of regional integration. Therefore, we must distinguish between (1) primary determinants that vitally affect the integrative process in all regions concerned and (2) helpful factors that are not essential to bring about integration.[10] Within the scope of this study, only the primary determinants can be considered.

Attempts at integration to date give reason to believe that the following factors are the primary determinants of the integrative process: as far as *pre-integration conditions* are concerned, a common culture cannot be considered a basic prerequisite, nor do cultural similarities necessarily lead to a high level of integration. The rate of transaction in the pre-integration period does not appear to be decisive. Regional integration has occurred between states which previously had

[9] Three different models of regional community formation have been presented: (1) Philip Jacob, regional community formation as a learning process; (2) Karl W. Deutsch, regional community formation as increasing preference for intra-group communications; (3) Ernst B. Haas, regional community formation as sector integration and spillover. Amitai Etzioni provides us with a more general theory; see Etzioni, *Political Unification* (New York 1965), 290-95.

[10] Morton A. Kaplan, "Problems of Theory Building and Theory Confirmation in International Politics," *World Politics*, XIV, No. 1 (October 1961), 9.

little to do with one another. Until 1960, intra-regional transactions in Latin America and especially in Africa were extremely limited, but lack of contact did not prevent the establishment of the Latin American Free Trade Association and the Organization of African Unity. Nor is democracy, pluralism, and the consent of citizens a prerequisite for the initiation of regional integration.[11] While the support of majority parties, powerful pressure groups, and politicians is important in an industrialized Western area, equivalent rather than identical conditions may make integration possible in a developing area. Haas and Schmitter found a functional equivalent of pressure groups and politicians in the Latin American *technicos*.[12] A small but vocal African elite, with an ideology of pan-Africanism, played an important role in the establishment of the OAU.

What is important, in all regions, is *the realization, by a significantly vital elite, that certain problems can no longer be solved by states acting independently*. The perception by this elite of common or converging interests, and their expectation of benefits thought to be obtainable through integration, are then the critical pre-condition for the establishment of a regional organization. This elite might conceive of the benefits in the following terms: the promise of more power as a result of integration, the promise of greater social, economic, or political equality and additional specific rights to individuals or groups, and the strengthening and defense of a sense of regional unity and solidarity. If this elite succeeds in transmitting the message of the promised rewards of integration to the nerve centers of the governments of the region, the process of integration can be initiated unless powerful regional or international forces prevent such a development from taking place.

Once the regional organization has been established, the following variables appear to be decisive:

1. Institutional Factors

a. *The decision-making process provided for by the constitutive treaty of the organization* will have an impact upon the integrative process. The treaty may provide for a supranational or an intergovernmental structure of competence or for a mixture of both. A supranational structure of competence provides for the establishment of a

---

11 According to Deutsch, the conditions and consequences associated with democracy and pluralism in modern Western society emerge as crucial elements in the process of integration. See *Political Community*.

12 Haas and Schmitter have been looking for functional equivalents for those factors favoring regional integration in Western Europe, but absent in other regions. See Ernst B. Haas and Philippe C. Schmitter, *The Politics of Economics in Latin American Regionalism*, Monograph Series on World Affairs, University of Denver (1965), 5.

regional center of power above the member states and a deliberate transfer of authority, if in limited amounts, to this center. It permits a redefinition of the interests and needs of the member states so as to work out a solution at the regional level. An intergovernmental structure of competence limits the regional system to direct interaction between the power centers of the member units and results in classic diplomatic negotiations. While the latter structure may slow down integration, it does not necessarily determine its outcome. A certain amount of supranationalism tends to develop in any well-established regional organization, as exemplified by the appearance of a certain corporate spirit and a regional orientation within both the Executive Committee of the Council for Mutual Economic Assistance and the Executive Council of the Central American Common Market.[13] In addition, the dynamics of regional integration have been to a large extent pragmatic, with an emphasis on the achieving of successful integration of governmental functions. There is a tendency to modify the original structure of competence of the regional organization through the use of new techniques of coordination and new institutional arrangements. If a certain measure of supranationalism does not develop, however, integration is unlikely to proceed.

b. *The character of the regional secretariat* has an impact upon the integrative process. Such a secretariat can be either the executive organ of the organization or merely an administrative organ with little power of independent initiative.

A responsible regional secretariat, exercising some executive power through its expertness, can play a vital role in the decision-making process. It can serve as a center of power around which transnational groups of actors can be formed. Working permanently on the regional level, the regional bureaucracy tends to become increasingly regional in outlook. Its view of policies tends to become more system-oriented than that of member governments who continue to remain primarily interested in gaining their own national ends within the framework of the organization. Integration will fail in the long run if no such regional secretariat is established or develops.

The secretariats of most of the regional organizations have, in recent years, tended to assume greater executive powers—a trend which has been carefully controlled by the member states, which see in it a real threat to their own sovereignty.

[13] The term "corporate spirit" was made familiar by Leon N. Lindberg in "Decision Making and Integration in the European Community," *International Organization*, XIX (Winter 1965). See also Edward McWhinney, "Classical Federalism and Supra-National Integration or Treaty-Based Association," *Proceedings of the American Society of International Law*, 57th Meeting, April 1963, 244-45.

2. *Functional Factors*

An important variable is *the functional scope of the regional organization*. Multi-functional organizations, providing for expansive tasks—their institutions are charged with specific tasks that continually involve other tasks with which the member governments are concerned—are more effective agents for regional integration than single-purpose organizations.

While the Covenant of the League of Arab States and the Charter of the Organization of African Unity provide for both political and economic cooperation, the constitutive treaties of the European Community, the Council for Mutual Economic Assistance, the Central American Common Market, and the Latin American Free Trade Association refer primarily to economic cooperation.

Both types of organizations, however, are multi-functional and do engage in economic as well as political activities. The economic activities of the League of Arab States and the OAU are becoming increasingly important. Definite political implications can be associated with most regional economic organizations even when their constitutive treaty does not include such notions. In Western Europe, economic integration is looked upon by most governments as a deliberate pathway to a regional political community. All the governments of Central America, with the exception of Costa Rica, have the same view with regard to the Organization of Central American States. The Council for Mutual Economic Assistance, while at present primarily an economic arrangement, is at the same time part of a larger plan for a regional political community. The majority of the members of the Latin American Free Trade Association, however, while accepting the basic necessity of economic integration, are as yet not ready to commit themselves to the establishment of a political community.[14]

Although economic in substance and techniques, economic integration is also in essence a fundamentally political process. This does not mean that there will be an "automatic spillover" from the economic sector to the political sector. Theorists of functionalism have pointed out that:

a. The scope-broadening effect of functional integration depends on which sectors are selected and how much is integrated. "The critical questions are what sectors are tackled first and how extensive the functional effort in each of these sectors is. If they are low spill-over sectors, or if integration in high spill-over sectors is below the take-off point, a broad-scope unification process will not be primed."[15]

[14] See Sidney Dell, *A Latin American Common Market?* (New York 1966), 36-49.
[15] Etzioni, *Political Unification*, 309.

b. While the spill-over process "assumes the continued commitment of major participants to the process of integration, it does not presume passionate enthusiasm and takes for granted opposition to specific items in the catalogue of integrative ventures. The support for given steps rests on the convergence of expectations of the participants; competing expectations and goals can be compromised on the basis of swapping concessions from a variety of sectors, all under the generalized purview of supranational institutions and processes."[16] The extent to which functions are denationalized and transferred to the regional organization is a matter for mutual political agreement, starting with the constitutive treaty and continuing throughout the existence of the organization.

The transfer of functions to the regional organization should not upset the equilibrium with respect to its functional scope and institutional machinery. The functions and jurisdictions which the regional organization actually exercises should correspond to the extent of the needs relevant to its purpose and the capabilities of the system. When burdens exceed capabilities, the system weakens. The questions of larger community police forces and law enforcement, and of the coercion of member states, for example, would clearly exceed the capabilities of a regional system during the early stages of the integrative process.

The extent of integrative capabilities and the further increase of these capabilities, both political and administrative, in the course of the integrative process are determined by the integrative capabilities which exist in the member states as well as in the regional organization itself. Such capability is related to the capacity of the members to respond effectively to each other's actions and needs and to adapt themselves and the system to changing circumstances. The presence or absence of growth in such capabilities plays a predominant role in every integrative process.

3. Political Factors

a. *The orientation of the politically relevant strata of the member states* plays an important role in the integrative process. One of the reasons for the slow growth of regional integration in some areas of the world lies in the fact that effective domestic pro-integration coalitions have not as yet developed. Certain elites may not have become sufficiently oriented toward their regional system.[17] The main sources

[16] Ernst B. Haas, "Technocracy, Pluralism and the New Europe," in Stephen R. Graubard, ed., *A New Europe?* (Boston 1964) , 73. For a criticism of the theory of functionalism, see, for instance, Stanley Hoffmann, "Discord in Community: The North Atlantic Area as a Partial International System," *International Organization* (Summer 1963), 530.

[17] This argument is fully developed in Etzioni, *Political Unification*, 47-51.

of opposition to early integration movements are various groups in the rural population and privileged groups, classes, or regions whose members fear some loss of their privileges as a result of integration, groups such as supernationalistic politicians, old-time bureaucrats, and small, antiquated industrial firms. Any major failure on the part of a formerly strong elite to adjust to its loss of dominance as a result of changed conditions may have a disintegrative impact.

Certain elites may continue to expect benefits from ties and obligations with outside powers and refuse to cooperate with the regional organization. Whole sectors of the regional system may remain controlled by an outside power. In the case of the EEC, for example, the formerly outer-directed elites have gradually rejected American control of the economic sector. More recently, they have attempted, with only partial success, to free European foreign policy and defense policy from American control.

Further, some states are simultaneously members of two or more regional or inter-regional organizations, whose basic aims may not be compatible, thus giving rise to disagreements among elites and weakening their commitment to the region. Both the African and Mid-Eastern systems, for instance, include the Sudan, the Maghreb, and the United Arab Republic; the Latin-Americans are members both of LAFTA and the OAS.

It is only after relevant elites have become sufficiently regionally oriented that regional integration can gain momentum. The emergence of pro-integration elites in a number of political units that can form the cores of strength around which the integrative process can develop is important. Pro-integration coalitions of politicians, technocrats, economists, new domestic industrial enterprises, and some indigenous bankers can effectively overcome the negative impact of the opposition forces.

In addition, there must be broad enough consensus, mutual communication and responsiveness, and cooperative interaction between the relevant regional and national elites and between the elites of the various member units. This requires a certain compatability of the major values held by these elites, a sense of "we-feeling," and a partial self-identification with the region in which they are living—although they may differ over some of the policy consequences to be drawn from this identification.

b. *The satisfaction of some of the initial expectations of key elites* is an important variable. Some tangible gains for a substantial part of the supporters of integration soon after the establishment of the regional organization seem necessary. So long as elites discover in the regional system the actual fulfillment or expectation of fulfillment of important needs, they will not cut off or reduce their support.

Whenever elites perceive real or alleged hardships attributed to the regional system and the promised rewards of integration are not forthcoming, the momentum of the integrative process will probably decline. This will be the case especially if the gains of some members are not matched by others, as illustrated by the Rumanian opposition to an increase of CMEA's regional planning powers, and the dissatisfaction of Uruguay with LAFTA.

To be successful, any integration scheme should give to each participating country the conviction that it will obtain a fair share of the ensuing benefits and that the existing distribution of benefits is the best possible one relative to its power position and could not be substantially improved by unilateral efforts at redistribution. What seems to be decisive in a country's evaluation of advantages of an integration scheme is whether it would result in a more rapid political and economic development than if the development took place within a strictly national framework.

It is not essential that the flow of benefits should balance at any given moment. Insistence on strict equality in the distribution of advantages could seriously retard the process of integration. Especially in the developing countries, a certain measure of unbalanced growth is unavoidable, and some parties will gain more than others; but it seems essential that there should be some balance over a longer period of time.

This gives rise to the complicated problem of how to avoid intraregional conflicts between the stronger and the weaker members that would undermine the objectives of integration and of the intended regional community. It calls for continuous adaptation in terms of new and more extensive expectations and benefits for all members. If these adaptive steps are not undertaken, serious political friction might arise, paralyzing the process of integration or even resulting in a total collapse of the integrative efforts. The developing countries have had such regrettable experiences in their relations with the rest of the world that they would not be willing to remain a party to an agreement in which they would run the risk that inequality within the region would become even more pronounced.

4. National and Regional Environmental Factors

The integrative process is affected by *the political and economic climate* of the region.

It has been suggested by some scholars that integration can be accomplished in industrialized but not in developing regions.[18] The in-

---

[18] For a discussion of the validity of integration in developing areas see, for instance, Lincoln Gordon, "Economic Regionalism Reconsidered," *World Politics*, XIII (1961), 231-53.

dustrial society of Eastern and Western Europe does provide a favorable setting in which regional integration can flourish. But while there are serious obstacles to regional integration in nonindustrialized areas, underdevelopment does not necessarily prevent integration from taking place.

Regional integration in the nonindustrialized world is influenced by the revolution of modernization which is taking place in the majority of developing states. The outcome of this revolution depends upon the will and capacity of a society to modernize its political, economic, social, and psychological systems and "to generate and absorb continuing transformation."[19]

In most of the developing states the major structural transformation and reform required for modernization has not as yet taken place. Approximately half of these states are still primarily concerned with the consolidation of modernizing elites. The leaders of the more traditional forces, often supported by foreign elements, are fighting to maintain their positions. Under these conditions, no decisive break with the institutions associated with a predominantly agrarian way of life, permitting the transition to a modern way of life, can be made.

But even in those states where the modernizing elite has firmly established itself, purposeful action has often been lacking. A rapid surmounting of domestic barriers to modernization would require the mobilization of all social groups in the direction of generally accepted economic and social targets. Consistent national programs to this end exist only in a limited number of developing states. There is considerable antagonism between the various social groups in most developing countries with the result that unity of purpose and action has not been achieved. The dependence primarily upon a colonial type of economy founded on the export of food products and raw materials to the industrialized world makes economic modernization difficult. In addition, the lack of skilled managerial and planning talent, the lack of financial resources, and the deficiencies in infra-structure create major problems.

The above factors do present a handicap to regional integration. No regional integration program can do much for developing countries in the long run unless it forms part of an overall strategy for development.[20] Politically organized societies with an effective government and a reasonably stable basis of support for the modernizing elite must be created. National states are the only agencies available to undertake many important aspects of the modernization process. *Sound*

[19] Manfred Halpern, "Toward Further Modernization of the Study of New Nations," *World Politics*, XVII (1964), 173.

[20] For a full exposition of this line of thought see Dell, *Trade Blocs and Common Markets*. See Miguel S. Wionczek, "Requisites for Viable Economic Integration," in *Latin American Economic Integration*, Wionczek, ed. (New York 1966).

national plans for the modernization of society are a basic requirement for the development of regional integration. Provided that the energies of the constituent states are directed effectively toward development goals, the concerting of their efforts on a region-wide basis could significantly accelerate the attainment of these goals.

Regionalism could be of great value in removing the serious obstacle to industrialization posed by the very small size of so many new countries and a fair number of the old ones. The International Economic Association, for instance, concludes that a population of from 10 to 15 million generally constitutes the minimum size of nation suitable for the development of heavy industries and that the major industrial economies of scale are unlikely to be achieved by a nation without a relatively high income and a population of at least 50 million.[21]

The developing states will be unable to carry out their development plans unless they make a sustained effort to produce within their own region the capital goods industries of which they are in such urgent need today and which they will require on a large scale during the next decades. In order to produce these capital goods and develop all the intermediate goods industries, the developing countries need a common market.

An integration program founded exclusively on the freeing of trade within the region is not sufficient. It would be equivalent, in most cases, to concentrating development on the more advanced countries within the region and would not ensure reciprocity of integration benefits for all participants. An integration program aimed at accelerating development will have to incorporate the following elements: a treaty for the gradual establishment of a customs union; a supranational planning agency; a regional development bank; a regional financial agency; an instrument that promotes industrial specialization by agreement; and a compensation fund for the weaker members.

The Central American experience shows that a program of this nature is possible. The CACM program contains almost all the mechanisms enumerated above. The new treaties for East African and Middle Eastern economic cooperation equally incorporate most of the above elements.

The social and economic attitudes and structures of the modernizing state seem to have their own inner logic which may favor integration. Underdevelopment creates major regional ideological affinities, especially among radical modernizing elites. The fact that all countries within a certain developing region have embarked on a course

---

[21] E.A.G. Robinson, ed., *The Economic Consequences of the Size of Nations* (New York 1960), XVII-XVIII. See also UN Doc. ST/ECLA/CONF.23/L.2/Add.1, *Latin American Symposium on Industrial Development*, Vol. II (December 1965), 145-64.

of modernization, facing much the same enemies and the same problems, produces regional ties. Despite a very emotional attachment to nationalism, the developing countries are aware that there can be no solution for many of their problems apart from integration, which may be delayed but must come to pass within the next few decades if modernization is to occur. Seen in terms of modernization, regional organizations in the developing world may well turn out to be vital centers of economic and social development.

5. *International Environmental Factors*

The growth of regional integration is also influenced by the international political and economic environment. Regional communities are open communities which operate under the evergrowing influence of external elements that are sometimes beyond their control. Outside forces can encourage or prevent the establishment of a regional community. In most existing regional communities, an outside factor has played a role in the community's formation or later development. The big powers have decisively affected developments within regions in which integration has taken place. Regional communities also influence each other. The EEC, for example, provided an incentive for the evolution of Eastern European, Central American and South American economic integration.

Once a regional community has been established, external forces operate to a far greater extent in an unstable community than in a stable one. A stable community, like the EEC and CMEA—with a sufficient degree of autonomy, institutional maturity, and regional consensus—can insulate itself successfully against the negative impact of outside forces. In an unstable community, lacking a sufficient degree of autonomy, such as CACM, LAFTA, the League of Arab States, and the OAU, external forces can set off a chain reaction which will change the tempo and direction of the integration process.

Where the capabilities of an unstable community are overburdened and the community can no longer perform its functions, it is opened to foreign penetration. The low capability of the Middle Eastern, African, and Latin American communities of controlling civil war situations and their lack of sufficient resources to achieve modernization have led to outside intervention. Experience has shown that Western interference in the affairs of the above communities has considerably weakened them and reduced their autonomy.

Regional integration in the developing world is also affected by the economic attitudes and behavior patterns of the industrialized states. The evidence so far seems to point to the fact that the industrialized world does not really intend to provide a viable international framework for the developing regions. It is impossible to discern anything like a genuine strategy for aid to economic and political development projects.[22] Policy-makers in the industrialized world appear more aware of the limited leverage provided by outside aid and seem less optimistic about the prospect of making political gains. One cannot expect much of an increase in the unilateral assistance programs to the developing world. Almost every aspect of Western trade policy discriminates against the developing countries. Communist trade policies, in different ways, also often handicap the developing countries. These countries have encountered increasing difficulties in obtaining the export earnings required to finance the imports they need for development. Part of the difficulty lies in the fact that world demand for primary commodities tends to grow much more slowly than the demands of the latter countries for the finished manufactures that form the major part of their imports. Although the cumulative force of the process of confrontation launched at the United Nations Conferences for Trade and Development is bound to have some impact upon the attitudes of the industrialized world, in the meantime, the slow rate of progress on virtually every recommendation of the first UNCTAD Conference is discouraging.

Another problem is that foreign capital has now gained considerable influence over the basic industries of many developing countries and is determining their patterns of development. The classical colonial relationship is changing and a new type of vulnerability and control is emerging. Foreign capital is increasingly important in the manufacturing sector of many developing countries, while retaining its influence in the mining and agricultural sectors. Not only can this hamper independent economic development, but it also often acts as a basic source of political stagnation. A new middle class essentially dependent on foreign-controlled, large-scale industrial enterprises, is supporting conservative ruling elites. The countries that are trying to implement progressive national and regional development policies are suffering strong internal and external political and economic pressures.

Autonomy, a condition where intra-community actions and responses predominate over external control, must be considered a minimum condition for the success of the integrative process. It enables the countries of the region to unify their criteria and policies over against other centers of the world.

For the time being, the regional communities in the developing world can be, at best, subsystems, autonomous but not independent; that is, not free of certain negative influences involving outside states. But even this minimum condition is often not fully met in these com-

22 W. Brandt, "To a New World Economy," *International Spectator*, xx (September 1966).

munities today. They do not appear as yet to possess a sufficient level of integration, independence of other systems, and internal interdependence among the constituent states.

The developing countries are aware of this lack of autonomy and of the external challenge to their emerging new way of life. So far it has not driven them closer toward unity, but it has separated them from each other instead. It has produced a basic split between those accepting and those rejecting dependence on the industrialized world. This diversity of national positions operates as a major obstacle to continued integration.

A continuation of the present policies of the industrialized countries will make the developing states increasingly aware of their subordinate position within a highly stratified international system. It will probably compel them, within the near future, to fall back on their own collective resources. It will increase, above and beyond the differences in national situations, the general feeling of a mutual threat, and also the hope of a common future. It may, therefore, also trigger the behavior patterns which will make acceleration of regional integration and the establishment of a more autonomous system possible.

The expanding economies of the socialist countries will provide new opportunities for coping with the change-resisting pressures exerted on developing countries from the Western industrialized states. Of particular importance is the availability of markets and other economic resources of the socialist countries that can be utilized in undertaking an effective solution of the developing world's economic crisis.

The essential conditions for integration outlined here, whose exact interrelations remain unknown, do not come into existence all at once and are not established in any particular fixed order. Rather, they may come into being very slowly and in almost any sequence. This does not mean that they are all of equal importance. A comparative study of regional integration suggests that, in all regions concerned, the internal political factors are the most important ones, followed by the environmental factors, and only after that the institutional and functional factors. Varying regional political, economic, and social contexts do not seem to alter significantly the relationship between these factors. A far more detailed examination of data, over a long period of time, will be required to draw more definite conclusions.

For integration to proceed, a stable equilibrium with respect to the institutional structure, functional scope, and commitment of the members should be maintained. Once most of the necessary conditions are present, the tempo of the integrative process quickens and a full regional political community will probably develop.

II

Efforts to forecast the prospects of regional integration confront considerable difficulties. The development of regional systems is determined by an interaction between national, regional, and international elites and forces. The results of this interaction are not easily predictable. It is impossible to predict the actions of each individual actor within the regional system because there are too many variables and the interaction problem is too intricate. Decision-makers may not follow the rules of means-ends-rationality and may respond in terms of nonrational considerations. It is difficult to identify the relative influence of the internal factors—born within the regional system itself—and that of external factors—born totally or partially out of the regional system. The latter may act with the same strength that the former does in the definition of the system's state and its process. To date, they form a continuum that can be considered separately only for analytical reasons.

One should also not underestimate the span of time that is required for major changes in the political, economic, and social fabric of the regional system to unfold. The system will be influenced by future conditioning factors, some of which may be integrative and others disintegrative. Some systems might spend decades wavering uncertainly within the zone of transition from minimal to full regional political community. A forecast can, therefore, only attempt to give a rough estimate of probable developments within a particular regional system, of the conditions under which the system will be altered, and of changes that may be expected to take place. It can identify certain regions of the world where the potential for further integration is high, and point out other regions where, despite the existence of regional institutions, some primary conditions seem weak or absent.

Within the next twenty years, some of the regional organizations (the European Community, the Council for Mutual Economic Assistance, the Arab League, and the Organization of Central American States) are likely to reach the level of full political community; others may not go substantially beyond the level of minimal political community (the OAU and LAFTA).

The seven-month boycott by France in 1964 of the institutions of the European Community produced a severe crisis. Agreement among the six member states was finally reached at the Council of Ministers' meeting of January 1966. This agreement will slow down Community integration to a certain extent since it has been decided that: "When in the case of decisions which could be taken by a majority vote, very important interests of one or more partners are at stake, the members of the Council will try to achieve within a reasonable period solutions which can be adopted by *all* the members of the Council."[23] A divergence of views persists about what should be done in cases where conciliation cannot be achieved. In addition, the ministers approved a series of seven points concerning relations between the Council and the Commission. While the Commission's right of initiative in making proposals to the Council was not reduced, the agreement reflects a desire to decelerate the expansion of the supranational powers of the Commission. This move was to be expected in view of the replacement of the executive bodies of the three European communities—the Coal and Steel Community, the European Atomic Energy Community, and the European Economic Community —by a single European Commission creating an increasingly powerful European executive organ. The Commission is a dynamic organ, with strong supranational tendencies, and these tendencies have been carefully controlled by the Council from the beginning.

The above agreement does not signify a turning away from the supranational to the intergovernmental pattern of decision-making. The existence of "a certain corporate spirit" distinguishes the Council from a mere intergovernmental body.[24] The unanimous consent of six ministers, or their representatives, is also more easily obtained than the separate approval of a particular decision by the six member states in accordance with their constitutional processes. The decisions of the Council do have the direct binding effect of law on natural and legal persons in the member states; i.e., a binding effect without implementation by national legislative organs.[25] The Commission will continue to play an important role in the decision-making process. When the Council debates a proposal, the Commission plays an active part. It is free to amend its proposals at any stage of the procedure and thus can play a constructive role in suggesting possible compromises between six national positions as conceived from an independent, regional standpoint.

The "Treaty Establishing a Single Council and a Single Commission of the European Communities," signed on April 8, 1965, by the representatives of the six member states, is the most important constitutional development since the Treaty of Paris and the Rome Treaties were signed. This Merger Treaty is intended to be the first step toward the ultimate merger of the ECSC, the EEC, and Euratom. The revision of the three treaties will provide the opportunity for a general review of the objectives and policies of the European Community and the establishment of a single Community. This re-

[23] *European Community*, No. 89 (February 1966), 1-2.
[24] Lindberg, "Integration in the European Community," 62.
[25] See Article 189 of the Treaty of Rome.

view, implying a confrontation of differing national policies, is going to be decisive in the development of European integration.[26]

In spite of the political and institutional disagreements, the Community institutions and organs have shown themselves competent to deal with the tasks laid upon them by the Treaties. The Community has penetrated the political life of each member unit and has developed such powerful support among economic and political elite groups that it is now an established and irreversible part of the European environment. The prospects for success of the European Community remain good. The consolidation of the Community and its transformation into a political as well as an economic entity will continue. In the course of the next decade or so, Western Europe is almost certain to move further toward some institutionalized form of political consultation and some common defense arrangements. It will hence be an increasingly important force with an emerging identity of its own. The level of a maximum political community will probably be approached within the near future.

Until 1962, CMEA was ill-equipped to implement any plans for integration. By then, however, largely as a result of the evolution of the EEC, the majority of CMEA members were in favor of establishing a unified intergovernmental planning organ empowered to issue binding decisions when unanimous agreement was arrived at. This organ would draw up regional plans for the rational allocation of resources and for the specialization of agriculture and industrial production. In addition, an enlarged secretariat, acting independently of the national governments and responsible to the collective regional planning organ, would be established.[27]

In 1964, CMEA went through a crisis when Rumania rejected the Charter amendments drafted to implement the above changes. The Rumanian position that a notification of lack of interest by one member removed the matter from the CMEA Council agenda had to be accepted, and the idea of a supranational planning organ had to be abandoned. The CMEA agreement of February 1964, however, provided a partial solution to the above crisis. Procedures were formalized to deal with cases in which complete accord could not be reached within CMEA.

1. In case of a veto where a multilateral problem is concerned, the interested parties may use the CMEA framework for research and negotiation.

2. A state which declares itself "non-interested" cannot veto an action agreed to by others. It can only refuse to participate. In most

26 Gordon L. Weil, "The Merger of the Institutions of the European Communities," 61 *American Journal of International Law*, 57-66 (1967).

27 *New Times*, No. 12, March 27, 1963.

cases, collaboration on the action program will then be effected outside CMEA. Since 1964, research and the initial stages of planning have taken place within the framework of CMEA, but a number of action programs have been administered independently of it. For example, in the case of a proposition to set up a programming center for iron and steel production, Rumania declared lack of interest. Seven members (i.e., all save Rumania and Mongolia) therefore set up their own agency, Intermetall, in July 1964, with headquarters in Budapest.[28] Eventually, these separate programs will probably be integrated into the central structure.

As far as the present structure of authority is concerned, the Council of Ministers determines the most important matters of policy. The practical role of the Council has been reduced since 1962, when the Executive Committee was established. This committee is both a policy-making and an executive agency. It was created to translate discussion at the council level into practical measures, and to continue, in the interim between council sessions, rapport among the participants. It consists of government representatives, but the existence of a regional orientation and of a certain corporate spirit distinguishes it from a mere intergovernmental body. It is increasingly becoming the real center of power within CMEA.

The CMEA permanent commissions are playing an increasingly important role in the preparation of politics and programs. The secretariats of the commissions are gradually being merged with the corresponding divisions of the CMEA Secretariat in Moscow, with the aim of achieving a comprehensive and coordinated administrative machinery required for the implementation of the increasingly complex tasks.

The CMEA recommendations and decisions are binding only on the governments which have agreed with them. They are not directly binding on national agencies and individuals, but must first be ratified by members and then incorporated into the national law of the member states. While the principle of sovereign decision is maintained, CMEA is more than a mere intergovernmental organization. It can vitally affect the independent sovereignty of member governments by forcing upon them various policies and action programs essential for achievement of the regional goals. The consequences of noncompliance are such that resistance is gradually becoming more difficult.

The CMEA, in comparison with other regional economic arrangements, is in a favorable position since it does not have to deal with the activities and projects of numerous economic units, as in the case of private enterprise economies, but with the centrally planned and

28 Michael Kaser, Comecon, *Integration Problems of the Planned Economies* (London 1965), 104. Also UN Doc. E/CONF.46/17, 8 January 1964, 5.

directed economies of its member countries. Once a recommendation has been agreed upon, transformed into binding agreements, and made a part of the national plans, economic integration proceeds at a fairly rapid speed.[29]

The national plans, however, also create a number of obstacles to speeding up the pace of regional integration. The lack of flexibility in introducing corrections into the national plans has had some negative effects on the economic structure of the Eastern European states. Certain conceptions about socialist methods of reproduction and the conduct of economic affairs under socialism have been retained even after they had begun to obstruct economic development.

It has become evident that if the CMEA members are to advance they must eliminate dogmatic attitudes and adapt planning methods to the process of material production. The basic producing units in the CMEA countries have been cut off almost entirely from market impulses, both domestic and foreign. The degree and effectiveness of integration within CMEA depends in many ways on a more active participation of its members in the world economy. It requires the development of new forms of economic relations between the CMEA countries and other parts of the world.

A problem arises from the fact that the Eastern European countries, because they are at different levels and in different phases of industrial development, adopt different attitudes toward CMEA. The more heavily industrialized northern members want to promote stronger regionwide planning controls. The less developed members are afraid that with continued integration they might be kept at the present level of industrialization; and the more advanced countries, in turn, are not inclined to eliminate the disparities in economic development at their own expense. While certain members look upon their central problem as a need for raw materials or further industrialization, others, like Czechoslovakia, find that their most important need is to redirect their trade westward. As a result, controversies within the economic community exists among members at similar levels of development, as well as between the industrially advanced and the less developed members.

Despite these disagreements, the search for new economic principles and techniques that are relevant to advanced, socialist, technological societies is a fundamental feature of present trends in the CMEA

[29] See Draginja Arsíc, "Certain Problems of Economic Development and Co-operation within the Comecon," *International Problems* (1967), 136-137; Jozef Bognar, *Co-Existence*, No. 2 (Nov. 1964), 94; A. Kashin, "The Communist Bloc, Rumania and Polycentrism," *Bulletin*, Institute for the Study of the U.S.S.R., XIII (October 1966) No. 10; John Pinder, "EEC and Comecon," *Survey*, No. 58 (January 1966); UN Doc. E/CONF.46/17 (January 1964), 5-10; UN Publication, Sales No. 66 II.B.4, *Economic Integration and Industrial Specialization among the Member Countries of CMEA*; *Proceedings of the UN Conference on Trade and Development*, Vol. VII, Part 2 (New York 1964).

countries. The basic principles of the Czechoslovak reform of the economy were in accordance with tendencies in other socialist countries, including the Soviet Union.

The growing popular demand for consumer goods and economic reform has created a new, pragmatic and anti-dogmatic attitude toward economic problems among a group that Billington has called "the efficiency-seeking intelligentsia."[30] This elite faces substantial opposition and arouses fears among certain dogmatic party officials. It is becoming an increasingly vital force, however, and may be considered an effective agent of change. Assuming that the reform, although gradual and long-range, will continue, important obstacles to the development of productive forces in the CMEA countries will be eliminated and socio-economic relationships transformed.

The developments within CMEA remain, of course, to a large extent dependent on the attitude of the Soviet Union. During the early years, this country completely dominated the organization, and used it exclusively for its own purposes. Between 1957 and 1962, the Soviet Union gradually moved from direct control over the Eastern European states to rule through consultative bodies. While the area remained a Soviet sphere of influence, the position of the Eastern European members was strengthened and the principles of national sovereignty, cooperation and mutual assistance were accepted. From 1962 on, each party claimed the right to govern its own people and define its own interests within a rather loose pledge of allegiance to Marxism-Leninism and to proletarian internationalism. Long-quiescent Eastern European states, such as Rumania and Czechoslovakia, were able to start moving toward independence. Within CMEA, the general strategy of the organization was no longer set purely in terms of Soviet estimates of what will benefit the region. The Eastern European members developed a vested interest in the organization and participated actively in the process of defining its goals and policies. CMEA became the testing-ground for demonstrations of independence. Socialist leaders sought to match their new political autonomy with increased economic power through a restructured CMEA. The growing multilateral ties among the Eastern European states afforded them an opportunity to act in concert against specific Soviet actions. As a result of joint pressure by Poland, East Germany and Czechoslovakia, the Soviet Union was forced to make some major concessions. Most Eastern European countries, at one point or another, jointly or separately, successfully opposed the Soviet position in CMEA in order to protect their own economic positions from what they regarded as Soviet interference.

[30] James H. Billington, "Force and Counterforce in Eastern Europe," *Foreign Affairs*, Vol. 47, No. 1 (October 1968) , 33.

This period of decentralization and indirect rule through consultative bodies seems to have been interrupted in August 1968, as a result of the military intervention by some Warsaw Pact members in Czechoslovakia. The predominant position and overwhelming physical power of the Soviet Union was once more underlined. A small but determined coalition of radical members of the secret police establishment and the military seem to have been able to gain new power, weakening the position of the more moderate, centrist party leaders. The Czechoslovak experiment scared certain vacillating moderates, converting them into advocates of a forceful course of action and driving them into a coalition with the hard-line extremists. The much larger community of intellectuals and technocrats was unable to merge into a sufficiently united counter-pressure group in support of the remaining moderate forces in the Politburo and Central Committee.

It is hard to predict the immediate and long-range impact of the invasion on relations within the regional community. Several conflicting forces are at work in the political processes of the Soviet Union. The exact importance of these forces and their interaction remain unknown. The more hard-line political leaders are in favor of an activist approach in Eastern Europe, which would forcefully consolidate the regional power orbit, reimpose tighter control over most parties and create a new socialist state community. Varying political issues, both national, regional and international, contribute to the present indecision of the moderate, centrist party leaders. They fear that a Czechoslovak defection from Communist orthodoxy would imperil their own position and weaken the solidarity of the socialist alliance. Extremist political leaders, especially in Eastern Germany, Poland and Bulgaria, exert pressures on the Soviet leadership in favor of continued intervention in Czechoslovakia. The prospect of a reorientation of Czechoslovak trade westward intensified the Soviet leaders' distrust of Germany. They look upon West Germany's current eastern policy, which seeks to open trade and diplomatic contacts with the Socialist countries of Eastern Europe, as an attempt to detach these states from the Soviet alliance. Finally, they fear the pressures they see developing simultaneously from a capitalistic Western Europe, dominated by the U.S. and West Germany, and a revolutionary activist China.

It seems unlikely, however, that developments in Eastern Europe in the immediate future will again provoke military intervention. The present leadership has already learned that the negative impact of military intervention against one of its allies outweighs the gains. The consequences of military intervention in Czechoslovakia are likely to make the hard-line party leaders more hesitant about repeating this step in the future. Part of the indecision of the more moderate leaders is explained by the fact that they remain the product of the radical tradition of the thirties. A younger, more pragmatic group of moderates will rise to power in the party in the near future. This group will, most likely, be more interested in the effective exercise of political power than in the use of the overwhelming Soviet military power.

It may be expected that the Eastern European leaders will continue to wield influence on the Soviet Union as far as regional and international relations are concerned. Various developments in early 1969, point to the creation of a new subregional coalition of moderate forces which will, in time, learn how to resist the Soviet tactic of opening up divisions within any force that challenges their dominance. For example, there has been a favorable response on the part of younger party members to the report of the Czechoslovak Academy of Sciences, published in October 1968. This report attacked the August intervention and pointed out that: "The metaphysical conception of socialism as a perfect system leads logically to the conclusion that any criticism of deficiencies and contradictions is considered indiscriminately as anti-socialist." It further stated that "If we shift the traditional Marxist concept of counter-revolution from the sphere of action to the realm of opinion, any opinion not entirely in conformity with a certain up-to-date conception may be interpreted simply as being counter-revolutionary. This is a dangerous logic, paralyzing the party and Marxist theory."[31] The Soviet Union, faced by a united group of moderate leaders, can win support from the socialist states only on condition that it avoids conflict in the military and economic sphere.

The growing power of CMEA itself will be a vital factor contributing to a balance of power within the region. The independent authority of CMEA, the development of a tradition of debating major problems that come within CMEA's purview and the effective right of members to oppose Soviet recommendations will make Soviet domination of the organization unlikely in the future. The Eastern European countries will probably press gradually toward even further erosion of Soviet dominance within CMEA.

Favorable developments within the Eastern European regional community will remain dependent upon the political situation in Western Europe. Any apparent rise in power of the Nazi-led right wing radicals in West-Germany would most likely weaken the moderate forces in the Socialist community. The present coalition of Christian and Social Democrats in Germany seems to be looking for a common ground where Germans and Russians can meet each other and overcome their traditional mistrust. If West Germany succeeds in its aim of engaging in a peaceful dialogue with the Socialist states, this would

---

[31] See "Report of the Czechoslovak Academy of Sciences," *New York Times* (October 24), 1.

reduce tensions and assuage the belligerency of the Soviet leadership. An all-European detente would improve and promote relations of mutual benefit between the member states of the Eastern European regional community, as well as facilitate the development of a cooperative relationship between the EEC and CMEA.

The future of regional integration in Eastern Europe will also be influenced by the force and direction of Eastern European nationalism. Tendencies at work within the region seem to pull two ways: toward closer economic and political integration and interdependence, and toward assertion of separate national interests. National aspirations, political and economic, have been released in the area, and special national interests with regard to regional and international foreign policy have been defined. The rebirth of nationalism has also accelerated the search for new political and philosophical ideals and the drive for economic efficiency. The long-term effect of the new nationalism will almost certainly be to erode some of the authoritarian features of the socialist system in Eastern Europe. It is unlikely that the conflict between autonomy and integration will paralyze the integration efforts. As in other regions, nationalism and regionalism exist side by side. It is widely recognized in Eastern Europe that it is not possible for countries ranging in population from 30 million down to 7 million, with low purchasing power, to enjoy a full development of modern industries on the basis of their separate markets. Eastern Europe is already moving toward some subregional cooperation, exclusive of Soviet participation but within the larger framework of CMEA. It may be expected that this trend will continue, creating by the mid-1980's a community of about 130 million people with a G.N.P. of about $215 billion. The subregional integration of Eastern Europe would be profitable to the Soviet Union and would provide it with a stable and secure partner.

The future of CMEA will continue to depend to a large extent on the aims and perceptions of a small elite of officials, party leaders and technicians. While real dissension has marked recent conferences of the CMEA Council of Ministers, and of the Party and Government leaders of the CMEA countries, there seem to be no signs of a deep and lasting disunity. Even Rumania and Czechoslovakia have called, on several occasions, for new forms of regional political and economic cooperation, and both regimes have asserted their continued loyalty to the Socialist regional community. Unless circumstances change, it is unlikely, though possible, that either of these regimes will follow the Yugoslav example and leave the community.

It is impossible to predict exactly how far the processes of change in Eastern Europe and the Soviet Union will lead. What is clear is that, so far, these processes have not destroyed the regional community-building process. The Communist elite remains united by the common bonds of converging interests, similar goals, and shared convictions as to the political and economic aims of integration. The next decade will probably see continuing erosion of the more militant, doctrinaire aspects of Marxism-Leninism. New, more independent, technologically-oriented elites are likely to be strongly interested in regional and sub-regional cooperation. The many successes achieved by these countries, in a relatively brief period, in spheres on which they concentrated their efforts attest to their ability to solve problems.

The consolidation of the EEC will remain a factor in the further integration of the European Communist states. In order to strengthen its position not only vis-à-vis the West but also the opposing Communist branch, they will probably, within the immediate future, seek a tighter regional organization, resulting in a decrease in polycentrism. The present phase may be looked upon as a transitory period for a further development toward the establishment of a full regional political community.

The new Charter of the Organization of Central American States (ODECA), which came into force on March 30, 1965, states that the five countries constitute an economic and political community aiming at Central American integration. The organs of the Central American Common Market (CACM), established in 1960, will be incorporated into ODECA.

In terms of limiting the sovereignty of the member governments, the Central American States have given little power to the regional institutions. Decisions on substantive questions in the two main organs, the Meeting of Heads of State and the Conference of Ministers of Foreign Affairs, have to be adopted unanimously. Decision-making is still carried out by traditional diplomatic instruments, treaties, and protocols to treaties, which must be submitted to a legislative ratification in each state.

One of the main reasons for the success of integration in Central America so far was the existence of a degree of separability of economic matters from the mainstream of political debate.[32] This enabled the existing modernizing elite, working in the regional institutions and in the governmental or private sectors of the member states, to bring about economic integration quietly. The expansion in regional trade has been impressive, and there has been effective cooperation in the construction of roads, telecommunications systems, railways, and air navigation. All that is lacking to complete the integration mechanism is the smooth functioning of specialization by agreement

---

[32] For an excellent projection see J. S. Nye, "Central American Regional Integration," *International Conciliation*, 562 (March 1967). Also "Situation of the Central American Integration Programme," UN Doc. E/CN.12/708, 1-5.

and the equitable distribution of new industrial activities. Extremely slow changes have occurred in the industrial structure of the area, still mainly limited to light consumer goods, by the absence of new large-scale domestic industries dependent on the total market. The emerging new domestic entrepreneur cannot match the financial and technological resources available to large international corporations entering the Central American market area. The available information suggests that a negative attitude on the part of the United States is partly responsible for the unimpressive performance of the Regime for Integration Industries. United States lending agencies have refused to sanction the use of their funds for loans, to firms designated as "integration industries." This is to be regretted since it may well be that the Regime, containing as it does a specific clause with respect to the participation of domestic and regional capital in "integration industries," is the only mechanism capable of preventing an undue share of the benefits from integration from continuing to fall into the hands of foreign industrial enterprises.

A projection of future success of Central American integration is difficult. With the addition of new functions and the development of new institutions, integration has become more difficult for politicians to ignore. As the integration process becomes more complex, the political conditions for further acceleration will change. Many of the new political and economic tasks of integration can only be viable if the governments fully support them. The main problem is that in the majority of states—El Salvador, Guatemala, Honduras, and Nicaragua—the transition from a political leadership committed to the traditional system to one that favors thoroughgoing modernization has not as yet been completed. The traditional elite feels threatened by the national and regional pro-integration elite and resists attempts to accelerate integration. Only in Costa Rica has the development of social and political change needed for modernizing reached a sufficiently high level.

The frictions resulting from the tendency for industrialization to center in three of the five member states, El Salvador, Guatemala, and Costa Rica, have had a weakening effect on the common market's institutional functioning. A compromise is still being sought by the less developed partners, Nicaragua and Honduras.

On the positive side, the economic distance between the five republics is relatively short, and Central America does not appear to need a compensation fund for the weaker members. This will make it easier for the CACM authorities to continue cooperation in the field of industrial integration and to extend the regional policy of industrialization to consumer-goods industries, as well as to those supplying raw materials, semifinished products, and capital goods.

A considerable degree of regional consciousness exists among modernizing elites in Central America. Most of the officials who staff the regional institutions are firmly committed to some form of Central American political union. In addition, a growing number of Central Americans belonging to the new middle sectors of the urban population are in favor of integration. Although this sector has only recently been mobilized into national life and is not a cohesive group, it has a modernizing impact upon the political system. As a result of the joint pressures of these various groups, modernization within Central America will probably be speeded up. A full regional political community may well be established within the next twenty years. The area, however, will remain a United States sphere of influence, and cannot be expected to play a truly independent role in world politics.

The limited scope and powers of LAFTA reflect the original consensus of member governments that the organization was not supposed to be a forerunner of political integration.

The major impetus for the formation of a regional market came from ECLA and its support group of *technicos*, not from the governments themselves. The final draft of the treaty represents a compromise among generally conflicting aims.[33]

LAFTA is an intergovernmental organization. The Conference is the decisional body of LAFTA. Decisions of the Conference in the form of recommendations or requests are adopted when affirmative votes are cast by at least two-thirds of the contracting parties and providing that no negative vote is cast. The Permanent Executive Committee is the permanent organ of the Association. The Committee can make suggestions to the Conference, but it cannot make any decisions directly binding on member states.

The Secretariat's duties are purely administrative. The Secretariat is not interpreting its role dynamically and has made no attempt to implant a distinctive regional ideology or to program the association's activities.[34]

One of the main weaknesses of the LAFTA Treaty is that no dynamic regional center of decision-making was established. The ultimate power to opt for accelerated integration has continued to rest with the governments themselves. The responsibility for carrying out the functions involved in the existing agreements has been entrusted to the system's political organs: The Conference and the Permanent Executive Committee. The task of these organs is above all to represent and defend the interests of the individual countries. The Conference is weak and refers even the most trivial decisions to the mem-

[33] Dell, *A Latin American Common Market?*, 25-26.
[34] Raul Prebisch, *Toward a Dynamic Development Policy for Latin America*, UN Doc. E/CN.12/680/Rev. 1 (1964), 102-07.

ber governments. The LAFTA negotiating machinery is, at present, unsuitable for the effective carrying out of the broader functions required for a new stage of integration. The adoption of policies aimed at the promotion of regional integration calls for the reconciliation of national interests with the overall aims of development of the area, and this may be difficult for bodies that by their very nature do not represent the interests of the Community as a whole and do not have real powers of practical action. The integration mechanism in LAFTA is a much weaker one than that operating in Central America. LAFTA is only a free trade area and does not have most of the agencies required for successful integration. As a result of the above, the powers of the organization have not increased to any extent and its general record over the past nine years is disappointing. Stipulated tariff reductions on behalf of the member countries were fulfilled, and there was a slight increase in trade, but in no way did LAFTA have a real influence on the industrialization of the member countries. Economic integration under such conditions, benefits primarily the firms best suited to take advantage of tariff liberalization—the large Western corporations.

Among most experts on Latin American integration there is a surprising degree of agreement regarding what must be done in order to make LAFTA an efficient integration instrument. It is generally accepted that in order to accelerate integration in the Latin American area, it is necessary that the permanent authorities of LAFTA, duly reorganized and strengthened, should study what kind of precise measures might be undertaken to solve problems common to the area. It is doubtful that these measures can be undertaken without recourse to regional-development planning. In this regard, it is discouraging that very few at the government level are willing to face up to this integration program requirement.

Almost all that LAFTA has done to date has been to pass resolutions expressing the intention to achieve effective economic integration. In December 1966, LAFTA ministers meeting in Montevideo approved a resolution to establish a permanent Council of Ministers as the organization's top policy-making body, together with a Technical Commission, fully empowered to put forward proposals; but this agreement was not translated into positive action by the most recent meeting of the LAFTA Conference. At the summit meeting held in April 1967 in Punta del Este, the main emphasis was put on trade liberalization. The Latin American governments committed themselves, however, to continued integration and to the modernization and reform of national and regional political and economic institutions. It was decided to promote joint meetings at a ministerial level of the participating countries in both LAFTA and CACM and to transfer to these meetings the responsibility of adopting decisions regarding the creation of a Latin American common market, to be set up before 1985. It is too early to see in what way this decision will affect the integration process.

There are various causes for the slowness in achieving integration in Latin America. LAFTA, with very few exceptions, does not enjoy decisive political support within and without the region.

In some countries such as Paraguay, Colombia, Ecuador, and Peru, a modernizing elite is still engaged in the consolidation of its position. While modernizing elites are established in such countries as Uruguay, Brazil, Argentina, Chile, Venezuela, and Bolivia, they lack the power to modernize all levels of society.[35] Small groups which have achieved a level of adequate political participation coexist alongside masses of population which have not done so, producing societies without a stable middle sector. The unpredictable uses of power by corrupt politicians create a climate of dissatisfaction and uncertainty. Inexperienced bureaucrats form a major obstacle to sound long-term governmental planning. With rare exceptions, no progressive national modernization programs, committed to independent economic development and the welfare of the masses, exist in Latin America. Ruling elites are unable or unwilling to respond to the requirements of a regional integration program. There is opposition to integration on the part of agricultural and economic vested interests. Until Latin American political underdevelopment is corrected and modernizing elites are firmly established in the majority of states, regional integration will be able to proceed only at a slow speed.

Another reason for the slow advance in achieving integration in Latin America is that it is a continent comprising countries in very different stages of development. The more advanced countries are hesitant to take part in a process of integration which might endanger advances which are possible for them through their own efforts. The poorer and smaller countries show an evident fear that the main benefits of integration may go to their more advanced neighbors. The LAFTA Conference has adopted many resolutions that define and broaden the special preferential regime for the less-developed LAFTA members. Nonetheless, they have not been implemented as yet to a degree which would compensate the weakest LAFTA members for their inability to produce goods for export to the region. In order for integration to proceed, it is necessary to create conditions which will allow all countries to feel confidence in integration as a joint undertaking.

Latin American integration is also considerably weakened by the tendency of some Latin American elites to continue to be primarily

[35] Black, *The Dynamics of Modernization*, 91-92.

outer-directed. Their awareness of an interest in other Latin American countries is limited. Their primary contact is with the centers of industrialization, above all with the United States. They permit certain large foreign investors, and foreign corporations whose operations in Latin America are based on dividing the regional market among their branches, to receive the major benefits from Latin American integration. The more inner-directed, modernizing elites do not receive sufficient support from the U.S. since the modernization program they advocate all too often collides with American interests.

From the short-range point of view, any forecast has to be pessimistic. It is doubtful that those sectors of society associated with modern industry, the industrialists and entrepreneurs, will be able to carry out the economic integration process by themselves. In most of the Latin American countries they constitute a class without much political power. Their interests tend to conflict with those of the national bourgeoisie of other Latin American countries. Finally, rather than oppose the extraregional interests, they seem more willing to cooperate with them.

With the exception of Mexico, reformist governments, willing to harmonize their national development policies with the aims of regional integration, do not seem to have a long life span in Latin America. Evidently these governments can maintain power only to the extent that the landowning and industrial bourgeoisie do not feel threatened by movements based on the masses, and to the extent that foreign interests favor them. In many respects, the present military governments of Argentina and Brazil demonstrate this fear of the advance of the masses and reject any reformist "alliance" of the bourgeoisie with the working classes. Both governments have also rejected an integrationist policy.

From the more long-range point of view, however, there are some hopeful signs for the Latin American integration movement. New social groups with an ideology favorable to change and with developmental and integrationist attitudes are rising to power. They do not, as yet, have enough influence to make their interests really felt. But slowly they are becoming important agents of economic and political integration. Integration has the support of some of the most dynamic elements in the Latin American societies. A new reformist type of Pan-Latin Americanism is developing among certain intellectual and reformist circles. Pro-integration elites are found among members of the new managerial elite, the economic bureaucracy, the military, and labor unions.

Pan-Latin Americanism is becoming, also, a living reality to an increasing number of Latin American politicians. The establishment in 1964 of the Latin American Parliament, with headquarters in Lima,

Peru, reflects the interest in integration of certain regionally oriented members of political parties. The new parliament is intended to act as a catalyst in spurring governments and peoples toward Latin American integration. Unfortunately, it probably will not have too much impact since the parliamentary system has not been very successful in Latin America even at the national level.

The pro-integration elites are convinced that social and political change in Latin America cannot be deferred any longer; pressure for modernization will increase at the rate at which the masses of peasants and workers make themselves felt. They realize that many of the complex problems of modernization cannot be solved in isolation, but do require regional collective action. They are losing confidence in outside alternatives in the form of increased U.S. assistance, commodity stabilization agreements, and lowered tariffs on industrialized products from developing countries. They feel that it is necessary for Latin America to adopt a common, practical, and effective development policy which would specifically benefit Latin American interests.

The pro-integration elites are convinced that the basic condition for the development of Latin American political potential is that it assert its own personality. As one of them has pointed out: "Pan-Americanism has been negative for Latin America, especially because it has represented the greatest obstacle to the creation of that authentic international community which rests on real and national factors, that is, the Latin American community. Pan-Latin Americanism is the only hope of creating an organic community in the future."[36] These common views in regard to the future of Latin America may encourage the pro-integration elites to cooperate in the goal toward regional and subregional integration. In Latin America, much would seem to depend on whether the U.S. can come to terms with these elites within the immediate future. If it does, it should be possible to achieve more regional integration than has proved possible so far. In that case, the pro-integration elites will probably succeed in defeating the interests opposed to integration and in effecting not only an upgrading of the LAFTA institutions but also in establishing new channels for the development of a minimal regional political community.

If, however, the U.S. continues to control most of Latin America, through closed, conservative, military or pseudo-democratic regimes, armed revolt by the masses may be the only way out of stagnation and underdevelopment. Combined national action by urban working classes and student cadre units, mass peasant organizations, and mobile guerrilla movements would then provide the only real solution for Latin America.

[36] Jorge Castaneda, *Mexico and the United Nations* (New York 1958), 172. See also Octavio Paz, *The Labyrinth of Solitude* (New York 1961).

The Pact of the League of Arab States makes no reference to eventual political unity. The League is an intergovernmental cooperative association whose major role is that of a coordinating agency in the fields of common political and functional activities. No supranational decision-making organ has been established. According to the Pact, the principal organs of the Arab League are the Council and the permanent Secretariat. An Economic Council and a Joint Defense Council were later provided by a special treaty, in 1950. The Arab League Council is the principal decision-making body of the League. Unanimity is required as a voting rule except as specified by the Pact. The decisions of the Council take the form of resolutions which "recommend," "urge," and "request" member states to take joint action. The Political Committee, one of the permanent committees established under the Pact, has taken over the functions of the League Council in all but name. The Committee discusses the recommendations of the various League organs. Its decisions, adopted by simple majority, are submitted to the League Council, where they are normally approved without serious debate.

A promising development from the point of view of the future of regionalism in the Arab world is the continued growth in importance of the Arab League Secretariat. The Arab League Pact gives the Secretariat only administrative functions. From the beginning of the organization, however, it has assumed an important role in the decision-making process. The permanent committees have come to rely on the Secretariat for the long-range studies which the committees consider in annual meetings. As a result of the effective cooperation between the Secretariat and the Political Committee, the League Council has been able to reach decisions covering a wide range of subjects. The Secretariat has now become the center of gravity of the League, partly because it is the only permanently functioning organ of the organization. The staff of the Secretariat are mostly young regionalists, impatient with the slow-moving political leadership. They are committed to regional unity and support recent proposals to amend the Pact of the League in order to increase the authority of the regional organs and to give them some supranational attributes.

How much regional integration can be expected within the framework of the League of Arab States?[37] The effectiveness of the League is strongly influenced by the existing political and economic divisions of the Middle East. Some of the states in this area, such as Libya, Yem-

[37] Black, *The Dynamics of Modernization*, 92-93. For a general discussion of the Arab League see Robert W. Macdonald, *The League of Arab States* (Princeton 1965). See also E. Kanovsky, "Arab Economic Unity," *The Middle East Journal*, XXI, No. 2 (Spring 1967); Kamel S. Abu Jaber, *The Arab Ba'th Socialist Party History, Ideology, and Organization* (Syracuse 1966); and J. H. Thompson and R. D. Reischauer, eds., *Modernization of the Arab World* (Princeton 1966).

en, and Saudi Arabia, are still in the early stages of the process of modernization, characterized by the gradual consolidation of the modernizing elite. Others, such as Algeria, Lebanon, Syria, Iraq, Egypt, Tunisia, Jordan, Sudan, and Morocco, have already entered the more advanced stage during which the economic and social transformation of society takes place. The great differences in circumstances and ideologies among these states produce divergent and often conflicting solutions to the complex problems of modernization. Jordan, Kuwait, and Morocco, for example, remain more traditional, adhering to their monarchical structures. Egypt, Algeria, Iraq, and Syria represent the radical, or revolutionary socialist regimes, with variations on the theme of "socialism." Lebanon and Tunisia pursue the more intermediate, or "moderate" and "liberal" path toward modernization. As a result, a lack of unity of purpose exists between the modernizing elites.

While the more radical modernizing elites of Army officers, technocrats, and professionals adhere to the ideal of a united Arab community, they are, at present, unable to accelerate the integration process. They are faced, at home, with the almost impossible task of eradicating corruption, forging effective political machinery, furnishing the requisite leadership, and instituting essential reforms to carry out modernization programs. Rapid population growth, unresolved power struggles, costly prestige projects, heavy military spending, and conflicting national goals slow down development. In addition, they are not sufficiently united in their Pan-Arab aims. There is no cooperation between the two Pan-Arab movements which have general influence in the Arab world: Ba'thism and Nasser's Arab Socialism. A deep-seated divergence in the Ba'th party has weakened its impact and has created several important splits. The Party has gained adherents in most Arab countries, especially among the young, educated, urban Arabs, but never seemed to take root in Egypt. Nasser and the Ba'thists could not agree on how to go about reaching their goal of Pan-Arab unity. When the United Arab Republic was formed early in 1958, it seemed that, finally, a powerful center of the Pan-Arab movement had been established. When the union collapsed, three-and-one-half years after it was established, Arab unity became a dream once more. The division of the Middle East into radical and more conservative states also has an impact upon the choice of relationship with the big powers. Jordan and Saudi Arabia have been closely associated with the U.S. Lebanon, Tunisia, Morocco, Kuwait, and Libya, for varying reasons, have pursued a moderate, "neutralist" course of action, while the "revolutionary socialist" regimes in Egypt, Syria, Iraq, and Algeria have adopted a position of "positive neutralism," at times in violent opposition to the Western world.

Economic realities in the Arab countries weaken the integrative process. While Syria, Lebanon, and Jordan (and to a lesser extent Egypt and Iraq) carry on a sizeable inter-Arab trade, the other states in the region have little economic contact with each other. The Maghrib region is closely tied to the economies of Western Europe. Algeria, Morocco, and Tunisia retain very strong ties with France. French economic aid is crucial for their development plans, and a significant part of their foreign trade is carried on with France. Since the middle of 1966, a movement toward greater Maghribi economic cooperation can be observed. The Sudan, Kuwait, and Saudi Arabia are equally closely tied to the economies of Western Europe and are not interested, for the time being, in Pan-Arab economic integration.

As of now the only Arab country which has developed industry to a significant degree is Egypt. But the Egyptians have had trouble in exporting their industrial wares. This is one of the reasons Egypt has been pressing for greater regional economic unity. While Lebanon, Jordan, Syria, and Iraq have not reached the Egyptian level of industrial development, their development plans lay great stress on speeding up industrialization. The latter three countries are in favor of economic integration, but afraid of Egypt's greater economic and political power. Lebanese attitudes toward Arab unity have always been tempered by the almost equal division between Muslims and Christians.

As a result of the above factors, the Arab League has not been able to function as a strong community builder. The recently established Arab Common Market is ambitious and far-reaching in its scope. It envisages the eventual establishment of a unified and integrated economy encompassing all member countries. However, only four out of the fourteen Arab League members have, so far, ratified the Common Market agreement—Iraq, Jordan, Syria, and the UAR. Algeria, Libya, Morocco, and Tunisia began preparing their own Maghrib Economic Community in November 1964, thus partly reasserting their earlier detachment from the problems of the Arab East.

No one can safely predict the future of regional integration in the Middle East. Within the immediate future, the Arab world will remain restless, sometimes at strife with itself and with the outside world. The differences among the contending leaderships in the Arab world are such that the establishment of a common Pan-Arab front seems out of the question for the time being.

There are, however, also some more encouraging developments. Despite conflict and disunity, one can detect a genuine long-term trend toward some form of unity in the Arab world. The differences between the more revolutionary and the more traditional regimes are narrowing. The forces of modernization are having a fundamental impact, whatever the formal structure of society. The salaried middle class and industrial workers are gaining steadily in the nonrevolutionary countries. The traditional elites are yielding to the demands of modernization, while the more radical elites are becoming more moderate and pragmatic. In practically every country of the area there are groups, usually among students, young technicians, and government officials, who believe that only a Pan-Arab solution will suffice for the problems of the Arab world. A variety of professional interest groups are doing much to expand the scope of programs of regional cooperation and to increase the participation of individual Arab citizens in regional activities. There is increasing awareness that the political boundaries of the Arab countries, the legacy of European colonial rule, are often at odds with the economic and political interests of the Arab states. Pan-Arab pressures are becoming more pronounced.

One should remember that it was only with the end of World War II and the revolution in mass communications that the Arab world was brought closer together. Up till then, the political pressures of the European powers and their open-door policy to European goods effectively defeated any attempts at regional integration and industrialization. It seems likely that with further modernization a greater degree of unity will come about, and a visible mutuality of economic interests will develop.

Egypt, Algeria, and Iraq in particular are strongly in favor of Arab socialism and Arab unity. These three countries have, for a long time, had a deep impact upon the political and economic development in the eastern and western parts of the Arab world. It seems likely that they will suceed in the near future, if supported by a sufficiently powerful regional pro-integration elite, in speeding up the integrative process in the Arab world. This may eventually result in a sufficient convergence of aims to permit the evolution of a vital regional integrative effort, administered by supranational techniques. In that case, a full regional political community will probably develop.

Like the League of Arab States, the Organization of African Unity is a loose, intergovernmental, cooperative association. No integrating mechanism standing above the separate policies of its members exists. All substantive resolutions of the Assembly of Heads of State and Government are in the form of recommendations and require a two-thirds majority of all the members of the Organization. The Council of Ministers was conceived to function as a permanent center for the peaceful resolution of conflicts among African states. In practice, the Council has developed a habit of shelving major decisions and passing them on to the Assembly. The Secretariat of the OAU has not as yet developed into a dynamic center of regional activity, and remains primarily an administrative organ. Under the leadership of its Administrative Secretary General Diallo Telli, it is trying to find a more central place for itself within the structure of the organization.

The contemporary regional political and economic climate in Africa does not seem to favor any immediate acceleration of the process of regional integration. Since 1963, the forces tending toward economic and political fragmentation have minimized a regional and Pan-African perspective.

The attentions of the modernizing elites in Africa south of the Sahara are bent toward internal development, in particular toward the consolidation of their own position in society. While they are relatively successful in some states, in others they are faced by the powerful opposition of a conservative elite. Especially in former French Africa, this conservative elite is opposed to a rapid, widespread and sustained development effort. Only in North Africa has a modernizing elite firmly established itself and it is directing the economic and social transformation of their respective societies.[38] Until more stable and secure national political communities are established under the leadership of modernizing elites, the main focus of attention of most African states will remain inward.

The Pan-African movement is not powerful enough any longer to act as a unifying agent for regional integration. It contains within itself serious tensions produced by the divergent ideological outlooks and the differing interests of its protagonists. Despite disagreements, almost unanimous support existed for Pan-Africanism until 1960. Then the situation changed. The main events associated with this change are the independence of Nigeria and the 13 French territories and the breakdown in the Central Government in the Congo. These events transformed the political life of the African continent and intensified the differences beneath the apparent solidarity of the African states. Three groups of states grew up: the conservatives, the moderates, and the radicals, reflecting basic positions concerning the important issues of African politics.

The resolution of the Congo crisis made possible the compromise of Addis Ababa. The second Congo crisis and the Rhodesian crisis led to a renewed open confrontation within the OAU of the competing outlooks of African governments. The result was an almost complete collapse of the Pan-African movement, and a weakening of the OAU.

At present, a majority of conservatives and moderates see the OAU as embodying an intergovernmental alliance, one of whose functions is to inhibit revolutionary ends and radical modernization programs. They support a slow, functional approach to Pan-Africanism and feel

---

[38] Black, *The Dynamics of Modernization*, 92-94.

that the OAU should concentrate on economic, technical, and cultural cooperation, acting as a mediator in inter-state conflicts, but leaving most of the political initiative to individual nations. A minority of radicals remain the promoters of an all-African political community. They hold that only a supranational body with extended powers of decision and action can solve Africa's problems. They are, however, split in their view of the OAU. Some feel that the OAU serves primarily as a restraint on revolutionary activity, and are not worried about the possibility of a breakup of the OAU. Others feel that such a breakup would make it more difficult for the radicals to put pressure on African governments to take more militant positions in world affairs. These different views are found among countries as well as within countries.[39]

In the domain of economics, the obstacles to African unity are no less serious. Most of the African states are small and large at the same time—small in population numbers and total income, large in area. The majority of them have less than 5 million people. The predominantly small states turn into micro-states as soon as one attempts to measure the size of their internal markets. The economic consequence of these facts is that they are even more economically dependent than most countries in other developing areas.

The contrast between rich and poor nations is an impediment to economic integration. The Francophone countries especially have their fears that the stronger industrial poles, such as Ghana and Nigeria, may reap the major benefits of integration. Economic rivalry is created between the African states as a result of their competition with each other for foreign aid and for the export of their predominantly agricultural resources.

The division of the states into Francophone and Anglophone has a long-lasting political and economic impact on African unity and development. One of the main reasons for the regrouping, in 1965, of the formerly French colonial areas into the Organisation Commune Africaine et Malgache (OCAM) was the outer-directed orientation of elites in these areas. As a result of this division, the efforts of integration meet many difficulties in West and Central Africa. To the many internal political and economic problems must be added the strong economic and political presence of the EEC and France in the area. France is yielding slowly in relative shares of trade, contracts, and finance to other EEC countries, and the U.K. and the U.S. are showing a growing political interest in Francophone Africa. The Secretariat of

---

[39] Pan-Africanism is perceptively explored by Immanuel Wallerstein, *Africa, the Politics of Unity* (New York 1967), 18-25. See also René Dumont, *False Start in Africa* (New York 1966); Ali A. Mazrui, *Towards a Pax Africana* (Chicago 1967); and William Zartman, "Africa As a Subordinate State System in International Relations," *International Organization*, XXI, No. 3 (Summer 1967).

the ECA has time and again expressed its concern that this special relationship between the EEC and its associates may separate them from their more natural partners in Africa.

The continued dependence on the former colonial powers acts as a serious constraint on united action by the OAU and tends to complicate freedom of choice with respect to purely intro-African affairs. President Nyerere is reported to have remarked at the 1966 Heads of State Meeting of the OAU: "I think the African countries will have to make up their minds whether they will give priority to Africa or to their association with their former masters." He added: "At present what the OAU Conference demonstrated more than anything else is that France and Britain have more power in the OAU than the whole of Africa put together."[40] Finally, the efforts of the U.S. and the U.S.S.R. to establish and maintain their influence in the African states introduced the divisions of the cold war into African politics.

It is difficult to predict the future of African regional integration. If the radicals should succeed in establishing themselves as the stronger force in Africa, this would speed up the modernization process and accelerate integration. But the contemporary climate does not seem to favor such a development. Since 1960, the U.S.S.R. has ceased or diminished its active support of radical forces on the African continent, whereas U.S. support to more conservative elements has been growing steadily.

No longer protected by the U.S.-Soviet competition for their favor, the African states are now more fully exposed to pressures arising from the Western world. It is to be expected that the Western world will continue to discourage the OAU from becoming an effective and independent regional and international force. Through direct and indirect political and economic manipulation, and through the division of one nation from another, the Western control in Africa can be easily perpetuated. Whether acceleration will take place within the immediate future will depend to a large extent on whether the world situation again moves in a direction that will allow more freedom of action to African forces. China has not yet developed the resources or central world position needed to place itself in the role the U.S.S.R. had played up until 1960. Eventually, when China becomes an active great power, the more radical African forces might find a new opportunity to develop their own position and to lead African regionalism into new, more political channels. In the meantime, certain trends are in existence which might have a more gradual impact upon the integrative process.

[40] *East African Reporter*, November 18, 1966.

1. The OAU has attempted, with some success, to assert its organizational preeminence. The Organization has been accepted as the collective agent of Africa. It has also had success in the assertion of its primacy vis-à-vis single member states or group of member states.

2. The African integration movement is gradually becoming more pragmatic and functional. Since it is generally agreed that for the time being regional integration can find only limited realization on the continental level, efforts are being made on the subcontinental level for the integration of economic and social functions. These efforts found sanction in a compromise resolution passed by the OAU Council meeting in Dakar in August 1965, which accepted the establishment of subregional groupings provided they were in accordance with OAU principles; that they were based on geographical realities and economic, social, and cultural factors common to the participating states; and that their aim was to coordinate economic, social, and cultural activities peculiar to the states concerned. A provisional division of Africa into four subregions—North, West, Central, and East Africa—has been approved.

The East African countries, Kenya, Tanzania, and Uganda represent a very special case of African cooperation based on certain unique advantages at the time of independence, such as a high degree of economic integration and close contact between the political elites. The Treaty for East African Co-operation which came into force on December 1, 1967, can be expected to bring about an increased rate of growth in the region as a whole and in each of the countries.

In Central Africa we find the Economic and Customs Union of Central Africa (UDEAC) with Cameroon, Gabon, Congo (B), Chad, and the Central African Republic, but the decision of the latter two in April 1968, to form a Union of Central African States (UEAC) together with Congo (K) has made the present and future of UDEAC uncertain.

The ECA has been very active in getting all West African states to join a West African economic community. In 1966 a new West African customs union was established and the representatives of all the West African countries recommended to their governments the setting up in 1967 of intergovernmental machinery for economic cooperation. In January 1968, the president of Niger, acting as president of OCAM, underlined the difficulties of this broader cooperation. A ministerial council met in Monrovia in April 1968 with no representation from the Entente countries (Ivory Coast, Upper Volta, Niger, Dahomey, and Togo).

Since the development of these countries depends on their participation in a subregional division of labor, the present economic boundaries can be expected to disappear within the near future. Integration will then be implemented gradually, starting in the subregions and moving up to the region at large, until the ultimate objective of an African Common Market and an African political community is ensured.[41]

3. In Africa, as in most other developing areas, new, energetic, regionally oriented elites are openly expressing their discontent with the existing state of affairs. They are to be found in a number of segments. One such segment consists of the inter-African organizations, such as the African trade union movement, especially AATUF, the Pan-African Student Movement, and the Pan-African Union of Journalists. These organizations with membership in many African states, create a force in favor of modernization and integration. Another powerful segment is comprised of young army officers and members of the civil service in the majority of African states. Most of the officer corps are newly recruited and trained and enjoy a relatively high level of education. They are essentially modern in their outlook and can be expected to attempt to activate programs of modernization. Another segment is made up of members of the opposition parties in conservative states, often living in exile.[42] These elites are impatient with the existing state of affairs and want to free themselves from colonialism, neocolonialism, and backwardness. They are losing confidence in the West's willingness to help them solve the many and serious problems of modernization facing them. They are in favor of truly nonaligned socialist governments and believe in Pan-Africanism. If these new elites succeed in building a bridge between the African radicals and conservatives, the result very well might be the emergence of a minimal regional political community.

III

As regional integration proceeds, certain accompanying, interrelated and to some extent conditioning changes take place in the style and structure of interaction among the actors involved in the integrative process:

a. Behavioral changes

The intensity of the regional orientation of national elites increases; mutual communication and responsiveness and cooperative interaction develops among the relevant national and regional elites; a consensus on major issues of intraregional and international affairs develops among elites, and common positions are adopted.

[41] Economic Commission for Africa, *Annual Report*, 3 (March 1964-23 February 1965), UN Doc. E/C/CN.14/343/Rev. 1.
[42] Colin Legum, *Pan-Africanism* (New York 1965).

b. Operational changes

The regional public and private organizational scene becomes rationalized as the organs of the regional system create a central role for themselves; the range and volume of intraregional transactions increases; the legal systems of the member states are harmonized; the bilateral basis of conflict resolution between the member states becomes multi-lateralized and power relations within the regional system are restructured; the likelihood that conflict among states within the region will be resolved by violence decreases markedly.

The following consequences of these changes shall be discussed in some detail below: (1) The development of a community of regionally oriented officials. (2) Increasing regional orientation on the part of pressure groups and political parties in the member states. (3) Improved techniques for the settlement of disputes. (4) Harmonization of laws of the member states. (5) Development of balancing techniques and equilibrium between the member states.

1. The integrative process has played an important role in the creation of a community of regionally oriented officials.[43] The role of the regionally oriented bureaucracy within the European Community has been described by many observers. But it is often overlooked that the role and power of the regionally oriented officials within CMEA have also grown continuously. The Standing Commissions and their Secretariats and the Conference of Commission Chairmen have been working closely together with the CMEA Secretariat in Moscow, with the Bureau of the Executive Committee, and with the various committees set up by the Council to deal with specific problems. This cooperation has stimulated increasing contact between regional and national experts and officials, a contact which was virtually nonexistent before 1956. Much of the progress CMEA has made has been accomplished, not in the high-level plenary sessions of the Council of Ministers, but in these more functional organs, where regionally oriented technical experts rather than political authorities are the chief participants. These organs are becoming the central planning authority within the CMEA context, affecting the organization of economic life in the entire area.[44]

The Central American integration program also owes its dynamic spirit to the existence of a group of individuals whose work is inspired by regional rather than national considerations. The officials of the Central American Economic Cooperation Committee, assisted by the ECLA Secretariat, have been the driving force behind integration in

---

[43] Lindberg, "Decision Making and Integration in the European Community," 71.
[44] Besides the 19 Standing Commissions, 3 other specialized agencies have been created: The International Bank, the Central Office of the Power System, and the Institute for Standardization.

the region, and the forum in which solutions are found for the problems presented by the creation of a common market. A community of functional specialists is developing here also.

This trend is much less pronounced in South America, the Middle East, and Africa (with the possible exception of the subregional African economic communities). In these areas effective intraregional functional cooperation is just starting. Contact between national and regional technical experts and officials has been too limited to create any real community consensus. Regionally oriented officials have not yet established themselves as an independent driving force and are still, to a large extent, dominated by national politicians. Penetration of regional thinking into the national administrative structures of these regions remains limited. In Latin America, for example, each member country has a national LAFTA Commission, but these bodies have little influence on national policy.

2. The integrative process has also had an impact upon interest groups and political parties. While this development is most pronounced in the European Community, a similar trend can also be detected in other regions. In general, a majority of interest groups in the member states of a regional organization continue to place primary emphasis on national governments. They consider efforts aimed at the national government more likely to be successful than those made directly to the regional institutions. With the exception of the European Community, the direct approach to regional institutions is limited. Whenever a national pressure group does seek contact with the regional institutions, the tendency exists to maintain direct access instead of working through the umbrella organizations that may have been formed on the regional level.

In the case of the European Community, regional pressure groups are gradually becoming more important. Their creation and reinforcement is supported by the Commission, which consults them in order to obtain a common opinion, rather than separate sets of national positions. Their most lucrative targets are the Commission and the Committee of Permanent Representatives. Regional business and agricultural groups appear to be effective and do have an impact upon the regional system. Regional labor unions remain disunited and unable to protect the interest of European workers in the community setting.

In Latin and Central America, there is a little contact between national pressure groups and regional institutions. There has been a proliferation of regional business interest groups, but the commitment of these groups to regional integration cannot be measured as yet. Most of them seem primarily interested in larger market and cartel agreements. They have all encountered tremendous difficulties in fusing the divergent interests of their members into a regional policy. The traditionally powerful agricultural interest groups in these countries have paid little attention to the regional institutions. Labor unions have only recently shown an interest in integration.

In the Middle East, interest groups have little impact upon the integration process. The International Confederation of Arab Trade Unions (ICATU), is the only active regional interest group with a Pan-Arab ideology. It is closely associated with the Arab League Secretariat and offers itself as an alternative to both the Communist dominated World Federation of Trade Unions and the Western oriented International Confederation of Free Trade Unions. Several professional societies with regional scope, such as the Federation of Arab Lawyers, the Arab Scientific Federation, the Federation of Arab Physicians, and the Arab Teachers' Federation have been established as a result of Arab League sponsorship.

In Africa, pressure group participation in the integration process is almost completely nonexistent. The All-African Trade Union Federation is the only regional group which has established permanent contact with the OAU. Other groups, such as the Pan-African Union of Journalists and the Pan-African Student Movement, do support integration. As long as the developing states remain in a transitional stage of political development, the role of the few existing pressure groups as actors in the regional system will remain limited.

The direct impact of regional institutions upon national political parties has been minimal. The European Community has established a regional parliament as part of its institutional framework, but it is an advisory body only, having little impact upon the development of the regional system. Regional political parties have been organized, but only the European Socialists consistently show cohesion. They are also the only force whose long-range dominant goal is the establishment of a supranational economic and political community. There is no consistent structural opposition to the Community system. Only the Gaullists question the expanding authority of the regional institutions. The Communists have so far been eliminated from representation in the European Parliament.[45]

The situation in CMEA is unique, because of the basic character of the political structure within the region. In this setting, the pragmatic value-sharing of allied Communist parties takes the place of interaction among kindred democratic parties in Western Europe. The Conference of the Leaders of the Communist and Workers' parties often functions as a regional policy-making body, a role which was not envisaged under the CMEA statute. The Conference intervenes when a change is desired in either the structure or the powers of the

[45] Gerda Zellentin, "Form and Function of the Opposition in the European Communities," *Government and Opposition*, 2, No. 3 (April—July 1967).

organization and usually gives added impetus in a particular area. During the past ten years, the Conference has met six times to reassess the tenets of regional economic cooperation.

In the other regions there is little or no regional cohesion among political parties. One of the purposes of the Latin American Parliament and the Legislative Council of ODECA is to encourage political parties to incorporate in their programs the objective of the integration and unity of Latin America. In the Middle East, the majority of the members of the Ba'th Party are Pan-Arab, but for political reasons the party has remained aloof from direct contact with the headquarters of the Arab League in Cairo.

The very existence of regional institutions will eventually compel interest groups and political parties to become aware of regional problems and force them to engage in united efforts beyond the limits of national frontiers. Intensification of the activities of interest groups and political parties can therefore be expected in all regions.

3. The interaction pattern of a regional organization is determined by two categories of interest: (a) member states attempt to achieve their national goals through the mechanism of the organization; (b) in order to maximize the rewards of the regional system, member states promote the collective goals of the organization. These two categories of interest are not always mutually exclusive, but the interaction between them often creates conflict, and calls for continued adjustment and redefinition of national and regional goals.

Each regional organization has its own basis of internal division and agreement and must accommodate itself continuously to a certain amount of internal tension. Alignments are often unstable and compromise patterns unpredictable, but some habits of continuous intrasystem adjustment are likely to emerge. The establishment of a cooperative pattern of interaction among the actors encourages the creation of a consensus concerning intraregional and international affairs and the use of peaceful methods to resolve conflict.

The legal basis in constitutive treaties for the regional settlement of disputes or disagreements varies from one organization to the other. Both regional economic and political organizations provide specific machinery for the settlement of disputes. In addition, the political groupings provide, to a limited extent, for methods to control the use of force within the region.

In the case of the European Community, the open expression of political disagreement within its institutional framework has increased mutual understanding of the problems involved, facilitated settlement, and created a consensus on regional and foreign policy issues. In certain areas, foreign policy powers have been transferred to the Community. Community organs have the authority to determine the direction and substance of some of the relations between the Community and third countries. They are empowered to open negotiations with third countries and can conclude appropriate trade agreements in the name of the Community. This can be considered an important grant of power that has far-reaching economic and political implications. The question of trade relations with the U.S., for example, was tied up with the future of the NATO Alliance and the Atlantic Community in general. Consideration of the question of trade relations with the CMEA countries resulted in a general discussion of a common policy toward the centrally planned economies. Discussion of the contents of the proposed second treaty of association with African states involved a clarification of the attitude of the six member states toward the developing world. The discussion of British membership involved a consideration of future relations with the members of the British Commonwealth. A certain measure of harmonization of policy was achieved in all these areas. Within the framework of the Community, a common European foreign policy is slowly evolving.

Like the European Community, CMEA operates in an advantageous political and economic environment for conflict resolution. From 1958 on, the Eastern Europeans seem to have been able to overcome much of their traditional, political, economic, and ethnic antagonism. Several formal arrangements for the peaceful settlement of disputes have been used. The Council of Ministers of CMEA is a prominent organ for the peaceful settlement of disputes. Other procedures include resort to arbitral tribunals, mediation or conciliation by a third party, and mixed commissions on which authorities directly involved in the dispute are represented. In most cases, a combination of concessions and coercion is sufficient to settle the dispute and to re-establish unity.

CMEA plays a limited role in the creation of an overall regional foreign policy. One area in which the organization is active is in the determination of the direction and substance of the economic relations between CMEA and the industrialized as well as developing countries. As far as foreign policy direction is concerned, many factors still tend to predispose Eastern European leaders to follow Soviet foreign policy lines. The tendency is probably enhanced by the relatively greater expertise of Soviet in comparison with many Eastern European leaders of foreign policy. At present, Eastern Germany and Poland seem to be most active in the formulation of a CMEA foreign policy, while Hungary, Czechoslovakia and Rumania play a more secondary role.

Regional organizations in the developing countries are less successful in the peaceful settlement of disputes. The most highly publicized disputes in the Middle East and Africa are colonial ones. In addition, regional organizations deal with conflicts resulting from a breakdown of law and order in member states, as well as border problems and other inter-state disputes.

In the case of the colonial situations, the African and Middle Eastern states have been able to present a more united front to the outside world by concerting their views through regional machinery. The regional organizations have been accepted as entities directly involved in the conflicts; as such, they have been able to put continuous diplomatic pressure on outside powers.

The organizations have not been able, however, to take really effective action in any of these situations. This is partly due to the limited number of feasible regional responses to such situations. Border-sealing procedures, for instance, while isolating a disorder, would also prevent the external assistance needed to overthrow a colonial government. The wide range of positions, from moderate to extremist, held by the members of the organizations, prevent regional bodies from playing a more interventionist role. Moreover, the political weakness of the developing states—even when acting together as a bloc— places a severe limitation upon the organizations. As a result, change in colonial situations remains dependent on shifts in the goals and policies of Western states.

The anti-colonial activities of the OAU clearly illustrate this weakness. Within the framework of the UN, the OAU has been fairly effective on a number of occasions. During its first year, 1963-1964, it was able to get the Security Council to meet twice on the South African case. In response to demands from the members of the OAU, the Security Council, for the first time, went beyond merely condemning South Africa and called on UN members to put an embargo on certain goods for South Africa, including arms, ammunition, and military vehicles. Later, as a result of similar pressures, both the General Assembly and the Security Council passed resolutions dealing with the Portuguese territories, Southern Rhodesia, and South West Africa.

In the Rhodesian case, the OAU anticipated the unilateral declaration of independence by the Smith regime and attempted to prevent it from coming about. Although an enthusiastic response was given to Nkrumah's assurance in his opening address to the Assembly of African Heads of State in 1965 that "the OAU will take whatever steps are necessary," the resolution voted on October 22, 1965 was moderate in tone. The Assembly did not consider a motion passed by the preparatory meeting of foreign ministers, recommending that an OAU peace-keeping contingent be set up. The final resolution placed the greatest responsibility on Great Britain—which it urged to use force to prevent a unilateral declaration of independence—and on the UN. When Rhodesia declared her independence three weeks later,

On November 11, OAU members were unanimous in condemning the move. But the split in African ranks continued, and while some states spoke in terms of African military preparations, others felt that all initiative should be left to Great Britain.

The Council of Ministers and its Defense Commission met in Addis Ababa from December 3 to 5, 1965. Here the radicals won the day and the African states announced that if the revolt had not been crushed by December 15, they would declare war on Rhodesia, impose economic sanctions, and sever all communications. It was also decided to bring pressure to bear in the UN to secure an economic embargo, and to break off diplomatic relations with Britain. Although this last measure was voted unanimously, only ten states, representing the radical camp, carried out the terms of the resolution.

The split in the African ranks continued throughout 1966. Although the African delegates to the UN stepped up their diplomatic activity in 1967, it was clear that the failure of the OAU to establish a consensus on Rhodesia had weakened African efforts to work for a swift overthrow of the Smith regime. United in their opposition to the white Rhodesian government, the African states disagreed over details of strategy, such as what aid to give nationalist movements and whether to break relations with Great Britain.

The same split between the radical and conservative camps has weakened the support given by the Liberation Committee to Africans in territories which have not yet gained independence. The assumption that the struggle for liberation was one on which conservative and radical Africans could agree proved to be incorrect. Assistance for liberation involved a decision as to who should receive this assistance —a collective political decision that might determine the future political complexion of the countries involved. Under these circumstances, the efforts of the Committee to unify nationalist movements and give them effective aid met with small success.

For most of the more radical Africans, the operations of the Committee were inherently ambiguous because the Committee allowed a large voice to those who did not share their revolutionary aspirations. As one example, an Algerian proposal to "intensify the organization . . . of the nationalists in Rhodesia with a view to launching armed action within the country and to recognize the ZAPU as the only liberation movement in Rhodesia" was rejected at the February 1966 session of the Assembly. The OAU attempted instead to reconcile the Zimbabwe African National Union (ZANU) and the Zimbabwe African People's Union (ZAPU) so that both parties could develop a unified stand in Rhodesia. However, no such reconciliation came about.

The Liberation Committee also supervises the training of "freedom fighters" for eventual operation against the Rhodesian, Portuguese, and South African forces. The Committee is advised by the OAU's Section for Military and Sabotage Training for African Countries, which directly runs the training camps located in Tanzania, Algeria, and the UAR, and channels supplies and instructors. There are now perhaps several thousand trained "freedom fighters" available for commando action. But because of political disagreement among African states, only a very few have been used so far, in Mozambique and Rhodesia.[46] It is generally accepted that force will be used to liberate colonial areas only if it does not jeopardize the position of the already independent states.

In the case of the Arab League, mediation in colonial questions, such as the dispute between Yemen and British authorities in Aden, the Muscat and Oman question, and the Buraimi oasis question between Saudi Arabia and the United Kingdom, has been equally unsuccessful.

Civil wars, especially those involving charges of external aggression or subversion, confront regional organizations with demands they are not well equipped to meet. The transition from traditional to modern leadership is generally violent, causing breakdowns of law and order. The gradualist approach of mending existing social structures often leaves political agencies in a backward stage and is not likely to promote those indigenous forces that are necessary to sustain modernization. In most cases, the more revolutionary approach of destroying and replacing traditional structures is required.[47] Civil wars and other forms of domestic unrest may be expected in most states belonging to regional organizations in the developing world.

In some cases, a civil war is fought over the occupancy or the arrangement of the roles in the structure of political authority, but no profound domestic or foreign policy alterations are envisioned by any of the parties. In the majority of cases, however, civil war involves major struggles over the substructures of society as well as over domestic and foreign policies. It is the latter type of civil war which can have the greatest impact upon the regional and international system, and which is therefore most exposed to foreign intervention. This intervention may take the form of: (1) helping the weaker party— usually the insurgents; (2) helping the stronger party—usually the incumbents; (3) working for a conciliatory solution through mediation or otherwise. The agents engaged in such intervention may be governments within or outside the region, public or private organiza-

---

[46] Wallerstein, *Africa the Politics of Unity*, 153-75.
[47] Irving Louis Horowitz, *Three Worlds of Development* (New York 1966), 195-225.

tions, or members of political or ideological movements affiliated with the parties in the civil war.[48]

The regional organizations have attempted to play a role in the settlement of certain civil wars. In these efforts, they have been limited by inadequate means and by the conflicting attitudes of their various member states in regard to the desirable outcome of internal strife. Regional consensus is made very difficult by the existence of fundamental differences in political systems and disparities in the level of political and economic development within the region. Some members of regional organizations are so intent upon securing a particular outcome in a civil war that they ignore the disruptive effects of that war, or of their reactions to it, upon regional relations. Even where the regional interest would be best satisfied by an effort at reconciliation, the differing views of its members may make it impossible for the organization to function as a successful third party.

The members of a regional organization often disagree on the nature of the outside threats or external control in particular situations, and some of them withhold the support needed to promote collective action against foreign intervention. For the more conservative sovereignty oriented members, "noninterference in the internal affairs of States" requires that states, regional and nonregional, refrain from active support for opposition movements in other states.

The more radical members are also opposed to intervention by outside states, but for them intervention is any action taken in the region by nonregional powers for neocolonialist purposes. They propagate revolutionary norms of international relations, in which the real enemies of the developing countries are held to be the Western states that continue to control the developing world by their economic power. According to this view, the concern of a genuinely independent developing state about the affairs of another state that is controlled by neocolonialism cannot be considered an act of intervention. Within the region, all are brothers and one can give assistance to brothers.

Despite many disagreements, a new principle of legitimacy has emerged in both the Arab League and the OAU to justify certain limited, noncoercive regional interventions in the affairs of war-torn countries. During the second Congo crisis, and again in relation to the Nigerian civil war, the OAU asserted that national reconciliation within a member country was a legitimate concern of the organization. The Arab League has equally claimed, in relation to the Yemen situation, that regional intervention is legitimate when peace has to be restored and order maintained. Both organizations have also tried to help

[48] See James Rosenau, "Internal War as an International Event," in *International Aspects of Civil Strife*, James Rosenau, ed. (Princeton 1964), 14-15. Also George Modelski, "The International Relations of Internal War," same, 14-15.

their members avoid the kind of civil war that is brought about less by internal political weakness than by external aggression or subversion.

In the case of the first Congo crisis in 1960, African leaders, lacking a regional organization through which to act, endorsed a UN peacekeeping operation as a means of preventing the superpowers from exploiting the situation. The impotence of the OAU in circumstances of intraregional civil strife was demonstrated during the second Congo crisis, which was brought before an extraordinary meeting of the Council in Addis Ababa in September 1964. The situation was critical: On July 23, Gaston Soumialot had announced the formation of a Provisional Government of the National Committee of Liberation, and on August 5 the rebels had won control of Stanleyville. The Council adopted a resolution asking for the withdrawal of mercenaries, requesting a cease-fire and establishing a nine-nation Congo Conciliation Commission. The Council also attempted to find an African solution to the Congo dispute which would exclude non-African intervention, and requested countries interfering in the Congo to desist.

The rhetoric of protest at the September 1964 Council meeting came from what I. Wallerstein called the radical "core" of the movement for African unity. Many Africans considered the Congo crisis a case of unwarranted interference by external powers in the affairs of an African country, with implications for peace and stability in the whole continent. Two factors helped build a consensus in the OAU against foreign intervention in the Congo. The first was the personality of Prime Minister Tshombe, who was identified by many Africans as an advocate of neocolonialism. The second factor was the use of white mercenaries by the central government of the Congo. Many normally moderate states joined the ranks of the radicals in regarding the internal situation in the Congo as a legitimate concern of the OAU. Even the conservative states acquiesced in the views of the radical "core."

As the leader of the Conciliation Commission, Jomo Kenyatta decided to hold preliminary consultations in Nairobi beginning September 18, 1964. The Commission had decided that it would go to the Congo to hold talks with the rebel leaders as well as with the government. It offered to assist in organizing a round-table discussion with all Congolese leaders and to supervise national elections. It also sent a delegation to Washington to ask the Americans to withdraw their military aid as an essential prerequisite to ending external intervention. When the delegation arrived in Washington, it was not even received by President Johnson—an incident interpreted by the delegation as a serious affront to the OAU.

Soon, however, the consensus in the OAU was to collapse. On September 23, President Kasavubu protested the OAU's "manifest interference in the Congo's internal affairs" and announced the Congo's withdrawal from the OAU. The joint American-Belgian Stanleyville operation in November 1964, hardened the lines of division which had already become evident between African states which supported the rebels and those which favored the central government. The operation also demonstrated the vulnerability of Africa to the power of their former colonial masters and the U.S.

From February 26 to March 9, 1965, the Council of Ministers met at Nairobi for its fourth ordinary session, with the Congo question at the center of its preoccupations. A split among the delegations soon made itself felt, and neither Tshombe's advocates nor his opponents were able to command a majority. The Council rejected, in a vote in which 14 states abstained, a Sudanese proposal demanding that the representatives of the rebel movement be heard. Two resolutions proposing that white mercenaries be replaced with African troops failed to win the required majority. The Council finally decided to shelve the issue rather than to resolve the deadlock, by passing the question on the Assembly of Heads of State.

The initiative was thus handed back to the individual countries and, implicitly, to the groups of states which had confronted each other in pre-OAU Africa. On May 23, 1965, the reconstituted organization of French-speaking states, the Organisation Commune Africaine et Malgache (OCAM), welcomed Tshombe's Congo as a member of the organization. This happened before the OAU had worked out an "all-African" attitude toward Tshombe's regime, and so had a tremendously controversial impact. The radical states, nonetheless, abandoned neither their opposition to the OCAM nor their condemnation of Tshombe.[49]

When the army mutinied in Tanganyika, Kenya, and Uganda in January 1964, the three countries appealed for British forces to restore order. An emergency meeting of the Council was held at Dar-es-Salaam in February 1964, at the request of President Nyerere of Tanganyika, to seek an African alternative to the British troops which he had been obliged to call in. On this occasion the OAU proved capable of finding an acceptable solution to a delicate situation. An agreement was reached providing for the replacement of the British troops by three battalions of African troops and an air wing. The Council agreed that Tanganyika had the right to choose from which African states she should seek this aid, and that the troops were to be placed

[49] For an excellent discussion of the role of the OAU in the settlement of civil wars see Linda B. Miller, "Regional Organization and the Regulation of Internal Conflict," *World Politics*, XIX, No. 4 (July 1967).

under the direction and control of the Tanganyika government. Algeria, Ethiopia, and Nigeria were asked to supply forces for Tanganyika. However, only Nigerian troops arrived, replacing the British troops in March 1964 and playing a role in the restoration of order.

Also before the Council at that time was the French intervention in Gabon. In February 1964, a military coup had succeeded in Gabon, when French paratroopers landed and restored the pro-French President Léon M'ba to power. President de Gaulle's decision to restore M'ba was intended to prevent a series of coups throughout the UAM states that would move their governments toward a more revolutionary position on African affairs. In addition, President de Gaulle's decision was also intended to safeguard Gabon's rich uranium supplies. The French action was openly applauded by (6) UAM states, with only Dahomey making a mild demurral. The Council did not discuss the issue and France went virtually uncriticized. The revolutionary movement in French-speaking Africa was sharply curtailed as a result of this intervention.

The OAU has heard relatively few cases involving accusations of intervention by regional states. Among these were the protest of the central government against alleged interventions by African states in the Congo in 1964-1965, and the protest by French-speaking states against Ghana in 1965. As under traditional international law, the OAU Charter leaves the door open for states in Africa to render assistance to an incumbent regime, while obliging them to refrain from assisting rebellious elements in a member country. And yet, more African assistance was rendered in 1964-1965 to "national liberation" forces in the Congo than to the central government. The UAR, Algeria, the Sudan, Congo-Brazzaville, and Uganda offered the rebels various types of assistance. Other states, including Ghana, Guinea, Mali, Morocco, and Tunisia, declared themselves against Tshombe. On the other hand, the French-speaking states maintained either a neutral silence or called for a condemnation of the rebel movement. Any collective decision on the status of the civil war and the resulting rights and obligations of the third-party member states of the OAU was impossible in the Congo case, and the protest of the central government was ignored.

In June 1965, the OAU Council of Ministers attempted to mediate in the quarrel between Ghana and its neighbors—Togo, the Ivory Coast, Upper Volta, and Niger. The Francophile countries had accused Ghana of engaging in subversive activity against them and had announced their intention of boycotting the next Assembly of Heads of State, to be held at Accra. The Ghanaian Foreign Minister denied these charges. The Council unanimously passed a resolution asking all members to attend the summit conference. It also set up a five-nation subcommittee to mediate the conflict. By June 13, the subcommittee elicited from President Nkrumah assurances that he would expel all refugees who were considered undesirable by any member state. Both Ghana and the OAU were prepared to take the step of denying the generally recognized right of sovereign states to grant asylum to political refugees in order to placate the Francophile states and to save the Accra summit conference.

Despite Nkrumah's effort to placate his neighbors, the Entente states reiterated their decision to boycott the Assembly. They were joined by Togo, Gabon, Chad and Madagascar, while nine other states sent only ministerial delegations. The Assembly thus opened on October 21 with the presidents of half of its member states absent. The problem of refugees and subversion was examined and two resolutions were passed, engaging the participants to refrain from subversive activity and to encourage political refugees to return to their own countries. Nevertheless, the boycott by so many states cast a shadow over the conference.

The OAU has been involved in several frontier disputes. Some of these led to armed conflict and remain unsettled, including disputes over the borders of Somalia and of Morocco. Others erupted into clashes but were subsequently resolved, or at least temporarily discontinued; among these were disputes between Mali and Mauritania, Egypt and the Sudan, Tunisia and Algeria, Dahomey and the Niger, and Ghana and several of her neighbors. Territorial questions were at issue in all these disputes, but the deeper causes were political and economic differences between the states involved. In the cases of Morocco and Somalia, both states sought initially to attain their aims by diplomacy; but having failed to obtain satisfaction, they attempted to advance their objectives by guerrilla-type military pressures. In both cases, their policies led to armed conflict involving their regular armies. Morocco fought a brief war with Algeria in October 1963 over the possession of certain frontier regions. Somali and Ethiopian forces clashed in January and February 1964 as a result of the escalation of guerrilla incidents. Both disputes have since subsided, but both Somalia and Morocco remain committed to their irredentist objectives.

The OAU played only a limited role in these two disputes. When hostilities escalated between Morocco and Algeria, the Algerian government requested an extraordinary meeting of the OAU Council to effect an African settlement. Before the Council met, however, President Ben Bella and King Hassan met in Bamako with two mediators, Emperor Haile Selassie and President Modibo Keita of Mali. They established a cease-fire committee which was influential in obtaining a cease-fire agreement in February 1964. They also agreed on a procedure to bring about a disengagement of forces, and that too was accomplished without the help of the OAU. A seven-nation commission appointed by the OAU Council in November 1963 helped to check tension between the two countries but failed to bring about a definitive settlement.

When fighting broke out between Ethiopia and Somalia, the Council called for an immediate cease-fire but was unable to help put the cease-fire into effect. That was done by President Abboud of the Sudan, who mediated between the parties. President Abboud later arranged for a Somali-Ethiopian conference in Khartoum, at which it was agreed to create a demilitarized zone along the border. The OAU refrained from appointing a commission to help solve the dispute. Instead, in February 1964, the Council called on the parties to negotiate directly with each other.

The failure of the OAU to effect final settlements of these border disputes highlights the limited usefulness of its conciliation and mediation efforts. The most important reason why the two disputes have not had more dangerous consequences appears to be the military weakness of Morocco and Somalia, and the absence of an economic base to sustain a military effort. The failure of Somalia and Morocco to gain African or other sympathy for their revisionist ambitions was another reason why the disputes did not become more dangerous. Despite its limitations, the OAU had some effect in containing the disputes. The existence and prestige of the organization, the principles of its Charter calling for peaceful settlement of disputes and respect for the territorial integrity of states, and a 1964 resolution asking respect for borders—all exercised a restraining influence.[50]

Among the Arab states, a difference of views has similarly contributed to the paralysis that often prevails when the Arab League deals with civil wars, subversion, charges of external aggression, or more general inter-state disputes.

As one example, the split within the League membership on the issue of the Yemen revolution in 1962 paralyzed the Organization and led to action by the UN. Since 1963, the League's Secretary-General has been involved in the Yemen situation, mediating between the UAR on the one hand, and Jordan and Saudi Arabia on the other.[51] The Arab summit conference of August 1967, played a more active role in restoring peace to Yemen. President Nasser reached an agreement with King Faisal of Saudi Arabia to work for an end to the Yemen civil war. Both agreed to stop their intervention in the civil war and to cooperate with mediation efforts by a tripartite committee compris-

[50] Saadia Touval, "Africa's Frontiers," *International Affairs*, 42, No. 4 (October 1966). See also Nora McKeon, "The African States and the OAU," *International Affairs*, 42, No. 3 (July 1966).
[51] Macdonald, *The League of Arab States*, 157-158.

ing officials from Morocco, Iraq, and the Sudan. But this may well turn out to be only a temporary agreement, since it was motivated largely by needs arising from the military defeat suffered by the UAR in the June 1967 war with Israel.

The Kuwait incident of 1961 showed that crisis situations tend to paralyze the League Council. When Iraq seemed to be about to take possession of Kuwait, the decisive action was taken not by the Arab League, but by the British, who occupied the Sheikdom through a well-timed coup. Several weeks later, the League decided to send a joint Arab force to Kuwait to replace the British. The first troops arrived in Kuwait on September 10, 1961. The 3,300-man force, coming from the UAR, Saudi Arabia, the Sudan, Jordan, and Tunisia, led by a Saudi commander, stayed in Kuwait until February 1963, by which time the crisis was over.

The League was also prevented from taking action in the border dispute between Algeria and Morocco in October 1963 because Morocco was not willing to cooperate with a league mediation commission.

On the more positive side, the League played a significant part in getting American and British forces out of Lebanon and Jordan after the interventions of July 1958.

The Secretary-General of the Arab League has frequently been successful in mediating disputes between member states. Secretary-General Hassouna mediated a dispute involving Jordan and the United Arab Republic in 1959. Mediation efforts resulted in Iraq's rejoining the League Council in September 1960, after a two-year boycott. In 1961, Hassouna was influential in solving the crisis that developed after Iraq claimed Kuwait. Late in 1961, he successfully negotiated an agreement between Syria and the UAR for an exchange of national military forces interned after Syria's break with the UAR in September.[52]

Like the OAU, the Arab League has not served as an effective regional arrangement against external intervention. The location of the League in a contested geopolitical area with considerable strategic importance and resources presents a major problem. The League is in no position to take effective action to settle the Arab-Israel conflict, one of the main sources of tension in the area and a persistent magnet for outside intervention. Certain intraregional disputes have been handled by the League, while others have been settled by secret negotiation, carried on without League involvement.

The above cases indicate that:

(1) If vital interests of the big powers are involved, any regional action, if it is to have any chance of success, must be favored by the big powers.

[52] Same, 158.

(2) Regional organizations will be able to deal with foreign interventions only to a limited degree, and it will be largely up to third-party states to exercise greater restraint in using internal conflict for the achievement of national goals.

(3) While foreign interventions in the affairs of the developing states are unavoidable at present, regional organizations can play a restraining role by defining the norms of intervention and by distinguishing between permissible and nonpermissible types of intervention.

(4) Regional organizations may have some success in containing civil wars and intra-state disputes before they have time to develop international ramifications and before nonregional powers intrude. They can maximize pressures that will restrain nonregional powers from escalating local or intra-state violence into superpower conflicts.

(5) When foreign powers have not intruded and competing governmental interests converge, a consensus may emerge on appropriate regional responses to civil wars and inter-state disputes. Even in such situations, the regional organization can play only a limited role in the settlement of important disputes between the more powerful regional states. But whenever small and middle powers are involved, the regional machinery can be effectively employed for the settlement of disputes.

(6) Experience with regional organizations has shown that only limited, nonmilitary regional actions, undertaken with the consent of the parties involved, have been accepted as desirable. The patterns of response have developed pragmatically in each case and have remained cautious. The following conclusions can be drawn about peaceful settlement techniques used by regional organizations:

a. Regional organizations have attempted to foster negotiations between disputants through various mediation techniques. The organizations themselves have served as centers for debate, negotiation, and mediation.

b. Conciliatory intervention has been avoided in most cases since this technique may antagonize the parties to the conflict. If an attempt is made to impose a solution that is not suited to the situation, tensions may be increased rather than eased.

c. The organizations have examined the claims and counterclaims made by the parties to the conflict, undertaken missions of investigation, and engaged in other fact-finding procedures. In civil wars, acting as a fact-finding body and determining that a situation involves only warring factions within a single country, the organizations have occasionally made it more difficult for outside powers to justify their own intervention by arguing that their adversaries are already involved.

d. Regional organizations have asked for a pause in fighting, during which parties could move toward negotiations. They have attempted to insulate internal conflicts and to discourage intervention by regional powers.

e. They have engaged in limited peace-keeping operations, such as the use of cease-fire commissions, observer groups, and border control bodies. Large scale peace-keeping operations have been avoided.

f. Any form of coercive military action is clearly beyond the present capabilities of the regional organizations.

Notwithstanding their deficiencies, the existing regional organizations in the developing world seem to be the only institutionalized forms for the peaceful settlement of disputes which are now feasible in those regions. In the near future, internal and external limitations, such as circumscribed jurisdictions and resources and ideological splits, will continue to restrict their responses to conflict. Eventually, stronger, more autonomous regional organizations can be expected to play a more vital role in the regulation of conflict on a subglobal basis.

4. One of the most important aspects of the European Community, and to a lesser extent of the Organization of Central American States, is the effort to reduce the differences among the national laws of the member states. The closer cooperation envisaged in the plans for Arab, Latin American, and African common markets will necessitate progress in harmonizing laws within these regions.

Harmonization of at least part of the national legal systems within a regional community is an integral part of any plan for progressive integration of the national economies and the political structures of the member states. The idea is to remove those differences among national laws which retard the process of integration.

The process of harmonizing laws in the European Community may well become the model for future developments in other regions. Therefore the techniques used by the Community for the gradual creation of Community law deserve further attention.

The institutions of the Community have the legal authority to order national governments to make changes in their legal systems to the extent necessary for the functioning of the EEC. In most cases where the Rome Treaty provides for harmonization,[53] the Commission has the authority to propose directives which the Council is competent to enact. The directives are drafted by expert working groups of national and regional civil servants and are approved by the Commission, which submits them to the Council. In most cases, the Council is required to obtain formal advice from the national parliamentarians

---

[53] The Treaty of Rome devotes two of its articles to what it calls "Approximation" of laws: Articles 100 and 101. See also Article 3 (h) .

assembled in the European Parliament and from the interested groups organized in the Economic and Social Committee. Unresolved issues are decided by the Ministers in the Council, mainly through a compromise of national interests. The directives, which set forth the results to be achieved, bind any member state to which they are addressed, though decisions as to form and means are left to the discretion of domestic agencies. The Commission supervises the execution of the directives. If it is not satisfied with the action taken, it may institute proceedings which can result in a declaratory judgment by the Court of the Community against the delinquent member. The Court has the final authority to review the legality of directives and to interpret them.

Only when a proposed harmonization measure exceeds the limits of the law-making power of the Community do the member governments resort to the process of creating new European law, valid throughout the Community. This is done through the conclusion of multilateral treaties, effecting the desired changes in the national laws.

Interest in creating new European law has recently increased. In a memorandum submitted to the Council of Ministers on April 22, 1966, the Commission concluded that the Rome Treaty offered only partial solutions to the problems arising from the existence of six autonomous juridical systems. The Commission pointed out that many problems could more readily be solved by developing new European law, established by convention, rather than enacting uniform national laws in each member state.[54]

In addition to the effort to harmonize national laws, the Community organs are generating large quantities of regional international cooperation law that directly affects the member states, their enterprises, and their citizens. The Court has made it clear that it regards the Community as having sovereign rights of its own, based on an independent, regional legal order which operates directly upon its subjects.

The function of the Court is to safeguard the rule of law in the interpretation and application of the basic treaties of the Community, and to review the legality of the legislative acts of the Commission and the Council of Ministers. States, the Commission and Council, enterprises, associations, and individuals may be parties before the Court. The Court has in large measure afforded effective legal recourse to eligible parties who complain that others have violated Community law.[55]

[54] *European Community*, No. 91 (April 1966) . See also Eric Stein, "Assimilation of National Laws As a Function of European Integration," 58 *American Journal of International Law*, 30-36 (1964) .

[55] Werner Feld, *The Court of the European Communities* (Amsterdam 1964)

Member states are not fully agreed on the relationship between Community law and national legal systems. They differ on the extent to which Community law takes precedence over conflicting provisions of national laws. The constitutions of most of the six member states provide for the transfer of certain sovereign powers to international organizations. Some of the constitutions recognize the supremacy of international law over national laws. Only in the case of the Netherlands is the supremacy of Community law over both national law and the constitution guaranteed. A complex relationship exists between the Community institutions and the member states, and occasional conflicts between Community and national norms cannot be avoided. Nevertheless, the Community slowly proceeds toward a common institutional order.

The process of legal unification in CMEA started during the first years of Soviet control of Eastern Europe. To facilitate Soviet domination, the Eastern European countries were forced to accept a massive dose of Soviet constitutional law and legal institutions.

The Polish and Hungarian revolts of 1956 indicated the desire of the Eastern European Communists to be free from Soviet control. From then on, the Communists focused on regional law instead of Soviet constitutional law. A new regional system of legal relationships was developed among the members of CMEA. Existing similarities between national legal principles and legal institutions made it easier to harmonize laws. The common use of centralized planning, national ownership of means of production, and similarity of the social systems served as a further impetus to legal integration.

The process of legal integration, supported by a system of regional treaties covering specific aspects of intraregional relations, has produced an advanced community of law among the members of CMEA, which differs from that of other regional systems.[56]

Legal integration is especially important in the developing countries. Different internal conditions in each of these countries have led to the development of different economic and financial institutions, legal structures, and governmental planning policies. Some have worked better than others in stimulating industrialization. Legal integration with respect to financial and economic institutions may be relevant to improving the rate of industrialization and progress toward achievement of a more efficient regional economic structure. To give some specific examples: (1) Harmonization of law facilitates the formation of public or private regional or subregional financial and economic institutions not now in existence, such as regional development banks; (2) Harmonization of substantive and procedural differ-

[56] Theofil I. Kis, *Les Pays de l'Europe de l'Est. Leurs Rapports Mutuels et le Problème de leur Intégration dans l'orbite de l'URSS* (Louvain 1964).

ences as to protective devices encourages transactions across national lines; (3) Harmonization of varying national savings incentives and instruments for directing investment facilitates a more efficient deployment of capital. It makes it increasingly attractive for savings to seek most productive use in investment in industrial development in a part of the region less well supplied with funds.

The makers and administrators of law in the developing countries have to cope with innumerable tasks. These tasks are too many and too complex to be attacked separately by each developing country. The number of skilled legislative draftsmen is limited. Joint discussion and research, and exchange of experiences are needed in order to prepare many laws. Questions such as how the intended legal innovation will affect the economy and the social structure of a developing country have to be answered. The answer seems to lie in the establishment within the region of central training and research institutions. Regional conferences, such as the African Conferences on the Rule of Law, held on several occasions since 1961, are to be viewed as important first achievements in a long-range program to promote legislative drafting within the framework of specific African cultural traditions, political institutions, and socioeconomic realities. Professional legal societies enable lawyers from different developing countries to familiarize themselves with the varying viewpoints of their colleagues, to examine common grounds for regional legal development, and to develop closer personal and organizational ties between them. The Arab Lawyers Federation, for instance, in cooperation with the Arab League Secretariat, is engaged in the unification of Arab legal codes and procedures.

As an outgrowth of regional institutions, diplomacy in both the industrialized and the developing world appears increasingly to recognize two levels of law. One level is that of international law to govern relations between nations at large. The other level is a kind of regional law to govern relations between the members of the regional organization. The latter is less codified, but has found expression in the constituent and other treaties, agreements, and legislative acts of the regional organizations. Despite many disagreements, some consensus is emerging on the rules of inter-state behavior. Repeated violations of these rules have not deprived them of their legal and political significance. At least they provide the members of a regional organization with some basis for the peaceful settlement of conflicts.

5. It has been argued that there is a tendency for regional organizations to fall under the domination of one or more of the larger powers located in the region. However, experience up to now does not seem to support this view. Once a minimum regional political community has been established, and a certain measure of interdependence has

developed among the member states, the integrative process tends to generate an equilibrium among its unequally powerful members and to prevent the absolute domination or dictation by the more powerful states in the region.

This equilibrium is not static.[57] It is a state of relative temporary stability, recurrently upset by factors causing change and replaced eventually by a new temporary balance. The balancing process is a persistent feature of regional politics. It is a dynamic process continuously varying as crucial features of regional relations and the national, regional, and international environment change.

The regional organization is likely to have a moderating influence on the regional power struggle, in accordance with the norms and sanctions of its functional scope and commitment and its institutional structure. Within its own sphere of competence, it acts as a mediator between the main states and the rest of the member nations and provides a protective, multilateral framework for the solution of conflicts of interest. Once the equilibrium among member states is controlled by means of an effective regional organization, the distribution of power ceases to be the result only or even primarily of competition and conflict.

In addition, all member states seek to secure for themselves by various balancing techniques the best possible position in the regional equilibrium. At the same time, those states firmly committed to the survival and growth of the system deliberately equilibrate forces for and against stability.

The equilibrium remains relative and does not preclude the existence of one or more states that are preponderant over the rest. Regional political communities are actually often created around one or several political units, or a composite of units. If a minimum regional political community has already been established, the existence of such core powers might be viewed with some suspicion but does not tend to arouse fear or cause disintegration. The acceptance of such core areas is made easier by the decline in the expectations of the use of force between the member units. A regional organization may be established specifically in order to create a kind of equilibrium of power within a certain area, and during its existence the policy decisions of some of its members may continue to be conditioned by the desire to maintain that equilibrium. France and Belgium, for instance, were interested in the creation of the European Coal and Steel Community to check the economic power of Germany, and this has remained one of their aims within the framework of the European Community.

[57] See George Liska, *International Equilibrium: A Theoretical Essay on the Politics and Organization of Security* (Cambridge, Mass. 1957).

Several balancing techniques can be detected in the operation of existing regional organizations:

a. The unanimity rule on substantive issues enhances the equilibrium of a regional organization and serves to prevent the permanent authoritarian control of the system by a single powerful member or bloc. Simple majority voting procedures can easily destroy the equilibrium if they are utilized too early during the integration process. The requirement for unanimous decisions, while slowing down the integration process, necessitates much more of a consensus among member states. Persuasion and cooperation become the mode of interaction between member states, and imperial tendencies are repressed.

b. Where a weaker member of a regional organization concludes that its interests are not adequately protected against the more powerful members, it may withhold the delegation of its sovereignty and its cooperation. As an example, the fear that Egypt would dominate the Arab League led Tunisia to boycott League activities on several occasions.

c. By organizing as a unit, smaller members can defend their interests against those of the larger members. This is illustrated by the experience within the European Community, where the interests of the three smaller members—Belgium, the Netherlands, and Luxembourg—are reasonably well protected through the effective functioning of their own union. The use of this technique is especially important in those areas, like Eastern Europe, Central and South America, and the Middle East, where some countries are at a lower level of development than others. By their joint insistence on a fair amount of equality in the distribution of benefits, the less developed states have been attempting to protect their interests. This, for instance, was one of the main reasons the governments of Chile, Colombia, Venezuela, Ecuador, and Peru signed the Declaration of Bogota, in August 1966. The declaration forms the basis for a program of immediate action in the field of economic integration to be undertaken by the five signatory states, in order to put them into a better bargaining position with the more developed Latin American states.[58]

d. Where two or more powers strive for active political control of a regional organization, the integrative process is likely to be accompanied by competition for the support of the smaller states. The operation of several power blocs within a regional organization, each one checking the other, has tended to maintain a balance of power.

e. The rivalry between two or more countries for leadership in a regional organization may also induce the other member states to disengage from the influence of the principal rivals. The resultant formation of neutral blocs may then tend to promote regional equilibrium.

[58] UN Doc. A/6410 (September 1966), 2-15.

The North African members of the Arab League have tended to form a neutralist bloc between Egypt and Iraq. The two dominant members of the League cannot ignore the position of member states uncommitted to either member at any given time.

These joint protective measures have not always been successful and economic and political gains have tended to gravitate toward the more advanced states in all regions. But the permanent domination of the regional organization by the more powerful states has been avoided.

The distribution of power in a regional system may be highly diffused rather than being hierarchically structured. In the African system, for example, there is little chance for a polar pattern of relations with power concentrated in one or two states. Countries like Algeria, Egypt, and Ghana have enough power, but for the time being, do not present a threat to the regional system. Other states, such as Nigeria, Kenya, and the Congo, will probably play a more powerful role in the future. Even within alliances, relations are between more or less equals rather than centered about single states. The existence of a conservative and more radical grouping does not create a rigid bipolar situation. The OCAM group remains quiescent and no closely knit radical counteralliance seems to be forming. A number of unaligned states serve a mediatory function between the two groupings.

IV

Before turning to a discussion of the existing relationship between the UN and the regional organizations, some attention should be given to the constitutional theory of the UN Charter in relation to regionalism.

During the first planning stages of the organization, regionalist conceptions of world order had considerable support. In 1943, Prime Minister Churchill presented his views for postwar organization. He envisaged the establishment of regional councils, with a superimposed world organization having somewhat secondary functions. President Roosevelt and Under-Secretary of State Welles seem also to have favored the regional approach. Within the Department of State, however, the view prevailed that a more centralized, universal peace organization should be created.

The Dumbarton Oaks Proposals incorporated the universal approach, giving regional organizations a clearly subordinate place. The proposals did not provide for the primacy of regional organizations over the UN in pacific settlement, as presently expressed in Articles 33 and 52 (2), nor the right of individual and collective self-defense as set out in Article 51. The present Article 53, giving the Security

Council precedence over regional organizations in the field of enforcement action, was included in the proposals.[59]

At San Francisco, the Latin American states, the Arab states, and Australia and New Zealand expressed dissatisfaction with the Dumbarton Oaks proposals. They wanted a more explicit recognition of regionalism and an acceptance of the exclusivity of regional agencies in peaceful settlement of disputes.

The split between the regionalists and universalists continued throughout the San Francisco Conference, until in the end a compromise was reached. The present Article 51 was inserted into the Charter, and the present Articles 33 and 52 (2) were reworded.[60]

Some of the delegates at San Francisco wanted to have the Charter endorse comprehensive political and functional regional organizations. However, this position did not receive much attention. Since maintenance of peace and security was the primary purpose of the United Nations, the main attention at San Francisco was given to the place of the regional organizations in this field,[61] and the provisions of Chapter VIII are in fact exclusively concerned with this aspect.

The Charter does not touch upon the legality of the *existence* of regional arrangements. What it does contain is a set of principles bearing upon the *activities* of regional organization:[62]

1. Regional organizations are specifically recognized as devices for maintaining peace and security on the regional level (Article 52.1).

2. Article 52.2 and Article 52.3, read in conjunction with Article 33, give regional agencies priority with regard to the settlement of disputes of a purely regional character. States involved in local disputes are encouraged to utilize regional agencies in their attempts to work out an amicable adjustment before referring the disputes to the Security Council. The Security Council is instructed to encourage the pacific settlement of local disputes through the relevant regional arrangements (Article 52.3).

3. These arrangements, however, in no way impair the right of any member of the United Nations to bring a dispute, or any situation which might lead to international friction or give rise to a dispute, to

[59] See Asbjorn Eide, "Peace-Keeping and Enforcement by Regional Organizations," *Journal of Peace Research*, No. 2 (1966). Also Francis O. Wilcox, "Regionalism and the United Nations," *International Organization* (Summer 1965).

[60] Leland M. Goodrich, "Regionalism and the United Nations, *Columbia Journal of International Affairs*, III (Spring 1949), 8.

[61] Leland M. Goodrich and Edward Hambro, *Charter of the United Nations; Commentary and Documents* (Boston 1949), 311. Also Norman J. Padelford, "Recent Developments in Regional Organizations," *Proceedings of the American Society of International Law* (April 28-30, 1955), 20.

[62] Eide, "Peace-Keeping and Enforcement by Regional Organizations," 125-27.

the attention of the Security Council or of the General Assembly (Article 35.1 and Article 52.4).

4. The regional activities in the pacific settlement of disputes are subordinated to the overriding jurisdiction of the Security Council, which may investigate any dispute and recommend settlement measures (Articles 34, 36 and 37). The parties to such a dispute must refer it to the Security Council if they fail to settle it through regional or other channels (Article 37.1). The regional organizations must at all times keep the Security Council informed of activities undertaken or in contemplation by them for the maintenance of international peace and security (Article 54). The General Assembly also has the right to discuss any question relating to the pacific settlement of any situation, including, presumably, the activities of regional agencies (Article 14).

5. In the field of enforcement action, regional agencies are integrated into the universal system as adjuncts to the UN. The Security Council can "utilize regional arrangements or agencies for enforcement action under its authority. But no enforcement action shall be taken under regional arrangements or by regional agencies without the authorization of the Security Council." (Article 53). In the case of an armed attack against any member of the regional agency, that agency has the right to invoke Article 51, dealing with individual or collective self-defense.

6. At all times, the activities of regional organizations have to be consistent with the purposes and principles of the UN. (Article 52.1). "In the event of a conflict between the obligations of the Members of the U.N. under the present Charter and their obligations under any other international agreement, their obligations under the present Charter shall prevail." (Article 103.) The activities of regional organizations are, therefore, subject to the main obligations undertaken by the members of the UN. These are to be found in Article 2.3, which imposes a duty to solve disputes peacefully, and Article 2.4, which prohibits threats to the peace or the use of armed force.

The framers of the UN Charter sought a compromise which could give regional organizations some autonomy but still keep them subordinate to the universal organization. In retrospect, it is fairly clear that Article 51 and the provisions of Chapter VIII did not result in a successful equilibrium. The lack of an effective balance between the principles of regionalism and universalism is partly due to the vagueness of some of the related Charter provisions.[63]

An additional factor responsible for the vague relationship between regional organizations and the UN is the weakness of the constitutional commitments of most of these organizations to the UN. This

63 C. Wilfred Jenks, "Co-ordination: A New Problem of International Organization," *Recueil des Cours*, II (1950).

is true not only of the collective security arrangements, but also of organizations whose activities fall under Chapter VIII of the Charter (with the exception of the OAS treaty), as well as the common market arrangements. While the need for coordinating regional action with the UN is mentioned in most of these treaties, no specific machinery is provided for. The vagueness of their langugage has made it possible for the parties to rely less and less on the UN.

The constituent instruments vary widely in their provisions concerning relations with the UN. They bear the stamp of markedly different political considerations and backgrounds. The OAS Charter, in its Preamble, reaffirms the principles and purposes of the UN. Article 1 provides that the OAS is a regional agency within the framework of the UN. Article 4 sets forth certain purposes in fulfillment of the regional obligations of the OAS under the Charter of the UN. It states that all international disputes which may arise between American states are to be submitted to the peaceful procedures set forth in the OAS Charter before being referred to the UN Security Council. The Council of the OAS is to promote and facilitate collaboration between the OAS and the UN. The organs of the OAS Council are to establish, in agreement with the Council, cooperative relations with the corresponding organs of the United Nations. The specialized inter-American organizations can conclude agreements with the specialized agencies of the UN. The article also provides that none of the provisions of the OAS Charter shall be construed as impairing the rights and obligations of the member states under the Charter of the UN.[64]

The Arab League and the OAU, while intended to operate within the general framework of the UN were not conceived of by their founders as regional agencies of the UN system. Their constituent instruments provide less elaborate arrangements for cooperation, and make no attempt to create a clear-cut relationship between these organizations and the UN.

The Covenant of the League of Arab States, which was established in March 1945, provides that a further concern of the Council of the League shall be to decide upon methods of collaboration with the international organization which may, in the future, be created for the preservation of peace and security and the regulation of economic and social relations.[65]

The OAU Charter affirms in its Preamble the faith of the African states that "The Charter of the UN provide (s) a solid foundation for peaceful and positive cooperation among states." Article 2 (1) states as one of the purposes of the organization the promotion of "in-

---

[64] C. G. Fenwick, "The Organization of American States," 59 *American Journal of International Law*, 315-20 (1965).

[65] Art. 3. See Macdonald, *League of Arab States*, 320.

ternational cooperation, having due regard to the Charter of the UN and the U.N. Declaration of Human Rights."

The EEC, CMEA, LAFTA and CACM treaties place even less emphasis on the U.N. The United Nations Charter does not define "Regional arrangements or agencies" under Chapter VIII, except to imply that they exist primarily for the purpose of safeguarding international peace and security.

Neither the Security Council nor the General Assembly has taken any decision intended to define the scope of Article 52 (1), nor has either of them expressly decided that a given regional arrangement did or did not fulfill the requirements stated therein.[66]

There have, however, been some instances in the proceedings of both the General Assembly and the Security Council when decisions were taken which have a bearing on the provisions of Article 52 (1). In 1948, the General Assembly issued a permanent invitation to the Secretary-General of the Organization of American States to be present at meetings of the Assembly. A similar invitation was extended to the Secretary-General of the League of Arab States in 1950 and the Administrative Secretary-General of the Organization of African Unity in 1965.[67] The General Assembly refrained from making any pronouncement on whether these organizations fell within the purview of Article 52 (1). On December 30, 1964, the Security Council gave implied recognition to the OAU as a regional organization under Chapter VIII when, in a resolution on the Congo situation, it expressed its conviction "that the OAU should be able, in the context of Article 52 of the Charter, to help find a peaceful solution to all the problems and disputes affecting the peace and security in the continent of Africa."[68]

The majority view today seems to be that the Arab League, OAS, and OAU are regional organizations in terms of Chapter VIII of the Charter.

The changing character of the UN system further upset the theoretical balance achieved in San Francisco between regionalism and universalism. During its first phase, from 1945 until 1958, the UN reflected to a large extent a world political environment of powerful, industrialized Western states and their political and/or economic dependencies. The dominant power within the world political system, the U.S., controlled the UN, and could in most cases mobilize a sufficient number of Latin American and Western European nations to support its position. The UN was largely used for the realization of the military and political aims of the U.S., and as a tool in the cold

[66] For a discussion of existing practice see *UN Repertory of Practice*, esp. Vol. II (1955), 280-320, 443.

[67] GA Res. 253 (III), 477 (V), 2011 (XX).

[68] UN Doc. S/2988, S/3232, A. 4543, A/4701.

war with the Soviet Union. During this phase, the collective security arrangements were established as independent entities asserting full autonomy in the conduct of their activities. The Western sponsors of these arrangements argued that they were in conformity with Article 51, but could not be considered regional agencies under Chapter VIII of the Charter. The control techniques of Articles 53.1 and 54, therefore, did not apply to such groupings.[69] The ultimate supremacy and control of the UN over regional organizations coming under Chapter VIII of the Charter was, however, not as yet challenged.

By 1958, a new phase started. The Western European states gradually came to play a more independent role in the UN. The Soviet Union became a more active participant in the world organization and a more effective critic of the U.S. role in the world organization. An increasing number of developing states were using the General Assembly as the forum for the expression of their dissatisfactions. General Assembly resolutions and discussions focused to a greater extent on problems that were of no immediate interest to the U.S. The U.S. was no longer the automatic determinant of UN decisions, but could exercise its predominance only if it won a sufficient measure of support from the Afro-Asian group.

During this second phase, new legal claims developed in support of far-reaching freedom of regional organizations from UN control. These claims evolved slowly, largely as a reaction to the complex pattern of interaction between the OAS and the UN.

The freedom of regional action by the OAS within the scope of pacific settlement and peace-keeping operations has been discussed or touched upon by UN organs in the following two categories of cases: (1) some Latin American countries have taken disputes with the U.S. to the Security Council and the General Assembly instead of the OAS; (2) others have attempted to bypass the OAS by taking disputes among themselves to the UN.

Disputes with the U.S. have been appealed to the UN by Guatemala in 1953 and 1954, by Cuba in 1960 and 1961, and by Panama in 1964. In 1960, Ecuador brought a dispute with Peru to the attention of the General Assembly, and in 1963, Haiti brought a dispute with the Dominican Republic before the Security Council.[70] In all of these cases, the U.S. succeeded in controlling the action taken by the UN organs and the disputes were turned over to the OAS or settled bilaterally. Neither the Security Council nor the General Assembly, however, admitted any lack of authority to deal with these matters, nor did they accept the argument that the OAS had exclusive jurisdiction.

[69] *UN Repertory of Practice*, Vol II (1955), 215-40.
[70] UN Doc. S/2988, S/3232, A. 4543 and A/4701.

The U.S. advanced the following claims: (1) The OAS had initial and exclusive jurisdiction over regional disputes; (2) a member of the OAS had no right to exercise its preference by turning instead to the UN.

These claims were partly challenged by a majority of other states, who held that (1) Pacific settlement comes fully within the jurisdiction of the regional organization and requires no UN supervision. It involves nonmandatory recommendations to the parties involved in a dispute, with the purpose of helping them to find a peaceful solution to their conflict. (2) A regional organization has priority in peaceful settlement of disputes and an attempt should be made by the UN and the parties involved in the dispute to use the regional organization first; (3) If the regional organization has already begun consideration of the dispute, it is preferable for the UN to wait for its outcome; but the regional organization does not have exclusive jurisdiction and the Security Council has the authority to intervene at any time it sees fit. (4) A member of a regional organization can, at all times, choose between recourse to the United Nations and recourse to the regional organization. The provisions of Article 35.1 is not invalidated by membership in a regional organization. (5) The principles of the regional system can never be invoked to deprive states of the protection of the UN; the legal protection afforded by both systems should be combined, never substituted for one another.

These views were apparently shared by Secretary-General Dag Hammarskjold, who, in his annual report for 1953-1954, wrote: "The importance of regional arrangements in the maintenance of peace is fully recognized in the Charter and the appropriate use of such arrangements is encouraged. But in those cases where resort to such arrangements is chosen in first instance, that choice should not be permitted to cast any doubt on the ultimate responsibility of the UN."[71]

Regional enforcement action has also been discussed by the UN in a number of other cases. When, in May 1948, Arab forces entered Palestine and engaged in hostilities with Jewish forces, the Arabs contended that this action was in accordance with Article 52 of the UN Charter. At that time there was no discussion in the Security Council of whether a regional organization was free to take coercive action. In 1956, the Soviet Union invoked the Warsaw Pact Treaty as part of its justification for intervening in Hungary.

The first time that regional enforcement action was extensively debated in the Security Council was in 1960, in relation to measures

[71] *Annual Report of the Secretary-General on the Work of the Organization,* (July 1, 1953-June 30, 1954), *(General Assembly Official Records,* 9th Session), Suppl. No. 1, p. XI.

taken by the OAS against the Dominican Republic. The OAS Council of Ministers of Foreign Affairs had condemned the Dominican Republic for intervention and aggression against Venezuela and had voted diplomatic, economic, and financial sanctions. The OAS informed the Security Council of its action, in accordance with Article 54 of the UN Charter. The Soviet representative asked for a meeting of the Security Council on the case, contending that the sanctions were enforcement action which, according to Article 53, could not be taken without the authorization of the Security Council. The debate in the Security Council was not conclusive. The Soviet Union argued against freeing regional organizations from the overall control of the Security Council and expressed the fear that this could create a precedent for future action by regional organizations. Some states, in particular the U.S. and U.K., argued that the action was not enforcement under Article 53 of the Charter. Other states did not want to take a stand on the issue. The resolution finally adopted merely "took note of" the OAS action.[72]

Another case arose in 1962 when the OAS voted to exclude Cuba from participation in the inter-American system and decided to apply economic and diplomatic sanctions against it. Cuba, in March 1962, challenged the legality of that action before the Security Council. However, the Council refused to place the question on its agenda.

Some weeks later, Cuba asked the Council to seek an advisory opinion from the International Court of Justice on the interpretation of Article 53. After a prolonged debate, the majority decided against the request.

In the "missile crisis" of the autumn of 1962, the Security Council briefly discussed the legality or otherwise of the quarantine against Cuba, but most delegates were more concerned with finding effective measures to end the highly dangerous situation.

The case of the U.S. intervention in the Dominican Republic, in April 1964, provoked the most far-reaching discussion yet of UN relations with a regional organization. In that situation, the U.S. attempted to legitimize its military action by securing approval of the OAS. It pressed for a transformation of the U.S. force into an OAS force. This was accepted by the OAS Council on May 6, by a very narrow vote. Six Latin American countries were unsympathetic to the U.S. intervention and only a few fully accepted it.

This time, the Security Council was much more divided. France, Uruguay, and the African and Asian members were openly critical, considering the action as a violation of Article 53 of the Charter. The U.S. lost a long battle to make the Security Council recognize the pri-

---

[72] Security Council Doc. S/4476 and 4477, and meetings 893-895, 992-998 and 1022-1025.

mary role of the OAS in the handling of the conflict. In May 1965, the Council passed a resolution calling for a cease-fire and asked the Secretary-General to send an observer to the Dominican Republic for the purpose of reporting to the Security Council. The Secretary-General's representative remained in the Dominican Republic until October 1966, reporting on the activities of the OAS force until it was withdrawn in September. This was the first instance in which the United Nations took action parallel to that of a regional agency.

The claims presented by the U.S. concerning the legality of OAS actions are complex.[73] The U. S. held that:

1. Regional efforts to maintain peace would be diluted if they were subject to the direction of the Security Council. If prior authorization was necessary, then enforcement action by a regional organization would become impossible because of the inhibitory effect of the veto power in the Security Council. The OAS therefore, had rightful and appropriate peace-keeping functions within the hemisphere and could apply certain types of enforcement action on a regional basis.

2. Enforcement under Article 53 did not include coercive measures short of military force, such as were applied in both the first Dominican and first Cuban cases. The UN Charter did not restrict the freedom of states to employ nonmilitary coercive measures, such as severance of diplomatic relations and economic boycott, and regional organizations were entitled to do whatever was legal for individual states. The OAS had fulfilled its obligation to the UN by keeping the Security Council informed of whatever enforcement action was being taken.

3. In the Cuban quarantine case in 1962, the measures taken did not constitute "enforcement" because the decision to apply the measures was only "recommendatory," not "mandatory." Therefore, the members of the OAS were not legally bound to participate in the quarantine.

4. In the Dominican case, military force was used for peace-keeping purposes only and not for enforcement action. Therefore, Article 53 did not apply and the OAS action was legal. Even in the absence of outside intervention, military force could be used to keep the peace and to prevent civil strife from resulting in a pro-Communist takeover.

The latter argument was based upon a resolution adopted by the 10th Inter-American Conference, held in Caracas in March 1954. This resolution declares that: "the domination or control of the political institutions of any American State by the international Communist movement, extending to this Hemisphere the political system of an

---

[73] Security Council Meetings 893, 1200-1221. See also Charles O. Lerche, Jr., "Development of Rules Relating to Peacekeeping by the OAS," *Proceedings of the American Society of International Law: 59th Annual Meeting* (April 1965), 60-67.

extracontinental power, would constitute a threat to the sovereignty and political independence of the American States."[74]

In response to the U.S. position, it was pointed out by a number of states that:

1. Any member of the UN had the right to ask for UN protection against what it considered unjust coercive action.

2. Limited, nonmilitary, regional peace-keeping operations, undertaken with the consent of the parties involved, could be undertaken without involving the world organization. Such operations should be noncoercive in character and their purpose should be to assist in achieving a peaceful settlement.

3. It could not be claimed that military force was being used for "peace-keeping" and not for enforcement. Any use of military force, no matter what the purpose, had to be considered as enforcement under Article 53 of the Charter.

4. Nonmilitary enforcement action, in the form of *limited* economic and diplomatic sanctions would normally not require Security Council authorization. Such coercion could, however, reach such a high level of intensity that it might constitute a threat to peace or might, from the perspective of world order, be considered unjust. Any form of *complete* boycott by a regional organization should be undertaken only when prior authorization by the Security Council had been given.

5. Any form of military coercion by a regional organization was illegal. Unless Article 51 was invoked, no blockades or other operations by air, sea, or land forces could be undertaken by regional organizations without prior authorization by the Security Council. No matter how "just" the cause, such a form of decentralized coercion could no longer be tolerated in the present world society.

Despite growing opposition to the U.S. attitude, the UN has been placed in a position of inferiority, unable to control enforcement action by the OAS. The main purpose of the UN is to monopolize the legal use of force and to prevent or reduce the decentralized use of force. As a result of OAS action, "a dangerous trend has come to the fore as regards the principle of nonintervention in America. It is the idea that the principle of nonintervention is to be opposed to the action of other states, but not to the collective action which a regional organization may adopt. Thus . . . the measures decreed by the OAS would not be considered intervention."[75]

The U.S. view of the legality of collective intervention is contrary to the principles of the Charter of the UN and of the OAS Charter. The

[74] 10th Inter-American Conference, Caracas, Venezuela, March 1-28, 1954, Final Act (Washington, Pan American Union), 94-95. See also Eide, "Peace-Keeping and Enforcement," pp. 129-30.

[75] Jorge Castaneda, "Pan Americanism and Regionalism," 382.

Caracas resolution authorizes collective action against member states in the event of the domination or control of their political institutions by Communism, an issue which clearly belongs within the domestic jurisdiction of states. The majority of the delegates disliked the idea of collective intervention. Mexico tried to change the intent of the resolution by specifying that the premise for collective action should be subversive action by *foreign* agents. The Mexican amendment was rejected, however. The Latin Americans voted for the Caracas resolution (with Guatemala voting against and Mexico and Argentina abstaining) only "because it was made plain that consideration by Washington of Latin American economic, financial, commodity price, and technical assistance aspirations would not otherwise be forthcoming."[76]

On May 6, 1965, the meeting of consultation of Ministers of Foreign Affairs passed a further resolution which was even more explicit. It stated that the OAS, "being competent to assist the member states in . . . the re-establishment of normal democratic conditions, is also competent to provide the means that reality and circumstances require . . . as adequate for the accomplishment of such purposes."[77]

The primary role of the Latin American members of the OAS in most collective security cases has been to provide a multilateral legitimacy for essentially unilateral U.S. action. The OAS serves to carry out the extracontinental objectives of the U.S., free from any control by the UN. It can be expected that the OAS will continue, at least in the immediate future, to be misused as a means to intervene against regimes of states which do not meet with the approval of the U.S.

The working relationship between the Organization of African Unity and the UN in the field of peaceful settlement and enforcement action has not presented any real difficulties so far. OAU members have been successful in getting many African-sponsored resolutions through the General Assembly and occasionally through the Security Council, although often in watered-down versions. They have taken the lead in promoting the use of nonmilitary collective action by the UN against South Africa, Portugal, and Southern Rhodesia.

The extensive utilization of the UN by the members of the OAU, acting collectively, is directly related to the existence of certain colonial and neocolonial threats. These states have recourse to the UN in order to compensate for their political, military, and economic weakness. They meet often while the General Assembly is in session to discuss matters of common interest. The chief purpose of these group meetings is to create a consensus within the limitations imposed by independent sovereignties and intraregional diversity. Since many small African states place their confidence in their regional

---

[76] Same, 399.
[77] 59 *The American Journal of International Law*, 987-88 (1965).

group, active members of the OAU can influence their less informed colleagues.

Resolutions by the OAU Assembly of Heads of State and Government afford one important means of focusing African opinion on a consensus. The Assembly considers the important agenda items of the UN General Assembly, and then instructs the permanent representatives of the member states to the UN to take appropriate action to implement their resolutions in the world organization.

This does not mean that the African group acts as a permanent voting bloc in the sense of a rigidly disciplined unit. But there is a large measure of agreement within the OAU voting bloc and the dissenting members usually abstain rather than vote against the majority of other members.

There has been active, if not notably effective, cooperation between the OAU and the UN in the cases of the Congo, Southern Rhodesia, South Africa, and Portugal, where the Security Council appealed to the OAU on several occasions to help find a peaceful solution, in conformity with Chapter VIII of the UN Charter. The UN Special Committee on Colonialism has cooperated with the OAU coordinating Committee for the Liberation of Africa.[78]

The OAU has not been involved in any jurisdictional dispute with the UN in connection with regional collective measures. It has approved many nonpeaceful measures against South Africa, Portugal, and Southern Rhodesia, often going beyond UN resolutions. In all these cases, however, it is clear that the OAU cannot as yet apply any effective sanctions within the region. Therefore, in the near future, no jurisdictional problems with the Security Council are likely to arise. Eventually, the OAU may be expected to adopt a more independent attitude with respect to regional enforcement action, and violations of Article 53 may then occur.

The OAU cooperates closely with the Economic Commission for Africa. The secretariats of the two bodies signed a formal agreement on November 15, 1965. ECA has placed its facilities at the disposal of the OAU and the new African Development Bank was planned under its auspices. Since the Commission can operate unaffected by political and constitutional changes on the continent, it is able to act as an effective clearinghouse and center for consultation for all African countries.

Cooperation between the League of Arab States and the UN has been limited and not particularly successful. One of the main reasons

[78] See, for instance, Res. S/6129 and S/217 and UN Doc. E/CN.14/343/Rev.1. Also Robert Owen Keohane, "Political Influence of Regional Groups in the General Assembly," *International Conciliation* (March 1966), 8-11.

is that many of the disputes in the Middle East have involved a non-member of the League, Israel.

During the war in 1948, Count Folke Bernadotte found it expedient to include the Arab League in his discussions and held frequent conferences with the League Secretary-General and other officials of the League. During the war in 1967, contact between representatives of the UN and officials of the Arab League was, once more, established and frequent meetings were held. In the many past and present disputes between the Arab states and Israel, the UN did not address itself directly to the League, but called upon: "the parties involved in the dispute" to do all in their power to assist in the implementation of a certain resolution. The Arab League has applied sanctions against Israel without even notifying the Security Council.

The League Council was instrumental in bringing colonial questions, such as the Moroccan, Tunisian, Algerian, and Oman questions, to the General Assembly and the Security Council. Like the Assembly of the Heads of State of the OAU, the Arab League Council considers General Assembly agenda items of direct interest to the Arab states, and attempts to add items to the agenda. There is a large measure of consensus within the League on most UN issues and, as in the case of the OAU, the dissenting members of the Arab League tend to abstain rather than vote against the majority of other members.

One of the few examples of successful cooperation between the Arab League and the UN on regional questions is the cases of Lebanon and Jordan, in 1958. When the League Council found itself unable to act, the dispute was referred to the UN Security Council. When the Security Council found itself deadlocked, it called an emergency session of the General Assembly. Before the Assembly could take action, however, the League Council was able to reach a decision. The League, working with the UN Secretariat, helped secure an agreement which was ratified by the General Assembly.

On several occasions, the Arab League Council has acted successfully on regional questions when the UN Security Council was deadlocked. As an example, the Security Council met in 1961 to discuss Kuwait at the request of the United Kingdom, but it submitted the dispute to the Arab League, which thereupon decided on action.[79]

The contacts between the UN and the Arab League have been primarily on an *ad hoc* basis. Four United Nations agencies and an information center have offices in Cairo where, with the exception of UNRWA (the relief agency for Palestine refugees), they have gen-

[79] Macdonald, *League of Arab States*, 251, 99. See also Benjamin Schwadran, "The Kuwait Incident," *Middle Eastern Affairs*, XIII (January and February 1962), 2-13.

erally operated with little or no reference to the activities of the Arab League.

The exclusion of Israel from the Arab League has made it impossible to establish a UN Economic Commission for the Middle East. The UN and the specialized agencies have undertaken programs in the member states of the Arab League, but direct cooperation between the UN and the Arab League for the purpose of coordinating regional development programs has seldom taken place.

The UN Economic Commission for Latin America has a good working relationship with LAFTA and CACM, both of which it helped to establish. The Commission is to a large extent insulated from the power political pressures exerted upon the main organs of the UN. Its action programs and research activities have contributed in building a more sophisticated approach to the requirements for economic development and the ways and means of promoting it. ECLA has been trying to influence the Latin American States to "break the closed circle of underdevelopment with new ideas—ideas that were regarded with hostility or reserve by people in financial circles in the U.S."[80]

The relationship between the UN and the regional economic organizations in the industrialized world is limited. Both the EEC and CMEA have established cooperation with the Economic Commission for Europe and the UN Conference on Trade and Development. Recently, the EEC Council of Ministers has decided to "proceed to consultations on the advisability, methods, and nature of links which the Commission might establish with international organizations."[81] But an active cooperation between the UN and these economic organizations cannot be expected.

As has been pointed out above, no clear-cut pattern of working relationships between the regional organizations and the UN has been established, except on the secretariat level in specialized fields. The policies of governments with respect to their regional institutions remain pragmatic and reflect changing interests. With the exception of the OAS, and the Warsaw Pact Treaty organization after the invasion of Czechoslovakia, there is no tendency as yet for regional organizations to challenge the ultimate responsibility of the Security Council.

Future regional involvement in the maintenance of peace may take a variety of forms, ranging from mere discussion of a dispute to regional military enforcement action. From the point of view of world order, and in harmony with the principles of the UN Charter,

[80] Alberto Lleras Camargo, "The Alliance for Progress: Distortions, Obstacles," *Foreign Affairs*, 42 (October 1963) , 27. For a detailed report on ECLA see UN Doc. E/CN.12/731/ Rev. 2.

[81] *European Community*, No. 89 (February 1966), 2.

the higher the level of intensity and the broader the scope of action, the stricter should be the requirements for UN initiation and supervision.

The future cooperative pattern between the UN and regional organizations will depend to a large extent upon what the regional groupings expect of the UN.

Within the immediate future, the UN will probably continue to be hampered by the power political environment in which it operates. It will reflect primarily the existing plutocratic system and will be able to uphold only to a limited extent the principles of general interest and interdependence. It will fail to provide an effective channel through which the new states can make themselves felt on the world stage.

It seems unlikely that the operational scope of the UN will expand quickly enough to cope with the many disturbances in the political, economic, and social environment. Actual needs will tend to outrun the functions and powers of the UN. If, at the same time, regional integration is realized in the developing world, and regional organizations succeed in satisfying the needs of the constituent states, their focus of attention may shift inward, away from the UN.

This does not mean that regionalism will destroy universalism. Regionalism is a frank concession of the limited reach of the UN at this point of history. Regional organizations have an ordering role to play in the present international system because of the nature of the system and the limitations it imposes upon both the UN and individual states to promote international order. Regionalism will permit a more effective equilibrium between the older states in the Western world and the new states in Asia, Africa, the Middle East, and Latin America. Eventually, if the UN responds to the new political environment, a new phase in the history of the organization can begin, and harmonization and integration of the world at large can proceed. A balance can then be established between universalism and regionalism, and universal and regional forms of international cooperation will then become inseparable, compatible, and mutually supporting.

V

In attempting to determine the importance of regional organizations to world order now and in the future, first it is essential to try to discern the basic structure of the present and future political environment.

Several conceptions of the contemporary distribution of world power have been advanced by careful observers. According to the unipolar view, the U.S. is presently the predominant power. The bipolar conception holds that the Soviet Union and the United States control present-day international affairs and balance each other. The multi-polar views perceives the existence of several rival centers of international power. Finally, there is the view that the contemporary period is one of gradual "atomization," in which a large number of states pursue their national interests independently from the super-powers.

Each of these views has a certain validity, depending upon which power factors are selected for analysis. The contemporary system can best be explained by a combination of elements of all the above views. The dominant trends today point to the development, in the near future, of a loose, multi-polar system, in which a redistribution of power among national and regional actors will have been accomplished. The remaining colonies and the traditional societies will be transformed within a few decades, while at least half a dozen nations or regional groupings are likely to advance into the "big power" group.

A multi-polar system would provide for a deconcentration of power and a more rational and democratic pattern of international relations. The stability of a multi-polar system appears *likely* to be substantially greater than that of a bi-polar system, with its tendency to ignore the needs of small and middle powers. If the spread of nuclear weapons could be slowed down or controlled, a transition to an increasingly multi-polar system might give mankind a chance to search for a more dependable form of world political organization.[82] A movement toward regionally integrated units *could* contribute to the development of such a loose multi-polar world system.

An important question is whether such a multi-polar system would remain loose and flexible. Regionalism might well create several units closer to an equality of economic and political power than now exists. But if this would result in a rigid polarization between several highly autonomous regional communities the stability of the international system would be threatened.

At present, the political and institutional ties between the constituent states are too weak to permit the regional communities to act in a cohesive and highly unified way on very many regional or international issues. But increased political integration resulting in the establishment of several large, autonomous communities with a sharpening of regional boundaries in the world, might produce rigidities and increased conflicts between these communities and damage global abilities for the promotion of peaceful change.

If not accompanied also by a strengthening of the global ties that

---

[82] Karl W. Deutsch and J. David Singer, "Multipolar Power Systems and International Stability," *World Politics,* XVI (April 1964), 406.

bind states across regions, regional integration might become a negative force. Without global "integration" above it, a "balance of power" system of several regional communities and superpowers would almost surely have to fail.[83]

Evidence so far points against the conclusion that continued regional integration will take place at the expense of greater worldwide integration. An increase in the institutional and behavioral ties that join states across regions can be observed. Many states associate with several regional communities and can help prevent the emergence of sharp conflicts between them. Behavioral ties across regions result in shifting political alignments of the major regions on different issues. Despite many problems and disagreements, there is a slow, but continuing progression toward the integration of the entire global system.

The world today presents two main sets of problems. The first one arises out of the friction between the private enterprise and centrally planned economies—a friction which may lead to general nuclear war. The second set is a result of the relationship between the Western industrialized world and a large number of new and relatively underdeveloped countries. Regionalism can play a role in the solution of these problems.

Regionalism is contributing to a more stable and cooperative relationship between Eastern and Western Europe. The Soviet attitude toward European integration has been ambivalent from the beginning. In the late fifties, Soviet spokesmen looked upon the European Community as an American plot to dominate Europe. In the early sixties, the emphasis shifted to the political threat represented by a joint American-German control of Europe. From mid-1962, the Franco-German alliance was identified as the nucleus of integration, and the viability of the European Community was recognized. "The Seventeen Theses" on Western integration, worked out in 1957 in Moscow to guide the struggle of international Communism against the EEC, were replaced by a new document, "The Thirty-two Theses." This document gave credit to the achievements of the EEC and foresaw collaboration not only between different states having different social systems but also between their economic unions. The strengthening of CMEA in the early sixties was a response to the growing power of the EEC.

The present state of economic and political contacts between the industrial states of Western and Eastern Europe indicates that they have entered a new, more cooperative phase. While the Soviet govern-

[83] For advocacy of a "balance of power" system see Roger D. Masters, "A Multi-Bloc Model of the International System," *American Political Science Review*, 4, No. 55 (1961), 780-98. For criticism of such a system see, for instance, Bruce M. Russett, *International Regions and the International System* (Chicago 1967), 218-34.

ment still continues some of its attacks on the European Community, the smaller Eastern European governments have accepted the existence of the Community. They watch with respect the integrative effort which has united onetime enemies through functional cooperation, led to the virtual abolition of frontiers, and laid foundations for the real independence of Western Europe. They believe that the Community will continue to grow in economic strength and will eventually take on significant political functions, and they are working hard to develop closer relations with the Community. There are also substantial tendencies in the countries of the European Community to intensify political and economic cooperation with the Socialist states.

The growing prosperity in both Eastern and Western Europe, the increasing restlessness with the division imposed on it more than twenty years ago, the Sino-Soviet split, and the decline in the solidarity of NATO are creating the conditions for a harmonious and cooperative relationship between European countries in the immediate future. For the time being, relations between Eastern and Western European governments are likely to continue on a predominantly bilateral basis. In 1964, the European Commission initiated a strong effort to speed up the introduction of a common policy toward the members of CMEA. In the next several years it is likely that the European Community will become more active in developing East-West economic, technical, and scientific cooperation. Step by step a cooperative relationship between the two organizations and common all-European institutions and ventures can be expected to develop.[84]

Regionalism has also brought about a better distribution of power between the U.S. and Western Europe. While it is not yet clear whether the Paris and Rome Treaties have created a rival or an ally for the U.S., it seems most likely that Western Europe will become an increasingly independent force in the world, with its own foreign and military policy. From the point of view of world stability, this can only be looked upon as a positive development. This, of course, does not prevent the continuation of certain cooperative military and economic relationships between the U.S. and Western Europe.

The existence of a more independent Europe might also contribute to better relations between Eastern Europe and the U.S. A lesser American military involvement in European affairs would facilitate a rapprochement between the U.S. and the Soviet Union, especially if the Soviet military threat is no longer made the major motivation for the Western alliance. This will perhaps induce a greater realiza-

---

[84] Rudolf Schlesinger, "Is the Cold War Inherently Necessary?," *Coexistence*, 4, No. 1 (January 1967). See also: Zbigniew Brzezinski, "Russia and Europe," *Foreign Affairs*, 42 (April 1964), 428-35.

tion of their mutual responsibility in world affairs and create a co-operative relationship between them.

The success of regionalism in the industrialized part of the world can endanger international stability if it is not counterbalanced by a steady growth of regionalism in the underdeveloped world. The EEC and CMEA, by reinforcing the overall position of some important in-dustrialized countries, tend to emphasize the imbalance in the world economy and intensify the conflict between developed and developing states.

That Western forms of regionalism can adversely affect the devel-oping world is apparent from an analysis of the association of 18 Afri-can countries with the EEC. While it is generally assumed that this as-sociation will benefit its African members, the consequences of some provisions of the 1963 Association Convention are extremely dubious.

The efficiency of the less-developed partner is hardly stimulated by this type of preferential arrangement. The effect of opening its do-mestic market to imported manufactures is more important than the extent to which its export industries can benefit from preferential treatment. As far as raw materials are concerned, the participating developing countries have been able to obtain price and volume ad-vantages in their export of raw materials to the European Commu-nity. But as long as the Community discourages the establishment of processing facilities in developing countries, these advantages are not very significant. In addition, most of them accrue to the benefit of European nationals and companies that operate in the beneficiary developing country. The Convention grants to nationals of Euro-pean Community member states establishment rights in African as-sociated states, and provides for the free flow of capital. It has proved almost impossible for Africans to buy into the ownership of certain European corporations operating on their soil. The managers of these corporations have insulated themselves from the Africans; at the same time, they are able to exert varying degrees of influence over the national policy of the countries involved. Finally, while the Convention is supposedly based on the philosophy that the economies of the associated states must be diversified as much as possible, fi-nancial aid from the European Development Fund is used mainly for infrastructure investments, and plans of a directly productive and in-dustrial character have been discouraged.

The real advantages and disadvantages of the system depend on the conditions under which it operates. The procedure of consulta-tions under the Convention, and the balance of political and eco-nomic power within the association, make it difficult for the asso-ciated members to take full advantage of the theoretical possibilities

inherent in the Convention. Unless appropriate new policy measures are adopted, it seems likely that the association will continue primarily to benefit its European members—especially France—and in
the long run will have mostly negative implications for the associated
states. The whole idea of the closed association is an outdated attempt to extend European influence to what is in effect a group of
client states. Unless the United Kingdom joins the Community, it
is also highly probable that the association will keep Africa divided
into two separate areas along the lines of former colonial affiliation.

The 18 associated states seem increasingly dissatisfied with both
the trade and aid aspects of the Convention. Most of them feel that
the European Community has failed to deal with their problems of
modernization and has not helped to correct the imbalance in their
terms of trade. There is also a growing awareness that the Convention affords the Europeans a degree of control over their economic
and political life that is unparalleled in any other system.

It seems that, if present tendencies continue, the associated states
may seek to disengage themselves to some extent from the special
Eurafrican relationship represented by the Convention. They increasingly favor a more open, limited type of association, such as the one
outlined in the Lagos agreement of July 16, 1966, associating Nigeria with the EEC and in the ARUSHA agreement of July 26, 1968,
associating the East African community with the EEC. The negotiations for a new association agreement between the EEC and the African associates that started in June 1968 are going to be important for
the future of African integration.

By the early seventies, the political and economic pressures working
against the closed association both in Africa and in Western Europe
will probably have gathered enough momentum to terminate the
association agreement. If the policies of the closed association continue much beyond 1970, they may become both the target and the
irritant of a more violent nationalism in Africa and actually increase
the instability of that continent.

Not only the association of a limited number of African states
with Europe, but the whole concept of a "Eurafrica"—an Africa associated by close vertical relationships with Europe—undermines African integration and development. Eurafrica still suggests the subordination of Africa to Europe—of poor primary producers to rich, developed
industrial powers. A sounder political aim would be to develop unity
on two parallel lines, the steady rapprochement between the ex-British
and ex-French territories in Africa being matched by the absorption
of Britain into Europe. Then between the two regional groupings,
Western Europe and Africa, there could be a fruitful and close cooperation.

Only through the effective use of their own regional institutions will the African and other developing countries be able to improve their economic and political bargaining power vis-à-vis the industrialized world.

Regional integration in the developing world can also have an important impact upon world order. The area of potential instability is dangerously great in a continuously interacting world society made up of a poor majority and a rich minority of states. There are some 110 developing countries, of which more than 90 have populations below 15 million. The majority of these states have obtained their independence since the Second World War. They have little or none of the cohesiveness that characterizes older states, and are often artificial products of colonial rule. Most of them are not yet viable entities which successfully discharge political, economic, and military functions associated with the exercise of national sovereignty. About half of them are actively engaged in the modernization of their societies, while in the other half modernizing elites are still consolidating their position.[85] It will take many decades for most of these societies to complete the main tasks of modernization. They will soon be joined by other states of varying size and importance that are still under colonial rule. The rate at which these countries move toward more stable political and economic conditions may depend to a large extent on their ability to form more viable regional and subregional communities.

The weakness of the developing states invites intervention and counterintervention by outside powers in their internal affairs. The Western powers have a strong desire to exert their influence upon the former colonies and have made use of covert and overt forms of coercion to accomplish these objectives. As a consequence of their weakness, some new states have become mere dependencies of the West.

In recent years, Western countries have developed elaborate counter-guerrilla strategies and capabilities intended for use against "revolutionary" movements in the developing world. The new arsenal of civil war strategy includes a capacity to airlift troops quickly into battle anywhere on the globe. In 1966, for example, the French organized an elite military division whose role is summed up in its official designation: La Force d'Intervention. The division is intended to strike at short notice to support shaky pro-French governments in the former African colonies. It was used for the first time in November 1967 to give support to President Jean Bedel Bokassa of the Central African Republic, who had been facing increasing hostility within his officer corps. France has defense pacts with 12 former African colonies, including the Central African Republic. The

85 Black, *The Dynamics of Modernization*, 147-57.

treaties permit French intervention, if invited, in times of "anarchy." It is the "anarchy" clause that gives Paris the option to support governments it favors and to thwart opposition movements viewed as too leftist or overly independent of French policy.

Western intervention in the developing states often provokes counterintervention on the part of the Communist leadership. Although the Soviet government proclaims its support for all "wars of liberation," in practice it is engaged in a cautious effort to further its foreign policy objectives. Soviet hopes of quick political conquest and a vastly expanded political and strategic role in the developing world have been tempered by experience. The paramount criterion for the USSR in supporting "wars of liberation" seems to be whether or not this support will weaken the position of the Western powers. "National Liberation" forces fighting for their countries' independence from the West are regarded as appropriate recipients of material support. The attitude of these recipients toward indigenous Communism and their socio-political orientation seem to be looked upon as matters of secondary importance.

While the Chinese leaders are attempting to draw every possible advantage from their outwardly more revolutionary attitude in order to capture the leadership of the most militant wings of the "national liberation" movements, in practice they seem equally cautious. At this stage at least, the Chinese leadership is not exporting revolutions by armed force, but is supporting selected "national liberation" forces engaged in a course that leads away from dependence on the West.

Conflict among the Communist and Western powers has been increasingly confined to struggles for influence in certain parts of the developing world. Some new states have become the battleground on which this competition for dominance is taking place. Such big-power confrontation in civil wars renders the international system more unstable and always carries with it the danger of escalation.

From the point of view of world stability, it is important that the developing states learn how to limit intervention in their internal affairs by both the Western and Communist states. In the case of South East Asia, for example, regional economic and political cooperation among the countries of the area might temper the present extreme nationalistic feelings and create a sense of regional solidarity and interdependence. In the case of Vietnam, Vietnamese Communists and non-Communists would find cooperation easier in a broad South East Asian framework than if they were left to face each other directly. North Vietnam's dilemma would be reduced if it could have some guarantee that the end of the war would lead to a form of regional integration not controlled by U.S. political interference. Despite many problems, effective regional cooperation, if supported by the relevant political elites, could probably evolve over the next decade.

As has already been pointed out, existing regional organizations are still too vulnerable to play a vital role in the control of foreign intervention and their influence upon the big powers is bound to be minimal. The contemporary imbalance in military-political power factors favors the industrialized nations and hinders the effective functioning of regional organizations in the developing areas.

The developing states are well aware of their subordinate position within a highly stratified international system. They know that their isolated voices do not command a receptive world audience and that, disunited, they do not have the capacity to influence the international system in any meaningful way. Within this context, they are becoming increasingly interested in developing their own regional organizations.

These organizations enable them to define their own regional goals and common interests. They can be used as instruments of action in order to: (1) increase their economic and political status and prestige within the international system; (2) create ideological and political cohesion within the region and promote the evolution of regional autonomy as a means to avoid the reassertion of power by the industrialized nations; and (3) correct the distribution of power within the international system in order to democratize it. The activities of these organizations already have had the result that the strategy of the "Latin American group," the "African group," and the "Arab group" is being considered by the world's decision-makers.

Once the regional communities have reached greater maturity and institutional stability, they will be able to control more effectively the influence of external factors on the politics and economy of their member states and to place more effective restraints upon the use of force and intervention by states. This may impel the industrialized powers gradually to work out a consistent and mutually profitable policy of noninterference. Both the West and the Soviet Union, and eventually China, can then become an important constructive factor in the political and economic development of the new states.

Some observers have held that regional organizations with an integrated military sector would present a threat to world peace. It should not be forgotten, however, that a sufficient amount of community building must take place before a fully integrated regional command structure with authority to act in the name of the region can be established. At best, only a partially integrated military sector can be expected within the immediate future. It may seem at first sight that such a limited regional military capability would enable a regional organization to commit aggression against a target state.

However, it seems improbable that these groups can wage war at this stage of their development, if only because their members are not yet sufficiently integrated to agree on the means of organizing an aggressive undertaking.

The history of the Arab League has shown that while a united front has been manifest in verbal attacks on Israel, the League has been less than successful in its attempts to coordinate action against that country. In 1964, the League decided to create a permanent joint Arab military planning staff in the Secretariat to deal with such problems as joint contingency planning, the standardization of training, and joint military maneuvers. It seems unlikely, however, that a permanent Joint Arab Command of any importance will be established in the foreseeable future. Only in the case of the economic boycott of Israel has coordinated action been successfully employed.

Most of the developing states will not possess a nuclear capability for many decades. Continued nuclear proliferation may, however, encourage some of the more important new states to acquire nuclear weapons. South Africa and Israel, for example, have an industrial base that might encourage them to acquire nuclear arms to deter their neighbors. India, Egypt, Ghana, Mexico, Brazil, and Argentina might also emerge as regional nuclear powers. The acquisition of nuclear capability by a member of a regional organization, or by a nonmember located within the same geographic area, would create or aggravate many problems and would affect the stability of the regional and international system. This makes the speedy development of stable and sufficiently integrated regional communities, with a more tolerant attitude toward target states, even more urgent.

Regional organizations can contribute to the development of international law. As has often been observed, modern international law is developed on both the universal and the regional level.[86] The lack of a closely knit world community of values, purposes, and interests represents a severe limitation on the growth of law on a universal level. On the regional level, however, legal integration and the evolution of common legal substantive laws can proceed successfully. The members of a regional organization often share common interests and affinities in their social and legal structures. The existence of such a common way of thinking facilitates the unification of law on a regional basis.

The multi-national regional communities are not only developing their own regional law, but are also making specific contributions to the development of international law. One such contribution is the

---

[86] See: Wolfgang Friedmann, *The Changing Structure of International Law* (New York, 1964). Also Philip C. Jessup, "Diversity and Uniformity in the Law of Nations," 58 *American Journal of International Law*, 341-59 (1964).

breaking up of the rigid separation of national and international law. The "communities" create intermediate types of law that are neither international in the traditional sense, nor national. Guggenheim finds that developments in the EEC may lead to the creation of a new "droit public européen distinct de l'ordre juridique étatique."[87] De Visscher refers to the Court of the European Community as applying a "droit international spécial."[88] The jurisprudence of the Court states that "notre cour n'est pas une jurisdiction internationale, mais la juridiction d'une communauté créée par six Etats."[89]

This type of regional law and lawmaking process may furnish a model of integration that may be used first on a regional level and later on a universal level when the world society has reached a requisite degree of common interests and values.

The most important contribution of the regional communities to international law lies in the values and goals which they provide to the international community. The regional institutions are reformulating the character and the basis of international law. Their policies and activities accelerate the evolution from the traditional rules of abstention to positive principles of cooperation for common interests.

Regional institutions enable the developing state to participate more effectively in the process of reconciling the competing claims of states and other participants. These states hold differing views as to what is permissible and desirable international behavior. While the more conservative governing elites in the new states are basically satisfied with the existing state of affairs and do not seek to transform the world community, the more radical elites challenge the present world system and question its values. The latter's demands for reform of the international legal order reflect changing positions of interest dictated by economic and political circumstances. They want a new world system that would provide for both wealthier and more powerful non-Western societies. They believe in an aggressive assertion of this policy and are willing to force the pace of change by direct national and regional pressures. Regional institutions permit them to adopt a common strategy of participation in the international legal and political order and to secure support for changes in the structure of international society.

[87] "Droit International Général et Droit Public Européen," *18 Annuaire Suisse de Droit International*, 9, 28 (1961).

[88] *Rapport de Paul de Visscher, Actes officiels, congrès international d'études sur la communauté européenne du charbon et de l'acier*, 2 (1957), 36.

[89] Fédération charbonnière de Belgique C. Haute Autorité, *Recueil*, 2 (1955-1956), 263. See also: Peter Hay, "The Contribution of the European Communities to International Law," *Proceedings of the American Society of International Law, 59th Annual Meeting* (April 22-24 1965), 195-201.

The case of Latin America illustrates the importance of a regional expression of international law. The imperialistic domination exercised by the U.S. over the Latin American states aroused their resentment. As a result, since World War I, these states have developed various doctrines upholding their freedom from interference—such as the Calvo, Drago, Tobar, and Estrada doctrines. The Calvo doctrine, for instance, was designed to govern conflicts with governments of outside states over investments by their citizens. These Latin American legal views are similar to the challenge to Western legal principles by some African and Asian states since 1945.

Regional organizations can contribute to harmonizing the many differences in legal views and interests of states. They can also facilitate the reorganization of the structure and rules of international law in order to increase their applicability to new situations throughout the world.[90] Only when international law has the capacity to serve the interests of all states can it operate as a viable basis for a democratic world order.

In general, regional efforts to achieve security, peaceful change, and higher standards of living seem to hold out the prospect for increased international stability. In the immediate future, regional organizations can achieve a degree of integration not possible in a universal organization. Activities of the worldwide organizations will remain limited, while the management of important problems of worldwide import, such as the control of nuclear testing and the policing of outer space, will remain the responsibility of the few countries that are capable of participating in these activities. Regional organizations are likely to remain the principal agencies of integration.

As already has been pointed out, regional integration without concurrent deliberate effort toward integrating the entire international system would be a highly questionable solution. Regional integration and universal integration are not mutually exclusive "strategies of world order." The choice about what to do about global unity may well determine the importance of regional organizations to world order now and in the future.

Conflict between national, regional, and international actors will continue to pose complex problems. Regionalism unites the participating countries, but in the very process of doing so, it tends to accentuate the factors that divide the new group from the rest of the world. Since individual states and major groupings of states will continue to differ greatly in goals and power, a new pattern of peaceful

[90] For a discussion of the national and international process of democratization of the legal community, see B.V.A. Roling, *International Law in an Expanded World* (Amsterdam 1960), 56-86.

relations between them will have to be worked out. It will take skill-ful and creative leadership to negotiate these problems in the dec-ades ahead and to devise a stronger world political system than we now know how to construct. Regionalism can be a powerful tool for good or for evil. What use man will make of it is impossible to foretell.

CHAPTER 10

The Prospects for Order through
Regional Security

LYNN H. MILLER

I. INTRODUCTION

ALTHOUGH regional organizations of all descriptions have received the attention of scholars during recent years, most of the best work in this area has been centered either upon problems of transnational integration and community-building or on the "functional" activities of regional associations.[1] Studies dealing specifically with the peace and security role[2] of regional organizations—at least in any generalized fashion—have been fewer. Some commentators on this aspect of regionalism have tended to dichotomize regional and universal approaches to international security in the abstract—usually as a

[1] These two foci are, of course, generally considered to be related. Ernst B. Haas has led in the study of the functional integration of regional groupings. See, for example, his "Regionalism, Functionalism, and Universal International Organization," *World Politics*, VIII, 2 (January 1956), 238-63; "International Integration: The European and the Universal Process," *International Organization*, XV, 3 (Summer 1961), 366-92; *Beyond the Nation-State* (Stanford 1964). See also Ben T. Moore, *NATO and the Future of Europe* (New York 1958), 263 pp. Karl W. Deutsch has made a unique contribution in this area with his elaboration of the idea of the security-community. See Deutsch and others, *Political Community and the North Atlantic Area* (Princeton 1957).

Analyses of particular regional groupings and their activities are much too numerous for an exhaustive listing. Some of the better, recent studies in this category dealing primarily with political aspects might include the following: Inis L. Claude, "The OAS, the UN, and the United States," *International Conciliation*, No. 547 (March 1964); J. Lloyd Mecham, *The United States and Inter-American Security, 1889-1960* (Austin 1961); B. Y. Boutros-Ghali, "The Arab League: 1945-1955," *International Conciliation*, No. 498 (May 1954); Robert W. Macdonald, *The League of Arab States* (Princeton 1965); George Modelski, ed., *SEATO: Six Studies* (Melbourne 1962), 302; M. Margaret Ball, *NATO and the European Union Movement* (London 1959), 486; John C. Dreier, *The Organization of American States and the Hemisphere Crisis* (New York 1962), 147; Charles G. Fenwick, *The Organization of American States: The Inter-American Regional System* (Washington 1963), 601; Jerome Slater, "The United States, the Organization of American States, and the Dominican Republic, 1961-1963," *International Organization*, XVIII, 2 (Spring 1964), 268-91; Zbigniew K. Brzezinski, "The Organization of the Communist Camp," *World Politics*, XIII, 2 (January 1961), 175-209; B. Y. Boutros-Ghali, "The Addis Ababa Charter," *International Conciliation*, No. 546 (January 1964).

[2] The terms "peace and security role" or simply "security role" will be used throughout this chapter to denote (1) the potential of a regional organization, through its peacekeeping machinery or diplomatic techniques, for controlling the forceful settlement of disputes among its own members, and (2) the potential of the organization to present a common military front against an outside actor or actors. Variations in this role are treated more fully in Part III of this chapter.

prelude to asserting that the former principle is incompatible with and inferior to the latter for the organization of peace. Often, however, they have not explored satisfactorily the question as to whether or not, or to what extent, the dichotomy actually exists in the practice of states since World War II.

On the other hand, proponents of effective regional organization as a pathway to order have been inclined to dismiss the multilateral treaty organizations of the postwar period as not "genuine" regional agencies of the type accounted for in Chapter VIII of the United Nations Charter. Both views may be essentially correct, but neither seems to take adequate account of the likely effects of regional security activity—through whatever agencies it has been expressed—that has been characteristic of much international conduct during the past twenty years. Empirical analysis that focuses upon this regional security activity, regardless of the instrumentalities used, should provide the base for sounder judgments as to its compatibility with the goals of universal order.

Any attempt to determine the prospects for international order through regional efforts to achieve security must consider two distinct, though clearly related, issues. One is basically a normative concern, i.e. whether or not the regional approach to security characteristic of much current international practice is compatible with the goals of universal order. The other, a problem for empirical analysis, concerns the trends currently operating that can suggest whether the amount and quality of current regional security activity will become either more or less significant in the future.

The approach to be undertaken here will begin by analyzing relevant tendencies discernible in the structure and conduct of international politics during approximately the past twenty years. The year 1945 is taken as a rough bench mark since the phenomenon of regionalism discussed here is almost exclusively the product of the postwar world. This is not to say, of course, that regional security activity was unknown prior to the war; indeed, as the experience of an earlier period may be seen to have relevance to the behavior of the present or near future, it will be drawn upon. The fact remains, however, that the post-1945 period differs in many fundamental respects from previous eras of political history: bipolarity and bloc politics, the creation of new nation-states out of the ashes of colonial empires, the threat of atomic devastation—these and other factors are essentially new ones in the international system (certainly so in combination). More importantly, they are not factors which can be expected to vanish overnight. They undoubtedly will continue to affect international political structures and behavior for some time into the future. Thus, the first part of the analysis which follows will emphasize the recent historical developments that have helped to shape and alter the parameters of regional security activity. The primary focus of attention will be upon both the changing and the comparatively constant relationships among national actors and international institutions.

Secondly, attention will shift more specifically to the developments in patterns of political behavior and normative standards as they apply to regional security activity. This section, too, is empirical-analytical, but discussion will deal primarily with the types and functions of recent regional security activity as seen within the environmental framework presented previously. Finally, extrapolation from those tendencies drawn from analysis of the operation of the international system and those working at present at the regional level in particular then should permit a sketch of the likely security role of regionalism in the future, and, thus, of its potential contribution or noncontribution to international order.

II. Postwar Politics and the Organization of International Security

With the close of World War II and the development of plans for a new international organization to replace the defunct League of Nations, there was discussion within the governments of both the United States and the United Kingdom as to the principle of order which should be incorporated into the organization's Charter, regionalism or universalism. Although Winston Churchill and Sumner Welles were the two principal spokesmen for the regional security approach, the proposals which emerged from the Dumbarton Oaks conference clearly favored a universal security attempt, somewhat on the pattern of the collective security scheme of the League of Nations. Nonetheless, regional arrangements were granted a rather conditional endorsement on the grounds that they be consistent with the purposes and principles of the universal organization. The draft provided that enforcement action by regional agencies could be taken only with the authorization of the Security Council.

At the San Francisco conference, however, many of the Latin American delegates in particular objected to this clear subordination of regional organizational activity to the UN, presumably on the grounds that it would give an already powerful Security Council even more authority. Such additional authority, too, would be granted by apparently denying permission to small states in regional groupings the chief responsibility for their own security. As the result of these objections, the UN Charter which emerged from the conference contained two provisions that seemed to grant regional organizations somewhat more authority than had been envisaged at Dumbarton Oaks.[3] Yet, in doing so, the prescribed relationship between regional organizations and the United Nations was left somewhat more ambiguous than it had been in the earlier draft proposals. Even so, the implication of Chapter VIII as a whole was relatively clear in its suggestion that even though regional groupings might play a more positive role in the peace and security field than had been anticipated by the leaders of the great powers, still, such activity was meant to be subordinate, in the final analysis, to the directives of the Security Council. On paper, at least, the Charter was far more explicit than the Covenant had been in attempting "to relate the regional organizations to the world organization and to reconcile the principles of universalism and regionalism."[4]

What manner of security system had the framers of the Charter attempted to devise? In their determination to make the Security Council the effective authority of international security, the participants in the San Francisco conference had partially abandoned the "pure" collective security rationale of the League of Nations, but only partially so. As Claude has argued cogently, grant of the veto power to the Council's permanent members ensured that they would be able to prevent any enforcement action being taken against their will. "The veto rule is an explicit declaration that the framers of the Charter rejected the idea of making . . . the United Nations an instrument of collective security in cases involving aggressive action by great powers."[5] Nonetheless, implicit in the international police powers granted the Security Council was the assumption that genuine collective security action could and, no doubt, would be undertaken against any other members guilty of aggressive action. It was in this kind of action that regional arrangements might play an important security role—not as the focal points of great power opposition but as either (a) the agents of universal collective action under the supervision of the Security Council, or (b) the instruments of settlement at the stage of a conflict when the involvement of the entire world community is not required.

[3] First, Article 52 (2) provided that members of regional organizations "shall make every effort to achieve pacific settlement of local disputes through such regional arrangements . . . before referring them to the Security Council." Secondly, the first Article of Chapter VI, dealing with the pacific settlement of disputes, listed the resort to regional arrangements among the other techniques contained in the Dumbarton Oaks proposal which should be explored before resorting to the Security Council (Article 33/1) .

[4] Gerhard Bebr, "Regional Organizations: A United Nations Problem," *American Journal of International Law*, XLIX, 2 (April 1955) , 168.

[5] Inis L. Claude, Jr., "The United Nations and the Use of Force," *International Conciliation*, No. 532 (March 1961) , 329.

The transformation of international politics that followed hard on the heels of the San Francisco conference soon undermined most of the assumptions built into the UN Charter about the way in which peace should be organized in the postwar world. Although most of the changes wrought in the security functions of regional groups can be traced directly to the onset of the cold war, this was not the only factor responsible for altering the structure of world politics. Several rather diverse factors have been at work within the international system since San Francisco to alter the role of regionalism in the ordering process. Although any extraction of certain historical trends as of greater explanatory value than others is in some sense arbitrary, those to be considered here are regarded as of primary importance (a) because of the persisting quality of the political problems they have induced and (b) because of their clear impact upon the conduct of politics in regional groupings.

Bipolarity and International Organization

The chief, immediate consequence of bipolarity for regionalism was the creation of a new kind of regional association in the cold war period, one apparently not anticipated by the framers of the Charter. Beginning with the creation of the North Atlantic Treaty Organization in 1949, several multilateral security organizations came into existence which, while meant to act as "regional" instruments of mutual defense (primarily in the sense that their membership was limited), deliberately avoided describing themselves as "regional arrangements" under the terms of Chapter VIII of the Charter. Instead, their adherence to the principles of the Charter was expressed through the provisions of Article 51. That article, included in Chapter VII rather than Chapter VIII of the Charter, guaranteed members "the inherent right of individual or collective self-defense." Adherence to Article 51 was designed to eliminate the control of the Security Council over the responses of regional agencies to armed attack.

This development could be read at first as specifically the Western response to the implacable hostility which now divided them from the Soviet camp. With the permanent membership of the Soviet Union in the Security Council, the West recognized the impossibility of directing regional security activity in their interests through the medium of that UN organ. Thus, Western leaders created three new multilateral pacts during the next several years which could operate outside the scope of Chapter VIII—NATO, SEATO, and the Baghdad Pact (later CENTO).[6] The United States also encouraged the

---

[6] The Baghdad Pact arrangement, which did not include the United States as a member, was the alternative pursued by the West after their suggestion of a Middle East Defense Pact, to be tied to NATO in some way, was summarily rejected by the Egyptians.

adoption within the OAS, heretofore a regional organization of the type whose relationship to the UN was specified in Chapter VIII, of a new defense pact for the Organization which likewise invoked Article 51 of the Charter for its authority.[7] But then, in 1950, the Arab League—whose operations like those of the OAS, previously had been accounted for by Chapter VIII of the Charter—also invoked Article 51 in drawing up its collective defense pact.[8] What originally had been a Western ploy to avoid Soviet involvement in regional security activity in which the Western powers had a stake was adopted by the "original" regional organizations as well, thus altering their legal relationship to the United Nations.

However much the functions of the original regional organizations and the new multilateral security organizations might differ in practice, they could now be regarded as comparable instruments of security in their relationship to the United Nations. The slight ambiguity of the Charter regarding the place of the original regional groupings within the UN system was not, thereby, resolved. On the contrary, that ambiguity was intensified, at least so far as the original regional groupings were concerned. Now they had set themselves up as agencies independent of Security Council control in matters regarding threats to their security from outside their membership, while they apparently remained bound by the provisions of Chapter VIII in other activities. This question of the legal relationship between the regional body and the universal one was to become further entangled, as will be seen in the next section, when these regional security pacts came to be applied to peace-threatening action by members of the group.

[7] Inter-American Treaty of Reciprocal Assistance:

"*Article 2*: As a consequence of the principle set forth in the preceding Article [condemning war], the High Contracting Parties undertake to submit every controversy which may arise between them to methods of peaceful settlement and to endeavor to settle any such controversy among themselves by means of the procedures in force in the Inter-American System before referring it to the General Assembly or the Security Council of the United Nations.

"*Article 3(1)*: The High Contracting Parties agree that an armed attack against an American State shall be considered as an attack against all the American States and, consequently, each one of the said Contracting Parties undertakes to assist in meeting the attack in the exercise of the inherent right of individual or collective self-defense recognized by Article 51 of the Charter of the United Nations."

[8] Macdonald argues, in his *Arab States* that Arab and Latin American delegates at UNCIO had supported the provisions of Article 51 on the assumption that they would be incorporated into Chapter VIII. Then he adds, "inexplicably, the result of the maneuver has been that the original regional organizations . . . and the newer collective-defense organizations . . . both invoked Article 51 and not Article 52 when they drafted their security treaties" (p. 222). Such a move may have been nearly "inexplicable" so far as the Arab League was concerned, but with regard to the Rio Treaty, U.S. membership in the Organization and U.S. leadership of the West in the cold war certainly encouraged the decision to remove the security activity of the OAS from the veto power of the Soviet Union.

The development of bipolarity, in addition to destroying all hope of great power concert, also served to alter the assumptions present at San Francisco as to the limited applicability of Council-directed collective security measures. Here one can discern at least three shifts in attitude toward the utility of universal collective action to maintain the peace in the UN period. The first such shift took place at the beginning of the cold war, prior to the clash of arms in Korea in 1950. This was the period of the formation of NATO, when the Charter's peace-keeping and enforcement provisions were rather suddenly and widely regarded as almost totally irrelevant to the political cleavages which had developed among the former Allied powers. The East-West split was seen as so pervasive it seemed unlikely that any aggressive action by a lesser power could be taken without cold war ramifications. Even the limited collective security provisions of the Charter had assumed that the great powers would have a common interest in preventing aggression by other states; now however, the tendency was to try to bring all other states into the spheres of interest of the superpowers and, thus, to incorporate most of the world into an area of vital concern to one or the other of the polar powers. The practicality of any sort of collective security action was questioned seriously.[9]

In the West, these assumptions as to the potentialities of collective security action were reversed rather suddenly at the time of UN entry into the Korean War. In that case, the fortuitous absence of the Soviet delegate from the Security Council permitted the Council to undertake a collective enforcement action somewhat similar in character (albeit directed against the satellite of a great power) to that which may have been anticipated at San Francisco. Even though a single member, the United States, became the chief agent of the military operation undertaken in the name of the organization, it was significant that most other members were willing to associate themselves with the official position of the Council. It was recognized that the circumstance which had permitted Security Council action in Korea would not

---

[9] By "collective security," I of course mean the idea of a universal or nearly universal commitment to thwart aggression no matter what state undertakes it. See Claude's excellent discussion of the theoretical suppositions of Wilsonian collective security in his *Power and International Relations* (New York 1962). The issue is confused by the fact that many commentators and statesmen, particularly in the West, have insisted upon dubbing the multilateral alliances of the postwar period "collective security organizations." Perhaps they have done so in the deliberate attempt to cast a greater aura of legitimacy upon the new arrangements by implying that they were simply variations on the accepted principle for maintaining peace and security. As Claude has noted, application of the term to these two very different approaches to the problem of security has served the unfortunate purpose of rendering extremely unclear the original, and essential, principles it was meant to describe.

likely be repeated. The surge of enthusiasm for collective security which grew in the first weeks of the UN action soon was expressed in the Uniting for Peace resolution, which was passed in the General Assembly in November 1950.[10] The resolution was intended to restore, insofar as possible, at least an approximate collective security system to the UN—this, at any rate, was the gist of many of the comments favoring passage recorded in the General Assembly at the time.[11] Specifically, of course, it provided General Assembly action in the event of Security Council deadlock over a peace-threatening situation. Authorizing the Assembly to designate the aggressor on the basis of a two-thirds majority vote, the resolution then provided for collective action—although necessarily on a voluntary basis—somewhat similar to that which the Charter had authorized the Council to direct. Growing as it did out of the Korean experience, it was clear that the Uniting for Peace resolution was meant to provide the machinery needed for universal collective action even against a great power involved in a situation of aggression.

This was a step beyond what had been agreed upon at San Francisco, and it soon became clear that the Western powers that sponsored the resolution did so on the assumption that it probably would only come into play to permit collective action against the expansionist tendencies of the Communist states.[12] Although the United States, in particular, remained a strong champion of the resolution, it was opposed bitterly by the Soviet Union and her allies. Moreover, as the fighting in Korea dragged on, the enthusiasm for collective security action which had been expressed in the resolution in 1950 gave way to greater feelings of caution and the recurrent, if not strengthened, conviction on the part of many that the United Nations—and perhaps the General Assembly in particular—really was not a very appropriate instrument for enforcement action against the major cold war antagonists. The resolution's suggestion that member states designate military units to be available for future collective security action under the General Assembly was virtually ignored in the aftermath of Korea. Still, even though the Uniting for Peace resolution never became the instrument of organization-wide collective security hoped for by its most ardent supporters, it nonetheless was to remain the effective instrument for greater General Assembly involvement in UN enforcement action in the future. This sec-

[10] "Uniting for Peace" resolution. General Assembly Resolution 377 (V).

[11] See GAOR: 5th Session, 299th-302nd Plenary Mtgs., November 1, 1950-November 3, 1950. See also the address of the President of the General Assembly, Nasrollah Entezam, at the 295th Mtg.

[12] See Claude's discussion of the Western rationale behind the Uniting for Peace Resolution in his "The United Nations and the Use of Force," *International Conciliation*, No. 532 (March 1961), 361.

ond phase of predominant UN attitudes toward the utility of collective security, then, was characterized by a temporary commitment to expanding the scope of such action well beyond that thought feasible at San Francisco, followed by an increased reluctance to implement such a scheme very effectively.

A third shift in attitude and practice originated, perhaps, in the UN action surrounding the creation of UNEF at the time of the Suez crisis in 1956. That case, and several since then, have illustrated a UN approach to peace and security matters that constitutes a rather novel adaptation of collective security theory to deal with one type of threat to the peace that is characteristic of the loose bipolar period. In the Suez affair—as later in the Congo and in Cyprus —UN intervention took the form of sending in an international military contingent, not to wage war on behalf of the international community against a designated "aggressor," but to try to stabilize a troubled political situation and ward off countervailing interventions by outside great powers. In 1960, Dag Hammarskjold described the rationale for UN action of this sort which would attempt to localize conflicts before they became entrenched within an inflamed cold war context, labeling such a role "preventive diplomacy."[13] As Claude has noted, preventive diplomacy "was conceived by Hammarskjold as an international version of the policy of containment, designed not to restrict the expansion of one bloc or the other, but to restrict the expansion of the zone permeated by bloc conflicts; it was put forward as a means for containment of the cold war."[14] The evident difficulties of the attempt to make this conception of the role of the UN fit the intricacies of the Congolese situation—especially in its later phases—must be granted. Nonetheless, there was a growing awareness by the 1960's that it was precisely this kind of UN action, whereby the organization became involved in a situation to prevent a dangerous confrontation, which was essential to international security.

Preventive diplomacy, in containing the cold war, thereby helps to stabilize and perhaps even encourage neutralism on the part of states not members of the polar blocs. Moreover, at the operational level, it must rely upon the political support of neutrals to be effective. As a partial theory of international security, it has both contributed to and been based upon the growing respectability of neutralism in the postwar period. Thus, it is not bipolarity in its early cold war manifestation—a period characterized in the West by the Dulles

[13] *Introduction to the Annual Report of the Secretary-General on the Work of the Organization, 16 June 1959-15 June 1960,* GAOR: Fifteenth Session, Supplement No. 1A (A/4390/Add.1).

[14] Inis L. Claude, Jr., *Swords into Plowshares,* 3rd rev. edn. (New York 1964), 286.

strictures against neutralism—that gave rise to the preventive diplomatic role for the United Nations; rather, that role has been made
possible in the period of superpower stalemate and the growth in the
number of national adherents to an uncommitted position in the cold
war contest. Although by no means all of the conditions of bipolarity
had been eliminated by the late 1960's, the structure of international
politics was once more in the process of change.

I leave to the next section a consideration of the extent to which this
shifting emphasis upon ways to stabilize the conditions of loose bipolarity has been paralleled in the security action of regional organizations. First, it is necessary to consider the impact of other factors
at work in the postwar international system upon the security role
of regionalism.

Nuclear Technology

Until the current period, most of the impact of nuclear technology
upon international politics could be subsumed under that of bipolarity. Since the U.S. and Soviet arsenals of atomic and nuclear weapons
were the only ones that were competitive from the point of view of
their military or deterrent quality, these capabilities of the superpowers simply contributed to the bipolarity of the international political structure. More precisely, even in the period before Soviet nuclear strength came to match that of the United States, the effective
monopoly over the use of atomic and nuclear weapons that each
of the superpowers possessed within its own bloc had far-reaching consequences both within and outside their spheres of interest. (1) Within each bloc, this effective monopoly of the ultimate instruments of
warfare produced a *de facto* dependence of their middle and small
power allies upon the two atomic giants that called into question
their very sovereignty as independent states. It is true that the effect of nuclear monopoly was considerably less compelling within the
Soviet bloc than in the West because of Moscow's political control
over the governments of the satellite states; indeed, some of the Eastern European states have somewhat increased their freedom to maneuver as Moscow's nuclear strength has grown. Nonetheless, they remain dependent upon the Soviet Union for large-scale military protection and vulnerable to Soviet military encroachment. In the Atlantic area, however, where no overt attempt has been made by the
United States to abridge the sovereignty of its allies, the nuclear weapons issue is more clearly the chief source of the radically altered political relationships among this group of states.

When the North Atlantic Treaty came into being, it constituted
primarily a unilateral guarantee by the United States to oppose the
destruction of the weakened nations of Western Europe by the power-

ful Soviet army. Because of their vastly inferior strength vis-à-vis the Soviet bloc even in this early period before the Soviet Union developed its own atomic capacity, it is questionable whether the Western European nations were faced with a rational alternative to an alliance with the United States. Since America was the only power capable of restraining the imperialistic tendencies of the Soviet Union, and because opposition to Soviet expansion was the only means perceived as leading to the avoidance of conquest by the Soviet army, an alliance with the United States became the goal of Western European governments. It was felt on both sides of the Atlantic that only by binding the United States to aid the Europeans in their defense through such an alliance could Europe safely count on U.S. support. Unable to foresee the long-range implications of deterrence for the alliance structure, however, the basic assumption of the NATO members was that they could cooperate on European military matters while maintaining, indeed, strengthening, their independent political systems.

In fact, however, almost from the beginning, NATO's deterrence goal demanded the creation of extensive organizational machinery. Whether or not these organizational structures that developed were the most important distinguishing feature of the new alliance, the fact that they were required as a matter of course if the business of the alliance were to be done served to indicate something of the alterations that had taken place in the security sphere of the changed international system.[15] As was recognized generally at the time of NATO's creation, the new alliance differed radically from the general pattern of alliances of the pre-war period in the matter of its ideological unity. With the creation of NATO, the operation of the classic balance of power principle upon alliance formation and behavior seemed an impossibility for the foreseeable future. Two implacably hostile groups of states now confronted each other, each avowing its own peaceful intentions and the defensive qualities of its alliance, but both sides

---

[15] NATO's purpose "is that of defending Western Europe's independence without any resort to war. NATO will fail in its fundamental purpose at the moment the nuclear war comes to Europe . . . ," Norman A. Graebner, "Alliances and Free World Security," *Current History*, xxxviii, 224 (April 1960), 216. But the credibility of the U.S. deterrent as applied to the NATO area depends upon the creation of devices making retaliation to an attack on any member state as nearly automatic as possible. Since the raison d'être of NATO is to deter aggression against the members, rather than to "defend" the territory in traditional terms once hostilities have broken out, the advance planning on the part of the alliance members requires altogether more complex a multilateral arrangement than did "defensive" alliances in the pre-atomic period. Most simply put, in the absence of a need to fight together once nuclear war breaks out, there is a greater impetus to work together to provide an effective deterrent force.

showing a considerable desire to see the enemy grouping eliminated.[16] In short, the complex *organizational* structure characteristic of NATO could be regarded as the consequence of the loose bipolar system that had emerged, combined with the deterrent requirements of the atomic age.

Yet neither in NATO nor in NATO's alliance counterparts in other areas of the world was the complex organizational structure ever transformed into an integrated unit.[17] Only one member state had the "sovereign" capability to undertake effective nuclear warfare; its allies have been forced to rely, for the most part, upon that power's professed intentions to defend the alliance, and have not acquired an institutionalized guarantee that such a decision will be made. The nuclear factor set in an organizational context has made it nearly impossible for alliance members to calculate with reasonable accuracy what could be expected from its partners in the event of an enemy attack. The issue was stated unequivocally by Hans Morgenthau when he insisted that "the availability of nuclear weapons to the United States and the Soviet Union has administered a death blow to the Atlantic Alliance, as it has to all alliances. . . . In the prenuclear age a powerful nation could be expected to come to the aid of a weak ally provided its interests were sufficiently involved, risking at worst defeat in war, the loss of an army or of territory. But no nation can be relied upon to forfeit its own existence for the sake of another."[18] One logical response to this dilemma has been that characterized by de Gaulle's *force de frappe*, which attempts the restoration of national military "sovereignty" in an atomic age. An alternative response would be the genuine transformation of the NATO organization into a supranational military authority—an alternative which had not

---

[16] Of the numerous statements—both official and unofficial—indicating the hostility on both sides of the Iron Curtain at the time of the creation of NATO, reports in the Soviet and American press of the time probably were most vitriolic.

[17] Although there has long been talk in NATO of the "integrated command structure" of the alliance, this does not mean, of course, that ultimate authority over use of nuclear weapons has been "integrated." By "integrated unit," then, I mean a genuinely supranational military body.

[18] Hans J. Morgenthau, "The Crisis in the Western Alliance," *Commentary*, xxv, 3 (March 1963), 187. Clearly, this view of Morgenthau's as to the obsolescence of all alliances is not one that he has developed fully in his writings. Elsewhere, his observations on alliances reveal a bias in favor of alliance formation and alliance policy that conforms to a balance of power international system (cf. his "Alliances in Theory and Practice," Arnold Wolfers, ed., *Alliance Policy in the Cold War*), and he pays little attention to any systemic changes that may have taken place as the result of a nuclear technology. The implication of the *Commentary* article—which analyzes the rationale of the French *force de frappe*—is that the "proper" response to this problem today is the abandonment of alliance for the construction of national independent nuclear arsenals, rather than the military integration of the alliance to restore calculability to military policy without encouraging nuclear proliferation.

been effectively dealt with in NATO circles before General de Gaulle's growing challenge to the alliance in 1965 and 1966.

Although it is NATO which exemplifies, *par excellence*, the challenge wrought by nuclear deterrence upon regional alliance organizations at the present time, that challenge lurks in the background in the other regional groupings in which the United States is a member as well. Neither in SEATO nor the OAS have the members consistently perceived a real Soviet atomic threat to the territories concerned in anything like the degree to which NATO members were preoccupied throughout with this threat during the 1950's. Moreover, neither the Latin American states in the OAS nor the smaller Asian members of SEATO were in the position a decade ago, in contrast to some Western European states, to develop even limited atomic capabilities of their own. Nonetheless, when Soviet missiles were emplaced in Cuba in October 1962, Latin American acquiescence in the demands of the United States that they be removed was clear indication of the total dependence of these states upon U.S. policy where nuclear issues were involved.

Outside the spheres of interest of the two superpowers, two regional security organizations exist, none of whose members possess atomic weapons. In both the Arab League and the Organization of African Unity the tendency developed (and in fact was made explicit in the OAU's Charter[19]) to make the organization a vehicle for preventing the intrusion of the cold war into the area. Such a policy was both demanded and made possible by the fact that no member states had access to atomic or nuclear weapons. But this nonatomic status of all the members may also have contributed to the capacity of those members to oppose each other. Thus, it may have made more difficult the creation of an effective police power to seal off the area from outside interference. Nonetheless, this "containment" role for the Arab League and, a bit later, the OAU developed perceptibly in the late 1950's, as the theory and practice of "preventive diplomacy" grew within the United Nations. The role just ascribed to the Arab League and the OAU is clearly a concomitant of preventive diplomacy from the regional perspective—a fact with important implications for world order.

The Rise of New States

The growth of regionalism in the uncommitted areas of the world was, of course, made possible by the achievement of national independence in many regions long under the colonial domination of Euro-

---

[19] Article III of the Charter of the Organization of African Unity lists the "principles" of the Organization, the last of which reads "affirmation of a policy of nonalignment with regard to all blocs."

pean powers. Two points need to be made in this connection. First, both the Arab League and the OAU could be described at least to some extent as vehicles for the solidification of national independence within the region as well as instruments of cooperation and regional order. Thus, almost since its inception, Arab League policy has been directed toward abetting the national independence movement of Arab regions still under the domination of foreign powers.[20] Similarly, the OAU Charter looks to the liberation of the remaining African colonies as one of the fundamental aims of the organization.[21] As the case of Kuwait within the Arab League indicated, this policy may be as much the result of rivalries among the membership (and their corresponding unwillingness to permit one power to annex a new territory at the expense of other members) as it is the product of an abstract dedication to the right of self-determination. Nonetheless, one result of the policy has been to emphasize the form of the grouping as the instrument of *national independence* rather than of *regional integration*.

Secondly, as the anticolonial movement has come to fruition throughout most of the world, the "neo-colonial" rationale of a continued Western hegemony in SEATO and CENTO has become increasingly less acceptable. Since nonalignment on cold war issues has become virtually the official doctrine of the new states, the continued alignment of a few Asian states with the Western powers in these two organizations now appears somewhat anachronistic; not simply to leaders of the third world, I would suggest, but even within Western circles.[22] Even at the time of the Iraqi-Turkish alignment in the Baghdad Pact, the move was so ill-received in the rest of the Arab world

---

[20] Cf. Macdonald, *Arab States*, 94-96.

[21] The Charter's preamble includes affirmation of the conviction "that it is the inalienable right of all people to control their own destiny," adding that the signatories are "determined to safeguard and consolidate the hard-won independence as well as the sovereignty and territorial integrity of our States, and to resist neo-colonialism in all its forms." Under Article II, the "purposes" of the Charter include those of promoting "the unity and solidarity of the African and Malagasy States," and eradication of "all forms of colonialism from the continent of Africa." Finally, one of the Organization's "principles" is listed (Article III) as "absolute dedication to the total emancipation of the African territories which are still dependent."

[22] Any number of American commentators have taken this line in recent years. Typical is an article by C. L. Sulzberger in the *New York Times*, June 3, 1964, which criticizes the Dulles conception of SEATO as an extension of Western influence and protection into Southeast Asia: "SEATO was a classic example of closing the barn door on a missing horse. In this case the horse was the Anglo-French empire. SEATO was written on the assumption of British and French armed strength that didn't exist. . . .

"During the pactomania phase of American policy-making, we allowed ourselves to be deceived by shadowy illusions. We believed such organizations as SEATO and CENTO were realities, but they weren't. . . ."

as to make Iraq something of a pariah within the membership until a *coup d'état* in that country brought Iraq's withdrawal from the Pact. Within SEATO it appears that only Thailand and the Philippines, of the Asian membership, remain generally willing to accept the anti-Communist orientation of the Pact.

Trans-National Integration Movements

Although this study attempts to focus on regional organization rather than regional integration, the two phenomena are inextricably linked in some respects at the empirical level. First, it seems clear that because integration movements have been relatively powerful throughout most of the postwar period, this process has served especially in Europe as a parallel legitimizing norm for the development of regional organization in the peace and security area. Although a maze of contradictory purposes and programs with unexplained and perhaps unintended ramifications has so far inhibited the development of an integrated community in the North Atlantic area, there can be little doubt but that the integrative aspirations of many leaders within this area have helped to make acceptable (in their own eyes as well as those of their followers) the growth and development of NATO. For them, the North Atlantic alliance has been not simply a coalition of powers whose only function is a firm military posture in the bloc politics of the cold war but rather an instrument providing for the military and political integration of the member states. The current challenge of de Gaulle, as already indicated, has brought into sharp relief the contradictions inherent in lip service to community-building and policy that is organizationally oriented. Still, the fact that an inchoate integrative aspiration lay behind the work of the alliance has helped make it appear as a legitimate instrument of regional order to those disinclined to look with favor upon the creation of a limited-member alliance.

On the other hand, the ideal of integration sometimes has served to inhibit realistic assessments of the utility of the multilateral organization as an end in itself. This seems to be at least as true in the case of the Arab League as it is with NATO (and it is within these two regional security organizations that the integrative aspiration most often is verbalized). Although it is easy to show that in both cases the constitutional document provides for an international organization and not a supranational community, nevertheless, both organizations sometimes are criticized by integrationists for not having accomplished what apparently they were not intended to accomplish. This would be largely irrelevant to the questions under investigation here except that it may help to focus upon a real issue for regional international organization in the current period—an issue already touched upon in the discussion of the impact of nuclear weapons: Is the organizational level within a region a practicable stopping place in the quest for security once the decision has been made (presumably for practical security reasons) to move beyond the principle of national self-sufficiency for the protection of desired values? If the current experience of NATO is now indicating that the return to national self-sufficiency appears a more practical alternative in some cases, it also must point up the impossibility of such a move—at least for the short run—for states that do not possess the resources for a large military establishment even in conventional terms. Otherwise put, the question at issue is whether or not the organizational dynamic is sufficient to provide the security demanded by member states (and this may entail security from other members as well as from external actors, it should be remembered), or whether and to what extent regional organization must be regarded as necessarily a temporary, half-way house between national independence and supranational integration.

III. The Dynamics of Regional Organization

One of the premises of this study is that the multilateral alliances of the postwar period have been as deeply involved, in some respects, in regional security activity as the "original" regional organizations that were treated in Chapter VIII of the UN Charter. Now, however, it will be useful to distinguish the security roles of these two types of organizations somewhat more clearly than was done in the previous section. This is not a distinction which can be made fruitfully solely on the basis of the differences in authoritative structures of each type of grouping; yet, such an examination can indicate the general *security orientation* of the grouping. Then it will be necessary to consider differences in types of *security activities*, which may or may not coincide with the group's distinctive orientation.

Original Regional Organizations[23]

Here are included those organizations which have arisen as the expression of some sort of regional solidarity vis-à-vis the outside world, and which possess the machinery, at least in embryo, to maintain security within their own region. In the most fully developed of these groups, the OAS, the machinery involved permits both (1) the settle-

[23] This is a shorthand phrase to denote the kind of regional organization in existence at the time the UN Charter was adopted and, thus, the type referred to in Chapter VIII of the Charter. The term is, of course, misleading if taken literally, since one extant organization of this type—the OAU—was not "original" in the sense that it existed when Chapter VIII was written. Rather, it is regarded as "original" because it is basically like the OAS and the Arab League in its conception.

ment of disputes among member states, and (2) the development of a common policy in the face of intervention from outside the region. For the other two groupings which fall into this regional type (the Organization of African Unity and the Arab League), the provisions for settlement of intramember disputes are less fully developed than are those for the second provision above. Characteristic of this group, however, is the fact that they are not alliances in the traditional sense, but are "ostensibly more permanent groups whose professed first aim is to keep the peace within a given area."[24] Their raison d'être, then, springs from territorial unity, made coherent by at least a modicum of recognized ideological or ethnic common ground.

In groupings of this type, the desire to maintain security among the members seems to have been the chief impetus to the creation of the organization. Thus, both the legal structures and political practice are likely to emphasize the aspect of the state actors-in-organization. Moreover, the language of Chapter VIII of the UN Charter seems to assume that the proper security activities of regional associations would be confined to issues involving conflicts among the member states.[25] Still as indicated above, both the OAS and the Arab League took steps in the years after the San Francisco conference to strengthen the security role of the organization-as-actor.[26] At the diplomatic level, all three of these groupings have experienced some measure of effectiveness in the elaboration of organizational policy vis-à-vis external actors. Thus, the primary orientation of these organizations toward the resolution of intra-group conflicts has been counterbalanced somewhat in practice through the elaboration of a more important role for the organization-as-actor.

Regional Alliance Organizations

This type of regional grouping includes many of the alliances of the postwar world, such as NATO, the Warsaw Pact, SEATO, and CENTO. The treaty arrangements containing a common defense pledge that do not fall within this category are those which are bilateral and not multilateral. These lack the so-called permanent insti-

[24] Peter Calvocoressi, *World Order and New States* (New York 1962), 59.

[25] Cf. Article 52 (2): "The Members . . . entering into such [regional] arrangements . . . shall make every effort to achieve pacific settlement of local disputes through such regional arrangements . . . before referring them to the Security Council."

It is true that the discussion in Article 53 (1) of measures which may be taken by a regional agency against former enemy states seems to reveal that the organization may deal as a single actor with external threats to its members. Nevertheless, the main thrust of the chapter's provisions is in the direction of internally directed security action.

[26] See notes 7 and 8 above.

tutions of the multilateral arrangements, such as secretariats, councils, and the like, and generally make no provisions at all for a coordination of military policy prior to outright military involvement with a third power. As to the multilateral arrangements which can be classed as regional organizations, however, their very strong emphasis has been upon united organization-wide policy—especially military policy—in the face of challenges from external actors. These are "outer-directed" associations which came into being expressly as the result of a felt threat from a common external enemy, and their concern with the intra-organizational relations of the members is largely subsumed within their concern for developing an effective security role for the organization-as-actor.

The external orientation of regional alliance organizations was, at the time of their creation, considerably more dominant than was the internal orientation of the original regional groupings. Nor has the emphasis shifted back toward the other security orientation as strongly in the alliance groupings as in the original organizations. Nonetheless, and particularly as disagreement has grown among the members of alliance groupings as to the nature and quality of the external threat to the region, the attention of the members inevitably has turned in greater measure to use of the organization to help resolve these issues which divide them. In both types of regional organizations some attempt has been made to ensure the inviolability of the area of jurisdiction in security issues.[27] In other words, the tendency in all regional security organizations has been to attempt to make the regional agency the primary, if not the only, authoritative structure for dealing with security issues in the area. Thus, both types of organizations have had to deal with internally divisive issues as well as with external challenges to regional security.

Hegemonial Action and "Good Neighborliness"

Turning next to a consideration of types of security activities engaged in by regional groupings, the crucially important distinctions in practice correspond roughly to the dual view of regionalism that has long been characteristic of the literature on the subject. On the one hand, most commentators who have looked with favor upon the regional approach to security have described a regionalism

[27] However, the U.S. reservation to its adherence to the SEATO Pact—that it would undertake to defend the territory of the Southeast Asian members and protocol states only in the event of *Communist* aggression—underscores the limitations, and perhaps the ambiguity, of the SEATO security role in the area. Since the function of the organization-as-actor has always been somewhat less clear than in the case of NATO, it is reasonable to suppose, not only that the actors-in-organization role may have suffered in consequence, but also that there is less than total agreement among the members as to making SEATO the sole authoritative structure for dealing with security issues in the area.

wherein motivation for common action arises out of mutual interest in the problems of the area and from a recognition of the value of good neighborliness. This is the sort of regionalism that might emerge as the logical extension of the provisions on the subject in the UN Charter, where the attempt is made to demonstrate the way in which the regional and universal organizations can work together harmoniously—each in its proper sphere. On the other hand, other commentators clearly have regarded the regional approach to security with disfavor, suggesting that such activity is in fact detrimental to international order. Clearly, however, what they have had in mind is the use of regionalism either as a means of asserting the hegemonic domination of a major power, or as a feeble attempt on the part of small-power neighbors to forestall or regulate such domination. According to the extreme form of this view, regionalism "is the establishment of the paramountcy of a Great Power in a defined geographical region."[28]

In fact, of course, both views of regional security activity are partially accurate perceptions of reality; all existing regional security organizations would seem to contain elements of both kinds of activities. Although it appears that the regional alliance organizations in particular were conceived as instruments for making explicit the hegemony of a great power in a specific geographical region, this aim has not been entirely absent in the formation of the original regional groupings. The dominant role of the United States within the OAS is perhaps the clearest example in groupings of this type, but in the Arab League, the Egyptian desire for leadership of the Arab states—and the continuing opposition of successive Iraqi governments to a dominant Egyptian role—also illustrates the hegemonic principle in a regional organization.[29] Moreover, in the Organization of African Unity, even though no single member has yet established itself as the dominant or decisive force in organizational affairs, it seems clear that several statesmen with ambitions of Pan-African unity under their leadership concluded that such aspirations could be pursued more effectively through the creation of an African organization.

At the risk of oversimplifying the complex varieties of relationships among states members of the various regional organizations, it can be said that the real dynamic in effective regional security activity is provided by the coexistence within each grouping of the opposing tendencies of "good neighborliness" on the one hand, and the hegemonic domination of the region by a powerful member on the other. This

[28] K. M. Panikkar, "Regionalism and World Security," in Panikkar and others, *Regionalism and Security* (Bombay 1948), 1.
[29] Macdonald, *Arab States*, 74-82.

is not to say, of course, that these dual tendencies are contained in effective balance in all existing regional associations; rather it suggests that in each such grouping members must continually come to terms with both demands if the organization is to function effectively as an instrument of security and regional order. Generally it has been appreciated that regional stress on "good neighborliness," i.e. upon the actors-in-organization, is conducive to the settlement of international disputes on a basis of cooperation rather than coercion. Ideally, the equal rights of participating states are emphasized and just settlements are the product of a mutual willingness to accept those rights. It is less often acknowledged, however, that in practice such emphasis may lead, not to cooperation but to fragmentation, and not to just settlements so much as anarchy. Thus, the inclination toward hegemonic domination of a regional grouping, i.e. toward stress upon the organization-as-actor, may be a necessary antidote to fragmentation. Moreover, when external considerations are included, the tendency toward hegemony on a regional organizational basis is at least useful in delimiting spheres of great power interest.

This analysis suggests that a "proper" balance must be maintained in each regional grouping between these dual tendencies (a) to dwell upon security issues among the members at the expense of effective concerted policy, and (b) to make the regional institution an instrument of the hegemony of one powerful member. Where the emphasis becomes wholly one-sided, it seems to be impossible to maintain the organization as a viable agent of security even for the limited purposes proclaimed for it. For example, when CENTO and SEATO were created, their emphasis was almost exclusively upon the organization-as-actor. Western powers sought to solidify their spheres of influence, thereby making clear to their opponents that these areas of the Middle East and Southeast Asia constituted legitimate regions of Western hegemony. The refusal of neighboring states in these areas to join these alliances cast doubt upon the assertions of the Western powers from the beginning. Still, had it been possible (not that it was even seriously attempted) to make of these organizations instruments for the settlement of regional problems, these organizations might, over time, have solidified Western ties to these areas, thereby making credible the assertion of Western hegemony. Instead, in ignoring the possibilities of these groupings in the area of intra-regional security, the Western powers involved found their claims to hegemony regarded as increasingly tenuous: by the 1960's CENTO was nearly moribund and SEATO was almost without credibility as an effective anti-Communist alliance.

In NATO, a one-sided emphasis upon the organization's security role did not have such drastic short-range consequences because the claim of a community of interest binding these member states together was perceived both by participants and by many nonparticipants as a legitimate claim. With NATO at the very core of the Western bloc, the issue seemed less one of extending Western hegemony than of consolidating Western interests, and those interests, for the most part, were conceived as sufficiently strong as to make unnecessary concern with intra-group security. Even so, by the 1960's NATO's role as the instrument of organization-wide security was threatened seriously by fissures within the membership. Although it may be questioned that an *organizational* approach (as opposed to an integrational one) to intra-regional cooperation and conflict resolution could have resolved the issues of military independence which threaten to split the alliance, still, such an added emphasis from the beginning might have laid the groundwork for greater political unity when the external threat to the area was seen to be diminishing. In the most serious war-threatening issue to divide the members of NATO—the Cypriote conflict, particularly as it was rekindled in 1963-1964—the attempt to make NATO the instrument of regional order was challenged successfully by Archbishop Makarios and Premier Khrushchev, and the issue was turned over to the United Nations.[30] It could be argued, of course, that even had NATO had a record of intra-regional security practice of this type, the option of UN treatment would have remained open. Indeed, it would have, but the experience of the OAS shows that where this type of security role is firmly established, the regional organization is likely to maintain its claim to jurisdiction.

On the other hand, the "original" regional groupings—with their clearer orientation toward the actors-in-organization—have managed to survive the strains of intra-regional conflict, and even to ameliorate it in some cases, while in the process they have developed a framework for common organizational policy. The experience of the Arab League is perhaps most illustrative here. Polarization of power between Egypt and Iraq has afflicted the League since its inception, preventing the effective cooperation of League members on mutual problems in many cases. Of the major recurring issues which confront the League, these two Arab states have been generally in agreement only in their opposition to rapprochement with Israel.[31] In spite of the inability of either state to establish its hegemony over the organization, however, the Arab states have joined increasingly

[30] See the *New York Times*, January 27-February 9, 1964. Considered in terms of spheres of influence, the outcome of the jurisdictional issue in the Cyprus case marked an indication on the part of Britain and the United States that, in acquiescing in UN action there, they no longer would regard Cyprus as coming under the protective umbrella of NATO.

[31] Macdonald, *Arab States*, 84-85.

in playing an identifiable role vis-à-vis external actors. The League has consistently supported the independence movements of the Arab territories in North Africa, has caucused and voted *en bloc* in the United Nations, and while under the leadership of Egypt's President Nasser, the policy of Arab nonalignment with the cold war blocs has been accepted widely.[32] While lip service still is paid to the idea of Arab political unity, intra-Arab rivalry continues to prevent any real progress in this respect. More significantly, however, this rivalry has been channeled through the organizational framework successfully enough to ensure the solidification of Arab independence movements and the growth in strength of an Arab bloc, as opposed to an Arab state.

The OAS is the only "original" regional organization to have one of the superpowers as a member. Yet in spite of the overwhelmingly dominant role of the United States in the Americas (or rather, perhaps, because of it), the actors-in-organization aspect of the grouping remains strong and important. In fact, most of the history of regional organization in this hemisphere can be read as the continuing attempt of the Latin American states to secure U.S. adherence to standards of nonintervention and noninterference in political affairs south of the Rio Grande, and, conversely, of the continuing U.S. attempt to make the inter-American organization a vehicle for the assertion of North American hegemony. U.S. acceptance of the nonintervention doctrine by the 1930's undoubtedly encouraged Latin American statesmen to champion the cause of the organization at San Francisco; they were persuaded that it was now "their" organization, in large measure, and that it could be utilized to prevent the arbitrary intrusion both of the United States and of other great powers into Latin American affairs. In the context of the cold war, however, the United States set about the task of utilizing the reorganized regional organization to attempt to strengthen the U.S. hold on the Western hemisphere. If U.S. hegemony in the area could no longer be exercised effectively by means of "Big Stick" diplomacy, it could, nonetheless, be maintained by upholding OAS primacy in hemispheric security, where U.S. policy demands almost always could be made to prevail. Thus, within a few years after San Francisco, Latin and U.S. roles were nearly reversed, and the United States took the lead in insisting upon the right of OAS primary jurisdiction in all inter-American disputes.

Secondly, and concurrently, the United States urged the elaboration of a more clear-cut organization-as-actor role for the OAS—specifically, one which would transform the organization into an anti-Soviet coalition. For a time in the 1950's, the United States seemed to be suc-

[32] Same, 105-18.

ceeding in this attempt almost entirely to the neglect of hemispheric problems and Latin American interests. The Caracas Declaration of 1954 was conceived as the chief instrument for exorcising Communism from the hemisphere, and was prompted specifically by the fact that a left-leaning government had come to power in Guatemala.[33] In the end, however, the United States chose to take covert unilateral action to secure the ouster of the Arbenz regime, and as a result, was hard-pressed to secure the support of the Latin Americans and of its other allies in insisting upon the right of the OAS to deal with the Guatemalan issue.[34] In effect, the attempt by the United States to assert the autonomy of the regional grouping was read by many as a subterfuge for what appeared to entail the unilateral accomplishment of U.S. policy goals through the guise of a multilateral agency.

In the years since the Guatemalan crisis, the United States has worked somewhat more assiduously to encourage development of the principle of collective intervention in the Americas for purposes of promoting democratic goals, thereby attempting to escape the onus of a thinly disguised unilateralism. The relatively democratic Latin American governments generally have been most willing to elaborate such a doctrine, for they have recognized increasingly that it is dictatorial regimes which have had the most to gain from a rigid doctrine of nonintervention.[35] U.S. support and even leadership of the OAS intervention in the Dominican Republic in 1960 and 1961—a policy urged on the OAS by certain Latin statesmen following Generalissimo Trujillo's attempted assassination of Betancourt of Venezuela—provided the United States with an effective *quid pro quo* for Latin American support of the U.S. demand to isolate the Castro government in hemispheric affairs. These two operations mark what have been perhaps the most effective multilateral interventionary ac-

[33] John C. Dreier, *The Organization of American States and the Hemisphere Crisis* (New York 1962), 53. See also C. Neale Ronning's discussion of the Caracas Resolution in similar terms in his article, "Intervention, International Law, and the Inter-American System," *Journal of Inter-American Studies*, III, 2 (April 1961), 249-71. An ironic element of the Caracas Declaration was, however, as Dreier has pointed out, that by stipulating that the "domination or control" of the "political institutions" of an American state by the Communists was the prerequisite to OAS action, it actually may have made such action under its terms more difficult by requiring proof of Communist domination.

[34] SCOR: 9th Yr., 671st-686th Mtgs. In the Security Council debate over the jurisdiction issue, only two states—Colombia and Turkey—were willing to back the U.S. unequivocally in its contention that the Security Council need not endorse OAS consideration of the case before such action could be regarded as legal under the terms of the Charter. Of the other states which voted with the U.S. in opposing the adoption of the agenda, the Brazilian delegate implied that the Council might take action once it had heard a report from the Inter-American Peace Committee.

[35] Jerome Slater, "The United States, the Organization of American States and the Dominican Republic, 1961-1963," *International Organization*, XVIII, 2 (Spring 1964), 287, gives evidence of these differences in attitude among Latin American elites.

tions undertaken in the spirit of organization-wide cooperation.[36] When, in 1965, the United States government again reverted to unilateral action in sending the Marines into the Dominican Republic, it was faced once again with the considerable reluctance of most Latin American governments to endorse such a move. Again, U.S. officials were reminded almost immediately of the deficiencies of unilateral intervention of this kind, and, as in the case of Guatemala, experienced difficulty in translating that action into one that was ostensibly regional in scope.

In sum, the two contrasting concerns of regional security are visible most clearly within the OAS. There, experience has indicated that the two approaches are not, or need not be, mutually exclusive ones, that, in fact, their healthy coexistence gives the regional organizational approach much of its dynamism. At the same time, the OAS experience reminds us that the hegemonic power in such a grouping must be able to perceive the long-range advantages of multilateral

---

[36] Definitive action against the Castro regime was taken finally at the Eighth Meeting of Consultation of Ministers of Foreign Affairs of the OAS at Punta del Este, Uruguay, from January 22 to 31, 1962. As reported in *International Organization*, XVI, 3 (Summer 1962), 654-55:

"After many consultations, conferences, private meetings . . . and compromises, the foreign ministers adopted seven main resolutions. (1) The adherence of any member of the OAS to Marxism-Leninism was incompatible with the . . . American system . . ; the vote was 20 for, 1 against (Cuba), no abstentions. (2) On the grounds of the first point, the present Cuban regime was incompatible with the principles and objectives of the inter-American system; the vote was 20 for, 1 against (Cuba), no abstentions. (3) Such incompatibility excluded Cuba from participation in the inter-American system, and the OAS was instructed to adopt . . . the measures required to put this resolution into effect; the vote was 14 for, 1 against (Cuba), and 6 abstentions (Argentina, Bolivia, Brazil, Chile, Ecuador and Mexico). The exclusion of Cuba had to be referred to the OAS Council . . . before being put into effect. The six abstaining delegations . . . took their action on the legal grounds that existing inter-American law did not provide the basis for such exclusion. . . . On February 14, 1962, Cuba's exclusion from inter-American affairs was made formal when the OAS Council received the resolutions aimed against Cuba that had been approved at the foreign ministers' meeting. The Council's meeting fulfilled the instructions of the foreign ministers for action. . . . For all practical purposes, the Cuban regime of Premier Fidel Castro ceased to be a member of the principal organ of the OAS. The other bodies of the OAS were subsequently to act separately to make formal the exclusion of Cuba."

In the case of OAS action in the Dominican Republic, the Sub-Committee of the Inter-American Peace Committee justified OAS intervention on these grounds:

"Taking into account the existing relationship between the violation of human rights and the lack of effective exercise of representative democracy on the one hand, and the political tensions that affect the peace of the hemisphere on the other, the Sub-Committee considers that there must be evidence of more progress than has thus far been attained before it can be concluded that the Dominican government has ceased to be a threat to the peace and security of the hemisphere."—Council of the OAS, *Second Report of the Sub-Committee of the Special Committee to Carry Out the Mandate Received by the Council Pursuant to Resolution I of the 6th Meeting of Consultation*, OAS Document CE/RC V-26, 1961.

as opposed to unilateral security action, just as the smaller-power members must be willing to use the organization for something more than simply the containment of the regional great power. If the shibboleth of nonintervention can render the organization impotent to deal with many of the practical regional problems that arise in this age of interdependence, so can the periodic unilateralism of Santo Domingo.

The United Nations and Regional Security

The elaboration of a preventive diplomacy approach to security in the United Nations can be regarded, in part, as a response to the claims of regional organizations to primacy in certain kinds of security issues. One of the postulates of preventive diplomacy is that the UN may take effective security action in areas where the claims of interest by cold war antagonists are recognized to be in conflict. Put in terms of regionalism, this is to say that UN action is required where effective regional action is not possible. To illustrate, the Suez crisis of 1956 was characterized by the attempt of two Western powers to reassert their lost hegemony in an area then controlled by governments in the process of constructing a doctrine of nonalignment. The claim to Western hegemony was challenged not only by the Arabs themselves and the Soviet Union, but even—tacitly—by the United States, which refused to accept the legitimacy of Anglo-French claims to an interventionary right in the area. Almost concurrently, however, the Soviet intervention in Hungary reminded the world—as had the U.S. intervention in Guatemala two years earlier—of the near impotence of the universal organization to counter the unilateral intrusion of a superpower in the affairs of one of its own bloc members. If effective restraints were to be exercised over this kind of hegemonic action, they had to originate within the regional grouping whose members were most directly affected.

There was frustration with these limitations upon the United Nations' ability to secure orderly and just settlement of issues that took place within the orbit of a superpower. Nonetheless, the little authority that the UN did possess in such cases could be marshaled, if not to ensure just solutions, at least to discourage the hegemonic state from flouting in such blatant fashion the principle of sovereignty and noninterference. The UN role in the Guatemalan situation is particularly instructive here. As indicated previously,[37] the fact that the U.S. insistence on regional settlement was made to prevail in this case did not disguise the fact that almost all other Security Council members were unwilling to accept the U.S. interpretation of the outcome as providing the regional organization with a *carte blanche* to take

[37] See note 34 above.

exclusive jurisdiction in such cases in the future. According to one commentator on the Guatemalan incident, "the victory of the United States was Pyrrhic, as well as incomplete. The United States had its way in Guatemala, but instead of establishing a precedent that the United Nations would be inclined to follow, it stimulated a persistent wariness against allowing the recurrence of such episodes."[38] While the Guatemalan case did not provide an effective United Nations alternative to the intervention of a hegemonic power in the affairs of a member of its own bloc, it may, at least, have encouraged such powers to secure the cooperation of their regional associates in advance whenever possible. At least, the United States was considerably more aware of the need for the genuine support of the Latin Americans by the time the issue of Castroism came to the United Nations. Even so, the jurisdiction issue was resolved somewhat more equivocally than it had been in the Guatemalan case, and an increased number of Latin American governments had by this time recognized that the doctrine of the absolute primacy of the OAS in hemispheric security affairs served no useful purpose to themselves.[39] Latin American support for U.S. sponsored regional settlement was becoming a commodity which had to be bargained for.

Within the Communist orbit, the prospects were somewhat less encouraging that the United Nations could help persuade the Soviet Union to seek genuinely multilateral solutions to intra-bloc conflicts. The questionable sovereignty of the East European states seemed to make unilateral Soviet interventions efficacious in a way that their counterparts by the United States in Latin America could not be. Yet, an important fact stands out in the post-Hungarian development of the Soviet bloc: the "satellite" status of the East European states—once an accurate description—must be questioned increasingly today, as the former "puppet" governments of Moscow display varying degrees of independence. The change is obvious even in the attempted reassertion of monolithic control from Moscow. When the Soviet Union invaded Czechoslovakia in the summer of 1968, a much greater effort was made than a dozen years earlier in Hungary to cloak the operation in multilateral legitimacy. Soviet troops entered the country with contingents from four Warsaw Pact allies, while the Soviet government strove to make credible the fiction that the invasion was car-

---

[38] Inis L. Claude, Jr., "The OAS, the UN, and the United States," *International Conciliation*, No. 547 (March 1964), 34. A full discussion of the case is included in Claude's article, 21-34.

[39] For the debates on the Cuban question in the Security Council, see SCOR: 15th Yr., 874th-876th Mtgs., 18-19 July, 1960; SCOR: 16th Yr., 921st-923rd Mtgs., 4-5 January 1961. General Assembly consideration of the Cuban complaints is contained in GAOR: 15th Sess., 872nd, 909th, and 995th Plenary Mtgs., in the 131st Mtg. of the General Committee, and in the 1149th-1161st Mtgs. of the First Committee.

ried out at the behest of Czechoslovak authorities. In spite of these efforts, it is by no means clear that Soviet officials have had reason to be satisfied with the outcome of their intervention. An interim assessment suggests that they have paid a high price both politically and economically. The reasons for the loosening of ties within the Soviet bloc are many and complex, and it is not suggested here that condemnations in the UN of Soviet behavior in Hungary and Czechoslovakia have figured very importantly among those reasons. Nonetheless, it is apparent that unilateral "solutions" by the Soviet Union to the security problems of Communist states become increasingly hard to sustain while the loosening of ties within the Soviet bloc continues.[40] It is doubtful that the Soviet Union yet needs to be as responsive to the wishes of her allies in most issues of security as the United States must be to hers; still, the challenge of Peking China to the dominant role of Moscow does require that the Soviet government make cooperation rather than coercion the basic principle of her relations with other Communist powers.

It goes without saying that so long as great power rivalry exists, the United Nations will be seized upon as the principal forum of opposition to hegemonic interventionary action—whether undertaken unilaterally or under the guise of a regional organization. The Soviet Union has never championed the principle of universal collective action so vigorously as when opposing OAS jurisdiction in the Guatemalan and Cuban cases, nor has the United States paid greater lip service to the principles of the Charter than in the Hungarian and Czechoslovak interventions.

Since the idea of preventive diplomacy assumes that UN action is called for in those marginal areas between spheres of great power interest, where countervailing interventions by those powers could result in a serious threat to world peace, a logical corollary of the theory would be that nonhegemonic regionalism be strengthened in those areas, both to inhibit interventions from external actors and to bolster UN security action when it is required. The emergence of the Organization of African Unity is a hopeful development in this direction, even though it would be naive to assume that its existence will automatically strengthen orderly security procedures in Africa. Two

[40] Haas has noted of the Soviet bloc that:
"Integration was *least* successful when the Communist Party of the Soviet Union possessed an organizational monopoly over the process. . . . The Stalin period witnessed a minimum of military cooperation, no joint economic planning, no exchange of information apart from the slavish imitation in Eastern Europe of Soviet examples, and no successful value-sharing among fellow-communists. Integration was a one-way process in which the aims of the European satellites were simply subordinated to those of the Soviet Union. . . . Now, there is little central direction, but, paradoxically, a good deal of practical integration."

conditions often may exist in practice which will serve to qualify the theoretical assumption that such an organization will harmonize with the preventive diplomatic approach. The first is the unlikelihood that such a grouping would be sufficiently united politically or strong militarily to prevent the determined intrusion of a superpower. Neither the Arab League nor the OAU has been successful in developing a genuine security arrangement for the use of the organization-as-actor. On the other hand, world order would not likely be better served if these groupings were to acquire atomic weapons with which they could threaten external states. So long as they remain weak militarily but cohesive in regional security activities, they should be able to help deter the incursions of external actors into their affairs.

This latter suggestion, however, points to the second, and probably more serious, practical qualification that needs to be noted. It is probably utopian to expect such nonhegemonic groupings consistently to bolster UN preventive diplomatic action within their regions. Where the interests of neighboring states are involved in a regional issue, the intervention of a United Nations force into the area may come to be regarded as an unwarranted intrusion by some of the regional states just as it may be welcomed by others because of national advantages they may hope to attain from it. Again, however, at the risk of oversimplifying the real problems which may develop in this respect, it may be that the "threat" of UN security action in an area nominally under the jurisdiction of a nonhegemonic regional organization may act to encourage the states of the area to develop effective techniques of settlement at the regional level, so that UN intrusion becomes less necessary, just as the cost to external great powers of their intervention becomes too high for the risks involved. So long as a "political vacuum" exists which the regional organization is unable to cope with, it must pay the price of UN involvement to achieve settlement.

It is no accident of history that during the past several years the most persistent and intractable international conflicts have taken place in Southeast Asia, for this is an area where neither regional nor universal techniques of settlement are politically appropriate. And they are not appropriate because of the current confusion and disagreement as to the proper place of the area within the international system. While the claim of Western hegemony in much of the area is increasingly difficult to justify on the basis of an objective appraisal of the political facts there, it is not a claim which has been relinquished by the United States government. Competing Western and Communist claims to influence in Southeast Asia—combined, perhaps, with the continuing refusal of India to associate herself with, much less lead, a regional security movement in the area—have prevented the development of a nonhegemonic regional organization on the Asian subcontinent to deal with the problems of local security. By the same token, the preventive diplomatic role of the United Nations has been inapplicable, since no way has been found to bring about effective UN intervention that would be acceptable to both the superpowers.[41]

Regardless of the outcome of the current conflict in Vietnam, it would appear that any effective long-range approach to security in the area must proceed from a recognition of the interests of the states located in the region. Such an approach would necessarily include China, although to admit this much is not to suggest that the smaller states in the vicinity must inevitably fall under Chinese tutelage. An organizational approach conforming to the patterns of the "original" regional associations could be made to contribute to orderly conflict resolution in approximately the same way that similar organizations elsewhere in the world are able to make such a contribution. No doubt, justice would not be done in every dispute that might arise, any more than it is done when powers external to the region seek to control the destinies of the area. Yet, the Asian solution of Asian problems—tempered by the right of appeal to the universal forum to prevent the harshest of regional solutions from being attempted—would do much to eliminate the nearly constant threats to world peace that will remain so long as *external* great powers continue to compete for influence there. But this brings us to the question of the prospective future of regional security.

IV. FUTURE PROSPECTS FOR REGIONAL PATTERNS OF ORDER

The norms of regional security action that have been taking shape during the past twenty years are the product of an international system which was rather rigidly bipolar during the first years of this period, and which had evolved into a "tripolar" or "multipolar" system by the mid-1960's. Thus, the crucial question for the future is whether the system itself is not changing to the point that the patterns of regional behavior appropriate to the present may be utterly inappropriate to the conduct of international politics ten or twenty years from now. Therefore, it is essential to attempt to determine what will be

---

[41] It is true that on January 31, 1966, U.S. Ambassador Arthur J. Goldberg addressed a letter to the president of the Security Council requesting an urgent meeting of the Council to consider the situation in Vietnam. Simultaneously a draft resolution was submitted by the United States to the Council calling for immediate discussions to arrange a peace conference, with participation by "the appropriate interested governments." Three days later, nine Security Council members voted to inscribe the resolution on the agenda, two opposed the move and four abstained. Once inscribed, however, the resolution was left undebated and the United States rested content, apparently, with having got the issue onto the agenda.

the basic features of the international system during the next few decades.

Of course, no such projection can be genuinely descriptive of reality at any given point in time in the future; rather, it must constitute a partial model whose basic form is determined by extrapolation from what are seen to be the dominant and dynamic trends at work today. Therefore, its construction must assume a basic continuity in the conduct of international politics from the present into the near future. For example, if widespread nuclear devastation were to occur, the system quite likely would be so transformed as to render such a model of the future nearly irrelevant to reality. Certainly there is no desire in what follows to propound a deterministic view of the future of world politics; neither current nor past history forecloses the way in which the future will unfold, even though it surely helps to delimit it. The dangers of deterministic analysis and the fallacies of models might well render useless and even harmful the attempt at prognostication if the projected period of study were a very long one. But in assuming the more modest goal of projecting certain current trends into the immediate future, it is submitted that these problems —while they cannot be eliminated—can, at least, be controlled.

The International System of the Future

My general view of the near future is one of a loosely multipolar system in which international coalitions and alignments will be relatively durable although, perhaps, not until after a continuing period involving some readjustments and shifting allegiances. Thus, this model of the future is not that of the "balance of power" system as Kaplan has described it,[42] even though it envisages the coexistence of several actors—whether individual states or groups of states—of approximately comparable strength and influence. Due in part to the comparatively more rigid and durable alignments than were characteristic of the "balance of power" system, transnational actors can be expected to play an important role. These would include both the universal international organization and lesser groupings of states, most of which would form partially integrated security-communities.[43]

The most obvious reason for viewing the international system of the near future as multipolar is the patent fact of the crumbling of bi-

[42] Cf. Morton A. Kaplan, "Balance of Power, Bipolarity and Other Models of International Systems," *American Political Science Review*, LI (1957), 684-93. For a full treatment of the normative patterns that were produced by the historic balance of power and loose bipolar international systems, see also Kaplan's work (with Nicholas deB. Katzenbach), *The Political Foundations of International Law* (New York 1961).

[43] The term is that of Karl W. Deutsch and others, *Political Community*: "The pluralistic security-community (a group of people which have become 'integrated') . . . retains the legal independence of separate governments." (p. 6)

polarity at the present time.[44] The Russo-Chinese split, which until quite recently may have appeared as a temporary aberration which could be healed with a change of personnel in the governing elites, now can be regarded as a long-term feature of the international landscape. Competition between these two Communist giants has intensified and the breach between them has widened steadily during the 1960's. Moreover, as the Chinese increase their economic and military strength and develop an atomic arsenal and delivery capability during the next few years, the incentives for their return to a bloc role subordinate to the Soviet Union can only decline in number and importance. Meanwhile, in the West, the incongruities of the idea of Atlantic partnership become more obvious with each passing month. Without attempting to predict in detail the shape of Western area politics in the years ahead, it can be safely ventured that the trend is not toward the monolithic unity of the area, but is rather in the direction of the bifurcation of the grouping so far as integrated units are concerned (which is not necessarily to say that wide-ranging cooperation and coordination of policy may not continue in important areas). This division conceivably could take one of several forms, e.g. between the "Anglo-Saxon" powers and those of continental Europe, as seems to be suggested by the Gaullist vision; between Europe, including Britain, and North America; or even on the basis of a Washington-Bonn, London-Paris dual axis. This analysis is not meant to foreclose the possibility of the eventual amalgamation of, say, the entire Atlantic area or the Soviet and Chinese states; rather, it concludes that for the short run, the dynamic tendencies are producing greater intra-bloc autonomy than has been characteristic of the recent past.

[44] Richard N. Rosecrance has argued cogently that neither the bipolar nor multipolar model of the international system constitutes a "relevant utopia" for the near future (see his "Bipolarity, Multipolarity, and the Future," *The Journal of Conflict Resolution*, x (3), 314-27). Instead, he suggests that the attractive features of each be combined in a systemic model of "bi-multipolarity": (p. 320) "Bipolarity provides for well-nigh automatic equilibration of the international balance; in addition, while reinforcing conflict between the two poles, it at least has the merit of preventing conflict elsewhere in the system. Multipolarity reduces the significance of major-power conflict by spreading antagonism uniformly through the system. What we should wish for . . . is to combine the desirable facets of each without their attendant disabilities."

The bi-multipolar concept which Rosecrance then describes constitutes a more deliberately deductive attempt than I have made to construct a model of the system's hoped-for future. Nonetheless, in general, what I project here in the way of future trends is compatible with the bi-multipolar model. I have eschewed use of the term, however, because I am not engaged here in rigorous model-building. Thus, it has seemed more useful in this empirical context to describe the future system as "loosely multipolar, in which international coalitions and alignments will be relatively durable."

There are good reasons for concluding that this trend toward greater autonomy will not soon be carried to the point of genuine state equality, however. Perhaps the most important of these is the atomic weapons factor. Although the principal nuclear powers have agreed upon a nonproliferation treaty, it is still possible that a few other states will become atomic powers during the next few years. The costs, however, of developing atomic and nuclear arsenals appear to be so great that it is doubtful that many of these states could enter the ranks of the first-class nuclear powers without a considerable co-operative effort. "Competitive" atomic powers, then, may be expected to remain few, and if more actors are to achieve superpower status in the near future, very few individual states will be able to do so. A more feasible pattern may be the military integration of more than one existing political unit.[45] The atomic factor has introduced the requirement of long-term and relatively close-knit alignment into coalition policy that was not present in the pre-atomic age. Nor does the trend away from bipolarity eliminate that requirement. An atomic or nuclear deterrent that is both credible and competitive with the capabilities of existing superpowers cannot be constructed by the temporary coalescence in a short-term alliance of small national arsenals. Credibility of the deterrent demands an integrated command structure with undivided authority to act in the name of the unit or units to be protected, while a competitive capability will entail, for most states, the joining of independent national forces under a single authority. The relatively long-term alignments of the future must, like those of the bipolar period, place much greater emphasis upon their internal organization than did those alliances of the more distant past.

A second reason for insisting upon the multipolarity of the near future, characterized by rather stable groupings of states, is the likely continuation of relatively great disparities among the major potential groupings of the world in the goals which they seek, the styles of their politics, and their levels of political and economic development. If the dominant issue of world politics is no longer perceived as a simple contest between Communism and non-Communism, other kinds of divisions have come into focus elsewhere, but these, too, are characteristically differences between groups of states rather than between individual states. Whereas nationalism in the European context can only be regarded today and in the future as a reactionary movement, in many of the underdeveloped areas of the world the over-

---

[45] This at least seems a possibility in the case of Western Europe, where the amalgamation of British and French atomic forces combined with the conventional military capabilities of these and other continental states could conceivably produce a unified military capacity that would make these states militarily competitive with the United States and the Soviet Union and, in this sense, "independent" as a single actor in questions of ultimate security.

whelming need to construct national political units where they have not existed before tends to make the ideology of nationalism a progressive and even a revolutionary doctrine. In these areas, nationalism is not likely to become a justification for the preservation at all costs of existing state boundaries so much as it will become the vehicle of the trans-state integration of a larger "nation," however defined. The marriage of national liberation movements to the doctrine of Pan-Africanism is particularly instructive here.[46]

While much of the West must devote increasing energy to coping with the problems of affluence and automation, much of the rest of the world will be involved in a life-and-death struggle for physical survival. While a part of the world—including, no doubt, some of the Communist states—will be engaged in the effort to democratize and liberalize the conduct of politics within their state systems, elsewhere authoritarian and totalitarian forms of government may be expected to wax strong. None of this is likely to encourage the formation of a world polity or a universal community in any meaningful sense of the term. Many of these disparities simply were camouflaged by the working of bipolarity, at least in its early days, and only now are they coming to be recognized as having been there all along.

This discussion is not meant to discount the fact that inter-state conflicts in the traditional sense will continue to form much of the basic stuff of international politics. The point is, rather (a) that limited groupings of states—and often of states that are relatively close geographically—will find that the numerous problems which they face in common will encourage them to take cooperative measures for their resolution; and (b) that these are not issues which can be treated meaningfully through constantly shifting, ad-hoc coalitions. Moreover, it is not implied here that the factors working toward greater regional solidarity are so overwhelming that the splendid isolation of regional blocs will be the result. While the diversity of political issues just alluded to should encourage the growth of regional efforts to provide for the security of the area, in functional terms the problems of development and democratization require the continuing cooperation of states in the Northern and Southern hemispheres.

The Organization of Security in a Multipolar World

As was seen in Part III the gradual loosening of the bipolar structure during the past decade has been accompanied on the one hand by the declining utility of the multilateral alliance *per se*, and on the other by the increased importance of regional security activity that

---

[46] Cf., Immanuel Wallerstein, "Pan-Africanism as Protest," in Morton A. Kaplan, ed., *The Revolution in World Politics* (New York 1962), 137-51.

focuses on intra-group problems. With the evolution of a more clearly multipolar system, the factors which have encouraged this trend should continue to operate. Thus, we can expect to see fewer attempts to extend the protective hegemony of great powers over distant territories and a greater effort to consolidate the interests of local powers in the more limited areas of their greatest interest.

It should be added immediately, however, that such an evolution will scarcely be smooth or simple. The revolutionary, transnational ideology of Marxism undoubtedly will continue to guide the elites of the Communist world in their foreign policies, encouraging them to promote revolution in distant countries and to maintain strong political ties with like-minded political cadres around the globe. Similarly, even though Western leaders seem to have learned that their former colonial subjects do not become automatic allies with independence, the diverse ties which have remained between many of them after nationhood no doubt will persist into the immediate future. There will, then, continue to be conflicting claims to the protection of various elite groups in far-flung areas, even though it is true that an increasing amount of security activity will rest with the groups most immediately involved in the vicinity.

Still, with the decline of bipolarity and the increased importance of new states in the international system, why should not an expanded security role for the United Nations be developed? The new states are, after all, among the most ardent champions of a dynamic universal organization, and the fact of bipolarity long has been regarded as the chief obstacle in the path of genuine collective security. In fact, however, there is little reason to assume that the principle of great power concert on which the security provisions of the Charter were built will be any more applicable to the realities of politics in the near future than it has been in the past two decades. Even if it be assumed that a rapprochement between the United States and the Soviet Union will extend to the point that these two powers may see eye to eye on measures of peaceful settlement and enforcement to be undertaken by the United Nations, the admission of Communist China to a seat on the Security Council—an event which surely will take place within the near future—does not portend great harmony among the permanent members. The current demands of the Peking regime upon the world are, perhaps, somewhat akin in quality to those of the Soviet Union in the immediate postwar period. If so, we may expect Chinese behavior in the Security Council to resemble that of the Russians during much of the recent past.

Given this situation, it is likely that the principal security role left to the UN will be some variation on that currently described as preventive diplomacy. Expansion of this role, however, will be fraught

with difficulties from two quarters: In the first place, it will be necessary to secure the acquiescence in UN action of several permanent
members that will be more nearly equal in their *de facto* relationships
than the current members have been heretofore. To do so need not depend upon the willingness of these states to accept the status quo in all
cases so much as it will require from them realistic appraisals of the
limitations of their own power in extended areas. Experience indicates that such appraisals may not come readily to states unaccus-
tomed to their role as great powers. Secondly, if even this limited security role is to be maintained for the United Nations, concrete steps
must be taken soon to ensure its acceptance on a regularized basis.
There was healthy recognition in the Twentieth General Assembly
that world order could be better served than by permitting preventive diplomacy to continue to grow "like Topsy," on an ad hoc and
uneven basis without due regard for the most effective means of financing such activity. Even though steps were undertaken beginning in 1965-1966 to reexamine the existing peace-keeping machinery
of the organization, no specific proposals have yet emerged for strengthening the UN role in this area.

These facts, taken together, should induce a certain pessimism as to
the short-range possibilities for a more extensive UN security role than
now exists. On the other hand, they help emphasize the need, if not
the likelihood, that much of the attempt to secure a more orderly
world should be directed to the regional level. From a normative
point of view, it is essential that the regional approach to security be
strengthened by the construction of viable regional organizations
whose members are viewed objectively, i.e. by actors external to
those organizations, as forming a unified and responsible grouping
for purposes of treating some security issues. Yet, the qualifier "some"
must be emphasized here, for an effective universal organization will
be required that is capable of responding to the need for peace-
keeping action where regional intervention would be unacceptable
to the international community as a whole. If United Nations preventive diplomacy can be regarded as complementing rather than opposing the regional approach to security, then the regional approach
must be made to conform to acceptable standards of international
behavior.

Regionalism and Political Order

It should not be impossible to set down general guidelines which may
help to ensure the evolution of regional security activity that conforms with the goals of human dignity. At the same time, any attempt
to specify the precise forms of regional security organization that
should be developed in all such groupings must be regarded as chi-

merical. What follows, then, is simply an attempt to make explicit the primary social and political requisites to the orderly development of a transnational, subsystemic organization.

Although it may be possible to regard political authority built wholly upon the use or threat of force as ensuring "order" within the social structure, that is a superficial kind of order which inevitably breeds chaos over the long run. Genuine order permits the ever-greater realization of goals based upon shared values that are sought by members of the group, and not rigidity of social and political structures. Authority that is firmly built upon "a consistent pattern of shared value realization" is itself productive of order, whereas tension and conflict can only result when authority is maintained by a resort to power that inhibits the goal-gratification of members of the group.[47] Considered in terms of regional politics, this proposition is, of course, the principal explanation of the fact that the unrestrained exercise of hegemony by a great power over lesser ones is so likely to have disorderly and destabilizing consequences. At the same time, it assumes the necessity of authoritative structures if coherent policy is to be produced. The requirement, then, is for an organization at the regional level that can act effectively without permitting it to become the instrument of the monolithic imposition of a single state's demands upon the wider area.

By any exacting definition, the regional association remains as the *organization* of "sovereign" states, rather than a single polity and, as such, may be regarded as an intermediate level of political integration between the (theoretically) fully integrated state units and the largely unintegrated international system as a whole. The proposition of orderly development sketched in the preceding paragraph, however, assumes as the ultimate norm of social and political life the fully integrated unit, where authority rests upon a consistent pattern of shared value realization. Thus, it cannot be regarded as accurately descriptive of the aims of transnational, subsystemic organization. Since regional organizations constitute a half-way house of transnational association, their authoritative structures are the creation of the states which comprise them, and their purpose is to help realize some of the goals of states rather than the values of individuals. The characteristic tensions (described in Part III) between hegemonic and nonhegemonic tendencies constitute—in the language of the present analysis—tensions which arise from the requirements of authoritative action on the one hand, and preservation of the relevant values of all associated states on the other.

[47] The quotation is from Kenneth S. Carlston, *Law and Organization in World Society* (Urbana 1962), 85-86.

Insistence upon the requirement of regional organizations to deal with some of the important security problems of the future does not stem from an inclination to hypostatize political development at the regional level. The goal of world order must be predicated upon the realization of human values, and should refuse to give absolute allegiance to particular political forms and structures as the only ones conducive to order. By the same token, our concern must be to fit the political structures which are available to the realization of those goals. Fully recognizing the tentative quality of regional organization in a world where universal order is demanded, I would posit as a normative goal of regional organizational development in the future what might be called the pluralistic unity of the organization, based upon the national "independence" of the constituent members. Such a goal attempts to account realistically for the apparently contradictory phenomena of current international politics, i.e. (a) the continuation of the nation-state as the basic unit of world politics (even though it can no longer be the final arbiter or ultimate protagonist in all international conflictual situations) and (b) the technological and political developments which, in large measure, render the nation-state as traditionally constituted unable ultimately to protect its own national values. However contradictory the demand may seem to be, the governing principle of regional organizational development should account for both the continuing "sovereign" independence of the nation-state and for the breakdown (or transformation) of national "sovereignty."

In part, then, the goal of pluralistic unity for the regional organization is posited on the assumption that a fuller scale political amalgamation of constituent member states is not a realistic goal for the near future—at least not in many areas of the world. But it is also suggested that, in the absence of genuinely democratic integrative processes, such a goal is more acceptable for the short run because it would entail restraint upon the violation of national values through a centralized authoritative structure. The existence of a pluralistic structure can prevent the unilateral expansion of the values of a particular elite at the expense of other members of the group; at the same time, however, it can encourage the harmonization of interests through a sharing of the instruments of power by which values are realized. A nonhierarchical regional grouping, in which diverse interests are recognized in the decision-making process, is far likelier to impose restraints upon its own security activity than is a body that is hierarchically structured. The result may, of course, merely be ineffective action or no action at all, but recognition of such a possibility itself encourages agreement on a common policy where such a policy is possible, without sacrificing values held vital by important members of the organization.

The Challenge of the Future

It is, of course, one thing to suggest the guidelines which ought to govern the operations of regional security organizations so that they are not disruptive of basic human values and quite another to suppose that they will be adhered to in practice. Undoubtedly, it would be utopian to suppose that the kind of pluralistic unity at the regional level set forth as a goal in the preceding discussion will be realized throughout the world in the near future. In some areas, and particularly where the locally dominant power combines expansionist goals with authoritarian methods, the pluralistic unity of the regional powers will be virtually impossible. For the short run, hegemonic domination in those regions probably must go nearly unchecked; lesser regional powers will scarcely have the capabilities to do so and external actors will find that any such attempt on their part would be too costly in terms of their own security and that of the international community generally. External actors will be well advised to contain expansionist tendencies, but not to attempt seriously coercive action within the area dominated by a locally hegemonic power. The realization of shared values through authoritative political structures must be postponed, in such instances, in the interests of general international security.

On balance, however, most of the lessons and developments of the recent past support the case for regional action that is conducive to order at both the regional and universal levels in the near future. First, the attempt to maintain alliances essentially like those of the past — wherein emphasis upon the common external threat has taken precedence over the attempt to harmonize mutual relations authoritatively—must be regarded as inadequate for purposes of preserving an effective coalition in a multipolar world. Since it will be in the interests of the great powers to maintain as effectively as possible the allegiance and the loyalties of other national actors within their blocs, these powers should be encouraged to take the lead in building pluralistic unity in their regional associations through strong emphasis upon the functions of the actors-in-organization.

Secondly, experience has shown that action undertaken in the name of a regional body which has only a tenuous organizational development tends to be both ineffective in the immediate sense that it fails to increase importantly the capabilities of the major national actor involved, and in the more general sense of encouraging settlement that is acceptable to other national and universal actors. If this factor should discourage the great and superpowers from the attempt to form military alliances with states where the impetus to organizational or integrative development is lacking, it may encourage them, nonetheless, to concentrate their efforts upon the building of authority within those more restricted areas where the requisites for such development are present.

Finally, growing recognition of the futility to the great powers of attempting to maintain organizational commitments in areas of the world beyond those of their immediate interests already has encouraged the establishment, at least in one area, of a nonaligned regional body, potentially capable of dealing with the actors-in-organization in an orderly fashion. If the current level of conflict in Southeast Asia can be reduced before other major actors are pulled into the vortex, a similar approach may come to be recognized as the most feasible means of attaining greater security in that area. All three of these historical factors can be viewed as encouraging the potential contribution of regionalism to security that is compatible with order. All three developments hold out the prospect—although certainly not the promise—that international security can be promoted in a context which permits the increasing realization of many fundamental human values.

Index

Index

Abboud, Ibrahim, 520
Abi-Saab, 319n
ABM systems, in developing nations, 177-78
"absolute" rights, 434
abundance, in near-future image, 20
Academy of International Law, 89
Addis Ababa, Charter of, 358
Adelman I, 452n
ad hoc coalition, 201
adjudicative arena, 101-02
affection, of private associations, 90
Africa, civil wars in, 514; "conscience" in, 402; modernizing elites in, 502, 506; regional integration in, 502-04: See also Organization of African Unity
African blocs, 300-01
African Conference on the Rule of Law, 526
African Development Bank, 540
African nations, membership in UN, 298
Afro-Asian countries, new states in, 320; United Nations and, 202. See also Africa; Asia; Third World
aggression, collective security and, 256; fear of, 444; indirect, 121; victim state in, 391
agrarian life, transition to industrial from, 7-8, 11, 21
agriculture, economic growth of, 20; commercialization of, 8
Ahmed, M. Samir, 306n
Akexandrowicz, C. H., 305n, 409n
Alger, Chadwick, 199, 234n
Algeria, Arab unity and, 501
Algeria-Morocco hostilities, 519
Alker, Hayward R., Jr., 84n, 202n, 211-12, 251n, 315
All-African Trade Union Federation, 509
Allen, Philip M., 407n
alliances, in balance-of-power systems, 158-59; in international legal order, 54; in loose bipolar system, 161-62; party systems and, 216-18; in unit veto system, 168; world parties and, 184
Almond, Gabriel, 240n
Almond-Coleman scheme of polity, 234, 235n
Alur, 235
Amerasinghe, C. F., 327n
American Academy of Arts and Sciences, 18
American Institute of International Law, 89
analysis, in decision-making, 79

Anarchists International party, 208
Anciaux, P., 440n
Antarctic Treaty, 30
anthropology, cultural relativism and, 346-49
anticolonialism, 170, 405
antimissile system, 177-78, 306
antitrust legislation, 87
anti-utopias, 228
apartheid, 60, 439
application, context and outlines of, 147; in decision-making, 145-48; inter-state, 146; sequence of, 145
appraising, in decision function, 152-54
Apter, David E., 22n, 232, 236n, 240n
Aquinas, St. Thomas, 410n
Arab Common Market, 500
Arab-Jewish conflicts, 535, 542, 552
Arab Lawyers Federation, 526
Arab League, 38n, 59, 261n, 312-13, 482, 510, 541, 561n, 568-70, 583; as community builder, 500; effectiveness of, 521; Israel and, 535, 542, 552; professional societies and, 509; Secretary General of, 521; split in, 520-21; UN Charter and, 532
Arab League Council, 541
Arab League Pact, see League of Arab States
Arab Scientific Federations, 509
Arab states, in development world; modernization in, 499; revolutionary socialist regimes in, 499; trade within, 500. See also League of Arab States
arena (s), establishment and maintenance of, 100-07; geographical range of, 102-03; institutional structures and, 101; organization vs. application in, 147; in world community, 97, 100-08
Arens, R., 108n, 116n, 123n, 148n
Argentina, modernizing elite in, 495
armed force, downgrading of, 345. See also force
arms control, future of, 306; regional, 360n
arms race, in outer space, 307
Aron, Raymond, 36n, 45n, 184n, 329n, 331n
Arsic, Draginja, 486n
ARUSHA agreement (1968), 548
Arzinger, R., 358n
Asher, Robert E., 226n
Asia, communist blocs in, 300; "conscience" in, 402. See also Afro-Asian countries; SEATO

national identity, army life and, 242; source of, 241

nationalism, as luxury, 465

"nationalized" values, 428

national leaders, commitment of, 457

national liberation, societies seeking, 24

"National Liberation" fronts, 550

national parties, 85-86. *See also* party; party systems

national purpose, reevaluation of, 249

national security, capacity for, 62. *See also* collective security

national self-determination, *see* self-determination

nation-state, in balance-of-power model, 156-57; military strategy in, 128; global interdependence and, 186; integration of, 468; interaction of, 138; political parties in, 85-86; power of, 112-13; prescription and, 141; replacement of, 187; rectitude system and, 118-19; structure of, 83; supersession of, 464; United Nations and, 230; war and, 464; wealth of, 113; world party systems and, 219-22; world society and, 185

nations, freedom of action of, 411; as human beings, 418; interpenetration between, 334-36, 342

NATO (North Atlantic Treaty Organization), 112n, 113n, 286, 546, 560, 565, 570; bloc membership of, 163-65, 171; vs. Communist bloc, 167; decline of, 300; deterrence goal of, 566-67; ex-colonies and, 163-64; fissures in membership, 576; in four-bloc system, 171; political parties and, 217; survival of, 300-01; trade relations and, 511; in unstable bloc system, 175

natural law, "absolutes" in, 377; conscience and, 380-403; justice and, 373; meaning of, 413; promises in, 383

"natural" rights, 434

nature, state of, 413

near future, economic growth and, 20; images of, 11-23; instability in, 22-23; international government in, 29-31; national development in, 24-25; nuclear weapons in, 28

Negley, Glenn, 36n

negotiation, legal change and, 352

neocolonialism, new states and, 327

neutrality, in development world, 178, 436; and Westphalia conception, 44-45

"New Deal of International Trade," 88

new states or nations, "aging" of, 368-71; changed international legal order and, 350-68; cold war and, 321; concept of, 319; external influences on, 330;

impact of, 323-50; influencing of, 334; internal developments in, 326-28; international law and, 364; negotiations among, 361; participation in future legal order, 317-71; rise of, 568-70; "socialist" doctrines in, 366n; source materials in, 321-23; "unworthiness" of, 359

New York Times, 17n, 86n, 118n

New Zealand, in development world, 177

Niebuhr, Reinhold, 40n

Nigeria, independence of, 502; and organization of African Unity, 503

Nkrumah, Kwame, 188, 512, 519

Nollau, Gunther, 205n

Nomad, Max, 208n

noncentralized systems, 198-99

nonparticipation, as sanction, 344

nonrecognition, in bipolar system, 160-63

North, Robert, 105n

North Atlantic Treaty Organization, *see* NATO

North Vietnam, cooperation with South Vietnam, 550. *See also* Vietnam

Notte-bohm case, 144

nouveau venu, 406

nuclear balance of terror, 245, 306, 308

nuclear capability, as power, 243

nuclear catastrophe, 229

nuclear power, in developing states, 552

nuclear propulsion, 297

nuclear technology, 565-68

nuclear test ban treaty, viii-ix, 167

nuclear war, resort to, 401; social modification and, 38

nuclear weapons, and balance-of-power model, 156-57, 179; in bipolar world, 179; collective security and, 283; control of, 166; credibility and, 168; in development world, 177; future of, 229; global interdependence and, 186; in loose bipolar system, 161-62; orbiting, 56-57, 307; proliferation of, 39; retaliation with, 165; and "rules of the game," 68; security of mankind and, 28; Soviet threat in, 165; state system and, 46; in unit veto system, 168; in unstable bloc system, 173; world government and, 187; world party systems and, 222

Nuer, 234-35

Nuremberg Judgment, Principles of, 41, 64, 69, 374

Nussbaum, A., 92n, 118n, 419n

Nye, Joseph S., 312n, 464n, 491n

Nys, E., 419n

BOOKS WRITTEN
UNDER THE AUSPICES OF THE
CENTER OF INTERNATIONAL STUDIES
PRINCETON UNIVERSITY

Gabriel A. Almond, *The Appeals of Communism* (Princeton University Press 1954)

William W. Kaufmann, ed., *Military Policy and National Security* (Princeton University Press 1956)

Klaus Knorr, *The War Potential of Nations* (Princeton University Press 1956)

Lucian W. Pye, *Guerrilla Communism in Malaya* (Princeton University Press 1956)

Charles De Visscher, *Theory and Reality in Public International Law,* trans. by P. E. Corbett (Princeton University Press 1957; rev. ed. 1968)

Bernard C. Cohen, *The Political Process and Foreign Policy: The Making of the Japanese Peace Settlement* (Princeton University Press 1959)

Myron Weiner, *Party Politics in India: The Development of a Multi-Party System* (Princeton University Press 1957)

Percy E. Corbett, *Law in Diplomacy* (Princeton University Press 1959)

Rolf Sannwald and Jacques Stohler, *Economic Integration: Theoretical Assumptions and Consequences of European Unification,* trans. by Herman Karreman (Princeton University Press 1959)

Klaus Knorr, ed., *NATO and American Security* (Princeton University Press 1959)

Gabriel A. Almond and James S. Coleman, eds., *The Politics of the Developing Areas* (Princeton University Press 1960)

Herman Kahn, *On Thermonuclear War* (Princeton University Press 1960)

Sidney Verba, *Small Groups and Political Behavior: A Study of Leadership* (Princeton University Press 1961)

Robert J. C. Butow, *Tojo and the Coming of the War* (Princeton University Press 1961)

Glenn H. Snyder, *Deterrence and Defense: Toward a Theory of National Security* (Princeton University Press 1961)

Klaus Knorr and Sidney Verba, eds., *The International System: Theoretical Essays* (Princeton University Press 1961)

Peter Paret and John W. Shy, *Guerrillas in the 1960's* (Praeger 1962)

George Modelski, *A Theory of Foreign Policy* (Praeger 1962)

Klaus Knorr and Thornton Read, eds., *Limited Strategic War* (Praeger 1963)

Frederick S. Dunn, *Peace-Making and the Settlement with Japan* (Princeton University Press 1963)

Arthur L. Burns and Nina Heathcote, *Peace-Keeping by United Nations Forces* (Praeger 1963)

Richard A. Falk, *Law, Morality, and War in the Contemporary World* (Praeger 1963)

James N. Rosenau, *National Leadership and Foreign Policy: A Case Study in the Mobilization of Public Support* (Princeton University Press 1963)

Gabriel A. Almond and Sidney Verba, *The Civic Culture: Political Attitudes and Democracy in Five Nations* (Princeton University Press 1963)

Bernard C. Cohen, *The Press and Foreign Policy* (Princeton University Press 1963)

Richard L. Sklar, *Nigerian Political Parties: Power in an Emergent African Nation* (Princeton University Press 1963)

Peter Paret, *French Revolutionary Warfare from Indochina to Algeria: The Analysis of a Political and Military Doctrine* (Praeger 1964)

Harry Eckstein, ed., *Internal War: Problems and Approaches* (Free Press 1964)

Cyril E. Black and Thomas P. Thornton, eds., *Communism and Revolution: The Strategic Uses of Political Violence* (Princeton University Press 1964)

Miriam Camps, *Britain and the European Community 1955-1963* (Princeton University Press 1964)

Thomas P. Thornton, ed., *The Third World in Soviet Perspective: Studies by Soviet Writers on the Developing Areas* (Princeton University Press 1964)

James N. Rosenau, ed., *International Aspects of Civil Strife* (Princeton University Press 1964)

Sidney I. Ploss, *Conflict and Decision-Making in Soviet Russia: A Case Study of Agricultural Policy, 1953-1963* (Princeton University Press 1965)

Richard A. Falk and Richard J. Barnet, eds., *Security in Disarmament* (Princeton University Press 1965)

Karl von Vorys, *Political Development in Pakistan* (Princeton University Press 1965)

Harold and Margaret Sprout, *The Ecological Perspective on Human Affairs, With Special Reference to International Politics* (Princeton University Press 1965)

Klaus Knorr, *On the Uses of Military Power in the Nuclear Age* (Princeton University Press 1966)

Harry Eckstein, *Division and Cohesion in Democracy: A Study of Norway* (Princeton University Press 1966)

Cyril E. Black, *The Dynamics of Modernization: A Study in Comparative History* (Harper and Row 1966)

Peter Kunstadter, ed., *Southeast Asian Tribes, Minorities, and Nations* (Princeton University Press 1967)

E. Victor Wolfenstein, *The Revolutionary Personality: Lenin, Trotsky, Gandhi* (Princeton University Press 1967)

Leon Gordenker, *The UN Secretary-General and the Maintenance of Peace* (Columbia University Press 1967)

Oran R. Young, *The Intermediaries: Third Parties in International Crises* (Princeton University Press 1967)

James N. Rosenau, ed., *Domestic Sources of Foreign Policy* (Free Press 1967)

Richard F. Hamilton, *Affluence and the French Worker in the Fourth Republic* (Princeton University Press 1967)

Linda B. Miller, *World Order and Local Disorder: The United Nations and Internal Conflicts* (Princeton University Press 1967)

Henry Bienen, *Tanzania: Party Transformation and Economic Development* (Princeton University Press 1967)

Wolfram F. Hanrieder, *West German Foreign Policy, 1949-1963: International Pressures and Domestic Response* (Stanford University Press 1967)

Richard H. Ullman, *Britain and the Russian Civil War: November 1918-February 1920* (Princeton University Press 1968)

Robert Gilpin, *France in the Age of the Scientific State* (Princeton University Press 1968)

William B. Bader, *The United States and the Spread of Nuclear Weapons* (Pegasus 1968)

Richard A. Falk, *Legal Order in a Violent World* (Princeton University Press 1968)

Cyril E. Black, Richard A. Falk, Klaus Knorr, and Oran R. Young, *Neutralization and World Politics* (Princeton University Press 1968)

Oran R. Young, *The Politics of Force: Bargaining During International Crises* (Princeton University Press 1969)

Klaus Knorr and James N. Rosenau, eds., *Contending Approaches to International Politics* (Princeton University Press 1969)

James N. Rosenau, ed., *Linkage Politics: Essays on the Convergence of National and International Systems* (Free Press 1969)

John T. McAlister, Jr., *Viet Nam: The Origins of Revolution* (Knopf 1969)

Jean Edward Smith, *Germany Beyond the Wall: People, Politics and Prosperity* (Little, Brown 1969)

James Barros, *Betrayal from Within: Joseph Avenol Secretary-General of the League of Nations, 1933-1940* (Yale University Press 1969)

Charles Hermann, *Crises in Foreign Policy: A Simulation Analysis* (Bobbs-Merrill 1969)

Robert C. Tucker, *The Marxian Revolutionary Idea: Essays on Marxist Thought and Its Impact on Radical Movements* (W. W. Norton 1969)

Harvey Waterman, *Political Change in Contemporary France: The Politics of an Industrial Democracy* (Charles E. Merrill 1969)